# THE ASHGATE RESEARCH COMPANION TO FEMINIST LEGAL THEORY

ASHGATE
**RESEARCH**
COMPANION

The *Ashgate Research Companions* are designed to offer scholars and graduate students a comprehensive and authoritative state-of-the-art review of current research in a particular area. The companions' editors bring together a team of respected and experienced experts to write chapters on the key issues in their speciality, providing a comprehensive reference to the field.

# The Ashgate Research Companion to Feminist Legal Theory

*Edited by*

MARGARET DAVIES

*Flinders University, Australia*

VANESSA E. MUNRO

*University of Nottingham, UK*

Routledge
Taylor & Francis Group

LONDON AND NEW YORK

First published 2013 by Ashgate Publishing

2 Park Square, Milton Park, Abingdon, Oxfordshire OX14 4RN
52 Vanderbilt Avenue, New York, NY 10017

*Routledge is an imprint of the Taylor & Francis Group, an informa business*

First issued in paperback 2018

**British Library Cataloguing in Publication Data**
A catalogue record for this book is available from the British Library

**Library of Congress Cataloging-in-Publication Data**
Davies, Margaret, (professor)
  The Ashgate research companion to feminist legal theory / By Margaret Davies and
Vanessa E. Munro.
    pages cm
  Includes bibliographical references and index.
1.  Feminist jurisprudence. 2.  Women--Legal status, laws, etc.  I. Munro, Vanessa. II.
Title. III. Title: Research companion to feminist legal theory.

  K349.D38 2013
  340'.1--dc23

                                                                          2013007752

ISBN-13: 978-1-4094-1859-7 (hbk)
ISBN-13: 978-1-138-07570-5 (pbk)

# Contents

# Notes on Contributors

**Rosemary Auchmuty** is Professor of Law at the University of Reading, UK. She writes about property law, legal history, gender and sexuality, and children's literature, all from a feminist perspective. Among her recent publications are articles and chapters on marriage and civil partnership, early women law students and women lawyers, teaching property law using socio-legal and feminist resources, and one of the *Feminist Judgments* (in the book edited by R. Hunter, C. McGlynn and E. Rackley, Hart Publishing 2010).

**Samia Bano** is Senior Lecturer in Law at the School of Oriental and African Studies, University of London, UK. Her research interests include the practice of Muslim family law in the UK and Europe, multiculturalism, Islamic jurisprudence and human rights and issues concerning the rights of Muslim women. She has published widely in these areas of scholarship. For example, she is author of *Muslim Women and Shariah Councils: Transcending the Boundaries of Community and Law* (Palgrave Macmillan 2012) and has recently completed a research project for the Ministry of Justice in the UK, entitled, 'An exploratory study of Shariah Councils in England with respect to family law' (2012).

**Elsje Bonthuys** is Professor of Law at the University of Witwatersrand, South Africa. She teaches and researches in the areas of gender and family law. She is author (with C. Albertyn) of *Gender, Law and Justice* (Juta Publishing 2007). Her most recent work explores issues of sexual orientation in South African Muslim communities and the ways in which South African media addresses the intersection between gender and race. Recent publications include 'Modes of (in)tolerance: South African Muslims and Same-Sex Relationships' (with N. Erlank) (2012), *Culture, Health and Sexuality*, 14(3), 269–282; 'Conscientious Objection to Creating Same-Sex Unions: An International Analysis' (with B. MacDougall, K. Norrie and M. van den Brink) 2012, *Canadian Journal of Human Rights*, 1(1), 125–162; and 'Gender and the Chief Justice: Principle or Pretext?' *Journal of South African Studies*, forthcoming.

**Susan B. Boyd** is a professor in the Faculty of Law, University of British Columbia, Canada. She holds the research Chair in Feminist Legal Studies and has published widely in the fields of feminist legal studies and family law, especially child custody law and the legal recognition of same-sex partnerships. Her recent work focuses on legal parenthood and the possibilities for autonomous motherhood. Her books include *Child Custody, Law, and Women's Work* (Oxford University Press 2003), *Reaction and Resistance: Feminism, Law, and Social Change* (UBC Press 2007), *Law and Families* (Ashgate 2006), and *Challenging the Public/ Private Divide: Feminism, Law and Public Policy*. In 2012, she was elected a Fellow of the Royal Society of Canada.

**Joanne Conaghan** is Professor of Law at the University of Bristol, UK, having previously taught at the universities of Exeter, Kent, and San Diego. She has been researching and writing in law for over 20 years and has published widely in areas which include tort law, labour law and feminist legal theory. Her recent publications include a monograph on *Law and Gender* (Clarendon Press 2013), a four-volume edited collection, *Feminist Legal Studies* (Routledge 2009) and *The New Oxford Companion to Law* (OUP 2008) co-edited with Professor Peter Cane, Australian National University. Joanne is also an Academician of the Academy of Social Sciences.

**Sharon Cowan** is a Senior Lecturer in Law at the University of Edinburgh, UK. Her research interests include: gender, sexuality and the law; criminal law; criminal justice; and asylum and immigration. Along with Helen Baillot of the Scottish Refugee Council and Vanessa Munro of the University of Nottingham, she has recently completed a national empirical project funded by the Nuffield Foundation, investigating how women asylum claimants, whose appeals are based on a claim of rape, are treated by the Asylum and Immigration Appeal Tribunal. Her recent publications include 'To Buy or Not to Buy? Vulnerability and the Criminalisation of Commercial BDSM' (2012) *Feminist Legal Studies*, 20(3), 263–279 and 'Hearing the Right Gaps: Enabling and Responding to Disclosures of Sexual Violence within the UK Asylum Process' (2012) *Social and Legal Studies*, 21(3), 269–296.

**Margaret Davies** is Matthew Flinders Distinguished Professor at Flinders University, South Australia. She studied in Adelaide and the UK before joining the Law School at Flinders in 1992. Her areas of research interest include feminist legal theory and the philosophy of property. She is the author of *Delimiting the Law* (1996), *Are Persons Property?* (with Ngaire Naffine, 2001), *Property: Meanings, Histories, Theories* (2007) and *Asking the Law Question*, 3rd edn (2008). Margaret is a Fellow of the Academy of Social Sciences in Australia and a Fellow of the Australian Academy of Law.

**Marie Fox** is Professor of Socio-Legal Studies at the University of Birmingham. Her research focuses on how law regulates human and animal bodies. Recent publications include 'Realising Social Justice in Public Health Law' (with M. Thomson), *Medical Law Review*, forthcoming; 'The New Politics of Male Circumcision: HIV/AIDS, Health Law and Social Justice' (2012) *Legal Studies*, 32(2), 255–281; 'Law and Veterinary Ethics' in C. Wathes (ed.), *Veterinary and Animal Ethics* (Wiley Blackwell 2012); 'Embryonic Hopes: Controversy, Alliance and Reproductive Entities in Law and the Social Sciences' (with M. Jaccob, B. Prainsack, M. Murphy and T. Franklin) (2010) *Social and Legal Studies*, 19(4), 497–517; and 'Legal Embodiment: Analysing the Body of Healthcare Law' (with R. Fletcher and J. McCandless) (2008) *Medical Law Review*, 16(3), 321–345.

**Judy Fudge** is Professor and Lansdowne Chair in Law at the University of Victoria, Canada. She was a Fernand Braudel Fellow at the European University Institute in 2012, and in 2013 she takes up a Leverhulme Visiting Professorship at Kent Law School. In 2009, she received the Bora Laskin National Fellowship in Human Rights for her research project 'Labour Rights as Human Rights: Unions, Women, and Migrants'. Her recent publications include: *Blurring Legal Boundaries: Regulating Work* (with K. Sankaran and S. McCrystal, Hart 2012); *Constitutional Labour Rights in Canada: Farm Workers and the Fraser Case* (with F. Faraday and E. Tucker, Irwin 2012); 'Global Care Chains: Transnational Migrant Care Workers' (2012) *International Journal of Comparative Labour Law and Industrial Relations*, 28(1),

63–70; 'Precarious Migrant Status and Precarious Employment: The Paradox of International Rights for Migrant Workers' (2012) *Comparative Labor Law and Policy Journal*, 34(1), 94–131.

**Judith Gardam** is Emeritus Professor at the Law School University of Adelaide in South Australia and a Fellow of the Academy of Social Sciences in Australia. She is an International Lawyer and a feminist scholar. Her particular areas of expertise are international humanitarian law and the international law rules that regulate the use of force between States. She has researched and published widely on these topics. Key publications include *The Challenge of Conflict: International Law Responds* (co-edited with T. Dolgopol, Martinus Nijhoff 2006); *Proportionality, Necessity and Force in International Law* (Cambridge University Press 2004); and *Women, Armed Conflict and International Law* (with M. Jarvis, Kluwer 2001).

**Åsa Gunnarsson** works at the Forum for Studies on Law and Society, at Umeå University, Sweden. Her main field of research is tax law and gender studies. She has also led projects about social citizenship and welfare state law, and has extensive experience in cross-disciplinary collaboration. Her key publications include Gunnarsson, Å., Svensson, E. and M. Davies (eds), *Exploiting the Limits of Law: Swedish Feminism and the Challenge to Pessimism* (Ashgate Publishing 2007) and K. Brooks, Å. Gunnarsson, L. Philips and M. Wersig (eds), *Challenging the Inequality in Tax Policy Making: Comparative Perspectives* (Hart Publishing 2011).

**Nancy J. Hirschmann** is Professor of Political Science at The University of Pennsylvania, USA. She is the author of many articles and several monographs: *Gender, Class, and Freedom in Modern Political Theory, The Subject of Liberty: Toward a Feminist Theory of Freedom,* and *Rethinking Obligation: A Feminist Method for Political Theory*. She is also co-editor of *Feminist Interpretations of John Locke, Feminist Interpretations of Thomas Hobbes, Revisioning the Political: Feminist Reconstructions of Traditional Concepts in Western Political Theory* and *Women and Welfare: Theory and Practice in the U.S. and Europe*. She has held fellowships from American Council of Learned Societies, The Institute for Advanced Study, The Bunting Institute of Radcliffe College, and the National Endowment for the Humanities.

**Rosemary Hunter** is Professor of Law at the University of Kent, UK. Her research is in the area of feminist legal theory, with a current focus on family law, family dispute resolution, and feminist judging. She was one of the organizers of the UK Feminist Judgments Project and co-editor of the book *Feminist Judgments: From Theory to Practice* (2010). She is also Chair of the UK Socio-Legal Studies Association, and an editor of the online open access journal *feminists@law*.

**Karen Morrow** has been Professor of Environmental Law at Swansea University, UK, since 2007. She is co-director of the Centre for Environmental and Energy Law and Policy. Her research interests focus on theoretical and practical aspects of public participation in environmental law and policy. She is author (with S. Coyle) of *A Philosophical Foundation for Environmental Law* (Hart 2004), and co-editor of the *Journal of Human Rights and the Environment*. Her recent publications include 'Perspectives on Environmental Law and the Law Relating to Sustainability: A Continuing Role for Ecofeminism?' in A. Philippopoulos-Mihalopoulos (ed.), *Critical Environmental Law: New Environmental Foundations* (Routledge 2011); 'Risk and Public Participation in Decision-Making on GMOs' in L. Bogiguel and

M. Cardwell (eds), *The Regulation of Genetically Modified Organisms* (OUP 2010); 'Sustainable Development, Major Groups and Stakeholder Dialogue – Lessons from the UN' in D. French (ed.), *Global Justice and Sustainable Development* (Martinus Nijhof 2010); and a co-edited collection (with J.B. Boer, A. Benidickson and A. Herman Benjamin), entitled *Environmental Law and Sustainability After Rio* (Edward Elgar 2011).

**Vanessa E. Munro** is Professor of Socio-Legal Studies in the School of Law, University of Nottingham, UK. She has published widely on feminist legal and political theory, with a particular focus upon sexual offences, consent and the regulation of women's bodies. She is author of *Law and Politics at the Perimeter: Re-Evaluating Key Debates in Feminist Theory* (Hart 2007) and co-editor of *Law and Sexuality: Feminist Engagements* (Routledge 2007), *Demanding Sex: Critical Reflections on the Regulation of Prostitution* (Ashgate 2008) and *Rethinking Rape Law: International and Comparative Perspectives* (Routledge 2010).

**Thérèse Murphy** is Professor of Law and Critical Theory at the University of Nottingham, UK. Her books include *Health and Human Rights* (Hart 2013) and, with M.L. Flear, A.M. Farrell and T.K. Hervey, *European Law and New Health Technologies* (OUP 2013). Working with colleagues from Nottingham and from further afield, she has recently guest-edited special issues of the journals *Law, Innovation and Technology*, *Medical Law Review*, and *Human Rights Law Review*.

**Jennifer C. Nash** is Assistant Professor of American Studies and Women's Studies at George Washington University, USA. Her research focuses on black feminism, black sexual politics, visual culture, and critical race theory. Her work has been published in *Feminist Review*, *Social Text*, *Scholar and Feminist*, and *Yale Journal of Law and Feminism*. Her book, *The Black Body in Ecstasy: Reading Race, Reading Pornography*, is forthcoming from Duke University Press.

**Dianne Otto** is Director of the Institute for International Law and the Humanities (IILAH) at Melbourne Law School, Australia. She researches in the areas of public international law, human rights law and critical legal theory, with a current focus on gender and sexuality issues in the context of the UN Security Council, peacekeeping and international human rights law. Her recent publications include a bibliographic chapter, 'Feminist Approaches', in *Oxford Bibliographies Online: International Law*, ed. T. Carty (Oxford University Press 2012), the editing of three volumes on *Gender Issues and Human Rights* (Edward Elgar Publishing 2013) and an article in the *Jindal Global Law Review* special issue on 'Rethinking Queer Sexualities, Law, and Cultural Economies of Desire' (2012). Professor Otto has held visiting positions at Columbia University, the School of Oriental and African Studies, New York University, the University of British Columbia and Albany Law School. She has been active in a number of human rights NGOs including Women's Rights Action Network (Australia), Women's Economic Equality Project (Canada), International Women's Rights Action Watch Asia Pacific (Malaysia), and International Women's Tribune Centre (New York). She helped draft a General Comment on women's equality for the Committee on Economic, Social and Cultural Rights and a General Recommendation on treaty obligations for the Committee on the Elimination of Discrimination Against Women.

**Sarah Song** is Professor of Law and Political Science at the University of California, Berkeley, USA. Her fields of interest include contemporary political and legal philosophy, the history of American political thought, and immigration and citizenship law. She has written on issues of democracy, multiculturalism, feminism, migration and citizenship. She is the author of the book, *Justice, Gender, and the Politics of Multiculturalism* (Cambridge University Press 2007). She is currently working on a book on the ethics of immigration policy.

**Ann Stewart** is Reader in Law/Associate Professor at the School of Law, University of Warwick, UK. Her research interests are in the areas of gender, international development and global justice. She has worked on collaborative projects in a number of jurisdictions, particularly in Southern and Eastern Africa, and South and South East Asia. Her recent publications include: *Gender, Law and Justice in a Global Market* (Cambridge University Press 2011); 'From Family to Personal Responsibility: The Challenges for Care of the Elderly in England' (2012) *Journal of Social Welfare Law and the Family*, forthcoming; 'Engendering Responsibility in Global Markets' in A. Perry-Kessaris (ed.), *Law in the Pursuit of Development: Theories into Practice?* (Routledge Cavendish 2010); and 'Who Do We Care About? Reflections on Gender Justice in a Global Market' (2007) *Northern Ireland Legal Quarterly*, 58(3), 358–374.

**Patricia Tuitt** is Professor of Law and Executive Dean at Birkbeck, University of London. Her research interests span the fields of international refugee law and human rights, and postcolonial theory and law – with a particular focus on European constitutionalism and the development of the European Union. Recent publications include 'From the State to the Union: International Law and the Appropriation of the New Europe' in *Events: The Force of International Law*, edited by F. Johns, R. Joyce and S. Pahuja (Routledge 2010). She is also author of *False Images: Law's Construction of the Refugee* (Pluto Press 1996) and *Race, Law and Resistance* (Glasshouse Press 2004).

**Margot Young** is Associate Professor in the Faculty of Law at the University of British Columbia, Canada. Her scholarship focuses on issues of gender equality as they compound social and economic rights. This work involves critical examination of Canadian constitutional law, as well as the assessment of Canadian social policy and social relations using a social justice lens. Margot collaborates with a range of community activists and researchers on a variety of community based research and engagement projects, including her recent lead involvement in an initiative looking at local issues of affordable and adequate housing as instrumental to the just city. Margot has published in the areas of constitutional equality law, social justice litigation and social welfare. She has worked extensively on non-governmental organizations' written submissions for periodic human rights review of Canada. Her publications include the co-editorship of *Poverty: Human Rights, Social Citizenship, and Legal Activism* (UBC Press 2007) and 'Social Justice and the Charter: Comparison and Choice' (2013) *Osgoode Hall Law Journal*, forthcoming.

# Editors' Introduction

## Margaret Davies and Vanessa E. Munro[1]

## Landscapes of Feminist Legal Theory

While feminism as a philosophical, political and critical approach has a far longer history, as a distinct scholarly contribution to *law*, feminist legal theory (FLT) is now well over three decades old. Those three decades have seen consolidation and renewal of its central concerns as well as remarkable growth, dynamism and change. This Companion aims to celebrate the strength of feminist legal thought, which is manifested in this dynamic combination of stability and change, as well as in the diversity of perspectives and methodologies, and the extensive range of subject matters, which are now included within its ambit. It provides an authoritative and scholarly review of contemporary feminist legal thought, and seeks to contribute to the ongoing development of some of its new approaches, perspectives and subject matters.

The specificity of feminist *legal* thought is that it engages in a sustained and critical way with legal concepts, legal theory, legal practice and areas of substantive legal doctrine. But while law provides the central site and stimulus of analysis, the 'legal' in FLT is clearly not intended to imply any kind of bright line separating law from other areas of social and political life: indeed, the nature and uniqueness of the 'legal' is itself questioned by feminist (and other critical) thinkers. As a result, FLT remains – akin to other forms of feminist theory and practice – intrinsically interdisciplinary in its methods and approaches. As the chapters in this collection repeatedly demonstrate, insights from philosophy, political theory, sociology, psychology, ecology, human geography, anthropology and a vast array of other fields of knowledge are strategically deployed in feminist engagements with the law, and the fluidity of the relationship between legal mandate and social interaction is routinely insisted upon.

In substantive terms, feminist legal scholars have, over the years, engaged with a rather long list of subjects. Equality, public participation, sexual and other forms of violence, family relationships, working conditions and other aspects of the material lives of women have, for example, long been at the core of feminist legal thought. So too have the various frameworks of rights which at the very least constitute an official endorsement of the idea of gender equality, and which have been heralded by some commentators as offering the potential for radical transformation of the ways in which law mediates prevailing gender–power relations. But over its lifespan to date, feminist legal theory has extended its reach, and is now engaging with an extraordinary range of others areas, including the regulation

---

1    The editors would like to thank Katie Cruz for her invaluable help in formatting the chapters included in this collection.

of health, the environment, war, development, taxation and migration. Though it is not possible in any one collection to fully do justice to the breadth of contemporary feminist legal scholarship, we hope – through the chapters that follow – to provide some insight into its diversity and scope.

There has also been an increasing reorientation away from an exclusive focus upon national states and their domestic concerns towards a more global consciousness, where lines of engagement and tension cross geo-political boundaries. As demonstrated in this collection, this has resulted in a feminist legal theory which, while remaining attentive to national jurisdictional concerns, also looks beyond these horizons to a complex terrain of multiple, intersecting political dynamics and issues. The ways in which the rise of economic neoliberalism, which has been promoted by powerful economies as well as by agencies such as the World Bank and International Monetary Fund, has impacted upon the formal and informal regulation of women's daily lives has, for example, been explored. So too, the current preoccupation with, and politicization of, flows of people as refugees, migrants, or trafficked 'victims' has been examined, set against a context in which international borders are increasingly fluid, the disparities between developed and developing nations are acute, poverty is feminized and drivers for displacement (such as war or famine) are prevalent. The consolidation of (and recent crises within) the European Union, as well as the development and instantiation within national jurisdictions of regional human rights frameworks, have also drawn the attention of contemporary feminist legal theorists beyond the domestic level.

Over time, moreover, not only have the doctrinal areas of concern to feminist legal theorists and the reach of their application expanded, so too the theoretical concepts and debates which circulate through their analyses have become increasingly complex. Whatever form it takes, feminist thought is centrally about the modalities of power which produce gendered social existence – whether power is located in law and state, in discourse, ideology, cultural practices, material life, micro-interactions or, more commonly these days, a coalescing of all of these factors. But a large number of intersecting concepts and analytical tools have been brought to bear upon this analysis of power in its myriad forms. Within the legal sphere, feminists have especially critiqued the individualistic focus of law and its limited conception of agency, the public/private distinction, the pervasive assumption of legal neutrality, the ethics of rationality and the foreclosure of an ethics of care, and the assumption that social change is pursued most effectively through law reform. Indeed, such conceptual debates have provided the theoretical building blocks of feminist legal thought and are iterated in various forms throughout feminist research. Yet, the ways in which these critiques have been developed, the relative scope for change through law that has been envisaged, and the extent to which women are capable of exercising power within the constraints of patriarchal privilege have been contested among feminists. In consequence, while it was once possible to see the broad contours of, and differences between, radical, cultural, socialist, liberal and postmodern feminism – and many of the chapters in this book address or allude to this recent history of feminist ideas – it is no longer easy to categorize feminist approaches in a clear-cut way. While the analysis offered by these 'strands' of feminism remains important and influential, feminist thought is now increasingly a network of ideas and concepts which crystallize or recede according to context and strategy. Grand theory, including a thoroughgoing postmodernism, is arguably in retreat and within feminist legal theory there has been a growing – and now embedded – recognition of the ways in which distributions of power are determined by the interaction of gender with other axes of social and economic differentiation, including race, sexuality, nationality, socio-economic status and religion.

Feminist legal theory, then, is now comprised of complex histories and many lines of interdisciplinary engagement. It is applied and conceptual, international and local, as well as self-questioning and linked into the dynamics of social and political change.

## This Book

Within this complex terrain, the aim of this Companion is, as far as possible, to provide a comprehensive and authoritative review of current research and new developments in the area of feminist legal theory. Bringing together contributors from a range of jurisdictions and legal traditions, the chapters provide a concise but critical review of existing theory in relation to many of the core issues or concepts that have animated, and continue to animate, feminist legal thought. In this context, of course, the boundaries that distinguish the 'legal' from the 'social' and 'political' are porous and artificially constructed, and many of the chapters reflect upon the interconnections between feminist critique of law and broader social domains, as well as interdisciplinary synergies.

The Companion is divided into three parts, dealing with 'Theory', 'Concepts' and 'Issues'. While the strong thematic currents which run through feminist legal thought, and the fact that general theory, key concepts and particular legal issues are mutually constitutive, means that there is no watertight logic that separates these three parts, the division is designed for pragmatic purposes to reflect at some level a movement from the more general to the more particular. The first part addresses theoretical questions which are of central significance to law, but which also connect to feminist theory at the broadest interdisciplinary level. These chapters consider theoretical debates over liberalism, materialism, freedom and agency, the jurisprudential framing of feminist legal theory, and feminist legal knowledge construction. Meanwhile, the 'Concepts' part draws on general feminist theory, but with a more specific focus on theoretical issues arising in legal contexts. These include the way race and racism is dealt with by law, multiculturalism, gender and sexuality, religion, and the conceptualization of equality. Finally, the 'Issues' section considers a range of more applied areas of substantive legal controversy, for example in relation to citizenship, human rights, violence against women, marriage and labour rights. The chapters in this section illustrate in specific settings the theoretical concerns raised in Parts I and II, and pose new questions of those theoretical approaches in a way that brings this collection, and indeed the feminist enterprise, full circle.

## The Chapters

### Part I

The first part of the book explores some of the large theoretical questions which characterize feminist legal theory – the nature of the individual, the role of law, the need to understand material circumstances, freedom, power, agency and knowledge construction. All of these chapters engage with the struggles of legal feminism in finding a path (or paths) through the complicated terrain of contemporary gender–power relations, and the role of law in their creation and perpetuation. Undoubtedly, many of the complications arise because of our intense awareness that theory itself is inevitably inadequate to the feminist project: as

Helene Cixous said, it is a 'dangerous aid' because it solidifies our thought and allows us to advance our understanding, but it is always an approximation which can be falsified (Cixous 1994: 4). There is no 'model' which provides a satisfactory approach to the many imperatives of feminist engagement with law. Instead feminists have found a multitude of pathways to follow in pursuit of these sometimes quite disparate goals, which include reimagining law without reinventing it, reconnecting feminist theory and activism, promoting a female-centric law without essentializing the 'female', valuing the material in dialogue with the discursive, and understanding agency in a world of constraint.

Feminist legal thought therefore tackles the gendered nature and practice of law, and its differential effects, from a variety of angles. Nonetheless, some foundational themes have emerged over the years and many of these are considered in the first chapter, by Rosemary Hunter. Hunter's chapter addresses the elements of the liberal legal system, surveying in the process features of feminist critique which remain fundamental even after some decades of scholarship. At their simplest, these elements are the legal person and the role of law. Although technically an abstract entity which can take a number of practical forms, the person has been imagined in nearly every legal context as socially masculine: 'rational, autonomous, self-contained, self-possessed, self-sufficient, and formally equal before the law' (Hunter, this volume). Liberal law is conceptualized in a similarly unhelpful way for women and its central distinction – public–private – perpetuates precisely those values associated with the liberal and masculine person. Hunter's chapter highlights very clearly the tension between feminism's many efforts to critique and reformulate both elements of liberal legalism, with law's own resistance to any deep conceptual change.

As Hunter illustrates, liberal law's focus on abstract reasoning and an abstract person leads to its dissociation from women's lives and their relationships, and the need to challenge this along a number of fronts. It is ironic, then, that in some quarters feminist theory itself, under the influence of postmodernism and poststructuralism, became detached throughout the 1990s and beyond from the material lives of women. Joanne Conaghan's chapter challenges the over-emphasis on textuality, which was one factor leading to the displacement of materialist analysis in feminist theory and more broadly. Conaghan's chapter surveys the various meanings of materialism and in particular highlights what is undoubtedly a resurgence in materialist thought, emphasizing its ongoing concerns with physical matter, with the nature of the human, and with the economic conditions which are such a vital constituent of social life and its inequalities. She argues that it is important to develop an approach which is neither entirely materialist nor discursive, neither modern nor postmodern, as 'these are simply two sides of an intellectually contrived divide' (Conaghan, this volume), but rather 'hybrid', and attentive to the 'entanglement' of humanly-constructed meanings and material reality.

The challenge of moving beyond simple theoretical binaries is also explored, though from a different angle, by Nancy Hirschmann in her chapter on freedom, power and agency. Hirschmann opens with the compelling claim that 'freedom is arguably the central theoretical question of feminism' and that 'it has lain at the heart of feminism since its inception' (Hirschmann, this volume). She continues by illustrating in detail the complexity of the idea of freedom in a world of constructions and constraints. For instance, contemporary feminism sees women as produced as subjects within a gendered and patriarchal world, rather than as pre-existing beings who are simply socialized by a biased set of cultural messages. By contrast, traditional concepts of freedom draw on a much simpler notion of the subject – one who is 'naturalized and unified'. In consequence, feminism has re-evaluated how freedom operates and what agency is, and in particular how it operates in a context where power is not just about restraint, domination or manipulation, but also about the production of subjectivity and the already-constrained contexts of agency. Hirschmann considers in particular the example of domestic violence, which brings into sharp focus the many practical complexities of exercising agency within a highly constrained context. She finally emphasizes the need to develop theoretical positions which can interact with legal and policy reforms in such a way as to enhance freedom and agency in such circumstances.

And finally in Part I, Margaret Davies' chapter explores the ways in which feminism challenges law's constructions of truth. Distinguishing between several types of legal truth – substantive, jurisprudential and declaratory – she argues that feminism has been very successful at challenging some but not all modalities of legal truth. Feminists have successfully deployed standpoint epistemology and empirical methods to contest narratives about women and gender which have been imported unquestioningly into the courtroom and other legal contexts. Nonetheless, like Rosemary Hunter, Davies points out the resilience of 'the truth about law', that is, that the central legal mythology of what law is remains remarkably static. Davies completes her chapter with some thoughts about alternative ways of understanding law, which might be drawn from socio-legal thought and legal anthropology.

## Part II

Whereas the chapters in the first part of the book address feminist legal thought at a very broad level and open up some large questions about subjectivity, freedom, knowledge and materiality, those in Part II focus on more specific themes, in particular questions of identity and difference, which intersect with a number of legal doctrinal areas. The first chapter by Elsje Bonthuys sets out the terrain of equality theory and law, while the subsequent four chapters each focus upon racial, religious, cultural and sexuality-based differences in women's identities and the ways in which these complexities have been addressed by law and by feminist theory.

Equality has been a foundational as well as a highly problematic notion for feminism. As Bonthuys explains, although rhetorically persuasive, the liberal notion of formal equality has been very difficult both practically and theoretically: it can lead to endless debates about the nature of the similarities and differences according to which equal treatment is measured; it often results in simplistic accounts of difference which neglect race, culture, sexuality, and other matters; and it can obscure the social and economic sources of inequality. Even expanded emphasis on substantive equality, which brings out the sources and nature of disadvantage in concrete settings, can have limitations. As Bonthuys charts, this has led some feminists to argue for the adoption of strategies to supplement the notion of equality, such as models based in social justice and welfare-oriented reforms, which endeavour to ensure full inclusion and participation, and an improvement of women's socio-economic status.

Sharon Cowan's chapter considers the foundational ideas of sex, gender and sexuality as they have been theorized within feminism. Cowan traces in detail the theory which has conceptualized and problematized these terms and which has offered sometimes quite startlingly different views about the relationship between them. From the familiar and analytically powerful sex/gender distinction emphasized by second wave feminism, through a number of key theorizations of sexuality by Catharine MacKinnon, Adrienne

Rich, Luce Irigaray, Monique Wittig and Judith Butler, Cowan explores the dynamic and often contested interpretations of sex, sexuality and gender as well as the politics of different theorizations of these ideas. The chapter concludes with some reflections about the challenges posed by queer and transgender politics, and about fruitful directions for future efforts in the theorizing of sexuality.

Both Bonthuy's and Cowan's chapters explicitly recognize the complexity of identity constructions, and the tendency of some feminist thought to emphasize gender and sex to the exclusion of other aspects of identity such as race, culture and religion. The final three chapters of this part focus specifically on these related yet distinct issues. Jen Nash's chapter begins with a discussion of twentieth-century theory about race, and in particular its rejection of the notion that racial categories are natural or biological. Asking '*what kind* of social construction race is' (Nash, this volume), Nash unpacks the production of race as embedded in everyday practices and state-based policies, and as a process of ongoing struggle and contestation over the meaning and boundaries of racial categories. Such dynamics, combined with the rejection of biologically-based racism, have made space for a 'new racism' which relies on more subtle categorizations but which nonetheless enforces racial divisions. In this context, proving discrimination has become increasingly difficult in the US in particular, where discriminatory intent (rather than effect) must be shown. Nash finally considers a range of new interventions in race theory, which bring different disciplinary insights into scholarship on intersectionality, the sensory codes of race construction, and the relationship between race and pleasure.

Membership of a cultural minority is another marker of difference among women which has highlighted the essentialist nature of any simple focus on women's identity. Sarah Song's chapter canvasses the debates raised by cultural recognition, within both liberal and feminist theory. As Song explains, culture has proved very controversial for feminism because of the perception that non-Western cultures are more patriarchal and oppressive, and therefore that integration by women into the dominant culture is a positive step. As Song argues, such perceptions can be based on a limited understanding of cultural practices (such as veiling), neglect the dynamic and hybrid nature of culture, and downplay the embeddedness of comparable norms within Western culture. Fortunately there are alternatives to assimilation, and Song considers and critiques three: a form of legal pluralism which has opt-in and opt-out provisions, a deliberative model which represents the voices of women as a specific constituent of cultural minorities, and an anthropological approach which focuses upon localized normative practices.

As factors in group identity, culture and religion overlap and intersect, but are rarely completely co-extensive. As a result, feminist thought regarding culture and religion deals with some similar and some distinct issues. In her chapter on religion and feminist legal theory, Samia Bano examines a set of issues which have become immensely fraught and controversial. Such controversies have been evident since postcolonial feminists, such as Gayatri Spivak, challenged the cultural bias of feminist discourse, but have clearly intensified in recent years with the increased visibility of Muslim populations in Western political contexts. After outlining the trajectory which feminist accounts of religion have taken in the West, Bano turns to the religion–gender axis as an illustration of intersectional analysis, and in particular how this plays out in discussions about agency. The understanding of agency is fundamental in debates over veiling and forced marriage and in particular whether agency is opposed simplistically to coercion, or (as also outlined in Nancy Hirschmann's chapter) seen as a reflective reaction to environmental constraints.

# Part III

Among the key methodological commitments of feminist (legal) theory is an attention to contextual analyses of social phenomena. As a result, there is, and always has been, an iterative relationship between abstract theorizations and concrete engagements. Theories have been inspired by and developed on the basis of 'ground-up' experiences, while our understandings of, challenges and responses to, those experiences have been enriched and informed by overarching hypotheses regarding structural constraints and binary exclusions. To this extent, there cannot be – and should not be – a sharp distinction between the broader theoretical and conceptual discussions that have animated Parts I and II of this collection and the more applied, contextual explorations that take place within Part III. That said, the chapters in this section take as their starting point a more concrete focus on a range of applied points of feminist concern or contention. Though wide ranging in their engagement with women's experiences, these chapters are not intended to be exhaustive, but to reflect the diversity of subject matters with which feminist legal theory has to date engaged.

Grounding her analysis in the broader discussions about core feminist issues, such as equality/difference and public/private, which were explored in the preceding parts of this collection, Margot Young's chapter reflects Part III's more applied focus by considering the implications of these debates in the specific context of citizenship. Highlighting the limitations (at least for feminist purposes) of traditional conceptions of liberal citizenship, Young also reflects critically upon the challenges that modern, neoliberal notions of citizenship may pose to women's calls for inclusion, recognition and representation. Having done so, she examines the more productive avenues that may be opened up for feminism by linking political theories of citizenship with insights into the spacialization of women's rights and responsibilities. Such an approach, she suggests, can help to ensure an approach to citizenship that not only reflects its amorphous and multi-scalar operation but adds vigour to gender-based critique.

Like Young, Diane Otto, in her chapter, also seeks to reimagine the frames and contours of feminist engagement with a core political and rhetorical device, namely human rights. Otto takes the reader through a careful genealogy of feminist engagements with human rights, specifically in the international legal context – from their early beginnings to the present day. Echoing some of the concerns regarding the relationship between sex and gender that were outlined in Cowan's chapter, she focuses particularly on a tendency therein towards dualistic representations of sex/gender and an asymmetrical commitment to women's gender-specific entitlements. Otto suggests that this has promoted a biologically determinist and overly-protectionist approach that restricts women's flourishing and excludes those who do not neatly fit the male/female binary. Without turning away from legal reform or feminist commitments, Otto explores the potential of strategies of gender mainstreaming, for example, to reimagine sex/gender in international human rights law in more progressive ways.

Meanwhile, Judith Gardam, returning to do a stock-take of feminists' engagement with the field of international humanitarian law after a period of absence, charts what she sees as an ongoing preoccupation with sexual violence against women in conditions of armed conflict. While the experience of sexual violence represents a serious violation both of women's individual personal autonomy and their collective security and equal status, Gardam cautions that privileging it at the expense of engaging critically with the myriad (and often more mundane) challenges faced by women in times of conflict is a problematic strategy. Gardam warns against too much celebration of the fact that feminists have been applauded for influencing the development of international criminal law's treatment of wartime rape in the face of a far more limited impact in other arenas, and suggests that the positioning of law in a particular – and punitive – mode within these responses may present its own difficulties.

The potential downsides of the increased currency that has apparently been afforded in recent years to the feminist 'Violence Against Women' agenda are also explored by Vanessa Munro in her discussion of the domestic (non-war time) context. Taking the UK as an illustrative example, Munro sketches the scale and significance of violence in women's daily lives, whilst emphasizing the malleability and fluidity of the boundaries of what counts as 'violence' across different sociological indices, theoretical frameworks and practical interventions. Munro situates this discussion against the context of modern forms of neoliberal governance, problematizing the ways in which the law (and more specifically, the criminal law) has been increasingly constructed as the primary mechanism through which to respond to women's experiences of, and precarity in the face of, sexual violence, with women being disciplined more and more into the role of responsible risk managers and survivors.

In their chapter, Marie Fox and Thérèse Murphy engage further with the ways in which women's bodies have been subjected to, and become scripts for the exercise of, patriarchal power, through a reflective mapping of the trajectory of feminist scholarship on health. They chart the development of this emerging genre for feminist legal theory through its preoccupation first with the body, then with a multiplicity of bodies, and more recently with the concept of (female) embodiment. Without denying the significance of insights regarding the operation of disciplinary biopower – in and beyond law – upon women's bodies, Fox and Murphy conclude by highlighting some of the conceptually and pragmatically important challenges that are yet to be adequately addressed by feminist legal theorists in this area, for example, in relation to issues of public health, resource allocation, dependency and human vulnerability.

This is not to say, of course, that there are not specific contexts of (bodily) dependency in relation to which feminist theory has long had a presence, perhaps the most obvious of these being pregnancy and motherhood. In Susan Boyd's chapter, she provides a thorough exposition of the difficulties and dilemmas posed to feminism by motherhood, both as a biological condition and a social construction. Focusing particularly on case studies of criminalized 'unfit' mothers and child custody disputes, Boyd illustrates the ways in which, notwithstanding decades of feminist critique, the law continues to impose certain normative constructions of motherhood; and in the context of the neoliberal state, reduces the responsibility of public bodies to support mothers in achieving these norms. To the extent that constructions, and experiences, of motherhood are bound up with notions of masculinity, gender, fatherhood, heteronormativity and the division of labour, Boyd advocates a focus on more transgressive forms of motherhood (for example, lesbian or single parenting), which she argues will allow us to forge a more substantial feminist challenge – and one that, crucially, avoids reinstating essentialist narratives of women's care or of a biological/genetic impulse.

Rosemary Auchmuty, in her chapter on marriage, similarly emphasizes the disciplinary and normative nature of the spousal relationship – or, more accurately, of the social constructions of meaning and the material structures of support built around the institution of marriage. Auchmuty provides a rich account of the history of feminist engagement with marriage, particularly in the UK context, from the Victorian period through to the present day. She exposes the dilemma which continues to exist – and which also now pervades discussions around same-sex civil partnership – over whether the most promising way to move forward is to abandon altogether the institution of marriage (on the basis that it cannot be disaggregated from patriarchy) or to seek to transform it 'from the inside' by creating, living out and thereby instantiating new (and more progressive) marital norms. Auchmuty concludes her chapter with a sobering reminder that there is no clear demarcation between free and forced in the context of marriage. Echoing the calls for a more nuanced understanding of agency expressed by Hirschmann and Bano, for example, in earlier chapters, Auchmuty highlights the ideological and material reality within which women have barely had the choice not to marry (without adverse consequence) which the concept of 'freedom' necessarily entails.

The structure and content of taxation policy is, of course, one significant material way in which the institution of marriage is both normalized and rendered a more appealing 'choice' for its entrants. In Åsa Gunnarsson's chapter, the tax incentives associated with marriage constitute but one among many of the myriad ways in which structural choices in taxation policy contribute to gender inequality. Gunnarsson, drawing on comparative insights across a range of quite different contemporary taxation systems, illustrates the extent to which a consciously gendered perspective is required in order to highlight the gendered outcomes of fiscal policies, and in order to ensure more progressive budgetary decisions by the state.

Picking up from Gunnarsson's insistence that the decision between paid work in the public sector and unpaid work in the household is fundamentally gendered, Judy Fudge, in her chapter, provides a critical overview of conceptual shifts in feminist engagement with labour law over recent decades. Insisting that what counts as labour law is ideological rather than conceptual, Fudge charts key shifts: (i) away from a focus on women as a unified category towards a more nuanced analysis of gender as a social construction; (ii) away from a preoccupation with formal contracts of employment towards a broader engagement with the labour market (including arenas of unpaid labour); and (iii) away from a faith in the potential for law as a simplistic mechanism for change towards a more complex understanding of the relationship between legal mandate and social reform. Seeking out a more robust conceptual basis for feminist engagement with, and reinvigoration of, labour law, Fudge examines paradigms grounded in human capabilities, as well as in a modified ethics of care approach.

This type of ethics of care approach is in turn developed further by Ann Stewart who, in her chapter, juxtaposes concerns regarding the gendered distribution of material goods (including the remunerations and protections associated with paid labour) with the broader context of globalization and neoliberalism. Stewart charts what she sees as a recent merging of discourses grounded in rights and those grounded in development analyses, which has led to the increasing deployment of rights based claims. Though such claims have had strategic, political and some practical benefits, Stewart laments what she sees as their relatively limited impact in terms of delivering a more equal world. She suggests that the language of rights has been too easily accommodated within neoliberal economic policies, ensuring a recognition of claims that is never adequately matched by a redistribution of resources. Inspired by an ethics of care approach, and drawing upon the feminist application of Karl Polyani's work that was initiated by Nancy Fraser, Stewart uses the specific example of Kenyan agricultural production to depict the potential for more satisfying and more just redistributive outcomes.

Like Stewart, in her strategic use of Polyani's work, Patricia Tuitt, in her chapter, turns to the work of perhaps unlikely feminist allies – namely Franz Fanon and Carl Schmitt – both to deconstruct dominant narratives and to fashion alternative feminist imaginings. Against the backdrop of the constitution of the European Union – with its regional free movement imperatives – Tuitt questions whether the so-called 'feminization of migration', which has often been welcomed by commentators as reflecting the increasing empowerment and equality of women (as self-willing, capable and rational migrants), is in fact reflective of a more sinister moment within which women have become key players in a process of violence and imposition that sweeps away existing structures through 'law-creating' acts of migration and ensures these women's 'inclusion' as citizens at the expense of the inclusion – indeed, the recognition – of others. Without necessarily seeking to 'roll back' these empirical shifts in the patterns of migration, Tuitt calls for a more circumspect approach by feminists to the underside of their operation, and for a more expansive engagement with the vulnerabilities that provoke, and are provoked by, migratory movements, whether one is in the position of traveller, 'settler' or 'native'.

Just as migration (whether free or forced) can provide a peculiarly precarious moment in the lives of many women, so too the existence of environmental risks can render women particularly vulnerable, often as a result of forces ostensibly beyond their control. In her chapter, Karen Morrow explores the nature and extent of this precarity, and reflects critically upon the contributions that have been made to date by so-called 'ecofeminism(s)'. Focusing particularly on the dual challenges of climate change and sustainable development, Morrow highlights the limits of feminism's influence on law and policy-making to date and underlines the urgency with which women's interests must be mobilized in order to bring about change. As the final chapter in this collection, Morrow's account offers a sobering reminder both of what is at stake for all of us in these environmental debates, as well as of the ways in which women's voices and energies, though brought to the fore by feminist theorists (in law and beyond) for several decades, risk being dangerously splintered and strategically sidelined.

# References

Cixous, H. 1994. *Rootprints: Memory and Life Writing*. London and New York: Routledge.

# Part I:
# Theoretical Questions in Feminist Legal Theory

# Contesting the Dominant Paradigm: Feminist Critiques of Liberal Legalism

## Rosemary Hunter

The concept of 'liberal legalism' refers to a set of assumptions found within law in societies and regimes (such as the international legal order) in which liberalism is the dominant political philosophy. These assumptions broadly concern: (a) the nature of the legal person; and (b) the role of law. This chapter will provide an account of both of these aspects of liberal legalism, and the feminist critiques to which they have been subject. Feminist critiques have been mounted from a variety of positions, ranging from liberal feminists challenging law to live up to its promises, to radical and postmodern feminists who, for different reasons, trenchantly reject the validity of the assumptions of liberal legalism. The chapter focuses on feminist critiques of liberal legalism rather than on internal debates within feminism, although these debates are evident in the different diagnoses of and responses to the perceived problems of liberal legalism.

## The Legal Person

As Ann Scales explains, two of the central tenets of liberalism are that the basic unit of society is the individual, who exists prior to social organization, and that individuals are rational and self-interested, and use their rationality to achieve their needs and desires (2006: 64). Consistently with these tenets, the legal person envisaged by liberal legalism is rational, autonomous, self-contained, self-possessed, self-sufficient and formally equal before the law. This person relates to others at arm's length through the mechanism of contract. In the words of Anna Grear, 'the paradigmatic liberal legal subject' is 'a socially decontextualized, hyper-rational, wilful individual systematically stripped of embodied particularities in order to appear neutral and, of course, theoretically genderless, serving the mediation of power linked to property and capital accumulation' (2011: 44). This makes it possible for a corporation as much as a human being to be considered a legal person.

Despite the appearance of neutrality and genderlessness, however, feminist critiques of the liberal legal person have noted its inherent masculinity. This argument is sometimes historical and empirical, and sometimes symbolic and normative. In the first account, privileged white men have populated law, shaped it in their own image, and instated their experience and view of the world as the legal norm, which has then come to be seen as universal, neutral, objective, inevitable and complete (Finley 1989: 892, Davies 1996: 72). The second, symbolic, account draws attention to the systematic associations within the Western imaginary between the characteristics of the legal person – rationality, autonomy, self-interest, objectivity, assertiveness, self-sufficiency, self-possession – and masculinity (see, for example, Naffine 2002: 81). We can see this masculine norm in the reasonable man of tort law and self-defence doctrine; the rational, self-interested actor of contract law; the responsible person of criminal law; the unencumbered worker of labour law; the rights-bearing individual of human rights; and the standard comparator of equality law (Finley 1989: 893, 896). These legal persons operate autonomously in the public sphere – it is difficult to imagine them, for example, changing nappies, cuddling children or breastfeeding (Naffine 2009: 158).

A significant consequence of the masculinity of the legal person is that women struggle to attain legal subjectivity. Again, this point may be understood both empirically and symbolically. Empirically, to the extent that law is built around an ideal type to which they do not conform, it creates problems for women and fails to take into account their lived reality and experiences. As Ngaire Naffine has pointed out, for example, 'women's bodies [are] not susceptible to the sort of self-mastery required of a self-proprietor' (1998: 203), and indeed for centuries women's bodies were seen as men's property (Naffine 1998: 204, 208–211). Even today, liberal legalism's autonomous, responsible subject is never pregnant and is not a wife (Naffine 2003: 365). And to the extent that they are excluded from legal subjectivity, women are also diminished, since liberal legal theory treats persons not fitting 'the normal model of autonomous, competent individual' as marginal, inferior and different (Minow 1990: 9–10).

On a symbolic level, the construction of the masculine as rational, objective and universal is premised on a binary construction of the feminine as its opposite – as irrational, subjective and particular. Thus, the legal person exists in a symbiotic hierarchy with the devalued feminine – his existence and power depend upon the negation and exclusion of the feminine (Naffine 2002: 81, 87). And again, as Margaret Thornton has noted, liberal legalism's essentialist representation of 'woman' as less than rational has been disabling for embodied women attempting to exercise legal subjectivity (1996: 30–31). One response to this observation has been Luce Irigaray's call for a legal regime that recognizes two, differentiated sexes rather than only one, universal (that is, male) sex (Irigaray 1993, 1994, 1996).

In her recent work, Naffine has argued for a more complex account of the legal person than that presented above. In contrast to her own earlier position, she now rejects the notion that 'law adopts a monolithic or singular or static view of the person which … either forces women out or obliges them to conform to it if they are to be regarded as persons too' (2011: 16). Rather, she argues that '[w]e need to acknowledge that law's concept of the person changes according to the guiding scheme of interpretation; that legal persons are therefore multiple rather than singular' (2011: 16). In her 2009 book *Law's Meaning of Life*, she identifies four views of the legal person: rationalist, religionist, naturalist and legalist. The rationalist sees the legal person as a rational actor, as found in liberal philosophy and criminal and contract law, whose capacity for reason is their most important characteristic. The religionist sees the legal person as a sacred being, whose most important characteristic is their human sanctity and inviolability, as found in human rights and medical law. The naturalist emphasizes the sovereign subject, the embodied and bounded self with rights to bodily integrity; while the legalist understands the legal person as simply 'an abstract device for endowing a capacity to bear rights and duties', with no fixed or essential characteristics.

Nevertheless, Naffine concedes that each of these legal persons has 'a masculine flavour', and thus continues to make it difficult for women *as women* to be persons in law

(2011: 16). In relation to the rationalist position, as noted above, women have traditionally been constructed as the opposite of rational (2011: 17), and even though [white] women were admitted to full public citizenship by the late 1920s, pregnant women are still not recognized in law as fully rational – their capacity for self-government in matters such as abortion remains legally limited (2011: 20). One might add that rape law continues at least to compromise women's capacity for sexual self-government, and that family law restricts the ability of separated mothers to determine how and where they and their children should live. The religionist version of the legal person as sacred and inviolable also has difficulties accommodating pregnant women (Naffine 2011: 18). The naturalist version of the legal person as a sovereign and bounded subject similarly has problems accounting for women's sexual and reproductive bodies (2011: 19). And according to Naffine, the legalist view has difficulty maintaining the separation of the legal from the human person in one or other of its patriarchal manifestations (2011: 19). It might also be observed that within the binary hierarchy referred to above, abstraction is associated with masculinity while the feminine is associated with particularity. Thus it would be easier for a legalist to see a man than a woman as an abstract legal person.

The empirical masculinity of the man of law in the form of lawyers and judges has led to calls by some feminists for greater representation of women in the legal profession and in the judiciary. For liberal feminists, this is an argument for law to finish what it began with the formal recognition of women as legal persons and the removal of barriers to women's entry to the professions in the early twentieth century, and to finally accord equal recognition to women's rationality (see, for example, Malleson 2003). Other feminists have argued that law needs to incorporate both sexes rather than just one; that women have important, gendered experiences and perspectives to bring to bear that will ensure legal rules and norms respond to a wider range of litigants and are more fully human (see, for example, Wilson 1990, Hale 2001, 2005, 2008, Rackley 2006, 2007, 2008). More controversially, some have relied on the cultural feminist argument that women reason in a 'different voice' characterized by an ethic of care (discussed below), which again has something valuable to offer to a law previously focused excessively upon individual rights (see, for example, Menkel-Meadow 1986, Sherry 1986, Wilson 1990).

The notion that women bring something different to lawyering and judging may, however, be perceived negatively rather than positively. As noted above, in the Western imaginary, woman's 'difference' has been seen to reside precisely in her non-rationality. This has rendered embodied women, in Thornton's words, 'fringe-dwellers of the jurisprudential community', not fully accepted as agents of legality due to their association with irrationality (1996: 3–4, 31). Moreover, the fact that the masculine in law has been universalized and appears under the guise of impartiality and neutrality means that women's perspectives are understood not as equally universal, but as particular, biased, special interests, not providing the degree of objectivity required for authoritative judgement (Thornton 1996: 6, Graycar and Morgan 2002: 57–58, Munro 2007: 49–50, see also Graycar 1998 and 2008). Thus, women's underrepresentation in the senior judiciary is justified due to their lack of the necessary 'merit' required for appointment.

One recent development within this debate has been the advent of feminist judgment-writing projects, in which feminist academics and lawyers have written 'alternative' judgments in prominent cases, in order to challenge established modes of legal authority, to highlight the masculinity of existing judgments and to demonstrate the results that a more inclusive judiciary might produce (see http://womenscourt.ca, www.feministjudgments.org.uk,

Hunter et al. 2010). Notably, however, these projects have explicitly brought *feminist* perspectives to judging rather than claiming to represent *women*'s perspectives or voices. They show how feminist legal theory may be applied in a practical context and illustrate differences within feminism, but they do not conflate women with feminists. This approach is consistent with broader calls for judicial diversity which are premised on the notion that conversations among judges with a wide range of backgrounds, life experiences and intellectual predispositions are necessary for law to attain democratic legitimacy (see, for example, Etherton 2010).

Another feminist line of attack on the liberal legal person has been Jennifer Nedelsky's call to reconceive autonomy (Nedelsky 2011). While other feminist legal scholars have also engaged with the concept of autonomy, it is important to distinguish Nedelksy's work from theirs. Robin West, for example, in her early article 'Jurisprudence and Gender', argues that the 'separation thesis' – the notion that human beings are physically separate from other human beings, and that separateness is epistemologically and morally prior to the relationships and cooperative arrangements that an individual may choose to form – is not true of women (1988: 1–2). Rather, women are 'essentially connected' to others, both materially and existentially, through pregnancy, sexual intercourse[1] and breastfeeding (1988: 3). She thus posits the 'connection thesis', which holds that '[w]omen are actually or potentially materially connected to other human life. Men aren't' (1988: 14). This view of a fundamental gender difference based on the presence or absence of connection locates West within the school of cultural feminism which seeks both to assert and to valorize women's difference from men.

Martha Fineman, by contrast, argues that all humans are dependent at some stage in their lives – in childhood, illness and old age – but caretaking for dependents is seen as a family responsibility and is usually undertaken by women. Because of this universal dependency, however, caretaking should instead be seen as a collective responsibility and care work better valued and resourced (2000, 2004: xiii–xvii). A 'societal commitment to the provision of basic social needs' would enable the achievement of true autonomy for all individuals based on a position of meaningful and widespread equality (2004: 29–30). In her later book, *Caring for Justice*, West comes closer to this position in acknowledging that connectedness is not unique to women, but that the beneficial work of maintaining care and connections is both disproportionately performed by women and insufficiently supported by law and society (1997: 1–5).

Nedelsky goes further than both of these theorists in arguing that liberalism is empirically wrong about autonomy in relation to all human beings all of the time. While liberal political and legal theories take atomistic individuals to be their basic unit, they fail to recognize 'the inherently social nature of human beings' (1989: 8). Social relations with others are *constitutive* of the human, not an optional add-on (1989: 8). In Nedelsky's view, however, this insight does not entail abandoning the concept of autonomy, which she argues remains valuable for feminism (1989: 7). Rather, it is necessary to reconceive autonomy not as an inherent quality of human beings but as a capacity that must be developed and sustained, and which can develop only in the context of relations with others (1989: 10–11). Relationships with others 'provide the support and guidance necessary for the development and experience

---

1    By contrast, as Nedelsky notes, the radical feminist view of sexual intercourse as the violation of a woman's bodily integrity is premised on the classical liberal notion of the bounded self (1990: 169–170).

of autonomy'; thus, relatedness is not the antithesis of autonomy but a precondition for it (1989: 12). This feminist version of relational autonomy then focuses attention on the kinds of relationships that promote (or diminish) autonomy, both interpersonal relationships and relationships with the bureaucratic state. We need to consider how to structure constructive relationships so that they foster rather than undermine autonomy (1990: 168).

Finally, postmodern feminists have critiqued the way in which liberal legalism's account of the legal person does not merely function as a representation of reality, but actively contributes to the construction of gender as a binary system, and of limited meanings and characteristics for 'masculine' and 'feminine' subjects and subjectivity (see, for example, Ahmed 1995: 58, Davies 1996: 4, Hunter 1996: 160, Naffine 2004). Mary Joe Frug, for example, notes that law produces differences and hierarchies between the sexes, and moreover produces these essentialized sexual differences and hierarchies as 'natural' (and hence as unquestionable) (1992: 128). Through an analysis of employment discrimination law, family law, and laws relating to sexual assault and prostitution, Frug (1992: 15–18, 32–33, 129–134) demonstrates how law produces the female body as terrorized ('a body that has learned to scurry, to cringe and to submit'), maternalized ('a body that is "for" maternity') and sexualized ('a body that is "for" sex with men', that is, both desirable and rapable) (1992: 129–130). This construction of the female body in turn affects how we dress, have sex, and regard ourselves and others (1992: 132). Similarly, Carol Smart argues that 'law operates as a technology of gender', 'a process of producing fixed gender identities', rather than merely applying to already gendered subjects (1992: 34). According to Smart, law brings into being 'both gendered subject positions as well as ... subjectivities or identities to which the individual becomes tied or associated'; thus 'Woman is a gendered subject position which legal discourse brings into being' (1992: 34). Smart, too, charts the rise of compulsory motherhood, showing how successive legislative provisions have constructed motherhood as 'natural' and unavoidable for heterosexually active women (1992: 37–39).

Continuing this theme, Sara Ahmed illustrates the way in which child support legislation constructs women as dependent on men and normalizes the heterosexual family, rendering women who have chosen to parent alone or in a lesbian relationship invisible and illegitimate (1995: 66–67). Ratna Kapur shows how the Indian courts' interpretations of sexual harassment prohibitions have reintroduced notions of sexual morality, chastity, and the cultural idealization of pure, modest Indian womanhood, with women claimants not conforming to these norms being denied protection (2005: 39–40). Sally Sheldon (1999) analyses law's gendered constructions of masculine and feminine reproductivity, demonstrating how UK foetal protection legislation, judicial endorsement of foetal protection policies, and legislation providing different degrees of civil liability of women and men for pre-natal injuries caused to children, construct the female reproductive body as weak, penetrable, volatile and uncontrollable, by contrast with the masculine heterosexual reproductive body which is constructed as strong, impermeable, stable and invulnerable. Within this legal discourse, too, men are constructed as breadwinners and women as primary carers. Thus, for instance, it is seen as acceptable for women to be excluded from workplaces involving high levels of exposure to environmental toxins, since the porous female body constitutes a potential danger to the foetus and thus requires control, surveillance and management, and since women are always potentially pregnant and their primary role is to nurture and care for children. The idealized, heterosexual male body, on the other hand, is not excluded from such workplaces, because it is considered strong and impermeable, and because of men's primary breadwinning role, even though men's sperm are equally if not more vulnerable to mutation as a result of environmental toxicity (Sheldon 1999: 133–134). Sheldon also contrasts the legal construction of the heterosexual male body with that of the gay male body which, in its obvious susceptibility to invasion and its consequent dangerousness to other bodies in the context of HIV/AIDS becomes 'feminized' (1999: 140), and notes also the differential racial and class constructions of potentially dangerous mothers in US and UK law, which account for differential forms of legal regulation (1999: 142).

As a consequence of this analysis of law's operation, both Frug and Smart argue that 'legal discourse should be recognized as a site of political struggle over sex differences' (Frug 1992: 126, Smart 1992: 39), and that feminist strategy should both contest the legal production and perpetuation of rigid identity categories that constrain women's ways of being in the world and 'construct an alternative version of reality' (Smart 1989: 2, 164, see also Cornell 1991: 151–152, Ahmed 1995: 69, Hunter 1996: 160). The feminist judgment-writing projects referred to above take up this challenge, albeit perhaps not in a way Smart might have envisaged (Hunter 2012), by rejecting naturalized gender differences, attempting to open up broader spaces for women to inhabit within law, and writing alternative understandings of women's diverse realities into the text of the law. The Canadian and UK projects offer, for example, 'alternative versions' to the limited, dismissive, uncomprehending or punitive accounts in the original judgments of infertile women (Harris-Short 2010), pregnant workers (Horton and James 2010), caring mothers (Bridgeman 2010, Hastings 2010), surrogate mothers (Ashenden 2010), lesbian 'other' mothers (Diduck 2010), lesbian marriage (Harding 2010), surety wives (Auchmuty 2010), young widows (Women's Court of Canada 2006b), women with learning disabilities (Bibbings 2010, Barker and Fox 2010), young unemployed women (Women's Court of Canada 2006c), elderly women (Carr and Hunter 2010), rape complainants (McGlynn 2010), Canadian Aboriginal women (Women's Court of Canada 2006a), Muslim schoolgirls (Malik 2010), and abused women in varying cultural contexts (Bano and Patel 2010, Munro and Shah 2010, Edwards 2010, Monaghan 2010).

Just as law constructs gender and gendered subjects, however, so too does feminist discourse. There is a danger, therefore, that feminist representations of women may be or become as rigid, limiting, constraining, totalizing and oppressive as legal representations. In other words, feminists risk creating our own normative Woman in place of law's version (see, for example, Frug 1992: 137, Smart 1992: 39, Hunter 1996, Kapur 2001, 2005, Halley 2008, Kotiswaran 2011). In order to mitigate this risk, feminists need to remain aware of our own historical location, avoid one-dimensional representations, present subjects as complex and multi-dimensional and focus on subjects and actions which have the capacity to disrupt existing norms (Kapur 2005: 128–131). Feminist counter-narratives – in judgments or otherwise – must ideally arise from a diversity of feminist voices and must remain contingent, contextualized, subject to discussion and debate, and open to critical scrutiny and revision (Hunter 2012). These desiderata would appear to be contrary to legal method, however, with its quest for certainty and predictability and its projection of apparently common sense and immutable truths. They suggest both a more transformative and a more modest potential for law than liberal legalism would traditionally endorse. It is to this question of law's role that the chapter now turns.

## The Role of Law

Liberal legalism posits law as an essentially benign, neutral and autonomous institution. It is connected to society in that its function is to assist in the coordination of social activities and the resolution of social problems. It does so according to shared moral values and political ideals, universal principles, rational argument, doctrine and logic. Law reform is seen as a valuable tool for resolving new or newly-discovered social problems and thus, legal change reflects social change. At the same time, liberalism imposes limits on the permissible scope of legal intervention in the social, particularly in relation to spheres of activity designated 'private', in order to maximize individual freedom (O'Donovan 1985: 2, Scales 2006: 64–65). Feminists have rejected this image of law as objective, impartial, progressive and self-limiting and have instead highlighted its tendencies to maintain and exacerbate inequality, exclusion and oppression (Munro 2007: 44, 50).

One key element of feminist critique has centred on the public/private distinction within liberal legalism and its construction of the 'private' as a sphere of legal non-intervention and one in which 'universal' norms such as equality and human rights do not apply (see, for example, Charlesworth 1995: 250, Philipps 2002: 45). Frances Olsen identifies three strands to this critique: first, arguments about where the boundary between 'public' and 'private' is drawn; secondly, arguments that the public/private distinction is incoherent; and thirdly, arguments that the appeal to privacy is both political and gendered; that private freedom belongs only to those with power (mostly men), and without it, privacy connotes insecurity, fear and oppression (often for women) (1993: 322–325). In practice, these strands of critique tend to overlap, with the third being a constant refrain.

In relation to the boundary between public and private, Olsen notes that the concept of 'privacy' 'is not a natural attribute nor descriptive in a factual sense, but rather is a political, contestable designation' (1993: 319). Since law plays a crucial role in constructing and maintaining the division between 'public' and 'private' (O'Donovan 1985: 3), it thus operates in a way that is inherently political (Olsen 1985: 836). So, for example, when law designates 'the family' as a zone of privacy into which the state does not intrude, it effectively refuses to regulate and thus permits and reinforces power differentials within families, manifested in internal hierarchies and inequalities (Okin 1991, Olsen 1985: 837, Auchmuty 2010), and in harms to women and children such as domestic violence (see, for example, Graycar and Morgan 2002: 12, Fineman and Mykitiuk 1994), marital rape (Graycar and Morgan 2002: 13) and child sexual abuse. Likewise, when the state promotes mediation and other forms of private ordering in family law, it tacitly sanctions the continuation of gendered power relations within the family (see, for example, Neave 1994, 1995, Graycar and Morgan 2002: 17).

Other examples of law's public/private distinctions include the refusal to allow tax-deductibility of childcare expenses, thus constructing those expenses as a matter of 'private' rather than state responsibility (Graycar and Morgan 2002: 18–19), a responsibility that falls primarily upon women. In the international law of armed conflict, a distinction is drawn between rape as an official policy of genocide or subjugation, and 'private' rapes in war which are not the subject of regulation, thus leaving many victims of wartime rape without redress (see, for example, Charlesworth 1995: 244). Moreover, the dividing line between public and private tends to be drawn differently according to one's race, class and sexuality (Boyd 1997: 12); so for example, Indigenous women and their children and those dependent on welfare enjoy considerably less family privacy than do white, middle class families (Boyd 1997: 20, Graycar and Morgan 2002: 14, 20).

Olsen's second strand of critique – that the public/private distinction is incoherent – is based on two arguments. The first is that law in fact intervenes equally in the 'public' and 'private' spheres; it simply does so in different ways in order to maintain the ideological distinction between the two. The private sphere is the subject of negative regulation and boundary definition. For example, failing to criminalize domestic violence influences behaviour within the family just as surely as positive criminalization would do. Contract law's presumption that there is no intention to enter into legal relations between family members and thus that agreements made within the private sphere of the family are unenforceable clearly regulates the nature of the relations that family members can (and cannot) have with each other (Graycar and Morgan 2002: 15). Legal policies concerning parental responsibility, parental authority, which groupings constitute a family and so on affect how people form families and how power and roles are distributed within them (Olsen 1985: 837). Far from being unregulated, 'the family is a major concern of the state' (Pateman 1983: 297); the notion of 'non-intervention' simply obscures state policy choices (Olsen 1985: 837). The second argument that the public/private distinction is incoherent is based on the observation that, despite the illusion of separation between them (O'Donovan 1985: 160), the public and private spheres are interdependent and mutually constitutive. Structures in the 'public' world of work produce power inequalities within the family, and the gender division of labour within families affects women's participation in the labour market (Pateman 1983: 282, 293, O'Donovan 1985: 12, 106–107). Likewise, '[t]he guarantees of justice and equality held out to citizens in the "public" sphere are worth systematically less to those who are pre-politically disadvantaged' (Lacey 1993: 97). Thus, attempts to reform either the public sphere or family relations are doomed to fail if they do not acknowledge the interconnections and challenge the dichotomy between the two (Olsen 1983: 1529–1530, O'Donovan 1985: 159).

The ideological function of the public/private distinction is seen clearly in the neoliberal 'turn' in political philosophy, governance and regulation, which has seen a shift:

> in the political orientation of the liberal state, whose role and responsibilities in relation to the life chances of its citizens [has been] reconfigured. Responsibility for individual welfare is less and less considered to be a matter of collective, social, or public obligation and is increasingly regarded as a private, individual or, at most, a family or charitable matter. (Fudge and Cossman 2002a: 3)

Neoliberalism embraces the notion that the state has inappropriately taken over a wide range of activities which are better left to the 'private' sector, in the form of the market, the community and the family (Kline 1997: 330, 336). Its central claim is 'that private choice is better than public regulation as a mechanism for allocating resources and ordering social affairs' (Philipps 2002: 41, Fudge and Cossman 2002b: 416). Thus, we have witnessed the retrenchment of the welfare state, the dismantling of social programmes, the privatization of public assets and services, and the expansion of the market and voluntary sector to take over many welfare state functions (Boyd 1997: 19, Kline 1997: 332, Philipps 2002: 70), but under significantly different conditions (see, for example, McDermont 2010, discussing the English case of *YL v Birmingham City Council* [2007] UKHL 27).

Feminist critiques of neoliberal privatization constitute an important recent development in feminist legal and political analysis. Feminist scholars have observed and documented the 'highly gendered implications' (Boyd 1997: 19) of privatization, which has simultaneously involved the reconfiguration of the gender order in relation to paid work (women's increased workforce participation and the demise of the male breadwinner), while the gender division of labour in relation to social reproduction has remained largely intact and arguably intensified (Fudge and Cossman 2002a: 25–26). Lisa Philipps notes, for example, that Canadian tax reforms since 1993 have reinforced the emphasis on individual, family and community responsibility to secure their own welfare, impacting on women as market actors, caregivers and contributors to the voluntary sector (Philipps 2002: 41–42). At the same time, pension reforms have shifted the locus of investment risk from the collective to the individual, which has exacerbated long-term disadvantages for non-standard workers, the majority of whom are women, who take time out of the workforce, work part-time, and/or are in temporary and precarious employment (Condon 2002). Family law and social welfare law increasingly emphasize the enforcement of private support obligations within families, via child support, spousal maintenance obligations, imputed financial support between adults sharing a household, and workfare for single mothers (Cossman 2002). These provisions enable society to benefit from women's social reproductive labour, while disallowing women and children's dependency on the state and enforcing their dependency on individual men, thus reinforcing male power and women's economic vulnerability (Barker 2012: 160–161).

Indeed, the focus of neoliberal family policy on the family's responsibility for the welfare of its members has encouraged a widening of the scope of 'family' in order to cast the net of responsibility more widely (Fudge and Cossman 2002a: 29, Barker 2012: 160). Thus, Nicola Barker argues that legal recognition of same-sex relationships 'fits seamlessly into a neoliberal privatizing agenda' (Barker 2012: 162), as lesbians and gay men are encouraged to take on the burdens of care, financial support and social reproduction (160). The differential impacts of privatization policies on racialized women, immigrant women, women with disabilities, and so on have also been identified (Fudge and Cossman 2002b: 409). Clearly, too, law continues to play a central role. The neoliberal privatization project is not one of deregulation, but of reregulation in the service of a new political agenda (Fudge and Cossman 2002a: 33, 2002b: 416, Philipps 2002: 41).

While some feminists have argued that the damaging effects of the public/private distinction for women may be overcome by extending the 'public' values of justice, rights and equality to areas traditionally designated as 'private', others have made the reverse argument, that values traditionally associated with the 'private' such as care, connection and empathy, should be extended to the public sphere. A prominent argument here has been the feminist ethics of care, which contends that liberal law's ethics of justice – based on the supposedly universal values of rights and formal equality – is both impoverished and founded on false premises (White and Tronto 2004). Human beings are not abstract, disconnected entities but are embodied subjects situated in particular social contexts and in complex relationships of interdependence with others (Gilligan 1982: 74, Tronto 1993: 162, Held 2005: 13). This is similar to Nedelsky's argument discussed earlier, but unlike Nedelsky, feminist care ethicists are not interested in rescuing liberal concepts such as autonomy for feminism, but in positing an alternative moral approach based on the value of caring.

Different versions of the ethics of care have been elaborated over the years. Earlier (1980s) versions posited the ethics of care as a specifically feminine ethics, derived from women's experience of maintaining relationships (Gilligan 1982) or, more specifically, from women's experience of mothering (Noddings 1984, West 1988). Later versions have tended to eschew such essentialist foundations and have described the ethics of care as a feminist ethics (Tronto 1993, Sevenhuijsen 1998, Held 2005, though compare Drakopoulou 2000), which better reflects the realities and diversity of women's as well as men's lives and concerns, and offers prescriptions for moral action which are capable of attending to and addressing gendered power differentials and inequalities (Sevenhuijsen 1998, Stewart 2011).

According to Selma Sevenhuijsen, the ethics of care as a moral activity requires judgements about 'what is the best course of action in specific circumstances', a question which engages situated, contextual reasoning rather than abstract reasoning or the application of a set of predetermined principles (1998: 59, 107). Moral problems are approached from an attitude of caring (Sevenhuijsen 1998: 83), a willingness to deploy emotions such as sympathy, empathy, sensitivity and responsiveness (Held 2005: 11), and a 'commitment to see issues from differing perspectives' (Sevenhuijsen 1998: 83). Caring involves sustaining relationships (Gilligan 1982: 30, 32), 'an ability and willingness to "see" and "hear" needs, and to take responsibility for those needs being met' (Sevenhuijsen 1998: 83), and recognition of differences in need (Gilligan 1982: 164). Joan Tronto has usefully distinguished four aspects of care: 'caring about', 'taking care of', 'care-giving' and 'care-receiving' (1993: 114). Notably, the first two tend to be performed by the more powerful in society, while the last two are more often done by the less powerful, and are socially devalued (1993: 114, 117, see also Smart and Neal 1999). Tronto further identifies four core values corresponding to these aspects of care: attentiveness (to the needs of others), responsibility (to care), competence (in care-giving) and responsiveness (of the care-receiver to care) (1993: 127–134).

In the legal context, the ethic of care might be put into practice in a number of ways. Reforms to family law, social security law and employment law could invest the work of nurturing and care with greater value (West 1997: 37, Finley 1989: 896, Tronto 1993: 165–166). In the field of child custody, Sevenhuijsen notes that men and women are in a position of mutual dependency and hence mutual vulnerability as parents (1998: 108). Instead of 'guaranteeing men authority rights to protect them from a (potential) dependency on women' (1998: 111) or maintaining 'the patriarchal view that, for men, connections can only be achieved by enforceable rights' (1998: 112), the law could seek to ensure that men develop greater competence and responsiveness as carers for their children and as receivers of care. At a more conceptual level, law could take a different approach to familiar dilemmas, constructing them not as issues of competing individual rights or interests to be resolved by the application of hierarchical normative principles, but as issues of conflicting responsibilities to be resolved by a contextual analysis that pays attention to relationships, needs, dependency and care (Gilligan 1982: 19, Finley 1989: 899–902, Tronto 1993: 164, Sevenhuijsen 1998: 107, see also McGlynn 2010). It should rely less upon abstract rules, principles and presumptions such as the 'right to family life', 'equality' or the priority of biological ties (Sevenhuijsen 1998: 120–121), and place more emphasis on justice as a process (Sevenhuijsen 1998: 115, 145) 'that is more cognizant of context and that focuses on particularity, cooperation and connection' (Munro 2007: 47).

This last point gives rise to the possibility of judging as a practice of care. In its liberal conception, '[j]udging with authority assumes that one stands above a situation, free of relationships and intimate ties' (Sevenhuijsen 1998: 113). By contrast, West argues that the goal of adjudication should not only be to achieve justice but also to exercise compassion, or care, for litigants (1997: 23; see also Sevenhuijsen 1998: 114). She contends that '[t]he judge-litigant relationship imposes caring constraints on decisions' (West 1997: 59, 52), including the requirement to take into account the individual circumstances and particularity of the parties rather than universalizing or commodifying them (1997: 54–55). According to West, many instances of glaring injustice in judicial decision-making could and should have been avoided by a more compassionate interpretation of the applicable law (1997: 48). West's argument and those of the other care theorists noted above bear many resemblances to the practices (if not always the stated intentions) of feminist judging identified in my analysis of the feminist judgment-writing projects and preceding literature (Hunter 2008, 2010).

The discussion of what the ethic of care might mean for law gives rise to the question of the relationship between the ethic of care and the ethic of justice. Some theorists have maintained that the two are simply incompatible, and the ethic of justice must give way to the superior ethic of care (Noddings 1984, Sevenhuijsen 1998: 34). Others have tried to find some accommodation between the two, by according them more or less salience in different fields (Held 2005), or seeing them as compatible, interrelated, and/or a necessary corrective to each other (Tronto 1993: 166–167, 171, White and Tronto 2004, Munro 2007: 27). At one extreme, West insists that justice and care are necessary conditions of each other – 'justice must be caring if it is to be just, and … care must be just if it is to be caring' (1997: 24) – and she provides numerous illustrations from case law of justice without care (which is ultimately unjust), and care without justice (which is ultimately uncaring). On the other hand, Anne Stewart, in a recent analysis of the gendered effects of globalized commodity chains and the marketization of care, takes the view that a care or relational analysis is more useful than a rights analysis in revealing global gender inequalities, and indeed provides a useful critique of both trade and rights discourses which have tended to prevail in discussions of globalization (2011: 7–8). According to Stewart, the care approach offers greater potential to recognize 'the way in which social and economic relations create injustice' (2011: 63–64), and also enables us to see how market, institutional, family and community relationships may be changed to avoid injustice (2011: 64).

The notion of an ethic of care has, however, been dismissed by radical feminists as simply women attempting to value 'what male supremacy has attributed to us for its own use' (MacKinnon 1987: 39). In the radical feminist view, exemplified by the writings of Catharine MacKinnon in the 1980s, the reality of social life is a gender hierarchy of men's power and domination and women's subordination and submission, imposed by force and marked in particular by men's control over, appropriation and objectification of women's sexuality (MacKinnon 1982: 529, 1983: 644, 1987: 3, 5, 1989: 51–52). Law, in this view, is one of the institutions of male power (1983: 645, 1989: 170). 'The law sees and treats women the way men see and treat women' (1983: 644). Liberal legalism's objectivist epistemology reflects the male perspective and legitimizes and reinforces existing distributions of power (1983: 645, 1989: 162–163, 237). Thus, when the state 'is most ruthlessly neutral, it will be most male'; when judges stick most closely to precedent and legislative intent they will most rigorously enforce male norms (1983: 658). In particular, liberal law fails to recognize and compensate the harms suffered by women under male supremacy, and instead ideologically justifies the harmful activities and defines them as not-harm (MacKinnon 1987).

Feminism's role, then, is to expose and try to change the social reality of women's subordination, placing 'women's experience, and the perspective from within that experience, at the center' of analysis and activism (MacKinnon 1989: 38, 1982: 536, see also 1989: chapter 5). Given the centrality of the appropriation of women's sexuality to the system of male power, radical feminist lawyers have been particularly concerned with laws relating to rape, sexual harassment, abortion, pornography and prostitution (see, for example, MacKinnon 1983: 646–655, 1987, 1989). While liberal legalism constitutes these issues as being about consent, morality, free speech and privacy, radical feminists see them as being about systemic sex discrimination. Radical feminist reforms would claim women's concrete reality of social discrimination and exploitation by men, such as sexual assault, pornography and prostitution, as forms of sex inequality – '[t]he main question would be: does a practice participate in the subordination of women to men?'– and would enable women to define and control their own sexuality (MacKinnon 1989: 244–248, 1987: 92).

This agenda achieved some tentative success in the 1980s with the introduction of the legal claim for sexual harassment, a claim which involved taking women's experience of violation seriously and marking 'the first time in history, to my knowledge, that women have defined women's injuries in law' (MacKinnon 1987: 105, 103). However, local ordinances enacted in Minneapolis and Indiana defining pornography involving 'the graphic sexually explicit subordination of women' as a violation of women's civil rights, and providing remedies for those injured by pornography (MacKinnon 1987: 175, 201, 210), were ultimately defeated by the assertion of the masculine value of constitutionally-protected free speech. Subsequently, radical feminist law reform efforts have extended to, and enjoyed somewhat greater success within, the international arena with a focus on violence against women as a violation of women's human rights (see, for example, MacKinnon 2006, United Nations General Assembly 2011), rape in the context of war and genocide (see, for example, McGlynn and Munro 2010), and action to end the international trafficking of women and girls for the purposes of sexual exploitation (see, for example, Barry 1979, Coalition Against Trafficking in Women 2012).

A final feminist challenge to liberal law's account of itself – and also to feminist law reform projects – has come from feminist legal theorists influenced by post-colonialism and post-structuralism, who have focused on the power of law to define and exclude its Others. Kapur, for example, has noted that in both the colonial encounter and the post-colonial era, Third World women have been constructed in law as victims of backward and uncivilized cultures, who exist outside the 'universal' liberal project. In order to attain liberal personhood and thereby obtain equality and rights, they require rescue from and must therefore abandon the oppressive cultural practices in which they are mired. But this definition is itself extremely oppressive for Third World women, rendering gender and cultural relations rigid and immutable and depriving women of the ability to act as agents within their own societies (2005: 2, 109–120).

Smart has observed the way in which law disqualifies other knowledges, including feminist knowledge (1989: 2, 11, 21) and has also argued that by continually looking to law to remedy harms to women, feminists simply legitimate law itself, endorsing its claims to be a force for good when this is far from empirically evident. Rather than seeking to extend the regulatory reach of law, feminists should 'resist … the creeping hegemony of the legal order' (1989: 5). While she has been careful to point out that this is not a prescription for feminists to disengage from law altogether (matters already in the legal domain cannot be abandoned, for example), Smart warns that instead of automatically assuming law's value and efficacy, the potential costs and benefits of deploying law in particular situations should be weighed up, recognizing that in some cases it may not be the best resource available (1995: 213). The structures of liberal law and the neoliberal restructuring of the state may severely limit the transformative potential of law reform efforts (Smart 1989: 115, 160, Thornton 1991: 456–458, Fudge and Cossman 2002b: 405, Hunter 2002). The costs of calling upon law may include the risks of reproducing and reinforcing limiting and constraining views of women, and of cooptation into conservative law and order, nationalist, religious and/or national security agendas (Thornton 1991: 464, Kapur 2005: esp. 120–128). On the other hand, as discussed earlier, by focusing on law not in its own (instrumental) terms but as a discourse which constructs knowledge and subjects, feminists ought to engage with law as a site of discursive struggle upon which to contest meanings about gender, culture and other normative categories (Smart 1989: 88, 165, 1992, 1995: 213, Kapur 2005: 3, 49, 129–131).

In postmodern times, however, the results of any feminist legal engagements will be uncertain. Law itself cannot be understood as having an essential character. It is neither simply an instrument of social coordination nor one of oppression. It is 'a complex and contradictory force', hence 'engagements with law do not produce certain outcomes, a stable subject, or clear victories' (Kapur 2005: 50, see also Sandland 1995). None of this means, according to Smart, that 'we have to abandon politics. But it does mean that we cannot make promises about what our politics will achieve' (1995: 214).

## Conclusion

Feminist politics clearly has not achieved the displacement of liberal legalism as the dominant legal form in nation states and international regimes which have inherited the Anglo-American legal tradition. While some concessions have been made to feminist critiques, liberal legalism's core claims about the role of law and the nature of the legal subject remain largely intact, and thus continue to impact adversely on women's lives and gendered subjectivities. The extension and reconfiguration of national and international legal orders in the interests of neoliberalism and globalization have occurred substantially within the same framework, and with obviously gendered effects. Feminist challenges are, therefore, also likely to continue.

This chapter has demonstrated that the nature of feminist critiques and the prescriptions offered have varied widely according to broader differences within feminist theory, ranging from calls from liberal feminists for liberalism fully to live up to its ideals (recent examples include Nussbaum 1999, Mullally 2006, Munro 2007: 51–61), to postmodern concerns to grapple with law at the level of discourse. Feminists have responded to changes in the political and legal environment, but have also been inventive, as seen, for example, in the hybrid blend of activism and critique represented by feminist judgment-writing projects (Hunter 2012). For all its disappointments and frustrations, then, it appears that for feminist legal scholarship, the encounter with liberal legalism has been and is likely to continue to be immensely productive.

## References

Ahmed, S. 1995. Deconstruction and law's other: Towards a feminist theory of embodied legal rights. *Social and Legal Studies*, 4(1), 55–73.

Ashenden, S. 2010. *Re N (A Child)*, in *Feminist Judgments: From Theory to Practice*, edited by R. Hunter et al. Oxford: Hart Publishing, 89–95.

Auchmuty, R. 2010. *Royal Bank of Scotland Plc v Etridge (No 2)*, in *Feminist Judgments: From Theory to Practice*, edited by R. Hunter et al. Oxford: Hart Publishing, 155–169.

Bano, S. and Patel, P. 2010. *R v Zoora (Ghulam) Shah*, in *Feminist Judgments: From Theory to Practice*, edited by R. Hunter et al. Oxford: Hart Publishing, 278–291.

Barker, N. 2012. *Not the Marrying Kind: A Feminist Critique of Same-Sex Marriage*. Basingstoke: Palgrave Macmillan.

Barker, N. and Fox, M. 2010. *Sheffield City Council v E*, in *Feminist Judgments: From Theory to Practice*, edited by R. Hunter et al. Oxford: Hart Publishing, 351–362.

Barry, K. 1979. *Female Sexual Slavery*. New York: New York University Press.

Bibbings, L. 2010. *R v Stone and Dobinson*, in *Feminist Judgments: From Theory to Practice*, edited by R. Hunter et al. Oxford: Hart Publishing, 234–240.

Boyd, S.B. 1997. Challenging the public/private divide: an overview, in *Challenging the Public/Private Divide: Feminism, Law and Public Policy*, edited by S.B. Boyd. Toronto: University of Toronto Press, 3–33.

Bridgeman, J. 2010. *R v Portsmouth Hospitals NHS Trust, ex parte Glass*, in *Feminist Judgments: From Theory to Practice*, edited by R. Hunter et al. Oxford: Hart Publishing, 369–378.

Carr, H. and Hunter, C. 2010. *YL v Birmingham City Council and Others*, in *Feminist Judgments: From Theory to Practice*, edited by R. Hunter et al. Oxford: Hart Publishing, 318–328.

Charlesworth, H. 1995. Worlds apart: Public/private distinctions in international law, in *Public and Private: Feminist Legal Debates*, edited by M. Thornton. Melbourne: Oxford University Press, 243–260.

Coalition Against Trafficking in Women. 2012. www.catwinternational.org. Accessed 8 August 2012.

Condon, M. 2002. Privatizing pension risk: Gender, law and financial markets, in *Privatization, Law, and the Challenge to Feminism*, edited by B. Cossman and J. Fudge. Toronto: University of Toronto Press, 128–165.

Cornell, D. 1991. *Beyond Accommodation: Ethical Feminism, Deconstruction and the Law*. New York: Routledge.

Cossman, B. 2002. Family feuds: Neo-liberal and neo-conservative visions of the reprivatisation project, in *Privatization, Law, and the Challenge to Feminism*, edited by B. Cossman and J. Fudge. Toronto: University of Toronto Press, 169–217.

Davies, M. 1996. *Delimiting the Law: 'Postmodernism' and the Politics of Law*. London: Pluto Press.

Diduck, A. 2010. *Re G (Children) (Residence: Same-Sex Partner)*, in *Feminist Judgments: From Theory to Practice*, edited by R. Hunter et al. Oxford: Hart Publishing, 102–113.

Drakopoulou, M. 2000. The ethic of care, female subjectivity and feminist legal scholarship. *Feminist Legal Studies*, 8(2), 199–226.

Edwards, S. 2010. *Attorney-General for Jersey v Holley*, in *Feminist Judgments: From Theory to Practice*, edited by R. Hunter et al. Oxford: Hart Publishing, 297–307.

Etherton, T. 2010. Liberty, the archetype and diversity: A philosophy of judging. *Public Law*, 2010, 727–747.

Fineman, M.A. 2000. Cracking the foundational myths: Independence, autonomy, self sufficiency. *American University Journal of Gender, Social Policy and Law*, 8(1), 13–29.

Fineman, M.A. 2004. *The Autonomy Myth: A Theory of Dependency*. New York: New Press.

Fineman, M.A. and Mykitiuk, R. (eds), 1994. *The Public Nature of Private Violence: The Discovery of Domestic Abuse*. New York: Routledge.

Finley, L.M. 1989. Breaking women's silence in law: The dilemma of the gendered nature of legal reasoning. *Notre Dame Law Review*, 64(5), 886–910.

Frug, M.J. 1992. *Postmodern Legal Feminism*. New York: Routledge.

Fudge, J. and Cossman, B. 2002a. Introduction: Privatization, law, and the challenge to feminism, in *Privatization, Law, and the Challenge to Feminism*, edited by B. Cossman and J. Fudge. Toronto: University of Toronto Press, 3–37.

Fudge, J. and Cossman, B. 2002b. Conclusion: Privatization, polarization and policy: feminism and the future, in *Privatization, Law, and the Challenge to Feminism*, edited by B. Cossman and J. Fudge. Toronto: University of Toronto Press, 403–420.

Gilligan, C. 1982. *In a Different Voice: Psychological Theory and Women's Development*. Cambridge, MA: Harvard University Press.

Graycar, R. 1998. The gender of judgments: Some reflections on bias. *University of British Columbia Law Review*, 32(1), 1–21.

Graycar, R. 2008. Gender, race, bias and perspective: Or, how otherness colours your judgment. *International Journal of the Legal Profession*, 15(1–2), 73–86.

Graycar, R. and Morgan, J. 2002. *The Hidden Gender of Law*. 2nd edn. Sydney: Federation Press.

Grear, A. 2011. Sexing the matrix: Embodiment, disembodiment and the law – towards the re-gendering of legal rationality, in *Gender, Sexualities and Law*, edited by J. Jones et al. Abingdon: Routledge, 39–52.

Hale, B. 2001. Equality and the judiciary: Why should we want more women judges. *Public Law*, 2001, 489–504.

Hale, B. 2005. Making a difference? Why we need a more diverse judiciary. *Northern Ireland Legal Quarterly*, 56(3), 281–292.

Hale, B. 2008. Maccabaean lecture in jurisprudence: A minority opinion? *Proceedings of the British Academy*, 154, 319–336.

Halley, J. 2008. *Split Decisions: How and Why to Take a Break from Feminism*. Princeton, NJ: Princeton University Press.

Harding, R. 2010. *Wilkinson v Kitzinger*, in *Feminist Judgments: From Theory to Practice*, edited by R. Hunter et al. Oxford: Hart Publishing, 430–442.

Harris-Short, S. 2010. *Evans v Amicus Healthcare Ltd*, in *Feminist Judgments: From Theory to Practice*, edited by R. Hunter et al. Oxford: Hart Publishing, 64–82.

Hastings, G. 2010. *Re A (Children) (Conjoined Twins: Surgical Separation)*, in *Feminist Judgments: From Theory to Practice*, edited by R. Hunter et al. Oxford: Hart Publishing, 139–146.

Held, V. 2005. *The Ethics of Care: Personal, Political and Global*. New York: Oxford University Press.

Horton, R. and James G. 2010. *Mundon v Del Monte Foods Ltd*, in *Feminist Judgments: From Theory to Practice*, edited by R. Hunter et al. Oxford: Hart Publishing, 407–413.

Hunter, R. 1996. Deconstructing the subjects of feminism: The essentialism debate in feminist theory and practice. *Australian Feminist Law Journal*, 6, 135–162.

Hunter, R. 2002. The mirage of justice: Women and the shrinking state. *Australian Feminist Law Journal*, 16, 53–74.

Hunter, R. 2008. Can *feminist* judges make a difference? *International Journal of the Legal Profession*, 15(1–2), 7–36.

Hunter, R. 2010. An account of feminist judging, in *Feminist Judgments: From Theory to Practice*, edited by R. Hunter et al. Oxford: Hart Publishing, 30–43.

Hunter, R. 2012. The power of feminist judgments? *Feminist Legal Studies*, 20(2), 135–148.

Hunter, R., McGlynn, C. and Rackley, E. (eds), 2010. *Feminist Judgments: From Theory to Practice*. Oxford: Hart Publishing.

Irigaray. L. 1993. *Je, tous, nous: Toward a Culture of Difference*, translated by A. Martin. New York: Routledge.

Irigaray, L. 1994. *Thinking the Difference: For a Peaceful Revolution*, translated by K. Montin. London: Athlone Press.

Irigaray, L. 1996. *I Love to You: Sketch for a Felicity Within History*, translated by A. Martin. New York: Routledge.

Kapur, R. 2001. Post-colonial economies of desire: Legal representations of the sexual subaltern. *Denver University Law Review*, 78(4), 855–885.

Kapur, R. 2005. *Erotic Justice: Law and the New Politics of Postcolonialism*. London: Glass House Press.

Kline, M. 1997. Blue meanies in Alberta: Tory tactics and the privatization of child welfare, in *Challenging the Public/Private Divide: Feminism, Law and Public Policy*, edited by Susan B. Boyd. Toronto: University of Toronto Press, 330–359.

Kotiswaran, P. 2011. *Dangerous Sex, Invisible Labor: Sex Work and the Law in India*. Princeton, NJ: Princeton University Press.

Lacey, N. 1993. Theory into practice? Pornography and the public/private dichotomy. *Journal of Law and Society*, 20(1), 93–113.

MacKinnon, C.A. 1982. Feminism, Marxism, method, and the state: An agenda for theory. *Signs*, 7(3), 515–544.

MacKinnon, C.A. 1983. Feminism, Marxism, method, and the state: Toward feminist jurisprudence. *Signs*, 8(4), 635–658.

MacKinnon, C.A. 1987. *Feminism Unmodified: Discourses on Life and Law*. Cambridge, MA: Harvard University Press.

MacKinnon, C.A. 1989. *Toward a Feminist Theory of the State*. Cambridge, MA: Harvard University Press.

MacKinnon, C.A. 2006. *Are Women Human? And Other International Dialogues*. Cambridge, MA: Harvard University Press.

Malik, M. 2010. *R (Begum) v Governors of Denbigh High School*, in *Feminist Judgments: From Theory to Practice*, edited by R. Hunter et al. Oxford: Hart Publishing, 336–345.

Malleson, K. 2003. Justifying gender equality on the bench: Why difference won't do. *Feminist Legal Studies*, 11(1), 1–24.

McDermont, M. 2010. Commentary on *YL v Birmingham City Council*, in *Feminist Judgments: From Theory to Practice*, edited by R. Hunter et al. Oxford: Hart Publishing, 311–317.

McGlynn, C. 2010. *R v A (No 2)*, in *Feminist Judgments: From Theory to Practice*, edited by R. Hunter et al. Oxford: Hart Publishing, 211–227.

McGlynn, C. and Munro, V. (eds), 2010. *Rethinking Rape Law: International and Comparative Perspectives*. Abingdon: Routledge.

Menkel-Meadow, C. 1986. The comparative sociology of women lawyers: The 'feminization' of the legal profession. *Osgoode Hall Law Journal*, 24(4), 897–918.

Minow, M. 1990. *Making All the Difference: Inclusion, Exclusion, and American Law*. Ithaca, NY: Cornell University Press.

Monaghan, K. 2010. *EM (Lebanon) v Secretary of State for the Home Department*, in *Feminist Judgments: From Theory to Practice*, edited by R. Hunter et al. Oxford: Hart Publishing, 449–458.

Mullally, S. 2006. *Gender, Culture and Human Rights: Reclaiming Universalism*. Oxford: Hart Publishing.

Munro, V. 2007. *Law and Politics and the Perimeter: Re-Evaluating Key Debates in Feminist Theory*. Oxford: Hart Publishing.

Munro, V. and Shah, S. 2010. R v Dhaliwal, in *Feminist Judgments: From Theory to Practice*, edited by R. Hunter et al. Oxford: Hart Publishing, 261–272.

Naffine, N. 1998. The legal structure of self-ownership: Or the self-possessed man and the woman possessed. *Journal of Law and Society*, 25(2), 193–212.

Naffine, N. 2002. Can women be legal persons? in *Visible Women: Essays on Feminist Legal Theory and Political Philosophy*, edited by S. James and S. Palmer. Oxford: Hart Publishing, 69–90.

Naffine, N. 2003. Who are law's persons? From Cheshire cats to responsible subjects. *Modern Law Review*, 66(3), 346–367.

Naffine, N. 2004. Our legal lives as men, women and persons. *Legal Studies*, 24(4), 621–642.

Naffine, N. 2009. *Law's Meaning of Life: Philosophy, Religion, Darwin and the Legal Person*. Oxford: Hart Publishing.

Naffine, N. 2011. Women and the cast of legal persons, in *Gender, Sexualities and Law*, edited by J. Jones et al. Abingdon: Routledge, 15–25.

Neave, M. 1994. Resolving the dilemma of difference: A critique of 'The role of private ordering in family law.' *University of Toronto Law Journal*, 44(1), 97–131.

Neave, M. 1995. Private ordering in family law – will women benefit? in *Public and Private: Feminist Legal Debates*, edited by M. Thornton. Melbourne: Oxford University Press, 144–173.

Nedelsky, J. 1989. Reconceiving autonomy: Sources, thoughts and possibilities. *Yale Journal of Law and Feminism*, 1(1), 7–36.

Nedelsky, J. 1990. Law, boundaries and the bounded self. *Representations*, 30(Spring), 162–189.

Nedelsky, J. 2011. *Law's Relations: A Relational Theory of Self, Autonomy and Law*. New York: Oxford University Press.

Noddings, N. 1984. *Caring: A Feminine Approach to Ethics and Moral Education*. Berkeley: University of California Press.

Nussbaum, M.C. 1999. *Sex and Social Justice*. New York: Oxford University Press.

O'Donovan, K. 1985. *Sexual Divisions in Law*. London: Weidenfeld & Nicolson.

Okin, S.M. 1991. *Justice, Gender and the Family*. New York: Basic Books.

Olsen, F.E. 1983. The family and the market: A study of ideology and legal reform. *Harvard Law Review*, 96(7), 1497–1578.

Olsen, F.E. 1985. The myth of state intervention in the family. *University of Michigan Journal of Law Reform*, 18, 835–864.

Olsen, F.E. 1993. Constitutional law: Feminist critiques of the public/private distinction. *Constitutional Commentary*, 10, 319–327.

Pateman, C. 1983. Feminist critiques of the public/private dichotomy, in *Public and Private in Social Life*, edited by S.I. Benn and G.F. Gaus. London: Croom Helm, 281–303.

Philipps, L. 2002. Tax law and social reproduction: The gender of fiscal policy in an age of privatization, in *Privatization, Law, and the Challenge to Feminism*, edited by B. Cossman and J. Fudge. Toronto: University of Toronto Press, 41–85.

Rackley, E. 2006. Difference in the House of Lords. *Social and Legal Studies*, 15(2), 163–185.

Rackley, E. 2007. Judicial diversity, the woman judge, and fairy tale endings. *Legal Studies*, 27(1), 74–94.

Rackley, E. 2008. What a difference difference makes: Gendered harms and judicial diversity. *International Journal of the Legal Profession*, 15(1–2), 37–56.

Sandland, R. 1995. Between 'truth' and 'difference': poststructuralism, law and the power of feminism. *Feminist Legal Studies*, 3(1), 3–47.

Scales, A. 2006. *Legal Feminism: Activism, Lawyering and Legal Theory*. New York: New York University Press.

Sevenhuijsen, S. 1998. *Citizenship and the Ethics of Care: Feminist Considerations on Justice, Morality and Politics*. London: Routledge.

Sheldon, S. 1999. Reconceiving masculinity: Imagining men's reproductive bodies in law. *Journal of Law and Society*, 26(2), 129–149.

Sherry, S. 1986. Civic virtue and the feminine voice in constitutional adjudication. *Virginia Law Review*, 72(3), 543–616.

Smart, C. 1989. *Feminism and the Power of Law*. London: Routledge.

Smart, C. 1992. The woman of legal discourse. *Social and Legal Studies*, 1(1), 29–44.

Smart, C. 1995. *Law, Crime and Sexuality: Essays in Feminism*. London: Sage.

Smart, C. and Neale, B. 1999. *Family Fragments?* Cambridge: Polity Press.

Stewart, A. 2011. *Gender, Law and Justice in a Global Market*. Cambridge: Cambridge University Press.

Thornton, M. 1991. Feminism and the contradictions of law reform. *International Journal of the Sociology of Law*, 19(4), 453–474.

Thornton, M. 1996. *Dissonance and Distrust: Women in the Legal Profession*. Melbourne: Oxford University Press.

Tronto, J.C. 1993. *Moral Boundaries: A Political Argument for an Ethic of Care*. New York: Routledge.

United Nations General Assembly. 2011. *Report of the Special Rapporteur on Violence against Women, its Causes and Consequences*. UN Doc. A/66/215.

White, J.A. and Tronto, J.C. 2004. Political practices of care: Needs and rights. *Ratio Juris*, 17(4), 425–453.

Wilson, B. 1990. Will women judges really make a difference? *Osgoode Hall Law Journal*, 28, 507–522.

West, R. 1988. Jurisprudence and gender. *University of Chicago Law Review*, 55(1), 1–72.

West, R. 1997. *Caring for Justice*. New York: New York University Press.

Women's Court of Canada. 2006a. Native Women's Association of Canada v Canada. *Canadian Journal of Women and the Law*, 18, 76–119.

Women's Court of Canada. 2006b. Law v Canada. *Canadian Journal of Women and the Law*, 18, 147–188.

Women's Court of Canada. 2006c. Gosselin v Québec (Attorney General). *Canadian Journal of Women and the Law*, 18, 193–249.

# Feminism, Law and Materialism: Reclaiming the 'Tainted' Realm

## Joanne Conaghan

## Introduction

> … *the guiding rule of procedure for most contemporary feminisms requires that one distance oneself as much as possible from the tainted realm of materiality by taking refuge within culture, discourse, and language. (Alaimo and Hekman 2008: 1)*

Over the last three decades it has become commonplace in critical scholarship to regard materialism as a discredited theoretical tradition which has been superseded by postmodernism, social and linguistic constructionism, and what is often referred to as 'the cultural turn'. This narrative of eschewal is familiar and closely linked to the widespread rejection of 'totalizing' theoretical projects, usually described in pejorative terms as 'grand theory' or 'metanarratives'.[1] In turn this stance is associated with critiques of Marxism, and to a lesser extent, radical feminism. However, the scope of anti-materialist denunciation is often wider, encompassing all forms of structuralism, modernism, or any adherence to the notion of objective access to a real/natural world or to the divisibility of language and reality (Alaimo and Hekman 2008: 2).

The reasons for the 'eclipse of materialism' (Coole and Frost 2010: 3) are complex and rarely subject to close scrutiny. They include a desire to avoid deterministic accounts of the social world that leave little room for resistance or human agency, challenge analyses of social inequality privileging economic or distributive concerns, and ensure proper recognition of other aspects of social relations and identity and the intersectional dimensions thereof. A postmodern suspicion of any invocation of 'the real' combined with enthusiastic endorsement of social constructionist approaches to the same has resulted in a critical tradition which is less grand and ambitious, more contingent and localized in its attentions. This has affected the content of theoretical engagement, encouraging the discursive decentring of the state, the reconceptualization of political space in less bounded, more fluid terms, and the relegation of class – a central concept in traditional social theory – to a 'bit part' in a series of endlessly dissolving analyses of identities, subjectivities and intersectionalities.

Nancy Fraser, neatly if controversially summed up these developing trends in the late 1990s when she observed a 'shift in the grammar of political claims-making' (Fraser 1997: 2). Fraser argued that the focus of political struggle had moved away from issues of redistribution towards a new politics of recognition, resulting in the 'decoupling of cultural politics from

---

1    Both terms coined by Lyotard (1984).

social politics and the relative eclipse of the latter by the former' (2). While Fraser's tone was tinged with regret, for many feminists the decimation of materialism affords little cause for lament. Moreover, in a legal context, the feminist attitude to materialism is best evidenced by its conspicuous absence from most contemporary accounts of feminist legal theory (see, for example, Munro 2007, Fineman 2011). On the rare occasion materialism *is* acknowledged (albeit obliquely as 'Marxism'), it is dismissed as having little to do with the role of law in society and therefore of no interest to feminist legal theory (Levit and Verchick 2006: 8). Thus has materialism been consigned to the twentieth-century archives of late modernism.

My purpose here is not expressly to disrupt this narrative or challenge its explanatory power although, like any account offering a broad-brush characterization of theoretical trends over different spatial, temporal, and disciplinary domains, it is vulnerable to charges of distortion, overgeneralization and unfounded assumptions. Moreover, it is never wise to pronounce the demise of a theoretical tradition; experience reveals a disconcerting cyclicity to theoretical endeavours not always apparent in the heat of the intellectual moment (as we shall see, materialism barely had time to succumb before it revived). However, acknowledging the fallibility of the narrative of eschewal does not mean it does not have wide academic purchase. I would suggest it does; in fact, it pretty much serves as the 'received' version of critical theory's past and present. This is the broad history of critical scholarship into which most new scholars are inducted, producing a generation of academics for whom materialism is at best a suspect tradition and at worst a theoretical field that has completely bypassed their consciousness.

This is no less the case within feminism. It is perhaps no coincidence that feminist theory began to achieve academic legitimacy during the intellectual maelstrom marking the transition from structuralist to poststructuralist, modernist to postmodernist theoretical paradigms. Indeed, feminism helped to precipitate the paradigmatic shift this transition represents. The discrediting of Marxism, for example, was aided by the failure of Marxist categories to provide an adequate account of women's subordination. The often convoluted efforts of a generation of feminists raised in the tradition of grand theorizing to offer a coherent analysis that simultaneously encompassed capitalism and patriarchy served only to underline the limitations of Marxism: feminists confronted a theoretical approach in which class and relations of production systematically trumped gender and relations of reproduction within an overarching, highly prescriptive framework leaving little apparent room for challenge or adaptation. It is hardly surprising that after extensive but largely unsatisfactory engagements within the received theoretical tradition (see, for example, Sargent 1981, Young 1997), many feminists raced to embrace the multiple potentialities of new modes of theorizing offered by postmodernism (see, for example, Nicholson 1990).

By the early 1990s, cultural theorist, Judith Butler (1990, 1993), was emerging as a particular influence in feminist legal theory. In theorizing sex and gender as cultural constructs in which sex is positioned as an *effect* of gender not its biological precondition (Butler 1990: 10), Butler's work is perhaps the most notable intervention marking the shift in theoretical attention away from the causes and consequences of women's disadvantage – in their many concrete, material contexts – towards engaging with the discursive processes and practices through which gendered subjectivities and identities are produced and the modes of and possibilities for disrupting or resisting them. Given the authority and cultural pervasiveness of law, Butler's approach lent itself remarkably well to feminist legal deployment (see, for example, Murphy 1997, Loizidou 1999). At the same time, while many of the reasons for this shift in feminist focus are well understood – indeed, were the outcome of a necessary and broadly progressive interrogation within feminism at the time (Drakopoulou 2000) – it soon became apparent that this theoretical reorientation did not come without costs.

As a framework for political, social and legal transformation, postmodernism has presented feminism with particularly pressing and seemingly irresolvable challenges: if knowledge is always situated and notions of truth, reason and objectivity are but the discursive creations of a foundationalist epistemology which must be jettisoned, how can feminists propound a positive programme for women's emancipation? If sex and gender lack any fixed or biological essence, indeed if gender categories are always suspect, upon what basis can women's identity as *women* be constructed? If women's experiences are so diverse as to preclude any appeal to commonality that does not inappropriately privilege some women over others (usually white, middle-class, Western women), who or what can feminism represent? Finally, if everything is the product of discourse, including our very selves – how are we to act as autonomous agents let alone as a political movement?

These are the kinds of questions with which academic feminism has been beset and as we struggle to answer them, we confront the many limits of the cultural turn. These include: the discursive disaggregation of subjects from their physical, biological, environmental and material contexts, producing the neglect of actual, living bodies; the repositioning of those bodies as scripts upon which discourse acts; and the loss of attention to the materiality of sex and sexed identity. Moreover, once the body as a living breathing entity falls out of the picture so also does the need to feed and clothe that body, put it to work, reproduce it daily and over the life cycle. As a result of the cultural turn, certain key concerns around the sexual division of labour, the interconnectedness of relations of production and reproduction, and the scale and persistence of women's economic disadvantage simply disappeared from the feminist theoretical agenda, notwithstanding their continued urgency in the 'real' world.

This led some legal feminists, including myself, to caution against the gap emerging between feminist scholarship and activism, a gap which was all the more acute in the context of law as a key site of feminist political struggle (Conaghan 2000: 354, Munro 2007: 2). Expressing my concerns at the millennium, I urged a change of direction in legal feminism on the grounds that '… close attention to the material lives of oppressed groups is a necessary task of any political project and … an important dimension to the intellectual goal of furthering our knowledge and enhancing our understanding of the world' (Conaghan 2000: 385). My call echoed that of others: Susan Boyd speculated that 'something is missing' from contemporary analyses of law and the family, producing the neglect of 'wider trends of globalisation, privatisation, and economic privation' (1999: 370). Margaret Thornton accused feminist legal scholarship of coming across as 'arcane and remote' and in the ideological grip of neo-liberalism (Thornton 2004: 16). To a number of academics then, feminist legal scholarship seemed to be approaching a theoretical and political dead end.

This sense of unease and lack of direction is not confined to law or feminism. Perhaps the best known articulation of critical *ennui* comes from Bruno Latour in 2004 expressing regret about the disengagement with reality occasioned by constructionism. Speculating that critical theory had 'run out of steam', Latour observed that:

> A certain form of critical spirit has sent us down the wrong path, encouraging us to fight the wrong enemies and, worst of all, to be considered as friends by the wrong sort of allies … The question was never to get **away** from facts but **closer** to them, not fighting empiricism but, on the contrary, renewing empiricism … the critical mind,

> if it is to renew itself and be relevant again, must cultivate a **stubbornly realist attitude** … (2004: 231)

How though, within a predominantly constructionist framework, *does* one cultivate a stubbornly realist attitude? Susan Hekman suggests that postmodernist scholars 'don't like to talk about reality because of its modernist association. So they simply ignore it' (Hekman 2010: 3). The result of this avoidance is an idea of reality as wholly absorbed by discourse, compelling no further interrogation other than constructionist terms. This is precisely what Latour warns us against. How can feminists and other critical scholars afford to ignore or theorize away the concrete material concerns of 'real' people? Is it possible or desirable theoretically to re-engage with reality without sacrificing the substantial insights of the linguistic turn? What might a postmodern materialist feminism look like and what would it entail for feminist legal scholarship and practice?

The purpose of this chapter is to offer a framework for exploring these questions by investigating the potentialities presented by ideas of materialism and materiality. The chapter draws, inter alia, from a burgeoning 'New Materialist' literature, spanning multiple disciplines and contexts, including but not limited to feminism. This literature seeks to counter the tendency to erase materiality from theoretical discourse while at the same time highlighting new understandings of the material in light of scientific and technological advances. Revisiting materialism, it is argued, offers new radical potentialities – ethical, conceptual, theoretical and political – in the wake of the postmodernist failure to provide an adequate theoretical base for an activist, politically transformative and materially grounded feminism. It offers a route out of what Stacy Alaimo and Susan Hekman describe as the 'impasse caused by the contemporary linguistic turn in feminist thought' (2008: 1). To this end, I want first to consider what we mean by the material and materialisms.

## Mapping the Material

> We live our everyday lives surrounded by, immersed in matter. We ourselves are composed of matter … How could we ignore the power of matter and the way it materializes in our ordinary experiences or fail to acknowledge the primacy of matter in our theories? (Coole and Frost 2010: 1)

The term 'material' is used in everyday conversation in various ways: it may refer to a fabric, for example cotton or silk, or it may be applied more generically to encompass any raw material from which things are made – wood, plastic and so on. In this sense, material denotes 'stuff' or 'matter', the constituent elements of 'things.' More generally, this notion of material tends to correspond with the physical or earthly world.

Another sense of material is linked to immersion in the everyday practical activities which contribute to human sustenance. For example, Margaret Davies characterizes materialism as attention to the 'everyday conditions of women's lives, particularly in relation to work, reproduction and caring responsibilities' (2008: 214). Given the contemporary theoretical preoccupation with the cultural and symbolic, some feminists call for *more* attention to be paid to the everyday conditions of women's lives. Martha Nussbaum, for example, censures Butler for 'turning away from the material side of life, towards a type of verbal and symbolic politics that makes only the flimsiest connections with the real situation of real women' (Nussbaum 1999). Nussbaum exhorts feminists to abjure the focus on language and discourse and turn to the situations of actual women, understood as living, breathing beings with practical material needs.

'Material' in this context often also assumes an economic or distributive hue. When Fraser observes that 'material inequality is on the rise in most of the world's countries' (Fraser 1997: 11), we know she alludes to economic or wealth-based inequality. In a related context, materialism may mean consumerism, as when Madonna sings about being a 'material girl living in a material world'. All these notions of material draw upon ideas of the real and they are often accompanied by a commitment to the existence of a reality unmediated by discourse, culture or intellectual abstractions.

A further common usage of material is in terms of significance or substantiality. This sense is evident in law; for example, in the requirement that an employer produce a genuine *material* factor other than sex to justify pay differences between men and women.[2] This meaning is also linked to a usage of 'matter' as in 'what's the matter?' or 'this issue really matters'. Etymologically, the word 'matter' derives from the Latin *materia*, meaning stuff from which things are made. However, it has also been linked to *mater*, the Latin for 'mother', and it is possible that the association of matter with importance, and relatedly, with origin or source, stems from this derivation. In any event, it is clear that 'material' and its various cognates, matter, materiality, and materialize (as in 'to give material substance to') are closely linked, both to each other and to the range of meanings which their ordinary usage denotes.

How do we get from meanings of matter and the material to an understanding of *materialism*? There are at least two core strands of theoretical materialism. The first is the philosophical tradition traceable back to the work of the Ancient Greek philosopher, Democritus, an early atomist in the fifth century BC.[3] This strand of materialism is concerned with the nature of matter, or, more broadly, with the composition of the natural/physical world and its relation to human thought. The *Oxford Companion to Philosophy* describes materialism as 'the view that everything is made of or derives from matter' (Honderich 1999: 530). This is often contrasted with idealism understood in Hegelian terms as the belief that ideas (or more broadly the mind/*geist*) constitute reality. In fact, viewing materialism through the crude idealism/materialism polarity is not helpful and it is perhaps not insignificant that in the new materialist literature, explanations of materialism tend to be less prescriptive and more open-ended than the *Companion* account. In their anthology of *New Materialisms*, Diana Coole and Samantha Frost explain materialism simply as 'ways of thinking about matter and processes of materialisation' (2010: 2). Similarly, Myra Hird describes (new) materialism as 'a keen interest in *engagements* with matter' (2009: 330). In both these contexts the key focus is on matter and theorization but without any particular allegiance to the idea that matter is theoretically predetermining. Not surprisingly, much of the scholarship in this tradition, particularly recently, engages with philosophies of science and nature.

By contrast, materialism in social theory and historical materialism in particular, turns the spotlight on the social: social relations, structures, processes, practices and the power dimensions therein. Historical materialism, the theoretical underpinning of Marxism,

---

2    Equal Pay Act 1970, s. 1(3), now incorporated in the Equality Act 2010, s. 69.
3    'Atomism' here can be understood as the idea that the world is composed of small indivisible particles, i.e., atoms.

begins with people and their practical needs – to feed, sustain and reproduce: our 'species needs' require us to work to subsist, producing over time a division of labour, its social organization and the development of technologies of production (Colebrook 2008: 60). In this sense, historical and philosophical materialism can be said to be similarly attentive to natural and/or biological concerns. Indeed, one reason why historical materialism has fallen from general favour is that it is often accused of presenting an essentialist conception of human nature (Edwards 2010: 282). However, it can be argued that, at least in some of his writings, for example, *The Economic and Philosophical Manuscripts 1844*, Marx resisted the idea of an essential, pre-social human nature and located nature firmly in the social (see further Kamenka 1983: 131–146).

In any event, from a starting point of basic human needs, Marx derives a theory of the materiality of history and the development of consciousness:

> *Men are the producers of their conceptions and ideas – real, active men as they are conditioned by a definitive development of their productive forces … Consciousness can never be anything other than conscious existence, and the existence of men is their actual life-process. (Kamenka 1983: 169)*

Attending to the 'life-process' requires engaging with 'real individuals, their activities and the material conditions in which they live' (163), specifically with those activities and relations necessary to subsistence. In this way, labour, and the institutions, processes and relations which structure labouring activities, emerge as the primary focus of study, including, Marx argues, historical study:

> *The first historical act is … the production of the means to satisfy [men's basic] needs, the production of material life itself. The first necessity therefore in any theory of history is to observe this fundamental fact in all its significance and all its implication and to accord it due importance. (171)*

Historical materialism then is a theory of history but one with descriptive and normative implications: as Marx famously remarked, historical materialism seeks not just to explain the world, but also 'to change it' (158). This aspiration to social transformation must, first and foremost, acknowledge the importance of materiality to the human condition. Thus, in his Preface to the *Critique of Political Economy*, Marx observes: 'It is not the consciousness of men that determines their being, but on the contrary, their social being that determines their consciousness' (160). Turning away from Hegelian idealism, Marx seeks to offer an account of historical and political change rooted in the practicalities of everyday life. From this core insight historical materialism has evolved primarily as a critique of capitalism but more broadly as an approach to analysing social change.

Historical materialism is frequently criticized for having 'totalizing' aspirations, a concern famously expressed in the slogan: 'Let us wage war on totality' (Lyotard 1984: 46).[4]

---

4   Kathi Weeks draws a useful distinction between 'totalizing theories' which tend to erase agency by 'reduc[ing] subjectivity to some functional effect of an abstract, determinable and monolithic system of structures' (1998: 4) and 'the aspiration to totality' which she describes as 'the methodological mandate to relate and connect' (71). Weeks argues that the aspiration to relate and connect individual subjectivity with wider, structural features of

Historical materialism is also routinely accused of privileging an economic 'base' over a social, political and cultural 'superstructure',[5] and of offering an essentially teleological view of history.[6] Such crude characterizations do little justice to such a rich and venerable tradition. It is important to remember that historical materialism did not spring full-grown and immutable from Marx's writings. It has had nearly two centuries to ferment and mature, yielding a range of diverse and sophisticated analyses, many of which simply do not warrant the kind of censure to which the tradition as a whole has been subjected. Far from forsaking contingency and complexity in favour of sweeping generalizations, grand axioms or universal postulates, there is a significant body of historical materialist literature in the tradition of E.P. Thompson and Ellen Meiksins Wood characterized by careful and painstaking study, fully attuned to the intricacies of particular social and historical contexts and the tensions and counteracting political forces therein (see, for example, Thompson 1980, Wood 1986, 1995). In these analyses, the theoretical focus remains firmly fixed on those social relations and processes imbricated in 'the production of life' (Hennessy and Ingraham 1997: 2) and their connection and relation to the 'immaterial' world of language, subjectivity, ideas and beliefs, imagination, value and affect (what is sometimes described as the relation between being and consciousness). In this sense and in contrast to the epistemological emphasis of the cultural turn, historical materialism – and materialism in general – is better understood as an ontological project. Indeed, one of the characterizing features of new materialism is the advocacy of a shift in theoretical focus from epistemology to ontology.

## New Materialism

> *Unprecedented things are currently being done with and to matter, nature, life production and reproduction. (Coole and Frost 2010: 4)*

Notwithstanding the theoretical aversion to materialism, recent years have witnessed the rise of a 'New Materialism' which is cross-disciplinary and encompasses a wide range of ideas and concerns.[7] Renewed engagement with materiality is the result of a wide combination of factors including: new scientific and technological developments requiring us to rethink our understandings of and relations to the physical world; a surge of academic interest in notions of embodiment (particularly in feminism); and increasing anxiety about the tenacious grip of neoliberalism and its far-reaching economic, political and cultural consequences.

---

social organization, for example, class or gender, does not require the adoption of a closed theoretical system or the denial of human agency.

5　　The base/superstructure metaphor actually plays only a limited role in Marx's writing. Ellen Meiksins Wood (1990) points outs that it owes more to Engels than to Marx and was taken up and reified in a Marxist–Leninist dogma which elevated a self-contained economic sphere over all others. Wood describes this as a 'distortion' of Marx's original insights (126). E.P. Thompson also challenges the base/superstructure metaphor, describing it as 'wrong' and 'radically defective' (1994: 218–220). Thompson emphasizes the marginality of base/superstructure in Marx's writing, pointing to alternative analogies used by Marx, for example, in the *Grundrisse*.

6　　Again a charge strongly disputed by, among others, Wood (1995: ch. 5).

7　　The account that follows draws from a range of sources, particularly Alaimo and Hekman 2008, Hekman 2010, Coole and Frost 2010, Hird 2004, 2009, Hird and Roberts 2011.

Much of new materialist scholarship concerns rethinking the materiality of the human body and conceptualizations of the physical world. Indeed, some new materialists explicitly distance themselves from the social theoretical tradition. Within feminism, a distinction is sometimes drawn between 'material feminism' and 'feminist materialism'. Myra Hird and Celia Roberts explain material feminism in philosophical terms as 'a critique of the ontological conditions that separate nature from culture' (2011: 211). By contrast, they see feminist materialism as concerned with 'women's material living conditions – labor, reproduction, political access, health, education, and intimacy – structured through class, race, ethnicity, age, nation, ableism, heteronormativity, and so on' (Hird 2009: 329). This distinction may be of practical help in identifying different foci or emphases within the new materialist literature, but mindful of the normative and conceptual constraints such classificatory exercises impose, I am inclined not to follow it and prefer to view the scope of new materialist writing as broadly as possible. Coole and Frost provide what I consider to be a far more useful and less prescriptive ordering of the literature around three core themes:

1. new scientific conceptualizations of matter;
2. new challenges to understandings of life and the human condition; and
3. new engagements with political economy in the context of the pressing urgency of contemporary socio-economic and political realities (2010: 7).

These three themes are united by a common aim – 'to give materiality its due' (329) and by a concern to move beyond the theoretical stalemate of the cultural turn.

## Rethinking the Physical World

A lot of new materialism takes its cue from recent scientific developments, specifically from newly emerging understandings of matter. Within science and philosophies of science, matter has traditionally been conceived as solid, tangible and inert, stuff which is acted *upon*:

> The predominant sense of matter in modern Western culture has been that it is essentially passive stuff, set in motion by human agents who use it as a means of survival, modify it as a vehicle of aesthetic expression, and impose subjective meanings upon it. This [is a] view of inert matter as inherently devoid of agency. (Coole 2010: 92)

This conception of matter has a long pedigree and corresponds to an essentially Newtonian conception of the physical world in which discrete objects are thought to tend naturally towards inertia, moving only when an external force or agent is applied to them (Newton's First Law of Motion). Inertia then is a core property of Newtonian matter. A similar conception of matter as solid and inert underpins the Cartesian dualism of mind and body (Gatens 1996: 109). Descartes defined matter as a corporeal substance constituted of length, breadth and thickness: so viewed, matter is fixed and measurable. More importantly matter defers to mind: in Cartesian terms, the mind is master of the body, and, by extension, man dominates nature. This yields a particular conception of cause and effect in which inert material substances are subject to external causal forces. Matter is without agency or spontaneity and causation is straightforwardly linear.

New Materialism seeks to conceive of matter in quite different terms, to encourage understandings of the material which are much less fixed and determined, much more ambiguous and complex. Much of this new thinking about matter derives from developments in theoretical physics.[8] To take two examples: Einstein's theory of relativity, by asserting that time and space are relative and not fixed, challenges the basic premises of Newtonian mechanics; similarly, advances in nuclear physics around the existence, configuration and activities of atomic and sub-atomic particles defy understandings of matter as solid, passive and inert. The particles which comprise matter, viewed through the lens of modern physics, are active, unstable, self-producing and mutating *agents*, a far cry from conceptions of matter as lifeless, inanimate 'stuff'.

I am sadly ill-equipped to offer any detailed account of the nature and implications of modern scientific developments.[9] However, one cannot fail to be intrigued by the way in which advances in modern science compel a transformation in the way in which we think about and imagine the physical world. Coole and Frost put it thus:

> *Conceiving matter as possessing its own modes of self-transformation, self-organization and directness, and thus no longer as simply passive or inert, disturbs the conventional sense that agents are exclusively humans who possess the cognitive abilities, intentionality and freedom to make autonomous decisions and the corollary presumption that humans have the right or ability to master nature. Instead the human species is being relocated within a natural environment whose material forces manifest certain agentic capacities and in which the domain of unintended or unanticipated effects is considerably broadened. (2010: 10)*

In this brave new world, the nature and effects of materiality cannot be ignored in our theoretical efforts to make sense of things. Matter *matters* because it plays an active role in processes of meaning and apprehension. In this sense, epistemology, as currently understood, must give some ground to ontology, including new investigations of the ontological premises upon which critical thinking, particularly that characterized by the cultural or linguistic turn, has been based. At the same time, the relation between being and consciousness, between nature and culture, emerges as much more complex and harder to grasp than any crude dichotomy between materialism and idealism would have us believe.

## Be(com)ing Human

What is the relation between bodies and selves? Who or what is an agent? What are the ontological and ethical underpinnings of distinctions between human and non-human, living and 'dead' matter? While materialism places 'man' and his 'species needs' at the heart of theorization, the cultural turn is often credited with turning its back on humanity, killing off the subject and with it any theoretical conception of human beings not premised on discursive construction: 'People are reduced to nodal points through which messages pass, and the self becomes dissolved into discursive structures' (Archer 2000: 3).

---

8    Although Gatens (1996: 55–58) argues that similar ideas can be found in the work of seventeenth-century philosopher, Baruch Spinoza.
9    For two excellent analyses of the philosophical implications of developments in scientific knowledge, see Pickering 1995 and Barad 2007.

Within this resolutely constructionist framework, material life has been almost completely overlooked. For example, it is striking that while the human body has attracted huge attention within postmodernist feminist theory, the focus for the most part has not been on the body per se but on discourses *around* and *about* the body. Within this theoretical frame the body is (re)presented as a product of discourse, its materiality ignored or treated as a 'brute given' upon which discourse acts (Bray and Colebrook 1998: 42). Thus are the realities of corporeality reduced to mere linguistic artefacts.

The case against postmodernism here is easy to overstate. As Hekman (2010) observes, some scholars we would most associate with the cultural or linguistic turn, for example, Wittgenstein and Foucault, interrogate the relationship between language and the real in more complex and multifaceted terms than is commonly acknowledged (Hekman 2010: Chapter 2 and 3). Moreover, feminist scholar, Donna Haraway, was probing the interface between discourse and materiality using the trope of the cyborg just as the postmodernist fascination with all things discursive was starting to take hold (Haraway 1990). Even Butler, who is perhaps most associated with the cultural turn in feminism, recognized the need to engage with the material, although some feminists have argued that Butler (1993) does not so much engage with materiality as theorize her way round it (Bray and Colebrook 1998, Barad 2007). The gist of Butler's argument is that materiality is a product of discursive practices, and that bodies, as we understand them, come into being – materialize – through the reiteration of regulatory norms, inter alia, of sexual difference. It follows that our perception of bodies as 'exterior', that is as outside or prior to discourse, is itself a discursive creation. Moreover, 'sex' is not a fact or a 'bodily given'; it is as much a cultural construct as 'gender'. The matter of bodies, Butler argues, is:

> indissociable from the regulatory norms that govern their materialization and the signification of those material effects … What constitutes the fixity of the body, its contours, its movements, will be fully material, but materiality will be rethought as the effect of power, as power's most productive effect. (Butler 1993: xii)

The difficulty with Butler's approach here is not so much that it is wrong; Butler is right to insist that our apprehension of the material world is discursively infused. However, the form her analysis takes permits us *only* to apprehend matter as construction. While Butler seems to acknowledge that matter is not wholly discursive – 'To claim that sexual differences are indissociable from discursive demarcations is not the same as claiming that discourse causes sexual difference' (xi) – in its *materializations*, she is effectively arguing, it is always so.

As a result, her analysis does not really allow us to 'get at' matter. Butler does not invite engagement with the *stuff* of bodies. Her approach forecloses exploration of what bodies *do* – how they come about, operate, act, mutate and expire – other than in constructionist terms. It encourages no consideration of how the discursive and material might 'intra-act'[10] in corporeal constitution and representation. In short, Butler's analysis affords no *agency* to the materiality of bodies. By contrast, many new materialists have explored ideas of agency

---

10    'Intra-action' is a term used by Barad (2007) to describe the 'entanglement of matter and meaning'. She uses 'intra' rather than 'inter' to avoid the presupposition that matter or meaning exist independently of each other: 'to be entangled is not simply to be intertwined with one another, as in the joining of separate entities, but to lack an independent, self-contained existence' (ix).

that encompass the agentic capacities of the natural/physical/material world. For example, Alaimo and Hekman claim that 'we need to talk about the materiality of the body itself as an active, sometimes recalcitrant force' (2008: 4). Andrew Pickering argues that 'human agents manoeuvre in a field of material agency' (1995: 7), that indeed we spend much of our everyday lives coping with such agency in the form of climatic variation, natural bodily processes and so forth. Karen Barad describes matter as 'a congealing of agency' (2008: 139). Barad advocates an understanding of discursive practices which goes beyond human-based activities to take proper account of the role of matter in conferring and configuring meaning. In so doing, Barad troubles the distinction between ontology and epistemology, arguing for a notion of 'onto-epistemology' which she explains as 'the study of practices of knowing in being' (Barad 2008: 147):

> There is an important sense in which practices of knowing cannot be fully claimed as human practices, not simply because we use nonhuman elements in our practices but because knowing is a matter of part of the world making itself intelligible to another part. Practices of knowing and being are not isolatable but rather they are mutually implicated. (147)

One of the most interesting features of this approach is that it allows us to acknowledge and engage with matter without at the same time reverting to modernist reaffirmations of dichotomous thinking that yield strict boundaries between the world and our knowledge of it. Returning again to Butler's work, Abigail Bray and Claire Colebrook (1998) have argued that notwithstanding Butler's best intentions, *Bodies that Matter* fails to escape the modernist dualities of mind and body, matter and its signification.[11] While Butler's focus on the body is an attempt precisely to challenge Cartesianism by arguing that the sexed body is an *effect* of gender rather than its precondition, her preoccupation with the discursive means that she fails to engage with corporeality other than as a *representational effect*. In this way she ends up perversely re–inscribing the mind/body dichotomy by positioning the body as a blank script upon which discourse acts.

By contrast, new materialism represents a genuine effort to give matter its due and to theorize the entanglement of mind and body, nature and culture, human and non-human forms of agency.[12] This is especially pertinent in the context of technological development. As technology fuses with human bodies to replace 'natural' bodily functions; as it is deployed to create human life in circumstances in which 'nature' would hitherto have denied; as, industrialized technologies effect the transformation, indeed threaten the very existence, of the 'natural world', how do we theorize the relation between nature and culture, between mind and matter, between the signifier and the signified? How do we account for natural disasters – not just scientifically but ethically and politically? How do resolve the difficult and seemingly irresolvable ethical – and often legal – dilemmas which new bodily technologies present? Coole and Frost put it thus:

> As scientists succeed in bridging species, artificially creating and extending human and animal life, and manipulating and synthesising genes to create new life forms,

---

11    Barad (2007) and Hekman (2010) offer a similar critique.
12    Actor Network Theory (ANT) is another way of acknowledging and theorizing non-human agency, see Latour 2005.

> *they muddle the concepts and boundaries that are the grounds for much ethical and political thinking. (2010: 22)*

Put simply, the conceptual and ethical map by which we have been navigating these issues requires substantial redrafting.

Once again this highlights the importance of ascribing agency. To whom or what do we attribute agency in these difficult, problem-solving contexts? While in a theoretical context agency has been most commonly understood as a feature of the human subject, new materialist perspectives clearly point towards a notion of agency – understood as active or agentic rather than intentional – which is far broader, encompassing much of what we might otherwise dismiss as 'dead' matter. Within this framing, it is no longer sufficient to attend only to discourse. We urgently require a practical theoretical accounting of the complex relation between the material world and human knowledge of that world which encompasses the creative and causative effects of material agency. We are also in need of a new conceptual and ethical vocabulary to aid our efforts to comprehend the nature and status of the human condition. That our notion of agency should embrace non-human agentic capacities, particularly in our analyses of causation and responsibility, does not mean we should discard those important values with which *human* agency is traditionally associated – values such as freedom, autonomy, integrity, identity and resistance. It does mean that we need to think much harder about how we frame such values, theoretically, ethically and in terms of our conceptions of social life.

## Political Economy after the Cultural Turn

> *"Late capitalism" is not just a vague abstraction; it is an array of contradictory global and local structural adjustments in the organization of production and consumption that is altering the way life is lived. (Hennessy 2000: 5)*

One of the most pernicious effects of the cultural turn is that it has encouraged a theoretical neglect of economic concerns at a time of rapid, radical economic transformation. Against the backdrop of new technological developments (especially in information and communication), growing international competitiveness, global economic restructuring, enhanced capital mobility, the irrepressible rise of flexible labour markets and new forms of (often precarious and low paid) work, dramatic growths in levels of wealth and economic inequality worldwide, all snugly embraced within the warm glow of neoliberal rhetoric and ideology, the critical academy turned away from any engagement with what was widely perceived as the economic determinism of Marxism and historical materialism. Unfortunately, with the abandonment of a theoretical framework in which economic considerations had always been foregrounded, came a theoretical *volte face* in which it was difficult to make any kind of theoretical assertion about the significance of economic relations and processes or to draw connections between economic conditions and exercises of power. It is within this context that Fraser drew attention to the demise of redistribution as a basis for political claims-making (Fraser 1997). More generally, the conceptual currency which emerged as dominant and which was preoccupied with matters of language, consciousness, subjectivity, identity and meaning, did not lend itself to analysis of the large scale, structural and systemic, economic, political and cultural changes taking place. Capitalism and class, labour and productive relations, the causes, course and consequences of severe and intensifying economic and wealth inequality simply fell for a while from academic view. From a feminist perspective, this was nothing short of disastrous for as Rosemary Hennessy points out: 'Women provide most of the world's socially necessary labour, that is, labour necessary to collective survival' (2000: 6). To abjure a focus on those activities necessary to our individual and collective survival was to disregard what is central to most women's lives.

This is increasingly recognized. There is evidence of real and pressing concern within the feminist academy and more generally to re-engage with issues of political economy (see, for example, Bedford and Rai 2010). But how do we do so without losing the benefits and insights of the cultural turn? How do we fashion a theoretical landscape for talking about the nature and functioning of contemporary capitalism that avoids the trap of economic determinism, is sensitive to temporal and spatial specificities, and takes full account of culture and signification in material contexts?

One difficulty here is that many contemporary scholars are insufficiently attuned to the diversity and sophistication of positions within the existing historical materialist tradition. An aversion to materialism has resulted in a lack of awareness of materialist engagements which do not posit an economic sphere as separate from or prior to other spheres (social, cultural and so on) and are not determining in any absolute or overriding way. Indeed long before the cultural turn, E.P. Thompson repeatedly insisted that what we understand as the economic or material is *irreducibly social*, is, in fact, constituted by social relations and practices:

> *I am calling in question … the notion that it is possible to describe a mode of production in "economic" terms leaving aside as "secondary" (less "real") the norms, the culture, the critical concepts around which this mode of production is organized. … we cannot even begin to describe feudal or capitalist society in 'economic' terms independently of the relations of power and domination, the concepts of use-right or private ownership (and attendant laws), the culturally endorsed norms and the culturally formed needs characteristic of the mode of production. (Thompson 1994: 219)*

Here Thompson is maintaining that the 'economic' is always already culturally infused. Indeed in its narrow conceptualization as a privileged sphere, it is itself a product of capitalist ideology (221). This is not to deny that capitalism as a mode of production shapes social relations and practices in significant ways – is, in some sense 'determinative'. However, Thompson's notion of determination is not as closed or impenetrable as is traditionally understood in Marxist theory. Thompson is influenced in this regard by Raymond Williams, an early exponent of cultural materialism, that is, the idea that culture is deeply imbricated in social organization and the mode of production (Williams 1958). According to Williams, 'determination' is a term with multiple meanings:

> *There is on the one hand the notion of an external cause which totally predicts or prefigures, indeed totally controls a subsequent activity. But there is also from the experience of social practice, a notion of determination as setting limits, exerting pressures … there is clearly a difference between a process of setting limits and exerting pressures whether by some external force or by the internal laws of a particular development, and that other process in which a subsequent content is essentially prefigured, predicted and controlled by a pre-existing external force. (Williams 1977: 83–85)*

Adopting Williams' notion of determination as 'setting limits' and/or 'exerting pressure on', Thompson offers a cautious endorsement of the materialist claim that social being *determines* social consciousness (Thompson 1978: 8). He argues that the capitalist mode of production (which, recall, he does not understand as narrowly economic but as irresolutely social) yields 'a "kernel" of characteristic human relationships – of exploitation, domination and acquisitiveness' (Thompson 1961: 28–29) which find expression in multiple and diverging ways, are historically inflected, and socially and culturally mediated. This is far removed from versions of mechanical materialism in which economic relations are said to be the base upon which the ideological superstructure perilously perches. Nor is Thompson endorsing an Althusserian notion of determination 'in the last instance' (Althusser 1969). He *is* affirming the central importance of human activities around subsistence to an understanding of the social world, insisting on a view of the relationship between social being and consciousness as 'in dialogue' (Thompson 1978: 8) and an understanding of the natural/material as always expressed in social relationships.

Within this frame we are better able to understand the relentless commitment in Thompson's writing to the historical role of human agency. Human struggle, Thompson contends, will always make a difference: 'changes in material life determine the conditions of … struggle and some of its character: but the particular outcome is determined by the struggle itself' (Thompson 1994: 222). A pertinent example of this approach is Thompson's analysis of wife sale, an English social practice of the eighteenth and nineteenth century (Thompson 1991) which, Thompson maintained, often functioned as a customary form of divorce and remarriage, so that even in the context of this most degrading practice, women could sometimes turn the situation to their own account. The custom formally required a wife's consent and evidence suggests that it was at least sometimes instigated by her to escape a relationship she no longer found satisfactory. Finding himself the focus of feminist criticism for depicting wife sales as anything other than 'yet one more example of the miserable oppression of women' (458), Thompson defended his position by cautioning against a reading of women's history 'as one of unrelieved victimhood' (460). Instead, Thompson emphasized the importance of acknowledging how women could exercise agency even in circumstances of extreme constraint. This was not an analysis in which the author felt bound to follow any 'totalizing' narrative, whether of capitalism, patriarchy or otherwise. As a result, Thompson was able to find 'something at work within the form [of wife sales] which sometimes contradicted its intention' (459), allowing the sale to work to the wife's advantage.

Thompson's historical approach constituted a new brand of 'socialist humanism' (Scott 1999: 70) that contrasted with the economism and mechanical materialism characterizing much of Marxist writing at the time. Moreover, his emphasis on the active role of individual human subjects in shaping their own histories ensured an account which, while continuing to foreground the material, was much more contextualized and much more attentive to social, cultural, spatial and temporal specificity. Nor is Thompson alone in offering a less prescriptive and more nuanced interpretation of historical materialism. Feminist scholar, Hekman (2010) suggests that elements in Marx's writing lend themselves to something other than strict economic determinism and the sharp separation of the natural and the social with which he is usually accredited. Focusing in particular on a close reading of *The Economic and Social Manuscripts*, Hekman argues that Marx's conceptualization of the relation between man and nature may be better understood 'as moving freely between the material and the discursive and indeed focusing on their interaction and inseparability' (2010: 119). In placing the necessity of human labour at the heart of his analysis, Marx is clearly making a claim about human existence, but not necessarily an essentialist claim about human nature. Indeed, much of Marxist theory seeks to challenge philosophical conceptualizations which posit the individual as separate from or prior to community (for example, liberalism) rather than as produced by and simultaneously productive of social relations.

The real point here is that neither Marx nor Marxism has to be reduced to a single orthodoxy which is itself a product of particular historical interpretations and developments and is not, in any absolute sense, necessary. We are as free in our readings of Marx as we are with other texts. This is the great legacy of postmodernism. Thus, in returning to and re-engaging with the insights of materialism, we should not consider ourselves bound by particular versions of the theoretical past. Indeed, it is this willingness to revisit afresh ideas and understandings which we have perhaps unthinkingly discarded or ignored which most characterizes new materialist writing.

## Towards a Feminist Legal Materialism

I began this essay by highlighting a concern in contemporary feminism that a gap had emerged between feminist theory and activism. In many ways, the theory/activism divide replicates the language/reality dichotomy which is the focus of much new materialist scholarship. Within law, this tension between theory and practice – and between the discursive and material – often lurks beneath the surface of debates about the strategic gains and risks of feminist engagement in law reform. On the one hand, feminists argue that law is a crucial site of political struggle and that strategic legal engagement holds the potential to produce concrete outcomes for women, making a substantial difference to the material conditions under which they live. On the other hand, it is asserted that feminist-inspired law reform can produce mixed even counter-productive results for women and is generally characterized by a process of uneven development (Smart 1986: 117). As a consequence, some feminists advocate the abandonment or at least substantial curtailment of law reform activities. We are encouraged to 'decentre' law as a strategy of reform and engage with it discursively (see, for example, Smart 1989; Fineman 1990), to approach it as a site of the construction and legitimation of regulatory norms and values which shape and inform meaning and produce gendered subjectivities and identities. This position is strongly influenced by a Foucauldian analysis of power which Smart in particular deploys to argue that the role of law in modern society is changing from an 'old' form of sovereign or juridical (top-down, state-based) power to a 'new' disciplinary modality in which law functions effectively as a 'claim to truth' that is an authenticating discourse which disqualifies or devalues other ways of seeing (Smart 1989: 4–25).

One way to view these two contrasting models of feminist legal engagement might be in terms of modernism and postmodernism respectively. Alternatively, one might invoke the material/discursive distinction to intimate that while law reform seeks directly to address the material realities of women's lives by providing new remedies or rights upon which they can rely, feminist engagements with law as discourse are less/not concerned with the material lives of 'real' women, focusing instead on the realm of immateriality, of subjectivity, consciousness, identity, selfhood and so on. This of course is a crude and rather misleading characterization which fails adequately to acknowledge the role which discursive and linguistic processes can play – in law and otherwise – in shaping the material realities of people's lives. However, where there is some resonance, or certainly cause for concern, is in the risk that discursive legal analyses, by virtue of their detachment from any material or empirical grounding, lose any sense of strategic or political purpose. Equally problematic is the tendency within such frames to treat political and legal goals 'as if they could be accomplished through theoretical fiat' (Eichner 2001: 6). A further common feature of discursive detachment lies in a preoccupation with social identities and subjectivities and a neglect to attend to, indeed, even to grasp the significance of social *relations*. Indeed some feminist scholars, adopting an identity-based approach, assume a position of intolerance in relation to any categorical deployment of sex or gender (on the grounds that they are 'mere' discursive constructions) notwithstanding their very real and concrete relational, distributional and hierarchical effects. If, on the other hand, we understand sex/gender not as identity but rather, drawing on the insights of historical materialism, in terms of relations and processes, the view that emerges is one in which sex/gender clearly operate as categories of social ordering but do not necessarily take any fixed or immutable form. Within a materialist frame, sex/gender can be conceived as active and evolving, fluctuating and mutating over time, space and context while simultaneously interacting with other material and discursive phenomena, including complexly configured, hierarchically imbued relations and processes (based on sexuality, class, race and so on) which produce multiple, intersecting inequalities (Conaghan 2008).

This point deserves further elaboration as it has presented such a dilemma to feminist legal scholars concerned to address problems of inequality without relying on sex/gender essentialism. The rejection of sex and gender as viable analytical categories is based first upon theoretical recognition that both categories are discursive constructs with no fixed essence or core. To deploy them as analytical categories is to endow them with a stability and authority that they lack. Moreover, to deploy them as markers of identity is to treat identity as unitary rather than fragmented and/or to privilege some aspects of identity (sex/gender) over others (race/sexuality/class and so forth). On the latter point, a focus on relations and processes rather than identity allows for the easier deployment of sex/gender as aspects of such relations and processes, alongside and in conjunction with other aspects (race/sexuality/class), with no necessary implication of privileging or denial of complexity or intersectionality. At the same time, to eschew sex/gender as categories of analysis because they are discursively infused and conceptually unstable is to assume that our categories and concepts are generally otherwise. Language *is* ambiguous, meanings do changes over time and space, and the value of concepts and categories lies not in their 'authenticity', their correspondence or otherwise with the real, but on the work that they do, their utility as analytical tools in the context of our efforts to understand and respond to problems of inequality and disadvantage. In that context, what is important is theoretically to anchor our concepts and categories to materiality not as *representations* of the real (thus falling back into the linguistic/reality divide) but as materially situated and intra-active. This requires a new openness about material-discursive encounters and an acceptance that materialism, including some versions of historical materialism, does not require the adoption of closed conceptual frames or crude models of causation. Nor are we compelled to adopt rigid conceptions of class or gender frozen in time and with no possibilities for mutual apprehension. On the contrary, materialism is an insistence that we pay attention to context and detail precisely to understand processes of change and development.

Most important, materialism reminds us that matter matters. The scholarship of cultural theorists such as Judith Butler allows us to conceive of sex/gender in performative terms, that is, as the citational reiteration of regulatory norms producing sexed bodies and gendered subjects, but it offers no entry into the nature and significance of materiality. By contrast, Karen Barad (2007) has reworked Butler's theory of performativity to emphasize the conjunction of material-discursive practices in the production of meaning. Barad insists on the relevance of materiality – of non-discursive processes – to processes of meaning conferral. She offers the example of foetal imaging via ultrasound (sonogram) to reflect upon what it means to 'see' the foetus on screen. In one sense it is technology which makes the 'seeing' possible; in another sense it is the material presence of new matter in the woman's body which we then 'see' as a foetus by bringing to bear our political and ethical conceptions of autonomous human life. The consequences of this technological–material–discursive encounter are significant in terms of how we perceive pregnancy, childbirth, women's bodies and human life. These consequences cannot be explained wholly in terms of discourse; at the same time they cannot be understood in terms of any sharp separation of language from the real. Barad's analysis offers a glimpse, I believe, of the potential of materialist approaches to advance our understanding of the relation between the world and our knowledge of it. This in turn will provide us with better conceptual and evaluative tools to assess law's operations and potential effects.

What becomes clear here is the need to resist conceptualizations of feminist legal engagement as *either* material or discursive, modern or postmodern, reform-based or theoretical. These are simply two sides of an intellectually contrived divide. Indeed, a lot of current scholarship is far better understood in hybrid terms, recognizing both the discursive dangers of law and its emancipatory potential, and requiring 'a contextual analysis towards the utility of legal strategies and … a permanently unclosed perspective on their benefits and burdens' (Munro and Stychin 2007: xii). In addition, positing the value of law in stark 'either/or' terms – as either an instrument which feminists can usefully deploy or an oppressive hegemonic discourse which they should resist – is to miss the complex inter- (or intra-) action of the material and discursive in a legal strategic context. The outcome of law reform initiatives will be shaped both by 'language' and 'reality', that is, by discursively imbued regulatory norms (which may or not surface in the context of particular legal engagements) *and* by the material circumstances in which they operate; moreover, the relation between the material and discursive here is neither causally direct nor easily untangled.

This is not necessarily a prescription for making law better correspond to what we conceive of as 'real'. The argument that law fails to reflect women's lives and experiences is commonly rehearsed in feminist legal scholarship. However, it may be that feminists are wrong here to see the problem as one of representation. It has been one of the core tenets of postmodernism to reject the idea of an objective reality 'out there' which can be accurately and dispassionately 'represented' by language (or by law). Instead, it has been argued that language or more broadly discourse is constitutive of the real, that there is no objective 'reality' to be represented, that our perceptions, experiences, our very sense of ourselves is discursively construed. The difficulty with this approach, as has been repeatedly pointed out, is that it has foreclosed any further engagement with materiality, understood as an aspect of the real which has now been reduced to discourse. So we move from a position where there is an objective reality which law does or should represent (hence, for example, positing a need to engage in law reform better to *represent* women's needs) or there is no reality only discourse, in which context there is nothing there to represent and we are free to explore the discursive potential of law as much as we like.

But of course there is something 'there' though how and whether to *represent* it is another matter. Materialism offers us a way out of the all-or-nothing dilemma of representionalism. Positing the world as a complex field of human and non-human agency and material–discursive intra-actions and practices, offers us an approach which is not reducible to any simple matrix of reality represented or representation made real. It does however provide us with avenues of theoretical exploration which we have hitherto abjured and it allows us better to apprehend the social world in all its complexity and unpredictability. Most importantly, it invites a conceptual, ethical, and contextual refocusing of feminism, including legal feminism, around material–discursive practices, their intra-action, and their concrete consequences in terms of how they impact upon people's lives.

# References

Alaimo, S. and Hekman, S. 2008. *Material Feminisms*. Bloomington and Indianopolis: Indiana University Press.

Althusser, L. 1969. *For Marx*. Translated by Ben Brewster. London: Verso.

Archer, M.S. 2000. *Being Human: the Problem of Agency*. Cambridge: Cambridge University Press.

Barad, K. 2007. *Meeting the Universe Halfway: Quantum Physics and the Entanglement of Matter and Meaning*. Durham, NC: Duke University Press.

Barad, K. 2008. Posthumanist performativity: towards an understanding of how matter comes to matter, in *Material Feminisms*, edited by S. Alaimo and S. Hekman. Bloomington & Indianapolis: Indiana University Press, 120–154.

Bedford, K. and Rai. S. 2010. Feminists theorize international political economy: the state of the field. *Signs: Journal of Women in Culture and Society*, 36(1), 1–18.

Bordo, S. 1998. Bringing body to theory, in *Body and Flesh*, edited by Donn Welton. Oxford: Blackwell, 84–97.

Boyd, S. 1999. Family law and sexuality: feminist engagements. *Social & Legal Studies*, 8(3), 369–390.

Bray, A. and Colebrook, C. 1998. The haunted flesh: Corporeal feminism and the politics of (dis)embodiment. *Signs: Journal of Women in Culture and Society*, 24(1), 35–67.

Brown, W. 1995. *States of Injury: Power and Freedom in Late Modernity*. Princeton: Princeton University Press.

Butler, J. 1990. *Gender Trouble: Feminism and the Subversion of Identity*. New York: Routledge.

Butler, J. 1993. *Bodies that Matter*. New York: Routledge.

Colebrook, C. 2008. On not becoming man: The materialist politics of unactualized potential, in *Material Feminisms*, edited by S. Alaimo and S. Hekman. Bloomington & Indianapolis: Indiana University Press, 52–84.

Conaghan, J. 2000. Reassessing the feminist theoretical project in law. *Journal of Law and Society*, 27(3), 351–385.

Conaghan, J. 2008. Intersectionality and the feminist project in law, in *Intersectionality and Beyond: Law, Power and the Politics of Location*, edited by E. Grabham, D. Cooper, J. Krishnadas and D. Herman. London: Routledge: Cavendish, 21–28.

Coole, D. 2010. The inertia of matter and the generativity of flesh, in *New Materialisms: Ontology, Agency and Politics*, edited by D. Coole and S. Frost. Durham: Duke University Press, 92–115.

Coole, D. and Frost, S. 2010. *New Materialisms: Ontology, Agency and Politics*. Durham: Duke University Press.

Davies, M. 2008. *Asking the Law Question*. 3rd edition. Sydney: Lawbook Co.

Drakopoulou, M. 2000. The ethic of care, female subjectivity and feminist legal scholarship. *Feminist Legal Studies*, 8(2), 199–226.

Edwards, J. 2010. The materialism of historical materialism, in *New Materialisms: Ontology, Agency and Politics*, edited by D. Coole and S. Frost. Durham: Duke University Press, 281–298.

Eichner, M. 2001. On Postmodern feminist legal theory. *Harvard Civil Rights–Civil Liberties Law Review*, 36, 1–77.

Fineman, M. 1990. Challenging law, establishing differences: the future of feminist legal scholarship. *Florida Law Review*, 42, 25–43.

Fineman, M. 2011. (ed.), *Transcending the Boundaries of Law: Generations of Feminism and Legal Theory*. New York: Routledge.

Fraser, N. 1997. *Justice Interruptus: Critical Reflections on the "Postsocialist" Condition*. New York: Routledge.

Gatens, M. 1996. *Imaginary Bodies: Ethics, Power and Corporeality*. London: Routledge.

Haraway, D. 1990. A manifesto for cyborgs: Science, technology and socialist feminism in the 1980s, in *Feminism/Postmodernism: Thinking Gender*, edited by L. Nicholson. New York: Routledge, 190–233.

Hekman, S. 2010. *The Material of Knowledge: Feminist Disclosures*. Bloomington & Indianapolis: Indiana University Press.

Hennessy, R. 2000. *Profit and Pleasure: Sexual Identities in Late Capitalism*. New York: Routledge.

Hennessy, R. and Ingraham, C. 1997. (eds), *Materialist Feminism: A Reader in Class, Difference, and Women's Lives*. New York: Routledge.

Hird, M. 2004. Feminist matters: new materialist considerations of sexual difference. *Feminist Theory*, 5(2), 223–232.

Hird, M. 2009. Feminist Engagements with Matter. *Feminist Studies*, 35(2), 329–346.

Hird, M. and Roberts, C. 2011. Feminism theorises the nonhuman. *Feminist Theory*, 12(2), 109–117.

Honderich, T. 1999. (ed.), *Oxford Companion to Philosophy*. Oxford: Oxford University Press.

Kamenka, E. 1983. *The Portable Karl Marx*. Harmondsworth: Penguin Books Ltd.

Latour, B. 1999. *Pandora's Hope: Essays on the Reality of Science Studies*. Cambridge, Ma: Harvard University Press.

Latour, B. 2004. Why has critique run out of steam? From matters of fact to matters of concern. *Critical Inquiry*, 30(2), 225–248.

Latour, B. 2005. *Reassembling the Social: An Introduction to Actor-Network-Theory*. Oxford: Oxford University Press. Levit, N. and Verchick, R. 2006. *Feminist Legal Theory*. New York: New York University Press.

Loizidou, E. 1999. The trouble with rape: gender matters and legal 'transformations.' *Feminist Legal Studies*, 7(3) 275–297.

Lyotard, J. 1984. *The Postmodern Condition: A Report on Knowledge*. Minneapolis: University of Minnesota Press.

Munro, V. 2007. *Law and Politics at the Perimeter: Re-evaluating Key Debates in Feminist Theory*. Oxford: Hart Publishing.

Munro, V. and Stychin, C. 2007, *Sexuality and the Law: Feminist Engagements*. London: Routledge-Cavendish.

Murphy, T. 1997. Feminism on flesh. *Law and Critique*, 8(1), 37–59.

Nicholson, L. 1990. (ed.), *Feminism/Postmodernism: Thinking Gender*. New York: Routledge.

Nussbaum, M. 1999. The professor of parody: the hip defeatism on Judith Butler. *The New Republic*, 220(8), 37–45.

Pickering, A. 1995. *The Mangle of Practice: Time, Agency and Science*. Chicago: University of Chicago Press.

Sargent, L. 1981. (ed.), *The Unhappy Marriage of Marxism and Feminism: A Debate on Class and Patriarchy*. London: Pluto Press.

Scott, J.W. 1999. *Gender and the Politics of History*. 2nd edn. New York: Columbia University Press.

Smart, C. 1986. Feminism and law: some problems of analysis and strategy. *International Journal of Sociology of Law*, 14(20, 109–123.

Smart, C. 1989. *Feminism and the Power of Law*. London: Routledge.

Thornton, M. 2004. Neo-liberal melancholia: the case of feminist legal scholarship. *Australian Feminist Law Journal*, 20, 7–22.

Thompson, E.P. 1961. The long revolution (Part I). *New Left Review*, 1/9, 24–33.

Thompson, E.P. 1978. *The Poverty of Theory and other Essays*. London: Merlin.

Thompson, E.P. 1980. *The Making of the English Working Class*. Harmondsworth: Penguin.

Thompson, E.P. 1991. *Customs in Common*. Harmondsworth: Penguin.

Thompson, E.P. 1994. *Making History: Writings on History and Culture*. New York: New York Press.

Weeks, K. 1995. *Constituting Feminist Subjects*. Ithaca, New York: Cornell University Press.

Williams, R. 1958. *Culture and Society: 1780–1950*. New York: Columbia University Press.

Williams, R. 1977. *Marxism and Literature*. Oxford: Oxford University Press.

Wood, E.M. 1986. *The Retreat from Class: for a New True Socialism*. London: Methuen.

Wood, E.M. 1990. Falling through the cracks: E.P. Thompson and the debate on base and superstructure, in *E.P. Thompson: Critical Perspectives*, edited by H.J. Kaye and K. McLelland. London: Polity Press, 125–152.

Wood, E.M. 1995. *Democracy against Capitalism: Renewing Historical Materialism*. Cambridge: Cambridge University Press.

Young, I.M. 1997. Socialist feminism and the limits of dual-systems theory, in *Materialist Feminism: A Reader in Class, Difference, and Women's Lives*, edited by R. Hennessy and C. Ingraham. New York: Routledge. 195–206.

# Freedom, Power and Agency in Feminist Legal Theory

### Nancy J. Hirschmann

Freedom is arguably the central theoretical question of feminism; it has lain at the heart of feminism since its inception. Feminists, both male and female, have sought to free humans from the constraints of gendered roles, rules, expectations and stereotypes. Freedom is a 'concept' to be sure – hence one might argue this chapter would be better placed in the second part of the present volume – but the centrality of freedom to the very meaning of feminism makes it foundational to feminist legal theory, as it is to feminist political theory and feminist philosophy.

One might argue further that feminist legal theory in particular, like the law itself, is more concerned with justice, that justice is the fulcrum on which all matters turn. But freedom underlies even that concern: for what animates claims of justice are times when women are unfairly restrained from doing things they wish to do, whether that involves work, sexual reproduction, sexual expression, movement, travel, or bodily integrity (Hirschmann 2013). Freedom is thus the core of feminist legal theory, and extends to questions beyond the meaning of the concept to the panoply of questions raised throughout this book about justice, autonomy, equality, difference, and most significantly, power.

## The Meaning of Freedom

Despite my protestations, of course, the meaning of the concept 'freedom' itself must be articulated if these other questions are to be addressed. We cannot say anything *about* freedom unless we have settled on a shared understanding of what the term means. And although freedom is such a commonplace idea, particularly for those in the West, that its meaning might seem intuitively obvious, in fact freedom is a complex and complicated concept.

In the middle of the twentieth century, noted Oxford philosopher and political theorist Isaiah Berlin outlined 'two concepts of liberty' that he called 'negative' and 'positive' liberty, and this scheme has dominated contemporary understandings in philosophy, political theory and law. The differences between these two models is a difference between the 'external' factors of freedom – conditions that prevent me from, or enable me in, doing what I want – and the 'internal' factors of desire and will, which determine what it is that I want to do in the first place. According to Berlin, in negative liberty theory an individual is free to the extent that she is not restrained by external forces, primarily viewed as law, physical force and other obvious forms of coercion. So, for instance, if I wanted to leave the house but my husband blocked the door, he would be restricting my freedom. 'By being free in this sense I mean not being interfered with by others. The wider the area of non-interference, the wider my freedom' (Berlin 1971: 123). Berlin's general notion that restraints come from outside the self, that they are alien to the self, they are 'other', is an important basic tenet of negative liberty; specifically, other humans' direct (or, in some cases, indirect) participation 'in frustrating my wishes' is the relevant criterion in determining restraint. Certainly, a desire may be formed in reaction to external stimuli – I may want to leave the house because there's a terrific shoe sale at the mall – but the important fact that negative libertarians point to is that this desire is *mine*, and I am responsible for acting on or resisting the desire (the mall isn't forcing me to come to the sale). Similarly, they are *conscious* desires in the sense that I have to know I have them; my desire for shoes may be a subconscious expression of my memories of childhood poverty and of hand-me-down shoes that were always falling apart; or perhaps it stems from anxiety about my appearance, so that if I just had the right pair of shoes I would feel sexy and gorgeous. Neither of these motivations, feminists might say, are particularly 'liberating'. But the relevant point for negative freedom is *that* I want it, and that I *know* I want it, rather than *why* I want it. Thus negative liberty draws clear-cut lines between inner and outer, subject and object, self and other.

Negative liberty expresses the dominant conception of freedom we find in both law and political philosophy since at least the seventeenth century (Hirschmann 2008). Thomas Hobbes famously declared: 'By liberty, is understood, according to the proper signification of the word, the absence of external impediments: which impediments, may oft take away part of man's power to do what he would' (Hobbes 1985: 189). John Locke similarly noted that 'we must consider what State all Men are naturally in, and that is *a State of perfect Freedom* to order their Actions, and dispose of their Possessions, and Persons as they think fit, within the bounds of the Law of Nature, without asking leave, or depending upon the Will of any other Man' (Locke 1963: 2.4). And John Stuart Mill, in his well-known essay *On Liberty*, argued for the primacy of pursuing 'our own good, in our own way' (Mill 1991). These classic statements of liberty are so well-known because they cohere with how we think of freedom in our everyday lives: I am most categorically free when I can do as I like, and most obviously unfree when I am prevented from doing what I want to do.

And yet consider the possibility, for instance, that my husband blocked the door because if I went to the shoe sale I would run up thousands of dollars more on our credit cards, which we already cannot pay off; we have been forced to sell our house because I bankrupted us, and have had to move twice since then because we fell behind in our rent, all because of my compulsive shopping. The credit card I will use has been obtained only after months of careful and responsible spending. Do we still think that my husband restrained my freedom? After all, his freedom would seem to be impeded by my behaviour, and of course my interference with his freedom is a legitimate reason for his interfering with mine, as Mill adamantly declared. But might we also think that his actions were intended to help liberate me from my compulsive spending? What if, instead of a shoe sale, I was leaving the house to meet my cocaine supplier, after months of struggling to remain clean and sober? What if my husband tried to prevent me leaving not because my addiction was impoverishing us – and thereby affecting his individual interest – but simply because he loves me and is trying to help me beat my addiction? We certainly can understand the attractiveness of the position that in preventing me from snorting cocaine, my husband might be preserving my freedom rather than inhibiting it.

This is where positive liberty is relevant. Positive liberty makes three contributions to expanding negative liberty. The most common and basic idea concerns provision of the conditions necessary to take advantage of negative liberties, such as providing wheelchair access to buildings or scholarships for education. Adopting a more contextual and communal notion of the self, positive liberty is able to view individual conditions such as disability, as well as social conditions such as poverty, as barriers to freedom that can be overcome by positive action, or the provision of conditions the individual cannot create on her own. Affirmative action could qualify as such an example, in helping women get hired in jobs and professions where there is a bias favouring men; or Title IX to provide better funding for women's sports. Both such measures do not merely eliminate barriers for women, but provide resources to permit women to develop their talents and skills and compete with men on a more level playing field.

A second contribution positive liberty makes involves its focus on 'internal barriers'. According to positive liberty, we can have 'second order desires', or 'desires about desires. We experience our desires and purposes as qualitatively discriminated, as higher or lower, noble or base, integrated or fragmented, significant or trivial, good and bad' (Taylor 1979: 184). Because of these conflicting capacities, it is not enough to experience an absence of external restraints, because the immediate desires I have may frustrate my true will – like my desire to snort cocaine when I've been struggling to quit.

This, however, allows for the possibility that others can assess my desires better than I can, particularly when I'm in the grip of those 'enslaving' passions. As I struggle to get by my husband, shouting 'let me out!' he firmly believes that it is in my true interest not to snort cocaine or buy more shoes, and so continues to block me until I land in a sobbing heap on the floor. Charles Taylor (1979) called this the 'second guessing' problem, because others claim to know what you want better than you do yourself. It is the most troubling aspect of positive liberty: determination of the will by others – not just preventing you from doing what you want 'for your own good', but claiming that such prevention is actually what you want.

This second guessing is particularly problematic when it is done by the state, illustrated most infamously by Jean-Jacques Rousseau's (1973) general will. Rousseau argued that, since the laws embody the true will, then by forcing me to obey the law the state is only 'forcing me to be free'--that is, to follow my true will, whether I know it or not. This is the Soviet-era nightmare that Berlin particularly argued against in 'Two Concepts of Liberty.' Indeed, it is because of the context of Cold War politics that the internal dimensions of freedom were generally ignored by twentieth-century freedom theorists; they were associated with totalitarian mind control, whereas Western liberal democracy was seen as providing for the maximum amount of freedom from restriction to follow one's own mind.

Berlin's concern is one many people in the West share, and particularly feminists. Feminists from Mary Wollstonecraft to Simone de Beauvoir and Betty Friedan to any number of contemporary feminist critics of modern Enlightenment philosophers like Immanuel Kant and Rousseau have critiqued decades, if not centuries, of men's declaring that they know better than women what women really want, because women are supposedly too emotional and irrational to know what they want themselves (de Beauvoir 1974, Friedan 1963, Lange 2002, Schott, 1997, Wollstonecraft 1985). And of course law has been a key instrument in enacting such paternalism; in the realm of property, ranging from forbidding women's inheritance to laws giving control of married women's property to their husbands; in the realm of education and employment, where women were excluded from education and a wide variety of professions, and even at times from being allowed to work for money, particularly if married; and in the realm of the family, in which women's personhood was subsumed by their fathers and then their husbands, whom, in the marriage 'contract,' they were sworn to 'obey' and who entirely subsumed their wives' 'civil personality' (Blackstone 1786, Hirschmann 2008, Mendelson and Crawford 1998).

But what positive liberty contributes to our understanding of freedom is the depth to which I can have *conflicting* desires and a *divided* will: I really want to quit cocaine, but I really want to snort it, too. I really want some new shoes, but I really want a stable life with my husband where we aren't always in debt. Most people would probably agree that quitting (both cocaine and shopping) would be a better choice, a choice that would be more consistent with my continued freedom; indeed, one that would liberate me, and hence the choice I really prefer to make. So it is at least an open question whether the person who prevents me from pursuing such desires impedes my liberty, or enhances it.

At the same time, however, how do we know which desires are an individual's 'true' desires, or 'higher' desires? With examples like cocaine addiction, the answer seems straightforward, but in most other conflicts of desires, the process of 'second guessing' could lead to an infinite regress (Friedman 1986). For instance, perhaps my desire to leave the house to shop for shoes is really my subconscious need to get away from my controlling husband; I'm hoping that he will leave me if I do this often enough. But then, maybe my seeing him as controlling is just expressing my deep fear of commitment; because of an abusive childhood, deep down I don't believe that I deserve to be loved; and so on, turtles all the way down. Similarly, even addiction is less clear-cut than we commonly imagine; recent studies show that addiction is not an enslavement driven by the inability to withdraw, but rather driven by pleasure: we do the things to which we are addicted because we enjoy them, pure and simple, suggesting more autonomous control than commonly thought (Foddy and Savalescu 2010).

Additionally, feminist insight into the concept of 'difference' suggests that even if women and men occupy opposing interest positions in contexts such as domestic violence, the implication that 'women' is a unified category, and that 'women' thereby all want similar things, is problematic; when intersected with other categories like sexuality, race, class, ethnicity, religion and culture, it becomes quite problematic to assume what individuals want, or to say that what we would want must be what we imagine they want. Recent work on disability studies in particular brings out the stark failure of imagination in understanding bodily difference and how such difference may introduce a range of desires completely unimaginable to others different from them: many advocates for Deaf culture, for instance, see deafness as a good, a quality that they value, in strong contrast to the dominant able-bodied view that deafness is intrinsically disabling and undesirable (Davis 1995). So the standard assumptions that are made about what any 'rational' person must want can be called into question, and feminism has been a leader in helping us realize this.

Figuring out what an individual woman 'really' wants thus demands a working through of history, relationship and context, all of which requires the deep interrogation of the self. But understanding the self is a social process. It presupposes language, a conceptual vocabulary, a system of signs with which to formulate and represent my own experience to myself, let alone to others; and it requires others with whom I can be in conversation, to analyse and determine what desires are really mine, and really better for me. This raises the question of where to draw the line between the internal self and the external world, because our self-understandings, our desires and choices, always need to be understood in context. Without such specificity of context, the individual is an abstraction.

# The Social Construction of Freedom

This leads to the third way that positive liberty challenges negative liberty, namely the 'social construction' of the choosing subject, the person who is having desires and making choices. How is it that I have the desires I have? Why do I make the choices I do? The idea of social construction is that human beings and their world are in no sense given or natural; rather, they are produced by and through the historical unfolding and development of practices, customs, institutions, economic structures, social structures, gender relations, familial configurations, and various other kinds of relationships. Our desires, preferences, beliefs, values, indeed the way in which we see the world and define reality, are all shaped by the constellation of personal, institutional and social relationships that constitute our individual and collective identities. Understanding them requires us to place them in their historical, social and political contexts. Such contexts make meaning possible (Derrida 1972, Foucault 1977, Hirschmann 2003, Rabinow 1984: 381–382).

But of course the contexts that women and men live in – for all their cultural and historical variety – are shaped importantly, if not primarily, by patriarchy, sexism and male privilege, just as they are by racism and white privilege, capitalism and class privilege, as well as heterosexism. Feminism shows us the important role that this context plays in constituting the 'subjects' of liberty – the individuals who come to want, desire and will the very things they are 'supposed' to (Butler 1993, Hirschmann 2003, Mackinnon 1987, Marcus 1992). Social construction is vital to a feminist understanding of freedom because it accounts for the ways in which gender is socially produced to in turn create individuals we call 'women' and 'men', the meaning of which is closely tied up with having 'appropriate' desires. Women's 'free choices' to reproduce, to marry, to pursue particular lines of education and career rather than others, are all part of a process of the 'social construction' of gender.

There are several aspects of social construction, however. The first aspect might be called 'ideology', the large-scale generalizations and social norms that restrict or encourage particular behaviours. The idea that women should be wives and mothers, for instance, has been a central aspect of patriarchal ideology at least since the 'sentimental family' gained popularity in the eighteenth century (Okin 1982) – though at least upper class women were assigned this role in the seventeenth century and earlier (Hirschmann 2008, 45–47, 91–99). This ideology also produces declarations about social relations that are generally distortions of the truth; for instance, that women are naturally irrational, or that they are too emotional (or sexual) for the public sphere (Elshtain 1981). For instance, women who wanted to study law in the nineteenth century were considered unfeminine. The law was considered a man's profession because it required logical thinking, which, it was declared, 'true' women could not perform.

The second aspect of social construction is 'materiality', and it entails the ways that ideological norms and beliefs translate into concrete effects. For instance, if female irrationality is used as a justification for not sending girls to school, we are more likely to end up with females who do not learn how to think rationally. In other words, ideology makes itself true, it justifies the production of conditions that guarantees what it assumes. Accordingly, because of the ideological belief that women belonged in the home, or that women were too irrational to undertake the rigours of legal study, women's entrance to law schools was blocked, creating a concrete materiality of women untrained in the law and who could not, in fact, engage in the logical thinking the law requires because they had been trained to think otherwise and were not given the tools of 'legal reason'. Ideology becomes self-fulfilling.

This process of materialization, however, is made possible because of 'discourse', a third aspect of social construction. Discourse refers to the ways in which this ideologically-produced reality shapes how we see and understand ourselves, our desires, and our freedom in a broader, perhaps 'macro' sense. If 'women' cannot think rationally, then the rare woman who educates herself by reading the books in her father's library, and can engage in rational discourse with men, becomes 'unfeminine' or 'manly'. At the same time, if women are excluded from education, and particularly from legal education and the practice of law, it is logical to assume that many women did not develop a *desire* to become lawyers because of such practices and norms. Discourse follows from these material conditions because our understanding of femininity becomes embedded in culture and the ways in which men and women think of themselves and learn their gender. How did the notions of 'woman' and 'femininity' reinforce their meanings as being at odds with the practice of law such that it did not even enter into many women's imaginations that they could become lawyers or that it was even a plausible desire for them to have?

These three aspects of social construction are not only interactive, but mutually constituting. In my example here, for instance, the ideological claim (law and the legal profession are for men because women are too irrational) created the material conditions (women barred from law school, and from education generally) that reinforced a discursive understanding of gender (women should not wish to work in the professions, those who do are perversions of nature, they should want to get married and have children) that in turn legitimates and reinforces the ideology (law and the legal profession are for men; women should marry and raise children in the home). Understanding freedom from a feminist perspective requires cutting through the layers of desire, limit and possibility to understand the complicated ways in which women and men alike are simultaneously restricted from and compelled towards particular expressions of will and desire.

Social construction might seem similar to socialization; namely, the ways that individuals are made to conform to social categories like gender by adherence to norms. Like socialization, the notion of social construction opens up the possibility that the inner self – our preferences, desires, self-conceptions – is constructed by and through outer forces and social structures, such as patriarchy, colonialism, capitalism, and so forth. But social construction is more complicated and deeply layered than socialization, and the idea of 'discourse' is key. Socialization is conceived as specific psychological and behavioural responses to conditions that could be changed or avoided. It thereby assumes an essential natural self underlying these oppressive conditions which would emerge if they were removed: all we have to do is realize the falseness of the ideology, and change the practices that the ideology justified. By contrast, social construction helps us see why such change is so difficult, because of the way that the idea of 'woman' has developed over time through unfolding ideological beliefs and concrete practices to shape human desire and preference: why should we want to change our practices if we really believe that women are irrational? Where does the desire to reject the desire to be a wife a mother come from? As Kathy Ferguson puts it: 'It is not simply that [we are] being socialized; rather, a subject on whom socialization can do its work is being produced' (Ferguson 1993: 129). Social construction is thus aimed at understanding much less overt and more complicated forms of social production, and it recognizes that humans cannot exist without that production; it is something that inevitably happens to everyone, men as well as women, rich as well as poor, at all times and in multiple ways. By suggesting that people are *produced through* social formations, and not simply *limited by* them, social constructivism thereby calls into question the assumption of what is genuine or true to the self, and what is false.

So in this light, whereas as socialization theory would view patriarchy as an unmitigated restriction on women, the social construction argument that the context in which women's desires and preferences are produced, expressed, evaluated and either granted, denied, or ignored altogether is a patriarchal one, does not mean that women are simply 'unfree', restricted by that context. In developing the critique of naturalism and a theory of how women are who they are because they are socially constructed by patriarchy, a feminist perspective shows us how desire, preferences, agency and choice are as socially constructed as are the external conditions that enable or restrain them. But at the same time, if social construction characterizes our entire social identity and being, if everyone is always and unavoidably socially constructed, then not only our restrictions, but our powers as well must have been produced by this very same process. This is the paradox of social construction. Who we are – the 'choosing subject' – exists within and is formed by particular contexts; the ideal of the naturalized and unified subject utilized by most freedom theory is thus deeply problematic and simplistically overdrawn. The contexts in which we live, patriarchal, sexist, racist and classist though they may be, have produced women's, indeed everyone's, agency.

This might suggest something of a paradox, for it seems to imply that there is nothing to be done about social construction; if women happen to be constructed in ways that are different from (white) men, so what? How can feminism claim that this construction is worse than any other construction of identities? If patriarchy is not simply an unmitigated restriction on women's otherwise natural desires, however, neither is it a neutral or even positive productive source of powers and abilities. Avoiding the helpless relativism of a deconstructive post-structuralism, social construction first of all suggests that the dichotomy between negative and positive liberty, and between internal and external restraint, is itself artificially constructed; and moreover that this construction can be seen as motivated by particular power structures that favour men over women. The fact that these power structures themselves were socially constructed, in a seemingly endless devolution, does not prevent feminists from acknowledging the ways in which power operates within any given social context, and to make political evaluations of those power relations. Though our contexts make women's agency possible, they often simultaneously put restraints on women's freedom not suffered by men. This duality of social construction permits, even requires, a more complicated engagement of the question of freedom.

Social construction thus also suggests that freedom is intimately intertwined with power, which must also be conceptualized along multiple vectors. What has been dubbed 'the four faces of power' (Digeser 1992) involves power as restriction (preventing someone from doing as they like), power as domination (forcing someone to do as you like), and power as manipulation (getting people to do what you want them to do by making them think that it is what they want to do) (Bachrach and Baratz 1962, Lukes 1986). These three faces of power are straightforward and easy to understand. And they play an obvious and important role in law, which seeks to adjudicate instances of people's being restricted, coerced and manipulated, and which in turn restricts people from engaging in some sorts of behaviours like theft, murder, fraud, and so forth, and coerces them to engage in others such as honouring contracts and obeying speed limits. We could even argue that the law manipulates us into wanting to obey it. But it is the fourth face, power as production, that is the most complex, for it involves the totalizing constitution of selves such that the purposiveness and agency of manipulation is made invisible; we not only cannot see that we are being manipulated, the people using or behind the forces that manipulate us cannot see this either, they simply accept our desires as natural or given. And indeed, 'manipulation', with its implication of identifiable agents engaged in specific sorts of action, may itself be an inaccurate term, too strong and purposive. Instead, we all engage in a process of social interaction that constantly, in an ongoing manner, makes us who we are and produces our desires.

## Domestic Violence as an Issue of Freedom

The complexity that social construction adds to freedom can be illustrated through consideration of an issue that many feminist lawyers and legal scholars are familiar with, domestic violence. At first glance, domestic violence might seem an odd example to show that all three levels of social construction are needed to understand women's freedom, for physical abuse would seem to be a clear cut case of domination and interference. Accordingly, the negative liberty model obviously has a great deal to offer: when a woman is assaulted or barred from leaving her house, she is unfree to act as she wishes on a clear negative liberty model. The first two 'faces' of power would seem to be the primary ones at work here: power as domination, force and coercion.

But what if a woman has tried to leave but her attempts at escape have always failed? Studies show that many battered women try repeatedly to leave but are thwarted: police fail to arrest; prosecutors fail to prosecute; judges fail to try the cases adequately; juries fail to convict. Or consider the fact that shelters are too few and inadequately funded. None of these would seem to illustrate the use of force or restriction; indeed, because the state *fails* to act, the force of the state is withheld, not applied. The question of how to identify the barriers to her freedom, and who is restricting her freedom, is accordingly complex and roundabout: politicians who vote against funding for shelters may be directly accountable, but what if they had to vote that way in order to preserve funding for other equally important social programmes? Do we say that taxpayers who do not want to pay more taxes are to blame, that they infringe on battered women's freedom?

Or what if a woman does not want to leave? What if she is afraid of being on her own? Or what if, after repeated failed attempts to leave, a woman develops feelings of helplessness and hopelessness, either because of the 'learned helplessness response' that Martin Seligman (1975) theorized (and which Walker (1984) transformed into 'battered woman syndrome') or as a survival strategy in which she convinces herself that she deserves the violence, that it is always her fault? Such a situation particularly complicates freedom, because what her desire is, exactly, becomes difficult to say. Certainly she herself may state, when asked, that she wants the hitting to stop. But when faced with the facts of recidivism and the difficulty in ceasing the violence while remaining in the relationship, the almost certain decreased standard of living if she leaves, and the increased possibility that her separated partner will kill her if she leaves (Fleury, Sullivan and Beybee 2000), all of these will affect what she 'wants' and how she sees herself. If her mother, her pastor, the police, the courts, all suggest, either directly or indirectly, that this is something she needs to work out herself; if the law fails to protect her and suggests she has no rights in relation to her husband; if employers do not want to hire her except for jobs that pay too little to support her children because she has been out of the labour market too long: how can we not believe that such experiences will affect a woman's preferences, desires and choices? How can we believe that they do not construct her identity and self-understanding?

From a somewhat different angle, what if a woman, anticipating that her partner is building to a violent outburst, starts a fight to get it over with, so that it does not catch her by surprise? Here, she is to all intents and purposes expressing agency, and she has made a choice, but we would not normally say that she is free. She is instead negotiating the barriers to and restrictions on her freedom to produce a slightly less bad outcome, an outcome that she dislikes a little less than the only alternative on offer. In this example, the woman still has a clear preference – not to be injured – and she is trying to come as close as she can to achieving that outcome. Her underlying preference, however – not to be hit at all – is something that may escape her understanding of possible outcomes; she may have become so accustomed to the apparent inevitability of the violence that she gives up devoting any space in her imagination to desiring it any more. How, then, do we evaluate 'what she wants'?

Martha Mahoney suggests that a discursive shift can help us understand women's agency and choices more accurately. Rather than a conceptual dichotomization of agency and victimization, freedom and unfreedom, in which 'victimization implies the one-way exercise of power, harm without strength; agency implies freedom from victimization', she suggests rethinking agency as 'acting for oneself under conditions of oppression' (Mahoney 1994: 62–65). Generally, agency is defined as 'the absence of oppression', which for battered women usually entails a single option: leaving. This stress on leaving, however, ignores the multiple albeit indirect barriers to leaving that patriarchal society puts in the way, from economic dependence to an unsympathetic legal system to cultural norms stating women's responsibility for relationship. Through such thinking – such as when killing the abuser in self-defence is viewed as insanity or the 'helplessness' of a 'battered woman's syndrome', or going limp is seen as passivity rather than self-protection – we fail to see the agency of battered women. Mahoney's definition makes it easier to understand why the conceptual vocabulary and epistemological assumptions of the existing discourses skew our inquiries to emphasize certain questions (Why didn't she leave?) while obscuring others (Why is he violent? Why did no one help?). In turn, this discursive reconfiguration makes it possible to see the efforts of battered women to get restraining orders, to move out of state, to get divorces, or to defend themselves – even when such efforts fail – as movements to create freedom within a context of oppression.

Conversely, however, it makes it easier to identify women's complicity with patriarchy through the choices they make: the white heterosexual shelter worker who denies access to a lesbian or to a woman who speaks no English supports white heterosexist patriarchy just as much as she fights it by providing a shelter to some women in the first place (Crenshaw 1991, Renzetti 1992). To say that discriminatory actions within shelters completely negate feminism is to deny the difficult conditions that underfunded battered women's shelters must negotiate on a daily basis. Similarly, the battered woman's mother who advises her daughter to work it out by herself because she cannot admit to herself the unequal power dynamics in her own marriage helps support patriarchy even as her actions help her survive it. The choices that women make within the constricted parameters of patriarchy express women's agency within a context of oppression, but simultaneously undermine it, because of course the end result of such actions does not stop the violence. While it would serve no feminist purpose to declare women's agency where they in fact have none – or by implication to emphasize women's agency to the point of implicitly holding them responsible for their victimization – it is equally problematic to deny this agency altogether. But both errors are unavoidable by-products of the failure to see the interaction of individual, institutional and discursive oppression.

For instance, let us return to the woman who prompts an attack so it does not catch her by surprise. Her choice will likely have an impact on her partner. He may see her not as a weak and helpless victim but as an antagonist; he may, in fact, be less violent as a result. Sharon Marcus argues precisely this in terms of sexual assault. In her view, what makes rape possible is in part the social construction of femininity that makes women freeze, not resist or fight back, and not protect themselves. In the patriarchal rape 'script', women equate rape with annihilation and death, and see the rapist as all-powerful, the penis as indestructible, and rape as inevitable. These beliefs not only disempower women, but fuel the rapist's own perceptions of himself as powerful as well. That is, the power of rape is not simply a function of the biological difference between penis and vagina. Rather, the fact that 'the social script … succeeds in soliciting its target's participation' helps to 'create the rapist's power' (Marcus 1992: 391, 387).

This is not to 'blame the victim', nor is it to substitute discourse for the event; indeed, to do so 'occludes the gap between the threat and the rape – the gap in which women can try to intervene, overpower and deflect the threatened action' (Marcus 1992: 389). But discourse is an important framework for understanding and reacting to these events. In particular, by seeing rape differently, women who are attacked may be able to respond differently, and in ways that defend themselves more effectively. Indeed, Marcus even seems to reject legal reform, instead advocating actual self-defence as a better strategy, because relying on the state for protection furthers the script's message that women cannot fight for themselves. As feminist legal scholars should see, however, feminist efforts to prevent victim's sexual history being admitted into evidence, and from having to show bruises to demonstrate non-consent, have been important moves to undermine key aspects of the 'rape script'. Changing discourse is a vital entry point for changing the social construction of rape, and thereby of women as victims and men as predators. Material changes and discursive changes occur interactively and complementarily.

Marcus's argument seems particularly applicable to domestic violence, which is scripted in many ways: indeed, the discourses of romantic love can make a man's controlling behaviour such as frequent phone calls to see what a woman is up to, or insisting that a woman quit her job to devote more attention to him and the home, seem 'endearing' features that demonstrate his deep care and concern for every facet of her life (Lorber 1994: 71). The same scripts can lead women to make choices that undermine their power within the marriage, such as quitting school or jobs. These scripts and discourses come to constitute women's identities and desires, the way that they see and understand their options, and the choices that they make.

A social construction approach shows the interactive dynamic of how women's identities as choosing subjects are constituted to make the choices that patriarchy needs them to make. Control at the individual 'micro' level by individual batterers works interactively and complementarily with the social 'macro' level of courts, police and medicine to socially construct battered women's choices, desires and freedom. Such control is not a coincidental by-product of social structures, but rather motivates and founds them. Social construction as domination and ideological misrepresentation – the batterer's violence, his claims, endorsed by police and judges, that violence is the victim's fault and that she deserves it – bleeds into materialization as it effectively blocks escape. Because police fail to arrest, women stop calling the police; because courts do not convict, women become reluctant to press charges or testify; because emergency personnel either fail to help her adequately or report her abuse to state agencies, women stop seeking medical attention; because friends and relatives tell them that women are responsible for making relationships work, and because battered women themselves share these beliefs and hold themselves responsible for the welfare of their batterers, battered women are ashamed of their abuse and do not tell anyone or ask for help.

## Seeking Solutions

Given the intractability of these difficulties, what should feminists concerned with freedom do about domestic violence? The temptation to seek out positive liberty solutions is great, such as mandatory arrest, or even mandatory counselling. Yet mandatory arrest policies have had limited effect because police operate within specific discourses that work against feminist efforts, such as interpreting 'community property' laws to mean that a man could not be arrested for damaging his wife's property; equating a man's physical assault to a woman's yelling at him, resulting in no arrest because they could not determine who was at fault; and dismissing a woman's desire to press charges because she 'would cool down the next day and forget about charges' (Ferraro 1989: 68–71). Hirschel et al.'s (1992) US-based study found that prosecution followed arrest in only 35 per cent of cases, and of those, few were sentenced to additional jail time beyond time served awaiting trial.

Mandatory arrest also poses a paradox of forcing on women the conditions in which their freedom and autonomy can develop. Mandatory arrest and no-drop prosecutorial policies certainly protect women from the abuses of official power just mentioned; and women who are not permitted to drop charges against their abusers are at lower risk of subsequent abuse than women who choose to drop charges. But at the same time such policies take away choice and control from women, just as battering does; choice is important to a battered woman's ability to feel in control, the thing she has least and the thing she needs most. And indeed, the lowest risk of recidivism occurs when women are allowed to drop charges but do not do so (Smith 2000: 1386). In such a situation, a woman's ability to make choices enhances her freedom the greatest at the same time that it jeopardizes it the most.

That might suggest a therapeutic approach: leave women free to choose whether to drop charges, but 'help' them realize that they do not want to. After all, mandatory counselling is the most significant – if still unsatisfactory – way to get abusers to stop. But the emphasis on psychotherapy invokes the shadow of women's historical institutionalization for 'madness' when they violated traditional norms of femininity (Gilbert and Gubar 2000), except perhaps in reverse, in that such women would seem to be 'externally and internally occupied by patriarchy', and therapy will 'uproot this occupied wrong self, thereby liberating the real' or 'nonpatriarchal self' (Brückner 2001: 770), thus forcing women to be free.

Social constructivism offers our best, though still far from perfect, answer. In the first place, it reveals that a focus on external barriers will be weakened without attention to the internal ones, as well as to the larger social, institutional and cultural context in which such barriers are created and operate. We must acknowledge the interaction of 'inner' and 'outer' and see them as interdependent in meaning and in practice in order to interrogate the social construction of the choosing subject, the subject of liberty. This provides the means for identifying not only the ways in which power relations are structured, but why it is so difficult to see those relations and that structure.

The tension between seeing domestic violence as a tragedy for individual women and as a social formation constructed by and through discourses of gender and material obstacles such as economic inequality and discrimination by the legal system; between recognizing the systematicity of violence as an expression of institutionalized male privilege and the specificity and difference of the experience for each individual woman; between external and internal forces and factors means that freedom cannot follow either a positive or negative liberty model. And yet my discussion here has clearly borrowed from the important ideas that each model suggests about individual difference, choice, abilities, resources and relationships, which a feminist theory of freedom must draw on. Feminist discursive interventions in domestic violence help make us more aware of the dominant discourses that construct battered women and indeed all women, and specifically the exclusion of women's humanity from freedom's conceptualization: the 'subject' of liberty is male. It thereby enables us to be more self-aware and critically analytical about the choices we make.

But what this leaves us with is the rather uneasy conclusion that the best way to support women's freedom is grossly imperfect: providing social supports to allow women to make a genuinely wide array of choices, but standing back and letting them choose badly if that is what they wish. Battered women must themselves decide whether to separate from their abusers; nobody else can make this decision for them, in keeping with negative liberty ideals. Paradoxically, however, because of the trauma of violence, a battered woman may not realistically be able to do this. Women's exercise of agency and freedom thus requires the help of others; it is important also to retain the positive liberty focus on the potential for others to help one realize one's true self and desires.

A social constructivist approach makes it possible to understand the ways in which the world view of individual batterers converge with the sexist attitudes of police, politicians, judicial officials, and society at large. Such convergence means that battered women cannot effectively resist as isolated individuals. That may be why community-based programmes that coordinate efforts between police, prosecutors, judges, shelters and medical personnel are more effective in reducing domestic violence than simple mandatory arrest policies (Tifft 1993). Similarly, for all their faults and problems, battered women's shelters provide safe spaces in which women can reject their victimization and reconstruct their self-identity as choice-making agents; this can help them see themselves as strong and capable precisely because they have survived and coped with abuse, and because they took the difficult step of leaving their homes to seek out the shelter.

In understanding the freedom of women, social constructivism allows us to bring together the two otherwise conflicting models of positive and negative liberty to forge a new way of understanding women as choosing subjects. Social constructivism allows us to see how social institutions, practices, cultural values and roles create pictures of reality and languages for understanding that influence individual's behaviour and self-understandings. But at the same time, it is crucial to note that individuals are not determined by such constructions, that possibilities of movement, agency, consciousness and choice exist within these parameters, that multiple contexts co-exist with which individuals can identify and ally themselves, and that we create and participate in these constructions in more and less active and conscious ways. Moreover, although we exist within large social formations in which all knowledge, desires and options are constructed for everyone, some people (men, whites, the wealthy) systematically have more power than others, including power to affect the social formation itself and conditions within it. As long as we ignore the fact that the framework in which women live is constituted and produced with their particular restriction in mind, we will continue to attribute agency and freedom to women when they in fact have little or no choice, and fail to see choice and agency when it is exercised.

Moreover, by situating my discussion of freedom in terms of domestic violence, I am suggesting that in order to achieve an accurate understanding of the complexities of agency, power and freedom, feminist legal and political theory must work interactively with scholars and practitioners of policy and law. We must base our theories on the reality of women's experience; but the reality of that experience cannot be understood without the theoretical tools that I have identified here. It is through this interaction that we can develop new and better understandings of women's freedom.

# References

Bachrach, P. and Baratz, M.S. 1962. Two Faces of Power. *The American Political Science Review*, 56(4), 947–952.

Berlin, I. 1971. Two Concepts of Liberty, in Berlin, *Four Essays on Liberty*. New York: Oxford University Press.

Blackstone, W. 1786. *Commentaries on the Laws of England*. London: J. Murray.

Brown, W. 1995. *States of Injury: Power and Freedom in Late Modernity*. Princeton, NJ: Princeton University Press.

Brückner, M. 2001. Reflections on the Reproduction and Transformation of Gender Differences Among Women in the Shelter Movement in Germany. *Violence Against Women*, 7(7), 760–778.

Butler, J. 1993. *Bodies That Matter: On the Discursive Limits of 'Sex'*. New York: Routledge.

Crenshaw, K. 1991. Mapping the Margins: Intersectionality, Identity Politics, and Violence Against Women of Color. *Stanford Law Review*, 43, 1241–1299.

Davis, L. 1995. *Enforcing Normalcy: Disability, Deafness, and the Body*. London: Verso Press.

de Beauvoir, S. 1974. *The Second Sex*. Trans. H.M. Parshley. New York: Vintage Books.

Derrida, J. 1972. *Positions*. Chicago: University of Chicago.

Digeser, P. 1992. The Fourth Face of Power. *Journal of Politics*, 54(4), 977–1007.

Elshtain, J.B. 1981. *Public Man, Private Woman*. Princeton, NJ: Princeton University Press.

Ferguson, K. 1993. *The Man Question: Visions of Subjectivity in Feminist Theory*. Berkeley: University of California Press.

Ferraro, K.J. 1989. Policing Woman Battering. *Social Problems*, 36(1), 61–74.

Fleury, R.E., Sullivan., C.M and Beybee, D.I. 2000. When Ending the Relationship Does not End the Violence: Women's Experiences of Violence by Former Partners. *Violence Against Women*, 6(12), 1363–1383

Foucault, M. 1977. *Language, Countermemory, and Practice*. Ithaca: Cornell University Press.

Friedan, B. 1963. *The Feminine Mystique*. New York: W.W. Norton.

Friedman, M. 1986. Autonomy and the Split Level Self. *Southern Journal of Philosophy*, 24(1), 19–35.

Foddy, B. and Savulescu, J. 2010. A Liberal Account of Addiction. *Philosophy, Psychiatry, & Psychology*, 17(1), 1–22.

Gilbert, S and Gubar, S. 2000. *The Madwoman in the Attic: The Woman Writer and the Nineteenth-Century Literary Imagination*. Second Edition. New Haven: Yale University Press.

Hirschel, J.D., Hutchison, I.W. and Dean, C.W. 1992. The Failure of Arrest to Deter Spouse Abuse. *Journal of Research in Crime and Delinquency*, 29(1), 7–33.

Hirschmann, N.J. 2003. *The Subject of Liberty: Toward a Feminist Theory of Freedom*. Princeton, NJ: Princeton University Press.

Hirschmann, N.J. 2008. *Gender, Class, and Freedom in Modern Political Theory*. Princeton, NJ: Princeton University Press.

Hirschmann, N.J. 2013. Rawls, Freedom, and Disability: A Feminist Rereading, in *Feminist Interpretations of John Rawls*, edited by R. Abbey. University Park, PA: Pennsylvania State University Press.

Hobbes, T. 1985. *Leviathan*, edited by C.B. Macpherson. New York: Penguin.

Lange, L. (ed.), 2002. *Feminist Interpretations of Jean-Jacques Rousseau*. University Park, PA: Pennsylvania State University Press.

Locke, J. 1963. *Two Treatises of Government*, edited by Peter Laslett. New York: New American Library.

Lorber, J. 1994. *Paradoxes of Gender*. New Haven: Yale University Press.

Lukes, S. 1986. *Power: A Radical View*. Revised edition. London: Blackwell.

Mahoney, M.R. 1991. Legal Images of Battered Women: Redefining the Issue of Separation. *Michigan Law Review*, 90(1), 1–94.

Mahoney, M.R. 1994. Victimization or Oppression? Women's Lives, Violence, and Agency, in *The Public Nature of Private Violence*, edited by M.A Fineman and R. Mykitiuk. New York: Routledge.

MacKinnon, C. 1987. *Feminism Unmodified: Discourses on Life and Law*. Cambridge, MA: Harvard University Press.

Marcus, S. 1992. Fighting Bodies, Fighting Words: A Theory and Politics of Rape Prevention, in *Feminists Theorize the Political*, edited by J. Butler and J.W. Scott. New York: Routledge.

Mendelson, S. and Crawford, P. 1998. *Women in Early Modern England, 1550–1720*. Oxford: Clarendon Press.

Mill, J.S. 1991. On Liberty, in *On Liberty and Other Essays*, edited by J. Gray. New York: Oxford University Press.

Okin, S.M. 1982. Women and the Making of the Sentimental Family. *Philosophy and Public Affairs*, 11(1), 65–88.

Rabinow, P. (ed.), 1984. *The Foucault Reader*. New York: Pantheon.

Renzetti, C.M. 1992. *Violent Betrayal: Partner Abuse in Lesbian Relationships*. Newbury Park: Sage Publications.

Rousseau, J.J. 1973. The Social Contract, in *The Social Contract and Discourses*, edited by G.D.H. Cole. London: Norman Dent and Sons, Ltd.

Schott, R.M. (ed.), 1997. *Rereading the Canon: Feminist Interpretations of Immanuel Kant*. University Park, PA: Pennsylvania State University Press.

Seligman, M.E.P. 1975. *Helplessness: On Depression, Development, and Death*. San Francisco: W.H. Freeman.

Smith, A. 2000. It's My Decision, isn't it? A Research Note on Battered Women's Perceptions of Mandatory Intervention Laws. *Violence Against Women*, 6 (12): 1384-1402.

Taylor, C. 1979. What's Wrong with Negative Liberty, in *The Idea of Freedom*, edited by A. Ryan. New York: Oxford University Press.

Tifft, L. 1993. *The Battering of Women*. Boulder: Westview Press.

Walker, L. 1984. *The Battered Women Syndrome*. New York: Springer.

Wollstonecraft, M. 1985. *A Vindication of the Rights of Women: With Strictures on Political and Moral Subjects*, edited by M.B. Kramnick. New York: Penguin.

# Law's Truths and the Truth About Law: Interdisciplinary Refractions

## Margaret Davies

Feminism is not the product of any one academic discipline and indeed has often contested disciplinary boundaries in the interests of illustrating the presence of gender and its effects across all areas of social, symbolic, political and economic life. Feminist *legal* thought has, like most academic feminism, drawn extensively and productively on the feminist theory of other disciplines and, equally importantly, on continuing engagement with the lives of women in all contexts. This chapter will review and evaluate some of the interdisciplinary and critical influences within feminist legal thought. I will focus in particular on the ways in which feminist social science and philosophy have assisted feminist legal theorists to challenge narratives which reinforce law's power to construct truth, as well as the particular gendered truths that it has constructed. Feminist critique of law's power to construct truth has been very extensive and somewhat successful, but less attention has been directed at discourses which might allow us to see the entire edifice of law differently. While feminist and critical legal approaches have successfully challenged ideas about the closure, separation and special status of law, by and large they have remained focused on the positive state-based law. There are good disciplinary reasons for this focus, but legal thinking, under the influence of sociology, anthropology and regulation theory is also moving towards a much more pluralistic and less static conception of the nature of law.

From its inception, feminist legal theory has had to confront a matrix of interrelated and mutually reinforcing legal 'truths' which are substantive, jurisprudential and declarative (or performative) in nature. In a substantive modality, law relies upon particular representations of the world, and these 'truths' have included numerous false stereotypes and misunderstandings of women, as well as a normative structure skewed in favour of values associated with masculinity. In its jurisprudential modality, law's truth involves numerous ingrained presumptions about law, politics and identity: the presumption that social inequalities can be adequately addressed by legal reform; that power is outside law, not structured, channelled or mediated by law; that law itself is a closed or at least relatively bounded system separated from the complex realities of everyday life (Lacey 1998: 1–15); and that the legal subject is a rational and autonomous entity separate from and prior to the law.[1] Both substantive and jurisprudential truths are representational in the sense that they combine descriptive and normative elements in a construction of how things *are*: substantive

---

1    The individualism of the legal person is considered in detail by Rosemary Hunter in her chapter in this collection.

legal truth concerns the way law represents the world, while jurisprudential truth concerns the way law represents itself (or, more correctly, is represented by its agents).

Declarative truth is a different and possibly more resistant order of truth because it is the structure or framework through which other truths are made as such. Declarative or performative truth concerns the material practices of law which iterate and cement law's truths. In this modality, feminism has had to challenge the notion that law speaks the truth, not only that it is objective and capable of neutrality, but also that whatever law says *is* the truth, because law has the authority in all circumstances to define what truth is (Smart 1989, 1990). Feminist legal theory has been very successful at counteracting substantive and jurisprudential truths by showing essentially that they misconstrue reality or construct it with a bias – for instance, by showing that the 'neutral' standards in fact value masculine norms. However, such arguments do not directly challenge the performative power of law, that is, its power to define the truth in the face of reality, which is central to positivist conceptions of law that allow it to be completely fictional (Kelsen 1991: 254). As I will explain later, all truth is performative in the sense that it relies on material iterations of what 'is'. However, what I have termed 'declarative' legal truth, unlike substantive and jurisprudential truths, makes the performance explicit as there is little need for substance or logic.

The first part of this chapter will review feminist epistemology and its use in challenging 'law's truths' or the way law represents the world. I argue that legal feminism has developed methodologies which allow powerful critique of law's truths and which also often offer alternative, reconstructed, narratives about women, gender and law. I also argue that feminism, along with legal critique more generally, has successfully challenged many of the more general jurisprudential 'truths about law' (or how law represents itself and how it is represented in mainstream legal theory). However, this has not been accompanied by strong alternative narratives about the nature and power of law. Moreover, contestation of law's truths and the truth about law leaves open several questions: how do feminists challenge the power of law to declare the truth (and do we want to do this)? Perhaps less controversially, how do we interrupt the performance of truths in law with different performances/truths? The point here is that, unlike representations, legal performances cannot be 'disproved' by alternative data for the simple reason that the performance itself creates the truth, even if we don't like it. Performative truths can only be challenged by oppositional, subversive or alternative performances. In the second part of the chapter I turn to approaches in the social sciences which may help legal feminists to formulate alternative narratives of law. In this part of the chapter I will review and evaluate 'new' empirical methodologies and consider the potential contribution to feminism of methods which emphasize affect, dynamic conceptual schemes and relationality.

## Law's Truths

### Early Context

Feminist legal thought of the 1970s emphasized the question of equality, defined in an essentially liberal fashion as sameness to an existing male standard (Dalton 1987–88: 4–5, Menkel-Meadow 1988: 71–72, Fineman 1992: 8–9). Focus was on the legal techniques, in particular anti-discrimination legislation, which could be deployed to promote equality. At that time, however, a number of factors both within and outside the legal academy contributed to an environment in which more far-reaching challenges than law reform could be envisaged. Undoubtedly the relative significance of these factors differed according to national, political and scholarly contexts. First of course, the increasing profile, radicalism and theoretical sophistication of feminist thought across all disciplines provided political motivation, peer encouragement and scholarly tools for feminist legal scholars to question accepted truths about law. Second, in the US context in particular, the critical legal studies movement had provided a precedent for the critique of the politics of law, in particular its role in conserving privilege. Critical legal studies provided a variety of methods for understanding law as a politically embedded, rather than neutral, institution. Third, feminism could not of course make large gains in the legal academy until women were employed and recognized as legal scholars in sufficient numbers (see also Thornton 1996: 119–123). And finally, the emergence of postmodern forms of critique of law throughout the 1980s strengthened but immeasurably complicated many of the core messages developed by feminist legal scholars.

A review of some of the significant early feminist legal scholarship reveals just how strong the interdisciplinary connections were from the beginning. This is hardly surprising. Traditional legal scholarship provided no inspiration at all to theorists wishing to move beyond an analysis fixated on formal equality and law reform. And critical legal studies, like other male-dominated 'progressive' movements of the time, sidelined both feminism and the emerging race-based critiques: this may have been partly in response to the intellectual conflict between the critique of rights promulgated by CLS and the need for feminists and racial scholars to insist, at times, on rights (Menkel-Meadow 1988: 63, Williams 1987, Delgado 1987). But, at least in the case of feminism, it was undoubtedly also the result of more old-fashioned gendered attitudes about the relative value of women's and men's scholarship and political agendas (Menkel-Meadow 1988). Given this context within legal scholarship, feminist legal scholars looked to other disciplines and to the broader feminist movement for theoretical inspiration. The results were undeniably very productive. For instance, in her two most influential articles (1982, 1983) Catharine Mackinnon referred to an extraordinary range of feminist and other theory in the fields of science, philosophy, psychoanalysis, psychology, history, literary studies and politics, as well as work based in feminist activism and polemics. The pieces were published in a generalist feminist journal, *Signs*, and referred only very occasionally to critical legal and feminist legal scholarship. Other early articles display a similar level of inspiration from beyond the law (see, for example, Olsen 1983, Rifkin 1980).

## Alternative Legal Truths

One of the most obvious obstacles for early feminist legal theory was the idea that legal knowledge was somehow objective and – perhaps apart from obvious instances of bias – neutral as between different social groups. The liberal view of law as a disinterested arbiter was thoroughly integrated into legal thinking, both academic and practical. The disciplinary insistence on the singularity of truth and the objectivity of knowledge was not, of course, specific to law: it was perhaps even more prevalent in scientific disciplines, across the social sciences, and also in philosophy. The challenge to male-defined notions of singular and universal truth was therefore a general and pressing preoccupation of feminist theory in all disciplines. From its earliest appearance, second wave feminism sought – and found – alternative disciplinary narratives and experiential grounds for knowledge. More importantly, feminists co-opted and developed philosophical theory which grounded such experiential and narrative explanations of knowledge and which ultimately connected epistemology to power. By the mid-1980s these approaches had consolidated into three types: identified by Sandra Harding and others as rationalist/empiricist, standpoint and postmodern (Harding 1986, Hawkesworth 1989, Bartlett 1990).

Rationalist and empiricist feminism, for instance, endeavoured to make the accepted knowledge paradigms of rationalism and empiricism more accountable to their own methods and less susceptible to poorly theorized assumptions, biased research methods, or untested claims about women and gender relations. Such approaches often presumed the possibility of objective knowledge but showed that existing 'knowledge' about women in fact often misrepresented the facts, or seriously skewed them by making unjustified presumptions. Possibly the most famous example was Carol Gilligan's counter-experimental critique of Lawrence Kohlberg's stages of moral development in which males reached a 'higher' stage than females, associated with abstract reasoning and universal norms. Gilligan famously challenged the argument that this style of moral reasoning was more developmentally advanced than that of females, who tended to value care and relations with others (Gilligan 1982). As Maria Drakopoulou points out, Gilligan's work 'was in no way extraordinary' compared to the work of other feminists of the time which was fundamentally about 'exposing sexist or patriarchal bias' and 'intended to cure the maladies of male-defined knowledge and theory' (Drakopoulou 2000: 204). Methodologically, such work presumed the parameters of science, but tried to ensure that women's experiences and lives were centrally valued in scholarship and not just seen as a deviation from a male norm. On the other hand, as Drakopoulou says, Gilligan's work '*was* extraordinary' because it involved the 'valorisation of a female nature whose portrait, painted with privileged colours, transformed those values and qualities traditionally despised as signs of weakness and inferiority into sources of moral strength' (204) and turned a narrative of human connection and relationality into a positive normative value for politics, philosophy, sociology and other disciplines. In the context of law, Gilligan's reformulation of ethics – the 'ethic of care' – proved particularly appealing because the abstract, universal, unconnected style of moral reasoning mapped so well onto what feminists perceived as typical legal reasoning. But empirically-informed contests over legal truths were not always this conceptual: for instance the claim, repeated frequently and uncritically in textbooks, judgments and the media that rape was a crime which was easy to allege and difficult to refute was contested repeatedly by feminists from the 1970s onwards, who showed, on the contrary, that it is a crime which is very difficult to allege and relatively easy to evade. Empirical data showed clearly, and still shows, that the majority of rapes are unreported and that convictions are extremely rare. These fundamental untruths were perpetuated largely because of an extensive network of myths imported uncritically into investigations and trials (Smart 1989: 32–49).

A second and equally influential theoretical approach, standpoint epistemology, drew on Marxist theory to explain the 'epistemic privilege' of the view from below (Elliott 1994, Hartsock 1983). Standpoint theory was based on the argument that in any oppressive relationship the person or group which is disempowered or oppressed can have a better understanding of the relationship than the oppressor or dominant party. This is because a disempowered person understands the dominant perspective because it is part of the political discourse or is culturally taken-for-granted. At the same time their experience, coupled with reflection on that experience, furnishes them with a standpoint challenging that dominant understanding. The person in the privileged position in the hierarchy doesn't have the resources at hand to develop the alternative standpoint, since they lack the experience of oppression. Terri Elliott's simple example is clear and persuasive: one person approaches a building and sees the entrance; a second person approaches the same building and sees an *obstacle* to access rather than an entrance – a flight of stairs with no wheelchair ramp (Elliott 1994: 426). The privileged person might understand abstractly and intellectually that there will be a problem for the person with a disability, but they don't have to experience it and are not in the end obstructed by it. The person with the disability, on the other hand, understands immediately both that the door is *supposed* to be an entrance, and that in fact it does not fulfil this function. Similarly, in the context of gender and law, standpoint epistemology was used as a theoretical corrective to the idea that there is an objective truth to law and that it just happens to reflect values associated with masculinity (Bartlett 1990: 872–873). Standpoint theory and the qualitative research to which it gave rise was also used in detail and across a number of different doctrinal areas, to prioritize women's experiences and import alternative narratives into the analysis of law.

Feminist empiricism and standpoint epistemology originally assumed that truths could be grounded in some non-discursive and non-constructed experiential realm. Feminist empiricism countered accepted truths of male-defined knowledge with empirically-described truths about women's lives, while standpoint epistemology argued that – at least in limited contexts – such experience was a better basis for a truth claim than the more limited perspective from the position of power. The two approaches were not mutually exclusive: on the contrary, standpoint epistemology provided a good deal of inspiration to feminists engaging in qualitative empirical research, insofar as it explicitly valued the voices and perspectives of women. Thus, experiential and standpoint perspectives challenged accepted truths by offering different and allegedly more authentic truths. Both approaches have been and continue to be immensely important for feminist legal critique because they have provided grounded theoretical resources for challenging bias in law and – more importantly – its hegemonic views of social order.

## Dissolutions

As subsequent history has shown, the initial challenge to a dominant truth has ultimately led to a dismantling of the very idea of epistemic certainty or objectivity. In consequence, although feminism has developed many effective critiques of law's truths, it has been less successful, and even conceptually thwarted, in its efforts to develop a solid basis for the normative reconstruction of law (Drakopoulou 2000: 217). Experience is complex and *any* reduction to a singular narrative will contain choice and partial representation. Challenging law's truths with alternatives does have the desired effect of illustrating the complicity of certain legal narratives with social distributions of power, and indicating that these narratives are not only flawed but also contingent. However, it inevitably also leads to the generation of a multiplicity of possibilities for representing the 'real', depending on the choices of the researcher, especially concerning method and interpretation.

It very quickly became obvious, for instance, that if standpoint was to be valued, it could not be generalized into a collective and authentic truth for women, because the differences between differently-situated groups of women was sometimes vast. The truth-status of such approaches was challenged by the sheer diversity of possible perspectives and their equal authenticity. Most notably, African-American feminists challenged the singularity and hidden racial assumptions of privileged white feminism, but so also did lesbians, women with disabilities and Indigenous/First Nations women (Harris 1990, Robson 1990, Behrendt 1993). In one sense this development could be regarded as a dilution of feminist critique (as the masculinist 'truth' is pitted against not just against one robust feminist alternative, but a variety of competing 'perspectives' derived from the experiences of various identity categories). But the fundamental and lasting legacy for feminist scholarship was first that the notion of an adequate or authentic empirical 'representation' or 'reflection' of the real was subject to critical scrutiny and second, that subjectivity and knowledge became intertwined in the most practical ways and most intimate spheres. I will return to this point later, as it has had a very significant impact on feminist legal theory.

A somewhat different approach which arose at around the same time in legal theory,[2] and which is sometimes loosely associated with it because it also leads to the demise of truth as a singular, objective and existent reality, derives from the various theoretical approaches known collectively as postmodernism or post-structuralism. But whereas the diversity of knowledges derived from different identities relies on standpoints and narratives of existent groups and people, the narrative form of truth for postmodernism is primarily about text, signification, and discourse. Throughout the 1990s, the textual analysis of postmodernism inspired a retreat from empirical research in some disciplines in favour of more theoretical work (Smart 2009, Adkins and Lury 2009). Texts, rather than social life and relationships, became evidence and 'truth' became a concept which related to discursive constructions as much as (or more than) factual and material things. In feminist legal scholarship the emphasis therefore shifted, at least in some circles, to the ways in which gender is constructed by law, rather than on whether the law truthfully represents reality, as Joanne Conaghan succinctly explains:

> From such a perspective, the stock of characters (male and female) depicted by law are not simply "fictions" who fail to comply with the "reality" of men's and women's lives: they are, rather, constitutive of that reality, part of the process of gender identity formation. (Conaghan 2000: 363)

The constitutive and ideological role of law in shaping the 'real', including gender, relationships, families and heterosexual normality, has been very extensively examined in recent feminist legal scholarship. This approach to law has helped feminist theorists de-naturalize the 'real' and challenge the view that law simply responds (or not) to a pre-existent social sphere. Law and social life are intertwined and mutually constitutive.

## Epistemic Plurality in Feminist Legal Thought

The story of feminist approaches to knowledge is a story of loosening and eventually relinquishing our anxieties about grounded truth and epistemic certainty. Feminists have rather swiftly developed complex attitudes to truth and certainty which eschew simplistic dichotomies between objectivity and subjectivity, universalism and relativism, truth and falsehood. Rather, feminist and other critical methodologies recognize that any knowledge is produced within contexts in which meaning and experience cannot be simply distinguished.

---

2    The philosophical origins of postmodernism in continental philosophy are obviously much earlier than its appearance in Anglo-American legal thought.

Such a theoretical outlook strengthens our critical resources immeasurably, leaving the one-dimensional, unlayered and unexamined truths looking shaky and even naïve.

In terms of the relationship between our understanding of social 'reality' and law, feminist legal theory has made extensive use of all of the forms of feminist epistemology which I have described, and put them to varying purposes in the service of legal change. In some quarters there has certainly been a recent emphasis on textual analysis, and much valuable work has been done in pursuit of understanding the ways in which legal texts construct women's lives and 'truths' about women, gender and sexuality (see, for example, Morton 2011, Kim 2012). At the same time, feminist legal scholarship has never moved away from valuing the empirical as a way of correcting legal myths and the ingrained gendered assumptions which often support them. Feminist legal theory has therefore been able to accommodate, for strategic and theoretical purposes, a large number of methodologies, sometimes combining discursive and empirical approaches to understand the interplay between text and social reality (see, for example, Bedford 2011, Quilter 2011). While all of the approaches do not necessarily cohere theoretically, the plurality of methods allows for sustained critique and collectively promotes political shifts in legal thinking.

It is worth outlining some of the specific contributions of feminist empiricism in law. In the first place, feminist legal theory has used empirical methods simply to identify problems (and progress) with the operation of law: feminist scholars have constantly made powerful use of fairly straightforward quantitative data about, for instance, the prevalence of rape (Larcombe 2011), domestic violence and sexual harassment, the gap in earnings between women and men, the numbers of women in public office and the professions and labour segregation. Of course, quantitative research often needs to be contextualized by more nuanced approaches. Simple statistical data can lead to simplistic statistical goals: increasing the rape conviction rate may be a laudable ideal, but not if it is done simply by putting police resources into those cases which fit the stereotype of 'real' rape and sidelining the more difficult cases (Larcombe 2011). Second, more qualitative empirical research, often inspired by standpoint theory, has been used to counteract myths and stereotypes and to illustrate the falsity or partiality of certain social narratives uncritically imported into law. Legal doctrine and its surrounding discourse has often presumed a reality which is unfounded or blatantly false and prejudicial to women, and empirical and standpoint research remains important in correcting these presumed realities (see, for example, Ellison and Munro 2009, Elizabeth, Gavey and Tolmie 2010, Hoyle, Bosworth and Dempsey 2011). Third, empirical research has helped feminists to analyse the gendering effects and symbolism of law (Bedford 2011) while more personal narratives inspired by standpoint epistemology have been used to import alternative stories and present new narratives in law (Williams 1987, Abrams 1991, compare Matsuda 1987). Over time, this has allowed a much richer and more subtle account of social life to enter into legal scholarship and (hopefully) the telling of legal stories. Qualitative information about women's experiences and the experiences of other legally marginalized groups has allowed new narratives to be heard across the entire spectrum of legal scholarship, and exposed intimate and private areas of social life.

Finally, new normative values and new discourses based on empirical and theoretical work have been imported into feminist legal analysis, creating positive normative alternatives to the traditional legal values. Perhaps most spectacularly, Carol Gilligan's empirical work on the ethic of care has generated an entire normative discourse about valuing relationality and enshrining a more caring ethos in law (Gilligan 1982, see Hunter in this collection). What began as a rather simple correction to empirical work biased towards masculine identity became an entire counter-narrative about the factual substratum of social life and the potential to normalize female values and assimilate this narrative into legal discourse. And finally, all of these uses of empirical, standpoint, and textual research underline what feminist legal scholars know about law theoretically – that law reform does not necessarily achieve social change; that power is in fact internal to law; that law is not a closed or even relatively bounded system separated from the complex realities of everyday life (Lacey 1998: 1–15); and that our normative environments interact in a dynamic, not formal or 'operationally closed' manner. I will come back to these last, jurisprudential, issues in the next section of the chapter.

At the same time, it is not always clear how feminist legal critique makes a difference to the substance of positive law, let alone the entire edifice of law, because of the need to engage with the present law at the same time as we imagine the future. Feminist legal theory encounters this difficulty in part because of the constraints of legal discourse and its power to declare the truth. A feminist-inspired narrative, and in particular an experientially-based knowledge regarded as one among many possibilities for seeing the world, cannot straightforwardly be elevated to the status of legal truth: law remains a blunt, authoritative, and unsubtle filter which is by its nature exclusive and monological. Although 'law' (by which I mean the reified performances of judges, legislators, bureaucrats and so forth) has undoubtedly become more attuned to human diversity and the impact of power upon our social lives, it still demands that facts be 'found' as truths, that normative positions are clear and unified, and that decisions be made which end by imposing a particular set of values. Selecting one normative foundation for a legal agenda will lead to the exclusion of other, possibly equally compelling, foundations. Moreover, simply illustrating by empirical or other means that law's truths are in fact myths, does little to counteract the declarative mode of law, where truth and falsity are defined not by correspondence to a 'real' but by the fact that what the law says is by definition the truth.

This can be explained by returning to the threefold matrix of truth (substantive, jurisprudential, and declarative) which I outlined at the beginning of this chapter. Substantive and jurisprudential 'truths' are not only representations about law and the world but also (normatively laden) declarations or enactments of law and the world (see, for example, Smart 1990). To take a simplistic and out-of-date example,[3] if the law says (as it once did) that married women do not have the right to own property, then that is a truth, made by the law, for a particular society. Married women do not own property (because the law says so). Such 'truths' are often based on presumptions about the world, relationships, human natures and gender difference – for instance that the family is properly run by a male head, that men are the beings most suited to this role, that women have other roles because of their nature, and so forth. These presumptions, which are sometimes defensible but are often not when it comes to gender, are also part of law's substratum of real world 'truths.' In this modality, however, 'truth' is also self-fulfilling, constructing gender in a particular way helps form the basis for the presumptions upon which further truths are based. Women who cannot own property are *made* dependent upon their husbands, a 'truth' which could then be used to support the view that women *should* be dependent. Clearly, there is no clear separation here between truth as a factual correspondence with a real state of affairs, and a truth as a fictive or normative construction which mandates a particular set

---

3    This example is a variation on one offered by Nancy Hirschmann above (this volume) to
     illustrate the processes of social construction.

of beliefs. The former kind of truth may be disproved empirically and theoretically, while the latter requires a different kind of intervention altogether. In many cases, long after the factual substratum has been completely discredited, the declarative and self-fulfilling part of the truth remains. To take a more current example, any 'difference' which would justify different treatment of same-sex partnerships when it comes to marriage law seems now hopelessly irrational, but the declarative aspect of law and its constructive power are yet to catch up in many jurisdictions. Same sex partnerships *are* different (but only because the law says so). Feminist legal theory has therefore not been able to rely simply on disproving 'truth', but has also had to find alternative truths with the power to reconstruct law.

However, this is not to say that the methodologies which presented counter-interpretations of dominant forms of legal knowledge can or ought to be abandoned. In a context where partial truths and unfounded stereotypes are still being promulgated uncritically, there obviously remains a significant role for challenging and reconstructing legal 'certainties'. Thus Conaghan states:

> In this sense, feminism purports to offer **a better understanding** of the social world by addressing aspects which have hitherto been ignored or misrepresented, while, at the same time, countering the ideological effects to which such misconceptions give rise. (Conaghan 2000: 360, my emphasis)

The better understanding offered by feminist legal theory is arguably not only epistemologically better, but also normatively better: it arguably reflects more of our social life and at the same time constructs it in a way which helps to address problems of misrepresentation. I personally don't have any problem with saying that feminist epistemology can lead to a more truthful account, or one which better reflects a social situation, or one which is a more useful account of a state of affairs. The emphasis here is on the comparative not the absolute truth – and on the politics of seeing things one way rather than the other.

## The Truth About Law

Feminist legal theory has therefore made extensive use of feminist epistemology in challenging laws truths, or the view of the world promulgated and reinforced by positive law. It has been especially successful in counteracting misconceptions and stereotypes, and promoting alternative narratives which are both normatively and empirically better. It has also, as I have indicated briefly, helped us to see through law's jurisprudential mythologies and to back up theoretical and critical approaches which contest the positivist and statist formulation of law. Nonetheless, because the positivist version of law is not itself actually about the empirical 'truth' of law but is rather a fiction which legal actors perform, it cannot simply be disproved by a resistant material world, but must be counteracted by different, and better, performances of law. Feminist legal theory has not yet managed to construct such an alternative at the level of a general understanding of law. But is this even possible, and would we necessarily recognize such a view of law when we saw it? Perhaps it does already exist, but remains implicit in our more practical interactions with law. Is a new theory of law possible which would accompany and frame feminist insight into the substance of law? Or does this hope unduly separate the substance and the form of law? Any new theory or reconstruction of law will emerge in dialogue with material and substantial enactments of law, not as a reified or externally imagined theory. It may be, then, that the foundations for the jurisprudential reconstruction of a more inclusive and participatory law already exist and are incrementally being developed by feminists and other critical theorists. In this section I consider some methodological approaches from socio-legal thought and legal anthropology which might be useful to feminist legal theory in this reconstructive process.

## The 'New' Empiricism of Sociology

Recent years have seen a revitalization of empirical methods in sociology, in the form of a renewed questioning of the methods of empirical research and the relationship between the world of experience and the world of concepts. This revitalization does not represent a return to positivist empirical method and its assumption that knowledge was independent of the observer. Nor is it a rejection of the postmodern attention to text and discourse. Rather, the so-called 'new empiricism' (as it seems to me) involves a pluralization of the very ideas of method and of the empirical grounding of knowledge.[4] This does not lead merely to the external differentiation of a number of different methods (qualitative, quantitative and so on) which might cast different types of light on social facts, but rather recognition of the inherent dynamism, contingency, and inter-relatedness of 'facts' and 'methods'. So, for instance, empirical research might pay more attention to affect, movement, sensation and psychosocial factors than is found in traditional empirical analysis (Clough 2009, Büscher and Urry 2009, Roseneil 2006). It might pay closer attention to complexity, without first categorizing social life into an orderly system or limiting itself with a pre-defined conceptual system (Law and Urry 2004, Smart 2009). A higher degree of conceptual innovation might be evident (Gane 2009) or a greater prominence given to the constructive role of the research itself in shaping the 'truth' (Law and Urry 2004).

Do these approaches provide useful resources for feminist *legal* theory? As a preliminary point, it is important to recognize that new empirical methods already owe much to prior feminist epistemologies and their expression in the social sciences. The point is made by Carol Smart:

> In critiquing classical sociological approaches, feminist work challenged the distinctions between researcher and researched, incorporated narrative and literary genres, championed qualitative work, and promoted reflexive standpoint research. Most importantly, feminist research was its most trenchant critic; it would not be an exaggeration to suggest that feminist methodologies existed then in a state of constant challenge and continual reformulation … The merger of feminist methods with sociological research practices (at least in the qualitative domain) meant that many of the early feminist challenges became taken for granted or normal practice. (Smart 2009: 296–297, see also McCall 2005)

Arguably, feminist epistemology and feminist approaches to the empirical had already conditioned the space in which any new empiricism could be developed, and it is very important not to forget this fact in the face of new theorizations. And it seems unlikely, at

---

4    There are strong parallels between the new materialism discussed by Joanne Conaghan in this collection, and what sociologists have termed the 'new empiricism'. See Conaghan, above, and Barad 2007.

first instance, that the new approaches offer anything radically or qualitatively different from the type or style of empiricism which feminism has been developing over the past 40 years, at least in relation to the generation of truths which challenge hegemonic legal narratives: certainly, feminist legal theory can benefit from an empiricism which is more sensitive to affect, more attuned to the intimate and psychological aspects of existence, and more intersectional. They will also undoubtedly allow a greater appreciation of the normative complexity which surrounds and informs positive law. New empirical methods might offer a variety of new resources and new languages for representing the real, and undoubtedly extend and develop in more detail many of the particular directions of feminist thought. It cannot necessarily easily reify such truths or completely reconstruct law on the basis of them, but nor could it ever do so.

My sense is that these new resources offer more of a renewed commitment to and intensification of methods which were already available to feminism, as Smart seems to be implying. It is not my purpose to describe or critique them in detail here (but see Adkins and Lury 2009, Smart 2009, Cooper 2009, compare Conaghan in this collection). But I do want to consider what appear to me to be some further interesting features of this work, in particular regarding its theoretical dimensions and how these might contribute to feminist contestations of jurisprudential truths. For these purposes I would like to comment on two aspects of the new epistemological climate – an innovative approach to concepts and the idea that method is performative.

One of the key focal points of postmodernism was the idea that concepts are created in discourse, and do not precede it. There is no independent world of concepts informing the way we think and what we know. Concepts are necessarily dynamic, because they emerge in webs or networks and therefore cannot be self-contained or entirely self-referential. As I have indicated, the emphasis in one mode of postmodernism was on textuality and the discursive nature of concepts. In its first iteration in Anglo-American thought this emphasis arguably resulted in the sidelining of the 'real' as the material expression of meaning in practical settings. In the philosophy of Deleuze, however, the concept gains a thoroughly empirical relevance, in that it emerges from our engagement with objects, whether these 'objects' are physical or already complex material phenomena such as 'society' (Deleuze and Guattari 1994, see generally Gane 2009). Concepts are not givens which categorize or order the world of objects, but nor are they derived from a material world which speaks for itself. There is no completely coherent relationship between the conceptual and the material. Rather, thought and its objects are dynamically related (Gane 2009) and the researcher, by entering into dialogue with objects, creates – not arbitrarily, but reflexively – concepts which respond to the changing tensions in material. Concepts are in process and experimental (Gane 2009: 87), not fixed or fetishized. The relationship between researcher, discursive medium, and 'reality' become more intentionally motivated: empirical research does not just find the truth, nor invent it, but crystallizes inchoate formations from a material substratum. The potential significance of this for critical and feminist legal theory is that it provides considerable inspiration and some theoretical resources for engaging with law on a conceptual level in a way which is not tied to the conventional picture of law as a state-based, determinate and hierarchically legitimated entity. As I have indicated, it is not possible simply to abandon a concept of law which has attained the status of self-fulfilling truth. Yet feminist legal philosophers may nonetheless have the opportunity to create new concepts and practices of law which thoroughly recognize the intermingling of a complex social environment and legal 'order'.

This innovative approach to the process of conceptualization supports theoretically what John Law and John Urry have referred to as the performative nature of sociological method. Sociological method *makes* social reality. This is not to say that reality is arbitrary and can be made according to the wishes of the researcher: a bad performance of the real would be an obvious and transparent failure of knowledge. Nor does it mean that there is some unobtainable real which empirical knowledge approximates, always inadequately. Rather, as Law and Urry put it, 'reality is a relational effect. It is produced and stabilized in interaction that is simultaneously material and social' (Law and Urry 2004: 395). In consequence the 'political grammar' of knowledge production moves from one where politics is a response to a material state of affairs to one where knowledge production is consciously motivated by a politics. Again, to quote Law and Urry,

> The issue is not simply how what is out there can be uncovered and brought to light, though this remains an important issue. It is also about what might be made in the relations of investigation, what might be brought into being. And indeed, it is about what should be brought into being. (396)

As a methodological point, is and ought are not clearly distinct: knowledge is a process, not a thing. Of course, I would add that since our meta-discourse insists on the reification of knowledge, once produced, knowledge *is* a thing and it is this apparent solidity which gives it its power. Law and Urry characterize the performative understanding of method as a movement from epistemology to ontology: 'The shift is from epistemology (where what is known depends on perspective) to ontology (what is known is also being made differently)' (Law and Urry 2004: 397). I would prefer to say that the shift is from a view of the world where epistemology and ontology are separate, to one where they are not only interrelated but actually inseparable (see Barad 2007: 49, 185, see also Conaghan in this collection). As they say themselves, 'what is known is being made differently' (Law and Urry 2004: 397). Knowing and being are part of the one process.

Arguably, the notion of performative knowledge production is not particularly new, as some decades of feminist epistemology and postmodern theorizing about the subject suggest (Law and Urry refer to Donna Haraway in recognition of the feminist grounding of the idea). However, it may have a strengthened presence in the context of *empirical* work, which was arguably only abstract in postmodernism and possibly under-theorized in feminist epistemology. This is essentially the thought that knowledge as an analysis of the material world can be chosen reflexively. Feminists have insisted for some time that knowledge has a prefigurative and reconstructive dimension, but perhaps less has been done to apply this to the empirical world.

In the context of feminist legal theory, a performative empiricism may provide several avenues for reconstructing jurisprudential 'truths about law'. For feminist legal scholars, the 'empirical' consists of the social world, and women's diverse material realities. As I have indicated, it also includes the substance of law and how law meshes with social life. A performative empiricism can arguably replay and recreate this matter in order to bring out new substantive concepts and new ideas about law. That this is possible is illustrated by a number of feminist performances which explicitly take on and recreate the law in specific circumstances in order to give it renewed, more aware, and more responsive meanings. Well-known examples include the Women's International War Crimes Tribunal (Chinkin 2001), the Women's Court of Canada (Majury 2006) and the UK feminist judgments project

(Hunter, McGlynn and Rackley 2010). The significance of such work is that it re-enacts and reconstructs the empirical material of real cases, making it possible to renew the law in a way which both affirms its centrality to social ordering and contests its truths (Davies 2012), leaving a 'female-gendered mark on the law' (Hunter, McGlynn and Rackley 2010: 8). Such interventions perform the law differently and shift the conceptual agenda. They also, by highlighting law's performative nature, help us reassess ideas about agency and subjectivity in the law. In conventional legal discourse, those with power to construct the law are legal officials, while others are simply subjected to law. Feminist legal performances, by contrast, explicitly allocate at least some of the constitutive power of law to its subjects (see further Davies 2012: 173–174) and in this way engage directly with law's declarative truth aspect, as well as with its substantive and jurisprudential dimensions.

## Extending the Range of 'Law'

It is possibly the case that the main contribution of the 'new' empiricism in sociology is that it consolidates and adds theoretical depth to existing feminist approaches to epistemology. As I have indicated, while it may be innovative to use the language of performativity in this context, the reconstruction of distinctions such as that between is and ought, epistemology and ontology, have been significant in feminist thought for some time. Feminist judgments and other renewals of the factual substrate of positive law offer new methodological approaches to law which are consciously reconstructive at the practical level. Such approaches bring together the ontology and epistemology of legal feminism because they foreground the fact that knowing the law and making it are part of the one process (compare Barad 2007).

There remain, however, key questions about the nature and limits of law – its jurisprudential truths and in particular its positivist shape. Legal positivism has been subjected to enormous pressure by feminists and many other critical scholars for many years, but it remains the assumed form of law which is in fact 'true' because we act as if it is so (Davies 2008: 286–287). Feminist judgments are a powerful method of contesting law's truths in part because they work within the positivist frame – an approach which paradoxically allows its weaknesses to be highlighted and tested in factual situations.

Nonetheless, positivist thinking suffers from serious limitations in conceptualizing the nuances of gender, the complexity of social normativity and distributions of power. I think it is therefore also important to step outside this frame and try to imagine law differently, even if such imaginings have little practical application for lawyers and legal scholars. Interdisciplinary feminist research offers various resources for doing this, allowing law to be viewed from angles other than its normal positivist and state-determined frame. Socio-legal approaches offer a variety of methods for observing state-centric law in its interaction with other forms of normativity: for instance legal consciousness studies are based on the idea that law and legality are constituted in the dynamic, often contradictory, but patterned understandings of law formed in everyday life (Ewick and Silbey 1992: 741–742). Susan Silbey describes her own previous research with Patricia Ewick as taking a 'decentred' approach to consciousness,

> ... in that the research does not document chiefly what people think and do about the law but rather how what they think and do coalesces into a recognizable, durable phenomena and institution we recognize as the law. (Silbey 2005: 347)

Research based on this idea expands the notion of law beyond the set of norms determined by state institutions, and potentially illustrates empirically the ways in which power differences such as those relating to race, class and gender, are written into legal narratives and legal experiences (Ewick and Silbey 1992, compare Merry 1990). However, Silbey has also critiqued the recent trajectory of legal consciousness studies, arguing that it has lost its 'critical edge' by being used for simple analysis of the ways different groups of people experience mainstream law and various law-related issues (2005: 357–358). The idea of constituted legalities, and in particular the mutually constitutive dynamic between law and consciousness of law, has been sidelined according to Silbey in the interests simply of understanding people's subjective experiences of law, an approach which reinstates rather than challenges the law–society dualism. One obstacle may be that the positivist concept of 'law' is so entrenched that it is difficult to maintain a theoretical trajectory which holds it in suspension – how a social group understands and interacts with a singular 'law' is one thing, but how different conceptions of law materialize through that process is quite another. Silbey does not use this language, but it is possible that the empirical material of legal consciousness could be 'performed' by researchers in ways which bring out alternative legal constructions.

These possibilities have been explored from a different angle in the context of legal pluralism. In some of its forms, legal pluralism does not illustrate the highly fluid dynamic imagined by early legal consciousness theory, preferring to focus on the plurality of objective legal systems (Manderson 1996: 1060). Nonetheless, many pluralist approaches have begun to explore the variations in 'law' which arise as a result of people's material and everyday engagements with and constructions of their normative contexts (Kleinhans and MacDonald 1997, Tamanaha 2001, Davies 2006). In this context, Rosie Harding argues that legal consciousness studies carry an implicit (but underdeveloped) openness to the idea of legal multiplicity or plurality – that is, that law may take different forms and have different foundations in different contexts (Harding 2011: 25–26, 29). Harding develops this productive alliance between legal consciousness and legal pluralism, specifically in the context of sexuality and the various ways in which lesbians and gay men experience and construct multiple legal and regulative contexts. Though focusing on sexuality, Harding's approach is transferable to a more general feminist approach to law: understanding 'law' as a plurality of interrelated and highly dynamic normative fields which are constituted in part by material lives, can bring new insight to the fundamental feminist question of how law is gendered.

The empirical complexity of interconnected and plural normative fields has also been solidly demonstrated by the feminist legal anthropologist Anne Griffiths, whose studies of marital disputes concerning family property in Botswana depict 'cross-fertilization' of nominally different legal systems – 'rules in one system are shaped by and are shaping those in another' (Griffiths 1998: 613). Her research brings to the fore the ways in which gender is interwoven with legal interpretation in multiple spheres and that thinking of laws as plural and 'plastic' rather than as singular and static, helps us to understand the complexity of gendered interactions with law and the different paths of resistance and reconstruction taken by different actors within the system (see also Griffiths 2001: 119–120). The analysis applies equally to developed states (1998: 613), where predominance of the ideology of legal centralism gives anthropological and sociological perspectives a particular role in bringing out normatively plural angles on law.

The alternative depictions of law suggested by legal consciousness studies and legal pluralism give empirical support to feminist theoretical and doctrinal analysis of state law's embeddedness in more complex normative environments. Because these environments are all gendered, though sometimes in different ways, it is important to understand the dynamics which connect and separate them. It is also possible that in time views which contest the image of positive state-based law may lend support to imagining legal alternatives which are more participatory and which allow contestations of traditional hierarchical and formal understandings of law (see further Davies 2008).

# Conclusion

Feminist legal scholars have successfully drawn on feminist empiricism and feminist epistemology to challenge many of law's truths. Alternative narratives about women's reality have become integrated into some parts of the law, though others remain stubbornly resistant to any fundamental change. As I have argued, feminists have been especially successful at challenging the substantive truths of law, though law's power to tell the truth remains a key obstacle to widespread change. Nonetheless, some feminist methodologies, notably those of the various feminist judgments projects, directly confront this declarative aspect of law's truth by writing law differently. Furthermore, socio-legal and anthropological analyses of material and everyday experiences of law challenge abstract and positivist legal knowledges, leading to a broader understanding of the nature of law itself.

# References

Abrams, K. 1991. Hearing the Call of Stories. *California Law Review*, 79(4), 971–1052.

Adkins, L. and Lury, C. 2009. What is the Empirical? *European Journal of Social Theory*, 12(1), 5–20.

Barad, K. 2007. *Meeting the Universe Halfway: Quantum Physics and the Entanglement of Matter and Meaning*. Durham: Duke University Press.

Bartlett, K. 1990. Feminist Legal Methods. *Harvard Law Review*, 103, 829–887.

Bedford, K. 2011. Getting the Bingo Hall Back Again? Gender, Gambling Law Reform, and Regeneration Debates in a District Council Licensing Board. *Social and Legal Studies*, 20(3), 369–388.

Behrendt, L. 1993. Aboriginal Women and the White Lies of the Feminist Movement. *Australian Feminist Law Journal*, 1, 27–44.

Büscher, M. and Urry, J. 2009. Mobile Methods and the Empirical. *European Journal of Social Theory*, 12(1), 99–116.

Chinkin, C. 2001. Women's International Tribunal on Japanese Military Sexual Slavery. *American Journal of International Law*, 95(2), 335–340.

Conaghan, J. 2000. Reassessing the Feminist Theoretical Project in Law. *Journal of Law and Society*, 27, 351-385.

Clough, P.T. 2009. The New Empiricism: Affect and Sociological Method. *European Journal of Social Theory*, 12, 43–61.

Dalton, C. 1987–1988. Where We Stand: Observations on the Situation of Feminist Legal Thought. *Berkeley Women's Law Journal*, 3, 1–13.

Davies, M. 2006. Pluralism and Legal Philosophy. *Northern Ireland Legal Quarterly*, 57(4), 577–596.

Davies, M. 2008. Feminism and the Flat Law Theory. *Feminist Legal Studies*, 16(3), 281–304.

Davies, M. 2012. The Law Becomes Us: Rediscovering Judgment (Review Article). *Feminist Legal Studies*, 20(2), 167–181.

Delgado, R. 1987. The Ethereal Scholar: Does Critical Legal Studies Have What Minorities Want? *Harvard Civil Rights-Civil Liberties Law Review*, 22, 301–322.

Drakopoulou, M. 2000. The Ethic of Care, Female Subjectivity and Feminist Legal Scholarship. *Feminist Legal Studies*, 8(2), 199–226.

Ellison, L. and Munro, V. 2009. Of "Normal Sex" and "Real Rape": Exploring the Use of Socio-Sexual Scripts in (Mock) Jury Deliberations. *Social and Legal Studies*, 18(3), 291–312.

Elizabeth, V., Gavey, N. and Tolmie, J. 2010. Between a Rock and a Hard Place: Resident Mothers and the Moral Dilemmas they Face During Custody Disputes. *Feminist Legal Studies*, 18(3), 253–274.

Elliott, T. 1994. Making Strange What Had Appeared Familiar. *The Monist*, 77(4), 424–433.

Ewick, P. and Silbey, S.S. 1992. Conformity, Contestation, and Resistance: An Account of Legal Consciousness. *New England Law Review*, 26, 731–749.

Fineman, M.A.1992. Feminist Theory in Law: The Difference it Makes. *Columbia Journal of Gender and Law*, 2, 1–23.

Gane, N. 2009. Concepts and the New Empiricism. *European Journal of Social Theory*, 12(1), 83–97.

Gilligan, C. 1982. *In a Different Voice*. Cambridge, MA.: Harvard University Press.

Griffiths, A. 1998. Reconfiguring Law: An Ethnographic Perspective from Botswana. *Law and Social Inquiry*, 23(3), 587–620.

Griffiths, A. 2001. *Gendering Culture: Towards a Plural Perspective on Kwena Women's Rights, in Culture and Rights: Anthropological Perspectives*, edited by J. Cowan, M. Benedicte-Dembour and R. Wilson. Cambridge: Cambridge University Press, 102–126.

Harding, R. 2011. *Regulating Sexuality: Legal Consciousness in Lesbian and Gay Lives*. Abingdon: Routledge.

Harding, S. 1986. *The Science Question in Feminism*. Milton Keynes: Open University Press.

Harraway, D. 1988. Situated Knowledges: The Science Question in Feminism and the Privilege of Partial Perspective. *Feminist Studies*, 14(3), 575–599.

Harris, A. 1990. Race and Essentialism in Feminist Legal Theory. *Stanford Law Review*, 42(3), 581–616.

Hartsock, N. 1983. The Feminist Standpoint: Developing the Ground for a Specifically Feminist historical Materialism' in *Discovering Reality: Feminist Perspectives on Epistemology, Metaphysics, Methodology and Philosophy of Science*, edited by S. Harding and M. Hintikka. Dordrecht: D. Riedel, 283–310.

Hawkesworth, M. 1989. Knowers, Knowing, Known: Feminist Theory and Claims of Truth. *Signs*, 14(3), 533–557.

Hoyle, C., Bosworth, M. and Dempsey, M. 2011. Labelling the Victims of Sex Trafficking: Exploring the Borderlands between Rhetoric and Reality. *Social and Legal Studies*, 20(3), 313–329.

Hunter, R., McGlynn, C. and Rackley, E. 2010. *Feminist Judgments: An Introduction, in Feminist Judgments: From Theory to Practice*, edited by R. Hunter, C. McGlynn and E. Rackley. Oxford: Hart Publishing, 3–29.

Hunter, R., McGlynn, C. and Rackley, E. 2010. *Feminist Judgments: From Theory to Practice.* Oxford: Hart Publishing.

Kelsen, H. 1991. *General Theory of Norms.* Oxford: OUP.

Kleinhans, M.M. and Macdonald, R.A. 1997. What is a Critical Legal Pluralism? *Canadian Journal of Law and Society* / Revue Canadienne de droit et societe, 12, 25–46.

Kim, S. 2012. The Neutered Parent. *Yale Journal of Law and Feminism*, 24, 1–59.

Lacey, N. 1998. *Unspeakable Subjects: Feminist Essays in Legal and Social Theory.* Oxford: Hart.

Larcombe, W. 2011. Falling Rape Conviction Rates: (Some) Feminist Aims and Convictions for Rape Law. *Feminist Legal Studies*, 19(1), 27–45.

Law, J. and Urry, J. 2004. Enacting the Social. *Economy and Society*, 33(3), 390–410.

Matsuda, M. 1987. Looking to the Bottom: Critical Legal Studies and Reparations. *Harvard Civil Rights-Civil Liberties Law Journal*, 22, 323–399.

Nielsen, L.B. 2000. Experiencing Legal Consciousness: Experiences and Attitudes of Ordinary Citizens about Law and Street Harassment. *Law and Society Review*, 34(4), 1055–1090.

MacKinnon, C. 1982. Feminism, Marxism, Method and the State: An Agenda for Theory. *Signs*, 7(3), 515–544.

MacKinnon, C. 1983. Feminism, Marxism, Method and the State: Towards Feminist Jurisprudence. *Signs*, 8(4), 635–658.

Majury, D. 2006. Introducing the Women's Court of Canada. *Canadian Journal of Women and the Law*, 18(1), 1–25.

Manderson, D. 1996. Beyond the Provincial: Space, Aesthetics, and Modernist Legal Theory. *Melbourne University Law Review*, 20, 1048–1071.

McCall, L. 2005. The Complexity of Intersectionality. *Signs*, 30(3), 1771–1800.

Menkel-Meadow, C. 1988. Feminist Legal Theory, Critical Legal Studies, and Legal Education or, The "Fem–Crits Go to Law School." *Journal of Legal Education*, 38(1–2), 61–85.

Morton, C. 2011. When Bare Breasts are a "Threat": The Production of Women's Bodies/ Spaces in Law. *Canadian Journal of Women and the Law*, 23(2), 600–626.

Olsen, F. 1983. The Family and the Market: A Study of Ideology and Legal Reform. *Harvard Law Review*, 96, 1497–1578.

Quilter, J. 2011. Reframing the Rape Trial: Insights from Critical Theory about the Limits of Legislative Reform. *Australian Feminist Law Journal*, 35, 23–56.

Rifkin, J. 1980. Toward a Theory of Law and Patriarchy. *Harvard Women's Law Journal*, 3, 83–95.

Robson, R. 1990. Lesbian Jurisprudence? *Law and Inequality*, 8, 443–468.

Roseneil, S. 2006. The Ambivalences of Angel's 'arrangement': A Psychosocial Lens on the Contemporary Condition of Personal Life. *The Sociological Review*, 54(4), 847–869.

Silbey, S. 2005. After Legal Consciousness. *Annual Review of Law and Social Science*, 1, 323–368.

Smart, C. 1989. *Feminism and the Power of Law.* London: Routledge.

Smart, C. 1990. Law's Truth/Women's Experience, in Dissenting Opinions: Feminist Explorations in Law and Society, edited by R. Graycar. Sydney: Allen and Unwin, 1–20.

Smart, C. 2009. Shifting Horizons: Reflections on Qualitative Methods. *Feminist Theory*, 10(3), 295–308.

Tamanaha, B. 2001. *A General Jurisprudence of Law and Society.* New York: Oxford University Press.

Thornton, M. 1996. *Dissonance and Distrust: Women in the Legal Profession.* Melbourne: OUP.

Williams, P. 1987. Alchemical Notes: Reconstructing Ideals from Deconstructed Rights. *Harvard Civil Rights-Civil Liberties Law Review*, 22, 401–433.

# Part II:
# Concepts in Feminist Legal Theory

# Equality and Difference: Fertile Tensions or Fatal Contradictions for Advancing the Interests of Disadvantaged Women?

## Elsje Bonthuys

*Equality projects are in disarray. (Sommerlad 2008: 171)*

Expressing similar sentiments, Rosemary Hunter (2008) argues that although the rhetoric of equality and inequality remains valuable to frame and raise awareness of women's political and legal claims, and despite the increased credibility of equality claims in the international arena,[1] these concepts nevertheless fail to describe or explain women's oppression meaningfully. Nor are they capable of supplying accurate and practicable standards for alleviating oppression. Hunter's frustration is shared by many prominent feminists who suggest alternative, or at least supplementary, concepts to remedy the defects of equality as a legal concept and goal.

Are feminist lawyers therefore abandoning equality? Should they abandon it? This chapter investigates the reasons for the current feminist disenchantment with equality by focusing on the inherent and probably unsolvable tensions which it embodies. These tensions, I argue, flow from the essentially comparative nature of the claim that women are treated unequally because of their gender. This means that equality claims cannot ultimately be divorced, at least in the legal context, from questions of 'equal to whom?' and 'which women?' Issues of difference – different from whom, different in which way and questions about the consequences of differences – are therefore inescapable and provide opportunities for conservative courts and litigants who wish to preserve gendered privilege to formulate an equality jurisprudence which, at best, advances the interests of a small group of already privileged women and, at worst, could reverse feminist legal gains. The intractability of these problems and the goal of improving conditions for the most disadvantaged women may ultimately cause feminists to abandon the feminist project in favour of more broadly based progressive movements to alleviate disadvantage affecting both men and women.

The first section will highlight some feminist and other transformative alternatives to equality and draw attention to some common themes among them. In the second part I explore the reasons for the retreat from equality by way of a rough historical sketch of the problems with difference within feminist legal theory and practice. The final section deals

---

1   See for instance the description of the history of women's equality claims in international human rights law in Fraser 1999.

with feminist formulations of substantive equality – the more contextual and transformative understanding of equality developed as an alternative to the formal view of equality espoused by many courts. I conclude by returning to the alternatives to equality discussed in the first section and evaluate whether they represent true alternatives to equality and whether feminists should strategically retreat from equality. My argument is that, although they provide new insights and useful ways of conceptualizing women's subordinate positions in society, these theoretical positions nevertheless implicitly rely on notions of equality or at least include equality as a part of their analysis. I argue that, rather than constituting viable alternatives to equality, the insights offered could be, and have been fruitfully used to enrich equality concepts and to counteract conservative legal interpretations of equality.

At the outset it should be emphasized that different jurisdictions have divergent concepts of equality; they emphasize different elements and, of course, rely on their own jurisprudence and on widely different constitutional frameworks. In certain jurisdictions, equality debates are waged mostly on the terrain of the interpretation and application of domestic legislation, while in others constitutional principles and rules of public international law are invoked to deepen and enrich understandings of equality. Various political, economic and social contexts and histories further diversify the problems which equality seeks to address and the practical solutions adopted (Loenen 1995). Problems experienced in one country's equality law cannot therefore mean that the concept should be jettisoned everywhere. On the contrary, feminists have long used jurisprudence and scholarship from other countries to push the boundaries of equality and incorporate new legal concepts within their own jurisdictions. Globalizing economic and social pressures and the increased visibility and effectiveness of international legal institutions add impetus to the convergence of legal norms, including equality norms, across national boundaries.

I focus on jurisdictions rooted in the English common law tradition and on legal equality claims in liberal legal systems. Although, as will appear later in this chapter, equality can be interpreted in different ways, equality arguments in this context are generally linked to claims of gender discrimination which depend in turn on constitutional or international human rights norms.

## Alternatives to Equality?

As a result of feminists' dissatisfaction with the limited results of legal claims for equality, especially for the most disadvantaged groups of women (and men), they have begun to explore the potential of other concepts such as social justice and freedom as foundations for new descriptions and analyses to deal with problems which appear to be unresponsive to traditional equality analyses.

Particularly promising is a transformative model of social justice (Auchmuty 2008, Jhappan 1998) of which Iris Marion Young's work is an example. She advocates a focus on social structures and institutional contexts, culture, symbols, habits and beliefs, relationships and processes rather than the achievement of rights or legal claims for equality (Young 1990). This model recognizes that oppression is group based and structurally imbedded in everyday processes and institutions, rather than being the result of deliberate discriminatory choices by privileged groups. Oppression manifests not only in discrimination, but in exploitation, marginalization, powerlessness, cultural imperialism and violence. The aim of social justice is not to achieve formal equality of treatment for all, but to ensure 'the full participation and inclusion of everyone in a society's major institutions, and the socially supported substantive opportunity for all to develop and exercise their capacities and realize their choices' with special representation for especially oppressed groups.[2]

Nancy Fraser (2003) adds another facet to the concept of social justice by arguing that it requires simultaneous transformation of three dimensions: satisfying marginalized groups' claims for recognition, claims for redistribution and claims for political participation (Fraser 2010: 365). The first two dimensions are especially important to my argument. Fraser shows how 'misrecognition' or social and cultural devaluation of certain groups like women and racialized minorities usually goes hand in hand with 'maldistribution' of economic resources. Gender is an example of this 'two dimensional social differentiation' where women suffer from social and cultural patterns which exclude and devalue them, which leads in turn to, or accompanies, gender specific economic disadvantages (Fraser 2003: 21) Fraser's aim of social justice echoes that of Young, namely 'participatory parity', or 'social arrangements that permit all (adult) members of society to interact with one another as peers' (36) which would require transformation of both cultural and social systems of misrecognition and economic systems of maldistribution.

The emphasis on full social and economic participation in both of these theories of social justice resonates with recent feminist scholarship focusing on (especially marginalized) women's lack of full citizenship (see, for example, Young in this collection). This has allowed feminists to contextualize abstract equality debates (see, for example, Bock and James 1992, Lister 1995, Gouws 1999) and to focus on the ways in which state policies, especially around welfare and childcare and limited access to state-provided goods and services, affect women's abilities to fully participate as active citizens (see, for example Lister 1990, Breitkreuz 2005, Goldblatt 2005). Instead of focusing on the achievement of equality as an abstract priority, the aim is to examine the ways in which state services could be better allocated in order to enhance women's citizenship. A variation of this approach is research which focuses on how government policies disadvantage poor women together with poor men, rather than on the differences between men and women (Boyd 2008).

Martha Nussbaum's capabilities approach shares the citizenship scholarship's emphasis on goals or outcomes, the focus on the needs of the most disadvantaged women and the goal of wider social and economic participation (Nussbaum 2000). Her work builds upon Amartya Sen's theories of development which target enhanced individual freedoms and capabilities as the route to national economic development. Sen's argument (1999) is that rather than focusing on increasing individuals' income, states should extend the agency of its citizens by guaranteeing individual freedoms or capabilities – understood comprehensively to include for instance the freedom or capability to avoid untimely death or hunger, and so forth – thus driving national development.

Nussbaum has adapted this theory to extend the feminist focus particularly to the ability of poor women to claim a 'threshold level of capabilities' from their governments. Although the goal is ultimately to ensure full equality, Nussbaum (2000: 12) acknowledges that '[t]he notion of a threshold is more important in my account than the notion of full capability equality'. The argument is that for the very poorest women the aim of achieving equality may currently be a distraction, or at least, unrealistic. Instead, a focus on a minimum level of individual capabilities would be more beneficial in the short term and would contribute towards the achievement of full equality in the long term. Capabilities are formulated in

---

2    Young 1990 calls this 'democratic pluralism' at 184–191.

terms of real socio-economic conditions and the realization of second and third generation human rights. This approach to some extent turns the equality argument on its head. Instead of arguing for gender equality in order to improve women's socio-economic conditions, Nussbaum (86) advocates for the improvement of socio-economic conditions first, postponing the debate about equality to a later stage. Her work implies that gender equality could be at least partly promoted by improving women's real social and economic conditions alongside the similar conditions affecting disadvantaged men.

Other feminists have argued for the formulation of new descriptions, concepts and legal rules to capture women's disadvantage, without getting bogged down in debates of whether women are similarly situated to men or not (see, for example, Lacey 1998). They contend that issues which harm women are not always easily framed in terms of equality and that, especially where the harm is most pervasive, societies and judges will tend to see them as either 'natural' or resulting from the choices made by the women in question. Catharine MacKinnon (1991) has for instance pointed to the general tendency to regard women's vulnerability to sexual assault as a result of their difference from men, and thus not amenable to change, rather than the effects of gender inequality: '[T]he worse the inequality is, the more like difference it looks' (1296). New ways of articulating women's concerns may therefore be more persuasive than relying on equality or inequality in the legal context.

Feminists have frequently developed specific concepts which have sat alongside equality analyses to explain particular manifestations of gendered disadvantage. In family and labour law, for instance, the gendered division of labour and its consequences, the feminization of poverty and the public/private dichotomy have been used to explain why women are unable to enter into paid work in the same way as men, why they are underpaid and why this situation is iniquitous. Concepts like date rape, sexual harassment, domestic violence, and the battered women syndrome have done much to explain women's vulnerability and the inadequacy of legal responses to violence against women (see, for example, Munro in this collection).

More recently Hunter (2008) has attempted to circumvent arguments around sameness and difference in debates about gendered remuneration differences by exploring the undervaluation of typically female work. In the context of legal aid funding she has also suggested a concept of 'policy neglect' to critique the lack of legal aid to cases which would typically affect women. In family law Susan Boyd (2008, 1989) has shown how legal rules based on formal equality could operate to the detriment of women who occupy traditional gender roles and suggested the concept of 'primary caretaker' as a mechanism for allocating child custody. Martha Fineman (2000) has argued that women's caring work within families leads to 'derivative dependency' which in turn reduces women's ability to provide financially for themselves. She has extended the argument to contend that the state has a duty to ensure that systems which mitigate human vulnerability, like education, employment, healthcare and so forth, are available to all and to address the factors which create systemic disadvantage and privilege for different groups (Fineman 2011).

These feminist concepts have however not supplanted equality analyses, but have rather illustrated the limits of formal legal equality. Feminists, for instance, exposed the fiction of formal equality in the workplace by drawing attention to the real contexts of workers who are systematically exploited and harassed on the basis of their gender. Analyses of the gendered division of labour and of intimate partner violence similarly disrupted the complacent assumptions of gender equality and harmony within families. In turn, these special feminist concepts are often articulated as claims for substantive equality, for instance arguing that formally equal child custody and division of matrimonial property is insufficient to compensate for the effect of women's disproportionate burden of caring labour within the family (Boyd 2008). Rather than special concepts competing with equality, the relationship between them should be mutually enriching and supportive. Moreover, the uncomfortable truism is that those men and women who access greater social, economic and discursive power can use feminist legal concepts like domestic violence and sexual harassment to their advantage as they can the concept of equality (see, for example, Mehra 1998).

The other approaches – social justice, citizenship and capabilities – are likewise not true alternatives to equality, because they all contain intrinsic elements of equality or at least imply the goal of gender and other forms of social equality. The full social and cultural participation for everyone and the eradication of exploitation, marginalisation and violence as advocated by Young, for instance, implies a commitment to end domination of certain groups over others. Fraser's 'participatory parity' explicitly names equality of participation as the goal of social justice, while citizenship and capabilities both, although not focusing on equality, could not be ultimately satisfied where certain groups' citizenship rights or capabilities remain disproportionately dominant as compared to others. These approaches widen the lens of equality from a narrow focus on legal rules and norms to the wider social, political and economic contexts within which law operates. As a consequence they link gender equality to socio-economic equality, urge engagement with structures, institutions and practices which have not traditionally been regarded as 'legal', and suggest new strategies and pathways for feminist activists (see, for example, Davies 2008).

The insights developed by social justice theorists have enriched and contributed to the development of a concept of substantive equality. It may be, therefore, that the problem resides not in the concept of equality itself, but in the ways in which equality claims could best be pursued in liberal, individualistic Anglo-American and continental legal systems in which concepts of justice, as Robin West (2003) points out, are inextricably bound to the formal notion of an unbiased, neutral judiciary which decides like cases in a similar manner. A focus on justice within Anglo-American legal systems would therefore not necessarily escape the difficulties associated with equality. My point is that although all of these theories provide valuable insights, none can ultimately replace equality as a legal goal or value. Even if they do not focus on *rights* to equality – as legally understood and articulated – at least the *value* of equality remains central to them all.

The next section takes a closer look at the problems associated with legal approaches to equality which underlie the formulation of many of these alternative theories.

## Equal to Whom? Which Differences Matter?

I have pointed out that equality is, at heart, a comparative concept, involving the questions, equal to whom, and equal in which respects? This section will examine the history of feminist legal thought through the lens of equality claims. The theme of the first subsection is the way in which the comparator group – to whom women have been compared – and also the group 'women' who have been compared to others, have shifted over time and across various strains of feminist theory. A secondary theme is the way in which difficult and deeply contested debates around equality have been extremely productive for feminist theory by contributing to the development of several basic feminist concepts currently in use. The second subsection will highlight some of the problems associated with a focus on differences within equality theory.

## Different from Whom?

As indicated by others in this collection, we can analyse feminist approaches to equality by comparing the differences which they regard as central to inequality and which they attempt to remedy. I will focus both on the people or groups of people who are compared with one another and on the characteristics which form the basis of the comparisons.

It is generally said that eighteenth- and nineteenth-century feminists were primarily concerned with granting middle class women access to the public sphere on an equal footing with men. Issues included women's suffrage, access to university education and to the professions. Feminists took issue with the prevailing orthodoxy that (middle and upper class) women's physical, psychological and intellectual characteristics were so different from those of men that they were to be barred, or 'protected' from entry into public life (Rhode 1989, Lacey 1998). Contrary to the perception that all feminists during this period insisted that women were essentially similar to men (according to Rhode 1989 'the rhetoric of rights' or what could be labelled liberal feminism), feminist arguments for women's inclusion were often based on the extent to which public life would be enriched and improved by women's special moral characteristics, particularly the nurturing and caring qualities associated with motherhood (Auchmuty 2008) also known as 'the rhetoric of roles' (Rhode 1989) or cultural feminism. Many of the early legal struggles for women's admission into the public sphere involved the even more fundamental issue of whether women should be regarded as 'persons' in the legal sense (Schultz 2003). Women's struggles to be admitted to the legal profession in different countries provide probably the most notorious examples of the debates about women's legal personhood and their differences from and similarities to men.[3]

An important feminist concept which arose from these and similar debates was the extent to which differences between men and women were inherent or biological (sex-based) on the one hand, or the result of socialization (gender-based) (Rhode 1989, Lacey 1998), on the other, although this particular terminology was not initially used (see, further, Cowan in this collection). Despite women's admission into the privileges of legal personhood around the end of the nineteenth and in the early twentieth centuries, these same debates continue still, and often on the same terrain. In relation to the legal profession, for instance, it is argued that removal of formal barriers to women's participation has left exclusionary cultural, social and practical obstacles intact (see, for example, Hunter 2002, Thornton 1996), while feminists continue to explore the issue of whether there is a distinct female voice, method or approach to law which women contribute to the profession (see, for example, Graycar 1998, Bogosh 1999, Bonthuys 2008a). Another abiding feminist theme flowing from earlier versions of explicitly and exclusively male legal personality, is the gendered nature of legal subjectivity (see, for example, Naffine 1990, 2003), and the masculinity of the law and legal systems in general.

In addition to addressing women's access to the public sphere, early feminists also addressed middle and upper class women's legal disadvantages within marriage, focusing

---

3    See for instance on the Canadian situation Kay and Brockman 2003; in South Africa see *Incorporated Law Society v Wookey* 1912 AD 623 and for Australia see Thornton 1996.

on women's lack of rights in relation to children and marital property. Similar arguments about women's difference or sameness to men were used to attack legal restrictions on women's legal capacity and personality within the family as were used in the public sphere of waged labour, education and suffrage (Auchmuty 2008).

The focus on and the questions around the differences between men and women was sustained in the twentieth century, but the terrain of the debate shifted away from blatant forms of exclusion to persistent inequalities in waged labour (see, for example, Fudge in this collection), family law (see, for example, Boyd and Auchmuty in this collection) and legal responses to violence and sexual assault against women (see, for example, Munro in this collection). Because these problems were not as clearly caused by formal exclusion, feminists investigated the social, cultural, institutional and economic contexts which structured disadvantageous positions for women. Depending upon their explanations for women's subordinate position, various strains of feminist theory identified factors such as the exploitation of women's labour by capitalist society (Marxist and socialist feminists), women's ability to bear children and their nurturing behaviour, women's distinctive moral reasoning (cultural and relational feminists) and various forms of male violence and sexual exploitation of women (radical feminists) as the salient differences to be addressed by equality theory. These explanations lead in turn to socialist and Marxist feminist analyses, cultural feminism and radical feminism together with their associated conceptual tools. It was said at this time that feminists could be described as being either 'maximizers' or 'minimizers' of difference (McFadden 1984, Humm 1992), with the maximizers arguing that the differences between men and women were ineradicable and that women's particular abilities and contributions should be more highly valued (also called 'difference' feminism), while minimizers ('sameness' feminism) held that there are few real differences between the sexes and that the aim should be to treat men and women the same (see, for example, Okin 1990).

This heated and complex feminist debate about whether or not women are the same as men was however overtaken by the next set of feminist debates on equality and difference which questioned the racial and class aspects of the very category 'women'. Foreshadowed by Sojourner Truth and other African-American women in the late 1800s United States, the 'gender essentialism' (see, for example, Harris 1990) hitherto engaged in by white middle class feminists was subjected to strong academic criticism. African-American women illustrated the racism inherent in much white middle class feminism, which tended to exclude black and working class women from its ranks and its concerns. Indeed, the very problems defined as women's issues were those facing predominantly white, middle class, first world women (see, for example, hooks 1981). This essentialism entailed that,

> [w]hen black people are talked about the focus tends to be on black **men**, and when women are talked about the focus tends to be on white **women**. Nowhere is this more evident than in the vast body of feminist literature. (hooks 1981: 7)

The force and persuasiveness of this critique opened the way for similar views to be expressed on the basis of class, sexual orientation, disability and third world citizenship. These forms of critique lead to various important feminist concepts, such as intersectionality (see Harris

1990, Romany 1997),[4] or the idea that various forms or axes of disadvantage overlap and interact with one another to situate different women in different positions of relative social privilege or oppression. Claims that the standpoint of the most oppressed women should be privileged (see, for example, Minow 1987, Collins 1991), and promotion of multiple consciousness as an explanation for the way in which many women experience the different aspects of their lives (see, for example, Matsuda 1989, Wing 1997) were other key theoretical positions associated with intersectional analysis. Most importantly, the assumption of uncomplicated female solidarity became unsustainable in the face of women's differing and sometimes opposing interests. As Chandra Mohanty (1988: 77) put it,

> [b]eyond sisterhood there is still racism, colonialism and imperialism.

Given the existence of powerful structures of oppression beyond, or in addition to gender, a crucial question now facing feminist theory is whether gender is more fundamental to women's disadvantage than race, class, religion and other socially relevant categories of difference. Some have argued that gender somehow precedes other bases of oppression by being implicated in the very structures of thought and language, while others have conceded that, on the whole, gender may not be more fundamental than race or class in any particular context (see Lacey 1998). Flowing from this problem, feminists living in religiously, culturally and racially diverse societies must deal with the complexities of achieving gender justice without imposing 'Western' values on cultural, religious and racial minorities (see Cohen et al 1999; Bano and Song in this collection). The political and legal tensions around the wearing of headscarves by French Muslim women illustrate the contestation around and manipulation of gender equality in such circumstances. Other examples centre on the recognition of religious marriages on the one hand, and the goal of gender equality and non-discrimination on the basis of sexual orientation on the other hand. These dilemmas show the complex interaction between gender equality and other interests, such as rights to culture and religion.

Having once acknowledged some of the differences between women, feminism was next faced with a bewildering proliferation of differences in the form of postmodern or poststructuralist feminist theory, which can be described as radically anti-essentialist in its insistence that women's identities are not fixed by either gender, race, class or sexual orientation, but are continuously produced and re-produced by competing and contradictory discourses. In its emphasis on the particular, postmodern feminism denies the usefulness of grand theory, including grand feminist theory (see, for example, Nicholson 1990, Frug 1992). These ideas so radically destabilize the category woman, that many feminists feel the need to defend the idea of female solidarity as a basis for feminism, at least in the form of an aspiration or goal. Other feminists have welcomed the opportunity to focus on local, particular and contingent practices of domination, rather than trying to find universal explanations for women's subordination, especially because this approach also highlights opportunities for women's agency and resistance (Offen 1990, Conaghan 2000).

Feminist theory can therefore be said to have at first focused on the physical, intellectual and moral differences between men and women. It then moved to differences of class, race, sexual orientation, disability, religion between differently situated groups of women and

---

4    See however the argument by Conaghan 2007 that the concept of intersectionality fails to explain the complex positions occupied by most women.

acknowledged that various combinations of these factors would structure different interests and needs for various groups of women and would render some of them particularly vulnerable to certain forms of domination. Currently the emphasis is on even more limited social contexts and environments, where many micro factors interact in complex and sometimes contradictory ways to create both oppression and opportunities for resistance for small groups of women in specific contexts. The problems associated with this movement from 'women' to very particularly situated women have been encapsulated by Deborah Rhode (1989: 2):

> The more adequate the acknowledgement of differences among women, the more difficult it is to represent common perspectives or concerns.

## Difficulties with Difference

In addition to the potential of radical anti-essentialism to unravel the feminist project entirely, this section will also describe other 'dilemmas of difference' (Minow 1987). Because the issues are so well-traversed in the feminist literature, I will present only the broad outlines and some examples of the debates.

The importance of difference to the equality project flows from an Aristotelian view of equality as treating likes alike and 'unlikes' differently (Rhode 1989). This is the basis of a 'formal' understanding of equality and the one with which legal method is most comfortable. West has pointed out that, despite the persistent critiques of formal equality, we should acknowledge that it aims to distinguish legal decision-making from 'political' reasoning, which may favour particular interest groups (West 2003: 10) and that it may therefore

> be rooted in a universalist and humanistic inclination to define the human community broadly – to envision a community that includes all, and includes all because of a recognition of a shared humanity.

Nevertheless, feminists have pointed to several negative consequences of linking equality to the establishment of legally relevant difference.

Both in talking about the differences between men and women, on the one hand, and the differences between women, on the other, the tendency is to regard the disadvantaged group or the group claiming equality as being different, and to believe that these differences define and constrain them entirely (Minow 1987, Young 1990). The advantaged comparator group, however, remains the unspoken norm to which the differently situated should aspire, while themselves not having to change at all. Mohanty (1988: 80–81) has, for example, pointed to the belief that every third world woman:

> leads an essentially truncated life based on her feminine gender (read: sexually constrained) and being "third world" (read: ignorant, poor, uneducated, tradition-bound, religious, domesticated, family-oriented, victimized, etc.) This ... is in contrast to the (implicit) self-representation of western women as modern, as having control over their own bodies and sexualities, and the "freedom" to make their own decisions.

Such a dichotomous and oversimplified view of difference reinforces negative stereotypes of disadvantaged groups as lacking socially valued qualities (Smart 1989, Young 1990,

MacKinnon 1991). It also reduces legal equality solutions to either assimilating the disadvantaged group and treating them the same as the dominant group, or retaining their 'difference' and therewith their disadvantaged position (Minow 1987). A clear illustration of this problem is found in the early US labour law cases which held that employers who refused to grant maternity benefits were merely distinguishing between pregnant women and non-pregnant persons. There was, by implication no issue of gender discrimination, since employers treated differently situated people differently, not on the basis of gender, but on the basis of difference (Rhode 1989).

A further problem is that the principle about treating likes alike and unlikes differently doesn't establish which differences are appropriate for the purposes of comparison (Rhode 1989). This leaves the definition of legally relevant difference within the 'terrain of political struggle' (Young 1990) and, in a conservative and inherently patriarchal discipline like law, often to be defined in the interests of the powerful. Maintaining the status quo is usually achieved by focusing only on legal differences between groups and regarding the differences created by social, cultural, economic and institutional contexts as legally irrelevant or 'private' (Lacey 1998). However, these factors continue to shape people's behaviour and abilities and may exclude the majority of women from taking advantage of gender-neutral legal rules (Young 1990). So, for instance, were an educated middle-class woman to bring a successful challenge against educational policies which exclude her from tertiary education, her success would be meaningless for other women who may be excluded as a result of poor primary education, lack of resources, cultural norms favouring early marriage and so forth.

Another frequently used legal strategy is to argue that women's particular difficulties are not the result of their difference, but of choices voluntarily made. This is generally followed by the liberal exhortation that the legal system should give effect to these choices – together with their usually detrimental consequences.[5] Thus, for example, the South African Constitutional Court has held that heterosexual female cohabitants choose to relinquish the social and legal benefits associated with marriage[6] and that '[t]he stigma that attaches to prostitutes attaches to them … by virtue of the conduct they engage in',[7] implying that sex workers choose to be stigmatized. Such an understanding of choice not only deliberately evades the real issues of women's differences and disadvantages within sexual relationships, but it also disregards the real social, cultural and economic contexts which structure the choices open to the most vulnerable women.

Moreover, the result of holding that a particular group is differently situated from the comparator can be inconsistent and contradictory, as illustrated by the ways in which assumptions of women's difference from men was used to argue both for and against admitting them into all-male professions like the law and the army (Rhode 1989).

Legal equality claims would be further shaped by the requirements that an individual claimant proves an individual right and, if successful, receives an individual remedy. In some instances, such as blatant exclusion of women from education institutions, for instance, this approach would ameliorate the situation for women whose social circumstances mirror those of the particular complainant. However, this is not enough. It leaves the door open for men to be equally, if not more successful than women in claiming gender discrimination

---

5    See for Canada, Philipps 2004; for the US, West 1985; Lacey 1998 in the context of the United Kingdom; and for South Africa, Bonthuys 2008b.

6    *Volks NO v Robinson* 2005 (5) BCLR 446 (CC) at paras 55, 91–93.

7    *Jordan v S* 2002 (11) BCLR 1117 (CC) at para. 16.

(Smart 1989, Lacey 1998) whenever women's differences are reflected in different legal treatment. Feminists have noted, for instance, how men have been able to harness the discourse of equality to advocate gender-neutral family law rules which award the same rights and duties to parents of both sexes. However, because gendered social expectations continue to demand that women take primary responsibility for childcare, gender-neutral rules generally benefit fathers at the expense of mothers (see Smart and Sevenhuijsen 1989, Fineman 1991, Graycar 2003).

The essence of the feminist critique of formal equality and its concomitant focus on difference is that it fails to provide a satisfactory solution to the problems of social, cultural and economic structures of privilege and disadvantage, but instead often simply rationalises the status quo. Young suggests an alternative concept of difference which is relational – a function of the relationships between people, rather than an aspect of disadvantaged groups – structural in the sense that it is not just caused by individual prejudice, and contingent upon time and social context. She also warns that a fixation on differences should not obscure the similarities and commonalities between the groups of people who are compared (Young 1990).

## Moving Away from Difference – Substantive Equality

The insights of social justice theorists like Young and Fraser have informed the legal concept of substantive equality which aims to cure the effects of formal equality by moving away from an exclusive and formalistic focus on difference. Substantive equality renders explicit the relationships between difference and power – showing the disadvantages caused by socially relevant difference rather than considering difference as important in itself (Rhode 1989, MacKinnon 1991, Young 1990). Three features of this concept stand out.

First, it is effects-oriented in considering the impact of difference, rather than the differentiation itself and entails a commitment towards dismantling disadvantage rather than eradicating difference (Minow 1987, Rhode 1989). This recognizes, for instance, that arguments by men that women should stay at home to look after children are not equivalent to arguments by women who insist that childcare is work and that they should be entitled to do it full time (Rhode 1989). In the first instance the claim is made to exclude women from the public sphere of wage work, while the second constitutes a claim on society to recognize the value of the work that women do and they have different implications for the power relationships between women and the fathers of their children, their employers and so forth.

In considering the impact of difference and of possible solutions to ameliorate disadvantage, both the dimensions of distribution and recognition, as formulated by Fraser, should be considered. This would mean that a court should consider, for instance, whether or not a particular allocation of material resources would improve the status and social recognition of the disadvantaged group, in other words, have a socially transformative effect, or whether it would confirm oppressive social structures while admitting only a few disadvantaged people to existing privileges (Albertyn 2007). Simultaneously, the impact of measures designed to improve the status of disadvantaged groups on the distribution of material resources should be considered. Fraser (2003) calls this 'perspectival dualism'. The consequence is that equality is equated neither with sameness, nor different treatment, but the current and historical context of the problem determines which solution would best address the particular harm complained of (Fraser 2003).

This leads to the second characteristic of substantive equality, namely that differences and their effects are viewed in concrete social contexts, rather than by reference to abstract legal norms. This recognizes that people are socially situated and that their abilities and opportunities are determined by their relationships with other people (Young 1990, Lacey 1998). It also recognizes that people live in sexed and racialized bodies and that legal differentiation may have both physical and social consequences (Young 1990, Lacey 1998). Context would also include the history of past disadvantage, which may still have symbolic, material or social consequences for the disadvantaged group.

Finally, context extends beyond the personal circumstances of individual equality claimants to the structures or patterns of domination affecting groups of people (Rhode 1989, Young 1990). This recognizes that disadvantage goes beyond individual prejudice by members of the advantaged groups to structural social relationships which consistently favour certain groups in particular ways. These patterns or structures include the interaction between gender and other socially relevant factors such as race, class, religion, culture and sexual orientation (Rhode 1989).

## The Limitations of Substantive Equality

In Canada and South Africa, both regarded as having progressive legal systems committed to a substantive understanding of equality, feminists have nevertheless remarked upon courts' unresponsiveness to claims for gender equality. Feminists have shown that the most privileged women are more likely to lodge and succeed with equality claims (Lawrence 2004, Jagwanth 2005) and that courts very often fail to understand and apply substantive equality correctly and consistently (Graycar and Morgan 2004, Hunter 2008). Although gender equality claims typically succeed in relation to domestic violence and reproductive rights, judicial responses to sex workers, women's claims in family law and socio-economic rights are often rejected using formalistic, a-contextual reasoning (Majury 2002, Bonthuys 2008b). Judgments are often inclusive rather than transformative – protecting certain vulnerable women and admitting a few women into the fold of privilege, but failing to challenge gendered stereotypes or social norms and structures (Albertyn 2007, Bonthuys 2008b). Moreover, the use of substantive equality tends to be interspersed with episodes of formal equality reasoning (Brodsky 2001, Albertyn 2007, Douglas 2008, Boyd 2008). Judges often fail to apply elements of substantive equality like intersectionality correctly, resulting in essentialism and ignoring the position of the most disadvantaged women (Duclos 1993, Pothier 2001, Hannet 2003, Bonthuys 2008b). They also deflect gender-equality claims by espousing a liberal view of society in which individual women's life choices are unaffected by their social, economic and cultural contexts (Fudge 1987, Bonthuys 2008b). Feminist scholars have shown that courts easily understand and take account of typically 'male' contexts, for instance the rage and sexual jealousy which could lead to domestic violence, but fail to understand women's experiences and reactions, and require expert evidence of women's behaviour in the context of domestic violence. Even when courts accept such expert evidence, their interpretations may nevertheless strengthen stereotypes about women's emotional instability and need for protection (Graycar and Morgan 2004, Bonthuys 2008b, Douglas 2008).

There are generally three groups of explanations put forward for courts' inadequate application of substantive equality. They relate to courts' failure to understand substantive equality, issues inherent in the concept itself and, finally, limitations imposed by the nature of law and the legal process.

Reg Graycar and Jenny Morgan (2004) argue that judges and legal practitioners simply don't read academic literature, and that complex and sophisticated feminist analyses are not as easily understood and applied as the more familiar concepts of formal equality. Difficulties with substantive equality may also be due to the way in which it has been linked to the constitutional value of dignity, understood in an individualistic, liberal sense (Fudge 1987, Albertyn 2007). Finally, there are indications that some courts may be convinced by the neo-liberal rhetoric that women have already achieved equality and that they therefore assume that formal equality is appropriate (Graycar and Morgan 2004, Boyd 2008, Hunter 2008). These courts therefore do not apply substantive equality because they misunderstand, or are not informed of,[8] real social contexts of disadvantage.

The second group of criticisms point out that the concept of substantive equality may contain the seeds for its own misapplication and for the typical slippage into formal equality which occurs in legal arguments and judgments. Despite representing a great improvement on formal equality, substantive equality retains a comparative element which is embedded in legal equality jurisprudence worldwide (Jhappan 1998, Majury 2002). This means that the problems about the comparator figure, discussed in relation to formal equality, are never far away. It also means that, when women claim equality, the outcomes are constrained to what is already available to privileged men, thus limiting the transformative potential of equality claims. Graycar and Morgan (2004) argue, for instance, that if Australian gay and lesbian groups claimed only equal recognition of their relationships to those of heterosexual couples, admission to the sexist institution of marriage would have been the limit of their achievement. Moreover, the comparison between men and women required for equality claims fuel the 'gender wars' – the unhelpful assertion that women are always the victims and that all men deliberately oppress them. Boyd (2008) points out that, in the area of child custody, this fails to capture the ways in which both mothers and fathers of certain classes may be disadvantaged by government policies on childcare or other structural elements like workplace norms.

Another criticism relates to the fact that equality tends to be legally and constitutionally linked to a set of grounds, such as gender, race, religion and so forth. Joanne Conaghan (2007) argues that this allows courts to perceive the harm as emanating from the grounds themselves, rather than focusing on the conditions of oppression for certain groups of people. Nevertheless, the counterargument is that the grounds signify actual patterns of disadvantage within most societies and that without grounds to guide them courts would not necessarily have done more to alleviate inequality (Pothier 2001).

Perhaps the shortcomings of substantive equality proceed as much from the structure of legal reasoning and the processes and possibilities inherent in liberal legal systems as from conceptual deficiencies. Common law method notoriously relies on abstracting and classifying people, situations and relationships as being either similar to or different from a particular precedent (West 1985, Mossman 1987, Code 1991, Williams 1993). Lawyers therefore find the notions of sameness and difference in formal equality familiar, while the need to contextualize inherent in substantive equality runs counter to their understanding of what is legally 'relevant' (Smart 1989). In her analysis of women's access to the legal profession, Hilary Sommerlad (2008) has for instance demonstrated how values based

---

8    Feminist litigation strategies may contribute to this. See, for example, Lawrence 2004.

on status, race, gender and ethnicity continue to exclude certain 'outsiders' and reinforce hierarchies of privilege in the profession. These factors are not explicitly articulated, but disguised as a concern for 'merit', 'suitability' or choice. The persistence of such factors may be impossible to prove to a court, especially when the upper echelons of the legal system often embody the same values.

Law especially prizes its image as neutral, objective and impartial, yet feminists have repeatedly demonstrated the impossibility of legal neutrality and how the legal system and legal method are implicated in upholding the status quo based on systemic inequality (Young 1990, Lacey 1998). Some judges regard it as a hallmark of impartiality to treat sexism and feminism or racism and anti-racism in same way, for instance (Graycar and Morgan 2004). It is in this very flawed claim to neutrality that law grounds its promise to deliver equality.

Diana Majury (2002 at 316) speculates that gender equality has not been central to the legal advancement of Canadian women, possibly 'because equality is not central to the betterment of women's lives'. However, the problem may lie more with the limits associated with legal reasoning and litigation as transformative strategies, leading other feminists to conclude that 'the best law has to offer falls far short of solving the problem of inequality' (Conaghan 2007) and to look toward non-legal strategies rather than legal claims to realize gender equality (Smart 1989). This seems also to be the point of alternative concepts such as social justice which emphasize the need for engagement beyond traditional legal territory. However, the next section shows that there may be developments in relation to socio-economic rights which may tempt us to re-engage with law.

## New Frontiers of Equality:
## Positive State Duties and Socio-economic Rights

While the imperfect application of substantive equality has led some feminists to express exasperation with the concept, others have on the one hand been pushing the boundaries of substantive equality and, on the other hand, using a substantive concept of equality to expand understandings of other human rights, particularly socio-economic entitlements. Fraser's twin goals of social recognition and material redistribution play an important role in many of these theoretical formulations. The eradication of disadvantages relating to status and material wellbeing and the eradication of social, cultural and material systems of domination become the goals of substantive equality, which are, in turn, linked to the achievement of socio-economic rights. In this respect, new advances in substantive equality theory link to the literature dealing with capabilities and citizenship described above.

Sandra Fredman (2008) has used a concept of substantive equality to challenge the liberal legal view of human rights which requires states only to refrain from discrimination and infringement upon individual rights (negative state obligations). She argues that a purely negative concept of state obligations can never accomplish Fraser's goals of recognition and redistribution. Legal liberalism casts the state only as a potential adversary to the achievement of human rights, but ignores the ways in which positive state action can enhance the socio-economic conditions of citizens and thus counter structural disadvantage. In this view equality is a site of conflict between state and citizens, rather than the shared social goal (Fredman 2008).

Canadian feminists have warned of their experience that courts are most likely to fall back on a formal understanding of equality when asked to adjudicate on concrete socio-economic benefits (Majury 2002, Fudge 2007). Nevertheless, feminists like Beth Goldblatt, Sandra Liebenberg (2007) and Fredman (2007) have emphasized the connection between status-based inequality, or 'misrecognition' and inadequate access to material resources – 'maldistribution' in Fraser's work. From this premise Fredman has argued that without redistributive measures status inequalities cannot be effectively alleviated. For this reason states should be tasked with providing for the socio-economic needs of their citizens or 'the use of resources to create a sense of universal citizenship' (Fredman 2007: 226) and 'to facilitate full participation in society' (Fredman 2007 at 227). Legally enforceable socio-economic rights have therefore been linked to the theories of social justice via an expanded concept of substantive equality.

Socio-economic rights are explicitly included in the South African Constitution. Liebenberg and Goldblatt (2007) have drawn on the links between status inequality and the inability of low status groups to access socio-economic benefits on the one hand, and the interrelatedness of all human rights as articulated in international human rights law on the other hand. They have used these premises to argue for an 'interpretative interdependence' between rights to substantive equality and socio-economic rights. This would entail the mutual imbrication of substantive equality and socio-economic rights so that the allocation of socio-economic benefits is subjected to substantive equality, while equality itself cannot be achieved without socio-economic transformation.

Although these attempts respond to the limitations and opportunities within specific legal systems, they may provide inspiration to the equality project in general. Another model is provided by the Scandinavian welfare states in which structural issues, such as female responsibility for child and family care and women's full participation in the labour market, have been addressed by extensive welfare entitlements and social services, rather than relying on using legal rights to equality to address individual entitlements (Johansson and Jansson 1989, Nousiainen, 2009, however see Skjeie 2009). It has been argued that this has reduced women's economic dependency on men, but in turn created an overwhelmingly female reliance on the state (Johansson and Jansson 1989). Nevertheless, the success or failure of such alternatives strategies is strongly dependent on the legal and political context. It would be extremely difficult to argue for socio-economic rights or an expanded system of social welfare in those legal and political cultures in which liberalism and individualism are such entrenched values as, for instance, the United States.

## Conclusion: A Strategic Move Away from Equality?

I have shown two contrasting feminist engagements with equality. While there are those who seem to abandon the concept in favour of what they regard as more productive theories and models, others are engaged in expanding understandings of substantive equality in order to make states responsible for the eradication of systemic domination. I would contend that feminists can and should do both. Halley (2006: 8) argues that 'sustaining competing theories for describing the same social arrangements can expand our sense of the stakes at stake when we make our choices about what to see as a social good and a social bad'. The same could be said for equality. I have shown how insights and concepts from the theories of social justice, citizenship and capabilities have been creatively incorporated into models of substantive equality. At the same time, new formulations of substantive equality can provide impetus towards the practical goals articulated by the former group of theories.

Despite the limited gains of equality jurisprudence in Canada and South Africa not all feminists from these jurisdictions think that the concept should abandoned. In analysing South African jurisprudence, Saras Jagwanth (2005) has shown the usefulness of equality to inform the interpretation of legislation, to develop and expand common law rules and to justify positive legal duties on states. Progressive interpretations of equality are also crucial to protecting women's legal gains from conservative challenges which would erode them. These gains include purely formal rights of access to education and paid work which are nevertheless crucial to women's advancement (Offen 1990, Jagwanth 2005). Because law is 'too powerful to be ignored' (MacKinnon 1991: 1285), Carol Smart (1989) argues that it cannot be abandoned to those who wish to strengthen hierarchies based on racial, class and gender privilege. For the same reason feminists' continued engagement with equality is crucial (Rhode 1989).

Moreover, exasperation with the limits of equality may proceed from a desire to make one concept do all the work of social transformation. This is unrealistic and unnecessary, since there are many other human rights which could be harnessed to this task. For instance, Kamala Sankaran (2007) uses a broad interpretation of the right to life in the Indian Constitution to argue for the extension of women's socio-economic rights. In fact, mutuality between equality and other human rights, where each informs the interpretation of the other may be both progressive and more palatable to traditionalist judiciaries than radical concepts of equality (Majury 2002, Jagwanth 2005).

Finally, the meanings of equality and substantive equality are not fixed, but depend on the precedents, legal debates, constitutional regime and legislation found within particular jurisdictions (Fudge 1987, Albertyn 2007). In jurisdictions where substantive interpretations of equality are not yet accepted, conservative interpretations of formal equality must be engaged and the boundaries pushed towards a wider understanding and acceptance of substantive equality (West 2003). In jurisdictions where the space exists, substantive equality should be theoretically expanded, at the same time as alternative concepts and models are explored. In all jurisdictions equality retains its symbolic and political value as a rallying cry for women and other disadvantaged groups (Hunter 2008), and at least the potential to contribute to the advancement of women's interests.

# References

Albertyn, C. 2007. Substantive equality and transformation in South Africa. *South African Journal on Human Rights*, 23(2), 253–276.

Auchmuty, R. 2008. The Married Women's Property Acts: Equality was not the issue, in *Rethinking Equality Projects in Law*, edited by R. Hunter. Oxford and Portland, Oregon: Hart Publishing, 13–29.

Bock, G. and James, S. (eds), 1992. *Beyond Equality and Difference: Citizenship, Feminist Politics, Female Subjectivity*. London: Routledge.

Bogosh, B. 1999. Courtroom discourse and the gendered construction of professional identity. *Law & Social Inquiry*, 24(2), 329–375.

Bonthuys, E. 2008a. The personal and the judicial: Sex, gender and impartiality. *South African Journal on Human Rights*, 24(2), 239–262.

Bonthuys, E. 2008b. Institutional openness and resistance to feminist arguments: The example of the South African Constitutional Court. *Canadian Journal of Women and the Law*, 20(1), 1–36.

Boyd, S.B. 1989. Child custody, ideologies and employment. *Canadian Journal of Women and the Law*, 3(1), 111–133.

Boyd, S.B. 2008. Is equality enough? Fathers' rights and women's rights advocacy, in *Rethinking Equality Projects in Law*, edited by R. Hunter. Oxford and Portland, Oregon: Hart Publishing, 59–79.

Breitkreuz, R.S. 2005. Engendering citizenship? A critical feminist analysis of Canadian welfare-to-work policies and the employment experiences of lone mothers. *Journal of Sociology and Social Welfare*, 32(2), 147–165.

Brodsky, G. 2001. Constitutional equality in Canada, in *Equality Law: Reflections for South Africa and Elsewhere*, edited by S. Jagwanth and E. Kalula. Cape Town: Juta, 241–254.

Code, L. 1991. *What Can She Know? Feminist Theory and the Construction of Knowledge*. Ithaca: Cornell University Press.

Cohen, J., Howard, M. and Nussbaum, M. (eds), 1999. *Is Multiculturalism Bad for Women?* Princeton: Princeton University Press.

Collins, P.H. 1991. *Black Feminist Thought: Knowledge, Consciousness and the Politics of Empowerment*. 1st edition. New York: Routledge.

Conaghan, J. 2000. Reassessing the feminist theoretical project in law. *Journal of Law & Society*, 27(3), 351–385.

Conaghan, J. 2007. Intersectionality and UK equality initiatives. *South African Journal on Human Rights*, 23(2), 317–334.

Davies. M. 2008. Feminism and flat law theory. *Feminist Legal Studies*, 16(3) 281–304.

Douglas, H. 2008. The demise of the equality defence and the failure of equality concepts, in *Rethinking Equality Projects in Law*, edited by R. Hunter. Oxford and Portland, Oregon: Hart Publishing, 41–57.

Duclos, N. 1993. Disappearing women: Racial minority women in human rights cases. *Canadian Journal of Women and Law*, 6(1), 25–51.

Fineman, M.A. 1991. *The Illusion of Equality: The Rhetoric and Reality of Divorce Law Reform*. Chicago: University of Chicago Press.

Fineman, M.A. 2000. Cracking the foundational myths: Independence, autonomy, and self-sufficiency. *American University Journal of Gender, Social Policy and the Law*, 8(1), 13–30.

Fineman, M.A. 2011. Vulnerability, equality and the human condition, in *Gender, Sexualities and Law*, edited by J. Jones et al. Oxford: Routledge, 53–62.

Fraser, A.S. 1999. Becoming human: The origins and development of women's human rights. *Human Rights Quarterly*, 21(4), 853–906.

Fraser, N. 2010. Injustice at intersecting scales: On 'social exclusion' and the 'global poor.' *European Journal of Social Theory*, 13(3), 363–371.

Fraser, N. 2003. Social Justice in the Age of Identity Politics: Redistribution, Recognition, and Participation, in *Redistribution or Recognition? A Political-Philosophical Exchange*, by N. Fraser and A. Honneth. London: Verso.

Fredman, S. 2007. Redistribution and recognition: Reconciling inequalities. *South African Journal on Human Rights*, 23(2), 214–234.

Fredman, S. 2008. *Human Rights Transformed: Positive Rights and Positive Duties*. Oxford: Oxford University Press.

Frug, M.J. 1992. *Postmodern Legal Feminism*. New York: Routledge.

Fudge, J. 1987. The public/private distinction: The possibilities of and the limits to the use of Charter litigation to further feminist struggles. *Osgoode Hall Law Journal*, 25(2), 485–554.

Fudge, J. 2007. Substantive equality, the Supreme Court of Canada and the limits to redistribution. *South African Journal on Human Rights*, 23(2), 235–252.

Goldblatt, B. 2005. Citizenship and the right to child care, in *(Un)thinking Citizenship: Feminist Debates in Contemporary South Africa*, edited by A. Gouws. Aldershot: Ashgate, 117–136.

Gouws, A. 1999. Beyond equality and difference: The politics of women's citizenship. *Agenda*, 15(40), 54–58.

Graycar, R. 1998. The gender of judgments: Some reflections on "Bias." *University of British Columbia Law Review*, 32(1), 1–21.

Graycar, R. 2003. Law reform by frozen chook: Family law reform for the new millennium? in *Family Law: Processes, Practices, Pressures*, edited by J. Dewar and S. Parker. Oxford and Portland, Oregon: Hart Publishing, 455–474.

Graycar, R. and Morgan, J. 2004. Examining understandings of equality: One step forward, two steps back? *Australian Feminist Law Journal*, 20, 23–42.

Halley, J. 2006. *Split Decisions: How and Why to Take a Break from Feminism*. Princeton: Princeton University Press.

Hannet, S. 2003. Equality at the intersections: The legislative and judicial failure to tackle multiple discrimination. *Oxford Journal of Legal Studies*, 23(1), 65–86.

Harris, A.P. 1990. Race and essentialism in feminist legal theory. *Stanford Law Review*, 42(3), 581–616.

hooks, b. 1981. *Ain't I a Woman? Black Women and Feminism*. London: Pluto Press.

Humm, M. (ed.), 1992. *Feminisms: A Reader*. Hemel Hempstead: Harvester Wheatsheaf.

Hunter, R. 2002. Border protection in law's empire: Feminist explorations of access to justice. *Griffiths Law Review*, 11(2), 263–285.

Hunter, R. 2008. Alternatives to equality, in *Rethinking Equality Projects in Law*, edited by R. Hunter. Oxford and Portland, Oregon: Hart Publishing, 81–101.

Jagwanth, S. 2005. Expanding equality. *Acta Juridica*, 131–148.

Jhappan, R. 1998. The equality pit or the rehabilitation of justice. *Canadian Journal of Women and Law*, 10(1), 60–107.

Johansson, S. and Jansson, M. 1989. Vocabularies of citizenship and gender: Sweden. *Critical Social Policy*, 18(3), 397–415.

Kay, F.M. and Brockman, J. 2003. Barriers to gender equality in the Canadian legal establishment, in *Women in the World's Legal Professions*, edited by U. Schultz and G. Shaw. Portland, Oregon: Oxford, 49–75.

Lacey, N. 1998. *Unspeakable Subjects: Feminist Essays in Legal and Social Theory*. Oxford: Hart.

Lawrence, S. 2004. Feminism, consequences, accountability. *Osgoode Hall Law Journal*, 42(4), 583–601.

Liebenberg, S. and Goldblatt, B. 2007. The interrelationship between equality and socio–economic rights under South Africa's transformative constitution. *South African Journal on Human Rights*, 23(2), 335–361.

Lister, R. 1990. Women, economic dependency and citizenship. *Journal of Social Policy*, 19(4), 445–467.

Lister, R. 1995. Dilemmas in engendering citizenship. *Economy and Society*, 24(1), 35–40.

Loenen, T. 1995. Comparative legal feminist scholarship and the importance of a contextual approach to concepts and strategies: The case of the equality debate. *Feminist Legal Studies*, 3(1), 71–87.

MacKinnon, C.A. 1991. Reflections on sex equality under law. *Yale Law Journal*, 100(5), 1281–1328.

Majury, D. 2002. The Charter, equality rights and women: Equivocation and celebration. *Osgoode Hall Law Journal*, 40(3), 297–336.

Matsuda, M. 1989. When the first quail calls: Multiple consciousness as jurisprudential method. *Women's Rights Law Reporter*, 11(7), 7–10.

McFadden, M. 1984. Anatomy of difference: Toward a classification of feminist theory. *Women's Studies International Forum*, 7(6), 495–504.

Mehra, M. 1998. Exploring the boundaries of law, gender and social reform. *Feminist Legal Studies*, 6(1), 59–83.

Minow, 1987. Justice engendered. *Harvard law Review*, 101(10), 10–95.

Mohanty, C.T. 1988. Under Western eyes: Feminist scholarship and colonial discourses. *Feminist Review*, 30(Autumn), 61–88.

Mossman, M.J. 1987. Feminism and legal method: The difference it makes. *Wisconsin Women's Law Journal*, 3, 147–168.

Naffine, N. 1990. *Law and the Sexes: Explorations in Feminist Jurisprudence*. Sidney: Allen & Unwin.

Naffine, N. 2003. Who are law's persons? From Cheshire cats to responsible subjects. *Modern Law Review*, 66(3), 347–367.

Nicholson, L. (ed.), 1990. *Feminism/Postmodernism*. New York: Routledge.

Nousiainen, K. 2009. Utility-based equality and disparate diversities: From a Finnish perspective, in *European Non-Discrimination Law: Comparative Perspectives on Multidimensional Equality Law*, edited by D. Scheik and V. Chege. London and New York. Routledge Cavendish, 187–214.

Nussbaum, M.C. 2000. *Women and Human Development: The Capabilities Approach*. Cambridge: Cambridge University Press.

Offen, K. 1990. Feminism and sexual difference in historical perspective, in *Theoretical Perspectives on Sexual Difference*, edited by D.L. Rhode. New Haven: Yale University Press, 13–20.

Okin, S.M. 1990. Thinking like a woman, in *Theoretical Perspectives on Sexual Difference*, edited by D.L. Rhode. New Haven: Yale University Press, 145–159.

Philipps, L. 2004. Measuring the effects of feminist legal research: Looking critically at "failure" and "success." *Osgoode Hall Law Journal*, 42(4), 603–614.

Pothier, D. 2001. Connecting grounds of discrimination to real people's real experiences. *Canadian Journal of Women and Law*, 13(1), 37–73.

Rhode, D.L. 1989. *Justice and Gender: Sex Discrimination and the Law*. Cambridge, MA: Harvard University Press.

Romany, C. 1997. "Ain't I a feminist?" in *Critical Race Feminism: A Reader*, edited by A.K. Wing. New York: New York University Press, 19–26.

Sankaran, K. 2007. Special provisions and access to socio-economic rights: Women and the Indian Constitution. *South African Journal on Human Rights*, 23(2), 277–290.

Schultz, U. 2003. Introduction: Women in the world's legal professions: Overview and synthesis, in *Women in the World's Legal Professions*, edited by U. Schultz and G. Shaw. Portland, Oregon: Oxford, xxv–lxii.

Sen, A. 1999. *Development as Freedom*. Oxford: Oxford University Press.

Skjeie, H. Multiple equality claims in the practice of the Norwegian anti-discrimination agencies, in *European Non–Discrimination Law: Comparative Perspectives on Multidimensional*

*Equality Law*, edited by D. Scheik and V. Chege. London and New York. Routledge Cavendish, 295–309.

Smart, C. 1989. *Feminism and the Power of Law*. London: Routledge.

Smart, C. and Sevenhuijsen. S. (eds), 1989. *Child Custody and the Politics of Gender*. London: Routledge.

Sommerlad, H. 2008. That obscure object of desire: Sex equality and the legal profession, in *Rethinking Equality Projects in Law*, edited by R. Hunter. Oxford and Portland, Oregon: Hart Publishing, 171–194.

Thornton, M. 1996. *Dissonance and Distrust: Women in the Legal Profession*. Oxford: Oxford University Press.

West, R.L. 2000. The difference in women's hedonic lives: A phenomenological critique of feminist legal theory. *Wisconsin Women's Law Journal*, 15(1), 149–215.

West, R.L. 2003. *Re-Imagining Justice: Progressive Interpretations of Formal Equality, Rights and the Rule of Law*. Aldershot: Ashgate.

Williams, S.H. 1993. Feminist legal epistemology. *Berkeley Women's Law Journal*, 8(1), 63–102.

Wing, A. 1997. Brief reflections toward a multiplicative theory and praxis of being, in *Critical Race Feminism: A Reader*, edited by A.K. Wing. New York: New York University Press, 27–34.

Young, I.M. 1990. *Justice and the Politics of Difference*. Princeton: Princeton University Press.

# 'What a Long Strange Trip It's Been': Feminist and Queer Travels with Sex, Gender and Sexuality

## Sharon Cowan[1]

Rosemary Auchmuty has emphasized the risk of trying to define what is meant by feminism – that inevitably in attempting to pin it down one loses as many supporters as opponents (2003: 377, footnote 1). Nonetheless, it is fair to say that the feminist project is often understood as both descriptive and normative: it takes women to have experienced discrimination on the basis of sex, gender and/or sexuality; and it applies a gendered analysis to what are largely understood as gender neutral legal and social arrangements, in order to improve the lives of women (Conaghan 2000). However, the key concepts of sex, gender and sexuality that feminists have employed as frameworks or tools for analysis of inequality have been the subject of much debate and disagreement. The way in which sex, gender and sexuality – and even the term 'woman' itself – have been conceptualized by feminists is the subject of this chapter. I will trace the course of the debates over the meaning and significance of sex, gender and sexuality to feminist theorizing. In doing so, the intention is not to summarize the work of every feminist theorist who has offered an analysis of these key concepts, but rather to identify themes that have arisen as feminist theorizing has evolved. Thus, what follows is not a linear inquiry, but rather a thematic analysis, or 'history of ideas', of those who have contributed to feminist debates on sexuality, sex and gender. In so doing, I hope to demonstrate that shifts in thinking are 'connected and overlapping' rather than 'purely … action leading to acrimonious reaction' (Garber 2006: 82).

The chapter focuses largely on Western feminist thinking, and in particular Anglo-American feminist legal theory, although some contributions of theorists from continental Europe are taken into account. What we will see is that although gender, sex and sexuality have been analysed as discrete concepts, they have also been conceptualized as interwoven and interdependent. Writers from different traditions and theoretical backgrounds have taken distinctly different views on the conceptual relationship between gender, sex and

---

1    I would like to thank the editors, Margaret Davies and Vanessa Munro for their enduring patience and encouragement; Wendy Van Der Neut for excellent research assistance; Helen Buxton and Justina Molloy for proof reading and deleting the metaphors and long sentences; the amazing students and my inspiring co-teacher Gillian Calder in the 2012–13 class 'Sexual Orientation and the Law', University of Victoria, Canada, for poking and stimulating my brain; and Sean Morris for always listening.

sexuality; this chapter aims to show how these views developed and the tensions and moments of connection that exist across these debates.

Beginning with 'second wave' feminism, the chapter will offer an overview of key moments in the sex/gender and sexuality debates. In so doing, it will look at the contributions not only of feminists to these conversations, but also the interventions offered by queer theorists and others, acknowledging, of course, that often work is not easily classifiable as falling into one or other field(s) and that there are many commonalities and intersections between different theoretical positions (Richardson 2006).

# Sex, Gender and Sexuality: 'Second Wave' Feminism

## Sex and Gender

Sex and gender have been the bedrocks of feminist thinking since what has been termed the 'first wave' of feminism in the late nineteenth to early twentieth century. As explored by Elsje Bonthuys in this volume, first wave – that is, liberal – feminists claimed that women were discriminated against on the basis of their sex (where sex was understood to mean what we would now call biological sex, as well as those characteristics thought to arise 'naturally' as a result of sexual differences between men and women, such as temperament, physical capacities and so on). The proposition that women should have equal access to education and to public life more generally was a key contribution of first wave feminist activism and theorizing, and was the foundation of campaigns for women's right to suffrage, and equal access to ownership of property and higher education. It was not suggested that women were the same as men; rather women should have the same rights to public life that men enjoyed.

However, 'second wave' feminism brought with it a move to distinguish between sex and 'gender' (Oakley 1972, Kessler and McKenna 1978). The distinction, first developed in 1968 by the psychoanalyst Robert Stoller, was utilized as a way of describing the development of gender identity – 'sex roles' – as independent from physiology (Eisenstein 1983: 7). Feminists employed the distinction in a more critical way to argue against conventional sex roles, emphasizing the sex/gender opposition as a way of demonstrating that while physiological sex might be innate, gender differences between men and women (that is, femininity and masculinity), which were commonly thought to be 'natural' and inescapable, and which provided the basis for differential treatment of men and women, are socially constructed. This gave feminists a way of understanding and theorizing gender as a culturally inscribed practice rather than an inherent trait. Sex might be taken to be biological and therefore determined, but the parameters and content of appropriate gender roles could now be legally and politically challenged.

Building on this, second wave feminist legal theorists began to develop critiques of the law as gendered – that is, male oriented – not only in its formal exclusion of women on the basis of their biological sex (historically as lawyers, as judges, from the vote, and so on) but also in its substance. Because our social world is gendered, they argued, the very culture of the law is also gendered, not only in its concepts and substantive rules (see, for example, MacKinnon's 1989 argument about the honest belief rule in rape) but also with respect to legal methods, such as defining relevance, and legal reasoning (Mossman 1987). Second wave feminism challenged discrimination on the basis of gender, and brought a focus on issues such as marriage, employment, reproduction, sexual violence and harassment, prostitution and pornography. But the fundamental problem for feminists at this time was the legal and social construction of gender, and the oppression of women's sexualities.

## Gender and Sexuality

Second wave feminists began to theorize sexuality as a core part of the patriarchal oppression of women; as such, gender and sexuality had to be theorized together. Like gender, sexuality was understood to be socially produced – a 'social rather than natural' occurrence (Jackson 2006: 38). According to this view, both sexuality and gender emerge not through benign social processes but through the power of male dominance. Radical feminists, such as MacKinnon for instance, argued that categories of difference which are taken as given (such as gender) are often instituted through an exercise of power which leaves some (that is, women) in a less advantaged and more oppressed situation than those who benefit from the existence of such categories (that is, men); and that the division of individuals into categories may itself be the constitution or creation of difference rather than the recognition of 'real' difference (MacKinnon 1989: 237, Spelman 1988: 150).

MacKinnon's work, which was paradigmatic of this era, suggested that women's sexualities are completely defined and dominated by male sexual culture, a position referred to by Halley (2008: 41) as 'power feminism'. Women's sexuality is culturally prescribed and controlled by the (male) state by various social and legal means, through the 'seamless web of life and law' (MacKinnon 1989: 241). MacKinnon's early theories, which wove a unique tapestry of feminism and Marxism, were particularly influential in this regard, as she claimed that '[s]exuality is to feminism what work is to Marxism – that which is most one's own, yet most taken away' (1989: 3).[2] She also made an explicit link between the construction of gender and the construction of sexuality:

> Sexuality, then, is a form of power. Gender, as socially constructed, embodies it, not the reverse. Women and men are divided by gender, made into the sexes as we know them, by the social requirements of its dominant form, heterosexuality, which institutionalizes male sexual dominance and female sexual submission. If this is true, sexuality is the lynchpin of gender inequality. (1989: 113)

Gender is therefore a product of the way in which sexuality is constructed by and through social relations – it is a result of patriarchal oppression of women's sexuality. As we will see shortly, in some respects this echoes the approach taken by other social theorists, such as Michel Foucault; while he did not theorize gender oppression as such, for Foucault, sex itself was produced by discourses of sexuality. For both these approaches then, it is sexuality that plays the most crucial role in grounding our legal and social conceptions of sex and gender.

Other radical feminists, such as writer Andrea Dworkin (1981), also argued that the sexuality women experience is not their own but that which is fantasized by men; their fantasies (such as rape and pornography) become our reality. Pornography is therefore not only the eroticization of the domination/submission relationship that exists between all men and women, but also a 'means through which sexuality is socially constructed,

---

2    For in-depth and close readings of MacKinnon's position on sexuality and sexual difference, see Cornell (1993: chapter 5), Halley (2008: 41 and the following pages).

a site of construction, a domain of exercise' (MacKinnon 1989: 134). Despite Dworkin and MacKinnon's imaginative attempts to harness the law to change women's lives by regulating pornography through the civil law, their approach to the issue of women's sexualities has been critiqued as over-determinant in its totalism of the cultural effects of power, and underplaying women's agency (Brown 1995: 89, Smart 1989: 77). MacKinnon's work in particular has been said to under-theorize, homogenize and generally denigrate both male (homo)sexuality and women's heterosexual desire (Stychin 1995: 62, Halley 2008: 65, compare Richardson 1996); and to ignore the institutionally powerful and often negative impact of law upon feminist projects (Brown 1995: 131, Halley 2008: 57). Angela Harris (1990) submitted a powerful critique of the work of MacKinnon, and that of the radical feminist Robin West, as demonstrating a 'gender essentialism' that elided race and class, amongst other things. MacKinnon's thesis also did not seem to take into account, in any meaningful way, the construction of lesbian sexuality.

However, a distinct lesbian feminist analysis of gender and sexuality did begin to emerge during the second wave. Lesbian feminists challenged mainstream feminist legal theory as being inherently heterosexual in its erasure of lesbian sexuality (Cain 1990), arguing that women's sexualities were overshadowed by the cultural, legal and political institution of heterosexuality, and the status of *being* a lesbian was believed to be the antithesis of heterosexuality. Adopting the identity of a 'woman-identified-woman' was perceived as the political solution, whether or not women chose to express this identity in a sexualized way (Eisenstein 1983: 53–54).

Embracing this approach, in 1980, Adrienne Rich published a 'landmark essay' (Fuss 1989: 47) entitled 'Compulsory Heterosexuality and Lesbian Existence' in which she argued that much feminist scholarship assumed female heterosexuality and ignored lesbian existence (1983: 178–182), thereby also neglecting the reality that heterosexuality is, by a variety of means, 'forcibly and subliminally imposed on women' (1983: 195). Rich argued that compulsory heterosexuality also serves to ensure the invisibility or at least deviant status of lesbian experience in the social world (1983: 185, 191). Unlike MacKinnon, however, Rich does not overstate male power, or share her view of the inevitability of male (heterosexual) culture's impact upon women; Rich attempts to describe the many ways throughout history in which women have evaded heterosexuality: 'everywhere women have resisted it, often at the cost of physical torture, imprisonment, psychosurgery, social ostracism and extreme poverty' (1983: 195–196).

Rich claimed that all women's authentic sexualities and experiences appear on a 'lesbian continuum' such that each woman has a range of 'Woman-identified experiences' throughout her lifetime, experiences that are not confined to genital sexual contact between women (1983: 192) and that are undermined by the institutions of heterosexuality (1983: 201), institutions which in turn are maintained through both physical violence and psychological control or 'false consciousness' (1983: 192). The aim then is to challenge the 'lie' of *compulsory* heterosexuality (199). For Rich and other lesbian feminist theorists, it is the coercive imposition of heterosexuality that produces gender; but while heterosexuality is understood as socially enacted, lesbianism is implied as a possibility that exists innately in all women (Jackson 2006: 46).

This kind of lesbian feminist theory has been critiqued as essentialist and ahistorical in its portrayal of a fundamental and authentic lesbianism which is different to, and oppressed by, compulsory (male) heterosexuality. Furthermore, in its adherence to the gender binary, Rich's work distinguishes what it means to be lesbian from the gay male experience; Diana Fuss critiques Rich as 'curiously unable to theorize male homosexuality outside of its popular negative stereotypes' (Fuss 1989: 47). However, Cheshire Calhoun suggests that this reading back into history the existence of lesbian identities provides a 'useful essentialist fiction' in that it demonstrates that there is nothing natural about the way in which our contemporary heterosexual 'law' (both formal and informal) is constructed, and reveals the way in which women over time have broken heterosexual and patriarchal law (1993: 1872–1874).

Rich's redefinition of lesbian experience was certainly controversial (Eisenstein 1983: 56), and fundamentally challenged the heterosexual assumptions of mainstream feminism, as well as medical conceptions of lesbian sexuality, and fostered heterogeneity in the movement (Stein 1992: 39). However, as will be explored further below, and unlike later feminist and queer theoretical engagements with law, the analyses of key feminists such as Rich and MacKinnon have been said to wrongly prioritize sexuality as the primary site of oppression (Jackson 2006: 46–47). Over-privileging sexuality as the site of women's oppression, and therefore as the cornerstone of feminist analyses, is said to neglect other aspects of gender inequality (non-sexual social practices of heterosexuality) such as labour (Jackson 2006: 46). Stevi Jackson, for example, has argued that although the two are empirically interrelated, gender should be prioritized since logically it precedes sexuality, and is a binarised, hierarchical practice of social division, which, like class, is structurally 'embedded in both social institutions and social practices' (2006: 41).

The 'sexuality as constitutive of gender' theorists have also been accused of neglecting the ways in which sexuality and gender could usefully be analysed separately, and how sexual oppression could be said to be a site of power/resistance outwith the confines of its relationship to gender oppression. For example, Gayle Rubin argued in 1984 in her influential article 'Thinking Sex' for 'a radical separation of gender and sexuality' (McLaughlin et al 2006: 1). Indeed, Rubin has been credited with having 'shaped the field of sexuality studies' (Stryker 2011: 82). Having first coined the term 'sex/gender system' in 1975 to describe the processes by which women are caught in a nexus of expectations and constraints by way of both nature (biology) and culture (socialization), Rubin went on to critique the hegemonic, conservative 'orthodoxy' of feminist work on sexuality (Richardson 2006: 25). Rubin categorized the work of anti-pornography radical feminists (such as MacKinnon) as 'sex–negative', and in direct contrast to her own 'sex-positive' analysis of the systematic exclusion of non-normative sexualities and sexual practices. During the 'sex wars' of the 1980s, when feminists most vehemently disagreed over crucial issues such as pornography, prostitution and sadomasochism, debates around the appropriate regulation of sexuality became heated and divisive, and Rubin, along with other feminists such as Carole Vance, Pat Califia and Joan Nestle undertook critical engagement with radical feminist perspectives, the result of which was a movement cleaved into two distinct camps (Rubin 2011, Vance 1984). As Susan Ardill and Sue O'Sullivan recall (2005: 109), you were either for sexual liberation or for women's liberation, you could not be for both.

Although criticized as going 'too far in denying the empirical connections between gender and sexuality' (Jackson 2006: 47), Rubin's contribution was important in grounding later 'queer' and postmodern feminist work, discussed below, that argued for the analysis of sexuality that was not *necessarily* grounded in feminist theory (see also Halley 2008). Likewise, the work of Eve Kofoski Sedgwick foregrounded the development of queer perspectives on the particularity of sexuality as discrete from gender studies: 'the whole realm of what modern culture refers to as "sexuality" and *also* calls "sex"… is virtually impossible to situate on a map delimited by the feminist defined sex/gender distinction" (Sedgwick 1990: 29).

Notwithstanding the work of Rubin and others, aimed at undermining mainstream feminist orthodoxies, much of feminist work at this time was largely focused on sexuality as the dominant and oppressive force in women's lives. Rich's focus on (hetero)sexuality as the primary site of oppression and her suggestion that all women are potentially lesbians was said to over-generalize and elide differences *among* those women/lesbians, including differences of class and race (Fuss 1989: 44, Harris 1990). This charge – universalism – has also been made, as noted above, against other radical feminists including MacKinnon and Dworkin, and is based on the tendency of such feminist arguments to assume a universal experience of sexuality and gender without accounting for the ways in which women's experiences are mediated through other 'identity markers' such as race, class, disability, religion and so on.[3] However, as we will see shortly, the central question of *sexual* difference continued to preoccupy many feminists for some time to come.

## Emphasizing or Eradicating Sexual Difference?

### Sexual Difference Feminism: Luce Irigaray

MacKinnon's 'power feminism' (Halley 2008: 41) sees sexuality, and thereby gender differences, as constructed by and through male oppression, a view that Halley describes as 'a dark vision of wall to wall domination' (2008: 72). At the same time, however, another strand of 'second wave' feminism stresses the importance of *sexual difference* between men and women, arguing that women's accounts and experiences of the world have been repressed, ignored or devalued, and that more attention must be paid to this fundamental sexual difference, both in law and in the social world more generally.

The problems of recognizing and naming female sexuality in particular are discussed at length by the Belgian feminist, Luce Irigaray. Strongly influenced by (and critical of) psychoanalytic theories, particularly those of Lacan and Freud, Irigaray critiques the existing system of 'patriarchal law' (1994: 14–18), and develops the idea of a 'civil law for women' (19–63, 67–87), that includes 'a civil offence to depict women's bodies as stakes in pornography or prostitution' (75). This will allow women, among other things, the right to human dignity, including 'an end to commercial use of their bodies or images' (Irigaray 1994: 60).

For Irigaray, politics and social change must be based on the recognition that women and men are fundamentally different:

> The human species is divided into **two genders** which ensure its production and reproduction. To wish to get rid of sexual difference is to call for a genocide more radical that any form of destruction there has ever been in History. (1993: 12, emphasis added)

---

3    On how to avoid universalizing while maintaining political unity, see Young (1997). Feminist legal theorists have also turned to intersectionality to address the ways in which differences between and among women interact in complex ways: see Nash (this volume) and Bonthuys (this volume).

The legal system, then, must be grounded in sexual difference, and rights and obligations must be rewritten to reflect this (1993: 13); the current system does not promote equality because it does not take sexual difference into account (1993: 84). The oppression of women through law and other social and cultural forces is an important issue but legal change must be accompanied by changes to our 'symbolic codes' such as language and religion (1994: 112), particularly the former since 'the organisation of the law reflects that of the language and vice versa' (1994: 41). Language for Irigaray is sexed and is 'neither universal nor neutral' (1993: 30), but has a sexuality that is male-defined and reflects male desire (1994: 32–33); women therefore lack the ability to speak, think, desire or imagine for themselves (1985a: 224).

Language is to Irigaray what law is to MacKinnon: apparently neutral but inherently male, and a dominant force in the construction of women's sexuality. Irigaray argues that within a masculinist linguistic system, the feminine is altogether *excluded*: women are unrepresentable and unthinkable, comprehensible only within male terms (Butler 1990: 9). To define female sexuality, to try to discover and give voice to female sexuality within the existing language system would be dangerous. Irigaray would rather resist a definition of female sexuality within this system; to do so would be to 'speak like men' (1985a: 78). Any practical gains that women have made this century have been due to their ability to take on a kind of male identity and to make themselves as much like men as possible (Irigaray 1994: 79). For Irigaray, this is not equality. In emphasizing the value of all that is feminine, Irigaray can be described as what Halley calls a 'cultural feminist' (2008: 58–59).[4] In her call for a distinct female voice and language, she is 'trying to "imagine" the unimaginable' (Whitford 1991: 22).

While MacKinnon believes that women are portrayed as different to men, and that this difference is not only culturally constructed but is the bedrock of inequality and male dominance, the very point of Irigaray's work is to demonstrate the ways in which discourse 'sames' women – that is, makes them the mirror image of men – hence Irigaray's call for the creation of a language for women, in order that they might speak and be heard, and be recognized as distinctly *female* subjects. In this view of the world, woman is not 'other' as part of a symmetrical binary system which privileges the first term (for example, subject/object or masculine/feminine), but is what Braidotti calls 'radically and positively other' (1994: 121).

Since Irigaray's analysis appears to rest on a binary model of two-sexed sexual difference, it has been argued that her concentration on sexed difference operates to demote other differences such as race, ethnicity or sexuality (Davies 1997: 43, Lacey 1997: 70).[5] Margaret Davies suggests that although Irigaray's gesture may be 'strategically useful' it is not necessarily 'a solution' since 'two sexes are, in any case, as oppressive to those who do not simply identify with one sex or the other or whose identifications do not fit their bodies, in the same way that the archetypal legal man is, broadly speaking, oppressive to women' (Davies 1997: 44). Katherine O'Donovan claims that the value of Irigaray's work is rhetorical rather than definitional (1997: 52), but according to Nicola Lacey, even as a rhetorical strategy it is not sufficiently reflexive and can be read as essentialist rather than transformative (1997: 69, 71). This is because Irigaray's specific recommendations may echo ahistorical stereotypical

---

4    See also Eisenstein (1983) for an analysis of second wave 'cultural' feminists who adopted the view that female sexuality was superior to that of males.

5    Irigaray is sometimes labelled as essentialist; others have categorized her work as 'radical materialism'. For discussion of this claim, see Whitford (1994: 51).

notions of the feminine and 'resonate with a conception of woman which is uncomfortably close to that of patriarchal social institutions, and which feminism has generally sought to undermine' (Lacey 1997: 70).

Ultimately, however, Irigaray's work had a fundamental impact on feminism and the sex/gender and sexuality debates. Her belief in the possibility of women's subjectivity and sexuality, of 'the positivity of sexual difference' (Braidotti 1994: 121), has proved to be a major challenge to discourses of law, psychoanalysis, science, linguistics and beyond. On the other hand, feminists wishing to eradicate sexual difference altogether, such as Monique Wittig, have also made a significant contribution to the field.

## The Rejection of Sexual Difference: Monique Wittig

Rich's argument that all women could experience lesbianism to various degrees contrasts with that of Monique Wittig, a French materialist feminist theorist claiming a distinctly lesbian perspective, who controversially claimed in 1978 that lesbians were not women, primarily because '"woman" has meaning only in heterosexual systems of thought and heterosexual economic systems' (1992: 32). Analogizing sexuality and class, and echoing the work of Simone De Beauvoir, Wittig argued that women only exist in relation and opposition to men; therefore, lesbians are not women because they do not relate to men 'economically, politically or ideologically' (1992: 20; see also Delphy 1970). Both Wittig and Rich question heterosexuality as a political regime, one that is forced upon women though a variety of social and legal means, and which women have internalized. But Wittig resists what she sees as previous lesbian reliance on and celebration of women's 'difference' from men (1992: 10), maintaining that such an approach simply replaces patriarchy with a similarly oppressive matriarchy. Strongly influenced by Marxism, Wittig uses the analogy of class to suggest that the power struggle between men and women should lead to the abolition of the system of sexual difference. Similarly to MacKinnon, she believes that there is nothing ontological about difference, that dominance is not a product of difference. Rather, difference is that which disguises dominance: it is simply the (heterosexual) male interpretation of domination:

> What is the different/other if not the dominated? For heterosexual society is the society which oppresses not only lesbians and gay men, it oppresses many different/others, it oppresses all women and many categories of men, all those who are in the position of the dominated ... The function of difference is to mask at every level the conflicts of interest, including ideological ones. (1992: 29)

However, for Wittig, in direct contrast to MacKinnon's approach, it is *gender* that produces a binary system of sexuality. And while Irigaray celebrates the possibility of creating a positive femininity and female sexuality, for Wittig 'the task is ... to displace the binary as such through a specifically lesbian disintegration of its constitutive categories' (Butler 1990: 126).[6] Concepts such as sex, gender, man and woman all contribute as 'categories of oppression' to a heterosexual regime (Wittig 1992: 77). Wittig's goal is to eradicate the categories of sex and gender so that our language system – and therefore the construction of the subject – becomes gender neutral. Consequently, men and women as such have to disappear 'politically,

---

6    On the possibility of a distinctly lesbian legal theory, see Robson (1998).

economically, ideologically'. If lesbians and gay men describe themselves as men and women, 'we are instrumental in maintaining heterosexuality' (1992: 29).

The answer for Wittig, then, is not to harden the existing categories through establishing lesbian and gay communities with corresponding legal rights and identities but to destroy these very categories themselves. We must therefore go beyond sex, even so far as 'rejecting all sciences which still use these categories as their fundamentals (practically all social sciences)' (1992: 19–20). In Wittig's view then, there is no escape for women from this heterosexual bind, unless we replace the current social, legal, economic and political system with a completely different alternative, as defined by a lesbian perspective. Such an alternative system would not, however, be predicated on biological asymmetry. Since categories of sex/gender are forced upon us as social realities when in fact they are constructions, the only way to achieve change is to dismantle our discourses on sex and gender and to reconceptualize sex, gender and sexuality without relying on difference, particularly biological difference (Butler 1990: 113).

Fuss (1989: 44) suggests that both Wittig's contention that lesbians are not women, and Rich's suggestion that in effect all women are (potential) lesbians, are equally unconvincing. Rich's definition of lesbian is too vague and inclusive, while Wittig's is too exclusive and reified. Nonetheless, Wittig's radical, lesbian, social constructionist, materialist philosophy offers a unique perspective on the debate around the meaning of sex, gender and sexuality as well as 'an experience beyond the categories of identity, an erotic struggle to create new categories from the ruins of the old, new ways of being a body within the cultural field, and whole new languages of description' (Butler 1990: 127). Post-second wave feminism, however, has begun to more closely interrogate the meaning of sexual difference, as well as the taken-for-grantedness of the biological and legal basis of sex itself.

## Sex, Gender and Sexuality: After the Second Wave

### Sex and Sexuality

That the sex/gender distinction is now commonly accepted as part of mainstream legal thinking is aptly demonstrated by the following quote from the English Court of Appeal decision in the transgender case *Bellinger v Bellinger*:

> The words "sex" and "gender" are sometimes used interchangeably, but today more frequently denote a difference. Mrs. Cox [Mrs. Bellinger's lawyer] submitted that gender was broader than sex. Her suggested definition was that "gender" related to culturally and socially specific expectations of behaviour and attitude, mapped onto men and women by society. It included self-definition, that is to say, what a person recognised himself to be. ([2002] Fam. 150 at 160)

Notwithstanding the proliferation of feminist theorizing around gender and sexuality, the concept of sex has largely, until relatively recently, been left out of the picture. As the sex/gender distinction became 'mainstreamed', feminist legal and social theory moved on. Critics began to suggest that the sex/gender distinction implies a questionable biological essentialism and binarism about sex (McNay 1992: 22). Although gender roles and scripts were fundamentally challenged by the separation of sex and gender, the distinction left the body languishing in the 'natural' realm of biology. It also linguistically and conceptually separated sex from gender in a way that sits uneasily with many contemporary feminist theorists (McNay 1992: 23).

Much feminist scholarship has therefore now challenged the 'sex versus gender' approach, contesting not only the naturalness of sex, but the relationship between sex/gender, and their relationship to the concept of sexuality. However, in order to explain how this more recent strand of feminist thinking on sex–gender–sexuality has evolved, we must pause to first say a few words about the work of Michel Foucault, which has been enormously influential on subsequent feminist (and other) theories of sex, gender and sexuality.

## Foucault: The History of Sexuality

Foucault's impact on theories positing the construction, as opposed to naturalness, of sex and sexuality, has been widespread and profound. The first volume of his three-volume text *The History of Sexuality* was published in France in 1976, and translated into English in 1978. Foucault was one of the first to discuss the way in which sexuality is produced (as is all knowledge) through the exercise of different levels and types of power.[7]

Foucault argues that 'sexuality is the set of effects produced in bodies, behaviours and social relations by a certain deployment deriving from a complex political technology' (1984: 127). Sexuality is not what we think it is: it is not an inherent or innate drive or orientation which can be repressed by power, or is 'disobedient' to a power 'which exhausts itself trying to subdue it and often fails to control it entirely' (1984: 103). Sexuality is a production of and through power, a 'transfer point for relations of power' (1984: 103). It is a 'historical construct' rather than a 'natural given' or 'furtive reality'. The 'proliferation' of various discourses and knowledges on sexualities is evident, according to Foucault, within a wide range of fields such as medicine, law and psychiatry (1984: 103). He argues that sexuality became linked with what he calls the 'bio-politics of the population', through control of reproduction, marriage, health, morality and so on (1984: 139). Through the crucial notion of 'bio-power', Foucault explains how 'knowledge-power' has come to affect bodies (1984: 143), such that '[P]ower and sexuality are not ontologically distinct, rather sexuality is the result of a productive "biopower" which focuses on human bodies, inciting and extorting various effects' (McNay 1992: 29).

For Foucault, sex is the concept that binds together lots of different elements of our bodies: 'anatomical elements, biological functions, conduct, sensations, and pleasures, and it enabled one to make use of this fictitious unity as a causal principle, an omnipresent meaning, a secret to be discovered everywhere: sex was thus able to function as a unique signifier and as a universal signified' (1984: 154). Foucault rejects any distinction between sex as natural and sexuality as construction; rather sex is bound up with the way in which bodies (and therefore the species) are regulated through power. Sex is therefore a 'regulatory construct' (McNay 1992: 29).

According to Foucault then, not only is sexuality a product of (classed) power relations, but sex is too. Sex does not precede sexuality; rather the reverse is true – the deployment of sexuality is part of the exercise of power that produces sex. Therefore, we cannot say that

---

7    Note also the significance of the work of the UK-based scholar Jeffrey Weeks (1981, 1985) during this period. For discussion of the implications of Foucault's arguments for scholarship focusing on racialized sexualities and on critiques of capitalism, see Ferguson (2004).

sex is real and sexuality a construct; rather we must demonstrate that sex is a product of sexuality – 'sexuality is a very real historical formation; it is what gave rise to the notion of sex' (1984: 157).

Notwithstanding some robust feminist critiques of Foucault's failure to theorize gender, or women's inequality (Fuss 1989: 107, McNay 1992: 33–35, Sawicki 1991: 29), some theorists, building on this Foucauldian perspective, have argued that rather than juxtaposing socially produced gender with natural biological sex, we can begin to understand sex itself (the interpretation of bodies) as historically and socially constructed (Laqueur 1990). More than that, sex, or sexed bodies, are produced through discourses about gender and sexuality. For example, as we shall see shortly, Judith Butler applies a Foucauldian analysis to gender in order to show how the concept of gender produces sex – that is, that the practice of seeing only two ways of doing gender produces two biological sexes (see also Hird 2002: 588). These shifts in feminist thinking have been in part brought about by the advent of postmodern and distinctly 'queer' perspectives that posit a pluralistic rather than binary system of sex/gender and sexuality.

## Sexes, Genders and Sexualities

### Feminism and Queer Theory

Notwithstanding Jackson's claim that 'it is feminists for whom there is most at stake in emphasizing the connections between gender and sexuality' (2006: 46), 'queer' analyses of sexuality began to emerge in the late 1980s.[8] The roots of queer theory are in social construction theory (predominantly that of Foucault as described above), feminist theory and post-modernism, particularly the deconstruction of identity and subjectivity. The central theme is a challenge to rigid binaries and categories, and a move away from grand theory in favour of many local interlocking social and legal struggles and theories – or 'strange affinities' (Hong and Ferguson 2011). Queer theory as a discrete perspective developed also in answer to some of the critiques of second wave feminism as universalizing (Richardson 2006: 19). Richardson, among others, has argued that queer feminist perspectives on sexuality, particularly that of Butler, were born in part from the insights extended through Rich's focus on compulsory heterosexuality, and Wittig's deconstruction of gender (2006: 30, Garber 2006: 84–85). Stychin also attributes the emergence of queer at least partially to the defeat of the civil rights approach, epitomized by the defeat of pro-gay immutability arguments in the 1986 US case of *Bowers v Hardwick*, which upheld the criminalization of 'sodomy' in Georgia; when the assimilationist 'we are the same' argument failed so dramatically, some gays and lesbians began to re-appropriate 'otherness' (1995: 149, 151).

Queer theorists have challenged feminism to take the social constructionism of gender and sexuality one step further, to explore the ways in which all kinds of (elements of) identities, including sex are fractured and 'contingent', and to question the binary categories of male and female – that is, the assumption that gender was constructed but somehow sex was not. Queer also poses the possibility of a multiplicity of sexes, genders and sexualities, rather

---

8    Feminist analyses of gender have also broadened to include masculinity studies but this is beyond the scope of the present chapter. See, for example, Davis, Evans and Lorber (2006) and Dowd (2008).

than arguing simply for the destruction of sex/gender and sexuality altogether. However, multiplicity does not necessarily mean a wholesale dismissal of identity categories or rights-based claims. As Vanita argues with respect to sexuality-based civil rights claims in India, categories may still be necessary in some contexts despite (and alongside – see Butler 1993: 222 on the 'double gesture') the queer rejection of identity politics (2002: 5, cited in Garber 2006: 81).

The queer movement has had a significant impact on the theory and practice of sexual politics. Queer theorists have helpfully disaggregated sex/gender and sexuality in a way that allows them to be analysed separately, and thus for sexuality to be the focus of study beyond the question of sex/gender. One theorist who has had a remarkable influence in this area, weaving together elements of feminism, queer theory and a postmodern approach more generally is Judith Butler. Adopting a more fluid and pluralistic account of gender than the binary model of her feminist predecessors, Butler's central argument is that gender is 'performed'.

## Gender, Performance and Performativity

So how is gender performed? In the same way that 'woman itself is a term in process ... an ongoing discursive practice' (1990: 33), gender is not a natural trait but an effect of discourse, and performed in the sense that it is a *'stylized repetition of acts'* (1990: 140), that 'congeal over time' (1990: 33), rather than a concrete stable and immutable identity. Butler describes in detail the way in which gender is a construct, and is 'performed':

> *Because there is neither an "essence" that gender expresses or externalizes nor an objective ideal to which gender aspires, and because gender is not a fact, the various acts of gender create the idea of gender, and without those acts, there would be no gender at all. Gender is, thus, a construction that regularly conceals its genesis; the tacit collective agreement to perform, produce, and sustain discrete and polar genders as cultural fictions is obscured by the credibility of those productions ... the "construction" compels our belief in its necessity and naturalness. (1990: 140)*

According to Butler there is no biological pre-existing sex through which gender and sexuality emerge. Rather, 'gender is a performance that *produces* the illusion of an inner sex or essence or psychic gender core' (1991: 28). For her, 'sex is an ideal construct which is forcibly materialised through time ... thus ... one of the norms by which the "one" becomes viable at all, that which qualifies a body for life within the domain of cultural intelligibility' (1993: 1–2). Thus, compulsory heterosexuality and its accompanying gender norms produce, as effects, categories of sex and sexuality (1990: 139–140, 1991: 24). Sex and gender are both what she calls 'regulatory fictions' (1990: 33).

As Butler herself clarified in 1993, performance is not about taking on the garb of a particular elected gender at whichever moment one chooses – in fact it is not really about choice at all, since the range of garments – the language and tools of gender – available to us are already prescribed within society (1993: 187). Butler also explains (echoing Wittig) that without homosexuality, heterosexuality would not exist (Butler 1991: 13). In order to make clear their boundaries, categories must be defined in opposition to (constituted through) something and therefore those opposites are *necessary*; performativity therefore has normative force through both reiteration and exclusion (Butler 1993: 188).[9] However, unlike Wittig, Butler does not believe that existing heteronormative concepts of sex and gender can simply be destroyed; only the proliferation or parodying of sex/gender is possible (compare Jeffreys 1994) because there is no possibility of agency '*outside* of the discursive practices that give those terms the intelligibility they have' (1990: 148, emphasis added).[10]

Butler critiques MacKinnon's conflation of sexuality and gender as 'highly deterministic' since it inhibits the theorization of sexuality apart from gender difference, and the study of 'kinds of sexual regulation that do not take gender as their primary objects' (1993: 239, see also Halley 2008). On the other hand, Butler argues, it is not desirable to completely separate gender from sexuality (1993: 5). Both feminism and queer theory take sexuality as their primary point of analysis and accept their 'constitutive inter-relationship' (1993: 240). Butler recommends that this 'opposition' between sexuality and gender needs to be reconceptualized, as does the complex relationship between sexuality, gender and other fields of power such as race (1990: 240). So, while heterosexuality and gender norms are closely linked, sexuality does not determine gender and vice versa. It is important, therefore, to recognize the importance of gender as distinct from sexuality, but in a way that accepts its centrality to the regulation of sexuality: neither one should be privileged over the other, but we ought to recognize the 'non-causal and non-reductive connection between sexuality and gender' (1993: 238).

Butler argues here that emerging feminist and queer theories should not focus on whether sex/gender or sexuality is prior, or more important, but rather on the relationship between these concepts. But some feminists have questioned what they see as a universalizing tendency within queer theory/politics that ignores feminist concerns about gender, lesbian sexuality (Walters 1996: 845–846, Jeffreys 1994: 174) and race (Samuels 1999, Ferguson 2004); as well as the content and structure of heterosexuality (Jackson 2006: 39). These deep-seated issues of universalism versus particularity have been especially acute in recent conversations about transgender politics and gender pluralism (Monro 2007), which have also, importantly, posed difficult questions for feminism about what it means to be a woman.[11]

## 'Next Wave' Feminism, Transgender Feminism and Gender Pluralism

Contemporary transgender activism and theory dispute the finality and inflexibility of male/female boundaries, and hence categories of sexual orientation (Monro 2007). In Butler's words, '[t]here are humans ... who live and breathe in the interstices of this binary relationship, showing that it is not exhaustive; it is not necessary' (2004: 65).[12] However, feminism and transgender politics have not had an easy relationship. Surya Monro (2007: 125) suggests that this is in part because of an inclination among some feminists to adhere to dyadic female/male categorization. An absolutist commitment to a dual and rigid classification system has also expressed itself through law: as Sally Hines has argued,

---

9    See also Butler (1993: 249 at fn. 3), McNay (1992: 138), Halperin (1995: 44).
10   Jackson (2006) critiques Butler's reading of Wittig as neglecting her all-important materialism. For Butler's take on materialism, see generally Butler (1993). For discussion of whether queer theory general can address questions of materiality, see McLaughlin (2006: 63–64).
11   For an early discussion of these issues in the legal context, see O'Donovan (1985).
12   See also the important work of scholars examining ways in which the bodies and experiences of intersex people confound heteronormative binary sex/gender assumptions: Kessler (1998); Fausto-Sterling (2000).

'[a]lthough the law now allows for movement *across* the binary of male/female, the spectrums *in-between* male and female, such as transgendered, intersexed, bigendered and androgynous, remain outside current frameworks of citizenship' (2007: para 1.3).

What is more, some feminists have argued that transgender people's struggles to be socially and legally accepted have in fact undermined the foundational concept of womanhood, upon which feminist struggles for equality are based; some have gone as far as to suggest that trans women are in fact men who have attempted to infiltrate women-only spaces (Raymond 1979). Others have argued strongly against women's equality and rights campaigns as inclusive of trans women's rights, either on the basis of sex, that is, a rigid biological binary, or gender, because of the significance of socialization as a woman (Boyle 2004).

On the other hand, notwithstanding Susan Stryker's question as to whether or not queer can 'adequately account for the transgender phenomena' (2011), Monro (2007: 142) has argued that queer-inspired gender pluralisms and an 'alliance-based politics' offer alternatives to the sex/gender binary and single issue politics of feminisms of the past. Similarly, Halberstam (2006: 97) has posited the possibility of 'transgender feminism' as 'the exciting potential of a merger of trans and feminist politics'. Such a merger could enable 'next-wave feminists' (Halberstam 2006: 103) to establish or further common projects and goals that do not reify theory or practice (on the productive tensions and 'contradictory tendencies' of transgender politics see Halberstam 2012 and Cowan 2009).

That there are some common feminist/trans goals seems incontrovertible. The constraining heteronormative assumptions and ideologies about sex and gender that underpin the dominant medico-legal and social discourses on what it means to be trans also shape the sexed/gendered lives of cisgender (that is, non-trans) people. Maleness and femaleness, as medico-legally understood, seems always to implicate normative ideals of heterosexuality (not homo-, bi-, a-, or pan-sexuality); monogamy (not polygamy or polyamory); marriage (rather than non-marital relationships); conjugality (rather than intimacy or friendship); life-long commitment (rather than short-term, casual, or intermittent connections); dual (rather than solo or multiple) systems of partnership; and family life (based on the primacy of relationships with children, spouses, and relatives rather than friends, workmates, neighbours or non-spousal intimates).

Each of these ideals reflects the deeply embedded existing heteronormative social and legal structures that permeate not only legal and political debates about trans issues, but about the politics and lived experiences of sex/gender more broadly; as such, they raise crucial questions for all critical analyses of law and the material social world around us. Contesting gender is not (solely) about 'individual gestures of dissent' but involves 'a collective process (of) social struggle' (Connell 2009: 110). As the critical trans scholar Dean Spade has recently argued (and as Carol Smart also suggested in 1989), this often means decentring law, and instead employing, indeed centring, non-legal community based strategies and striving for a shared imagination of transformative change (2011: 156). Accordingly, as I have argued elsewhere (Cowan 2009), it is important for feminists – indeed everyone interested in theorizing sex/gender and sexuality and their intersection with other vectors of human experience – to fully engage with the questions and debates raised by the ways in which transgender people's lives are legally and socially regulated.

# Conclusion: Moving Forward and Gladly Beyond?

*No one term can serve as foundational. (Butler 1993: 240)*

This chapter has traced the emergence and evolution of feminist theorizing about sex, gender and sexuality. So how should contemporary feminists and others conceptualize sex/gender and sexuality? Butler has critiqued the ways in which gender discourse 'absorbs and displaces "sex"' (1993: 5), but although we may wish to avoid conflating the two, Lois Bibbings has identified how difficult it is '(linguistically and conceptually) to analyze the concepts "sex" and "gender". If they are so interwoven, would it not be more accurate to talk of sex and gender as one thing?' (2004: 223–224).

As we have seen, feminist and queer theorists have taken different views on whether or not sex and gender are separable, and which, if any, should take analytical precedence. The underlying message of more recent arguments seems to be that despite heuristic advantages of separation, sex, sexuality and gender cannot be completely disaggregated, and to attempt to do so 'may restrict rather than enhance our efforts to theorise the complex intersections' (Richardson 2006: 27). Moreover, as Harrison notes, 'there will never be any natural experiment in which we might find out what the sexed body entails entirely outside the ways in which it, and the person whose body it is, has been gendered' (2006: 43). And, as contemporary feminist and queer theorists have argued, sex/gender and sexuality are linked not only through the oppositional homo/heterosexual binary, but also because ambiguity about sex/gender throws our expectations about sexuality into confusion, and vice versa.

Initial concerns were raised that queer theory would neglect race or gender politics. Yet, queer theory has clearly had a major impact on contemporary feminism's treatment of sex/gender and sexuality, and race. Recent queer of colour analyses, for example, have brought questions of the racialization of desire more centrally into focus (Hong and Ferguson 2011, Holland 2012, Ferguson 2004). Likewise queer crip studies offer provocative and rigorous analyses of the intersection of heteronormativity and norms that discipline the disabled body (McRuer 2011, McRuer and Samuels 2003). Queer theories can therefore offer another set of tools, overlapping with, yet distinct from, feminism, to view the ways in which sex/gender and sexuality remain central features of contemporary social and political life, and how they are interwoven with other aspects of material embodment. Like feminism, queer theory may need to be continually rewritten, but both can offer a platform from which to make connections with other critical social theories such as critical race theory and crip studies. Moving away from the characterisation of feminism as the study of sex/gender and queer as the study of sexuality, then, we can see each theoretical enterprise as having overlapping territories (Richardson 2006: 26, Cossman 2003–4), where both have resonance and relevance for contemporary theorizing on sex/gender and sexuality and beyond.[13]

As feminism acknowledges the queer critique and tries to more readily accommodate an analysis of *sexuality* which cannot be reduced purely to *gender*, or vice versa, so will feminism encourage queer theory to acknowledge the relevance of gender politics to analyses of sexuality and desire (MacIntosh 1993: 49). The future for feminism and for queer theory may well lie in 'the articulation of *new ways of thinking* about how sexuality and gender' – and, we might add, sex, race, class and physical embodment – are profoundly interconnected (Richardson

---

13    On the question of the relationship between feminist legal theory, and 'Law, Gender and Sexuality Studies', see Conaghan (2009).

2006: 36, emphasis added). In turn this may lead us to consider the possibility of ways of being 'which we do not yet know how to name or that sets a limit on all naming' (Butler 2004: 74).

# References

Ardill, S. and O'Sullivan, S. 2005. Upsetting an Applecart: Difference, Desire and Lesbian Sadomasochism. *Feminist Review*, 80(1), 98–126.

Auchmuty, R. 2003. Agenda for a Feminist Legal Curriculum. *Legal Studies*. 23(3), 377–401.

Bibbings, L. 2004. Heterosexuality as harm: fitting in, in *Beyond Criminology: Taking Harm Seriously*, edited by P. Hillyard, C. Pantazis, S. Tombs and D. Gordon. London: Pluto Press, 217–235.

Boyle, C. 2004. The Anti-discrimination Norm in Human Rights and Charter Law: *Nixon v. Vancouver Rape Relief. University of British Columbia Law Review*, 37(1), 31–72.

Braidotti, R. 1994. Of bugs and women: Irigaray and Deleuze on the becoming-woman, in *Engaging with Irigaray: Feminist philosophy and modern European thought*, edited by C. Burke, N. Schor and M. Whitford. New York: Columbia University Press, 111–137.

Brown, W. 1995. *States of Injury: power and freedom in late modernity*. Princeton, New Jersey: Princeton University Press.

Butler, J. 2004. *Undoing Gender*. New York: Psychology Press.

Butler, J. 1993. *Bodies that Matter: On the Discursive Limits of 'Sex'*. New York: Routledge.

Butler, J. 1991. Imitation and Gender Insubordination, in *Inside Out: Lesbian Theories, Gay Theories*, edited by D. Fuss. New York: Routledge, 13–31.

Butler, J. 1990. *Gender Trouble: Feminism and the Subversion of Identity*. New York: Routledge.

Cain, P. 1990. Feminist Jurisprudence: Grounding the Theories. *Berkeley Women's Law Journal*, 4, 191–214.

Calhoun, C. 1993. Denaturalizing and desexualizing lesbian and gay identity. *Virginia Law Review*, 79(7), 1859–1875.

Conaghan, J. 2009. The Making of a Field or the Building of a Wall? Feminist Legal Studies and Law, Gender and Sexuality. *Feminist Legal Studies*, 17(3), 303–307.

Conaghan, J. 2000. Reassessing the feminist theoretical project in law. *Journal of Law and Society*, 27(3), 351–385.

Cornell, D. 1993. *Transformations: Recollective Imagination and Sexual Difference*. New York: Routledge.

Connell, R. 2009. Accountable Conduct: "Doing Gender" in Transsexual and Political Retrospect. *Gender and Society*, 23(1), 104–111.

Cornell, D. 1995. *The Imaginary Domain: abortion, pornography and sexual harassment*. New York: Routledge.

Cossman, B. 2003–4. Sexuality, Queer Theory, and "Feminism After": Reading and Rereading the Sexual Subject. *McGill Law Journal*, 49(4), 847–876.

Cowan, S. 2009. "We Walk Among You": Trans Identity Politics Goes to the Movies. *Canadian Journal of Women and the Law*, 21(1), 91–118.

Davies, M. 1997. Taking the inside out, in *Sexing the Subject of Law*, edited by N. Naffine and R. Owen. Sydney: LBC Information Services, 25–46.

Davis, K., Evans, M. and Lorber, J. 2006. *Handbook of Gender and Women's Studies*. London: Sage.

Delphy, C. 1970. The Main Enemy: a Materialist Analysis of Women's Oppression, reprinted in *Close to Home: A Materialist Analysis of Women's Oppression*, C. Delphy. 1984. London: Hutchinson, 57–77.

Dowd, N. 2008. Masculinities and Feminist Legal Theory. *Wisconsin Journal of Law, Gender and Society*, 23(2), 201–248.

Dworkin, A. 1981. *Pornography: Men possessing women*. London: Women's Press.

Eisenstein, H. 1983. *Contemporary Feminist Thought*. London: Unwin.

Fausto-Sterling, A. 2000. *Sexing the Body: Gender Politics and the Construction of Sexuality*. New York: Basic Books.

Ferguson, R. 2004. *Aberrations in Black: Toward a Queer of Color Critique*. Minneapolis: University of Minnesota Press.

Fineman, M.A., Jackson, J.E and Romero A.P. (eds), 2009. *Feminist and Queer Legal Theory: Intimate Encounters, Uncomfortable Conversations*. Farnham: Ashgate Publishing.

Foucault, M. 1984. *The History of Sexuality: An Introduction*. London: Peregrine.

Fuss, D. 1989. *Essentially Speaking: Feminism, Nature and Difference*. New York: Routledge.

Garber, L. 2006. On the Evolution of Queer Studies, in *Intersections between Feminist and Queer Theory*, edited by D. Richardson, J. McLaughlin and M.E Casey. Basingstoke: Palgrave Macmillan, 78–96.

Halberstam, J. 2012. Global Female Masculinities. *Sexualities*, 15(3/4), 336–354.

Halberstam, J. 2006. Boys Will be … Bois? Or, Transgender Feminism and Forgetful Fish, in *Intersections between Feminist and Queer Theory*, edited by D. Richardson, J. McLaughlin and M.E Casey. Basingstoke: Palgrave Macmillan, 97–115.

Halley, J. 2008. *Split Decisions: How and Why to Take a Break from Feminism*. Princeton, New Jersey: Princeton University Press.

Halperin, D. 1995. *Saint Foucault: Towards a Gay Hagiography*. New York: Oxford University Press.

Harris, A. 1990. Race and Essentialism in Feminist Legal Theory. *Standford Law Review*, 42(3), 581–616.

Harrison, W. 2006. The Shadow and the Substance: The Sex/Gender debate, in *The Handbook of Gender and Women's Studies*, edited by K. Davis, M. Evan and J. and Lorber. London: Sage, 35–52.

Hines, S. 2007. (Trans)forming Gender: Social Change and Transgender Citizenship. *Sociological Research Online* [Online], 12(1). Available at: www.socresonline.org.uk/12/1/hines.html [accessed 26 November 2012].

Hird, M. 2002. Out/Performing Our Selves: Invitation for Dialogue. *Sexualities*, 5(3) 337–356.

Holland, S. 2012. *The Erotic Life of Racism*. Durham: Duke University Press.

Hong, G. and Ferguson, R. (eds), 2011. *Strange Affinities: The Gender and Sexual Politics of Comparative Racialization*. Durham: Duke University Press.

Irigaray, L. 1985a. *Speculum de l'autre femme*. Paris: Les Éditions de Minuit, 1974. Translated by G.C. Gill as *Speculum of the Other Woman*. Ithaca, N.Y: Cornell University Press.

Irigaray, L. 1985b. *Ce sexe qui n'est pas un*. Paris: Les Éditions de Minuit, 1977. Translated by C. Porter and C. Burke as *This Sex Which is not One*. Ithaca, N.Y: Cornell University Press.

Irigaray, L. 1993. *je, tu, nous: pour une culture de la différance*. Paris: Grasset, 1990. Translated by A. Martin as *Je, Tu, Nous: Toward a culture of Difference*. New York: Routledge.

Irigaray, L. 1994. *Le temps de la différance: Pour une revolution pacifique*. Paris: Librarie Générale Française, 1989. Translated by K. Montin as *Thinking the Difference: For a peaceful revolution*. London: Athlone Press.

Jackson, S. 2006. Heterosexuality, sexuality and gender: Rethinking the intersections in *Intersections between Feminist and Queer Theory*, edited by D. Richardson, J. McLaughlin and M.E Casey. Basingstoke: Palgrave Macmillan, 38–58.

Jeffreys, S. 1994. *The Lesbian Heresy: A Feminist Perspective on the Lesbian Sexual Revolution*. London: The Women's Press.

Kessler, S. 1998. *Lessons from the Intersexed*. New Jersey: Rutgers University Press.

Kessler, S. and McKenna, W. 1978. *Gender: An Ethnomethodological Approach*. Chicago: University of Chicago Press.

Lacey, N. 1998. *Unspeakable Subjects: Feminist Essays in Legal and Social Theory*. Oxford: Hart.

Lacey, N. 1997. On the subject of sexing the subject, in *Sexing the Subject of Law*, edited by N. Naffine and R. Owens. North Ryde, NSW: LBC Information Services, 65–76.

Laqueur, T. 1990. *Making Sex: Body and Gender from the Greeks to Freud*. Cambridge, MA: Harvard University Press.

MacIntosh, M. 1993. Queer theory and the war of the sexes, in *Activating Theory: Lesbian, Gay, Bisexual Politics*, edited by J. Bristow and A. Wilson. London: Lawrence and Wishart, 33–52.

MacKinnon, C. 1989. *Towards a Feminist Theory of the State*. Cambridge, MA: Harvard University Press.

McLaughlin, J., Casey, M.E. and Richardson, D. 2006. Introduction: At the Intersections of Feminist and Queer Debates, in *Intersections between Feminist and Queer Theory*, edited by D. Richardson, J. McLaughlin and M.E Casey. Basingstoke: Palgrave Macmillan, 1–18.

McNay, L. 1992. *Foucault and Feminism*. Boston: Northeastern University Press.

McRuer, R. 2011. Disabling Sex: Notes for a Crip Theory of Sexuality. *GLQ: A Journal of Lesbian and Gay Studies*, 17(1), 107–117.

McRuer, R and Samuels, E. (eds), 2003. Desiring Disability: Queer Theory Meets Disability Studies. A Special Issue of *GLQ: A Journal of Lesbian and Gay Studies*, 9(1–2).

Mossman, M.J. 1987. Feminism and Legal Method: the Difference it Makes. *Wisconsin Women's Law Journal*, 3, 147–169.

Monro, S. 2007. Transgender: Destabilizing Feminisms?, in *Sexuality and the Law: Feminist Engagements*, edited by V. Munro and C. and Stychin. London: Routledge, 125–150.

Oakley, A. 1972. *Sex, Gender and Society*. London: Temple Smith.

O'Donovan, K. 1985. *Sexual Divisions in Law*. London: Weidenfield and Nicolson.

O'Donovan, K. 1997. With Sense, Consent, or Just a Con? Legal Subjects in the Discourse of Autonomy, in *Sexing the Subject of Law* edited by N. Naffine and R. Owen. Sydney, NSW: LBC Information Services, 47–64.

Raymond, J. 1979. *The Transsexual Empire: The Making of the She-Male*. Ann Arbor: University of Michigan Press.

Rich, A. 1983. Compulsory heterosexuality and lesbian existence, in *Powers of Desire: The Politics Of Sexuality*, edited by A. Snitow, C. Stansell and S. Thompson. London: Virago, 177–205.

Richardson, D. 1996. *Theorising Heterosexuality: Telling it Straight*. Buckingham: Open University Press.

Richardson, D. 2006. Bordering Theory, in *Intersections between Feminist and Queer Theory*, edited by D. Richardson, J. McLaughlin and M.E Casey. Basingstoke: Palgrave Macmillan, 19–37.

Robson, R. 1998. *Sappho Goes to Law School: Fragments in Lesbian Legal Theory*. New York: Columbia University Press.

Rubin, G. 1975. 'The traffic in women': Notes on the 'Political Economy' of Sex, in *Toward an Anthropology of Women*, edited by R. Reiter. New York: New York University Press, 157–210.

Rubin, G. 1984. Thinking Sex: Notes for a Radical Theory of the Politics of Sexuality, in *Pleasure and Danger: Exploring Female Sexuality*, edited by C. Vance. Boston: Routledge and Kegan Paul.

Rubin, G. 2011. Blood under the Bridge: Reflections on "Thinking Sex", *GLQ: A Journal of Lesbian and Gay Studies*, 17(1), 15–48.

Samuels, J. 1999. Dangerous liaisons: queer subjectivity, liberalism and race. *Cultural Studies*, 13(1), 91–109.

Sawicki, J. 1991. *Disciplining Foucault: Feminism, Power and the Body*. New York: Routledge.

Sedgwick, E.K. 1990. *The Epistemology of the Closet*. Berkeley: University of California Press.

Smart, C. 1989. *Feminism and the Power of Law*. London: Routledge.

Spade, D. 2011. *Normal Life: Administrative Violence, Critical Trans Politics and the Limits of Law*. South End Press: New York.

Spelman, E. 1988. *Inessential Woman: Problems of Exclusion in Feminist Thought*. Boston: Beacon Press.

Stein, A. 1992. Sisters and queers: the decentring of lesbian feminism. *Socialist Review*, 22(1), 33–55.

Stryker, S. 2011. The Time has Come to Think about Gayle Rubin. *GLQ: A Journal of Lesbian and Gay Studies*, 17(1), 79–82.

Stychin, C. 1995. *Law's Desire: Sexuality and the Limits of Justice*. London: Routledge.

Walters, S.D. 1996. From here to queer: radical feminism, postmodernism and the lesbian menace (or why can't a woman be more like a fag?) *Signs*, 2(4), 830–869.

Weeks, J. 1981. *Sex, Politics and Society. The Regulation of Sexuality since 1800*. London: Longman.

Weeks, J. 1985. *Sexuality and its Discontents: Meanings, Myths and Modern Sexualities*. London: Routledge.

Whitford, M. 1994. Reading Irigaray in the Nineties, in *Engaging with Irigaray: Feminist Philosophy and Modern European Thought*, edited by C. Burke, N. Schor, and M. Whitford. New York: Columbia University Press.

Whitford, M. 1991. *Luce Irigaray: Philosophy in the Feminine*. London: Routledge.

Wittig, M. 1992. *The Straight Mind and other Essays*. Boston: Beacon Press.

Young, I.M. 1997. *Intersecting Voices: Dilemmas of Gender, Political Philosophy, and Policy*. Princeton, New Jersey: Princeton University Press.

# Theorizing Race, Theorizing Racism: New Directions in Interdisciplinary Scholarship

Jennifer C. Nash

W.E.B. Du Bois's claim that the 'problem of the twentieth century is the problem of the color line' has become one of his most famous, and most frequently quoted, insights (Du Bois 1903). But what does it mean to read that sentence *now* – more than a century after Du Bois wrote it? How has 'the colour line' been redrawn and transformed in the century since Du Bois crafted a sentence that has become foundational to his legacy? How do scholars discern the 'problem' of the colour line in a new century marked by a national love affair with the rhetoric of colour blindness? And how is the 'colour line' complicated, re-routed, intensified, and intersected by other 'lines' – or structures of domination – including gender, sexuality and class?

This chapter draws on scholarly work produced across disciplines to make sense of what the 'colour line' is – or, perhaps more appropriately, what the colour lines are. I begin by unpacking the now-common scholarly refrain that race is a social construction. I endeavour to ask *what kind* of social construction race is, and to examine how race is a social construction that intersects with other constructions including gender and sexuality. In so doing, the chapter treats race not as a fixed construct, but as something that is actively produced, and whose production depends on gender and sexuality. The chapter then turns to an examination of scholarly work surrounding racism, particularly scholarship that examines the contemporary rhetoric of 'colour-blindness' as a new articulation of racism. The chapter ends by taking up new directions in the study of race and racism. I focus on three promising interdisciplinary endeavours: the birth of post-intersectionality scholarship, the rise of sensory accounts of race and racism, and the turn towards thinking about the pleasures minoritarian subjects can take in racialization.

This chapter is purposefully interdisciplinary, as work on race and racism is produced across the humanities, social sciences and natural sciences. Indeed, this chapter reveals that disciplinary promiscuity is a prerequisite for a robust understanding of race-making. By drawing on the insights of a host of disciplines, this review aspires to reveal the wide array of scholarly production investigating race and racism, and the panoply of questions scholars ask about race's persistence in the twenty-first century.

## Theorizing Race

Scholars across the disciplines increasingly advocate theorizing race, rather than allowing 'folk' or popular concepts of race to inform scholarly production (Wacquant 1997: 222). By actively interrogating race's historically specific contours and meanings instead of treating race as a transhistorical and transnational constant, scholars can investigate how racial regimes are crafted, transformed and toppled in different historical moments. Michael Omi and Howard Winant characterize this approach as one which treats race as an 'unstable and 'decentered' complex of social meanings constantly being transformed by political struggle' (Omi and Winant 1994: 55). The move towards treating race as a site of 'struggle' allows scholars to study *processes* of racialization, and to treat race-making as a dynamic, reiterative, contextual and deeply social project.

Race-making serves a political purpose: it 'signifies and symbolizes' the workings of power, but cloaks its politics in the language of the natural (Omi and Winant 1994: 55). That is, race *seems* to be a way of talking about real bodily difference when it is actually a historically contextual method for distributing resources, benefits and power. Historian Evelyn Brooks Higginbotham notes, 'perceived as "natural" and "appropriate", ... racial categories are strategically necessary for the functioning of power in countless institutional and ideological forms, both explicit and subtle' (Higginbotham 1992: 253–254). For Higginbotham, race's power comes from how it mobilizes the language of the 'natural' to hide its construction.

But if race is a social construct that lays a claim to the natural, how is race made and re-made from epoch to epoch? Omi and Winant advocate conceptualizing race's history as a *series* of racial formations through which 'racial categories are created, inhabited, transformed, and destroyed' (1994: 55). 'Racial formation' captures how seemingly fixed racial categories are produced and reproduced, and how racial categories are themselves sites of struggle and contest. Emblematic of the constant re-making of racial categories, many scholars have argued, is how whiteness has expanded in different moments (and contracted in others). Scholars including David Roediger (1999), Noel Ignatiev (2008), Thomas Guglielmo (2004), and Matthew Frye Jacobson (1999) have revealed the 'vicissitudes of whiteness' (Jacobson 2001) and documented how various immigrant groups have been ushered into – or excluded from – whiteness. In so doing, they reveal that whiteness is its own culturally contingent formation rather than a fixed category, and underscore how racial categories – even 'unmarked' racial categories like whiteness – are always sites of political struggle.

While a 'racial formation' approach reveals that racial categories are dynamic and contested, it also offers scholars tools for studying how race is crafted. Omi and Winant assert that race is formed at individual and social levels, making the work of 'racial projects' both quotidian and institutional. First, race is engendered through everyday 'racial projects'. At the individual level, we consistently 'notice' race and 'utilize race to provide clues about *who* a person is' (Omi and Winant 1994: 59). We are 'inserted in a comprehensively racialized social structure' and so race becomes foundational to the way we understand and interpret the social world and the subjects who inhabit that world (Omi and Winant 1994: 60). Race's effects on our everyday micro interactions, race's capacity to shape our judgments, perceptions, and interpretations means that race becomes a kind of every day 'common sense' (Omi and Winant 1994: 59).

One of the primary ways that race becomes 'common sense' is through visual culture. Indeed, there is now a burgeoning interdisciplinary literature on the visual politics of 'racial formation'. This work emphasizes how visual culture is deployed to entrench and naturalize racial hierarchy (and, at times, to disrupt it). Some scholars reveal that majoritarian visual culture repeatedly deploys 'controlling images', representations which entrench notions of black subjects' alterity (Collins 2000: 69). Patricia Hill Collins suggests that 'controlling images' are 'designed to make racism, sexism, poverty, and other forms of social injustice appear to be natural, normal, and inevitable parts of everyday life. Even when the initial conditions that foster controlling images disappear, such images prove remarkably tenacious because they not only subjugate ... but are key in maintaining intersecting oppressions' (Collins 2000: 69). While Collins's conception of 'controlling images' is particularly interested in the injuries that visual culture inflicts on black women – reducing black women to asexual mammies and matriarchs or hypersexual jezebels and welfare queens – it is clear that black men are also subjected to damaging 'controlling images' where they are reduced to criminals or hypersexual phalluses. Ultimately, 'controlling images' are representational devices that justify and entrench the dominant racial order, all the while masking their political work under the guise of 'entertainment'.

While race is reproduced through 'controlling images', some scholars have argued that the visual field – the very terrain on which images are projected and consumed – is itself structured by race. Judith Butler's analysis of the Rodney King video tape – one which captured incontrovertible evidence of racialized police brutality – asks how evidence of the brutalized black body could be interpreted as evidence of the dangerous black body. She concludes that we inhabit a 'racially saturated field of visibility', one in which race literally structures the parameters of what can – and can't – be seen (Butler 1993: 15). Images of King's prostrate black body beaten by police officers become literally *un*-seeable, or instead interpreted as evidence of King's violent black body. Ultimately, as Butler argues 'the visual field is not neutral to the question of race; it is itself a racial formation, an episteme, hegemonic and forceful' (Butler 1993: 17). If race shapes the visual field, structuring what can be seen and what is invisible, race is also tethered to the visual in other ways. Race is presumed to be visually legible, to make itself apparent on bodies. One of the recurring tropes in the burgeoning literature on mixed-race studies captures the cultural anxiety surrounding bodies that escape or undermine easy categorization. Race operates by enlisting our belief in our eyes: we come to believe that we can *see* race, that race will make itself known on bodies. Race quite literally plays a trick on the eye, allowing us to think that we *see* race when we never really do, and fuelling our anxiety about moments when race is particularly illegible.

If race is produced in a host of quotidian ways, it is also produced by what Omi and Winant term 'the racial state', through a set of juridical decisions and policies that serve to articulate and amplify racial categories. As David Goldberg notes, 'modern states are intimately involved in the reproduction of national identity, the national population, labor and security in and through the articulation of race, gender, and class' (Goldberg and Solomos 2002: 6). The 'racial state' decides which bodies can be naturalized, which bodies are 'worthy' of state support, which bodies to subject to hyper-surveillance and hyper-incarceration, and so on. While Omi and Winant focus on the social processes through which an American commitment to race making has been undertaken, the last decade has seen the emergence of a vibrant field of comparative work which examines the labour of 'racial states' globally. Most importantly, this work has disrupted the notion that America is the 'paradigmatic case for the sociological understanding of race' and has revealed the panoply of racial classification systems that are deployed globally in different moments to classify bodies (Telles 2004: 2).

Much of the comparative work on race-making has focused on Brazil, emphasizing (and sometimes celebrating) Brazil's elaborate racial taxonomy. Edward Telles details the host of ways that Brazilians racially classify themselves, including *branco* (white), mixed race (*mulato*), brown (*moreno*), and black (*negro*), clearly at odds with America's still-rigid black/white binary (Telles 2004: 1). He argues that 'unlike in the United States, race in Brazil refers mostly to skin color or physical appearance rather than to ancestry. This difference, and many others regarding race matters, between the two countries derive from two distinct ideologies and systems of modern-day race relations' (Telles 2004: 1). Yet this work also reveals that Brazil's relatively fluid racial classification system and its national mythology of racial democracy can coexist with racism (Sansone 2003: 4).

Attempts to *theorize* race increasingly focus on how race produces itself alongside or through *other* social categories, including gender and sexuality. A host of scholars and activists have examined how race and other structures of domination are intertwined and interlocking; indeed, black feminists have been articulating the connections among structures of domination for decades (Beale 1995, Combahee River Collective 1982, King 1988). The Combahee River Collective called for an analytic framework that would study the 'manifold and simultaneous oppressions that all women of color face' (Combahee River Collective 1982: 13), Frances Beale imagined black women's social positions as fundamentally linked to capitalism's unrelenting 'attempt[s] by many devious ways and means to destroy the humanity of all people, and particularly the humanity of black people' (Beale 1995: 146), and Deborah King analysed black women's distinctive 'multiple jeopardy' (King 1988). In recent years, the term 'intersectionality', what Leslie McCall calls 'the most important theoretical contribution that women's studies, in conjunction with related fields, has made so far', has focused interdisciplinary scholarly attention on how structures of domination are intersecting and mutually reinforcing (McCall 2005: 1771). More than that, the idea of intersectionality captures the particular invisibility of black women from anti-racist work, feminist work, and from legal doctrine which recognizes racial discrimination and gender discrimination but does not recognize how race and gender operate together to make black women's experiences of discrimination, at least at times, particular (Crenshaw 1989). In the spirit of the now-canonical anthology *All of the Women are White, All of the Men Are Black, But Some of Us Are Brave* (1982), intersectionality analysis exposes the ways that women has come to mean white, and black has come to mean men.

While intersectionality reveals how structures of domination are mutually reinforcing, a host of scholars have long asked *how* – and under what conditions – race has intersected with gender and sexuality to produce distinct effects (Hodes 1997, Hodes 1999, Nagel 2003). In so doing, these scholars have put into practice the promise of intersectionality, revealing the particular historically specific ways in which structures of domination lean on each other for support. Werner Sollors, for example, argues that the racial border has long been enforced by the policing of particular kinds of intimacies. He argues, 'one theme that has been pervasive in U.S. history and literature and that has been accompanied by a 300-year-long tradition of legislation, jurisdiction, protest, and defiance is the deep concern about, and the attempt to prohibit, contain, or deny the presence of black–white interracial sexual relations, interracial marriage, interracial descent, and other family relations across the powerful black–white divide' (Sollors 2000: 3). And yet, other scholars, including Martha Hodes, have been committed to examining the moments when racial borders become permeable (or more permeable). Her work on interracial intimacies between white women and black men reveals that 'in the antebellum South, white women and black men who engaged in illicit sex did not uniformly suffer swift retribution, for under slavery such liaisons did not sufficiently threaten the social and political hierarchy – as they would after emancipation' (Hodes 1999: 6). Hodes's work both underscores that race, gender and sexuality are inextricably intertwined *and* that the nature of their relationship is historically contingent.

While race has long been practiced as a bar against certain intimacies, racial domination has often taken the form of sexual domination, whether through the sexual control of black women during slavery (White 1999, Camp 2004, Morgan 2004), the forced implantation of the contraceptive Norplant in poor black women's arms (Roberts 1998, Smith 2002), or the ongoing demonization of poor black women (and the conflation of 'poor' with 'black') (Hancock 2004). In a hyper-visible example of Foucauldian bio-power, the state has taken a profound interest in regulating the reproductive choices and liberties of certain black women. Taking intersectionality seriously requires scholars to investigate how control of black subjects' sexuality – materially, representationally and physically – becomes a critical and elementary form of racial domination, one that has been practiced across time and space. More than that, it reveals that the very notion of race has sexual underpinnings: we can think of the racial border as a sexual border that prohibits (or permits) particular kinds of intimacies, and we can think of the construction of racial difference as indebted to gender and sexuality, and to fictions of black subjects' dangerous longings.

Ultimately, contemporary scholarship on race emphasizes that race-making is a socially contingent and contextual process; racial categories are subjects of constant debate, struggle and contestation, and they are constantly re-negotiated and re-made at both individual levels and institutional levels. The very crafting of race requires other structures of domination, like gender and sexuality, which often lend meaning to racial categories and/or help naturalize racial categories. As scholars continue to theorize the historical and geographical contingency of race, they also increasingly recognize the intimate relationship between race and other structures of domination.

## On 'the New Racism'

Much of contemporary scholarship on racism has grappled with a fundamental paradox: how do we explain the persistence of racism alongside the proliferation of colour-blindness rhetoric? How is it that in a moment when so many profess colour-blindness, claiming not to even 'see race', that race continues to fundamentally shape the social world from the quotidian to the institutional? What are the social, political and psychic structures that allow for this paradox to sustain itself? Of course, these questions are not distinctive to our post Civil Rights, Obama era, though they are amplified in new ways in a moment that is often hailed as 'post-race'. Indeed, in our 'post-race' moment, the 'new racism' works through paradox: evidence of racial inequality proliferates yet colour-blind race practitioners insist that racism is over (or that 'things have gotten better'); naming racial injuries and seeking redress is condemned as 'playing the race card'.

Some scholars explain the paradoxical co-existence of colour-blindness rhetoric and material racial inequality by using the term 'new racism'. Eduardo Bonilla-Silva argues that the 'new racism' – a colour-blind racial ideology that emerged in the late 1960s and flourishes today – is a way of 'explain[ing] racial inequality as the outcome of nonracial dynamics' (Bonilla-Silva 2010: 2). Unlike a Jim Crow racial regime, which used blacks' imagined 'natural' differences as an explanation for racial inequality, colour-blind racism uses 'the product of market dynamics, naturally occurring phenomena, blacks' imputed cultural limitations' and the language of choice to explain the continued persistence of racism (Bonilla-Silva 2010: 2). Colour-blind racism explains social phenomena like residential segregation as the result of a set of 'natural' choices about where people choose to live, rather than as an articulation of racial inequality.

Colour-blindness rhetoric is particularly problematic because it appropriates the language of racial progress and uses it to mask pernicious racial inequality. Indeed, colour-blindness *sounds* normatively desirable, and deploys the language of productive progress to mask persistent structural inequality. Ian Haney Lopez argues, 'colorblindness is a form of racial jujitsu. Co-opting the moral force of the civil rights movement, it uses that power to attack racial remediation and to defend structural racism, including the racism that infects the criminal law arena' (Lopez 2011: 54). Colour-blind rhetoric is deployed by its practitioners to assert that race-based remedies are no longer necessary (and, indeed, are *racist*) precisely because we live in a moment where subjects are colour-blind, where subjects readily claim not to even notice race. Indeed, 'one important dimension of the new racism is to cover over the harm done to victims and to mute their protest' (Collins 2004: 12).

If colour-blindness is the new dominant racial ideology, the 'new racism' uses distinctive mechanisms to ensure its power. As Patricia Hill Collins argues, the 'new racism' *depends* on gender and sexuality because it 'requires new ideological justifications, and the controlling images of Black femininity and Black masculinity participate in creating them' (Collins 2004: 122). Moreover, these 'controlling images' are increasingly supported by configurations of global capital and mass media that make the 'new racism' transnational (Collins 2004: 54). Images of black bodies move across time, space and national boundaries with greater ease – and with greater power – than ever before. Thus, strategies for toppling the 'new racism' will have to include a commitment to responding to visual culture's relentless circulation of images of black deviance and alterity.

While Collins suggests that visual culture is central to the 'new racism', other scholars suggest that our colour-blind era actually makes use of new machinery of racial domination, a set of institutions which *seem* inclusive but actually actively disenfranchise certain bodies. Loic Wacquant advocates considering our historical moment as marked by the emergence of a new 'peculiar institution': the prison. While the 'peculiar institutions' of earlier eras included slavery, Jim Crow, and the birth of the ghetto, Wacquant argues that the 'single greatest *political* transformation of the post-Civil Rights era in America is the joint rolling back of the stingy social state and rolling out of the gargantuan penal state that have remade the country's stratification, cities, and civic culture, and are recasting the very character of "blackness" itself' (Wacquant 2010: 74). The prison, Wacquant (and other scholars including Ruth Gilmore, Angela Davis and Michelle Alexander) argue, is a deeply racialized institution, one which ensnares more black bodies than at any other moment in our nation's history, and one which – like the 'new racism' is both omnipresent and invisible. In some ways, hyper-imprisonment (a term which Wacquant uses in lieu of 'mass imprisonment') is emblematic of how colour-blindness' rhetoric and politics work. While prison is a deeply racialized institution, as Michelle Alexander argues, 'rather than rely on race, we use our criminal justice system to label people of color "criminals" and then engage in all the practices we supposedly left behind. Today, it is perfectly legal to discriminate against criminals in nearly all the ways it was once legal to discriminate against any African American' (Alexander 2011: 24). By disguising racial discrimination in other forms of discrimination – discrimination against 'criminals' or against former-felons – the 'racial caste system' that is part and parcel of the 'prison industrial complex' is effectively masked.

While racism persists in a colour-blind era with new institutions – including the prison and global media – emerging to perform the work of race-making, racial discrimination is increasingly viewed narrowly: racism is viewed as an aberration, as the bad *intentional* actions of one particular actor, rather than something systemic, entrenched and quotidian. Indeed, the Supreme Court has made the litmus test of discrimination not discriminatory *effects* (is the outcome of a particular practice discriminatory?) but discriminatory *intent*, requiring a plaintiff to show the bad heart or corrupt mind of a particular actor, something notoriously hard to prove, particularly in an era where actors are increasingly unlikely to explicitly articulate racist intentions (*Washington v. Davis*). While intent continues to be the standard for 'proving' discrimination, scholars increasingly argue that racism is an *unconscious* structure, making racism's seething effects palpable, but proving its intent challenging. Charles Lawrence argues, '[t]o the extent that this cultural belief system has influenced all of us, we are all racists. At the same time, most of us are unaware of our racism. We do not recognize the ways in which our cultural experience has influenced our beliefs about race or the occasions on which those beliefs affect our actions. In other words, a large part of the behavior that produces racial discrimination is influenced by unconscious racial motivation' (Lawrence 1987: 322). Lawrence's work on unconscious racism has been supported by the intellectual production of social scientists, most notably social psychologist Mahzarin Banaji's work revealing that we all unknowingly harbour a set of implicit racial attitudes which shape our decision-making. If attitudes and biases are understood to be held *implicitly*, and yet racial injuries are supposed to be *intentionally* inflicted, it becomes increasingly hard, if not wholly impossible, to convincingly 'prove' racism.

While racism is increasingly defined in narrower terms, making it nearly impossible to 'prove', the notion of 'white innocence' has expanded to foreclose a host of remedial schemes which would remedy the lingering effects of past discrimination and the harms of continuing discrimination. Thomas Ross argues that the rhetoric of 'white innocence' is particularly evident in the affirmative action debate where 'it is presumed that the white victim is not guilty of a racist act that has denied the minority applicant the job or other position she seeks' (Ross 2000: 636). Ross suggests that the shift towards thinking about individual action, rather than structural racism, obscures important questions about privilege and dominance. He pointedly asks, 'what white person is "innocent," if innocence is defined as the absence of advantage at the expense of others?' (Ross 2000: 636). Ross suggests that a structure of unquestioned and unconscious white privilege acts as what Catharine MacKinnon calls 'an affirmative action plan for white men' (MacKinnon 2006: 75).

Because 'proving' discrimination has become increasingly difficult in a legal and cultural moment marked by incredibly high intentionality standards, and in a moment that views racism not as structural but as individual, the labour of critical race theory has been to use story-telling to document the ways that racism – or 'spirit-murder' as Patricia J. Williams poignantly calls it – continues to inflict itself on black bodies (Williams 1991: 73). Part of the labour of 'oppositional storytelling' is to reflect that law captures and enshrines particular stories; they just happen to be dominant stories, and so enjoy the label of 'knowledge' rather than 'story' (Delgado 2000). Other stories – stories about racial and sexist wounds – are called simply 'stories' which require additional evidence and proof to be credible. Through story-telling, critical race scholars both display the politics of knowledge and amplify the wounds of racism and patriarchy. For them, stories are 'powerful means for destroying mindset – the bundle of presuppositions, received wisdoms, and shared understandings' (Delgado 2000: 229).

If stories can disrupt the social world, challenging 'shared understandings', what are the stories critical race scholars tell about moments of racial progress? Some scholars, including Derrick Bell, explain racial progress through an 'interest convergence principle'. Bell first articulated his principle in an analysis of *Brown v. Board of Education*, asserting that the decision can not be understood without 'some consideration of the decision's value to whites, not simply those concerned about the immorality of racial inequality, but also those whites in policymaking positions able to see the economic and political advances at home and abroad that would follow abandonment of segregation' (Bell 1980: 524). Ultimately, interest convergence helps us understand how 50 years post-*Brown*, schools can continue to be profoundly segregated. *Brown*, Bell argues, benefited whites as much as blacks – though in different ways – and thus explains why the Supreme Court delivered a unanimous decision that seemed to usher in a dramatic shift and, instead, resulted in an ambivalent mandate to desegregate schools with 'all deliberate speed' (*Brown v. Board of Education*). Bell's conception of 'interest convergence' suggests that racial progress occurs when it is mutually beneficial to blacks and whites, rather than as an act of benevolence conferred upon blacks by whites.

Yet interest convergence is not the only device scholars use to understand moments of racial progress. The language of colour blindness suggests that the fact of *some* racial progress – for example, the now-iconic example of Obama's election – acts as proof that racial discrimination is over. In this way, the persistence of colour-blind racism seems to hinge on a few explicit examples that are called upon to stand for the end of racism. Indeed, colour-blind racism *requires* certain kinds of proof of racial redress to underscore the colour blindness of our own moment.

# New Directions

The study of race and racism proliferates in a wide array of disciplines. The remainder of this review traces three new directions in the study of race and racism: the advent of post-intersectionality studies, the turn toward sensory accounts of race and the emergence of scholarly work on pleasures in racialization. My interest in these three areas stems from their emphatic insistence on opening up new areas of scholarly conversation around race and racism, even prompting dialogue about questions that have long been thought of as taboo or unspeakable. I am also committed to these areas because of their insistence on meaningful interdisciplinarity. In moving across disciplinary borders, all three innovations draw on the theory and methods of the humanities and social sciences, crafting complex frameworks for exploring race and racism.

## Post Intersectionality

Two decades after Crenshaw coined the term 'intersectionality', intersectionality has been institutionalized. Indeed, intersectionality has become the primary analytic used across disciplines to theorize both identity and structures of domination. Yet, intersectionality has not been without its critics. In recent years, intersectionality has increasingly been subjected to critical scrutiny in myriad ways. Some scholars suggest that intersectionality can be expanded to act as a broad methodological innovation apart from 'women of color studies' (Hancock 2007); some critique the centrality of the race/gender intersection to intersectionality and instead highlight other intersectional identities (Kwan 1999), others suggest that intersectionality entrenches a liberal logic of diversity and inclusion (Puar 2005), and still others suggest that it problematically renders black women the quintessential intersectional subject (Nash 2008a). The post-intersectional turn emerging from the legal academy can best be understood as an attempt to re-orient intersectionality towards subjects whose experiences and identities continue to be under-theorized or ignored by feminist theory, critical race theory and/or queer theory.

Legal scholar Peter Kwan identifies a few shortcomings of intersectionality theory; first, he argues intersectionality 'does not pack much of an epistemological punch' (Kwan 1999: 686). While intersectionality illuminates that black female subjectivity is not simply the sum of race and gender, it does not necessarily tell us what the experience of black womanhood is. Kwan argues that narratives are 'often used to fill this gap. But narratives provide only the empirical data on which the theoretical work remains to be done' (Kwan 1999: 686). Moreover, as intersectionality is used to explore more and more categories – including nation, ability, immigration status – its ability to analyse all of these categories and their connections is compromised. More than that, as identities are constituted by a seemingly endless intersection of categories, intersectionality is required to select which intersections matter more, an approach which, Kwan argues, is 'theoretically no different than a pre-intersectionality approach' (Kwan 1997: 1277). Finally, Kwan argues that intersectionality does not provide an impetus for coalition building, for political organizing across or outside of identity categories.

In the wake of these critiques, a group of scholars who envision themselves as 'post-intersectionality' have emerged to craft new theories of mutually constitutive structures of domination. Using terms like cosynthesis (Kwan 1997), multidimensionality (Hutchinson 2001), and interconnectivity (Valdes 1995), these scholars all share an interest in thinking about identity categories with new complexity. Some are motivated by an attempt to centre the race/sexuality intersection generally, and the experiences of black queers specifically. Others hope to grapple with the intersections of privilege and subordination in more complex ways than intersectionality does (Ehrenreich 2002), or to examine how identity categories are 'sometimes themselves constructed or synthesized … and relies upon other categorical notions' (Kwan 1999: 689).

While post-intersectionality scholars actively seek ways to resuscitate intersectionality, other scholars have suggested jettisoning intersectionality all together, and instead think about the relationship between structures of domination and identity differently. Jasbir Puar's work contains a rigorous critique of intersectionality, asserting that the theoretical framework:

> *Demands the knowing, naming, and thus stabilizing of identity across space and time, generating narratives of progress that deny the fictive and performative of identification: you become an identity, yes, but also timelessness works to consolidate the fiction of a seamless stable identity in every space. As a tool of diversity management, and a mantra of liberal multiculturalism, intersectionality colludes with the disciplinary apparatus of the state – census, demography, racial profiling, surveillance – in that "difference" is encased within a structural container that simply wishes the messiness of identity into a formulaic grid. (Puar 2005: 128)*

Reading intersectionality as a regime which presumes that race, gender, class and other identity categories are fixed and knowable rather than fluid and constantly in motion – and which calls for visibility politics (for example, making black women's particular experiences of discrimination or injury legible), Puar advocates abandoning intersectionality. In its place she suggests moving toward a Deleuzian 'assemblage' or 'a series of dispersed but mutually implicated networks' which, rather than assuming that race, gender and sexuality are separate but intersecting vectors, 'is more attuned to interwoven forces that merge and dissipate time, space, and body against linearity, coherency, and permanency' (Puar 2005: 128). Ultimately, assemblage circumvents a liberal visibility politics and moves toward 'feeling, tactility, ontology, affect, and information' (Puar 2005: 128).

I flag the emerging and vibrant field of post-intersectionality scholarship because of its interest in thinking about new and under-theorized intersections and because of its commitment to thinking about how identities are always already marked by intersections of privilege and oppression. The labour of post-intersectionality has, at least in part, been de-centring the black female subject as the prototypical intersectional subject in ways that trouble the mythology that black women are always, necessarily the quintessentially oppressed subject. But I am also invested in post-intersectionality for its commitment to thinking about the shortcomings of the intersections metaphor, both theoretically and politically. Puar's work reveals not only intersectionality's easy institutionalization (one which has made intersectionality a synonym for diversity) but its fixity. Puar offers feminist legal scholars another framework for conceptualizing how subjects experience their bodies and the movement of those bodies through time and space.

## Beyond Visuality

Scholars have long argued for the centrality of the visual to both race and racism: the visual field is used to perpetuate racial violence and to entrench racial ideologies, race is presumed to be visually legible (and when bodies escape legibility they are the source of endless anxiety), and the visual field is structured by race. Recently, a number of scholars have advocated for thinking about how other registers become important sites through which racial difference is imagined. Mark Smith argues that 'modern discussions of "race" and racial identity are hostage to the eye. With few exceptions, popular writing as well as many academic works … tend to treat race as an exclusively visual phenomenon' (Smith 2007: 2). In place of the primacy of the visual, Smith advocates studying how the other senses became central to the construction of race and racial identity. His work, a 'sensory history', aims to analyse the production of 'sensory stereotypes about black people' (Smith 2007: 3). In shifting away from the supremacy of the visual, his analysis of the ways that other senses have been used to craft racial taxonomies is an important intervention into the host of ways – outside of the eye – that we 'see' race.

Similarly, Jennifer Stoever-Ackerman's work on the 'sonic color line' takes as a point of departure that 'sound is frequently marginalized within historical accounts and/or treated as ancillary to visual media' (Stoever-Ackerman 2010: 63–64). But Stoever-Ackerman argues for the centrality of sound, arguing that 'we hear race in addition to seeing it. Sonic phenomena like vocal timbre, accents, and musical tones are racially coded, like skin color, hair texture, and clothing choices. At one level, the sonic color-line posits racialized subject positions like "white," "black," and "brown" as historical accretions of sonic phenomena and stereotypes that can function without their correlating visual signifiers and can often stand in for them' (Stoever-Ackerman 2010: 65). Stoever-Ackerman's work reveals that race is heard as much as it is seen, and that the sonic and the visual are both significant registers where race is crafted and reproduced.

Both Smith and Stoever-Ackerman reveal that the scholarly focus on the visual has often obscured the centrality of other senses – smell, and sound, for example – to deeply held mythologies about racial difference. In moving beyond the visual, and recognizing the importance of other senses to racial myth-making, the move toward 'sensory histories' allows for a more complex analysis of the production of race.

## Race-pleasure

Scholars in a number of disciplines have recently begun to ask about the centrality of pleasure to race-making and to embodied experiences of racialization. Generally, when scholars have considered pleasures in race, their work has taken one of two directions: first, for decades, scholars have traced the cultural and political pleasures black subjects can take in racialization, using this 'pleasure' to explain the long-standing debates over appropriations of ostensibly black cultural production. Second, scholars have argued that white subjects take a kind of pleasure in racialization, a 'sadistic' enjoyment in inflicting race-making on black bodies and calling it natural (Farley 1997). Race, then, becomes something that confers pleasure on white subjects and pain on black subjects.

Yet, in recent years some scholars have become increasingly interested in other kinds of pleasures minoritarian subjects can take in racialization, focusing particularly on the aesthetic, erotic and sexual pleasures that minoritarian subjects can locate in racialization. Some of this work has emerged out of queer theory, which has long had an interest in the productive value of shame, of bottom positions, practices and pleasures (Bersani 1987, Crimp 1987, Sedgwick 1993, Stockton 2006). For these scholars, shame can be a space for identity formation, for pleasures of all kinds, and even a space for a kind of redemption.

New interdisciplinary scholarship on 'race-pleasure' (Nash 2008b) fuses queer theory's commitment to thinking about shame's value with a critical race theory interest in building a theory of 'race positive sexuality' (Shimizu 2007), a theoretical formation which examines how race generally, and racial fictions and stereotypes, can fuel and unleash the sexual imaginations of minoritarian subjects in precisely the ways they animate the sexual imaginations of majoritarian subjects. This approach – adopted by a wide range of scholars including Shimizu 2007, Nash 2008b, and Miller-Young 2008 – takes as a point of departure that aesthetic, erotic and sexual pleasures *in* racialization are not simply the domain of majoritarian subjects. Instead, Shimizu argues that race becomes a vehicle for naming pleasures and longings, and a profound 'political critique of the normal' (Shimizu 2007: 23).

## Conclusion

This chapter reveals that contemporary scholarship on race and racism insists on treating race as an iterative social process. Racial meanings are contextual and contingent, and racial categories shift in distinctive historical moments and locations. By underscoring race as a process rather than a trans-historical constant, recent work on race is able to treat racial categories as fluid, dynamic and contested rather than static and fixed. This chapter also underscores that racism is a contextual and contingent practice; it takes particular forms in distinctive moments, with our moment marked by what some scholars have termed the 'new racism', a colour-blind racism. Finally, the chapter has underscored that race's labour – classifying bodies and allocating power, resources and benefits accordingly – depends on gender and sexuality, so that race-making is a practice that relies on other structures of domination to maintain its hegemony.

As scholars continue to think about how it is that race is made – institutionally and individually, through law and policy, through quotidian practices and state mandates – they reveal that race is an American pastime, one of our unspoken obsessions. Indeed, race permeates not simply our social structures, but also our cultural representations, our collectively held fictions, and even our most intimate longings and pleasures. Yet, like Clifford Geertz's Balinese cockfight, race also becomes a terrain where we tell ourselves stories about ourselves, mythologies and fictions about progress, about equality and about colour-blindness despite the persistence of entrenched racial inequality.

# References

Alexander, M. 2011. The New Jim Crow: Mass Incarceration in the Age of Colorblindness, in *Race, Crime, and Punishment: Breaking the Connection in America*, edited by K.O. Lawrence. Washington, DC: Aspen Institute, 23–39.

Beale, F. 1995. 1970. Double Jeopardy: To Be Black and Female, in *Words of Fire*, edited by B. Guy-Sheftall. New York: Random House, 146–156.

Bell, D. 1980. *Brown v. Board of Education* and the Interest Convergence Dilemma. *Harvard Law Review* 93, 518–533.

Bersani, L. 1987. Is the Rectum a Grave? *October*, 43, 197–222.

Bonilla-Silva, E. 2010. *Racism Without Racists*. 2nd Edition. New York: Rowman.

Butler, J. 1993. Endangered/Endangering: Schematic Racism and White Paranoia, in *Reading Rodney King/Reading Urban Uprising*, edited by R. Gooding-Williams. New York: Routledge, 15–22

Camp, S.M.H. 2004. *Closer to Freedom: Enslaved Women and Everyday Resistance in the Plantation South*. Chapel Hill: University of North Carolina Press.

Collins, P.H. 2000. *Black Feminist Thought*. 2nd Edition. New York: Routledge.

Collins, P.H. 2004. *Black Sexual Politics: African Americans, Gender, and the New Racism*. New York: Routledge.

Combahee River Collective Statement. 1982. A Black Feminist Statement, in *All the Women are White, All the Blacks Are Men, But Some of Us Are Brave: Black Women's Studies*, edited by G.T. Hull, P.B. Scott, and B. Smith. New York: Feminist Press, 13–20.

Crenshaw, K. 1989. Demarginalizing the Intersection of Race and Sex: A Black Feminist Critique of Antidiscrimination Doctrine, Feminist Theory, and Antiracist Politics. *University of Chicago Legal Forum*, 1989, 139–167.

Crimp, D. 1987. How to Have Promiscuity in an Epidemic. *October*, 43, 237–271.

Delgado, R. 2000. Storytelling for Oppositionists and Others: A Plea for Narrative, in *Critical Race Theory: The Cutting Edge*, 2nd Edition, edited by R. Delgado and J. Stefancic. Philadelphia: Temple University Press, 60–70.

Du Bois, W.E.B. 2005 (1903). *The Souls of Black Folk*. New York: Simon and Schuster.

Ehrenreich, N. 2002. Subordination and Symbiosis: Mechanisms of Mutual Support between Subordinating Systems. *University of Missouri Kansas City Law Review*, 71–72, 251–324.

Farley, A.P. 1997. The Black Body as Fetish Object. *Oregon Law Review*, 76(3), 457–535.

Goldberg, D.T. and Solomos, J. 2002. Introduction, in A Companion to Racial and Ethnic Studies, edited by D.T. Goldberg and J. Solomos. Malden, MA: Blackwell, 1-13.

Guglielmo, T.A. 2004. *White on Arrival: Italians, Race, Color, and Power in Chicago 1890–1945.* New York: Oxford University Press.

Hancock, A. 2004. *The Politics of Disgust: The Public Identity of the Welfare Queen.* New York: NYU Press.

Hancock, A. 2007. Intersectionality as a Normative and Empirical Paradigm. *Politics & Gender*, 3(2), 248–254.

Higginbotham, E.B.H. 1992. African-American Women's History and the Metalanguage of Race. *Signs*, 17(2), 251–274.

Hodes, M. 1997. *Sex, Love, Race: Crossing Boundaries in North American History.* New York: New York University Press.

Hodes, M. 1999. *White Women, Black Men: Illicit Sex in the Nineteenth Century South.* New Haven: Yale University Press.

Hutchinson, D. 2001. Identity Crisis: 'Intersectionality,' 'Multidimensionality,' and the Development of An Adequate Theory of Subordination. *Michigan Journal of Race and Law*, 6, 28–50.

Ignatiev, N. 2008. *How the Irish Became White*. New York: Routledge.

Jacobson, M.F. 1999. *Whiteness of a Different Color: European Immigrants and the Alchemy of Race.* Cambridge: Harvard University Press.

Jacobson, M.F. 2001. Becoming Caucasian: Vicissitudes of Whiteness in American Politics and culture. *Identities: Global Studies in Culture and Power*, 8(1), 83–104.

King, D.K. 1988. Multiple Jeopardy, Multiple Consciousness: The Context of a Black Feminist Ideology. *Signs*, 14(1), 42–72.

Kwan, P. 1999. Complicity and Complexity: Cosynthesis and Praxis. *Depaul Law Review*, 49, 673–690.

Kwan, P. 1997. Jeffrey Dahmer and the Cosynthesis of Categories. *Hastings Law Journal* 48, 1257–1292.

Lawrence, C.R. 1987. The Id, The Ego, and Equal Protection: Reckoning with Unconscious Racism. *Stanford Law Review*, 39(2), 317–388.

Lopez, I.H. 2011. Structural Racism and Crime Control, in *Race, Crime, and Punishment: Breaking the Connection in America*, edited by K.O. Lawrence. Washington, DC: Aspen Institute, 39–65.

MacKinnon, C.A. 2006. *Are Women Human? And Other International Dialogues.* Cambridge: Harvard University Press.

Massey, D.S. and Denton, N.A. 1993. *American Apartheid: Segregation and the Making of the Underclass.* Cambridge: Harvard University Press.

McCall, L. 2005. The Complexity of Intersectionality. *Signs*, 30(3), 1771–1800.

Miller-Young, M. 2008. Hip-Hop Honeys and Da Hustlaz: Black Sexualities in the New Hip-Hop Pornography. *Meridians*, 8(1), 261–292.

Morgan, J.L. 2004. *Laboring Women: Reproduction and Gender in New World Slavery.* Philadelphia: University of Pennsylvania Press.

Nagel, J. 2003. *Race, Ethnicity, and Sexuality: Intimate Intersections, Forbidden Frontiers.* New York: Oxford University Press.

Nash, J.C. 2008a. Re-thinking Intersectionality. *Feminist Review*, 89, 1–15.

Nash, J.C. 2008b. Strange Bedfellows: Black Feminism and Anti-Pornography Feminism. *Social Text*, 97, 51–76.

Oliver, M.L. and Shapiro, T.M. 2006. *Black Wealth/White Wealth: A New Perspective on Racial Inequality*. 2nd Edition. New York: Routledge.

Omi, M. and Winant, H. 1994. *Racial Formation in the United States*. 2nd Edition. New York: Routledge.

Puar, J.K. 2005. Queer Times, Queer Assemblages. *Social Text*, 23(3–4), 121–139.

Roberts, D. 1998. *Killing the Black Body: Race, Reproduction, and the Meaning of Liberty*. New York: Vintage.

Roediger, D. 1999. *The Wages of Whiteness: Race and the Making of the American Working Class*. Revised Edition. New York: Verso.

Ross, T. 2000. Innocence and Affirmative Action, in *Critical Race Theory: The Cutting Edge*, 2nd edn, edited by R. Delgado and J. Stefancic. Philadelphia: Temple University Press, 635–647.

Sansone, L. 2003. *Blackness Without Ethnicity: Constructing Race in Brazil*. New York: Palgrave.

Sedgwick, E. 1993. Queer Performativity: Henry James' The Art of the Novel. *GLQ*, 1(1), 1–16.

Shimizu, C.P. 2007. *The Hypersexuality of Race: Performing Asian/American Women on Screen and Scene*. Durham: Duke University Press.

Smith, K.A. 2002. Conceivable Sterilization: A Constitutional Analysis if a Norplant/Depo–Provera Welfare Condition. *Indiana Law Journal*, 77, 389–417.

Smith, M.M. 2007. *How Race is Made: Slavery, Segregation and the Senses*. Chapel Hill: University of North Carolina Press.

Sollors, W. 2000. *Interracialism: Black–White Intermarriage in American History, Literature and Law*. New York: Oxford University Press.

Stockton, K.B. 2006. *Beautiful Bottom, Beautiful Shame: Where 'Black' Meets 'Queer'*. Durham: Duke University Press.

Stoever-Ackerman, J. 2010. Splicing the Sonic Color-Line: Tony Schwartz Remixes Postwar Nueva York. *Social Text*, 102, 59–85.

Telles, E.E. 2004. *Race in Another America: The Significance of Skin Color in Brazil*. Princeton: Princeton University Press.

Valdes, F. 1995. Sex and Race in Queer Legal Culture: Ruminations on Identities and Interconnectivities. *Southern California Review of Law and Women's Studies*, 5, 32–46.

Wacquant, L. 1997. For an Analytic of Racial Domination. *Political Power and Social Theory*, 11, 221–234.

Wacquant, L. 2001. Deadly Symbiosis: When Ghetto and Prison Meet and Mesh. *Punishment and Society*, 3(1), 95–133.

Wacquant, L. 2010. Class, Race and Hyperincarceration in Revanchist America. *Daedalus*, 139(3), 74–90.

White, D.G. 1999. *Ar'n't I a Woman? Female Slaves in the Plantation South*. New York: W.W. Norton.

Williams, P.J. 1991. *The Alchemey of Race and Rights*. Cambridge: Harvard University Press.

Wilson, W.J. 1990. *The Truly Disadvantaged: The Inner City, the Underclass, and Public Policy*. Chicago: University of Chicago Press.

Wilson, W.J. 2010. *More Than Just Race: Being Black and Poor in the Inner City*. New York: W.W. Norton.

# Feminists Rethink Multiculturalism: Resisting Essentialism and Cross-Cultural Hypocrisy

## Sarah Song[1]

'Multiculturalism' is sometimes used as a descriptive term to refer to culturally pluralistic societies. This chapter examines the idea of multiculturalism in its normative sense – as a set of moral, political and legal claims about the proper way to respond to cultural diversity. A basic premise of theories of multiculturalism is that mere toleration of group differences falls short of treating members of minority cultural groups as equal citizens. What is required instead is recognition or positive accommodation of group differences.

The philosopher Will Kymlicka (1995), a leading theorist of multiculturalism, coined the term 'group-differentiated rights' to refer to a range of legal and political exemptions, accommodations, and forms of assistance to cultural minorities. Some group-differentiated rights are held by individual members of minority groups, as in the case of individuals who are granted exemptions from generally applicable laws in virtue of their religious beliefs or individuals who seek language accommodations in voting or education. Other group-differentiated rights are held by the group *qua* group rather than by its members severally; such rights are properly called 'group rights', as in the case of limited self-government rights extended to indigenous groups and minority nations who claim the right of self-determination. In the latter respect, multiculturalism is closely allied with nationalism.

While multiculturalism has been used as an umbrella term to characterize the claims of a wide range of disadvantaged groups, including women, racial minorities, LGBT persons, and the disabled (see, for example, Taylor 1992), most theorists of multiculturalism tend to focus their arguments on immigrants who are ethnic and religious minorities (for example, Mexican Americans, Jews and Muslims in Western Europe and North America), minority nations (for example, Catalans, Basque, Welsh, Québécois), and indigenous peoples (for example, Native peoples in North America, the Maori in New Zealand).

Feminist scholars have turned their attention to the theory and practice of multiculturalism with an eye toward its effects on women and other vulnerable members of minority groups. This chapter explores feminist engagement with multiculturalism. It begins with a discussion of what claims of 'culture' consist of and how multiculturalism

---

1    For helpful comments on this chapter, I am very grateful to Sara Ludin and the editors of this volume, Margaret Davies and Vanessa Munro.

has been defended before turning to examine feminist critiques. Particular legal cases and political controversies will be discussed along the way.

## Claims of Culture

Multiculturalism is closely associated with 'the politics of difference' (Young 1990), 'the politics of recognition' (Taylor 1992, Fraser and Honneth 2003), and 'identity politics' (Gutmann 2003), all of which share a commitment to revaluing disrespected identities and transforming dominant patterns of representation and communication that marginalize certain groups. Contemporary theorizing about multiculturalism largely takes for granted that it is 'culture' and 'cultural groups' that are to be recognized and accommodated. If we look closely at the range of claims made in the name of 'culture', we see a broad range of claims involving religion, language, ethnicity, nationality and race. Culture is a notoriously overbroad concept, and all of these categories have been subsumed by or equated with the concept of culture (Song 2008).

Examples of cultural accommodations or 'group-differentiated rights' include exemptions from generally applicable laws (for example, religious exemptions); assistance to do things that the majority can do unassisted (for example, multilingual ballots, funding for minority language schools and ethnic associations, affirmative action); representation of minorities in government bodies (for example, ethnic quotas for party lists or legislative seats, minority–majority Congressional districts); recognition of traditional legal codes by the dominant legal system (for example, granting jurisdiction over family law to religious courts); or limited self-government rights (for example, qualified recognition of tribal sovereignty and federal arrangements recognizing the political autonomy of Quebec) (for a helpful classification, see Levy 1997).

Much scholarly discourse on multiculturalism revolves around religious examples: religious exemptions from generally applicable laws, the recognition of the traditional legal codes of religious communities, and limited self-government rights for territorially concentrated religious minorities.[2] Familiar examples of religious exemptions include the Amish who want to be exempt from schooling requirements, Sikhs who wish to be exempt from helmet laws, and Muslim girls and women who seek to wear the headscarf or burqa in public spaces. Following John Locke, contemporary liberal theorists tend to privilege a particular understanding of religion – as a matter of inner belief and conscience, which serve as a source of normative authority and are regarded by believers as binding ethical commitments (Cohen 1998, Scheffler 2007). Because religion, understood as inner belief and conscience, has this normative authority, liberal theorists privilege religion over more

---

2    The tendency to conflate culture and religion is not surprising. First, religious observance is shaped by local and national culture, as suggested by the great differences between, for example, the Indonesian, Indian and Iranian forms of Islam. Influence also runs in the other direction: religious practice shapes local and national cultures. For example, Amish religion shapes the Amish way of life, and Christianity has deeply shaped the modern cultural norms and practices in the West. Second, individuals and groups seeking legal accommodations may have incentives to blur the distinction between religion and culture. Most Western liberal states have strong legal protections for religious freedom, so individuals or groups seeking accommodation of particular practices may be compelled to present those practices as 'religious' rather than merely 'cultural'.

purely 'cultural' claims. Expressions such as 'cultural norms' or 'cultural values' are viewed as descriptions of convention, what people already do, not a source of normative authority in the way religious beliefs are.

Along with religion, language is at the centre of cultural claims-making (Kymlicka and Patten 2003). Each nation state typically establishes a common language in which to conduct its affairs. In the course of liberalization, Western states relinquished the notion that a common religion was integral to national integration, but the opposite occurred with respect to language, which moved to the fore as the single most important element in the construction of national identity. Nation-building has been fuelled by more malignant motives than the mere need for a lingua franca (not least racism and xenophobia) such that forging a common language has sometimes involved the domination and suppression of minority languages and identities. Consider the ethnolinguistic conflict in Eastern Europe after the fall of communism in 1989; the debate over official multilingualism in Canada and Spain; and the debate over bilingual education in the US.

In addition to religion and language, 'culture' also signifies the different rituals and customs involving food, dress, family roles, and musical and other artistic practices that constitute a way of life for a group. Ethnic minorities have sought exemptions from general rules that penalize or constrain their customs, as well as positive assistance from the state to pursue and preserve their group traditions (for example, funding for ethnic associations) and symbolic recognition measures (for example, national holidays, school curricula).

The cultural claims of immigrants and ethnic minorities comprise only a part of leading theories of multiculturalism. Another central claim of 'culture' has been the claim of self-determination by minority nations and aboriginal groups. It is no accident that many of the leading theorists of multiculturalism (Kymlicka (1989) and (1995), Taylor (1992) and (1995), Tully (1995)) are writing in the context of Canada where the cultural claims that loom large are those of Quebec and First Nations. In contrast to ethnic and racial minorities, minority nations have sought some measure of political autonomy through secession (for example, Slovenia) and federal arrangements (for example, Quebec, Catalonia, Native tribes).

Race has had a more limited role in multicultural discourse, and most theorists of multiculturalism have provided little guidance for thinking about the relationship between race and culture. For instance, Kymlicka (2001: 198) has written that his theory of multiculturalism is not intended to address the concerns of racial minorities, emphasizing that a *sui generis* approach is needed to overcome the racial exclusion of black minorities, 'the group which is most in need' among visible minorities in Canada and the US. In contrast, Charles Taylor includes African Americans in his discussion of multiculturalism when he discusses the 'canon wars' in the university and the issue of self-respect among racial minorities in light of demeaning images projected in the wider society (Taylor 1994: 26, 65). Antiracism and multiculturalism are distinct but related ideas: the former highlights 'victimization and resistance', whereas the latter highlights 'cultural life, cultural expression, achievements, and the like' (Blum 1992: 14). Claims for recognition in the context of multicultural education are demands not just for recognition of aspects of a group's cultural traditions and practices (for example, African American art and literature) but also for acknowledgment of the history of group subordination and its concomitant experience (Gooding-Williams 1998).

With these myriad claims of 'culture' in mind, let us turn to consider normative justifications and critiques of multiculturalism.

# Leading Theories of Multiculturalism

There are at least three prominent justifications for multiculturalism in the existing scholarly literature.

## Communitarian

One justification for multiculturalism arises out of the so-called 'communitarian' critique of liberalism. Liberal theorists have typically been committed to ethical individualism; they insist that individuals should be free to choose and pursue their own conceptions of the good life. They have tended to give primacy to individual rights and liberties over community life and collective goods. Some liberals are also individualists when it comes to social ontology, holding a view that some call methodological individualism or atomism. Atomists believe that you can and should account for social actions and social goods in terms of properties of the constituent individuals and individual goods. The target of the communitarian critique of liberalism is not so much liberal ethics as liberal social ontology. Communitarians reject the idea that the individual is prior to the community, and that the value of social goods can be reduced to their contribution to individual well-being. They instead embrace ontological holism, which views social goods as 'irreducibly social' (Taylor 1995). It is this holist view of collective identities and cultures that underlies Charles Taylor's argument for a multicultural 'politics of recognition' (1992). Diverse cultural identities and languages are irreducibly social goods, which should be presumed to be of equal worth. Recognition of the equal worth of diverse cultures requires replacing the traditional liberal regime of identical liberties and opportunities for all citizens with a scheme of special rights for minority cultural groups.

## Liberal Egalitarian

A second justification for multiculturalism comes from within contemporary liberalism. Partly as a response to the charge that liberalism cannot adequately account for the value of cultural membership and identity, Kymlicka has developed the most influential theory of multiculturalism based on the liberal values of autonomy and equality (Kymlicka 1989: 1995, 2001). In contrast to communitarian accounts of multiculturalism, Kymlicka's account is based on an instrumental defence of culture. Culture is instrumentally valuable to individuals for two reasons. First, it enables individual autonomy. One important condition of autonomy is having an adequate range of options from which to choose. Cultures provide contexts of choice, which provide and make meaningful the social scripts and narratives from which people fashion their lives (see Appiah 2005). Second, culture is instrumentally valuable for individual self-respect. Drawing on theorists of communitarianism and nationalism, Kymlicka argues that there is a deep and general connection between a person's self-respect and the respect accorded to the cultural group of which she is a part. It is not simply membership in any culture but one's *own* culture that must be secured because of the great difficulty of giving it up.

Relying on these premises about the instrumental value of cultural membership, Kymlicka makes the following egalitarian argument: because liberal democracies are committed to egalitarian justice and because members of minority groups are disadvantaged in terms of access to their own cultures (in contrast to members of the majority culture), they are entitled to special protections or group-differentiated rights. The idea of choice plays an important role here. Kymlicka suggests that inequalities stemming from membership in a minority culture are unchosen, just as inequalities stemming from one's native talents and social starting position in life are unchosen. Insofar as inequality in access to cultural membership stems from luck and not from one's own choices, members of minority groups can reasonably demand that members of the majority culture share in bearing the costs of accommodation. Minority group rights are justified, as Kymlicka argues, 'within a liberal egalitarian theory … which emphasizes the importance of rectifying unchosen inequalities' (Kymlicka 1995: 109).[3]

One might question whether minority cultural groups really are 'disadvantaged' or suffer a serious inequality as liberal theorists of multiculturalism suggest. Why not just enforce antidiscrimination laws, stopping short of any positive accommodations for minority groups? Egalitarian defenders of multiculturalism contend that antidiscrimination laws fall short of treating members of minority groups as equals. This is because states cannot be neutral with respect to culture. In culturally diverse societies, we can easily find patterns of state *support* for some cultural groups over others. Language is a paradigmatic marker of culture. While states may prohibit racial discrimination and avoid official establishment of religion, they cannot avoid establishing one language for public schooling and other state services (Kymlicka 1995: 111, Carens 2000: 77–78, Patten 2001: 693). Cultural or linguistic advantage can translate into economic and political advantage since members of the dominant cultural community have a leg up in schools, the workplace and politics. Cultural advantage also takes a symbolic form. When state action extends symbolic affirmation to some groups and not others in establishing the state language and public symbols and holidays, it has a normalizing effect, suggesting that one group's language and customs are more valued than those of other groups.

In addition to state support of certain cultures over others, state laws impose *constraints* on some cultural groups over others. Consider the case of dress code regulations in public schools or the workplace. A ban on religious dress burdens religious individuals, as in the case of Simcha Goldman, a US Air Force officer, who was also an ordained rabbi and wished to wear a yarmulke out of respect to an omnipresent God (*Goldman v. Weinberger* 475 US 503 (1986)). The case of the French government's ban on religious dress in public schools, which burdens Muslim girls who wish to wear headscarves to school, is another example (Benhabib 2002: ch. 5, Bowen 2007, Laborde 2008). Religion may command that believers dress in a certain way; this is what Peter Jones calls an 'intrinsic burden', a burden that must be born by the believers as a requirement of faith (Jones 1994). In Goldman's case or in the case of the French headscarf controversy, religion does not command that believers refrain from attending school or going to work. Yet, the burden on believers does not stem from the dictates of religion alone; the burden arises from the intersection of the demands of religion and the demands of the state (what Jones calls an 'extrinsic burden'). Intrinsic burdens are not of collective concern; bearing the burdens of the dictates of one's faith – prayer, worship, fasting – is an obligation of faith. When it comes to extrinsic burdens, liberal multiculturalists argue, egalitarian justice requires assisting cultural minorities through exemptions and accommodations.

While offered as a general normative argument for minority cultural groups, liberal multiculturalists distinguish among different types of groups. For instance, Kymlicka's

---

3    The discussion in this section draws on Song 2007: ch. 3.

theory of liberal multiculturalism offers the strongest form of group-differentiated rights (self-government rights) to indigenous peoples and minority nations because their minority status is unchosen; they were coercively incorporated into the larger state. In contrast, immigrants are viewed as voluntary economic migrants who chose to relinquish access to their native culture by migrating. Immigrant multiculturalism – what Kymlicka calls 'polyethnic rights' – is understood as a demand for fairer terms of integration through exemptions and assistance, not a rejection of integration (Kymlicka 1995: 113–115).

## Postcolonial

Some scholars have looked beyond liberalism in arguing for multiculturalism. This is especially true of theorists writing from a postcolonial perspective. The case for tribal sovereignty rests not simply on premises about the value of tribal culture and membership, but also on what is owed to Native peoples for the historical injustices perpetrated against them. Reckoning with history is crucial. Proponents of indigenous sovereignty emphasize the importance of understanding indigenous claims against the historical background of the denial of equal sovereign status of indigenous groups, the dispossession of their lands, and the destruction of their cultural practices (Ivison 2006, Ivison et al. 2000, Moore 2005, Simpson 2000). This background calls into question the legitimacy of the state's authority over aboriginal peoples and provides a *prima facie* case for special rights and protections for indigenous groups, including the right of self-government. The claim here is for restoring the right of self-government that colonial regimes took away.

A postcolonial perspective also seeks to develop models of constitutional and political dialogue that recognize culturally distinct ways of speaking and acting. Multicultural societies consist of diverse religious and moral outlooks, and if liberal societies are to take such diversity seriously, they must recognize that liberalism is just one of many substantive outlooks based on a specific view of the person and of society. Liberalism is not culture-free; it expresses a distinctive culture of its own. This observation applies not only across territorial boundaries between liberal and non-liberal states, but also within the territory of the liberal state to its relations with non-liberal minorities. The contention here is that liberal theory cannot provide an impartial or neutral framework governing relations between different cultural communities. British political theorist Bhikhu Parekh has argued instead for a more open model of intercultural dialogue in which a liberal society's constitutional and legal values serve as the initial starting point for cross-cultural dialogue but these 'operative public values' are open to contestation (2000: 269). Similarly, James Tully (1995) surveys the language of historical and contemporary constitutionalism with a focus on Western states' relations with Native peoples to uncover more inclusive bases for intercultural dialogue.

## Feminist Theorizing about Culture and Multiculturalism

While they share multicultural theorists' concern for the marginalized status of minority cultural groups, feminist theorists have cast a critical eye on multiculturalism out of a concern for its effects on women and other vulnerable members of minority cultural groups. Defenders of multiculturalism focus on inequalities *between* majority and minority groups in arguing for special protections for minority groups, but group-based protections sometimes have the effect of creating or reinforcing inequalities *within* the groups being accommodated.

## Tensions between Multiculturalism and Feminism

This concern was raised by Susan Moller Okin in her provocatively titled essay, 'Is Multiculturalism Bad for Women?' first published in the *Boston Review* ([1997] 1999). Okin argued that multicultural policies may come at the price of reinforcing the oppression of women. Okin's point about tensions between multiculturalism and feminism is part of a broader problem of 'internal minorities' or 'minorities within minorities' (Green 1994, Eisenberg and Spinner-Halev 2005). The term 'minority' does not necessarily refer to a group's numerical strength in the population but to groups that are marginalized or disadvantaged. Vulnerable subgroups include not only women but also children, sexual minorities, the poor, and religious and cultural dissenters. As Ayelet Shachar puts it, 'well-meaning accommodation by the state may leave members of minority groups vulnerable to severe injustice within the group, and may, in effect, work to reinforce some of the most hierarchical elements of a culture', a problem she called 'the paradox of multicultural vulnerability' (Shachar 2001: 3).

Few feminists have rejected Okin's central point – that multicultural policies can attenuate feminist goals – but Okin's underlying conception of culture and her generalizations about minority cultures have generated much critical commentary among feminist theorists. Okin's normative critique of multiculturalism was premised on two controversial claims. First, that 'most cultures have as one of their principal aims the control of women by men'. She pointed to the 'founding myths' of Judaism, Christianity and Islam as examples 'rife with attempts to justify the control and subordination of women' (1999: 13). Second, she posited that 'many (though not all) of the cultural minorities that claim group rights are more patriarchal than the surrounding cultures' in the West (17). To illustrate the latter, Okin pointed to cases involving immigrants in the West engaged in practices from polygamy and child marriage to clitoridectomy, kidnapping and rape, and 'wife murder by immigrants from Asian and Middle Eastern countries' (18). Okin thus concludes that members of minority cultures 'might be much better off if the culture into which they were born were either to become extinct (so that its members would become integrated into the less sexist surrounding culture) or, preferably, to be encouraged to alter itself so as to reinforce the equality of women – at least to the degree to which this value is upheld in the majority culture' (22–23).

## Rejecting Essentialist Notions of Culture

Okin's critique of multiculturalism seems to have provoked as much criticism by feminist scholars as multicultural policies themselves. In particular, many feminist theorists have taken issue with Okin's static, monolithic conception of culture. As Bonnie Honig (1999: 36) put it in her response essay: 'contra Okin, culture is something rather more complicated than patriarchal permission for powerful men to subordinate vulnerable women. There are brutal men (and women) everywhere. Is it their Jewish, Christian, or Muslim identity that makes them brutal ... or is it their brutality?' Cultures are not monolithically patriarchal in the way Okin suggests, and the practices she labels as sexist are more complicated than that label allows.

Take the example of veiling. Veiling might be a sign of women's subordination, as Okin contends, or it may be part of a broader effort aimed at both sexes to manage a community's personal and sexual relations. We need to know something about the meaning of veiling in a particular context before making a judgment about its being good or bad for women. Many Muslim feminists see veiling as an empowering practice. Veiling permits upwardly mobile professional women to, in Leila Ahmed's words, 'emerge socially into a sexually integrated' world that is 'still an alien, uncomfortable social reality for both women and men' (Ahmed 1992: 223–224). In the case of the headscarf controversy in France, Seyla Benhabib emphasizes the importance of asking the girls wearing the headscarf about their own understandings of the practice. Had their voices been listened to, it would have become clear that the meaning of wearing the headscarf itself was, in Benhabib's words, 'changing from a religious act to one of cultural defiance and increasing politicization' (2002: 117). These alternative interpretations of veiling emphasize its emancipatory potential for women and suggest the polyvocal nature of particular practices. While these interpretations are important challenges to Okin, it is also important to avoid a binary framework in which veiling is either an oppressive imposition or a form of emancipatory resistance. Saba Mahmood (2005: 9) frames this conundrum well: 'Does the category of resistance impose a teleology of progressive politics on the analytics of power—a teleology that makes it hard for us to see and understand forms of veiling and action that are not necessarily encapsulated by the narrative of subversion and reinscription of norms?'

Feminists have also taken issue with the 'enlightened West vs. barbaric East' binary implied by Okin's discussion. Leti Volpp has argued that Okin's failure to view cultures as hybrid and contested leads Okin to view feminism and multiculturalism as intrinsically opposed. Volpp brings the often neglected concept of race into theorizing about multiculturalism, and she identifies Okin's analysis as part of a larger tendency to assume that people from racialized minority groups are motivated by their culture whereas members of the dominant racial groups are motivated by choice (Volpp 2001). In comparing virtually identical acts by white Americans versus non-white immigrants, Volpp observes that behaviour we consider 'bad' is 'conceptualized only as culturally canonical for cultures assumed to lag behind the United States' (2000: 96). Volpp's critique forms part of a broader feminist critique of essentialism. While her focus is on cross-national discourses comparing dowry-murders in India and domestic-violence murders in the US, Uma Narayan (1997: 87) observes a similar dynamic at work *within* the boundaries of Western nation states: 'To put it bluntly, there is a marked tendency to proffer "cultural explanations" for problems within communities of color within Western contexts more readily than there is to proffer "cultural explanations" for similar problems within mainstream Western communities.'

Guarding against this 'us vs. them' binary is especially important if feminists are to be allies in the struggle against racism and ethnocentrism. In the current context of backlash against immigration and multiculturalism, feminist critique of minority cultural practices can play into the hands of those who deploy the rhetoric of gender equality in ways that demonize and exclude minority groups. As Anne Phillips has remarked: 'People not previously marked by their ardent support for women's rights seemed to rely on claims about the maltreatment of women to justify their distaste for minority cultural groups, and in these claims, cultural stereotypes were rife' (2007: 2).

## Cultures as Hybrid, Contested and Overlapping

Contra Okin, many feminist theorists writing on multiculturalism explicitly defend multicultural accommodations on grounds of equality and justice for minority groups (Shachar 2001, Deveaux 2006, Phillips 2007, Song 2007). Yet, they suggest the need for a multiculturalism premised on a more nuanced understanding of culture – one that is hybrid, contested and overlapping. Phillips articulates this need by calling for a 'multiculturalism without culture', which 'dispenses with the reified notions of culture that feed those stereotypes to which so many feminists have objected, yet retains enough robustness to address inequalities between cultural groups' (2007: 8). Phillips is right that many defenders and critics of multiculturalism have exaggerated the unity of cultures, but rather than remove or minimize the role of culture in debates about multiculturalism, I think feminist scholars ought to develop and defend more nuanced understandings of culture. Phillips' analysis actually suggests a more complex understanding of culture that might be identified as social contructivist.

A social constructivist account of cultures views cultures as the outcome of historical processes of internal contestation and intercultural interaction (Benhabib 2002, Song 2007). This approach takes what Benhabib calls a 'narrative view of actions and culture': analyses of culture begin by distinguishing the standpoint of the social observer from the social agent. It is the observer 'who imposes, together with local elites, unity and coherence on cultures as observed entities'; by contrast participants in the culture experience their traditions through 'shared, albeit contested and contestable, narrative accounts' (Benhabib 2002: 5). Some conflicts over cultural practices originate primarily within a group as a result of internal disagreement over the meaning and significance of particular practices.

In my own work, I have emphasized the role of intercultural interactions in shaping the identities and practices of minority cultural groups, not only ordinary social interactions between groups but also state action that imposes the dominant culture's gender norms and practices onto minority communities (Song 2005, 2007). Sometimes intercultural interactions have fuelled movements towards greater gender equality, but in other cases, intercultural interactions have reinforced unequal and oppressive norms and practices across cultures. State institutions reflecting the dominant culture's gender norms have long shaped the gender practices of minority cultures. For instance, majority institutions directly imposed mainstream gender biases onto minority communities, such as the 1887 Dawes Act, which subverted Native American women's roles in agricultural work by making Native American men heads of household, landowners and farmers (Cott 2000: 123). More common today are the indirect ways in which mainstream gender norms have resonated with and offered support for gender hierarchies in minority cultural communities, as in the 'cultural defences' in criminal law.

To demonstrate these interactive dynamics, let us consider in greater depth two cases that Okin mentions in passing.[4] In one case, a 23-year-old Hmong refugee, Kong Pheng Moua, abducted a 19-year-old Hmong woman, Xeng Xiong, and forced her to have sex with him. In his defence, Moua claimed that he was performing a traditional Hmong practice of matrimony called 'marriage by capture' in which a woman, even one who is willing to get married, should resist in order to establish her virtue.[5] Moua did not present cultural evidence to claim that he did not know rape was illegal in the US, nor did he argue that rape was not a category of offence in Hmong culture. Instead, he claimed that he did not understand Xiong's resistance as expressing non-consent. As Moua's lawyer put it, 'At the last minute the girl must say, "No, no, I'm not ready", and the boy must say, "Baloney, you'll be mine tonight." If those attitudes were not expressed, the girl would not appear

---

4    The following discussion draws on Song 2007: ch. 5.
5    *People v. Moua*, No. 315972–0, Fresno County Superior Court (February 2, 1985).

strong enough to the man, and he would not appear strong enough to her' (Song 2005: 479). The court dismissed the rape and kidnapping charges, and Moua was charged with false imprisonment and sentenced to 120 days in jail and a $1000 fine.

In another case, a Chinese immigrant, Dong Lu Chen, killed his wife after he discovered she was having an affair. In his defence, an anthropologist testified that 'in traditional Chinese culture, a wife's adultery is considered proof that a husband has a weak character, making him undesirable even after a divorce', and because of this stigma, a cuckolded man who reacts violently is behaving reasonably. The judge noted that Chen's cultural defence was integral to the reduction in criminal charges: 'Were this crime committed by the defendant as someone who was born and raised in America, or born elsewhere but primarily raised in America, even in the Chinese American community, the Court would have been constrained to find the defendant guilty of manslaughter in the first degree.' Chen was convicted of second-degree manslaughter and received a sentence of five years' probation with no jail time.[6]

Okin discusses these two cases to illustrate the tensions between feminism and multiculturalism and to cast doubt on the latter. She is right to be critical of the use of 'cultural defences' in ways that reinforce women's subordination, but she overlooks the ways in which the dominant culture's gender norms enable the accommodation of patriarchal practices within minority communities. Although the defence lawyers in both these cases emphasized cultural *differences* between immigrant and mainstream defendants, there is a striking *congruence* in the norms of the dominant culture and minority cultures when it comes to intimate relations between the sexes.

Consider the Chen case in light of the provocation defence in Anglo-American common law. American men who kill their wives or girlfriends have recourse to a criminal defence that, if successful, provides reduced charges and punishment. They are not called 'cultural defences', but they rely on deeply rooted cultural understandings about what constitutes reasonable behaviour between intimate partners. In her study of 15 years of American cases in which defendants invoked the provocation defence, Victoria Nourse found that courts have extended the provocation doctrine to include not only a wife's adultery but also the 'infidelity of a fiancée who danced with another, a girlfriend who decided to date someone else, and of the divorcée found pursuing a new relationship months after the final decree' (1997: 1333). Juries have returned manslaughter, instead of murder, verdicts in cases where the defendant kills his wife and claims 'passion' because she left him, moved the furniture out, planned a divorce, or sought a protective order. As Nourse puts it, 'one is as likely, if not more likely, to find a relationship that has ended, was ending, or in which the victim sought to leave, as one is to find an affair or sexual infidelity alone' (1343). The provocation defence continues to operate in ways that reinforce the possessive norms rooted in a code of male honour: a woman's infidelity, which in some jurisdictions includes her attempts to leave a relationship, betrays a loyalty expected of her. American courts have deemed such betrayal to be worthy of compassion by the law. This was precisely the logic at work in the *Chen* case.

We can see a similar intercultural dynamic of congruence at work if we consider the 'wife capture' case in the context of rape law. Not so long ago in the US, unless there was obvious evidence of coercion, a woman charging rape had to convince the court that she had resisted the defendant's advances 'to the utmost'. In the absence of such resistance, the defendant

---

6    *People v. Chen*, No. 87–7774, Supreme Court, NY County (December 2, 1988).

could claim that he had made a 'reasonable mistake' as to her consent. Many states have rewritten their laws minimizing the resistance requirement: 'reasonable' resistance is supposed to be sufficient. Yet, out of a concern that defendants would have fewer clues as to non-consent after the minimization of the resistance requirement, courts have been more willing than in the past to admit a 'mistake of fact' defence. Rape traditionally has involved two elements: force on the part of the perpetrator and lack of consent on the part of the victim. In most states, a defendant charged with rape can raise a 'mistake of fact' defence, which allows him to claim that his belief as to the other party's consent was honest and reasonable. Most rape statutes still use some combination of 'force', 'threat' and 'consent' to define the threshold of liability – the line between criminal sex and seduction (Estrich 1986). In giving meaning to those terms at the threshold of liability, rape law continues to draw on and accommodate very powerful mainstream norms of male aggressiveness and female passivity.

In Moua's case, the defence lawyer did not explicitly invoke the mistake of fact defence, but in response to the district attorney's assertion that he had 'never heard of any other cultures getting a break because they thought [rape or kidnapping] was okay', Moua's lawyer replied that 'in the California culture' defendants have been given some 'credit' by the courts and cited a case in which a kidnapping and rape conviction was overturned by the California Supreme Court on the grounds that in the absence of resistance, it was reasonable for the male defendant to believe the woman pressing charges against him had consented to sex. In nearly all American states, intimidation short of physical threats, including psychological pressure used by people in positions of authority, is treated as if it were mere persuasion. The old idea that women who say 'no' don't really mean no is still reflected in the dominant culture. Some Hmong men may engage in cultural practices that subordinate Hmong women, but there are similarly powerful norms of male aggressiveness and female passivity at work in mainstream legal doctrine and social practice. My point about congruence is that the latter has offered support for the former.

In order to understand and adequately respond to the problems raised by the 'cultural defence', feminists must resist essentialist 'us vs. them' notions of culture by broadening the scope of their critique and interrogating the norms and practices of the dominant culture alongside those of minority cultures. It is especially important to be attentive to the ways in which majority norms shape the practice of accommodation. As Anne Phillips (2003) has argued in examining the 'cultural defence' in English courts, the larger problem with its use is that it has proven the most effective when it resonates with troubling gender norms of the dominant culture.

## Toward New Feminist Approaches to Multicultural Dilemmas

How then should feminists approach the claims of culture and multiculturalism? Many feminist theorists seem to agree that multicultural accommodations should be permitted insofar as they enhance rather than undermine the freedom of individuals. Where the extension of a group-specific right threatens the agency of individual members of minority cultural groups, it should not be granted. Whether a particular claim for accommodation ought to be granted should be sensitive to contextual considerations. Recent feminist writing on multiculturalism emphasizes the importance of close attention to the particularities of context and the inclusion of the voices of those affected by particular dilemmas in their resolution. To conclude, I want to highlight three different approaches developed by feminist scholars writing about culture and multiculturalism and briefly consider the future challenges these approaches must address.

The first is a legal pluralist approach developed by Ayelet Shachar, which focuses on designing institutions to enable the transformation of group norms. Her 'transformative accommodation' approach divides jurisdictional authority between groups and the state. Legal pluralist arrangements, such as Shachar's, are most appropriate for groups whose members see themselves as bound by religious law, as well as groups that are territorially concentrated and already enjoy a measure of legal authority, but not for groups of immigrants or ethnic minorities who do not adhere to a comprehensive doctrine or who do not have separate jurisdictional authority. Jurisdictional authority should be divided such that neither the state nor the group has a monopoly of power over an entire 'social arena', such as family law, education, criminal justice or resource development. Instead, governance over each arena is divided according to different functions or 'sub-matters'. In the arena of family law, groups have the authority to determine membership rules while states govern the distribution of rights and duties among group members (Shachar 2001: 51–55, 119–122). In theory, this initial division of authority is not intended to be permanent; individuals can 'opt in' or 'opt out' of specific group positions by reversing jurisdictional authority in relation to a particular sub-matter. For example, if an individual member of a group dissents from some group rule or practice, she can 'opt out' and invite state intervention in defining group membership. This 'opt out' provision allows individual members to pose a credible threat of exit since groups want to avoid the reversal of jurisdiction that would bring state intervention, and this creates incentives for the group to serve its members better (122–126).

There are at least two feminist worries with Shachar's approach. First, as Oonagh Reitman has argued, group leaders may become more, not less, determined in their commitment to hierarchical practices as dissenters threaten to leave the group. Drawing on the example of Orthodox Judaism, Reitman (2005: 199) observes: 'Orthodox leaders want to ensure ideological purity and the pursuit of what is perceived to be God's command. They may have little interest in bolstering numbers as such, preferring to soldier on with those whose commitment is beyond question.' Second, in order for the incentive structure that Shachar envisions to have a truly transformative effect, members must be able to make credible threats of exit, and this will depend on their having *real* rights of exit. As feminists have long emphasized, exiting a relationship or community is incredibly difficult for vulnerable parties (see, for example, Okin 2002). Leaving means losing not just cultural or religious affiliations and the intrinsic value they hold for members but also the social relationships and material benefits associated with membership. In light of this difficulty, the state will have to intervene to ensure realistic rights of exit. The challenge is to be attentive not only to material conditions but also conditions of knowledge and psychology that enable individuals to exit. Feminists must attend to the forces that construct and constrain persons as subjects in the first place (Hirschmann 2002, Mahmood 2005, Cowan 2006).

A second approach to multicultural dilemmas is a democratic approach that gives a central role to deliberation. Liberal theorists tend to start from the question of whether and how minority cultural practices should be tolerated or accommodated in accordance with liberal principles, whereas democratic theorists foreground the role of democratic voice and ask how affected parties understand the practice at the centre of the cultural claim or dilemma. In a subsequent essay on multiculturalism, Okin argues (2005: 86–87), 'a state that values liberalism above all would have no more need to consult with the women of [a patriarchal] group than it need consult with slaves before it insisted upon their emancipation or with workers before it insisted upon their protection from deadly workplace hazards… [T]he liberal would stress that basic rights … should not be granted or withheld depending on the outcome of democratic procedures.' Like John Stuart Mill, Okin favours state regulation of conduct that harms individuals, with her definition of harm being more expansive than Mill's. For example, Okin points to the unequal treatment of women within the Catholic Church and suggests that the Church should no longer enjoy tax-exempt status 'so long as it radically discriminates against women in all of its most important hiring decisions and in the distribution of institutional power' (2005: 87).

In contrast to liberal feminists, feminists working within democratic theory have argued for drawing on the voices of those affected by the practices in question. They do so on the principled normative ground that the legitimacy of any decision depends on giving those affected by the decision a voice in the making of that decision. Democratic feminists also emphasize the epistemic advantages of a deliberative approach: deliberation can clarify the nature of the interests at stake and the complex sources of conflicts (Benhabib 2002, Deveaux 2006). Deliberation also provides opportunities for minority group members to expose instances of cross-cultural hypocrisy and consider whether and how the norms and institutions of the larger society, whose own struggles for gender equality are incomplete and ongoing, may reinforce rather than challenge patriarchal practices within minority groups (Song 2007: 74–75). Determining what constitutes gender subordination and how best to address it is a difficult matter, and interventions into minority cultural groups without drawing on the voices of minority women themselves will not best serve their interests.

One worry about a deliberative approach is that it may encourage the 'sedimentation of cultural groups and communities' such that specific spokespersons – generally male and more conservative voices – are positioned to privilege their own views of their community's practices as representative of the entire community (Phillips 2007: 161, see also Sunder 2001). But a deliberative approach does not say that *any* dialogue should be taken as representative. Feminist theorists who adopt a deliberative approach have emphasized that those who have basic rights and interests at stake should have a greater voice in the governance of the cultural claims. Deliberation requires certain substantive conditions to be met, including basic liberties and equal deliberative opportunities. These are demanding conditions, and aspiring to them may involve legal interventions as well as efforts at intercultural dialogue and persuasion to ensure that the voices of vulnerable parties are represented. Where such conditions are not met, we should be sceptical that women at the centre of gendered cultural conflicts actually embrace practices that appear to undermine their freedom.

A third approach to multicultural dilemmas comes from legal anthropology. While many political and legal theorists of multiculturalism have moved away from static, essentialist conceptions of culture, they tend to assume a static conception of law and rights. Law and legal institutions are taken to be neutral instruments by which religious and cultural norms and practices are to be corrected or transformed. In contrast, legal anthropologists blur the boundary between law and culture, and seek to show how law and culture produce and shape one another. As Jane Cowan, Marie Bénédicte Dembour and Richard Wilson suggest in their introduction to *Culture and Rights: Anthropological Perspectives*, the question is not whether universal values conflict with culturally particular norms and practices regarding women and if so, what to do about it. Rather, the central question is primarily empirical and local: how have particular normative frames (for example, 'feminism vs. multiculturalism') found their way into particular local struggles, and how do actors on all sides negotiate, resist and transform those frames? On this approach, searching for 'a single theory that would provide definitive guidance on the relationship between culture and rights is quixotic'; all efforts at universal theory-building are local and contestable. This approach suggests that we should give more attention to empirical, contextual analysis of particular struggles and conflicts, as well as be 'more skeptical of claims to culture, and to examine more closely the power relations and divisions they sometimes mask' (Cowan et al. 2001: 21). One worry about this approach is that the focus on particular struggles, coupled with an abdication of articulating general principles, may not provide as rich a basis for normative critique of the practices in question. If the aim is to hold up a mirror to existing practices through the method of thick description, where does the articulation of alternative normative visions come from? To be sure, feminist scholars should heed Cowan's call for 'an interdisciplinary dialogue' and more 'empirically grounded studies of rights and culture' (2006: 21), but we should also continue to articulate constructive normative alternatives drawing on the voices of those at the centre of multicultural dilemmas.

Feminist theorizing about culture and multiculturalism stands to benefit from greater interconnections between the normative theorizing of political and legal theorists and the local, empirical analysis of legal anthropologists and other social scientists. Just as feminist scholars have moved away from static, essentialist notions of culture, they must move more decisively away from static notions of law and legal institutions. Such interdisciplinary analysis will assist in fashioning more reflexive, critical approaches to culture and multiculturalism.

As I hope to have shown, feminist theorizing about multiculturalism has greatly enriched and advanced ongoing debates about culture and multiculturalism. The earliest feminist interventions focused on the tensions between valuing cultural membership and protecting the freedom and equality of women. More recent feminist interventions have suggested ways to get beyond the dichotomies suggested by the frame of 'multiculturalism vs. feminism' – through innovative reform of legal institutions, deliberative democracy and more fluid conceptions of law as well as culture. Many challenges lie ahead, especially in the context of the current political retreat from multiculturalism in the West. The retreat from multiculturalism is often justified in the name of feminism, but as many feminists have emphasized, complete rejection of multiculturalism is not in the best interests of women. If we are to pursue both feminist and multicultural goals, as I believe we should, feminist scholarship on culture and multiculturalism will continue to be indispensable.

# References

Ahmed, L. 1992. *Women and Gender in Islam: Historical Roots of a Modern Debate.* New Haven: Yale University Press.

Appiah, A. 2005. *The Ethics of Identity.* Princeton: Princeton University Press.

Benhabib, S. 2002. *The Claims of Culture: Equality and Diversity in the Global Era.* Princeton: Princeton University Press.

Blum, L.A. 1992. *Antiracism, Multiculturalism, and Interracial Community: Three Educational Values for a Multicultural Society.* Boston: Office of Graduate Studies and Research, University of Massachusetts.

Bowen, J.R. 2007. *Why the French Don't Like Headscarves: Islam, the State, and Public Space.* Princeton: Princeton University Press.

Carens, J. 2000. *Culture, Citizenship, and Community: A Contextual Exploration of Justice as Evenhandedness.* Oxford: Oxford University Press.

Cohen, J. 1998. Democracy and liberty, in *Deliberative Democracy,* edited by J. Elster. Cambridge: Cambridge University Press, 185–231.

Cott, N. 2000. *Public Vows: A History of Marriage and the Nation.* Cambridge, MA: Harvard University Press.

Cowan, J.K., Dembour, M.B. and Wilson, R.A. 2001. Introduction, in *Culture and Rights: Anthropological Perspectives,* edited by J.K Cowan, M.B. Dembour and R.A. Wilson. Cambridge: Cambridge University Press, 1–21.

Cowan, J.K. 2006. Culture and Rights after Culture and Rights, *American Anthropologist,* 108(1), 9–24.

Deveaux, M. 2006. *Gender and Justice in Multicultural Liberal States.* Oxford: Oxford University Press.

Eisenberg, A. and Spinner-Halev, J. (eds), 2005. *Minorities within Minorities: Equality, Rights, and Diversity.* Cambridge: Cambridge University Press.

Estrich, S. 1986. Rape. *Yale Law Journal,* 95(6), 1087–1184.

Fraser, N. and Honneth, A. 2003. *Redistribution or Recognition? A Political-philosophical Exchange.* London: Verso.

Gooding-Williams, R. 1998. Race, multiculturalism and democracy. *Constellations,* 5(1), 18–41.

Green, L. 1994. Internal minorities and their rights, in *Group Rights,* edited by J. Baker. Toronto: University of Toronto Press, 101–117.

Gutmann, A. 2003. *Identity in Democracy.* Princeton: Princeton University Press.

Hirschmann, N.J. 2002. *The Subject of Liberty: Toward a Feminist Theory of Freedom.* Princeton: Princeton University Press.

Honig, B. 1999. 'My culture made me do it,' in *Is Multiculturalism Bad for Women?,* edited by J. Cohen, M. Howard, and M.C. Nussbaum. Princeton: Princeton University Press, 35–40.

Ivison, D. 2006, Historical Injustice, in *The Oxford Handbook of Political Theory,* edited by J. Dryzek, B. Honig and A. Phillips. Oxford: Oxford University Press, 507–525.

Ivison, D., Patton, P. and Sanders, W. 2000. *Political Theory and the Rights of Indigenous Peoples.* Cambridge: Cambridge University Press.

Jones, P. 1994. Bearing the Consequences of Belief. *Journal of Political Philosophy,* 2(1), 24–43.

Kymlicka, W. 1989. *Liberalism, Community, and Culture.* Oxford: Oxford University Press.

Kymlicka, W. 1995. *Multicultural Citizenship: A Liberal Theory of Minority Rights.* Oxford: Oxford University Press.

Kymlicka, W. 1999. Liberal complacencies, in *Is Multiculturalism Bad for Women?* edited by J. Cohen, M. Howard and M.C. Nussbaum. Princeton: Princeton University Press, 31–34.

Kymlicka, W. 2001. *Politics in the Vernacular: Nationalism, Multiculturalism, and Citizenship.* Oxford: Oxford University Press.

Kymlicka, W. and Patten, A. 2003. *Language Rights and Political Theory.* Oxford: Oxford University Press.

Laborde, C. 2008. *Critical Republicanism: The Hijab Controversy and Political Philosophy.* Oxford: Oxford University Press.

Levy, J.T. 1997. Classifying cultural rights, in *Nomos XXXIX: Ethnicity and Group Rights,* edited by W. Kymlicka and I. Shapiro. New York: New York University Press, 22–66.

Mahmood, S. 2005. *Politics of Piety: The Islamic Revival and the Feminist Subject.* Princeton: Princeton University Press.

Moore, M. 2005. Internal Minorities and Indigenous Self-Determination, in *Minorities within Minorities: Equality, Rights and Diversity*, edited by A. Eisenberg and J. Spinner-Halev. Cambridge: Cambridge University Press, 271–293.

Narayan, U. 1997. *Dislocating Cultures: Identities, Traditions, and Third World Feminism*. New York: Routledge.

Nourse, V. 1997. Passion's progress: modern law reform and the provocation defense. *Yale Law Journal*, 106(5), 1331–1448.

Okin, S. [1997] 1999. Is multiculturalism bad for women? in *Is Multiculturalism Bad for Women?*, edited by J. Cohen, M. Howard, and M.C. Nussbaum. Princeton: Princeton University Press, 9–24.

Okin, S. 2002. Mistresses of their own destiny: group rights, gender, and realistic rights of exit. *Ethics*, 112(2), 205–230.

Okin, S. 2005. Multiculturalism and feminism: no simple questions, no simple answers, in *Minorities within Minorities: Equality, Rights, and Diversity*, edited by A. Eisenberg and J. Spinner-Halev. Cambridge: Cambridge University Press, 67–89.

Parekh, B. 2000. *Rethinking Multiculturalism: Cultural Diversity and Political Theory*. Cambridge, MA: Harvard University Press.

Patten, A. 2001. Political theory and language policy. *Political Theory*, 29(5), 683–707.

Phillips, A. 2003. When culture means gender: Issues of cultural defence in the English courts. *Modern Law Review*, 66, 510–531.

Phillips, A. 2007. *Multiculturalism without Culture*. Princeton, NJ: Princeton University Press.

Reitman, O. 2005. On exit, in *Minorities within Minorities: Equality, Rights, and Diversity*, edited by A. Eisenberg and J. Spinner-Halev. Cambridge: Cambridge University Press, 189–208.

Scheffler, S. 2007. Immigration and the significance of culture. *Philosophy and Public Affairs*, 35(2), 93–125.

Shachar, A. 2000. On Citizenship and multicultural vulnerability. *Political Theory*, 28(1), 64–89.

Shachar, A. 2001. *Multicultural Jurisdictions: Cultural Differences and Women's Rights*. Cambridge: Cambridge University Press.

Simpson, A. 2000. Paths toward a Mohawk Nation: narratives of citizenship and nationhood in Kahnawake, in *Political Theory and the Rights of Indigenous Peoples*, edited by D. Ivison, P. Patton, and W. Sanders. Cambridge: Cambridge University Press, 113–136.

Song, S. 2005. Majority norms, multiculturalism, and gender equality. *American Political Science Review*, 99(4), 473–489.

Song, S. 2007. *Justice, Gender, and the Politics of Multiculturalism*. Cambridge: Cambridge University Press.

Song, S. 2008. The subject of multiculturalism: culture, religion, language, ethnicity, nationality, and race?, in *New Waves in Political Philosophy*, edited by B. de Bruin and C. Zurn. New York: Palgrave Macmillan, 177–197.

Sunder, M. 2001. Cultural dissent. *Stanford Law Review*, 54(3), 495–567.

Taylor, C. 1994. The politics of recognition, in *Multiculturalism: Examining the Politics of Recognition*, edited by A. Gutmann. Princeton: Princeton University Press, 25–73.

Taylor, C. 1995. *Philosophical Arguments*. Cambridge, MA: Harvard University Press.

Tully, J. 1995. *Strange Multiplicity: Constitutionalism in an Age of Diversity*. Cambridge: Cambridge University Press.

Volpp, L. 2000. Blaming culture for bad behavior. *Yale Journal of Law and the Humanities*, 12(1), 89–116.

Volpp, L. 2001. Feminism and multiculturalism. *Columbia Law Review,* 101(5), 1181–1218.

Young, I.M. 1990. *Justice and the Politics of Difference.* Princeton, NJ: Princeton University Press.

# In the Name of God? Religion and Feminist Legal Theory

## Samia Bano

In this chapter, I ask how a feminist critique of current legal developments can contribute to our conceptual understanding of women's religious subjectivity and agency, and whether this can further our understanding of how religious women in the monotheistic religions – Islam, Christianity and Judaism – are being framed in relation to forced marriage and debates on veiling. In doing so, I start from fairly common premises within critical theory, which insist that traditional notions of legal objectivity and legal neutrality simply do not exist, and that the operation and effects of law cannot be understood in isolation from the social, moral and political context in which law operates (Williams 1988). I draw upon one such critical perspective, feminist legal theory, to better understand how specific ideas of religious women are mediated through the law in order to produce the dialectical representation of religious women both as agents and victims of their communities.

Historically, feminist scholars have focused on the patriarchal nature of religion and the limits that religious practice and belief impose upon women, thereby in effect limiting female autonomy, choice and women's rights in both the public and private spheres (see Sharma 1994). As Katherine Young (1987: 6) warns, however, studies of women and religion cannot 'be summed up by the descriptions of Chinese footbinding, Hindu *sati*, Muslim *purdah* and Christian witchcraft' but must instead seek to uncover the nuances in challenges to religious power and authority in order to explore alternative narratives. Current feminist scholarship maintains the critique of patriarchy, but has also moved beyond this concern, using a wide range of methodological approaches and conceptual frameworks in order to capture the experiences of religious women. Drawing upon the disciplines of theology, sociology, history and politics as well as notions of 'complementarity' and 'feminist standpoint theory', the emergence of religious thought and practice has been traced in order to uncover the unbiased experiences of women who belong to different religious communities and groups.

Today, in the West, there is a great deal of scholarly interest in understanding the nature of religion and the religious experience. Historically, women's religious experience has been measured by attendance at places of worship, frequency of prayer, study of religious texts and adherence to religious doctrines or texts. Much of this scholarship focuses not only upon issues concerning the rise and/or decline of religiosity and religious practice but the growing influence of secularism and secularization upon religion and its consequences. Woodhead and Heelas (2005), for instance, draw upon the emergence of 'co-existence' theory within Christianity which points to new and different forms of Christianity that have emerged under secularism, primarily evangelical and charismatic Christianity. It is beyond the scope of this chapter to provide an overview of women's experience in Islam, Christianity and

Judaism since 'the exercise of locating and tracing dominant religious ideas and institutions as they pertain to women or women to them is itself a generalizing activity' (Young 1987: 5). Instead, I focus on the discursive characteristics of debates about religion and women, addressing in particular the ways in which, in the West, liberal values govern and distort public consciousness and legal responses.

The right to religious freedom and religious expression underpins discussions on human rights, citizenship and equality in liberal democracies throughout the Western world. Further, the impact of secularization upon women's religiosity raises questions of personal autonomy, choice and consent while belonging to religious communities. Debates over the legal limits of state intervention into the private lives of individuals, and the extent to which liberal principles of equality, non-discrimination and individual autonomy are manifested in law also raise important questions regarding religious freedom and belief in the context of civic society. These discussions have interacted with feminist commentary in order to enable critical exploration of the ways, and extent to which, religious practice and belief limit women's lives, in both the public and private spheres. More recently, feminist scholars have documented and explored the tensions inherent in much Western political theory regarding the normative values that underpin the liberal state and the difficulties associated with the social and legal regulation of minority and majority communities (for example, Philips 2007). This literature conceptualizes our understanding of equality, difference and rights, while seeking to provide a clearer framework regarding the relationship between individuals' diverse systems of belief, religious activity and the state. Critiques focus on the boundaries between the rights enshrined in anti-discrimination legislation and individual demands to practice religious belief, which have come to the fore with conflicts over the right to wear the veil, rights in education, visible symbols of religious belief and employment rights. Some of these conflicts have resulted in legal disputes in Britain and elsewhere. In *EWEIDA v. British Airways* (2008), for instance, a Christian employee lost her claim to be allowed to wear a visible cross along with her BA uniform. In *Singh* (2008), Sakira Singh won the right to wear a Kara bracelet along with her school uniform and in *Begum* (2006), Shabina Begum lost her appeal to wear the jilbab at her local school.

In this chapter, I will tease out some of the complexities in contemporary debates about the relationship between religion, law and feminist social and legal theory, both in order to better understand how this relationship takes shape and to consider whether it produces specific outcomes for religious women. Is there a conflict between traditional and/ or orthodox religious belief systems and thought with secular values in Western liberal democracies? To what extent is there a clash between 'secular' values of human rights, in particular women's equality and autonomy, and religious ideas, norms and values? And how do concepts such as equality, dialogue, justice and autonomy operate within and between state law and minority religious groups? The significance of the shift towards the renewed assertion of a religious identity in Western societies raises the question of what 'should be the relation between religion and the state in liberal democracies today?' (Levey 2009: 1). The commonly-held idea that the spread of modernity, globalization and consumerism will inevitably lead to the decline of religion and religiosity in Western societies has largely been proven to be incorrect. As Inglehart and Norris (2004: 16) report, 'the world as a whole now has more people with traditional religious views than ever before – and they constitute a growing proportion of the world's population.' Does religion, therefore, act as a source of discrimination and disadvantage for its followers and adherents, in particular women? Such questions can also include the role of religious faith in the public spheres and forms of religious behaviours that may violate the principles of liberal democracies (namely liberty, tolerance, human rights and freedom of choice).

I consider these questions from three angles. First, I sketch the historical and current landscape of Western feminist engagements with religion, drawing attention in particular to an increased consciousness of multiculturalism and secularism in recent years. These factors add complexity to what started in feminist thought as a more simple critique of religious patriarchy. Second, I consider the ways in which (despite multiculturalism) core liberal values such as agency, autonomy and equality have dominated the agenda, both within Western feminism and in broader cultural contexts. Minority feminists have offered strong critique of the way in which these liberal values collapse into a simplistic binary analysis of, for instance, consent versus coercion. Such values also mask their own cultural heritage in the name of universalism, meaning that visibly non-complying *cultures* are seen as the source of the problem, rather than, for instance, male dominance. Finally, I look at the ways in which these debates have played out in the context of some specific and high-profile issues – namely, veiling and forced marriage. In this context, I suggest that alternatives to the binaries which have structured discussion about agency and equality are beginning to be replaced by more nuanced and reflective markers of autonomy.

## Religion and Western Feminism

Feminist scholars have long critiqued the position of women within religious ideology and practice and as conceptualized within church–state relations (for example, Sagal and Yuval-Davis 1997). Under the project of gaining equality, feminist scholars had historically charted the ways in which religious doctrine served to entrench the inferior legal status of women in Western societies in the eighteenth and nineteenth centuries (Wolstonecraft 1975, de Beauvoir 1946, Daly 1973). Others, such as the eighteenth-century feminist Mary Astell (1799), had drawn upon religious Christian doctrine to develop a more progressive relationship between religion and feminism (Astell and Springborg 2002). Similarly, Elizabeth Cady Stanton, seeking to document the experience of Christian women to church life, published the *Women's Bible* in 1898. Both Astell and Stanton are considered to be feminist theologians drawing attention to the marginalization of women in dominant patriarchal Christianity. It has been suggested, on this basis, that their primary impulse for demanding the rights of women was reform in religious doctrine, which manifested itself in personal devotion, serious theological reflection and a vision for moral renewal and social justice (Apetrei 2011). Thus, far from being a constraining influence on feminism, religion was depicted and understood for many as a stimulus to new thinking about the status of women in society and law.

Within mainstream non-theological feminism however, the focus has been upon the ways in which the institutions of the family, home and motherhood in monotheistic religions (Islam, Christianity and Judaism) can entrench patriarchal conditions for women members. More specifically, control of women's sexuality and reproductive roles is deemed crucial to promoting and preserving religious ideologies to the extent that any transgression by individual community members is deemed threatening and unacceptable. This critique intensified with the advent of second wave feminism in the 1960s and 1970s, which documented women's departure from traditional religions and the impact of secularization, leading to the emergence of new religions and spiritualities (Woodhead and Heelas 2005).

In Britain, the organization, 'Women Against Fundamentalism' was set up in 1989 following the 'Rushdie Affair'[1] to challenge the rise of religious orthodoxy and fundamentalism within minority religious communities. As member Julia Bard (1992: 1) explained:

> WAF's work from the start has been based on the conviction that while fundamentalism appears in different forms in different religions and in different political contexts, all of them have at the heart of their agendas the control of the lives, minds and bodies of women. This is expressed in terms of "family values" a constellation of supposedly immutable ideas which place men at the head of the family, bestowing on it its status as well as its income, and which define women as the conveyors of morality and tradition to the next generation. A non-conformist or rebellious woman, according to this view, will endanger the future of the community as a whole which is thus entitled to coerce her to "do her duty" or throw her out.

Male religious leaders' control of women, their denial of women's rights to freedom, choice and autonomy, and their role in defining acceptable patterns of female behaviour, therefore, underpin many feminist critiques and campaigns. These critiques have led to a new form of scholarship which casts new light on the relationship – both current and historical – between women, religion and society (Anderson 1998).

One of the key points of contention between the religious and secular is the argument that rights to equality and autonomy are enshrined in secular human rights principles and law, and that, in contrast, religious doctrine often fails to promote these rights or actively undermines them. This has generated conflict between the notions of secularism and the religious, a conflict which has been described as both permanent and intractable. Carole Christ, for example, maintains that the Bible's core message is based upon male domination and male authority mirrored on earth (1987: 59–60). Frances Raday explains,

> monotheisms are the hard core of culture for more than half the world's population. The distinctive marks of monotheistic scriptural religions are clear: transcendental authority, a canonical text with authoritative clerical interpretations, norms for regulation of daily life and punishment for transgression. Religion is, hence, an institutionalised aspect of culture, with focal points for political power within society. (2003: 3)

As a result, Rita Gross (1996) has argued that the relationship between religious and secular conceptions of women's role is 'too broken to be fixed' (140). As I will explain in the next two sections of the chapter, this conflict has been played out in relation to specific issues such as veiling and marriage as they come up against liberal values such as autonomy and equality.

In recent times, increased consciousness of cultural difference has also complicated the field. The relationship between secularism, multiculturalism and religion is problematic in its negotiation of relations between the state and ethnic and religious groups, but is also increasingly crucial to better understanding how such relations can be managed and

---

1    The 'Rushdie affair' is described as the controversy surrounding the publication of Salman Rushdie's novel, *The Satanic Verses* in 1989.

developed. In social and political theory, 'multiculturalism' is a relatively new concept that can be traced to the mid-twentieth century with the deployment of state strategies to manage ethnic difference generated by increased migration. Banor Hesse points out that multiculturalism has now become 'a contested frame of reference for thinking about the quotidian cohesion of western civil societies uncertain about their national and ethnic futures' (2000: 1). Homi Bhabha describes it as a 'floating signifier' where 'differentiation and condensation seem to happen almost synchronically' (1998: 45). Indeed the conflation of 'multiculturalism' with the related terms 'identity', 'race', 'ethnicity' and 'diaspora' has led to epistemological questioning over its precise meaning. Despite problems over its meaning and epistemological use, the term remains useful in understanding the different strategies and policies employed by the state in its attempts to 'govern' and 'manage' ethnic and cultural diversity (Hall 2000).

Today, feminist literature explores the relationship between feminism, multiculturalism and religion in the lives of religiously diverse women living in both majority and minority communities (Afshar 2008, Purkayastha 2009a). More specifically, the focus has been on the relationship between religion, women's issues, gender roles and culture; and feminism has been at the fore of attempts to understand the experience of religious women's lives in a complex and nuanced way. This is reflected in a recent special issue of *Feminist Review*, for example. In their introduction to this issue, Avtah Brah and Lyn Thomas explain that the emergence of 'secular spiritualities' challenge the old binaries of 'religion and tradition' versus 'modernity and secularism'. They insist that, in order to better understand what meanings women attach to these new developments, it is necessary to pay closer attention to the narratives of the women themselves (2011: 2). Feminist theology has also recently been a focus of possible reform in the monotheistic religions. For example, ideological developments embracing feminist principles of equality, non-discrimination and human rights have been expressed by Christian, Muslim and Jewish feminists. In Islam, for example, the emergence of Islamic feminism (Wadud 1991, Barlas 2006) has led to debates on reformulating Islamic principles from a universal human rights perspective. But, although there have been a number of family reforms in various Muslim majority societies (Welchman 2009), conflict remains over notions of equality and the persistence of patriarchy.

In Europe, the position of minority ethnic groups and the question of state responsibility for ensuring the successful integration of such groups into mainstream society have recently come under sustained attack from all sides of the political spectrum. This renewed questioning of religion is framed as part of a debate which analyses the benefits of multiculturalism versus its possible detrimental impact upon European society (Modood 2007). In Britain, multiculturalism has largely been framed and articulated around questions of cultural identity and the forging of a common national identity. It is not a singular doctrine and has been described as embodying three different forms: conservative multiculturalism that insists upon assimilation; liberal multiculturalism, which focuses upon integration in mainstream society while tolerating certain cultural practices in private; and pluralist multiculturalism, which affords groups rights for cultural communities under a communitarian political order (Parekh 2002).

The diversity of religious belief systems in European states has long raised critical questions about how far diverse religious practices can be accommodated in the public spheres, as well as the extent to which state and religion should be separated. Levey (2009) points out that Western democracies today are being challenged by religion along three intersecting fault-lines, namely 'religion-politics, religion-multiculturalism and Islam-Muslims/multiculturalism'. Each of these raises a number of pressing questions:

> *How should liberal democracies respond to their growing Muslim communities? What is the appropriate liberal response to a girl wearing a headscarf to a French school, or to an Islamic organisation's request for public funding in the UK, or to a request that images of the Prophet Muhammad not be published in newspapers? Should these cases be seen as instances of "multiculturalism" and "diversity", which contemporary liberalism should defend and celebrate? Or are they rather examples of a dangerously theocratic impulse, which threatens the social peace and the liberal separation of religion and the state? Should places like France, Germany and the UK adjust their legal codes in order to accommodate a religious tradition that was not party to the original peace compacts, and that may not accept some of the limiting terms of modern liberalism? (2009: 3)*

Such a list captures both the serious and the polemical nature of contemporary debates surrounding Muslims, religious identity, integration and multiculturalism. The emphasis lies on conflicts generated by the recognition of the rights of religious groups. In the following two sections, I deal with some of these conflicts in more detail, focusing in particular on the ways in which they have often been conceptualized through women's agency and women's bodies.

## Liberal Values and Religious Constraint

Throughout history, the circumscribed values that underpin Western conceptions of law and justice have strongly influenced how law is perceived and understood by contemporary feminist political and legal theorists. In describing how law deals with questions of justice, political philosophers analyse the fragmented nature of legality and the relations between normative orders and individual rights (Dworkin 1986). Law is an important potential source of power and the pursuit of justice in response to the challenges presented by diverse cultural and religious communities reveals contradictory practices. The *effects* of a plural and multicultural society upon the development of English law have been extensively documented over the past 20 years, by anthropologists, sociologists and increasingly legal scholars (Malik 2012). The debate over the nature of this interaction is often characterized as a clash of a given set of values, identity and interest claims by state law and the demands of minority religious communities. This in turn gives rise to central and difficult questions regarding the appropriate level and type of legal accommodation to be afforded and protected.

Contemporary liberal thinkers, shaping the terms of liberal values in Western societies and the postcolonial world, have advanced a rather conservative agenda. Significantly, they have done so in and through liberal rights discourse rather than in opposition to it (Kapur 2005: 19). For many of these thinkers, the focus on religious women serves as a yardstick to consider the conflict between the rights of religious communities and the rights afforded by the liberal state. As Sherene Razack (2008: 86) points out, *women's bodies have long been the ground on which national difference is constructed. When the Muslim woman's body is constituted as simply a marker of a community's place in modernity and an indicator of who belongs to national community and who does not, the pervasiveness of violence against women in the West is eclipsed. Saving Muslim women from the excesses of their society marks Western women as emancipated.*

Violence against women in the West is not seen as 'cultural' because of the universalism associated with Western values. Indeed, the heightened visibility of Muslim women only serves to underline the narrative of Western women's freedom.

The recent debates on honour crimes illustrate the ways in which UK law enshrines such a view of 'cultural' violence. In her work, Anna Carline problematizes the manner in which notions of honour, shame and 'honour killings' 'have recently been constructed as specific to certain cultural, ethnic and religious groups and as being "other" to the norms and standards of western society. This self/other construction enables law and society to condemn killings by ethnic-minority groups, or more specifically Asian (and frequently Muslim) men, whilst potentially rendering invisible the relevance of honour and shame to those homicides committed by western men' (2011: 80). She argues that the law of provocation, which is frequently used by men who kill their partners, is premised upon a 'white western notion of male honour' (80).

In theorizing these issues, it is important to begin with the recognition that religious women belong to many diverse communities and their lived experiences must therefore be understood as complex, strategic and at times contradictory (Afshar 2005). Over the past three decades, feminist theorists have grappled with the question of how to reconcile Western interpretations of sexual equality and the autonomy of women's agency[2] with cultural and religious difference. Debates have largely been focused on a clash of values scenario within which liberal notions of equality, free will and choice have been deemed 'progressively modern' and open to all, while the continued adherence of women belonging to minority communities to religious and traditional ties has been presented as illiberal, backward and a barrier to the enhancement of women's rights. In these debates, the law and juridical liberalism (for example, anti-discrimination legislation) serve as the starting point to enhance the rights of all women. Admittedly this dichotomous approach of Western liberalism versus traditional practice and the universal applicability of 'Western modernity' with the ideas of Enlightenment to non-Western traditions and in non-Western contexts has been the subject of intense critique. Post-colonial theorists such as Gayatri Spivak (1988) and Chandra Mohanty were among the first to challenge the ahistorical, overgeneralized constructions of Muslim women as members of minority religious communities. Basing themselves in both a post-colonial and feminist critique, they challenged the epistemological roots of Western scholarship that focused on the subordinated position of women belonging to minority, ethnic and religious communities. Going against the grain of traditional Western feminism, Spivak (1988: 25) highlights the hierarchical positions of power that Western feminists occupy and the need to critique feminist 'subject positions'. A failure to do so, she suggests, renders many pre-existing feminist arguments simply inadequate and limited.

2   The concept of agency is often understood in relation to concepts of the individual, the person and the self; discussion of these questions falls outside the scope of this paper, but see the chapter by Nancy Hirschmann, this volume.

Perspectives like these also emerge in the scholarship on agency. Framing the question of individual agency in terms of the extent to which Western democratic principles can be applied within non-Western societies (and the idea of human rights interconnected to Western liberal democracy) raises the rhetoric of a 'clash of civilizations'. A key debate in human rights literature is the conceptualization of cultural human rights. Bandana Purkayastha (2009b: 290) points out that:

> *The notion of cultural human rights has gotten mired, almost exclusively, on debates about the hijab, honour killings, stoning rape victims (along with genital mutilation, forced marriages, and polygamy). Cultural human rights were developed to protect minority cultures from extinction in the midst of a powerful majority culture. The world's indigenous people, for instance, have sought cultural human rights protection to revive and sustain their identities. Yet most discussions of cultural human rights do not focus on organized attempts to promote cultural extinction. Nor do many "transnational" feminist activists who claim to speak for "global women's rights" systematically consult with local groups that actually work on these issues.*

However, providing cultural rights is not simply a matter of making provisions for multiple sets of 'personal and family' civil laws based on the idea that religions and cultures are unchanging and non-diverse. These same laws have been used by men to subordinate women in their communities (Purkayastha 2009a: 292). It is therefore necessary to start from the perspective of diversity and more nuanced contestation *within* specific communities, rather than simply looking at conflict between broader (and male-defined) versions of culture. In turn, questions of agency and identity inevitably arise.

In the UK, for example, a number of legal issues have been addressed and policy measures introduced which have a particular relevance for Muslim women. Most prominent among these have been the right to veil at school, to wear the jilbab at the workplace, policies against forced marriage, and debates on the recognition of Islamic law. Underpinning each of these debates is the question of consent versus social coercion and the extent to which Muslim women are able to express their autonomy and agency while living within Muslim communities. For example, women's apparent consent to marriage in the face of coercive social, cultural and structural forces has often been broadly interpreted as acquiescence to patriarchal authority, whereas agency is equated with women's declared resistance (Goddard 2000: 3), often through the strategy of exit. Others have argued that the very idea of choice in the context of overarching systems and networks of power and domination is problematic (Wilson: 2006). Inter-generational changes among British Asian communities in the UK have been interpreted as evidence of the rational exercise of agency by young British Asian women through strategic manoeuvres, and through compromise and negotiation within structural constraints (Samad and Eade 2002). I will come back to some of these issues in the final section of this chapter.

Feminist writing provides many avenues for conceptualizing multiple identities and multiple forms of inequality (Cooper 2004). Feminist political theorists, such as Nancy Fraser and Iris Young, approach the question by considering a matrix of factors – both social and structural – which position women in particular contexts. Fraser (1989) links social relations to distinct economic and cultural societal structures and to related forms of redress (recognition and redistribution). She approaches oppression as a process whereby social collectivities operate along a spectrum from injustices of distribution to those of recognition.

For Fraser, therefore, the issue of multiple identity raises a number of key questions: 'Which identity claims are rooted in the defense of social relations of inequality and domination? And which are rooted in a challenge to such relations? ... Which differences ... should a democratic society seek to foster, and which, on the contrary should it aim to abolish?' (1989: 65). Meanwhile, Young, in her book *Justice and the Politics of Difference* (1990), provides five criteria of oppression: exploitation, marginalization, powerlessness, cultural imperialism and violence. While her analysis can be applied to various groups (such as the elderly, or gays and lesbians), she draws upon the social constituency of 'women' to reflect upon the different dimensions of oppression that they may experience on account of their gender. For both theorists, it is apparent that claims of cultural and religious difference – part of a pluralist model of power that affords minority groups limited yet significant autonomy – can be recognized only if they do not involve the oppression and subordination of women.

For many feminist *legal* scholars, the focus has also been squarely on the question of equality and subordination in the context of the ways in which legal regulations construct, and respond to, intersecting orders of inequality. This approach ultimately draws upon the work of legal feminists such as Catharine MacKinnon (1987) and others, who maintain that the law tends to reflect masculine values: many of the values around which the law is built, including its assumption of an individualistic 'reasonable' person, are those used and valued by men. Scholars such as Patricia Williams (1988) and Kimberley Crenshaw (1989) use the concept of intersecting identities (in this case race, class and gender) to illustrate how the law and legal relations fail to grasp the complexities of black women's lives. For example, juridical liberalism expressed via legislation such as anti-discrimination legislation remains inadequate in understanding the position of minority ethnic women who may be situated in multiple social locations. As such, these laws simply fail effectively to redress the claims of discrimination.

More recently, and as indicated above, postcolonial feminist legal scholarship has identified and critiqued the hierarchical positions of power that many Western feminists occupy in equality debates. For example, Spivak (1990) and Mohanty (1997) have challenged the representations of non-Western women made by both liberal inclusionists and structural bias approaches to women's human rights. As Sally Engle-Merry (2006: 61) points out, there is an urgent need to attend to cultural and religious differences and to see similar types of oppression in both majority and minority communities. In addition to questioning First World feminist understandings of culture and religion, such critics also challenge the structural bias, with its focus on culture, as the principal site of women's oppression. As Obiora Chinedu Okafor puts it, 'the truth of the matter is that, despite popular feminist discourses, culture may not be the dispositive influence on the responses of women' (quoted in Engle 2006: 62). So how does such postcolonial and feminist difference scholarship help us to better understand the question of religious difference and the expression of religious women's agency and choice as members of religious communities? This scholarship produces a critique of power relations in the public and private spheres to demonstrate how power operates both unevenly and strategically in order to disempower the weak and marginal within communities. The intersection of feminism with postcolonial analyses develops new forms of methodologies to produce 'new ways of seeing' and postcolonial knowledge. In particular, it centres the experience of women drawing upon political critique and analyses grounded in personal narratives.

Feminist interpretations of autonomy encourage women to make personal choices that include the autonomy of being and the right to go against what is considered as the norm.

This raises a number of important questions relating to how we understand autonomy, choice and agency and whether ultimately autonomy and equality can ever be reconciled. As Charusheela (2004:197) questions: 'Can we conceive of worlds in which women act differently from men, attain different outcomes based on criteria we do not ourselves agree with, and yet do so as autonomous choosing beings expressing a desired identity for themselves?' She goes on to list a number of questions that lie at the heart of current feminist debates:

> *What do we do when women in a foreign culture assert as a choice actions or behaviours that do not lead to equality? What do we do when women in asserting their right to autonomy of cultural identity and national self-determination do not attack a social construction of gender we deem patriarchal, nor seek to replace it with notions of human autonomy or choice that we consider marks of female emancipation?*
> *(2004: 197)*

As we can see from the brief discussion above, feminist engagements with issues of choice and definitions of agency can be underpinned by broad and sometimes false distinctions. It is too simplistic to contrast belonging to a religious group and the constraints this may bring, with the autonomy of opting out. The critique of such either/or choices is now well documented and for the past two decades feminist theorists have been grappling with the criticism that their analyses of women's oppression are ethnocentrically universalist. As Anne Phillips (2007) points out, while there is broad agreement in principle that ethnocentric universalism is to be avoided, there is also much disagreement about how this can be achieved without falling into debates on cultural relativism. Some of these matters have been addressed in the context of debates about Muslim women, in particular in relation to the questions of veiling and forced marriage. In the next section, I will unpack the discourse of agency and equality in a more applied fashion, by reference to these two issues.

## The Right to Veil and Forced Marriage Debates

In 2006, Jack Straw MP, then British Foreign Secretary, expressed his discomfort at meeting with Muslim female constituents who wore the veil (with their face covered), and stated that he was in the habit of asking women to remove their veil in his office. He further stated that women should not wear veils that cover their face. Characterizing the veil as 'a visible statement of separation and of difference', he said that, above all, his discomfort lay in the fact that the veil, in his view, prevented him from having a truly 'face-to-face' encounter with his constituent (Bhandar 2009). Drawing upon this example, and the Government Green Paper entitled *The Governance of Britain*, published in July 2007, Brenna Bhandar points out that Jack Straw's comments reflect anxiety about the issue of social cohesion and the perceived need for common British values. So, on what basis has this specific form of clothing become a symbol for constraint and disempowerment of Muslim women? As Charusheela quite rightly points out, 'unless one decides that all social markers of gender-difference are always and everywhere constraints, there is no intrinsic aspect of the veil that can make us decide to locate it as constraint while we leave out stockings and skirts and all other markers of female-male difference in apparel norms in other societies' (2004: 196).

Contemporary discussions on the right to veil go to the heart of current feminist concerns about whether veiling acts as a *constraint* that limits the choice of Muslim women. The majority of contemporary discussions on the veil and veiling in the UK focus on the autonomy of Muslim girls and women *freely* to veil themselves. Thus, such discussions embrace ideas that Muslim women have little choice but to veil and displace any notions of autonomy and decision making in the process of choosing to veil (Bhandar 2009). For Asma Barlas, the veil 'has become so overinvested with meaning that one can no longer speak of it in any simple way'; in western societies it has become a 'Muslim cultural icon' (2006: 57). As Stewart Motha (2007: 140) points out, 'the veiled woman troubles feminism and secularism in much the same way. Both feminism and secularism face a problem of finding a consistent position that respects individual autonomy, and simultaneously sustains a conception of politics freed from heteronomous determination.'

The problem of forced marriage within Muslim communities is another area in which agency has been understood narrowly in terms of liberal values. In 1999, a working group was established by the Home Secretary to investigate the extent to which forced marriage was practiced in England and Wales. In the same year, the Community Liaison Unit was set up by the Foreign and Commonwealth Office (FCO) and given responsibility for dealing with the international dimensions of forced marriages. In 2000, the report, *A Choice by Right*, was published by the working group. This focused on clarifying the arranged/forced marriage distinction and providing clear guidelines to public bodies such as the police, schools and social services as to what can be deemed a forced marriage. In line with this, in 2002, police guidelines were issued by the Association of Chief Police Officers to better equip members of the police force in dealing with forced marriage (Phillips and Dustin 2004: 535).

Most recently, the Forced Marriage (Civil Remedies) Protection Act 2007 was passed to provide protection specifically for people at risk of being forced into marriage. The Act enables the court to make 'forced marriage protection orders' to protect the individual. In deciding whether to make such an order, the court must have regard to 'all the circumstances including the need to secure the health, safety and well-being' of the individual, as well as 'his or her wishes and feelings (so far as reasonably ascertainable) and giving them such weight as the court considers appropriate given his or her age and understanding' (Herring 2009: 66).

In their work, Sundari Anitha and Aisha Gill (2009) note that, to date, the case law in England and Wales on forced marriage reveals that agency continues to be framed in terms of the individual's ability to choose freely. A thin notion of consent is thus used to differentiate between forced and arranged marriages. But, by considering the social and cultural construction of personhood, and especially womanhood, among South Asian communities, they argue that a considerably less clear-cut and far from dichotomous perspective on consent and coercion emerges. Consent and coercion in a marriage can be better understood as two ends of a continuum (arranged and forced marriage) between which lie degrees of cultural and social expectation, control, persuasion, pressure, threat and force. Within these constraints, South Asian women exercise their agency in complex and contradictory ways, which are not always recognized by the existing exit-centred state initiatives on this problem. In England and Wales, the cases of *Mahmood v Mahmood* 1993, *Mahmud v Mahmud* 1994, and *Sohrab v Khan* 2002 have involved acceptance by the courts that emotional pressure can take a variety of forms, from being made to feel responsible for bringing about a loved one's death to threats of suicide made by the coercer. Anitha and Gill (2009: 67) point out that:

*judgments indicate some engagement with the cultural contexts within which emotional pressure or threats are used to coerce. However, despite the extension of the definitional ambit of coercion to include such hazily defined "grey areas", the notion of "free will" remains central to the legal discourse on forced marriage in the UK, which is underpinned by opposing the concept of self-constituting, free individuals entering into a consensual marriage to that of a marriage contracted through coercion. The courts have long recognized the coercive power of direct threats of force, whatever their source, and have more recently been willing to accept that emotional pressure can also be coercive. But in either case, the fundamental issue at stake is the individual's free will. The problem is that this pre-occupation with the concept of "free will" obscures the contexts in which consent is constructed and the process through which this is done, especially in the absence of explicit threats: simply put, many coercive forces go undetected.*

Current initiatives in this arena focus, then, on the question of individual agency and the option of exit for vulnerable women being forced into marriage. Community attempts to persuade the state to adopt a dialogue-centred approach via the use of mediation services have, moreover, been met with resistance from women's organizations.[3] For example, proposals to challenge forced marriage included family-led mediation in order to allow victims of forced marriage to remain within the family context. However, it was argued by numerous women's organizations that in practice women's attempts to reconcile with families can lead to undue levels of social pressure in the face of a continued threat.

What has become clear in debates over veiling and marriage is that not all religious women seek to exercise their agency in a way understood by Western feminists to enhance their autonomy. Within the context of a patriarchal system, religious or not, women will often act to uphold gendered norms, such as beauty culture, or adopt disciplinary bodily technologies like elective cosmetic surgery (Frank 2006). Most feminist celebrations of women's agency are in the service of a politics of emancipation. Such accounts interpret women's lack of autonomous impulses as acquiescence to patriarchal power structures, and see women's desires as informed by 'oppressive norms of femininity' (Morgan 1991, Wolf 1991). But agency is not necessarily this clear-cut. Matt Waggoner (2005: 24) explores the question of ethics in discussions of agency and draws upon the notion of 'ethical embodiment'. He explains that what 'the idea [of ethical embodiment] … preserves is that a strong model of agency (as radically autonomous) is a fiction, since subjects are always formed and shaped by conditions not of their making, but there is nonetheless more to subjectivity than those conditions and their effects alone. Causal conditions are capable of giving rise to undetermined moments of self-reflection, self-interrogation, openness to the unforeseeable.' Agency, therefore, must be seen as shaped, but not determined, by external constraints. It is reflective and nuanced, rather than consisting of broad (and often uncritical) assertions of autonomy.

One argument that does not conceptualize agency as oppositional has been discussed extensively in Saba Mahmood's account of the women's piety movement in the mosques of Cairo (2004). This work uncouples agency from liberatory politics and highlights the ways

---

3    For example, the women's organization, Southall Black Sisters resigned from the working group on forced marriage in protest against the recommendation of mediation to reconcile victims of forced marriage with their families.

in which some women belonging to traditional, patriarchal and religiously conservative communities are able to negotiate and assert their agency within these highly 'structured' contexts, albeit in complex and intricate ways that cannot be ignored. She argues that the complexity of women's actions in different contexts can and must be understood in multiple ways. Susan Wendell (1990) also points to the role of structural inequalities while retaining a strong sense of respect for women's agency and responsibility to act within the constraints and possibilities presented by their context. That this agency, which has been defined as 'the socioculturally mediated capacity to act', can emerge in particular situations and places and at particular times has been noted in research examining the impact of education, employment, class and the perception and reality of racism on women's marriage choices (Ahmad 2007). However, there has been far less exploration of how personal histories, emotions, motivations and institutional arrangements, as well as practical concerns, such as access to information and perceived access to services, all have a bearing on women's agency and the language they use to talk about it.

Similarly, research on the marriage practices of South Asian Muslim women in Britain has also uncovered instances where young women have spoken about their need to uphold certain traditional norms out of a positive need to assert their belongingness within a community under siege (Bredal 2005). In her study, Fazila Bhimji (2009) examines the ways in which British born South Asian Muslim women engage with Islam through study circles. She argues that the religious spaces within which the women participate allow them to assert various identities, as well as agency, as they collectively search to comprehend Islam. In traversing these religious spheres, women transform them from male dominated sites to spaces wherein feminine, political and cosmopolitan identities are expressed.

Yet such non-oppositional demonstrations of agency have implications for the exit-centred state response to the problem of forced marriage. The primary state response to the problem of forced marriage is through the justice system, which has three aspects to it: a range of civil responses to protect women who have presumably left their abusive family or are seeking to do so; to render marriages based on coercion null and void; and to punish perpetrators under a range of existing laws. Women's groups have long recognized that not all women seek to leave abusive families through exit, and that an even smaller number want to initiate criminal or civil proceedings against family members in cases of forced marriage. However, the current state response in the UK is geared towards criminal justice intervention over any other, and the recent legislation on forced marriage has not been accompanied by any additional funds for specialist domestic violence services.

Women exercise their agency in complex and often contradictory ways, as they assess the options that are open to them, weigh the costs and benefits of their actions, and seek to balance their often competing needs with their expectations and desires. While there remains a need to recognize gendered power imbalances, there also remains a need to respect women's exercise of agency. In particular, rather than a simplistic assumption that agency is demonstrated by the exercise of individual free will, there is a need to develop consciousness of agency as a reflective response to circumstances, including those associated with religious belief and community.

## Conclusion

The complex relationship between women, religion and the law raises fundamental questions over the extent to which religious women are able to express their rights, autonomy and agency while living within and belonging to different religious communities. Feminist scholars have addressed these issues in relation to marriage, divorce, legal status, dress code and education. Furthermore the influence of culture, identity and state-law relations has affected the position of religious women within society and in the private spheres of family, home and local communities. The issue of gender roles and patriarchal relations underpins much of feminist critiques over the role and status of religious women belonging to diverse religious communities, yet Muslim, Jewish and Christian feminists have also drawn upon Western and secular critiques to seek equality, strengthen their rights and challenge patriarchal interpretations within religious thought. In this chapter, I have sought to highlight some of these conflicts and consider the ways in which the law has been utilized, evoked and applied to produce specific outcomes for religious women. As I have shown, there is a need to reformulate the reductionist binary conceptions of agency versus coercion, and to work towards a new discourse of personal freedom in order to encapsulate the actual experiences of religious women.

## References

Abu-Lughod, L. 2002. Do Muslim Women Really Need Saving? Anthropological Reflections on Cultural Relativism and its Others. *American Anthropologist*, 104(3), 783-790.

Ahmad, F. 2006, The scandal of 'Arranged Marriages' and the pathologisation of BrAsian Families, in *A Postcolonial People: South Asians in Britain*, edited by N. Ali, V.S. Kalra and S. Sayyid. London: Hurst & Co, 272–288.

Ahmad, F. 2007. Muslim Women's Experiences of Higher Education in Britain. *American Journal of Islamic Social Sciences*, Special Issue on Higher Education, 24(3), 46–69.

Afshar, H. 2005. Behind the Veil, in *Women and Islam: Critical Concepts in Sociology*, edited by H. Moghissie. London: Routledge, 56–72.

Afshar, H. 2007. Muslim Women and Feminisms: Illustrations from Iran. *Social Compass*, 54(3), 419–434.

Ahearn, L. 2001. Language and agency. *Annual Review of Anthropology*, 30, 109–137.

Ali, S. 2000. *Gender and Human Rights in Islam and International Law: Equal Before Allah, Unequal Before Man?* The Hague: Kluwer Law International.

Anderson, L. 1998. *Feminist Philosophy of Religion: Rationality and Myths of Religious Belief.* Oxford: Blackwell.

Anitha, S and Gill, A. 2009. Coercion, Consent and the Forced Marriage Debate in the UK. *Feminist Legal Studies*, 17(2), 165–184.

Anthias, F. 2002. Beyond Feminism and Multiculturalism: Locating difference and the politics of location. *Women's Studies International Forum*, 25(3), 275–286.

Apetrei, S. 2011. Women, Feminism and Religion in Early Enlightenment England. *Journal of British Studies*, 50(2), 465–466.

Astell, M. and Springborg, P. 2002. *A Serious Proposal to the Ladies*. Peterborough: Broadview Press.

Bard, J. Women Against Fundamentalism and the Jewish Community. *WAF Journal*. 1992–1993(4), 3–5.

Barlas, A. 2006. *Believing Women in Islam: Unreading Patriarchal Interpretations of the Qu'ran*. Austin: University of Texas Press.

Bhabba, H. 1998. Cultures in Between, in *Multicultural States: Rethinking Difference and Identity*, ed. D. Bennett. London: Routledge, 29–36.

Bhandar, B. 2009. The Ties that Bind: Multiculturalism and Secularism Reconsidered. *Journal of Law and Society*, 36(2), 301–326.

Bhimji, F. 2009. Identities and agencies in religious spheres. *Gender, Place and Culture*, 16(4), 365–380.

Bhopal, Kalwant. 1999. South Asian women and arranged marriages in East London. In *Ethnicity, Gender, and Social Change*, ed. Rohit Baror, Harriet Bradley and Steve Fenton, 117–134. Basingstoke: Macmillan.

Brah, A. and Thomas, L. 2011. Religion and Spirituality. *Feminist Review*, 97, 1–4.

Bredal, A. 2005. Arranged marriages as a multicultural battle field, in *Youth, otherness, and the plural city: Modes of belonging and social life*, edited by M. Andersson, Y. Lithman and O. Sernhede. Gothenburg: Daidalos, 67–89.

Carline, A. 2011. Constructing the Subject of Prostitution: A Butlerian Reading of the Regulation of Sex Work. *International Journal for the Semiotics of Law*, 24(1), 61–78.

Charusheela, S. 2004. Postcolonial Thought, Postmodernism, and Economics: Questions of Ontology and Ethics, in *Postcolonialism Meets Economics*, edited by S Charushleea and E Zein-Elabdin. London: Routledge, 40–58.

Chetkovich, C. 2004. Women's agency in a context of oppression: Assessing strategies for personal action and public policy. *Hypatia*, 19(4), 122–143.

Christ, C. 1987. *Why Women Need the Goddess*. San Francisco: Harper Row.

Cooper, D. 2004. *Challenging Diversity, Rethinking Equality and the Value of Difference*. Cambridge: Cambridge University Press.

Crenshaw, K. 1989. Demarginalizing the Intersection of Race and Sex: A Black Feminist Critique of Antidiscrimination Doctrine. *University of Chicago Legal Forum*, 1989, 139–167.

Daly, M. 1973. *Beyond God the Father: Toward a Philosophy of Women's Liberation*. Boston, MA: Beacon Press.

Davies, M. 2002. *Asking the Law Question: The Dissolution of Legal Theory*. Sydney: Lawbook Co.

de Beauvoir, S. 1946. *The Second Sex*, translated by H.M. Parshley. London: Vintage. Dworkin, R. 1986. Law's Empire. London: Fontana.

Fitzpatrick, P. 1992. *The Mythology of Modern Law*. London: Routledge.

Frank, K. 2006. Agency. *Anthropological Theory*, 6(3), 281–302.

Fraser, N. 1989. *Unruly Practices: Power, Discourse and Gender in Contemporary Social Theory*. Cambridge: Polity Press.

Goddard, V. (ed.), 2000. *Gender, Agency and Change: Anthropological Perspectives*. New York: Routledge.

Gross, R. 1996. *Feminism and Religion*. Boston, MA: Beacon Press.

Hall, S. 2000. Conclusion to the Multi-cultural Question, in *Unsettled Multiculturalisms: Diasporas, Entanglements, Transruptions*, edited by B. Hesse. London: Zed Books.

Hart, H.L.A. 1994. *The Concept of Law*. 2nd edn. Oxford: Clarendon Press.

Herring, J. 2009. *Family Law*. 4th edn. Essex: Longman.

Hesse, B. 2000. Introduction: UN/Settled Multiculturalisms, in *Unsettled Multiculturalisms: Diasporas, Entanglements, Transruptions*, edited by B. Hesse. London: Zed Books.

Home Office. 2000. *A choice by right: The report of the working group on forced marriage*. London: Home Office Communications Directorate. Available at: www.fco.gov.uk/Files/KFile/AChoiceByRightJune2000.pdf [accessed 12 December 2012].

Inglehart, R. and Norris, P. 2004. *Sacred and Secular: Religion and Politics Worldwide*, Cambridge: Cambridge University Press.

Kapur, R. 2005. *Erotic Justice, Law and the New Politics of Postcolonialism*. London: Glass House Press.

Levey, B.G. 2009. Secularism and Religion in a Multicultural Age, in *Secularism, Religion, and Multicultural Citizenship*, edited by B.G. Levey and T. Modood. Cambridge: Cambridge University Press, 1-24.

Mahmood, S. 2004. *Politics of Piety, The Islamic Revival and the Feminist Subject*. Princeton: Princeton University Press.

Malik, M. 2012. *Minority Legal Orders in the UK: Minorities, Pluralism and the Law*. London: British Academy.

Mayer, E. 1999. *Islam and Human Rights*. Boulder: Westview Press.

McKinnon, C. 1987. *Feminism Unmodified: Discourses on Life and Law*. Cambridge, MA: Harvard University Press.

Merry, S.E. 2006. *Human Rights and Gender Violence: Translating International Law into Local Justice*. Chicago: Chicago University Press.

Modood, T. 2007. *Multiculturalism: A Civic Idea*. Cambridge: Polity Press.

Modood, T. 2008. Multicultural Citizenship and the anti-sharia storm. [Online: Open Democracy]. Available at: www.opendemocracy.net/article/faith_ideas/europe_islam/anti_sharia_storm [accessed 14 December 2012].

Mohanty, C. 1991. Under western eyes: feminist scholarship and colonial discourse, in *Third World Women and the Politics of Feminism*, edited by C.T. Mohanty, A. Russo and L. Torres. Indianapolis: Indiana University Press, 51–80.

Mohanty, C. 1997. *Feminist Genealogies, Colonial Legacies, Democratic Futures*. New York: Routledge.

Mojab, S. 2006. In the Quagmire's of Ethnicity: A Marxist critique of liberal 'exit' strategies. *Journal of Ethnicities*, 5(3), 341–361.

Moore, S.F. 1978. *Law as Process: An Anthropological Approach*. London: Routledge and Kegan Paul.

Morgan, K. 1991. Women and the Knife: Cosmetic Surgery and the Colonization of Women's Bodies. *Hypatia*, 6(3), 25–53.

Motha, S. 2007. Veiled Women and the Affect of Religion in Democracy. *Journal of Law and Society*, 34(1), 139–162.

Norrie, A. 2005. *Law and the Beautiful Soul*. London: Glasshouse Press.

Okin, S.M. 1997. Is Multiculturalism Bad for Women? *Boston Review* [Online], Oct/Nov. Available at: www.bostonreview.net/BR22.5/okin.html [accessed 14 December 2012].

Parekh, B. 2002. *The Future of Multi-Ethnic Britain. The Parekh Report*. London: The Runnymede Trust.

Phillips, A. 2007. *Multiculturalism Without Culture*. Princeton and Oxford: Princeton University Press.

Phillips, A. and Dustin, M. 2004. UK initiatives on forced marriage: Regulation, dialogue and exit. *Political Studies*, 52(3), 531–551.

Purkayastha, B. 2009a. Transgressing the Sacred-Secular, Public-Private Debate, *Living Our Religions, Hindu and Muslim South Asian American Women Narrate Their Experiences*, edited by A. Narayan and B. Purkayastha. Sterling: Kumarian Press, 1–23.

Purkayastha, B. 2009b. Conclusion: Human Rights, Religions, Gender, in *Living Our Religions, Hindu and Muslim South Asian American Women Narrate Their Experiences*, edited by A. Narayan and B. Purkayastha. Sterling: Kumarian Press, 285–297.

Raday, F. 2003. Culture, Religion, and Gender. *International Journal of Constitutional Law* 1(4), 663–715.

Razack, S. 2004. Imperilled Muslim women, dangerous Muslim men and civilised Europeans: Legal and social responses to forced marriages. *Feminist Legal Studies*, 12(2), 129–174.

Razack, S. 2004. *Casting Out: The Eviction of Muslims from Western Law and Politics.* Toronto: University of Toronto Press.

Sagal, G. And Yuval-Davis, N. (eds), 1992. *Refusing Holy Orders: Women and Fundamentalism in Britain.* London: Virago Press

Samad, Y. and Eade, J. 2002. *Community Perceptions of Forced Marriage.* London: Foreign and Commonwealth Office.

Scott, J.W. 2007. *The Politics of the Veil.* Princeton: Princeton University Press.

Shachar, A. 2001. *Multicultural Jurisdictions, Cultural Differences and Women's Rights.* Cambridge: Cambridge University Press.

Shah, P. 2005. *Legal Pluralism in Conflict: Coping with Cultural Diversity in Law.* London: Glass House Press.

Sharma, A. 1994. *Our Religions: The Seven World Religions.* New York: HarperCollins

Spivak, G. 1988. Can the subaltern speak? in *Marxism and the Interpretation of Culture*, edited by N. Nelson and L. Grossberg. Chicago: Illinos UP, 271–313.

Spivak, G. 1990. *The Postcolonial Critic: Interviews, Strategies.* New York: Routledge.

Sunder, M. 2005. Enlightened Constitutionalism. *Connecticut Law Review*, 37(4), 891–906.

Wadud, A. 1991. *Qur'an and Women: Rereading the Sacred Text from a Woman's Perspective.* Oxford: Oxford University Press.

Wadud, A. 2006. *Inside the Gender Jihad: Women's Reform in Islam.* Oxford: Oneworld.

Waggoner, M. 2005. Irony, Embodiment, and the 'critical Attitude': Engaging Saba Mahmood's Critique of Secular Morality. *Culture and Religion*, 6(2), 237–261.

Welchman, L. 2009. Family, Gender and Law in Jordan and Palestine, in Cuno, Kenneth M. and Desai, Manisha (eds), *Family, Gender, and Law in a Globalizing Middle East and South Asia.* Syracuse, NY: Syracuse University press, 126–144.

Wendell, S, 1990. Oppression and victimization; choice and responsibility. *Hypatia*, 5(3), 15–46.

Werner, M. 2006. *Comparative Law in a Global Context, Legal Systems of Asia and Africa.* Cambridge: Cambridge University Press.

Williams, P. 1988. On Being the Object of Property. *Signs*, 14, 5–24.

Wilson, A. 2006. *Dreams, Questions, Struggles: South Asian Women in Britain.* London: Pluto Press.

Wolf, N. 1991. *The Beauty Myth: How Images of Beauty are used against Women.* New York: Doubleday.

Wollstonecraft, M. 1975. *Maria or the Wrongs of Woman.* New York. Norton and Co.

Woodhead, L. and Heelas, M. 2005. *The Spiritual Revolution: Why Religion is giving way to Spirituality.* Oxford: Blackwell Publishing.

Young, I.M. 1990. *Justice and the Politics of Difference.* Princeton: Princeton University Press.

Young, K.K. 1987. Introduction, in *Women in World Religions*, edited by A. Sharma. Albany: State University of New York Press, 1–22.

## Table of Cases

*Mahmood v Mahmood* [1993] SLT 589
*Mahmud v Mahmud* 1994, SLT 599
*Sohrab v Khan* [2002] SCLR 663
*R (Begum) v Governors of Denbigh High School* [2006] UKHL 15
*Sakira Singh* [2008] EWHC 1865 (Admin)
*Eweida v British Airways plc* [2010] EWCA Civ 80

# Part III:
# Issues in Feminist Legal Theory

# Gender and Terrain:
# Feminists Theorize Citizenship

Margot Young[1]

The notion of citizenship is a common frame for debates about justice, equality and liberty. These other concepts are themselves contentious and capacious but key, of course, to arguments for progressive social change. This chapter takes up the challenge of sorting through a remarkably broad and multidisciplinary literature on citizenship to pull out a few strands of thought. This sorting will, it is hoped, advance nuanced feminist understandings of the citizenship conversation, and in turn, appreciation of feminist contributions to studies of justice, equality and liberty. The chapter's purpose is both to recall and invoke feminist considerations of citizenship, as well as to provide a provocative context to continue thinking about ideas of citizenship from a place of feminist politics.

So this chapter has a modest goal: to replicate some of the significant feminist critiques and modifications to thinking about citizenship, and to situate these observations in the context of recent developments that recognize spatial organization as central to the experience of citizenship. A number of distinct discussions follow. The first provides an overview of examinations into citizenship, demonstrating that the concept is capable of capture from a range of perspectives and with a diversity of focus. The second section looks at traditional conceptions of liberal citizenship and maps important feminist responses to this understanding. This section links feminist commentary on the politics of difference to critique and remodelling of the concept of citizenship. Some consideration of the contrast between formal equality and substantive equality informs this argument. The third discussion considers the role that the divide between public and private spheres plays in this conversation. Reliance on this dichotomy suffuses traditional and patriarchal framings of citizenship rights and obligations. Feminist critiques are a powerful source of commentary on these central elements of liberal citizenship. The fourth section focuses on the challenge that neo-liberal notions of citizenship pose to feminist enlargements of the concept to include more historically disregarded groups including, but not limited to, women. The fifth, and final, section wraps these prior discussions in a more grounded (literally) consideration of citizenship in the context of the spatial arrangements of the city. The emphasis here is on linking political theories of citizenship with geographic insights into spatialization of rights

1     This chapter was written with financial assistance from a Community University Research Alliance grant from the Social Science and Humanities Research Council and a Peter Wall Solutions Initiative Grant from the University of British Columbia. Thanks to Jessica Fletcher and Alain Saint-Onge for their research assistance. Special thanks to Margaret Davies and Vanessa Munro for their thoughtful editorial suggestions and forbearance. Equally, a nod to Neve Ostry Young for her patience.

and the physical environment in which citizenship activities play out for so many women. The chapter's conclusion takes stock of what feminist understandings of citizenship must be if the notion is to retain effectiveness and political vigour for gender critique and progress.

## A Wide Conversation

The field of citizenship studies has situated citizenship as 'a vital political, social and cultural issue of our time' (Isin and Turner 2007: 16, Richardson 1998). Certainly, the identity – in both its legal and political forms – is a foundational preoccupation of liberal democracies and shorthand for our ethical obligations to each other (Song 2011). The focus has traditionally been on the legal relationship between the individual and the polity or nation state (Sassen 2002). However, political, economic, technological and cultural changes have catalysed challenges to, and necessitated re-examination of, the facts and conceptions of citizenship. As power diffuses beyond the edges of the nation state and accumulates outside the realm of government, issues of belonging multiply and fragment. There are operational and rhetorical opportunities for the articulation of 'new types of political subjects and new spatialities for politics' (Sassen 2002: 5). Thus, as Lynn Staeheli rightly notes, 'citizenship is a … messy concept' (Staeheli 2003: 97). It is a notion that, despite a possibly relatively simple *de jure* meaning, has been used in multiple and complex ways to capture forms of standing in the political community across times and places and for different groups (Staeheli 2003). Indeed, the concept risks 'mean[ing] very little since it can so readily mean so much' (Bosniak 2000: 487). But the failure in most countries of the normative project to achieve 'equal' citizenship makes its contemplation a worthwhile task (Sassen 2002).

Sculpting of the concept for the purposes of any one discussion is, therefore, necessary. But how to do this? Clearly, as some commentators pointedly argue, the designation is critically grounded in legal realities and consequences (Robson and Kessler 2008). These same commentators decry concentration on 'metaphoric' analysis for its elision of the harsh legal realities – 'deportation and confinement' – that confront those whose citizenship is challenged (Robson and Kessler 2008: 559). But, a purely practical and legal focus fails to capture so much that is rich and evocative about the debate. For example, the term can also extend more broadly to contemplate 'ideas, practices, and relationship' beyond the legal (Staeheli 2003: 99). Thus the notion of citizenship can denote actual political or legal rights and duties, or it can, alternatively, focus on primarily cultural aspects, facts of recognition or identity, political agency, or how belonging is conceptualized (Friedman 2005). The debates consider issues of social, political and legal inclusion in the community and, indeed, 'the very basis of community' (Staeheli 2003: 97). The term does often signal a legal and political status in that it confers national identity, but it also invokes social status, or placement in channels of distribution, recognition and participation (Isin and Turner 2007). Linda Bosniak, in a nod to this pixelated invocation of the term, sets out four understandings of citizenship: 'citizenship as formal legal status …, citizenship as rights, citizenship as political activity, and citizenship as identity/solidarity' (Bosniak 2000: 456). Regardless of context, the idea connotes 'a certain sense of entitlement' (Yuval-Davis 2011: 47). This is not to say that basic and formal features of the relationship between the individual and the state, such as passport issuance and legal residence, are irrelevant (Yuval-Davis 1991). But most conversations focus more on the citizen as 'a figure with political standing, a standing equal to that of other citizens' in a variety of contexts: legal, social, and economic (Pateman 1998: 192).

Theorists identify a number of general 'fault lines' along which traditional, dominant theories of citizenship abut (Bosco et al. 2011: 160, Moosa-Mitha 2005: 370). For example, notions of an individuated citizenship stand opposed to more relational or communitarian alternatives. These theories differ in terms of what the basis of citizenship is, and who, therefore, is entitled to or disentitled from citizenship. In the first group of theories – individuated citizenship – citizenship status lies with those who formally possess legal rights and privileges. Historically, private property ownership was the most significant of these indicators. This is the citizenship of classical liberalism (Bosco et al. 2011: 160) which, in its most extreme form, entails the notion of responsible citizenship that is characteristic of today's neo-liberalism. Contrasted to this is an understanding of citizenship that rests on group membership and that is relational. Here the central marker of citizenship is participation in civic responsibilities (Bosco et al. 2011: 160). A third variant is the idea of cosmopolitan citizenship: a citizenship that, while sited nationally, involves consciousness of and commitment to global humanity and community (Bosco et al. 2011: 160). This version reflects the attenuation of the link between territory and citizenship practices and identities (Sassen 2002). All of these variants in their traditional form fall within a rough category of liberal citizenship, although they have differing degrees and ways of recognizing social relations, community, the nation state and cosmopolitan focus.

As noted above, features that shape both the conception of citizenship and the communities to which individuals lay claim occur across a range of scales. Local, national and international processes, conditions and institutions cast formal and substantive form on citizenship (Jaggar 2005). Different levels of citizenship constitute different sets of resources for political resistance and action (Staeheli 2003: 99). Thus, in response to the effects of globalization, some citizenship studies realign the focus away from the nation state to the transnational or international level, attending to how international structures and institutions shape citizenship (Staeheli 2003: 97–98). Others go in the opposite direction, focusing on local forces and localities as the scale at which citizenship is given its meanings. Here the argument is that 'routinized, face-to-face contacts' of local sites forge the substratum of citizenship (Staeheli 2003: 98). Others insist that citizenship is inevitably about the relationship between individuals and the nation state, arguing that this is the most cogent site of regulation external to the individual (Robson and Kessler 2008: 543). It is also the case that citizenship under the neo-liberal modes of governance of the last decades has been rescaled both 'up' and 'down' and, consequently, one focus alone is insufficient. At the same time that the transnational has emerged as significant, states have employed 'governing through communities' such that the rights and responsibilities of citizenship are given at least formal expression at the civic level (Desforges et al. 2005: 440–441). The result is that citizenship is experienced by many as 'multi-scalar': it is appreciated and articulated in reference to a variety of contexts (some geographic, others not) in which an individual's citizenship is relevant: nation, city, ethnicity, religion, region, for example (Desforges et al. 2005: 441). In the face of this, Linda Bosniak understands citizenship as something that is 'multiple and overlapping' (Bosniak 2000: 450). Thus, the relationship between the citizen and the nation state is only one of the 'several layers of people's citizenship' (Yuval-Davis 2006: 207, Volpp 2011: 2). (Pointedly, this must be operative in thinking about the concept as it relates to Indigenous peoples (Moosa-Mitha 2005).) Equally, single faceted accounts of citizenship may limit the power of the concept (Song 2011).

Use of the notion of citizenship as a theme connecting other issues of political relevance is not to be embraced naively; the concept of citizenship has a number of political strikes against it from the start. Its politics are variable; indeed, as a number of theorists note, it is a notion critical to both progressive and conservative politics (Yuval-Davis 1991: 58). The attribution of citizenship functions as much to marginalize as it does to recognize: the concept 'relentlessly' (Isin 2005: 381) imports the idea of boundary – for example, physical, political, or social borders – that pairs inclusion with claims of exclusions (Lister 1997). Carole Pateman notes this, arguing that, in its practical consequences, citizenship has been exclusionary, 'both in terms of membership in nation states, and in terms of the inclusion and standing of various categories of inhabitants within those states' (Pateman 1998: 196). Here the reference is to those who, while resident in a nation state, have the status of non-citizens or are treated as second-class citizens (Moosa-Mitha 2005). Citizenship claims can be as much about who is out as who is in. In other words, they do 'the dirty work of boundary maintenance' (Yuval-Davis 2006: 204). Too frequently, as well, the idea assumes a 'naturalness' of the boundaries asserted, ignoring how the concept of community that citizenship evokes is an 'ideological and material construction' produced by political struggle and compromise (Yuval-Davis 1991: 59). It is a struggle over where and how boundaries are set and the 'theorizing [of] state and society' (Yuval-Davis 1991: 66).

While the concept is presented as gender-neutral, it has in fact been traditionally deeply gendered, encoding particular understandings about appropriate social placement and roles for women and men (Lister 2007, Pateman 1988, Yuval-Davis 1991, Walby 1994). There is, Patrizia Longo reminds us, no ungendered citizen (Longo 2001). To wit, the ideal citizen of traditional theory is, among other things, male: 'there is a dissonance between "women" and "citizen" that disturbs the would-be universal' (Thornton 1997: 487). The claims of traditional discussions of citizenship to universality, unconditionality and equality belie how citizenship – both in theory and in practice – has been very much gender-based and gender-exclusionary (Brodie 2008a, 2008b). Carole Pateman's formulation of the 'sexual contract' underpinning the current liberal state and its designation of citizens is a foundational moment in this feminist critique of traditional notions of citizenship (Pateman 1988, 1986). Grants of citizenship, further, have also been racialized and sexualized, attendant to and reflective of heterosexual, white, and patriarchal privilege. Indeed, like any major organizing concept of status, the idea of citizenship reflects dominant power hierarchies in its articulation of ideas of inclusion and exclusion. The concept of citizenship plays a significant role in the construction and maintenance of unequal social relations (Walby 1994). Consequently, its reference is fraught – pulling on sets of ideas and order that figure significantly in women's, and other groups', oppression and disempowerment.

Nonetheless, the idea of citizenship is powerful. Its formal promises – while only selectively and discriminatorily delivered in practice, and too complacently referenced in theory – speak meaningfully and evocatively to those most in need of them. As Ruth Lister argues, it can inform a range of progressive political arguments about social and political belonging, and so is a tool for many marginalized groups struggling for justice (Lister 2007, Yuval-Davis 2006). Citizenship is, moreover, a 'momentum' or 'mobilizing' concept (Hoffman 2007: 138): a notion under sustained expansion as claims about it are gathered in aid of a broader politics of inclusion, social justice and material well-being by more and more groups. Lauren Berlant powerfully notes that:

> the promise that the democratic citizenship form makes to people caught in history. The populations who were and are managed by the discipline of the promise – women, African Americans, Native Americans, immigrants, homosexuals – have long

*experienced simultaneously the wish to be full citizens and the violence of their partial citizenship. (Berlant 2002: 19)*

Iris Marion Young states simply that: '[a]n ideal of universal citizenship has driven the emancipatory momentum of modern political life' (Young 1989: 250). Nonetheless, the starting place for any conversation about citizenship that takes seriously a social justice and equality politics must be one of hesitation, caution and qualification.

## Expanding Citizenship: Encompassing Difference

Almost invariably, discussions of citizenship begin with reference to T.H. Marshall, a mid-twentieth century British sociologist responsible for the foundational, modern conception of citizenship as composed of three strands of rights: civil, political and social. As the base for much of liberal citizenship theory, Marshall's account therefore receives considerable attention from feminist theorists. In his most famous essay, 'Citizenship and Social Class', Marshall describes citizenship as 'full membership in a community, with all its rights and responsibilities' (Marshall 1950). Marshall's attentiveness to social condition reflects his contemporary society, where the struggle for redistribution in the development of the post-war welfare state followed 'over a century of discursive and political struggles around the inherent gap between liberalism's promise of citizen equality and the structural inequalities of capitalism' (Brodie 2009: 98, Isin and Turner 2007). His story is of expanding citizenship rights, and social rights are the most recent addition. These second generation rights attend to material and social interests and needs, including, according to Marshall, the right to economic well-being and the right to be included in the 'social heritage and to live the life of a civilised being according to the standards prevailing in the society' (Marshall 1950: 14).

Marshall's discussions of citizenship contain much that is viewed positively by feminist thinkers. Nina Yuval-Davis, for example, notes that Marshall's invocation of 'community' allows citizenship to be identified in terms broader than simply the nation state (2006). This reference fits well with current discussions of the saliency of citizenship across the different levels of the political and social worlds in which individuals are embedded. 'Community' can capture belonging within states and across nations, including both local politics and supranational groupings. Similarly, the notion of social rights as something critically provided by the state is a conceptual precursor to current feminist discussions around social assistance provision (welfare) and a guaranteed annual income (Young 2010b, Pateman 1989).

However, Marshallian citizenship, and the liberal citizenship theory it has spawned, have been criticized from many perspectives. Marshall's evolutionary view of citizenship and his failure to contemplate cultural and other aspects of citizenship are targeted. Critique most relevant to this chapter focuses primarily on Marshall's failure to contemplate a more complex and variable identity for the citizen (Isin and Turner 2007). His analysis fails to address factors other than class, most notably gender, but also race, ability, ethnicity, religion and sexuality, for example (Lister 2007, Robson and Kessler 2008: 540). Thus, Marshall's formulation is figured as inattentive to how race, gender and sexuality configure understandings of citizenship, including his own (Walby 1994, Richardson 1998, Yuval-Davis 2006, Walby 1994). This failure means that the social divisions that inform individual and group experience trigger and justify exclusion from citizenship norms and privileges;

difference and inclusivity are incompatible (Bosco et al. 2011). At the moment Marshall was articulating his notion of citizenship as a status bestowed on members of a community, women were excluded from full membership in the emerging welfare state. The 'masculinist character' of citizenship was, therefore, 'repressed' (Pateman 1989: 184, Jones 1990).

Though limited significantly in this regard, efforts have been made in recent times – as identity has increasingly emerged as the focus of modern social movements – to re-elaborate and deepen Marshall's social notion of citizenship, in order to enable it to reflect a greater sensitivity to identity and difference, to variety in social membership, and to the restrictions of understanding citizenship purely in terms of rights (Isin and Turner 2007, Richardson 2000, Cossman 2007). In forging this approach, the common concerns that debates around the idea of citizenship share with so many other areas of feminist thought and activism in terms of thinking about 'difference' become apparent. Indeed, a hallmark of feminist citizenship theory is the centring of 'difference' (Moosa-Mitha 2005). Liberal political theory elaborates a universal citizenship: all members of a given community, those inside, bear equal rights and the state is neutral as to individual differences or varying social contexts. 'Difference' marks those outside the designation of citizen, as distinct from those whose 'sameness' locates them within. Wrapped up in the idea of citizenship, therefore, is 'a politics of difference' (Yuval-Davis 1991: 59). Certainly, Marshall's conception of citizenship was not without its own 'notion of difference' (Yuval-Davis 1991). At least initially, social rights made sense in the context of class differences as social-welfare rights. But the range and scope of difference recognized was narrow. In a world marked by a 'multiplicity of social logics' (Laclau and Mouffe 2001: 188), attentiveness to how difference is recognized, shared and, ultimately, valued is argued to be essential. Observable, then, has been the feminist reformulation of theories of citizenship to both encompass and recognize difference, as difference is experienced within specific socio-economic contexts and as difference is 'invented/produced' (Richardson 1998, Yuval-Davis 2006, Moosa-Mitha 2005). Any adequate theory of citizenship, Yuval-Davis asserts, will assign central importance to issues of the stratified access of various categories of individuals to the state, and the effects of this difference on relations of domination and on power differentials (Yuval-Davis 1991: 58). Thus patterns of inclusion and exclusion are interrogated, with the purpose of identifying the institutional and social practices, norms and rules that might mete out full and effective citizenship status (Moosa-Mitha 2005).

Feminists' insights about difference make apparent various inadequacies in traditional, liberal and neo-liberal ideas of citizenship. These latter theories cannot contemplate difference in other than negative ways: they either '[burden] with excessive ascribed "difference" or ... [fail] to acknowledge ... distinctiveness' (Fraser 2000: 27). Differences are, in the words of Margaret Thornton, 'sloughed off' by the 'carapace of universalism' (1997: 486) or exceptionalized to render women unsuitable for citizenship (487). Either results in subordination and exclusion. Such is the 'gender-loadedness' of traditional citizenship (Longo 2001: 271).

Feminist scholars of all ilks have noted the challenge that thinking about sameness and difference poses. Martha Minow has coined the term 'dilemma of difference' (Minow 1990, Young 1989); Carole Pateman famously writes of 'Wollstonecraft's dilemma' (Pateman 1989: 197). These 'dilemmas' refer to the paradoxical dangers of either ignoring or focusing on difference. As Minow explains, 'the problem of inequality can be exacerbated both by treating members of minority groups the same as member of the majority and by treating the two groups differently' (1990: 20). Pateman notes that the extension of citizenship to women on the same (formally) equal terms upon which it is available to men denies the distinctiveness and value of women's activities and roles. Yet, entrenching those differences as women's route to full citizenship cements and naturalizes gender difference, losing opportunities to break out of discriminatory norms and reimagine institutions of patriarchy: for example, the gendered division of labour. '[E]ither women become [like] men and so full citizens; or they continue at women's work, which is of no value for [traditional] citizenship' (Pateman 1989: 197).

In light of these concerns, some commentators urge transcending this debate by thinking beyond the terms of 'sameness' or 'difference'. One approach is to discuss, instead, different notions of equality. Formal equality emphasizes the ideal of the liberal individual, unencumbered by any particularity of history, social location or circumstance, granted identical assignment of rights and opportunities (McIntyre 1993: 26–27). Very powerful critiques of liberal citizenship can be launched simply by the charge that women be accorded the identical rights and opportunities that men experience. Inequality that is obvious and of singular dimension is often appropriately addressed by a demand for formal equality. This idea has had powerful critical bite for such gendered citizenship issues as getting the vote, or arguing for equal pay. Assertions of universality deliver strategic traction or 'discursive space' to leverage claims to equality and citizenship in the name of citizenship (Brodie 2008a: 169). But, the more marginal groups are, the less a formal equality lens refracts their difference as unjust – exclusion seems justified by their difference. Deep and persistent inequality is left intact and unaddressable. Formal equality thus has a deep irony. It is justified by liberalism's radical but abstract commitment to full inclusion based on shared moral worth; but, in practice, it is condemned to justifying exclusion (Young 2010a: 193, Lessard 2010).

Substantive equality, by contrast, treats individuals as richly different, astride dense linkages of social and economic structural relations. It is sensitive to context and existing power arrangements. Difference is understood as historically and socially based, and as contingent and shared (Young 2010a: 196). Patrizia Longo takes up a similar refrain in relation to citizenship, emphasizing the need for transcending preoccupation with equality or different treatment. She argues for a wider notion of equality, one that is sensitive to difference and that addresses the ways in which difference matters through redistributive justice and radical inclusion (Longo 2001, Lessard 2010). Chantal Mouffe also argues for avoiding the back and forth between sameness and difference. But her discarding of this debate stems from an insistence on understanding this as a 'false dilemma': the figure of 'women' does not signify 'any unified and unifying essence' to compare with some 'homogeneous entity "man"' (Mouffe 1992a: 373). Instead, the focus should be on the 'multiplicity of social relations in which sexual difference is always constructed in very diverse ways' (Mouffe 1992a: 373). Subordination, not difference, should be named: 'To ask if women should become identical to men in order to be recognized as equal, or if they should assert their difference at the cost of equality, appears meaningless once essential identities are put into question' (Mouffe 1992a: 373).

The task is challenging. The category of women is, of course, not a stable one. Women are affected differently depending upon a variety of other social divisions. Gender-specific racisms, as so many have noted, for instance, fracture a simple divide between men and women. Thus, feminist post-modernist analyses, disallowing reference to grand narratives or universal signifiers (Yuval-Davis 1991: 65), render problematic any one abstract, general theory of citizenship equality. Yuval-Davis argues that the quest is 'to retain the multiplicity and multidimensionality of identities within contemporary society, but without losing sight of the differential power dimension of differential collectivities and groupings within the society and the variety of relationships of domination/subordination between them' (Yuval-Davis 1991: 67). Similarly, Iris Marion Young urges a theory that discards strict attentiveness to formally equal treatment in favour of recognition of group differences (Young 1989).

Marshall's theory of citizenship can thus start a long and complex trail, a path that leads through calculation or critique of the idea of citizen identity, to competing theories of how inclusion and exclusion understand difference, to feminist conversations about the best conceptualization of equality or subordination. At its heart, this is a conversation about broadening the constitution of citizenship through challenging why and how difference comes to matter, and how equality is composed (Moosa-Mitha 2005). But feminist thought also targets another classic metaphor of liberal citizenship – the juxtaposition of the public and the private spheres. It is to this that this chapter next turns.

## Public/Private: Targeting the Substance of Exclusion

Condemnation of the public–private dichotomy so central to liberal thought is a significant and lasting contribution of feminist writing and struggle. As Yuval-Davis notes, feminist critique 'demolished' this differentiation years ago (Yuval-Davis 1991: 63). Not surprisingly, then, critical reference to the public/private dynamic features centrally in feminist reconsiderations of citizenship norms and politics. Traditional discussions of citizenship reference the difference between the public and private spheres, and the public/private divide is frequently named by feminist theorists as the mechanism responsible for much of the long standing denial of women's full citizenship. Sylvia Walby, for example, argues that full public citizenship for women must necessarily rest on the destabilization of patriarchy and its institutions, including the idea of separate and ranked public and private realms (Walby 1994).

To repeat, the public and private spheres are central categories of liberal thought. Preoccupied with the legitimacy of the coercive exercise of collective, central power over the free and autonomous individual, liberalism anxiously draws a line between public and private spheres. The public is the sphere open to configuration and regulation by collective power, to state authority; preserved within the private are intimate and personal matters subject only to mastery by the individual: heart and hearth, kith and kin. The private is the realm of 'natural rhythms of material and biological necessity' (Prokhovnik 1998: 85) and of individual norms and choices. Exclusion of the state and collectively enforced rules from the private realm circumscribes the power of the collective. The 'picket fence' of the boundary protects individual freedom and shields private relations from political accountability.

The divide is slippery, but functional in its ambiguity and manipulability. Different categories – the family, the market, the state, civil society, government – figure across a range of pairs of concepts juxtaposed across this divide. How the roles of public and of private are cast varies according to the political purpose that motivates the formulation (Affolder 2009). For example, the market can figure as 'private' in conversations about justifying an absence of state regulation but as 'public' in contrasting traditional activities of women and men. Commenting on the variability of what stands in for 'public', Plummer charges that there are 'multiple, hierarchically layered and contested public spheres' (Plummer 2001: 243–244).

Boundaries of citizenship, and its relevant rights and responsibilities, traditionally lie across the division between the public sphere and the private sphere. Historically (at least in recent history), men have been positioned in the public realm of work and the market, women in the private arena of home, family and community (Staeheli and Clarke 2003: 106). The oppositions cited are 'the private and public, women and citizen, dependent and breadwinner' (Pateman 1989: 202). Such placement of the sexes influences and shapes the practices of citizenship typically available to and taken up by men and women. The activities of liberal citizenship – paid employment, voting, political participation, public service – take place in the public sphere and stand in opposition to the activities of the private sphere and to the activities of 'non-citizens', such as women, children, slaves and 'foreigners' (Prokhovnik 1998: 86).

Placement of women in the private sphere, as well as their association with nature, translates into the exclusion of women from politics and public life. The norms of the public – justice, rationality, law, autonomy – thus reflect the masculine citizen and affirm his life pattern. The range of activities typical of female participation is excluded from the public sphere (Prokhovnik 1998, Young 1989). Alongside the assertion of a rigid distinction between public and private spheres lies strict enforcement of a gender order, one that locates women within the private, domestic sphere of the home and the family (Brodie 2008a: 167). Women are incorporated in civil society not as citizens but as members of the family – a realm distinct from civil society (Pateman 1989: 182). This 'social imaginary', constituted by public policy and political strategies, blocks women's social and economic rights, their economic and legal independence, and perpetuates dubious stereotypes of the ideal woman (Brodie 2008a: 167–168, Lister 2007).

Pateman argues that the idea that society has the basic structure of a public world of the state and its policies, separated from the private, familial sphere, is both true and false (Pateman 1989: 183). It is true because many women continue to experience this separation as a feature of their daily lives. But it is false in that the public is never far from the private – state policies have always reached into the family. Feminist inquiry into social citizenship has strengthened appreciation of the extent of the interlarding of the public into the private. The two spheres are implicated in each other: the public very much shapes the private just as the private makes the public possible. As Longo points out, the assignment of women to the domestic sphere, and the attachment of specific (unpaid) labour to that assignment, creates the preconditions for men's activities in the public sphere (Longo 2001: 274). And, men have a legitimate place and authority in both (Pateman 1989: 183–184). 'Practices of citizenship involve both public-sphere narratives and concrete experiences of quotidian life that do not cohere or harmonize' (Berlant 2002: 10).

The absence of women, and of experiences and roles traditional for women, from the compass of citizenship is not mere oversight. A number of feminist theorists argue that this exclusion is, rather, integral to traditional and liberal understandings of citizenship (Jones 1990). As Ursula Vogel (1991) points out, women are not simply latecomers to the grant of citizenship; women cannot merely succeed to that status as part of an expansive straight line evolution of the original notion. The very calculation of the citizen references men in their capacity as household heads and paid workers. Women's economic dependency on active citizens (men) is assumed (Thornton 1997: 495, 499), such that women are, in general, 'cast as mere dependents', not full citizens (Brodie 2008a: 168, 2008b, Fraser and Gordon 1994, Walby 1994). Citizenship for women becomes an elaboration of private, domestic (unpaid) tasks (Pateman 1989: 127). The specificity of women is relegated to the private sphere (Young

1989). Thus, the terms on which citizenship is conceived require not merely the addition of women to the mix but rather a more profound and fundamental recasting of how citizenship is conceived and calibrated. Many feminist theorists accordingly argue that citizenship theory must be rejigged to recognize the activities and social relations that form the basis of women's citizenship (Lister 2007).

There is, however, no consensus among feminist theorists about the fix required in the face of the exclusionary functioning of liberalism's public/private split. Some argue for the erasure of the distinction between public and private and its implications for state action: some for drawing the line between the spheres in a different place. Others argue simply for the deconstruction of the hierarchical opposition the distinction sets up. An approach that retains the divide, but understands women's exclusion from the public as problematic, will argue for women's liberation from the private realm (Prokhovnik 1998: 89). Others, still operating within the divide, assert the promotion of the private side and its extension into the public realm. The maternal values of care and family are asserted as important renovations of more traditional and masculinist values of the public (Lister 2007). Here, ironically, as Brodie notes, the coding of women as the selfless caregivers of the family and home lent moral and political salience to women's claims for public citizenship in the early decades of the twentieth century (Brodie 2008a: 168). Some of these solutions thus retain the dilemma over difference: more of the same with women added or validation of difference through the 'maternalization' of politics. And the criticism then is that traditional conceptions of politics and gendered subjectivities go unchallenged (Prokhovnik 1998: 94). Lister, in particular, cites the problem of 'sexually segregated norms of citizenship' as a consequence of pushing private activities into public recognition, keeping intact the sexual division of labour (Lister 1995: 9, 12).

Most convincing, perhaps, are those who argue for doing away with the public/private divide. They assert that only by this move can the difference of, and between, women be recognized, such that activities of both realms become the stuff of citizenship (Prokhovnik 1998: 89). The goal is not to achieve a better, gender-neutral conception of citizenship but rather to expand what counts as citizenship such that women and their gender-specific experiences, their 'ethically-grounded activities' in both public and private, are part of the picture (Prokhovnik 1998).

Feminist reconsiderations of the public/private divide (as this notion figures in discussions of citizenship) are thus another route to consideration of issues of identity and difference. Young links these conversations in her assertion that traditional understandings of the public realm, the civic public, is exclusionary of groups for whom assumptions of sameness fail (Young 1989). The public sphere is spun as a realm of generality devoid of individual particularity; the private is home to the personal and the specific (Young 1989: 255). The universality of the public demands the suppression of differences. This is the mechanism by which universal grants of citizenship constitute selective exclusion of groups for whom differences from norms of the ideal citizen have social consequence. Young describes this as the 'paradox of citizenship': 'social power makes some citizens more equal than others, and equality of citizenship makes some people more powerful citizens' (Young 1989: 259). The solution Young proposes is a public that explicitly allows and ferments recognition and representation of the 'differences' of oppressed groups (Young 1989). She argues for a changed, more charged and diverse, civic sphere.

Of course, much feminist critique of traditional notions of a universal public citizenship extends beyond thinking purely about gender. However, in recent times, as modalities of governance shift increasingly in the direction of neo-liberalism, the line between the public and the private is further confounded, not through the extension of public morality to the private sphere, but through the application of market and private economic logic to all spheres. Postulation of a robust public, understood in this context as the social and the political, juxtaposed to the individual, has thus been muted. The next section examines this claim.

## The Neo-liberal Citizen: A Challenge to Feminist Politics

My purpose here is not to undertake an extensive unpacking of neo-liberalism and its market fundamentalism. Rather, I seek to look briefly at how some feminist theorists have engaged with the impact of neo-liberalism on women and current citizenship debates. This engagement touches on other themes already discussed in this chapter and shows a broad rethinking of what citizenship for many groups – but importantly women – can be in a neo-liberal era. This section, then, is concerned with how feminists have countered the emergent citizenship norms of the neo-liberal polity, setting out the ideological scenery that situates current feminist struggles over citizenship.

The ascendancy of neo-liberalism has seen governments move away from commitments to universal social rights and comprehensive state guarantees of welfare provision (Isin and Turner 2007). While the deployment of neo-liberal social policy across nations varies, a 'cluster of core assumptions' mark common departures from the post-war welfare state and its social liberalism (Brodie 2010: 1568). Even Marshall's simpler notion of social rights as a response to class inequities is imperiled. Theorists chart both the 'hollowing out' and, then, the 'filling in' of the state as part of neo-liberal policies (Desforges et al. 2005: 440). The role of government is both reduced and expanded to serve the 'rational, entrepreneurial, economic individual' (Kern 2010: 6). The idea of 'social' citizenship is eviscerated: social issues are viewed as essentially economic problems and the economic order reaches to include all human activities within its logic. Thus, the influential attachment of social rights to citizenship status, with the state as responsible for meeting these rights, taken up by Marshall and the tradition of liberal citizenship his thought initiates, are undone. Within neo-liberal governance rationales, the free market replaces government as the mechanism to meet human needs and guarantee freedom (Isin and Turner 2007). There is a dramatically reduced role for public services, and the institutionalization of an individualized structure to service delivery (Collins et al. 2011). Political and collective activity is stigmatized, regulated and restricted (Collins et al. 2011), with a refocus in civil society on service provision, and away from advocacy. These changes have had a disproportionate impact on women, exacerbating the socio-economic exclusion of individual women and sapping the economic resources of women's organizations (Collins et al. 2011).

More pointedly, in many nations, the late twentieth century and the early years of this century have seen a turn away from gender-sensitive ideas of the citizen. For example, Janine Brodie, a Canadian political scientist, chronicles an initial and gradual acceptance of gendered issues – such as equality, reproductive freedom, political representation and anti-violence campaigns – into the Canadian political mainstream during the 1980s. Using Canada as a case study, she notes that this more gender-aware public agenda challenged earlier norms of gendered behaviour segregated across the public and private spheres. This movement destabilized the previous era's assumptions of women's exclusion from the worlds of politics and business, of patriarchal rule in the home and community, and of selective grants of women's civil and political rights (Brodie 2008a: 167). The post-war widening of citizenship concerns, however, was quickly followed, in Canada and many other countries, by the triumph of neo-liberal strategies of governance. More gender-nuanced conceptions of the citizen (what Brodie calls 'the irredeemable gendered subjects' of the liberal post-war welfare state) were replaced with the single figure of the neo-liberal citizen-subject – a 'genderless and self-sufficient market [actor]', the wilful, self-biographer (Brodie 2008a: 165). With this reformulation comes a re-modelled idea of citizenship – one that is marked by the processes of 'invisibilization and individualization' (Brodie 2008a: 166, Dobrowolsky 2008). Groups marginalized by larger social and political processes of exclusion lose legitimacy and recognition; individual causes and solutions are asserted for collective social problems (Brodie 2009: 103). Women disappear as a distinctive constituency of concern for social policy. Jane Jensen writes of this as a shift in 'citizenship regime'. The neo-liberal regime, she argues, is characterized by four key features: different rights and responsibilities; new rules; a changed balance between the state, the citizen, the market, and the community; and different political identities of belonging (Jensen 2008: 188).

Thus, the economization of the social (Clarke 2008) within neo-liberalism, has recast citizenship, including, as noted, the relationship between citizens and the state. This market citizen, if in need of social assistance, accepts such assistance only in the short term, and contingent on the commitment to return to self-sufficiency (Collins et al. 2011, Jensen 2008, Jenson and Phillips 2001). Universal programmes are retooled as targeted assistance, available only when other processes of self-help fail. Two consequences ensue. First, restructured public services dilute the state's ability and intention to respond to social need. And, second, what resources are available are triggered by assignments of individual responsibility (Collins et al. 2011). These processes of residualization are productive of social exclusion and disempowerment (Sommerlad 2004: 367).

Within the neo-liberal paradigm, there is 'little tolerance for making "special" claims on the basis of difference or systemic discrimination', claims that recognize existing forms of gender inequality (Brodie 2008a). At least as an idea at the national level, 'citizenship is invoked to draw a mantle of sameness over those deemed to be members of the community' (Thornton 1997: 486). Citizenship ascriptions have 'reproduced a particular version of the responsible/ good citizen based on assimilationist norms and values, even while acknowledging the increasing power of the language of citizenship' (Richardson 2000: 264). The deeply etched patterns of gendered existence are denied by neo-liberalism (Brodie 2008a: 171). Formally gender-neutral policy and processes consistently, then, produce unequal, gender-specific outcomes and norms. The result has been, as theorists note, 'the simultaneous erosion and intensification of gender, both literally and metaphorically' (Brodie 2008a: 170). The political and social relevance of gender in public life is denied; policies treat men and women as if their gender was irrelevant. Yet, individuals continue to live and to understand their lives in very gendered ways, particularly in relation to the processes of social reproduction as they interact with the market economy. Formal ideas of genderless individualism are belied by the real experiences of women struggling with gendered responsibilities in both the private and the public spheres (Brodie 2008a: 171). Indeed, the experience of gender in the lives of women – particularly the most marginalized and oppressed – is sharpened (Brodie 2008a: 171). Ignoring the 'difference difference makes' renders more acute the material and political oppression of those who misfit the ideal of this neo-liberal citizen.

Angela McRobbie makes a series of specific points about emergent citizenship for young women, in particular, in the neo-liberal environment of Western liberal democracies. The grant of economic independence represents to (young) women the promise of liberation but it is, in fact, a freedom contained within the economic sphere, inscribing notions of consumer citizenship in place of political empowerment and identity. The result, McRobbie intones, is the 'fall of the public woman' (McRobbie 2012). Young echoes such a concern in her call to awake from 'privatized consumer slumbers' (Young 1989: 252). In the face of this shift in citizenship regimes (Jensen 2008), feminist theorists have challenged the distinction between active and passive citizenship, a contrast predicated on thinking about the real content and experiences of women's lives. Similarly, a number of feminist theorists focus on the 'performance' as opposed to merely the 'status' of citizenship (Lister 1997, Stasiulis and Bakan 1997, Yuval-Davis 1997). These insights have at least two important implications. First, the notion of participation is complicated, as a wide range of activities – such as provisioning or community maintenance (activities of the traditional private sphere) – register as citizen involvement. Second, the observation entails understanding citizenship as not merely the passive receipt of status, but rather to be represented and achieved through the acts of claiming a role in the important contexts of individuals' lives (Volpp 2011). Individuals marked by difference – as a result of gender and other identity features – have never been passive recipients of the privileges and liberties of society; to the extent these rights have been realized, they have been fought for.

As different nation states have seen the retrenchment of social service provision, the opportunities for, and forms of, political citizenship and social citizenship have been changed and challenged (Staeheli and Clarke 2003: 109). Moosa-Mitha points out that what counts as 'active' is itself selectively and normatively delineated (2005). Young, in a similar vein, writes of the destabilization of citizenship norms and identities creating spaces for new markers of citizenship and new identities as citizens (Young 1989). This results in women leveraging public citizenship status and impact through traditional private activities in proactive ways. Thus, formally non-political agents (say, housewives) may be understood to exercise actual significant political agency (Sassen 2002: 6). The contours of citizenship – that is, the experience and character of citizenship – can be actively reshaped through the daily activities of individuals. Research on provisioning in Canada, which I will discuss further in the next section, illustrates this (Collins et al. 2011). Groups traditionally socially and economically marginalized are active in the refashioning of citizenship practices of meaning in their own lives (Bosco et al. 2011). Marginalized groups, in the citizenship options available to them, reveal and reinforce important identity features such as gender, sexuality or race/ethnicity (Staeheli and Clarke 2003: 111) (thus rendering citizenship and difference compatible). Nancy Fraser has recognized the importance of the practice of citizenship to women's status as citizens, and to justice for women, through the addition of 'representation' – or political empowerment and participation – to her list of justice concerns (Fraser 2003). Significantly, this discussion is about what counts as participation and agency. And it is also a broadside to the public/private split as it governs citizenship status.

## Citizenship and the City: Recovering Place and the Everyday

This chapter began by noting the different scales at which citizenship is assigned and debated. There, the point was to illustrate the variability of sites of citizenship and to acknowledge the multiple scales at which individual and group citizenship registers. Discussion in this final section pinpoints the very immediate and local scale of the city. Citizenship theory is not unique in such a focus: the city has emerged as a site for research across a range of scholarly disciplines (Fainstein 2010). Saska Sassen argues that the global city has a dynamic that reflects direct interaction with other levels of community – the national, regional and global. The urban experience is uniquely a distinct formation of imperatives from these other levels (Sassen 2010) and cities provide terrain where new political, economic, cultural and subjective processes are emerging, particularly in light of the transformation and diminishment of the national level (Sassen 2002). For example, the large or global city locates possibilities of new forms of power and politics at the subnational level, creating new transnationality and translocality. More specifically, the current 'urban moment' offers insight into the materialization of the trends currently destabilizing the concept of citizenship – among other things, 'the presence and voice of … socio-cultural diversity' (Sassen 2010: 3) and growing urban concentrations of the disadvantaged and dispossessed (Sassen 2002). Interestingly, a return to the city also tracks early historical contexts for thinking about citizenship (Sassen 2002).

It is thus argued that cities occupy a place of recent, resurgent importance. Cities are 'key geographical sites' for the playing out of neo-liberal policies and programmes (Kern 2010: 7). The new modes of neo-liberal governance, outlined in the previous section, bear directly and powerfully on the shape of large cities. As cities reach for global city status, physical arrangements of public and private space, and notions of citizen and citizenship are enlisted in this goal (Kern 2010). The city is a physical manifestation of the social relations and norms that reflect and sustain this extension.

By way of illustration of this point, Leslie Kern, in a study of condominium development in Toronto, sees urban development in the cities of Western democracies as an important force in the neo-liberal reconstitution of urban citizenship and in the counter-struggles for social justice in the city. She argues, more specifically, that the marketing of condominiums to women, with its combination of urban space construction and consumerism, has reconfigured gendered urban citizenship in non-liberatory patterns. Women are enticed by the image of consumer agency into patterns of consumption that betray and sideline effective political agency (Kern 2010).

Most relevant, perhaps, to this discussion is the claim that cities provide concentrated illustration of inequalities and of citizens' responses to injustices as everyday practices of power (Sassen 2002). The destabilization of categories and identities of citizens catalysed by recent changes plays out most pointedly in cities. Cities are 'strategic terrain' (Sassen 2002: 19) for the conflicts, contradictions and openings of global capitalism, new transportation and telecommunication technologies, and the fracturing and multiplying of identity. As such, theorists also see the development of new progressive citizenship practices in the spaces of cities. Cities locate institutional innovation and creative individual and group agency (Sassen 2002). New political actors emerge (Sassen 2002), with fresh public practices. Cities thus are important spaces of inclusion and exclusion, of centrality and marginalization (Kern 2010: 7).

For the purposes of this chapter, discussion of this locality is useful for two other specific reasons. First, this focus is important because it allows a notion of spatiality to infuse the discussion: '[t]he struggles and practices of citizenship are powerfully shaped and conditioned by spatial relationships and the geography of the city' (Staeheli 2003: 99). Theorists argue that a positively radicalized citizenship for women – and other marginalized groups – must necessarily engage with the spacialization of politics and inequality in our built environments. Thus, feminist social geographers have contributed immensely to discussions of women and citizenship, arguing convincingly that citizenship is formed and experienced through engagements with particular social spaces (Desforges et al. 2005: 440, Klodawsky 2009: 594). Exciting discussions of the connection between citizenship and place, of citizenship and lived context, animate feminist literature in this area. Analysis looks at how gendered social relations are 'inscribed in, and shaped by, the built environment' and the effects of citizenship regimes 'traced through everyday life and the ways that people construct their identities in relation to the city' (Kern 2010: 5). The underlying precept is that commitments to social equity must engage with both a political and a physical landscape (Zukin 1991). For example, a Canadian study of single mothers on welfare in the city of Vancouver charts a very different physical reality of city spaces for these women (Gurstein and Vilches 2010). The shaping of urban opportunities affects how single mothers experience their membership in the urban community. These urban planner authors use the ideal of the just city to argue for more politically sensitive urban structures and opportunities to meet the distinctive needs of this group of marginalized people.

Second, a focus on cities emphasizes the immediate everyday environment in which citizenship is experienced. Urban citizenship reveals localized sets of social relations and practices core to our daily experiences. Here, for some feminist theorists, the focus is on the 'ordinary', a concept that encompasses both social and legal orders, and the standard, routine or average (Staeheli et al. 2012: 630). Urban citizen literature thus looks to the prosaic, not extraordinary, instances and experiences of citizenship: the 'humdrum' of daily life containing the unfolding of 'acts of citizenship' (Isin and Turner 2007: 16). Cities are 'a strategic arena for the development of citizenship because they engage the tumult of citizenship through the concentration of difference and the availability of public space' (Kern 2010: 11). Thus, how cities contemplate, order and recognize diversity in their built environments ground and make concrete, and pragmatic, more abstract discussions of the politics of difference.

Survival tactics at the level of the household, for example, provide insight into how everyday activities shape citizenship, particularly of women. Feminist discussions of provisioning illustrate a variant of such civic citizenship activity. Collins et al. argue that, as public services have shrunk, women's provisioning work has occupied the spaces that are left, constituting a key facet of women's lived citizenship and women's challenge to market citizenship. Understanding provisioning as 'the work of securing resources and providing the necessities of life to those for whom one has relationships of responsibility', these researchers detail Canadian women's low-income community group activities in a number of urban centres (Collins et al. 2011). The researchers observe that the collective activities of this marginalized citizenry, in both Canada and implicitly at least in other liberal democracies, 'keep alive feminist struggles in the face of the neo-liberal political and economic challenges of the twenty-first century' (Collins et al. 2011: 298). These activities are, it is claimed, an act of 'reclaiming, recasting and rethinking social citizenship' given the effacement of the social by neo-liberalism (Collins et al. 2011: 304). Women's agency exercised in traditional ways in fact constitutes important civic community maintenance and demonstrates how urban community and activism allow women to constitute themselves as active, not passive, and full, not partial, citizens in their everyday environments. 'In these strategies and in the routinized interactions that shape social relations and feelings of belonging, the spaces of the city are centrally important' (Staeheli 2003: 99). Small actions hold the potential to 'nudge' into place significant change in patterns of control and authority (Staeheli et al. 2012: 630).

This discussion of citizenship in the city brings together a challenging range of multidisciplinary feminist thought about citizenship. Cities have been revitalized as centres of struggle for a wide range of social justice groups and projects. Neo-liberalism has meant decentralization, downgrading and downloading of those aspects of citizenship fought for by feminists since Marshall first articulated his more limited notion of social citizenship. For many, the most meaningful acts of citizenship now occupy the spaces of the city: women's, and others', experiences of inclusion or exclusion take place in and reflect the constitution of the city. Thus, the turn to the social and physical geography of the environments in which so many of us in developed nations live, thickens consideration of the realization, expression and meaningfulness of feminist deployment of notions of citizenship.

## Conclusion

A journey through feminist thought on questions of citizenship is necessarily a tour of major aspects of feminist theory generally. A renewed interest in questions of citizenship, as a way to capture both concerns about and optimism for community in the twenty-first century, is marked in both feminist and in other ranges of critical thought. This chapter has been motivated by, first, a desire to link conversations about citizenship to important established moments of feminist thinking and, second, by interest in enlisting notions of space and the local to chart new opportunities for conceptualizing social justice engagement. Struggles over citizenship by marginalized groups can be ordinary and extraordinary. A focus on local agency importantly allows the large and dramatic instances of resistance not to overshadow the incremental and ordinary acts of creative agency that persistently erode and re-contour understandings – rhetorical, material, legal and conceptual – of women's citizenship.

## References

Affolder, N. 2009. The private life of environmental treaties. *American Journal of International Law*, 103, 510–525.

Anthias, F. and Yuval-Davis, N. (eds), 1989. *Women-Nation-State*. London: Macmillan.

Berlant, L.B. 2002. *The Queen of America Goes to Washington City: Essays on Sex and Citizenship*. Durham: Duke University Press.

Bosco, F.J., Aiken, S.C. and Herman, T. 2011. Women and children in a neighborhood advocacy group: Engaging community and refashioning citizenship at the United States–Mexico border. *Gender, Place and Culture: A Journal of Feminist Geography*, 12(2), 155–178.

Bosniak, L. 2000. Citizenship denationalized. *Indiana Journal of Global Legal Studies*, 7(2), 447–509.

Brodie, J. 2008a. Putting gender back in: Women and social policy reform in Canada, in *Gendering the Nation State: Canadian and Comparative Perspectives*, edited by Y. Abu–Laban. Vancouver: UBC Press, 165–184.

Brodie, J. 2008b. We are all equal now: Contemporary gender politics in Canada. *Feminist Theory*, 9(2), 145–164.

Brodie, J. 2009. Reforming social justice in neoliberal times. *Studies in Social Justice*, 1(2), 93–105.

Brodie, J. 2010. Globalization Canadian family policy, and the omissions of neoliberalism. *North Carolina Law Review*, 88(5), 1560–1592.

Clarke, John (2008). Living with/in and without neo-liberalism. *Focaal*, 51, 135–147.

Collins, S.B., Reitsma-Street M., Porter E. and Neysmith, S. 2011. Women's community work challenges market citizenship. *Community Development*, 42(3), 297–331.

Cossman, B. 2007. *Sexual Citizens: the Legal and Cultural Relations of Sex and Belonging*. Stanford: Stanford University Press.

Desforges, L., Rhys, J. and Woods, M. 2005. New geographies of citizenship. *Citizenship Studies*, 9(5), 439–451.

Dobrowolsky, A. 2008. Interrogating 'Invisibilization' and 'Instrumentalization': Women and current citizenship trends in Canada. *Citizenship Studies*, 12(5), 465–479.

Fainstein, S.S. 2010. *The Just City*. Ithica: Cornell University.

Fraser, N. 2000. Rethinking recognition. *New Left Review*, 3, 107–120.

Fraser N. 2003, Social justice in the age of identity politics: Redistribution, recognition, and Participation, in Redistribution or Recognition? *A Political-Philosophical Exchange*, edited by N. Fraser and A. Honneth. London: Verso.

Fraser, N. and Gordon, L. 1994. A genealogy of dependency: Tracing a keyword of the US welfare state. *Signs*, 19(2), 309–336.

Friedman, M. 2005. *Women and Citizenship*. Oxford: Oxford University Press.

Gurstein, P. and Vilches, S. 2010. The just city for whom? Re-conceiving active citizenship for lone mothers in Canada. *Gender, Place and Culture: A Journal of Feminist Geography*, 17(4), 421–436.

Howard, C. 2007. Introducing individualization, in *Contested Individualization: Debates about Contemporary Personhood*, edited by C. Howard. New York: Palgrave Macmillan.

Hoffman, J. 2007. *Citizenship Beyond the State*. London: Sage.

Isin, E. 2005. Engaging, being, political. *Political Geography*, 24(3), 373–387.

Isin, E. and Turner, B.S. 2007. Investigating citizenship: An agenda for citizenship studies. *Citizenship Studies*, 11(1), 5–17.

Jaggar, A. 2005. Arenas of citizenship: Civil society, the state, and the global order. *International Feminist Journal of Politics*, 7(1), 3–25.

Jensen, J. 2008. Citizenship in the era of new social risks: What happened to gender inequalities?, in *Gendering the Nation-State: Canadian and Comparative Perspectives*, edited by Y. Abu-Laban. Vancouver: University of British Columbia Press, 185–202.

Jenson, J. and Phillips, S. 2001. Redesigning the Canadian citizenship regime: Remaking the institutions of representation, in *Citizenship, Markets, and the State*, edited by C. Crouch, K. Eder and D. Tambini. Oxford: Oxford University Press, 69–89.

Jones, K. 1990. Citizenship in a women-friendly polity. *Signs*, 15(4), 781–812.

Kern, L. 2010. *Sex and the Revitalized City: Gender, Condominium Development, and Urban Citizenship*. Vancouver: UBC Press.

Klodawsky, F. 2009. Home spaces and rights to the city: Thinking social justice for chronically homeless women. *Urban Geography*, 30(6), 591–610.

Laclau, E. and Mouffe, C. 2001. *Hegemony and Socialist Strategy: Towards a Radial Democratic Politics*. 2nd edn. London: Verso, 2001.

Lessard, H. 2010. Substantive universality: Reconceptualizing feminist approaches to social provision and child care, in *The Legal Tender of Gender: Law Welfare and the Regulation of Women's Poverty*, edited by S. Gavigan and D. Chunn. Oxford: Hart Publishing, 217–248.

Lister, R. 1995. Dilemmas in engendering citizenship. *Economy and Society*, 24(1), 1–40.

Lister, R. 1997. *Citizenship: Feminist Perspectives*. London: Macmillan Press Ltd.

Lister, R. 2007. Inclusive citizenship: Realizing the potential. *Citizenship Studies*, 11(1), 49–61.

Longo, P. 2001. Revisiting the equality/difference debate: Redefining citizenship for the new millennium. *Citizenship Studies*, 5(3), 269–283.

Marshall, T.H. 1950. Citizenship and Social Class. Cambridge: Cambridge University Press.

McIntyre, S. 1993. Backlash Against Equality: The "Tyranny" of the "Politically Correct". *McGill Law Journal*, 38(1), 1–63.

McRobbie, A. 2012. Top girls?: Young women and the post-feminist sexual contract. *Cultural Studies*, 21(4), 718–737.

Minow, M. 1990. *Making All the Difference: Inclusion, Exclusion, and American Law*. Ithaca: Cornell University Press.

Mitchell, D. 2003. *The Right to the City: Social Justice and the Fight for Public Space*. New York: The Guilford Press.

Moosa-Mitha, M. 2005. A Difference-Centred Alternative to Theorization of Children's Citizenship Rights. *Citizenship Studies*, 9(4), 369–388.

Mouffe, C. 1992a. Feminism, citizenship and radical democratic politics, in *Feminists Theorize the Political*, edited by J. Butler and J.W. Scott. London and New York: Routledge, 369–384.

Pateman, C. 1986. Introduction: the theoretical subversiveness of feminism, in *Feminist Challenges: Social and Political Theory*, edited by C. Pateman and E. Gross. Sydney: Allen and Unwin, 1–10.

Pateman, C. 1988. *The Sexual Contract*. Cambridge: Polity Press.

Pateman, C. 1989. *The Disorder of Women*. Cambridge: Polity Press.

Pateman, C. 1998. Contributing to Democracy. *Review of Constitutional Studies*, 4(2), 191–212.

Plummer, K. 2001. The Square of Intimate Citizenship: Some Preliminary Proposals. *Citizenship Studies*, 5(3), 237–253.

Prokhovnik, R. 1998. Public and private citizenship: From gender invisibility to feminist inclusiveness. *Feminist Review*, 60, 84–104.

Richardson, D. 1998. Sexuality and Citizenship. *Sociology*, 32(1), 83–100.

Richardson, D. 2000. Claiming citizenship? Sexuality, citizenship and Lesbian/Feminist theory. *Sexualities*, 3(2), 255–272.

Robson, R. and Kessler, T. 2008. Unsettling sexual citizenship. *McGill Law Journal*, 53, 535–571.

Sassen, S. 2002. The repositioning of citizenship: Emergent subjects and spaces for politics. *Berkeley Journal of Sociology*, 46, 4–26.

Sassen, S. 2010. The City: Its Return as a Lens for Social Theory. *City, Culture and Society*, 1(1), 3–11.

Sommerlad, H. 2004. Some reflections on the relationship between citizenship, access to justice, and the reform of legal aid. *Journal of Law and Society*, 31(3), 345–368.

Song, S. 2011. Rethinking Citizenship through Alienage and Birthright Privilege: Bosniak and Shachar's Critiques of Liberal Citizenship. *Issues in Legal Scholarship*, 9(1), Article 6.

Staeheli, L.A. 2003. Introduction: Cities and citizenship. *Urban Geography*, 24(2), 97–102.

Staeheli, L.A. and Clarke S.E. 2003. The new politics of citizenship: Structuring participation by household, work, and identity. *Urban Geography*, 24(2), 103–126.

Staeheli, L.A., Ehrkamp, P., Leitner, H. and Nagel, C.R. 2012. Dreaming the ordinary: Daily life and the complex geographies of citizenship. *Progress in Human Geography*, 36(5), 628–644.

Stasiulis, D. and Bakan, A. 1997. Negotiating Citizenship: The Case of Foreign Domestic Workers in Canada. *Feminist Review*, 57, 112–139.

Thornton, M. 1997. The judicial gender of citizenship: A look at property interests during marriage. *Journal of Law and Society*, 24(4), 486–583.

Vogel, U. 1991. Is citizenship gender-specific?, in *The Frontiers of Citizenship*, edited by U. Vogel and Michael Moran. London: Macmillan, 58–85.

Volpp, L. 2007. The culture of citizenship. *Theoretical Inquiries in Law*, 8(2), 571–602.

Volpp, L. 2011. Denaturalizing citizenship: An introduction. *Issues in Legal Scholarship,* 9(1), 1–6.

Walby, S. 1994. Is citizenship gendered? *Sociology*, 28(2), 379–395.

Young, I.M. 2000. *Inclusion and Democracy*. Oxford: Oxford University Press.

Young, I.M. 1989. Polity and group difference: A critique of the ideal of universal citizenship. *Ethics*, 99(2), 250–274.

Young, M. 2010a. Unequal to the task: 'Kapp'ing the substantive potential of section 15'. *Supreme Court Law Review*. 2nd edn. 50, 183–219.

Young, M. 2010b. Women's work and a guaranteed income, in *The Legal Tender of Gender: Law, Welfare, and the Regulation of Women* edited by S. Gavigan and D. Chunn. Oxford: Hart Publishing, 249–276.

Yuval-Davis, N. 1991. The citizenship debate: Women, ethnic processes and the state. *Feminist Review*, 39(1), 58–68.

Yuval-Davis, N. 1997. Women, Citizenship and Difference. *Feminist Review*, 57, 4–27.

Yuval-Davis, N. 2006. Belonging and the politics of belonging. *Patterns of Prejudice*, 40(3), 187–198.

Yuval-Davis, N. 2011. *The Politics of Belonging: Intersectional Contestations*. London: SAGE Publications Ltd.

Zukin, S. 1991. *Landscapes of Power: From Detroit to Disney World*. Berkeley: University of California Press.

# International Human Rights Law:
# Towards Rethinking Sex/Gender Dualism

## Dianne Otto[1]

A growing number of accounts of the history of feminist engagement with international human rights law celebrate its victories while also endeavouring to shed light on its limited emancipatory effects (Gaer 1998, Fraser 1999, Engle 2005a). Previously, I have crafted one such history that examines the female subjectivities produced by this engagement with law, highlighting its propensity to reproduce, through a variety of imperial techniques and historical residues, conceptions of women that fail to constitute them as fully human (Otto 2006: 318). As revealed by this genealogy, one recurring problem is the resort to 'protective' responses to women in international human rights law's texts and practices, which assume women's vulnerability and dependency and therefore women's need for 'special protections', despite the commitment to equality. In turn, the interdependence of the male/female gender binary empowers and privileges corresponding male subjectivities which are constituted as fully human, which includes the expectation that they provide protection for women. The result is the continued naturalization of gender identities that normalize women's secondary status and men's power and authority. The representation of women as always lacking would seem to confirm Luce Irigaray's argument that women are 'unrepresentable' in masculinist discourses of identity (Irigaray 1985), although I am not prepared to reach this conclusion just yet. Instead, the conclusion that I draw from my historical account is that the feminist project in international law has 'barely begun' (Otto 2006: 356). I urge the need to reimagine sex/gender as multiple and shifting, rather than dualistic and always already asymmetrical, if we are ever to disrupt the persistent reiteration of protective stereotypes of women in the international legal lexicon.

In this chapter, I want to take up the challenge of re-imagination. In developing my argument, I am greatly indebted to Darren Rosenblum whose critique of the asymmetrical focus on women of the Convention on the Elimination of All Forms of Discrimination Against Women (CEDAW) has enriched my thinking about this issue (Rosenblum 2011). I am also grateful to Janet Halley for her useful schematization of 'sexual subordination feminism', which has been particularly influential in international law in recent years, as embracing the following characteristics: a commitment to treating gender as dualistic (m/f), which always works asymmetrically to women's disadvantage (m>f), and therefore necessitates that feminism 'carries a brief for f' (Halley 2006: 17–18). While Halley's analysis leads her

---

1    Professor of Law, Melbourne Law School, The University of Melbourne, Australia. Thanks to Margaret Davies, Vanessa Munro and Darren Rosenblum for their helpful feedback on earlier drafts.

to suggest that feminists need to 'take a break' from feminism, in order to 'see' what their analysis excludes, I think that she does not do justice to the diversity of feminist thought. This chapter provides, I hope, an example of rethinking gender dualism and asymmetry from within feminism, without taking a break. In my discussion, I use the terminology of 'sex/gender' because I want to reject the idea that either of these categories might be natural and thus immutable (Davies 1997), which is not a new insight, but one which remains deeply unacceptable to conservative thinkers, as well as to some feminists. As Simone de Beauvoir observed in her pioneering work on women's oppression, 'one is not born a woman, but, rather, becomes one' (de Beauvoir 1974: 295). Judith Butler has developed this idea, arguing that biological sex, like gender, is a performative category; that the 'naturalness' of bodies as well as of sex/gender is the effect of social expressions (performances) of gender which are restricted to a limited frame of possibilities by prevailing conceptions of gender normativity (Butler 1990: 24–25). To accept the idea of a sex–gender distinction that is reflective of a nature–nurture divide, as in the contemporary United Nations (UN) definitions (Secretary-General UN 1998), is to think of the body as already fixed by biology which is then interpreted culturally. Yet if we understand that bodies are also socially produced, the colonizing effects of the idea that there are inherent biological certainties can be resisted and the manifold creative possibilities for the expression of gender identity, desire and sexuality can surface.

I begin by retelling my earlier genealogy of feminist engagement with international human rights law, this time focusing on the story of the dualistic representations of sex/gender and the field's asymmetrical commitment to 'women's rights', showing how these tropes are implicated in the persistence of protective representations of women. This retelling also illustrates the exclusionary effects of gender dualism and asymmetry; how they silence gendered discrimination and human rights abuses suffered by men and others, whose gender expressions and identities fall outside the gender binary (m/f) system, such as intersex and transgendered people, gender transients, multi-gendered people, androgynes, butch lesbians, transvestites and others who may identify as an 'in-between' or third sex (Monro 2007: 125). Yet, as I argue, there are also opportunities, already present in the law, to challenge these exclusions by refusing both dualism and assumed asymmetry.

I then examine efforts over the last two decades, by feminists and others, to reimagine sex/gender as a fully social category in the context of international human rights law. These efforts draw to some extent on the existing opportunities to challenge the entrenchment of naturalized and exclusionary technologies of sex/gender, but they also reflect a curious reluctance to fully exploit those opportunities by challenging the understanding of gender as dichotomous. I focus on two developments: the adoption of the language of 'gender' to supplement the biological language of 'sex' and the implementation of 'gender mainstreaming' by the human rights treaty bodies. These developments, despite their cautiousness and mixed results (see, for example, Charlesworth 2005, Kouvo 2004), show that embracing sex/gender as a fully social category does not mean forsaking feminism's long-standing commitment to addressing women's disadvantage, as many feminists fear. On the contrary, I argue that they demonstrate that reframing sex/gender as multiple and shifting is necessary to strengthen the feminist project in law, because it offers the means to eliminate the relentless reproduction of protective representations of women and their associated privileged masculinities.

In expressing concern about gender dualism and asymmetry, I am not denying their usefulness in describing and explaining many everyday realities. However, the question that weighs increasingly heavily for me is whether accepting them as given, and thus carrying a brief only for women, provide the best means to pursue the emancipatory possibilities that are opened up by the recognition that gender is entirely a social category. One problem is that a relentlessly dualistic understanding of gender is so easily recolonized by naturalized accounts of biological sex. A second is that the asymmetrical reproduction of injured and vulnerable representations of women, which not only cast men as their protectors, but also as inevitable perpetrators, normalizes sex/gender hierarchies and protective representations of women. A third problem is that understanding sex/gender as operating dualistically and asymmetrically prevents an understanding of the diverse ways that sex/gender operates as a technology of power.

## A Brief Historical Backdrop to Sex/Gender Dualism and Asymmetry in International Human Rights Law

At least until the advent of international human rights law in 1945, sex/gender in international law was understood as m/f dichotomy, and the privileged status of men *vis-à-vis* women was considered natural. Women were invariably produced by international law as the dependents, property or extensions of men and therefore in need of legal 'protection' rather than legal 'rights'. Like colonized peoples, women were considered, by nature, incapable of full autonomy and agency. Thus, women were denied full legal personality and brought into being as the objects of international law, rather than as its subjects. For example, international humanitarian law implicitly affirmed women's dependent status by providing for the protection of '[men's] family honor and rights' during armed conflict and foreign occupation (CRLCW Article 46 1899, 1907).[2] Further, early treaties prohibiting trafficking in women for the purposes of prostitution denied women the capacity to 'consent' to sex work (IASWT 1904, ICSWST 1910, 1912, ICSTWC 1921, CSTWFA 1933) and international labour law banned women's employment in certain occupations that were deemed to be too dangerous for women or too disruptive of their domestic responsibilities (see, for example, ILO MPC Convention 3 1919, ILO CCNWWEI Convention 4 1919, ILO CCEWUWMK Convention 45 1935). In contradistinction to these stereotypes of women as vulnerable and familial by nature, men were produced as their protectors, supporters and saviours; as breadwinners and household heads in private life and as leaders, thinkers, workers, soldiers and everything else of value in the public sphere. This hierarchical scheme of dualistic sex/gender took women's inferiority to men as a given, and legitimated treating them protectively, rather than as bearers of rights.

During the era of the League of Nations, feminist engagement with international law gradually moved away from supporting protectionism, which was resisted by some feminists who defended protection as a form of affirmative action (Lake 2001: 254, 257). The shift refocused attention to contesting the denial of full legal capacity and subjectivity to women – questioning sex/gender as hierarchy, but not as duality. While a number of feminists continued to support the adoption of protective labour standards and anti-trafficking treaties, others were arguing instead for women's equality and rights (Gaer 1998: 5, Connors 1996: 147, 149). By 1935, the rights lobby was in ascendance and the League's 16th General Assembly considered a proposal to promulgate a convention that would

---

2    A list of Conventions, Declarations and Covenants appears below.

promote women's civil, legal and political equality with men (Galey 1995: 1, 7, Lake: 2001 259).[3] While the impending Second World War eventually halted what would have signified a momentous shift in thinking, away from protectionism to affirming women's equality and rights, the groundwork for the system's asymmetrical understanding of sex/gender inequality as negatively affecting only women had been laid, informed by the immediate need to challenge the gender hierarchy that was firmly instantiated in the law.

With the adoption of the Charter of the United Nations (UN Charter) in 1945, the anticipated new body of universal human rights law promised a transformation of the protective and colonial traditions that had preceded it. The Charter's prohibition of 'sex' discrimination (Article 1(3)) rather than discrimination against women, opened the possibility that gender asymmetry would not be automatically presumed. With Eleanor Roosevelt at its helm, a working group of the UN Commission on Human Rights (CHR) began drafting the Universal Declaration of Human Rights (UDHR) in 1947, which was to give content to the Charter's sketchy references to human rights and fundamental freedoms. However, the issue of how 'sex' discrimination would be approached had already arisen in the CHR, with women's rights advocates arguing for a specialized institution focused on improving the status of women, while others took the view that this would itself be discriminatory and reinforce the marginalization of women's questions (Fraser 1999: 887). Roosevelt initially supported the latter position, but she was eventually persuaded to the former (887). This led to the UN Economic and Social Council (ECOSOC) establishing the Sub-Commission on the Status of Women in 1946, which was elevated in 1947 to a free-standing Commission on the Status of Women (CSW) (Galey 1995: 8). The Danish Chair of the Sub-Commission, Bodil Begtrup, defended the importance of an upgraded women's body on the grounds that combining women's rights with those of men was 'unrealistic and academic' and that the distinctiveness of women's concerns needed to be studied separately (8). In line with this thinking, the CSW was given the brief to promote women's rights in all fields of human endeavour (Fraser 1999: 888). So by 1947, the asymmetrical approach to sex discrimination was already firmly cemented into the UN's institutional framework, justified, not without foundation, on the ground that women's specific disadvantage would be ignored or misunderstood by 'universal' human rights institutions.

One of the first tasks of the CSW was to participate in Roosevelt's working group, which was drafting the UDHR. Members pursued the CSW's asymmetrical brief, arguing for explicit reference to issues that were primarily or solely of importance to women, but within the framework of women's equality with men rather than as protective measures (Morsink 1999. For more critical analyses see Helen Bequaert Holmes 1983, Charlesworth 1998). Adding to her earlier justifications for separate treatment of women's rights, Begtrup explained that because 'sex equality was a right which had been acquired but recently, it would be necessary to emphasize it explicitly in certain Articles' (Fraser 1999: 888). The asymmetrical approach was again contested, this time by the majority of the working group, including Roosevelt who, despite her capitulation to the establishment of the CSW, felt that the general prohibition of discrimination based on sex (article 2) was sufficient to ensure women's equal enjoyment of universal human rights (Morsink 1991: 231–232). She feared that making reference to rights that were specific to women would weaken the position of women by undercutting the meaning of 'everyone' and introduce rights that were not

---

3    The states responsible for presenting the proposal were Argentina, Bolivia, Cuba, Dominican Republic, Haiti, Honduras, Mexico, Panama, Peru and Uruguay.

'universal' in nature (Lake 2001: 265). In hindsight, Roosevelt's concerns proved to be well-founded, as the institutions devoted to women's issues were quickly marginalized and the idea that women needed to enjoy specific human rights opened a space for protectionism to re-emerge.

Ultimately, the UDHR declared everyone to be entitled to the enjoyment of universal human rights and fundamental freedoms 'without distinction of any kind', including on the basis of 'sex' (UDHR Article 2). Like the UN Charter, this did not confine sex/gender discrimination to a particular 'sexed' group. Yet the asymmetrical influence of the CSW lobby is also apparent in the UDHR, which reiterates the principle of equality in the context of suffrage (Article 21) and marriage (Article 16(1)). Unfortunately, new footholds for protectionism also emerged with the granting of 'special care and assistance' (not parental rights) to mothers with young children (Article 25(2) and the recognition of rights to 'privacy', to 'just and favourable [workplace] remuneration' and to an 'adequate' standard of living, as held by men on behalf of their families (Articles 12, 23(3) and 25(1)). Following the lead of the UDHR, the International Covenant on Economic, Social and Cultural Rights (ICESCR) and the International Covenant on Civil and Political Rights (ICCPR), adopted in 1966, both rely on the general prohibition of 'sex' discrimination to ensure that men and women equally enjoy the rights they enumerate (ICESCR Article 2(2), ICCPR Article 2(1)), while also treating women protectively in the context of parenting (ICESCR Article 10(2)) and the 'natural' (presumed heterosexual) family (ICCPR Article 17(1) and 23(1), ICESCR Articles 7(a)(ii), 10(1) and 11(1)). Similarly, the International Convention for the Suppression of the Traffic in Women and Children, adopted in 1947, did nothing to alter the protective assumptions of the earlier anti–trafficking instruments (Kaufman Hevener 1978: 138–139), and the International Labor Organization re-endorsed the protective treatment of women in the paid workforce when it revised and updated its earlier conventions banning them from night work and underground work in mines in 1948 (136–137). How are we to understand the persistence of protective representations of women, and the biological certainties they rely upon, in the new era of universal human rights and rights-based feminism? It is surely pertinent to consider whether they are fuelled by dualistic conceptions of sex/gender and by feminists carrying a brief only for women.

Alongside these general developments, the CSW promulgated conventions promoting women's (formal) equality with respect to political and nationality rights (CPRW 1953, 1954, CNMW 1957, 1958, DeBehnke 1998: 181–182),[4] and prepared the first comprehensive international enumeration of women's rights, the 1967 General Assembly Declaration on the Elimination of Discrimination against Women (DEDAW). Yet once it became apparent that this work was having little impact on eliminating discrimination against women in practice, the solution was seen to be the development of more robust asymmetry by drafting a new convention that would promote women's substantive equality. Again, there were voices arguing for symmetry, proposing that the new convention should be called the 'Convention on the Promotion of Equality between Men and Women' and, further, that consideration should be given to renaming the CSW as the 'Promotion of Equality of Men and Women

---

4    Despite the formal affirmation of equality in the convention on women's political rights, a memorandum of the Secretary General still treated the granting of political rights to women as a grant of privilege or protection: see DeBehnke 1998.

Branch' (Rosenblum 2011: 23–24)[5] but again these views did not prevail. The CEDAW, adopted in 1979 and entering into force two years later, is concerned solely with addressing discrimination against 'women'. Although CEDAW was modelled on the *Convention on the Elimination of All Forms of Racial Discrimination* (CERD) (Reanda 1992: 267, 286, Burrows 1986: 86–88), which prohibits all forms of discrimination that fall under the umbrella of 'race', it focuses on eliminating discrimination suffered by only one sexed identity group (women), as Rosenblum observes (2011: 47–48). Reference is made to men, but mostly as the comparator against which women's (in)equality is to be measured. Men are also implicitly implicated as the putative discriminators, reinforcing traditional stereotypes of both women and men. Although it is hard to fathom in retrospect, even the drafters of CEDAW were unable to completely discard protectionism. In the field of employment, CEDAW requires states parties to provide 'special protection' for pregnant women in the workplace from types of work that may be harmful to them (Article 11(2)(d)), allowing for revision only in light of scientific knowledge (Article 11(3), which doubly removes the decision to undertake such work from women themselves. The treatment of women's reproductive rights is also protective, couched in terms of marriage and decision-making that is shared equally and 'responsibly' between spouses (Article 16(1)(e)), rather than as an individual human right. The survival of protectionism in CEDAW, in the heartland of international human rights law, demonstrates its alarming tenacity. It suggests that asymmetrical thinking is highly susceptible to capture by protective accounts of women's capacities, and colonization by the naturalized explanations for women's inequality (and men's superiority) that are nurtured by such accounts.

During the early 1990s, another rethinking of feminist engagement with international human rights law fostered a renewed emphasis on asymmetry by focusing on the neglected problem of violence against women (Bunch 1990). A global campaign successfully mobilized many local, regional and international NGOs, and prompted states to support the development of specialized instruments, including a General Assembly Declaration on the Elimination of Violence Against Women (DEVAW) in 1993 and three regional treaties, two of which focus solely on addressing violence against women (IACPPEVAW 1994, PACHPRRWA 2003, CECPCVAW 2011). Particular urgency was devoted to addressing sexual violence, which led to significant developments in international criminal law and in policies applying to post-conflict peace support operations, as well as in human rights law. As a result, the law has moved away from treating rape during armed conflict as an infringement of family honour (Askin 2003, Bedont and Hall-Martinez 1999), and sexual exploitation and abuse perpetrated by military and humanitarian actors involved in UN peacekeeping missions is no longer ignored (Secretary-General 2003). The human rights treaty bodies have also all taken steps to ensure that their treaty texts are interpreted so as to recognize violence against women as a human rights violation, following the lead of the CEDAW Committee by interpreting violence against women as a form of discrimination against women (CEDAWC 1992).

However, the increased focus on women as the victims of violence also led to a resurgence of protective representations in international law, confirming for me just how deeply problematic the assumptions of gender duality and asymmetry are. In international human rights law, women were increasingly defined primarily by their vulnerability

---

5    Quoting from ECOSOC, CSW, Report on the Twenty-Fifth Session, 267 UN Doc E/5451 (Supplement No. 4), 25 January 1974.

to men's violence (Scully 2009). In the context of armed conflict and its aftermath, sexual violence came to be represented as 'the worst' harm that can happen to women, even worse than death, newly justifying protective responses that deny women's (sexual) agency and autonomy (Miller 2004, Engle 2005b, Halley 2008, Otto 2007). Particularly pernicious has been the revival of protective stereotypes of women outside the west who are again, or still, at risk of being understood through a neo-imperial frame as 'thoroughly disempowered and helpless' and in need of rescue from their 'uncivilized' cultures, as Ratna Kapur has argued (2002: 10–18). It is these developments, among others, that led Halley to suggest the need for taking a break from feminism in order to understand why so many feminist undertakings in international law are rapidly losing ground, even as many are celebrating their apparent success.

Yet at the same time, and without taking a break, feminists have also promoted a number of other developments that have facilitated a new questioning of international human rights law's assumption of m/f dualism and m>f asymmetry, and the expectation that feminists will only ever carry a brief for women. Two of these developments are the use of the language of 'gender' and the adoption of the strategy of 'gender mainstreaming'. While feminists have generally supported these developments, there has also been some reluctance to pursue all the possibilities for rethinking sex/gender that they create for fear that this will undermine the feminist project (Loenen 1994). Some of these fears echo Begtrup's concern in the 1940s that the distinctiveness of human rights violations experienced by women will be lost and men's concerns will again dominate, unless women's issues are given separate treatment (Esperanza Hernandez-Truyol 2011). Other fears include the loss of the category of 'women' as an organizing focus (Esperanza Hernandez-Truyol 2011, Persram 1994) and the loss of 'credibility' if feminist demands expand to include those 'less respectable' others whose gender expression falls outside the m/f dualism (Miller 2004: 36–39). I will now turn to exploring these two developments in order to highlight some of the new opportunities for change they open and, in the process, challenge this feminist trepidation and dispute Halley's view that it is necessary to 'take a break' for this challenge to be effective.

## The Possibilities Opened by the Language of 'Gender'

With the admission of the language of 'gender' into international law in 1995, at the Fourth World Conference on Women in Beijing, a distinction between 'sex' (nature) and 'gender' (nurture) was formally accepted by states (Otto 1996). This acceptance was unquestionably a victory for feminist engagement with international law, as confirmed by the ferocious resistance staged by many Catholic and Islamic states, the Holy See, and fundamentalist religious NGOs, who feared (correctly) that the use of the language of gender would threaten the sanctified status of the 'natural family' and legitimate a host of 'unnatural' practices like homosexuality, lesbianism, bisexuality and trans-genderism (Buss 2004: 269). For feminists at the time, the importance of this shift was captured in a statement prepared by a group of women's NGOs in Beijing:

> We will not be forced back into the "biology is destiny" concept that seeks to define, confine and reduce women and girls to their physical sexual characteristics … The meaning of the word "gender" has evolved as differentiated from the word "sex" to

*express the reality that women's and men's roles and status are socially constructed and subject to change. (Women's Net, 1995)*

Looking back, it is easy to see that the feminist enthusiasm for this change was limited to the rejection of biology as solely determinative of women's and men's opportunities in life. Feminists were still prepared to accept that biology ('sex') provided the foundation for social conceptions of masculinity and femininity and that gender was a dualistic construction. This partial embrace of the emancipatory potential of the terminological change also meant that feminists did not challenge the homophobia and trans-phobia that was expressed by many of those antagonistic to the use of the term gender, who were clearly alert to its manifold possibilities. A lesbian NGO caucus was active in Beijing, campaigning (unsuccessfully as it turned out) to retain the four references to 'sexual orientation' in the draft Platform for Action (Otto 1995: 289). This caucus operated separately from the caucus that was promoting women's human rights, despite a significant overlap in membership of the two groups, including myself. As I recall, the rationale for the separation was the fear that association with lesbian rights might undermine support for women's rights. This rationale was not unique to the context of Beijing, but repeated a long-standing unwillingness of many feminists to promote rights associated with women's (homo)sexual freedom and autonomy, fearing that this would threaten the fragile 'respectability' of those promoting women's rights and thus limit their effectiveness (Rothschild 2000). For some, no doubt, this rationale was also driven by shame and homophobia. As a strategic response to the 'lesbian-baiting' that was in full evidence in Beijing, and is so often used by conservative organizations and states to impugn women's rights advocates as 'deviants' (Rothschild 2000: 13), some of the feminist reluctance to respond directly to the fear-mongering of the Vatican and others can perhaps be understood. But it backed them into a corner of silence and even denial of the potential of the language of gender to release everyone from the confines of sex/gender dualism and presumed heterosexuality (Case 2011).

The adoption of the language of gender in Beijing led to the promulgation of UN institutional definitions, which draw the same distinction between 'sex' (biology) and 'gender' (social) as the NGOs, and also treat gender as a dualism (see, for example, Secretary-General 1998). By anchoring social constructions of gender in a biological base, these definitions have continued to bolster those who insist that dualistic m/f is the 'natural' order. Feminist disagreement about how far to take social constructivism has often compounded the problem. Yet even within a framework of m/f duality, the shift to understanding gender as a social category opens many new opportunities for change, as illustrated by CEDAW which, despite its commitment to asymmetry, also emphasizes the social nature of conceptions of m/f and their interdependence. The CEDAW preamble lays the groundwork by noting 'that a change in the traditional role of men as well as the role of women in society and in the family is needed to achieve full equality between men and women' (1979: preamble para 14). Significantly, the need to promote social change is framed as a legal obligation in article 5(a), which requires that states parties 'take all appropriate measures':

*To modify the social and cultural patterns of conduct of men and women, with a view to achieving the elimination of prejudices and customary and all other practices which are based on the idea of the inferiority or superiority of either of the sexes or on stereotyped roles for men and women.*

In the context of CEDAW as a whole, and in contrast to the language adopted earlier in DEDAW which limited its call for abolishing discriminatory practices to those 'based on the idea of the inferiority of women' (Article 3), the symmetry of this obligation is almost breathtaking. Indeed, Rosenblum suggests that article 5(a) could be used to reinterpret CEDAW as prohibiting all forms of 'sex' discrimination (Rosenblum 2011: 95–96). There is scope, then, to read CEDAW as presenting a challenge to the asymmetrical scaffolding that has supported the separate development of women's human rights and the reinvigoration of protectionism, just as it is possible to read the prohibition of discrimination on the basis of 'sex' in other human rights instruments as not confined only to discrimination experienced by 'women'.

Yet there has been surprisingly little feminist focus on the CEDAW article 5(a). One notable exception is Kirsten Anderson who, in the context of the elimination of violence against women, argues that international human rights law imposes obligations on states to eliminate harmful notions of masculinity that lead to such violence (Anderson 2008). In her search for evidence of such obligations, she argues that the treatment of violence against women as predominantly an issue of women's equality conceptually excludes or reduces the space for addressing harmful masculinities. Sandesh Sivakumaran is also concerned with the 'male' side of the ubiquitous gender duality, but from the point of view of challenging the silences that surround sexual violence perpetrated by men against other men (Sivakumaran 2005). He argues that many feminists ignore sexual violence aimed at men because their view of gendered power is too polarized and static (m>f), which prevents an understanding of (performative) hierarchies of power within masculinity that would enable connections to be made between the gendered domination and the abuse of power that underlies all rapes (Sivakumaran 2005: 1281–1282). His view lends support to my argument that dispensing with dualism and asymmetry would strengthen advocacy for women's rights by situating women's inequalities within an understanding of gender as a technology of power that may also disadvantage men and other gender identities, and thus work against protective responses to women.

There are many feminists who would agree with Sivakumaran. Sally Baden and Anne Marie Goetz, for example, after canvassing the developments in Beijing, urge feminists to be consistent about 'women' being a socially constructed category, emphasizing the interdependence of concepts of masculinity and femininity which requires that changing ideas about women necessarily involves changing ideas about men (Baden and Goetz 1998: 19, 34). They call for the construction of a feminist politics that is not reliant on 'woman' having a determinate meaning, which would also allow for recognition of a range of masculinities (Baden and Goetz 1998: 32–33). Brenda Cossman, drawing on Butler and building on de Beauvoir's insight that gender is a process of becoming, urges understanding sex/gender as tenuously constituted by repeated and ritualized 'performances' (Cossman 2002: 282). Her approach opens gender analysis to a broad array of shifting identities and subjectivities.

Yet despite the emancipatory possibilities opened by the language of gender, it remains common for feminists to use gender as a synonym for 'women' (Charlesworth 2005), which undermines the idea that it is a social and relational category and threatens to reduce women again to biology. Many feminists remain wary of the new forays into thinking that performative and social conceptions of gender make possible. They are afraid that fully disengaging sex/gender from its biological moorings will mean the loss of the precarious spaces that have been carved out for attention to be paid to women's human rights issues.

This fear leaves these feminists clinging to gender dualism and asymmetry and the presumption of heterosexuality, rendering them ill-equipped to counter the conservative backlash led by conservatives and religious fundamentalists, which has gathered steam since Beijing, intent on reasserting the (biological) 'certainties' of gender. Testament to the success of the backlash is the definition of 'gender' proffered in the Rome Statute establishing the International Criminal Court, which was able to lay claim to some allegiance with feminism because of this continued commitment to dualism and asymmetry. The definition insists that gender 'refers to the two sexes, male and female, within the context of society' (RSIC Article 7(3)) described by Cossman as 'stunningly narrow' (Cossman 2002: 283), although there is still room for exploiting its 'constructive ambiguity' as Valerie Oosterveld argues (2005: 67–68). Clearly though, feminist reticence about fully embracing the social nature of sex/gender not only sustains biological accounts of sex/gender and protective reactions to women's human rights abuses, but also plays into the hands of the conservative forces that are driving this retrenchment.

## The Possibilities Opened by 'Gender Mainstreaming'

A related development, which also has the potential to challenge international human rights law's presumption of sex/gender dualism and asymmetry, was the adoption of 'gender mainstreaming' as a UN system-wide strategy for achieving women's equality. As with the adoption of the terminology of gender, the Fourth World Conference on Women provided the site for this development. A definition, which has since been widely accepted, was promulgated by ECOSOC as part of its follow-up to the Beijing conference. Gender mainstreaming is defined as 'a process of assessing the implications for women and men of any planned action ... a strategy for making women's as well as men's concerns and experiences an integral dimension ... of policies and programs ... so that women and men benefit equally and inequality is not perpetuated' (ECOSOC 1997). Although this definition remains within a dualist framework, its use of symmetrical language opens the potential to disrupt the orthodoxy of m>f asymmetry. For their part, the chairpersons of the human rights treaty committees rose to the challenge, agreeing to 'fully integrat[e] gender perspectives' into their working methods.[6] As a result, three of the human rights treaty bodies have adopted General Comments, which seek to provide authoritative interpretations of their treaty texts that are more gender inclusive. A fourth treaty body, the Committee that monitors the *Convention Against Torture and Other Cruel, Inhuman and Degrading Treatment or Punishment* (CAT 1984) has addressed the issue more briefly in a General Comment on implementation obligations. These soft law reinterpretations provide an opportunity for the treaty bodies to fully embrace sex/gender as a social category and address women's inequality as one aspect of a larger pattern of sex/gender hierarchies, rather than requiring special protections (Otto 2010).

The first two treaty bodies to take up the challenge of gender mainstreaming were the Human Rights Committee, which adopted General Comment 28 on the 'equality of [ICCPR] rights between men and women' (HRC 2000), and the CERD Committee, which adopted

---

6    Report of the Sixth Meeting of Persons Chairing the Human Rights Treaty, UN Doc. A/50/505 (1995) para 34(a)-(f).

General Recommendation[7] XXV on the 'gender-related dimensions of racial discrimination' (CERDC 2001). Both authoritative interpretations break important new ground in the conceptualization of women's human rights, although their approaches are quite different. General Comment 28 boldly reinterprets each ICCPR right to be more inclusive of women's experience, which has the important effect of feminizing mainstream human rights, rather than treating human rights violations that are specific to women as a special category. For example, states parties may be in violation of the right to life (Article 6) when the only way that women can prevent unwanted pregnancies is by resorting to life-threatening backyard abortions, or when women are living in extreme poverty and deprivation (HRC 2000: para 10). General Recommendation XXV takes a different approach. Instead of reinterpreting specific rights, the CERD Committee elaborates a methodology for 'fully taking into account the gender-related dimensions of racial discrimination' (CERDC 2001: para 5). The methodology aims to bring to light forms of racial discrimination against women that may otherwise escape detection (para 1), making it clear that CERD obligations extend to addressing intersectional forms of discrimination experienced by women.

Disappointingly, neither treaty body questions the convention of gender dualism and asymmetry. They both use 'gender' as a synonym for women (HRC 2000: para 8, 17, CERDC 2001: para 2).[8] The only references to men are either as the comparator against which to measure women's equality (HRC 2000: para 18, 20, 24)[9] or as presenting a barrier to women's enjoyment of equal rights (para 20–24).[10] It is assumed that men do not suffer gender-based harm. I am especially at a loss to explain why the CERD Committee fails to take the opportunity to recognize that sexual violence can also be directed at men because of their racial or ethnic identities, when examples of such violations abound. It is perhaps, as Sivarkumaran suggests, fear of the 'taint' of homosexuality that serves to maintain the silence about m/m sexual violence (Sivakumaran 2005). Further, the opportunity to fully embrace sex/gender as a social category, and thus clearly reject biological essentialism, is squandered by the failure of both treaty bodies to acknowledge any other gender identities or forms of gender expression, besides women and men. This is particularly puzzling with respect to the HRC, which has previously interpreted 'sex' discrimination under the ICCPR to include discrimination on the basis of 'sexual orientation'.[11] Why not take the even more obvious step of including 'gender identity' in its understanding of 'sex'? My final observation about the shortcomings of these two General Comments is that they both rely

---

7    The terminology of 'general recommendation' reflects language in the Convention on the Elimination of All Forms of Racial Discrimination, article 9(2). A General Recommendation is an authoritative interpretation, the same as a General Comment.

8    para 8 (referring to measures taken in times of armed conflict 'to protect women from rape, abduction and other forms of gender-based violence') and para 17 (referring to women's 'gender-specific violations of the Covenant').

9    para 18 (access to justice must be enjoyed by women 'on equal terms with men), para 20 (women's right to privacy must be enjoyed 'on the basis of equality with men') and para 24 (restrictions on remarriage by women are prohibited if they are 'not imposed on men').

10   paras 20, 21, 23 (men as husbands, fathers, guardians, brothers who control aspects of women's lives in families) and para 24 (men as rapists or as perpetrators of violence against women).

11   *Toonen v Australia* (488/1992), CCPR/C/50/D/488/1992 (1994; *Young v Australia* (941/2000), CCPR/C/78/D/941/2000 (2003); *Joslin v New Zealand* (902/1999), CCPR/C/75/D/902/1999, 30 July 2002, Individual Opinion of Committee Members Mr Rajsoomer Lallah and Mr Martin Scheinin (Concurring).

predominantly on illustrative examples that focus on violence again women (HRC 2000: paras 5, 8, 10–12, 16, 22, 24 and 31) – sexual violence, forced sterilization and abuse of women workers in the case of General Recommendation XXV (CERDC 2001: para 2) – which, as I have argued, invites protective responses. Relying too much, perhaps, on the framework of subordination feminism, and possibly also influenced by the shame of homophobia, the HRC and the CERD Committee miss the opportunity, offered by the language of gender, to radically rethink their approach, leaving them wedded to dualism and asymmetry and carrying a sex/gender brief only for women.

More happily, one of the conceptual leaps made possible by the language of gender was embraced in 2005, with the adoption of General Comment 16 by the Committee on Economic, Social and Cultural Rights (CESCR), which monitors ICESCR. General Comment 16 disrupts the long lineage of asymmetry by identifying men, as well as women, as potential victims of sex discrimination and gender inequality. For example, in defining direct discrimination, the CESCR refers to different treatment 'based exclusively on sex and characteristics of men or of women, which cannot be justified objectively' (CESCR 2005: para 12). Further, both boys and girls are identified as needing protection from practices that promote child marriage (para 27) and benefits, like parental leave, must be made available to both men and women (para 26). Yet, despite its symmetrical approach, the reality that sex/gender discrimination and inequality largely operates to women's disadvantage is clearly recognized, which should help to allay feminist fears that symmetry will lead inevitably to the elevation of the interests of men over those of women. General Comment 16 achieves this result by acknowledging, with respect to *specific* rights violations, that women are 'primarily' the victims (domestic violence) (para 27), 'particularly' affected (historical disadvantage) (para 8), 'generally' placed at a disadvantage (cultural assumptions and expectations) (para 14), and may require 'particular attention' (the right to form and join trade unions) (para 25). Thus, its method is to look to the specific situation to determine where the sex/gender disadvantage lies, rather than assume that it will always be suffered by women. The definition of 'gender' offered by General Comment 16 echoes CEDAW Article 5(a), but takes it a step further by emphasizing that gender disadvantage is 'generally' experienced by women:

> Gender affects the equal right of men and women to the enjoyment of their rights. Gender refers to cultural expectations and assumptions about the behaviour, attitudes, personality traits and physical and intellectual capacities of men and women, based solely on their identity as men or women. Gender-based assumptions and expectations generally place women at a disadvantage with respect to substantive enjoyment of rights, such as freedom to act and to be recognized as autonomous, fully capable adults, to participate fully in economic, social and political development, and to make decisions concerning their circumstances and conditions. Gender-based assumptions about economic, social and cultural roles preclude the sharing of responsibility between men and women in all spheres that is necessary to equality. (CESCR 2005: para 14)

As this definition illustrates, the CESCR breaks decisively with m>f. It makes visible the harm that men as well as women suffer because of sex/gender discrimination, while also acknowledging the reality that women are more likely to be disadvantaged than men. Also important is the recognition that m/f relies substantially on cultural norms and, thus, that realizing equal rights requires changing the way both men's and women's gender identities are imagined and practiced. The symmetry of the definition, aided by the reference to women's autonomy, works against protective responses to women's human rights abuses because men too may be victims, and because sex/gender equality involves change that affects both women and men. Yet General Comment 16 remains devoted to a dualistic conception of gender, despite the fulsome acknowledgment of its social nature. As indicated in its more recent General Comment 20 on article 2(2), the CESCR prefers to interpret prohibited discrimination on the grounds of 'other status' rather than 'sex', to include 'sexual orientation' and 'gender identity' (CESCR 2009: para 32). However, once sex/ gender is accepted as a social construct, it must surely follow that everyone has a 'gender identity', that identification as 'women' and 'men' are only two of the possibilities, and that discrimination on the ground of 'gender identity' is therefore 'sex' discrimination.

In 2008, the CAT Committee embraced a further conceptual leap, with its observations about the gender dimensions of its convention in General Comment 2, which elaborates implementation obligations (CATC 2008). Several references are made to gender in the context of emphasizing that special attention must be paid to protecting groups or individuals who are, as a result of discrimination or marginalization, 'especially at risk of torture' (para 21). A non-exhaustive list of characteristics and factors that may increase this risk is enumerated, including 'gender, sexual orientation, [and] transgender identity' (para 21) building on concerns the CAT Committee has previously expressed in concluding observations about the susceptibility of homosexuals to torture[12] and attacks against 'sexual minorities' and 'transgender' activists.[13] Although I am curious as to why it was felt necessary to identify both 'gender' and 'gender identity' as separate grounds of discrimination, this approach not only rejects the presumption of asymmetry, but also moves towards reading sex/gender as a performative category that is capable of multiple potential forms of expression and identification. The enumeration of risk factors is followed by the observation that 'gender is a key factor' that can intersect with other characteristics of a person to make them more vulnerable to torture or ill-treatment (para 22). The Comment then elaborates some of the specificities of risk that may be associated with gender, noting that 'women' are at risk in contexts that include 'deprivation of liberty, medical treatment, particularly involving reproductive decisions, and violence by private actors in communities and homes', and that 'men' may be subject to 'certain gendered violations of the Convention such as rape or sexual violence and abuse' (para 22). Further, it is observed that men and boys, as well as women and girls, may be subject to violations 'on the basis of their actual or perceived non-conformity with socially determined gender roles' (para 22). Again, it is important to note that the CAT Committee's recognition of gendered human rights violations suffered by men and other gender identities, does not lead to marginalizing the concerns of women. Further, this is achieved by the same method as the CESCR – by paying attention to the specificities that may variously increase the risk of women, men and other gender identities to torture. By treating everyone's experience as 'specific', this method achieves inclusivity and thereby helps to ensure that responses to human rights abuses experienced specifically by women are not protective.

---

12    See, for example, Concluding Observations of CAT regarding Argentina, CAT/C/CR/33/1, para 6(g), 10 December 2004; and Concluding Observations of CAT regarding Egypt, CAT/C/CR/29/4, para 5(e), 23 December 2002.

13    See, for example, Concluding Observations of CAT regarding Venezuela, CAT/C/CR/29/2, para 10(d), 23 December 2002.

In sum, while gender mainstreaming has the potential to challenge the protective legal representations of women that have survived well into the age of human rights, the treaty bodies, like many feminists, have been slow to develop this potential. The General Comments adopted by the HRC and the CERD Committee both treat 'gender' as a synonym for 'women', uncritically repeating the heritage of sex/gender dualism and asymmetry and the accompanying disposition to treat women protectively. More hopefully, the General Comments adopted by the CESCR and the CAT Committee break with the tradition of asymmetry, which enables the inclusion of gendered harms experienced by men, and promotes looking to the specificities of both women's and men's experiences to determine where the gender disadvantage lies. The CAT Committee takes a further step by disrupting gender dualism, with its recognition that gendered human rights abuses can be experienced by people of diverse gender identities. Importantly, the latter two General Comments show no signs of marginalizing women's human rights, while also presenting substantial barriers to protectionism. Despite failing to recognize the confluence of 'gender' and 'gender identity' – a development that still awaits – they make way for more performative, multiple and compound conceptions of sex/gender and foster more inclusive coverage of sex/gender discrimination and inequality by human rights law. Dispensing with the architecture of dualism and asymmetry may yet provide the means of overcoming the tenacity of biological determinism and its attendant protective representations of women.

## Conclusion

It is necessary to redraw the maps of feminist engagement with international human rights law in a way that fully grasps the social nature of sex/gender. To date, the dominant codes of m/f dualism and m>f asymmetry have sustained biological accounts of sex/gender and protective responses to women's human rights abuses, thwarting the recognition of women as fully human. While it is tempting to conclude that this production of women is the inevitable result of the masculine dominative logic of the law and that we need, instead, to pursue a specifically feminine imaginary outside the law, as Irigaray might argue, I am not convinced – at least, not yet. I prefer instead to employ a cartography that treats sex/gender as a fully social and performative category, which makes it possible to imagine that the discursive practices of international human rights law can re-conceive sex/gender as a fluid conception that has multiple possible forms of expression and identification. Such a re-conception, vertiginous as it may seem from the vantage point of the present, will go at least some way towards addressing the problems that have haunted feminist engagement with international human rights law – the tenacity of biological explanations for women's subordination, the continuing vitality of protective conceptions of women, and the failure to grasp the diverse ways that sex/gender operates as a technology of power. The adoption of the language of gender, and the related strategy of gender mainstreaming, present important opportunities to pursue such a remapping of sex/gender, as shown by the work of the CESCR and CAT Committee. In their gender mainstreaming General Comments, these two treaty bodies show that it is possible, within the language of law and without taking a break from feminism, to introduce definitions of sex/gender that do not presume duality or hierarchy. By paying attention to the detail of particular situations of sex/gender inequality, an open determination of the form the discrimination takes, and who is disadvantaged by it, is made possible. Far from leading to the marginalization of women's issues, or the loss of the category of women, the General Comments show that treating sex/gender as diverse and shifting creates new opportunities to enrich and strengthen efforts to ensure that women are represented as fully human in human rights law. Engaging sex/gender as an inclusive category has the additional advantage of enabling feminists to 'carry a brief' for everyone who experiences sex/gender harm, including those who do not identify as, or are not perceived to be, women. While this remapping will no doubt present feminists with new dilemmas, it promises to at least thwart the tenacity of biological determinism and protectionism. Let me say again, the feminist project in international human rights law has barely begun.

# References

Anderson, A. 2008. Violence Against Women: State Responsibilities in International Human Rights Law to Address Harmful 'Masculinities'. *Netherlands Quarterly of Human Rights*, 26(2), 173–197.

Askin, K.D. 2003. Prosecuting Wartime Rapes and Other Gende-Related Crimes under International Law: Extraordinary Advances, Enduring Obstacles. *Berkeley Journal of International Law*, 21(2), 288–349.

Baden, S. and Goetz, A.M. 1998. Who Needs [Sex] When You Can Have [Gender]? Conflicting Discourses on Gender at Beijing, in *Feminist Visions of Development: Gender Analysis and Policy*, edited by C. Jackson and R. Pearson. London: Routledge, 19–38.

Bedont, B and Hall-Martinez, K. 1999. Ending Impunity for Gender Crimes under the International Criminal Court. *Brown Journal of World Affairs*, 6(1), 65–85.

Bunch, C. 1990. Women's Rights as Human Rights: Towards a Re-Vision of Human Rights. *Human Rights Quarterly*, 12(4), 486–498.

Burrows, N. 1986. International Law and Human Rights: The case of women's rights, in *Human Rights: From Rhetoric to Reality*, edited by T. Campbell et al. Oxford: Blackwell Publishing, 80–98.

Buss, D. 2004. Finding the Homosexual in Women's Rights: The Christian Right in International Politics. *International Feminist Journal of Politics*, 6(2), 257–284.

Butler, J. 1990. *Gender Trouble: Feminism and the Subversion of Identity*. New York: Routledge.

Case, M.A. 2011. After Gender the Destruction of Man? The Vatican's Nightmare Vision of the 'Gender Agenda' for Law. *Pace Law Review*, 31(3), 802–817.

Charlesworth, H. 1998. The Mid-Life Crisis of the Universal Declaration of Human Rights. *Washington and Lee Law Review*, 55(3), 781–796.

Charlesworth, H. 2005. Not Waving but Drowning: Gender Mainstreaming and Human Rights in the United Nations. *Harvard Human Rights Journal*, 18, 1–18.

Connors, J. 1996. NGOs and the Human Rights of Women at the United Nations, in *The Conscience of the World: The Influence of Non-Governmental Organisations in the UN System*, edited by P. Willetts. London: Brookings Institution Press, 147–180.

Cossman, B. 2002. Gender Performance, Sexual Subjects and International Law. *Canadian Journal of Law and Jurisprudence*, 15(2), 281–297.

Davies, M. 1997. Taking the Inside Out: Sex and Gender in the Legal Subject, in *Sexing the Subject of Law*, edited by N. Naffine and R.J. Owens. North Ryde, Australia: LBC Information Services, 25–46.

de Beauvoir, S. 1974. *The Second Sex* (ed. and trans. H.M. Parshley). New York: Vintage.

DeBehnke, C. 1998. Introduction to Convention on the Political Rights of Women, March 31, 1953, in *The International Human Rights of Women: Instruments of Change*, edited by C.E. Lockwood, D.B. Magraw, M.F. Spring and S.I. Strong. Washington, DC: American Bar Association, 181–182.

Engle, K. 2005a. International Human Rights and Feminisms: Where Discourses Keep Meeting, in *International Law: Modern Feminist Approaches*, edited by D. Buss and A. Manji. Portland: Hart, 47–66.

Engle, K. 2005b. Feminism and its (Dis)contents: Criminalizing Wartime Rape in Bosnia and Herzegovenia. *American Journal of International Law*, 99(4), 778–816.

Fraser, A.S. 1999. Becoming Human: The Origins and Development of Women's Human Rights. *Human Rights Quarterly*, 21(4), 853–906.

Gaer, F.D. 1998. And Never the Twain Shall Meet? The Struggle to Establish Women's Rights as International Human Rights, in *The International Human Rights of Women: Instruments of Change*, edited by C.E. Lockwood, D.B. Magraw, M.F. Spring and S.I. Strong. Washington, DC: American Bar Association, 4–89.

Galey, M.E. 1995. Forerunners in Women's Quest for Partnership, in *Women, Politics and the United Nations*, edited by A. Winslow. Westport: Greenwood, 1–10.

Halley, J. 2006. *Split Decisions: How and why to take a break from feminism*. Princeton: Princeton University Press.

Halley, J. 2008. Rape in Berlin: Reconsidering the Criminalisation of Rape in the International Law of Armed Conflict. *Melbourne Journal of International Law*, 9(1), 78–124.

Hernandez-Truyol, B.E. 2011. Unsex CEDAW? No! Super-Sex It! *Columbia Journal of Gender and Law*, 20(2), 195–223.

Hevener, N.K. 1978. International Law and the Status of Women: An Analysis of International Legal Instruments Related to the Treatment of Women. *Harvard Women's Law Journal*, 1, 131–156.

Holmes, H.B. 1983. A Feminist Analysis of the Universal Declaration of Human Rights, in *Beyond Domination: New Perspectives on Women and Philosophy*, edited by C. Gould. Totowa NJ: Rowman & Allanheld, 250–264.

Irigaray, L. 1985. *This Sex Which Is Not One* (trans. C. Porter). Ithica: Cornell University Press.

Kapur, R. 2002. The Tragedy of Victimization Rhetoric: Resurrecting the "Native" Subject in International/ Postcolonial Feminist Legal Politics. *Harvard Human Rights Journal*, 15, 1–38.

Kouvo, S. 2004. *Making Just Rights? Mainstreaming Women's Human Rights and a Gender Perspective*. Sweden: Iustus Forlag.

Lake, M. 2001. From Self-Determination via Protection to Equality via Non-Discrimination: Defining Women's Rights at the League of Nations, in *Women's Rights and Human Rights: International Historical Perspectives*, edited by P. Grimshaw, K. Holmes and M. Lake. New York: Palgrave, 254–271.

Loenen, T. 1994. Rethinking Sex Equality as a Human Right. *Netherlands Quarterly of Human Rights*, 12(3), 253–270.

Miller, A.M. 2004. Sexuality, Violence Against Women, and Human Rights: Women Make demands and Ladies Get Protection. *Health and Human Rights*, 7(2), 16–47.

Monro, S. 2007. Transgender: Destabilising feminisms?, in *Sexuality and the Law: Feminist Engagements*, edited by V. Munro and C.F Stychin. Abingdon: Routledge, 125–150.

Morsink, J. 1991. Women's Rights in the Universal Declaration. *Human Rights Quarterly*, 13(2), 229–256.

Morsink, J. 1999. *The Universal Declaration of Human Rights: Origins, Drafting, and Intent*. Philadelphia: University of Pennsylvania Press.

Oosterveld, V. 2005. The Definition of Gender in the Rome Statute of the International Criminal Court: A Step Forward or Back for International Criminal Justice? *Harvard Human Rights Journal*, 18, 55–84.

Otto, D. 1995. Lesbians? Not in my Country. *Alternative Law Journal*, 20(6), 288–290.

Otto, D. 1996. Holding Up Half the Sky, But for Whose Benefit?: A Critical Analysis of the Fourth World Conference on Women. *Australian Feminist Law Journal*, 6, 7–31.

Otto, D. 2006. 'Lost in translation: re–scripting the sexed subjects of international human rights law', in *International Law and Its Others*, edited by A. Orford. Cambridge: Cambridge University Press, 318–356.

Otto, D. 2007. Making Sense of Zero Tolerance Policies in Peacekeeping Sexual Economies' in *Sexuality and the Law: Feminist Engagements*, edited by V. Munro and C.F. Stychin. Abingdon: Routledge, 259–282.

Otto, D. 2010. Women's Rights, in *International Human Rights Law*, edited by D. Moeckli, S. Shah and S. Sivakumara. Oxford: Oxford University Press, 345–364.

Persram, N. 1994. Politicizing the *Feminine*. Globalizing the Feminist. *Alternatives*, 19, 275–313.

Reanda, L. 1992. The Commission on the Status of Women, in *The United Nations and Human Rights: A Critical Appraisal*, edited by P. Alston. Oxford: Oxford University Press.

Rosenblum, D. 2011. Unsex CEDAW, or What's Wrong with Women's Rights. *Columbia Journal of Gender and Law*, 20, 1–65.

Rothschild, C. 2000. *Written Out: How Sexuality is used to Attack Women's Organizing*. International Gay and Lesbian Human Rights Commission and the Centre for Women's Global Leadership.

Scully, P. 2009. Vulnerable Women: A Critical Reflection on Human Rights Discourse and Sexual Violence. *Emory International Law Review*, 23(1), 113–123.

Secretary-General UN. 1998. Integrating the Gender Perspective into the Work of United Nations Human Rights Treaty Bodies: Report of the Secretary-General, UN Doc HRI/MC/1998/6, para 16, 3 September 1998.

Secretary-General's Bulletin. 2003. Special measures for protection from sexual exploitation and abuse, ST/SGB/2003/13, 9 October 2003.

Sivakumaran, S. 2005. Male/Male Rape and the 'Taint' of Homosexuality. *Human Rights Quarterly*, 27(4), 1274–1306.

Women's Net, 1995. NGOs Frustrated by UN Preparatory Meeting 4. *Human Rights Defender* 1–4.

## Conventions, Declarations and Covenants

CAT. Convention Against Torture and Other Cruel, Inhuman and Degrading Treatment or Punishment (CAT), adopted 10 December 1984, entered into force 26 June 1987.

CATC. CAT Committee 'General Comment No. 2: Implementation of article 2 by States parties' (2008), CAT/C/GC/2, 24 January 2008.

CECPCVAW. Council of Europe Convention on Preventing and Combating Violence Against Women, CETS No. 210, 11 May 2011.

CEDAW. Convention on the Elimination of All Forms of Discrimination Against Women, adopted 18 December 1979, entered into force 3 September 1981, 1249 UNTS 13.

CEDAWC. CEDAW Committee, General Recommendation No. 19, UN Doc A/47/38, 30 January 1992.

CERD. Convention on the Elimination of All Forms of Racial Discrimination, adopted by the UN General Assembly, GOAR 2106A(XX), 21 December 1965, entered into force 4 January 1969.

CERDC. CERD Committee 'General Recommendation No. XXV: Gender–Related Dimensions of Racial Discrimination' (2001), 56th Session, 2000, UN Doc. HRI/GEN/1/ Rev.5, 26 April 2001.

CESCR. Committee on Economic, Social and Cultural Rights, 'General Comment No. 16, The equal right of men and women to the enjoyment of all economic, social and cultural rights (art. 3 of the International Covenant on Economic, Social and Cultural Rights)' (2005), E/C.12/2005/4, 11 August 2005.

CESCR, Committee on Economic, Social and Cultural Rights, 'General Comment No. 20: Non–discrimination in economic, social and cultural rights' (2009), E/C.12/GC/20, 2 July 2009.

CNMW. Convention on the Nationality of Married Women, New York, 20 February 1957, in force 11 August 1958, 309 UNTS 65.

CPRW. Convention on the Political Rights of Women, New York, 31 March 1953, in force 7 July 1954, 193 UNTS 135.

CRLCW. Convention Respecting the Laws and Customs of War on Land (Hague Convention II), 29 July 1899, art 46.

CSTWFA. Convention for the Suppression of the Traffic in Women of Full Age 1933, 53 UNTS 13.

DEDAW. Declaration on the Elimination of Discrimination against Women, GA Res 2263 (XXII), 7 November 1967.

DEVAW. Declaration on the Elimination of Violence Against Women, UNGA Res 48/104, 20 December 1993.

ECOSOC. Agreed Conclusions, 1997/2 on gender mainstreaming, UN Doc A/52/3, chpt IV(a).

HRC. Human Rights Committee, 'General Comment No. 28: Article 3 (Equality of Rights between Men and Women)' (2000), UN Doc HRI/GEN/1/Rev 5, 29 March 2000.

IACPPEVAW. Inter–American Convention on the Prevention, Punishment and Eradication of Violence Against Women, 9 June 1994 (1994) 33 International Legal Materials 960.

IASWT. International Agreement for the Suppression of the White Slave Traffic, 1904 1 LNTS 83.

ICCPR. International Covenant on Civil and Political Rights, adopted 16 December 1966, entered into force 23 March 1976, 999 UNTS 171.

ICESCR. International Covenant on Economic, Social and Cultural Rights, adopted 16 December 1966, entered into force 3 January 1976.

ICSTWC. International Convention for the Suppression of the Traffic in Women and Children 1921, 9 LNTS 415.

ICSWST. International Convention for the Suppression of White Slave Traffic 1910, 1912 Gr Brit T S No.20 at 267.

ILO CCNWWEI. International Labor Organization, Convention Concerning Night Work of Women Employed in Industry, 1919 (Convention 4).

ILO CCEWUWMK. International Labor Organization, Convention Concerning the Employment of Women on Underground Work in Mines of All Kinds 1935 (Convention 45).

ILO MPC. International Labor Organization, Maternity Protection Convention 1919 (Convention 3).

PACHPRRWA. Protocol to the African Charter on Human and Peoples' Rights on the Rights of Women in Africa, Assembly/AU/Dec.14(II), 11 July 2003, art 20.

RSIC. Rome Statute of the International Criminal Court, UN Doc A/CONF. 183/9, article 7(3), 17 July 1998.

UDHR. Universal Declaration of Human Rights, GA Res 217A(III), 10 December 1948.

# A New Frontline for Feminism and International Humanitarian Law

## Judith Gardam[1]

For some years, I took a 'break from feminism' in the words of the American scholar Janet Halley (but in quite a different sense than she suggests) (Halley 2006). At that time, I thought that I had nothing particularly new to contribute towards the debate in my particular field of study, women and international humanitarian law (IHL). I wanted to allow time to refresh myself and see what avenues might open up in the future. Of course, in one sense, all our work as feminists is infused with our world view, and I mean by 'taking a break' merely that the word 'feminist' did not appear in the title or in the text of my writing. I was aware of the growth in scholarly literature on rape and sexual violence in armed conflict and the burgeoning jurisprudence of the two ad hoc international criminal tribunals established by the Security Council of the United Nations in the 1990s.[2] But my mind was on other aspects of IHL and I had not given a great deal of thought to where we were heading with this focus on criminal punishment of sexual violence against women in armed conflict.

Writing this chapter has required an overview of the existing feminist debates in the area of IHL. IHL is the modern term for what used to be known as the law of war. Nowadays, with the advent of the 1949 United Nations Charter outlawing war and the growing emphasis on human rights, this ancient, complex and highly detailed set of treaty and customary rules that regulates the conduct of armed conflict has become known as either IHL or the law of armed conflict. IHL with its emphasis on the humanitarian aspects of the rules is the preferred term of the International Committee of the Red Cross (ICRC), the Swiss based association with a special responsibility for the development and implementation of IHL. The law of armed conflict is the preferred term of the military that recognize the regime is not purely humanitarian but also serves the demands of military efficiency.

In focusing my mind on what had been happening in feminism and IHL I was somewhat dismayed to discover that the whole field of women and IHL seemed to have been consumed in recent years by the topic of sexual violence and its criminalization and punishment. To say this might suggest that there had been previously a wider focus, but that is not really the case. As I will explain later, in the early 1990s, there were only the glimmerings of a broader appreciation of the actual world that women inhabit during periods of armed conflict and

---

1     Thanks to James Krumrey-Quinn for his excellent research assistance.
2     The International Criminal Tribunal for the former Yugoslavia (ICTY) was established pursuant to UN Security Council Resolutions 808 (February 1993) and 827 (May 1993), and the International Criminal Tribunal for Rwanda (ICTR) pursuant to Security Council Resolution 955 (November 1994).

the sense that perhaps we needed to cast a critical eye over IHL. I think it accurate to say that international law feminists on the whole have sidestepped IHL (apart from the narrow focus of sexual violence and International Criminal Law (ICL)) in contrast to the vigorous, broad and multifaceted debate that has characterized the topic of women and Human Rights Law (HRL). Frequently this latter debate has encompassed issues involving women and armed conflict and it is true that the distinction between the two regimes is becoming less rigid (see, for example, Ben-Naftali 2011). Nevertheless, IHL remains the *lex specialis* during periods of armed conflict and occupation and it is a powerful and effective regime if you can fit into one of its categories (Gardam 2005: 212–216, discussing the limitations of HRL during periods of armed conflict). It is therefore disappointing, given the level of armed conflict experienced in today's world and its impact on women, that IHL as a whole has not been subjected to a broader scrutiny by feminists.

The focus on sexual violence in armed conflict and ICL has undoubtedly pushed into the shade what fragile developments there were that took a wider view of women and IHL. The abundant associated literature also reveals considerable unease among feminist scholars as to what has been achieved, where we have gone wrong, and what harm has been done by this narrow focus. This internal agonizing is nothing new for feminists, but I argue in this chapter that it is nonetheless very limiting in terms of going forward.

In providing a snapshot of feminist legal theory in the area of IHL I take as my overall theme one that is familiar territory for legal feminists, that is the extent to which engagement with the law has made any inroads into the prevailing representation of women in the IHL regime (see, for example, Otto 2005: 105, considering the same issue in the context of HRL). After assessing the outcome of two decades of feminist engagement with IHL, I conclude that our work has done nothing to disrupt existing stereotypes of women. But some will argue that such an assessment overlooks what should be seen as a feminist success story, albeit an imperfect one. A common perception among feminist international law scholars is that not only has their work been received with a wall of indifference from their academic colleagues but also that, despite high-profile strategies such as gender mainstreaming, little has really been achieved on the ground for women (Charlesworth 2011: 9).[3] A spectacular exception to this apathy is the synergy between feminist theory and practice that led to the criminal enforcement of the provisions of IHL dealing with sexual violence against women in armed conflict. We now have a thriving area of 'respectable' ICL scholarship (both feminist and non-feminist) focusing on this issue and unprecedented advances have been made in the interpretation and enforcement of the relevant provisions of IHL (see, for example, Chinkin 2003). One could see this as a great triumph of a remarkable partnership between scholarship and advocacy. These achievements, moreover, have received what is clearly regarded as the ultimate accolade from mainstream international lawyers, namely that the development of ICL 'testifies to the transformative potential of the adaptation of positive law to meet women's concerns' (Simma and Paulus 1999: 306). Anything more fundamental, however, such as asking whether 'the "new" international criminal law remains primarily a system based on men's lives' (Charlesworth 1999: 386) is seen as 'unhelpful'. Such an approach apparently lacks objectivity and neutrality and provides no basis for decision-makers to adopt general standards of human behaviour for holding accountable perpetrators of crimes

---

3    Charlesworth contrasts the failure of the Academy to engage with feminist ideas with the engagement from international institutions. However, she sees the latter as primarily lip service and having achieved no real change.

against women or indeed for more wide-ranging reforms outside ICL (Simma and Paulus 1999: 306, commenting on Hilary Charlesworth's contribution to a symposium on method, Charlesworth 1999).

To me this encapsulates the whole problem with so much of feminist engagement with this area of international law. I am not referring to the rather bewildering failure in this day and age to have persuaded our peers that reliance on so-called 'neutrality' and 'objectivity' traditionally has served to render women invisible in the law. Rather, it seems to me that what turned out to be not only acceptable in the mainstream but also successful in achieving normative change has driven the focus of feminist IHL scholarship and may continue to do so. It is understandable why this is the case as it is exhilarating to think that all one's hard work has not been in vain.[4] I am nevertheless somewhat alarmed at how readily and relatively uncritically the focus of feminist inquiry has turned to sexual violence against women in armed conflict and ICL as the preferred medium for change.

My main concern is that this focus on sexual violence has diverted feminists from confronting the more mundane, less high profile but fundamental issue of the role played by endemic discrimination in determining the ways in which armed conflict impacts on women and from attempting to have this reality reflected in IHL. Not only is criminal law an unlikely means of changing the status quo but it also has the effect of ensuring that the image of women reflected in the law remains one-dimensional – they are visible only as victims of sexual violence. As one Kosovar woman has been quoted as saying '[i]t is really amazing … that the international community cared only about Kosovar women when they were being raped – and then only as some sort of exciting story. We see now that they really don't give a damn about us' (Rehn and Sirleaf 2002: 125).

I am not, of course, the only feminist who is concerned that this focus on sexual violence fails to challenge existing stereotypes of women (see, for example, Engle 2005, Buss 2007). Moreover, some interesting and provocative recent feminist work in international law demands that we carefully examine the dilemmas and contradictions in these developments (see, for example, Engle 2005, 2008, Halley 2009). I see this debate, however, as having just about run its course and, despite it, feminist engagement with IHL remains centred on sexual violence and has failed to step outside that framework. I doubt whether we shall see much in the way of new ideas and the literature seems to have taken on a rather quarrelsome tone, which usually means that the topic is exhausted and all that is left is fighting over the crumbs.

The structure of the discussion in this chapter is as follows. First I trace the evolution of feminist encounters with IHL and reflect on what have been identified as the core issues. I then spend some time reflecting on the feminist engagement with sexual violence in armed conflict and ICL and on what we can perhaps learn from this. Finally I provide some tentative suggestions for further fruitful 'excavations', as Ngaire Naffine so aptly describes the feminist project (Naffine 1990). I am aware that in doing so I struggle to step outside the limits of the idea that if we could just get the law right things might improve for women. In my view the campaign to criminalize sexual violence against women in armed conflict is

---

4    It is also a reflection of the impoverishing impact of an endless focus on crises (see, for example, Charlesworth 2002 and Koskienemmi 2002). Both Charlesworth and Koskienemmi critique what gets to be defined as a crisis in international law and what is excluded. Janet Halley constructs a far more sinister agenda at work from this focus on sexual violence, namely the stifling of feminist dissenting voices in favour of what she terms 'radical feminist universalism' (Halley 2009).

a stark reminder of what Carol Smart has referred to as the easy seduction of feminists by law reform (Smart 1989: 160). It may be, therefore, that all that will be achieved, as Christine Chinkin puts it, is 'a triumph of form over substance' (Chinkin 1997: 18). Nevertheless, the powerful role that law plays in constructing the way we see the world and moulding reality, confers on it at the very least a significant symbolic role to play in any advances in the protection of women during times of armed conflict.

## The Development of a Feminist Voice in the Legal Regime Regulating Armed Conflict

Feminism came somewhat late to international law. Perhaps the fact that the discipline in general deals primarily with the relations between the abstract entities of States posed somewhat of a barrier to the investigations of feminists. It could be argued that all individuals are invisible in international law, not just women. After all, surely rules regulating such matters as the seabed, outer space, trade relations and disarmament are gender neutral? Consequently, there may have been the perception that this feature of the discipline made it inhospitable terrain for legal feminists (Charlesworth 2008: 164). Since this initial hesitation was overcome, however, the discipline has been subjected to ongoing, sophisticated and rigorous analysis using a range of feminist methodologies. Quite what this has achieved on the ground is another matter and the overall reaction has been described as 'a mass of passively resistant inertia' (Chinkin, Wright and Charlesworth 2005: 17–18).

The feminist project in international law commenced in the early 1990s with the work of Hilary Charlesworth, Christine Chinkin and Shelley Wright, who first proposed the heretical argument that international law was gendered and served to disempower and marginalize women (Charlesworth, Chinkin and Wright 1991, Charlesworth and Chinkin 2000). Their work over the next two decades was to go from strength to strength and has fundamentally influenced the direction of feminist scholarship in international law. I found myself somewhat hesitantly following their example and thinking about how feminist ideas could inform my work on IHL. I say 'hesitantly' only in the sense that this was a completely empty field of scholarship for international lawyers and this left me uncertain of where I should start (see, however, Khushalani 1982, Krill 1985, providing a non-feminist account of the provisions of IHL applicable to women).[5] I was also aware that always lying in wait in the background of any critique of IHL is the vested interest of the military and the nature of militarism that to a large extent determine the content and application of the legal rules. Confronting this institution is not a task for the faint hearted. The military functions in many ways as a 'masculinity cult' that serves to reinforce gender identification for men (see, for example, Enloe 1993: 73). According to a female cadet in the Australian Defence Force Academy that trains officers for the Australian military forces:

> ... amongst cadets there was a strong culture of commodification of women, particularly as sexual objects. Female cadets were often treated as "game" after hours,

---

5    Although neither of the works by Khushalani or Krill were feminist or critical, they were important early steps that at least recognized the existence of women in armed conflict.

*rather than as respected colleagues. Female cadets were often harassed by male cadets [and] these sorts of actions were simply part of the culture at ADFA. (AHRC 2011)*

Having said this I must acknowledge a recent positive reaction to feminist concerns with IHL from a somewhat unexpected quarter, the military itself. While feminist legal scholars have been preoccupied with some internecine bloodletting over how to deal with the criminalization of sexual violence in armed conflict, at least one senior US military officer has taken the feminist critique of IHL at face value and come up with some practical suggestions in response (Prescott 2012). I will return to this issue towards the end of the chapter.

In hindsight one can see three distinct, albeit somewhat haphazard stages in feminist engagement with IHL, although a search for methodological purity in this work will be a frustrating enterprise. However, for those interested in how a range of different feminist tools have been employed, and to what effect, then the literature is a rewarding illustration of feminist scholars at work and their interaction with activism. As detailed further below the first stage of engagement consisted of an investigation into whether the provisions of IHL had a gendered dimension. After all, IHL has the potential to be a particularly useful laboratory for gender analysis since it deals with armed conflict, the activity in which we find the 'warrior'. Such an entity must surely provide a fertile field of investigation for feminists. The focus then moved to a consideration of the IHL provisions that protect the civilian population. The third stage was the major project to ensure that feminist theory made its way into the world of the emerging ICL in the form of punishing sexual violence against women.

## The Gender of the Combatant/Civilian Distinction in IHL

The first feminist engagement with IHL, as I have said, was a classic feminist gender analysis. The starting point was the seemingly natural division drawn in the rules between combatants and civilians. 'Natural' because this is a regime to regulate armed conflict and combatants should logically be at the centre of these rules. This might have been a novel enterprise for feminist international lawyers but the gender of the civilian/combatant distinction had been for some time an integral aspect of the work of feminist international relations scholars (see, for example, Kinsella 2005, Sjoberg 2006).[6] Their insights about the 'male' warrior or combatant on whom falls the natural role of protector with all its attendant power and influence and the civilian population, who are correlated with the gendered, powerless feminine, were readily translated into IHL.

What we see in IHL is an assumption as to the value of lives and the privileging in its rules of the life of the combatant. It is true that individual combatants are frequently expendable in the interests of what is perceived as a military advantage. Overall, however, IHL prioritizes their protection over civilians and it does so on the basis of military necessity (Gardam 1993a, 1993b, 1990). 'Military necessity' is taken as a given within IHL. Military lawyers use this concept without further explanation to justify the impracticality of efforts to improve the protection of victims of armed conflict. However, it is not a neutral yardstick and incorporates a hierarchy of values. It assumes that military victory and the defence of

---

6    This dichotomy is alive and well in other areas of international law (see, for example, Heathcote 2010). Heathcote describes the association of women as a category of protected subjects in the responses to the events of the 11th of September 2001.

the State are pre-eminent and operates to prioritize the demands of national security over other factors, such as the protection of all civilians caught up in conflict.[7] Consequently the logic of IHL is that the life of the combatant is more important than that of the civilian, and this is even more so if that civilian belongs to the 'enemy' State.

It is beyond the scope of this chapter to outline in detail the evidence to support what is a damning critique of IHL on this point (see, for example, Gardam 1993a, Gardam 1997). It is unclear where this argument as to the gendered distinction between combatants and civilians in IHL could take us as feminist international lawyers. Does it advance the debate to recognize that in one sense all civilians are gendered 'female'? Would everything be all right if there were more rules protecting civilians or if they were better implemented? Be that as it may, feminist legal scholars appear to have paid little if any attention to the gendered nature of non-combatant immunity and probably with good cause as it requires fundamental and unlikely structural change in the regime of IHL.

## The Discrimination Argument

There was, however, a more limited canvas that perhaps had more potential for achieving change in relation to the rules that are intended to protect the civilian population during armed conflict. This was the second focus of feminist IHL scholarship. Whether the civilian population is gendered feminine or not, from a pragmatic perspective the majority are women. Politically, one of the major stumbling blocks to arguments that we needed to focus on the provisions of IHL that dealt with the civilian population from the perspective of women was that what happens to male members of the civilian population in armed conflict is appalling. To argue that women have been neglected arouses resistance and even hostility from many quarters as it is seen as suggesting that their experiences are worse than those of men, whereas the facts seem to belie this.[8] In fact this concern still resonates and has found its way into feminist work on sexual violence (see, for example, Engle 2005: 814 and see Carpenter 2006, arguing that the focus on women and children has in fact obscured the impact of armed conflict on men).

The point that must not be overlooked, however, is that the experience of women of armed conflict is not better or worse but that it differs from that of civilian men and the law does not recognize this. Civilian men in today's armed conflicts are most likely to be deliberately killed, tortured or detained. Women are less likely to be directly targeted in these ways but are nonetheless subjected to a wide range of other violent and traumatic events. From the legal perspective the killing, torture or the unlawful detention of civilians is a breach of the law and punishable as such. In contrast so much of what happens to women during such times is not prohibited, or where it is formally prohibited the legal provisions have historically been ignored.

What is particularly illuminating about this work is when the provisions of IHL relating to women are isolated so as to construct a picture of 'the woman of IHL' (see Gardam and Jarvis 2001: 95–100, Gardam 1997: 233). As with many regimes based on formal equality,

---

7     The gender attributes of the notions of national security and the State itself have been subjected to scrutiny by feminists (see, for example, Reardon 1985, Enloe 1993, Tickner 1992).

8     It is worth noting, however, the comment of Major-General Patrick Cammaert, Commander of UN peacekeeping forces in the Eastern Congo, that '[i]t has probably become more dangerous to be a woman than a soldier in armed conflict' (OHCHR).

there is some recognition in IHL of the limitations of this approach when the norm of the system is male. IHL has a number of 'special' provisions for women. These rules attempt to address the 'biological' differences of women and some of the consequences that flow from these characteristics (see Gardam and Jarvis 2001: 62–68).[9] For example, IHL includes rules addressing the situation of pregnant women, maternity cases and women as victims of, or at risk of sexual violence. Although some 42 provisions of the various IHL instruments deal specifically with women, they all do so from the perspective of women's relationship with others and not as individuals in their own right. The recognition of the vulnerability of women to the effects of armed conflict remains centred around these 'qualities'.

Apart from the protections contained in these special provisions that do seek to address valid concerns, women are largely invisible in IHL. Any indication that women's experience of armed conflict is distinctive and encompasses wider issues than their roles as mothers and objects of sexual violence is not discernible. The assumption is that the general provisions in relation to combatants and civilians perform this function. This in fact is not the case. These rules take an equally constrained view of the reality of armed conflict for the lives of women. The shortcomings of IHL are exacerbated by the fact that many provisions with the potential to encompass some aspects of women's experience have traditionally been interpreted in such a way as to exclude women from their scope (see, for example, Gardam and Jarvis 2001: 128–134). For example, the phrases 'inhuman treatment' and 'wilfully causing great suffering or serious injury to body and health', have not until recently been regarded as encompassing acts against women that are clearly capable of falling within their ambit.

In common with the gendered combatant/civilian distinction, this wholesale critique of IHL did not attract the level of debate among feminist international lawyers that, given its importance, one might have expected. The difficulty was that any meaningful response once again required fairly fundamental structural change.[10] What was needed was a reorganization of what was included and what was excluded in IHL. There was some engagement with the idea that discrimination worsened the impact of armed conflict on women but a stubborn resistance to the idea that there should be any commitment to real change in IHL (Gardam 2005).

The idea of reform was certainly strongly resisted by the International Committee of the Red Cross. Their approach has always been that there are already special provisions protecting women in IHL and that it is a question of better implementation of the existing law (Lindsey 2001: 213–214). Parts of the United Nations system have been a little more robust in their approach and there have been a number of broadly focused initiatives encompassing women and armed conflict, some of which place sexual violence against women in armed conflict in a wider framework of structural inequality (see, for example, Otto 2010: 102–103).

As an aside it is instructive to note that the debates about women and armed conflict in the Security Council are always conducted in open meetings whereas the practice nowadays is for any topic of any real importance for States to be conducted behind closed doors. What conclusion one should draw from this practice remains unclear. A somewhat world-weary view might well be that there is a tacit understanding among States that this is a topic on

---

9    One can argue that IHL merely reflects the patriarchal State's investment in women as the reproducers of nations (see, for example, Pettman 1996: 187).

10   There has been some quite intense debate on this issue, namely whether the provisions of IHL are satisfactory in relation to the protection of women in armed conflict or that what is needed is better implementation of the existing law (see, for a detailed discussion of the differing views, Oosterveldt 2009).

which there can be a general wringing of hands but no real engagement with the issues. Otherwise, there might well be some tension between States. By contrast, other 'real' issues on which States anticipate that some action may need to be taken are conducted at the high diplomatic level and behind closed doors.

## The Punishment of Sexual Violence Against Women in Armed Conflict

Against this background the third and, to date, final stage of engagement, which has secured changes in the legal responses to sexual violence against women in armed conflict, can be read as a major success story for the feminist IHL project. It was the horrific events of the armed conflict in the Former Yugoslavia that galvanized the international community into action. In response to international pressure in 1993, the Security Council established the International Criminal Tribunal for the former Yugoslavia (ICTY) to try persons suspected of having committed war crimes in that conflict. This was followed in 1994 by the establishment of the International Criminal Tribunal for Rwanda (ICTR). The Statutes and jurisprudence of these bodies resulted in not only the fundamental reinterpretation and enforcement of existing provisions of IHL protecting women against sexual violence but also new procedural and substantive law on sexual violence in armed conflict, now reflected in the Rome Statute of the International Criminal Court (ICC) (see, for example, Chinkin 2003).[11]

Feminist scholars played a significant role in these developments and have continued to make frequent and significant contributions to the literature in the area. This new battleground also attracted the attention of US domestic feminists like the indomitable Catharine MacKinnon, who gained a new international audience by arguing that rape and sexual violence in armed conflict was just a manifestation of the 'war on women' at the global level (MacKinnon 1994, 2006, Murphy 2005: 70–77).[12]

It is a relatively straightforward task to state the normative changes to the law regulating sexual violence in armed conflict and my purpose is not to go over that well-documented ground (see, for example, Chinkin 2003). What I want to trace here is how these changes have aroused considerable unease among feminist scholars. I want to suggest that, among other things, it demonstrates the richness of feminist scholarship in this area to study how various authors have dealt with their ensuing discomfort.

Some writers reiterated the concern frequently aired by human rights feminists that this relentless focus on women as powerless victims undermines their possibilities for sexual and political agency and, moreover, disguises the fact that women are in some cases complicit in wartime abuses, if not indeed perpetrators thereof (see, for example, Engle 2005: 780, 794–797, 806–807, Engle 2008, Kapur 2002). We are also cautioned against seeing only part of the picture if we do not take into account the intersection of gender and ethnicity that is a characteristic of much sexual violence in modern conflicts (Buss 2007, Engle 2005).

The particular concern for some feminists is the limited vision of the sexual agency of women that underlies the developments in the criminal punishment of sexual violence

---

11  A distinctly feminist initiative was the unofficial Women's International War Crimes Tribunal conducted in Tokyo in December 2000 dealing with the treatment of so-called 'comfort' women by the Japanese military during the period up to and including the Second World War.

12  Murphy discusses the recent phenomenon of domestic feminists moving into what she refers to as 'feminist internationalism'.

in armed conflict. Specifically, they seek a more nuanced approach to how issues such as consent are treated during wartime sexual contact (Engle 2005: 803–806, Halley 2006; Engle 2008). Accordingly Engle, for example, argues that the ICTY's approach to consent in what it deems inherently coercive circumstances such as detention, diminishes 'women's capacity to engage in sexual activity with the "enemy" during the war' (Engle 2005: 784, 794–797, 803–804, 806–807, see also Kapur 2002)[13] Along the same lines, it has been argued that perhaps we need to re-think the impact and aftermath for women of sexual violence in war. Is it a universal truth that rape 'breaks' and destroys women once and for all? (Engle 2005: 813–814, Engle 2008). Do we not further diminish women by this assumption? Other feminists (and I include myself among them) are alarmed by some of the implications of this way of conceptualizing the issue of agency and in particular the tendency to downplay the issue of systemic power (Grahn-Farley 2011). I find particularly problematic Engle's reliance on the depiction by a male author (Hemingway 1940) of female sexual agency during war as a possible way of reimagining the response to the experience of rape: '[a]lways I fought and always it took two of them or more to do me the harm' (Engle 2008: 946–948, 954). I think it is accurate to say that in such situations resistance will frequently worsen the violence. Moreover, what is the advantage of presenting a stereotypical male response – meeting violence with violence – as a manifestation of agency for women, along with an equally stereotypical masculine view of sex: '"[b]ut did thee feel the earth move". And indeed she said she did?' (Engle 2008: 948).

There may well be substance to some of these concerns but the argument about conceptualizing women primarily as victims is open to the challenge that it overlooks a significant distinction between IHL and HRL. It needs to be appreciated that IHL is a regime that only operates during times of armed conflict and occupation with the aim of protecting all those who are vulnerable during such times, be they combatants or civilians, male or female.[14] The use of the word 'victim' in IHL, that I agree is problematic in many situations, should take its meaning from its particular context. Everyone is a potential victim in this regime. It is, therefore, not surprising that women appear as victims in IHL and to talk of sexual and political agency for anyone during such times of social disintergration takes on a somewhat unrealistic air. The issue for feminists is whether the reality of women's lives is accurately reflected in the provisions of the regime. HRL in contrast, although of increasing relevance in times of armed conflict, is designed to operate during times of peace and serves both as a shield and a sword in the sense that it not only protects individuals but it does so by conferring on them enforceable rights. One can legitimately expect more from this regime in terms of empowerment than IHL. Consequently, to constantly elide these two regimes, as does much of the feminist scholarship in this area, can from time to time be problematic. We need to bear this in mind when we are considering applying critiques developed in other parts of international law into IHL.

Perhaps the most fundamental debate among feminist scholars and activists in the campaign to ensure the punishment of sexual violence against women in armed conflict, and one that still reverberates through feminist writings, was how to classify and prosecute

---

13   This approach to consent in cases of sexual assault is now contained in the Rules of Procedure and Evidence of the International Criminal Tribunal for the Former Yugoslavia (2008).

14   This is the purported aim of IHL and one can argue that it is in fact more about protecting the interests of the State but for the sake of argument in this article I assume IHL has a basically protective role. Jochnick and Normand provide an alternative vision (Jochnick and Normand 1994).

wartime rape and sexual violence (see, for example, Engle 2005, explaining the differing feminist positions, particularly the debate about classifying wartime rape as 'genocidal'). The processes that led to the resolution of these differences have been viewed with misgivings in some quarters. In particular, Halley sees the traditionally rich variety of feminist voices as having been silenced in this campaign by the ruthless pursuit of power by those dedicated to achieving a particular radical feminist agenda, one that is designed to eliminate the universal subordination of women by men and end the global 'war on women'. Criminal law, with its emphasis on prosecution and punishment, has the key role to play in this campaign (Halley 2009: 45, 46, 66, 74–75). Halley argues that as part of this agenda certain feminists (including myself as the co-author of an 'unreliable handbook' of 'literary fiction') are deeply implicated in an ongoing conspiracy that played out in the negotiations of the Statutes of the ICTY, ICTR and the ICC. The aim apparently is to subvert the distinction between the two legal regimes – IHL that applies in times of armed conflict and HRL, the so-called law of peace – in order to facilitate the punishment at the international level by the ICC of not just wartime rape but 'everyday' rape occurring in the domestic setting.

There is some truth in this claim insofar as some feminists, primarily from the US, are concerned (MacKinnon 2006). Sexual violence has always been a prime item on the feminist agenda. It is therefore not surprising to find the influence of this focus extending into the international context, particularly with the increased participation of feminist domestic criminal lawyers on these issues, whose agenda may well have been to bring developments at the international level to bear on domestic rape. It is also true that much feminist international legal scholarship has called for a re-drawing of its boundaries to more truly reflect the experiences of women (Charlesworth and Chinkin 2000). In the specific context of IHL, I have argued for the recognition that what is covered currently by that regime is gendered and neglects the different ways in which women experience armed conflict and its aftermath. However, the conspiracy theory of Halley is a simplistic and misleading assessment of the overall work of the majority of the scholars who were engaged in this debate. Their writing indicates a sophisticated understanding of the structure of male/ female power relations and an awareness of the limitations of criminal law to make a real difference. They acknowledge that if we do not address the conditions that make rape and sexual violence against women so prevalent, it is merely a 'band-aid' approach to prosecute sexual offences at the international, or indeed the national level (Chinkin, Wright and Charlesworth 2005: 28). They are thus far from the single issue/single approach zealots they are sometimes portrayed as, but are no doubt influenced by the thinking that if there is to be an unprecedented development in the punishment of breaches of IHL, it would be a lost opportunity not to insist that sexual violence against women is part of this new world.

Leaving aside feminist power politics and the accompanying scholarly debates that are all good grist for the feminist mill, why do I think this focus on sexual violence has a much more worrisome impact than, for example, potentially interfering with women's sexual autonomy in times of armed conflict? Surely after years of neglect we would be churlish not to greet with enthusiasm the recognition and punishment of some of the violence perpetrated against women in armed conflict, even if the process and outcome are far from perfect? To my mind, however, there are significant negative consequences for women from this single issue approach. Certainly, it perpetuates and reinforces the limited vision of women contained in IHL, as someone who only becomes visible through their sexual identity. Most importantly, in doing so it deflects attention from the myriad other pressing issues that women face during and after armed conflict that, if not caused, then at the very least are exacerbated by endemic discrimination. The so-called progress on the prosecution of sexual violence during armed conflict also gives credence to the claim that women are now being taken seriously by the legal regime. But are they? As Hilary Charlesworth has observed in the context of the inclusion of women in human rights institutions, it is easy to be 'dazzled' by appearances (Charlesworth 2011: 23).

## The Way Forward

As I have argued, apart from a focus on sexual violence against women, the vast inertia that Charlesworth has identified in relation to the insights of feminism and international law generally is even more pronounced in the case of IHL. Adding to this is reluctance on the part of those feminists who work in HRL to engage with IHL beyond sexual violence.

Despite the obstacles, in my view there is potential for progress by pressing for the interpretation and implementation of the whole range of existing provisions of IHL in ways that recognize the experience of women in armed conflict. In saying this, I find myself retreating from the position I have previously advocated, namely that we need to focus on law reform (Gardam 2005).[15] How simple it all seemed when it first became apparent that women's experience of armed conflict was not reflected in IHL. Following on from the precedent of the 1979 Convention for the Elimination of all Discrimination Against Women, a new Geneva Convention that dealt with the issue seemed the obvious answer. Irrespective of the relative advantages of such a strategy it has no hope of success (Gardam 2005). So we work with what we have.

My cautious optimism as to the usefulness of persevering with what law we have is based on the possibility of a new ally in this enterprise. It has always been clear that there will only be fundamental change when it becomes apparent to political and military leaders that recognizing and responding to the different impact of armed conflict on women due to their role in society can have positive outcomes in terms of military efficiency. In particular, that such an approach can serve to provide increased protection for combatants. The military are above all pragmatic. To take one example, as part of their gender mainstreaming action plan in response to Security Council resolution 1325, NATO forces in Afghanistan have been including in their operations Female Engagement Teams (FETs) comprised of women soldiers trained in gender issues. The FETs do not just sit back at headquarters and play token roles,[16] nor is their focus on sexual violence against women. They are involved in actual military operations in support of infantry units in the field such as information gathering, weapon searches and the distribution of humanitarian assistance (Pottinger, Jilani and Russo 2010). It is reported that this strategy has 'enhanced operational effectiveness through "improved information gathering, enhanced credibility and better force protection"' (Prescott 2012: 56 citing Dharmanpuri).

It is not the prospect of improved military efficiency from these initiatives that interests me but their by-products; their potential for increasing the visibility of women and their needs during and in the aftermath of armed conflict. Thus it has been reported that FETs can gain direct access to women in Afghan communities that is unavailable to their male colleagues.

---

15    See Oosterveldt 2009 for a full discussion of the differing views on the need for law reform.
16    This appears to be the case with the Gender Adviser appointed under BSI–SC Directive 40–1 (NATO 2009) (Prescott 2012, footnote 243 and accompanying text).

Consequently they can assist in the more equal implementation of the requirements of IHL that deal with essential supplies and services (Pottinger, Jilani and Russo 2010: 7).[17]

One should not, however, see such developments as the start of a brave new world. I suspect there is limited enthusiasm for such undertakings at the command level and among the troops who in all probability view the FETs and other such initiatives as something that just has to be done to placate the UN and its supporters.

Apart from cautiously welcoming these developments and being intrigued that Pashtun men apparently view foreign women troops not with hostility but as a kind of third gender (Pottinger, Jilani and Russo 2010: 2), what can feminist legal scholars add? Such programmes as the FETs are directly engaging with the interplay between gender and culture and I think this is a direction that is ripe for scholarly feminist analysis as we continue to argue for better recognition in IHL of the ways in which women experience armed conflict over and above their stereotypical roles as mothers and sexual objects. Unlike the situation with HRL, the influence of culture on the content and implementation of IHL has not aroused much interest among scholars (see, by contrast, Provost 2007). However, it is not as if culture is not acknowledged in IHL itself. Respect for cultural diversity is one of its foundational principles.[18] Moreover culture has a powerful impact on how IHL operates in that it has been used, in the main unthinkingly, in ways that have a negative impact on women. It is often the justification for why little can be done for women in many situations arising from armed conflict. As one Kosovo woman lamented in a somewhat different context: 'when it comes to real involvement in the planning for the future of this country, our men tell the foreign men to ignore our ideas. And they are happy to do so—under the notion of "cultural sensitivity". Why is it politically incorrect to ignore the concerns of Serbs or other minorities, but "culturally sensitive" to ignore the concerns of women?' (Rehn and Sirleaf 2002: 125).

Complicating this scenario is the fact that IHL itself, perhaps even more so than HRL, comes replete with cultural assumptions. Simple statements to respect cultural differences in treaty provisions cannot disguise the fact that it is a regime that reflects not only male but Western visions of women (Gardam 1997). Given this reality, any proposals, for example to adopt the strategy of better implementation or re-interpretation of existing law, run the risk of imposing such values on all women. These are very real issues as the vast majority of the armed conflicts that IHL deals with today take place on the territory of non-Western States such as Afghanistan and Iraq and it is the Western military that are implementing IHL. This is not to say that the needs of women in such times cannot be recognized and responded to but it requires a serious commitment and creativity from all actors including feminist scholars.

---

17 For example, article 55 of the *Convention (IV) Relative to the Protection of Civilian Persons in Time of War* provision for humanitarian assistance to civilians in occupied territories.

18 For example, article 27(1) of the *Convention (IV) Relative to the Protection of Civilian Persons in Time of War* provides: 'Protected persons are entitled, in all circumstances, to respect for … their manners and customs.' This provision is described as 'proclaiming … the principles on which the whole of "Geneva Law" is founded' and balancing 'the rights and liberties of the individual against those of the community' (Pictet 1958: 200).

# Conclusion

Reflecting over the last decade or so of the engagement with IHL it is apparent that feminist scholars and activists have brought an end to the prevailing impunity for those who commit sexual violence against women in armed conflict. I am in no position to judge what gains have been made on the ground for women through these developments. I am in a position to conclude that we seem to have sacrificed pursuing action to address the more mundane and seemingly intractable everyday experiences of women during such times. I suggest that feminists should revisit the broader challenge described in the second part of this chapter, namely thinking of ways in which the existing provisions of IHL can be applied and re-interpreted so that women's experiences of armed conflict and its aftermath can be more effectively addressed, but in ways that recognize that IHL takes a limited and Western view of women's lives.

We nowadays have a fairly clear picture of women's global experience of armed conflict. We can demonstrate that IHL in many ways fails to respond to this reality. What we really do not have a clear idea of is how to avoid making an effective response more difficult by automatically assuming that certain outcomes that may seem self-evident to Western feminists will work in all contexts.

# References

Australian Human Rights Commission. 2011. *Report on the Review into the Treatment of Women in the Australian Defence Force Academy: Phase 1 of the Review into the Treatment of Women in the Australian Defence Force*. Sydney: Australian Human Rights Commission.

Ben-Naftali, O. 2011. *International Humanitarian Law and International Human Rights Law*. Oxford/New York: Oxford University Press.

Buss, D. 2007. The curious visibility of wartime rape: gender and ethnicity in international criminal law. *Windsor Yearbook of Access to Justice*, 25(1), 3–22.

Carpenter, C.R. 2006. *'Innocent Women and Children': Gender Norms and the Protection of Civilians*. Aldershot: Ashgate Publishing.

Charlesworth, H. 1999. Feminist methods in international law. *American Journal of International Law*, 93(2), 379–394.

Charlesworth H. 2002. International law as a discipline of crisis. *Modern Law Review*, 63(3), 377–392.

Charlesworth, H. 2008. International law: a view from the antipodes, in *Regards du Génération sur le Droit International*, edited by E. Jouannet, H.R. Fabri and J.M. Sorel. Paris: Pedone, 161–167.

Charlesworth, H. 2011. Talking to ourselves? Feminist scholarship in international law, in *Feminist Perspectives on Contemporary International Law: Between Resistance and Compliance?*, edited by S. Kouvo and Z. Pearson. Oxford: Hart Publishing, 17–32.

Charlesworth, H. and Chinkin, C. 2000. *The Boundaries of International Law: A Feminist Analysis*. Manchester: Manchester University Press.

Charlesworth, H. and Chinkin, C. 2002. Sex, gender, and September 11. *American Journal of International Law*, 96(3), 600–605.

Charlesworth, H., Chinkin, C. and Wright, S. 1991. Feminist approaches to international law. *American Journal of International Law*, 85(4), 613–645.

Chinkin, C. 1997. Feminist interventions into international law. *Adelaide Law Review*, 19(1), 13–24.

Chinkin, C. 2003. Feminist reflections on international criminal law, in *International Criminal Law and the Current Development of Public International Law*, edited by A. Zimmermann. Berlin: Duncker and Humblot, 125–160.

Chinkin, C., Wright, S. and Charlesworth, H. 2005. Feminist approaches to international law: reflections from another century, in *International Law: Modern Feminist Approaches*, edited by D. Buss and A. Manji. Oxford: Hart Publishing, 17–47.

*Convention (IV) Relative to the Protection of Civilian Persons in Time of War.* 1949. 75 UNTS 287, Geneva.

Engle, K. 2005. Feminism and its (dis)contents: criminalizing wartime rape in Bosnia and Herzegovina. *American Journal of International Law*, 99(4), 778–816.

Engle, K. 2008. Judging sex in war. *Michigan Law Review*, 106(6), 941–961.

Enloe, C. 1993. *The Morning After Sexual Politics at the End of the Cold War.* Berkley and Los Angeles: California University Press.

Forsythe, D.P. 2005, *The Humanitarians: The International Committee of the Red Cross.* Cambridge: Cambridge University Press.

Gardam, J. 1990. A feminist analysis of international humanitarian law. *Australian Yearbook of International Law*, 12, 265–278.

Gardam, J. 1993a. Gender and non-combatant immunity. *Transnational Law and Contemporary Problems*, 3(2), 345–370.

Gardam, J. 1993b. The law of armed conflict: a feminist perspective, in *Human Rights in the Twenty-First Century*, edited by P. Mahoney and K.E. Mahoney. Dordrecht: Martinus Nijhoff Publishers, 419–436.

Gardam, J. 1997. An alien's encounter with the law of armed conflict, in *Sexing the Subject of Law*, edited by N. Naffine and R. Owens. North Ryde: LBC Information Services, 233–250.

Gardam, J. 2005. The neglected aspect of women and armed conflict: progressive development of the law. *Netherlands International Law Review*, 52(2), 197–219.

Gardam, J. 2010. War, law, terror, nothing new for women. *Australian Feminist Law Journal*, 32, 61–75.

Gardam, J. and Jarvis, M. 2001. *Women, Armed Conflict and International Law*, The Hague: Kluwer Law International.

Goldstein, J. 2001. *War and Gender: How Gender Shapes the War System and Vice Versa.* Cambridge: Cambridge University Press.

Grant, R. and Newland, K. *Gender and International Relations.* Bloomington: Indiana University Press.

Grahn-Farley, M. 2011. The Politics of Inevitability: An Examination of Janet Halley's critique of the Criminalisation of Rape as Torture, in *Feminist Perspectives on Contemporary International Law: Between Resistance and Compliance?*, edited by S. Kouvo and Z. Pearson. Oxford: Hart Publishing, 109–129.

Halley, J. 2006. *Split Decisions: How and Why to Take a Break from Feminism*, Princeton: Princeton University Press.

Halley, J. 2009. Rape at Rome: feminist interventions in the criminalization of sex-related violence in positive international criminal law. *Michigan Journal of International Law*, 30(1), 1–123.

Hemingway, E. 1940. *For Whom the Bell Tolls.* New York: Charles Scribner's Sons.

Jochnick, C. and Normand, R. 1994. The legitimation of violence: a critical history of the laws of war. *Harvard International Law Journal*, 35(1), 49–96.

Kapur, R. 2002. The tragedy of victimisation rhetoric: resurrecting the 'native' subject in international/post-colonial feminist legal politics. *Harvard Human Rights Journal*, 15, 1–37.

Keen, M.H. 1965. *The Laws of War in the Late Middle Ages*. London: Routledge and K. Paul.

Khushalani, Y. 1982. *Dignity and Honour of Women as Basic and Fundamental Human Rights*. The Hague: Martinus Nijhoff Publishers.

Kinsella, H.M. 2005. Securing the civilian: sex and gender in the laws of war, in *Power in Global Governance*, edited by M. Barnett and R. Duvall. Cambridge: Cambridge University Press, 249–272.

Koskienemmi M. 2002. 'The lady doth protest too much': Kosovo, and the turn to ethics in international law. *Modern Law Review*, 65(2), 159–175.

Krill, F. 1985. The protection of women in international humanitarian law. *International Review of the Red Cross*, 25(249), 337–363.

Lindsey, C. 2001. *Women Facing War*. Geneva: International Committee of the Red Cross.

MacKinnon, C.A. 1994. Rape, genocide and women's human rights. *Harvard Women's Law Journal*, 17, 5–16.

MacKinnon, C. 2006. Women's September 11th: rethinking the international law of conflict. *Harvard International Law Journal*, 47(1), 1–31.

Murphy, Y. 2005. Feminism Here and Feminism There: Law, Theory and Choice, in *International Law: Modern Feminist Approaches*, edited by D. Buss and A. Manji. Oxford: Hart Publishing, 67–86.

Naffine, N. 1990. *Law and the Sexes: Explorations in Feminist Jurisprudence*. Sydney: Allen and Unwin.

North Atlantic Treaty Organisation (NATO). 2009. *BSI-SC Directive 40-1: Integrating UNSCR 1325 and Gender Perspectives in the NATO Command Structure Including Measures for Protection during Armed Conflict*. Belgium/USA, 2 September 2009.

OHCHR. *Rape: Weapon of War* [Online: Office of the High Commissioner for Human Rights]. Available at: www.ohchr.org/en/newsevents/pages/rapeweaponwar.aspx [accessed: 22 April 2011].

Oosterveldt, V. 2009 Feminist debates on civilian women and international humanitarian law. *Windsor Yearbook of Access to Justice*, 27(2) 385–402.

Otto, D. 2005. Disconcerting 'masculinities': reinventing the gendered subject(s) of international human rights law, in *International Law: Modern Feminist Approaches*, edited by D. Buss and A. Manji. Oxford: Hart Publishing, 105–129.

Otto, D. 2010. Power and danger: A feminist engagement with international law through the U.N. Security Council. *Australian Feminist Law Journal*, 32, 97–122.

Pettman, J. 1996. *Worlding Women: A Feminist International Politics*. London: Routledge.

Pictet, J. 1958. *Commentary on the IV Geneva Convention Relative to the Protection of Civilian Persons in Time of War*. Geneva: International Committee of the Red Cross.

Pottinger, M., Jilani, H. and Russo, C. 2010. *Half-Hearted: Trying to Win Afghanistan without Afghan Women* [Online: Small Wars Journal]. Available at: <http://smallwarsjournal.com/blog/journal/docs–temp/370–pottinger.pdf> [accessed: 10 April 2012].

Prescott, J.M. 2013. NATO gender mainstreaming and the feminist critique of the law of armed conflict. *Georgetown Journal of Gender and the Law*, 14(1), 83–132.

Provost, R. 2007. The international committee of the red widget? The diversity debate in international humanitarian law. *Israel Law Review*, 40(2), 614–647.

Reardon, B. 1985. *Sexism and the War System*. Syracuse: Syracuse University Press.

Rehn, E. and Sirleaf, E.J. 2002. *Women, War and Peace: The Independent Experts' Assessment on the Impact of Armed Conflict on Women and Women's Role in Peace-building*. New York: UNIFEM.

Roberts, A. and Guelff, R. 1989. *Documents on the Laws of War*. 2nd edn. Oxford: Clarendon Press.

*Rules of Procedure and Evidence of the International Criminal Tribunal for the Former Yugoslavia*. 2008. U.N. Doc IT/32/Rev.41. The Hague: ICTY.

Simma, B. and Paulus, A. 1999. The responsibility of individuals for human rights abuses in internal conflicts: a positivist view. *American Journal of International Law*, 93(2), 302–316.

Sjoberg, L. 2006. The gender realities of the immunity principle: why gender analysis needs feminism. *International Studies Quarterly*, 50(4), 889–910.

Smart, C. 1989. *Feminism and the Power of Law*. London: Routledge.

Tickner, J.A. 1992, *Gender in International Relations: Feminist Perspectives on Achieving Global Security*. New York: Columbia University Press.

U.N. Security Council. 1993. *Resolution 808*, New York, 22 February 1993.

U.N. Security Council. 1993. *Resolution 827*, New York, 25 May 1993.

U.N. Security Council. 1994. *Resolution 955*, New York, 8 November 1994.

Wilde, R. 2010. Compliance with human rights norms extraterritorially: 'human rights imperialism'?, in *International Law and the Quest for its Implementation: Liber Amicorum Vera Gowlland-Debbas*, edited by L. Boisson de Chazournes and M. Kohen. Leiden: Martinus Nijhoiff Publishers, 319–348.

# Violence Against Women, 'Victimhood' and the (Neo)Liberal State

## Vanessa E. Munro[1]

Violence takes many forms, arises in diverse contexts and operates on multiple scales. It has political, social, economic, cultural and inter-personal dimensions that are often mutually supportive. While the specific phenomenon of violence against women obviously substantially predates the emergence of second-wave feminism, it was during the 1960s and 1970s in particular that its prevalence and political significance was most forcefully highlighted, at least in the Western context. Although, in many regards, the demands made by second-wave feminists remain unaddressed to this day, the campaigning which took place during this period drastically shifted the terrain upon which the issue was conceptualized, problematized and responded to. Pioneering feminist work highlighted, among other things, the 'mundane' nature of violence against women, uncovering the high prevalence of physical and sexual abuse, particularly within domestic settings, and exposing the powerful ideologies relied upon both by perpetrators and by the state in order to normalize and justify such conduct.

As an explanatory and critical concept, then, violence has been routinely deployed in prominent feminist accounts of the origins and perpetuation of patriarchy. As an empirical reality that has been, and continues to be, experienced (in physical, sexual or psychological forms) in the lives of many women, it has also provided a focal point for feminist activism. But despite its importance within feminist theorizing, the meaning and parameters of the concept of 'violence' are malleable and fluctuating; though grounded in a very real experience of harm or wrongdoing, they are heavily socially constructed, relating in complex and mutually-affirming ways to observers' normative responses. As a result, engaging effectively with the concept and role of 'violence', and of 'violence against women' in particular, necessitates a nuanced and critical approach.

In this chapter, I will examine these different levels of feminist engagement with the experience and concept of violence, and I will explore their (often complex and contested) relationship to designations of 'victimhood'. The expansion and contraction of the concept of violence within feminist theorizing, and the associated but distinct shift in register from 'violence against women' to 'gender-based violence' that has been evidenced in some quarters, will also be charted, and the opportunities and challenges which these developments present will be examined. Having explored the (patriarchal) foundations for

1  With the usual caveats, I am grateful to Katie Cruz for her excellent research assistance in the initial stages, and to Sharon Cowan, Margaret Davies, Clare McGlynn and Jane Scoular for their helpful comments on an earlier draft of this chapter.

violence against women challenged by feminist theorizing and activism, in the final stages of the chapter, I will reflect on the implications of this in terms of feminism's engagement with law. This discussion will be framed in particular by a contemporary context in which previously expressed concerns over the role of the state (and the law) in providing redress for, and protection against, violence have been re-engaged by the apparent co-option of a range of self-consciously feminist agendas in the service of neo-liberal strategies of surveillance, responsibilization and risk management.

## Violence as Lived Reality: Empirical Evidence of Violence in Women's Lives

In this section, I offer some wider context to the conceptual discussion on violence against women that follows by examining the current state of knowledge in relation to the scale of violence in women's lives. The empirical snapshot provided here is, inevitably, highly partial and particularized. It is not possible – and certainly not within this chapter – to provide a comprehensive account of the highly divergent experiences of violence encountered by women in different contexts. Manifestations of violence, as well as the meanings and significance attached to them, are highly culturally and personally specific. Indeed, as Chandra Mohanty (1988: 67) has put it, 'male violence (if that indeed is the appropriate label) must be theorised and interpreted within specific societies, both in order to understand it better, as well as in order to effectively organise to change it'. Thus, while violence can be, and is, experienced (albeit in different ways and in different circumstances) by women across the globe, for current purposes, I restrict my focus to giving a brief snapshot of prevalence in the context of the United Kingdom, the jurisdiction with which I am most familiar. Though generating its own idiosyncrasies, experience in the UK provides a lens through which we can also glimpse parallel experiences within many other Western European and Commonwealth jurisdictions.

Probably the two areas within which feminist engagement has been most persistent in the UK relate to domestic abuse and sexual assault. Focusing on domestic abuse pierces the veil of family privacy and provides a mechanism by which to challenge traditional familial structures within which wives were treated primarily as the property of their husbands. As Rebecca Dobash and Russell Dobash have explained (1994: 4), 'the sources of conflict leading to violent events reveal a great deal about the nature of relations between men and women, demands and expectations of wives, the prerogatives and power of husbands, and cultural beliefs that support individual attitudes of marital inequality.' Thus, by highlighting and problematizing domestic abuse, feminist advocates not only develop strategies to increase support to its victims (for example, through the establishment of dedicated shelters) but also lever (albeit with varying degrees of success) for broader social and attitudinal change. As a specific manifestation of domestic abuse, as well as a broader form of victimization outwith the context of prior relationships, sexual assault has similarly been a focus of considerable feminist activism and concern. Liz Kelly and Jill Radford (1998: 53) have suggested that feminist movements, nationally and internationally, have tended to direct so much attention to sexual assault for three reasons – first, it is 'one of the ugliest and most brutal expressions of masculine violence toward women'; second, 'rape and the historical discourses around it reveal a great deal about the social relations of reproduction'; and third, 'rape reveals a great deal about the way in which the woman's body is seen as representing the community'. But despite the attention that feminists have devoted to these topics, and the extent to which – through these efforts – the issues of domestic abuse and sexual assault have attracted growing official and social concern, in the UK context, there has to date been a lack of large-scale prevalence studies specifically addressing the topic of violence against women (Brown et al. 2010).

Our primary data comes instead from official statistics on reported offences or self-report responses to a specific module included within the broader structure of the annual British Crime Survey (BCS). Both sources are limited in their ability to capture incidence accurately. It is widely acknowledged that victims of domestic abuse and sexual assault may be reluctant to formally report their victimization to police, and may not even recognize what has been done to them as a crime (for discussion, see, for example, Kelly 2002, Regan and Kelly 2003, Jordan 2004). Self-report studies do little to identify victims in the latter category, and only enable partial glimpses at the former, since many will remain reluctant to disclose to any third party, let alone an unknown survey administrator. Moreover, the BCS's reliance on a postcode sampling method entails that communities who may be particularly vulnerable to sexual abuse, such as the homeless, are inevitably excluded, which in turn skews prevalence rates. In addition, there is often a significant disconnect between the definitions of violence adopted in official resources and those employed by self-consciously feminist researchers. While the former tend to rely on the reporting of discrete incidents – typically of physical violence – in order to chart prevalence, the latter often adopt a far wider definition, encompassing threats or fears of violence, emotional distress, economic hardship or structural disadvantage. As will be discussed further below, there are benefits and difficulties associated with each of these approaches; and such definitional divergence within contemporary discourses on violence against women can facilitate miscommunication between, and even manipulation by, different stakeholders.

Despite these cautionary concerns, it is, however, instructive to briefly explore the current state of official knowledge in the UK in relation to the scale of domestic abuse and sexual assault. It has been suggested that 45 per cent of British women will be subject to domestic violence or stalking at least once in their lifetimes (Walby and Allen 2004), with data from the 2009/10 BCS estimating that over 1.2 million women had been subject to domestic (including sexual) abuse in the previous year (Smith et al. 2011). Though it is increasingly acknowledged that men can be subject to domestic violence at the hands of female partners, evidence suggests that this is comparatively rare and that domestic abuse remains a form of male-to-female victimization in the majority of cases (Smith et al. 2011). Concerted efforts to encourage police to take seriously, and intervene in, domestic disputes have yielded improvements in UK reporting and conviction rates. Even in the relatively short period between 2003 and 2007, for example, the success rate on prosecutions for domestic violence in England and Wales increased from 46 per cent to 69 per cent (Home Office 2009). According to the UK Equalities Office, this was in large part due to the development of Specialist Domestic Violence Courts, which – although criticized by some feminists for ghetto-izing the issue of domestic abuse or diminishing its importance as a form of physical assault – have been praised by others for providing a more tailored, sensitive and holistic response (Cook et al. 2004, Home Office 2008).

In relation to sexual forms of abuse specifically, there were 54,982 sexual offences recorded by the police in England and Wales in 2010/11, of which 82 per cent were classified as 'most serious sexual assaults', including rape (Home Office 2011). The 2010/11 BCS estimated that 2.5 per cent of women aged between 16–59 years had experienced a sexual assault within the past 12-month period. Some 38 per cent of the victims of rape or serious sexual assault who reported to the BCS in 2009/10 had told nobody else about what had happened to them, and only 11 per cent had officially reported the incident to the police (Smith et al. 2011). While 65 per cent of the victims who contacted the police reported that they had found their response to be 'very helpful' or 'fairly helpful', a large proportion of complainants were less satisfied, notwithstanding a raft of measures in recent years designed to improve police and prosecutor responses (Smith et al. 2011). Although concern has recently been expressed regarding the tendency for (feminist) campaigners to become overly preoccupied with conviction rates in the abstract (Home Office 2010), attrition of rape complaints remains an ongoing concern within the UK criminal justice system. In England and Wales, the percentage of reported rapes that ultimately secure a conviction has languished at around 6 per cent, with many complaints being abandoned by police or prosecutors early in the process and often without adequate explanation. In those cases that make it to trial, moreover, dubious gender stereotypes are often still relied upon to discredit female complainants (Kelly, Temkin and Griffiths 2006, HMCPSI/HMIC 2007), tapping into a widely held public attitude that women who fail to conform to traditional gender roles – by dressing provocatively, flirting or drinking more than a moderate amount of alcohol – must bear some, if not all, of the responsibility for their sexual victimization (Finch and Munro 2007, Ellison and Munro 2009, Temkin and Krahe 2008).

As noted above, while this data on domestic abuse and sexual assault, and the feminist activism that has accompanied it, provide important insights into the scale of violence in the lives of women in the UK, they do not, and cannot, provide a complete picture. Aside from its methodological limits and the fact that it only maps incidence within one jurisdiction, often effacing important differences *between* communities in the UK in the process, this data is also inevitably limited by its focus on domestic abuse and sexual assault specifically. Although these may be viewed by many as paradigm examples of violence against women, there are myriad other forms in existence and a more comprehensive mapping must find a way to include them. At the same time, however, this is a complex and contentious task. The boundaries of what counts as 'violence' are themselves contested, socially constructed, malleable, and shifting over time, place and context. Broader, and more inclusive, approaches may include verbal or emotional abuse. In addition, they may include circumstantial force and constraints on agency that shape decisions by women to, for example, sell their sexual or reproductive services, to wear religious veils or to participate in cultural practices which others have considered harmful. Such approaches may throw better light onto the reach, and complexity, of violence in women's daily lives, and may allow for more careful consideration of the different modes and degrees of violence that can be experienced. At the same time, by troubling sharp distinctions between physical force and other, non-physical forms of coercion, and including all such manifestations within the overarching category of 'violence', they risk a level of conceptual confusion and may dilute the normative condemnation that violence attracts. They also engage difficult debates over victimhood/agency, and position what many regard as less serious forms of abuse on a par with extreme physical violation. In terms of securing tangible victories, such strategies may, therefore, be counter-productive, permitting a trivialization of experiences of violence and entailing the emergence *within* feminism of divided perspectives on how we define violence, on what counts as harmful, and on what role the state ought to play in intervening. In the rest of this chapter, I will examine these concerns further, exploring the ongoing challenges that they present.

# Understanding Violence Against Women:
## A Symbol and Strategy of Patriarchy?

Tracking the empirical incidence of, and calling for improved practical responses to, the domestic and sexual abuse of women were not, of course, the only contributions made by second-wave feminism. In the UK, as in the US, a related and equally important contribution came at the theoretical level, where the links between the personal and the political were exposed. Key to this approach was the insistence that violence in women's lives, in whatever form, could not be properly understood, let alone addressed, without acknowledging the mutually supportive relationship between its individual, ideological and institutional manifestations under conditions of patriarchy.[2] Building on this insight, throughout the 1980s and into the 1990s, British feminists like Kelly emphasized the existence of a continuum of violence linking heterosexual, and apparently consensual, practices and relationships with forced and abusive conduct (1988), whilst Dobash and Dobash insisted that 'violent men cannot be understood without understanding the immediate contexts of violent events and the wider social context in which such behaviour is more or less tolerated or rewarding' (1998: 168).

Expressing these ideas in radical form, in the US, Catharine MacKinnon insisted that violence against women, and sexual violence in particular, played a pivotal role in instantiating, preserving and supporting men's dominance. In this section, I will highlight the implications of this analysis for our understanding of the scale and meaning of violence, and of violence against women in particular. I will argue that this type of anchoring in structural analysis usefully highlights the interconnections between divergent contexts and experiences of violence, enabling us to see points of continuity between what might otherwise appear as distinct incidents and to acknowledge the broader symbolic consequences of what might otherwise appear as trivial encounters. At the same time, however, I will also explore the extent to which, to achieve this potential, it generates the need for a more nuanced and sophisticated understanding of violence than has typically been afforded in such feminist accounts.

In line with her broader, 'feminism unmodified' approach, MacKinnon provided a rhetorically striking critique within which violence against women is understood as a paradigmatic symbol and strategy of patriarchy. Its occurrence is neither random nor reducible to individual pathologies; it is systemic and systematic, reflecting and perpetuating a social structure within which men enjoy a position of power and privilege over women. Sexual violence has a particularly pivotal role in this framework, since, according to MacKinnon, sexuality is the 'lynchpin' of gender domination – 'that which is most one's own, yet most taken away' (1989: 3). By exerting control over women's sexuality, a control that in its most extreme form is manifest in coercive sexual assault, men bolster their position of dominance, creating what Susan Brownmiller (1975) has referred to as a 'male protection racket' which disempowers women and renders them increasingly dependent upon the vagaries of male protection. For MacKinnon, although it is important to highlight and attend to the elements of power and dominance thereby implicated in rape, it is equally

---

2    This, of course, is not an insight limited to feminists or feminism – see, for example, Žižek (2008: 1–2) for a discussion of the importance of stepping back from our fascination with directly visible forms of subjective violence, to consider both 'systemic violence' and the 'symbolic violence embodied in language and its forms'.

important not to conceptualize it purely as a form of violence, since to do so would eclipse its connection to 'conventional' forms of heterosexuality and preserve the conviction that (non-forced) 'sex is good' (1987: 134). The construction of a gender hierarchy is itself integral to the establishment of male sexual desire, and this eroticization of dominance and submission must be tackled, since otherwise the boundaries between acceptable seduction and force will continue to be determined by men, for men, imperilling the prospects for rape conviction in individual cases and blocking the path to sex equality.

Though often praised for its ability to problematize gender relations beyond the confines of a debate over equal versus special treatment by drawing attention to fundamental questions of power, dominance and vested interests (see, for example, Finley 1988, Cornell 1991), MacKinnon's work has also been the subject of substantial criticism. I have explored the nature of these criticisms elsewhere (see, in particular, Munro 2007) and it is not my aim in this chapter to recount them again in any detail. For current purposes, it is its potential for over-emphasizing what Janet Halley has referred to as the 'm>f' dimension of feminist analysis that may be particularly problematic (2006: 18). Within this frame, women are depicted as perpetually victimized and subordinated, while men are constructed as the inevitable oppressors. Not only does this risk marginalizing the experiences of women who do not consider themselves to be victimized, and/or flattening important distinctions in the grades and modalities of victimization that might be encountered by different women at different times, in different locations and in different contexts, it also sidesteps many of the more complex realities of gender relations, as well as contentious debates regarding what constitutes gender violence.

While providing crucial insights regarding the need to situate individual experiences of violence in women's lives within the broader context of gender–power relations, a more nuanced analysis is thus clearly required. Simply dismissing as 'false consciousness' the claims of women who, for example, insist that they engage in prostitution as a result of choice fails to take us very far in terms of understanding the complex ways in which social norms and structural conditions influence personal decision-making, blurring the clarity of the boundary between agency and victimhood. Likewise, while stubbornly positioning the female as the paradigm victim of violence supports the theoretical frame of the patriarchal dominance approach, it may diminish our capacity to fully acknowledge, understand and problematize those incidences of women's violence (including those targeted against men) which do occur, marginalizing the various complex ways in which violence is structured along axes other than gender.

More recent engagement by feminists has often sought to respond to these difficulties by providing mechanisms through which to offer more complex accounts, without losing sight of its interaction with broader, structural conditions of power and opportunity, and without reducing the phenomenon and practice of violence to the (inter-) personal level. In the context of domestic abuse, for example, the associations of passivity and helplessness conjured through the psychiatric labelling of the 'battered women' have been challenged for their tendency to pathologize what may be a perfectly rational response to systematic abuse, particularly in situations where the state authorities appear to offer little prospects for, or interest in providing, alternative resolution (O'Donovan 1991, Wells 1994). At the same time, commentators have emphasized the complex ways in which those within abusive relationships locate strategies of management and negotiation that, though not necessarily targeted at exit, are designed to increase their security and freedom (see, for example, Hirschmann in this collection). Similarly, in the context of sexual assault, efforts have been devoted to challenging the tendency to fix attention exclusively on the conduct of the complainant in order to assess the mentality and culpability of the defendant, by highlighting the irrelevance to consent of prior drinking, flirtatious behaviour or 'provocative' attire and by opening up to greater critical scrutiny the social and cultural norms through which engagement in sex is negotiated and communicated by both parties (see, for example, Ellison and Munro 2009).

In this way, then, the conventional binaries between coercion and freedom, victimhood and agency, dominance and equality, which have framed more radical feminist accounts, have been deconstructed, troubled and challenged, albeit rarely if ever entirely abandoned. Strategies, such as the distinction between responsive, 'episodic' choice and more long-term, 'programmatic' agency (Meyers 1989), have been invoked to promote a more nuanced analysis of the different ways, and different levels upon which, we as individuals make decisions, even in often difficult circumstances. At the same time, drawing on the work of Michel Foucault in particular, it has been acknowledged that constraint and power can never be transcended, but only negotiated and managed in ways that create greater or lesser opportunities for resistance and destabilization. As Susan Hekman explains, this 'redefines agency in a way that explodes the boundaries imposed by the constituting/constituted subject. It ... entails that subjects find agency within the discursive spaces open to them in their particular historical period' (1995: 202). This, in turn, has focused attention on the concrete narratives provided by those directly involved, and on how they do, or do not, manage to negotiate the constraints and pressures that are imposed upon them – both externally and internally – in order to make choices which can be reconciled with their goals, values and overall sense of self.

Though important, these have not been uncontroversial developments, and they have generated considerable disquiet among some theorists who have long engaged with violence against women, who argue that such postmodern influences have robbed feminism of its collective base for action on behalf of women and the normative platform from which it condemns the monolithic power of male dominance (Hester et al. 1996, Jeffreys 1997). Such commentators have insisted that the impulse to locate forms of agency even in the midst of constraint and coercion has paralyzed feminism and denied recognition and redress to victims. It has also, they suggest, generated a preoccupation with cultural issues of identity politics over material concerns, which has in turn done little to redress women's vulnerability, whether on the individual or collective scale.

In reality, it seems that both of these perspectives have some merit, and both provide important and necessary lenses through which to understand and engage with the issue of violence, specifically as it plays out in the context of women's lives. The challenge remains, however, in how to bring these positions into more constructive engagement. Nowhere perhaps has the magnitude of this task been more clearly evidenced than in the context of responses to prostitution, where divisive debates continue to rage between feminists over the extent to which the selling of sexual services – by women for men's satisfaction – is, fundamentally and inherently, a form of violence against women. Such debates have marked recent international and regional engagements, and while, at the national level, they have interacted with the peculiar socio-economic conditions, social policy environment and composition and scale of local sex markets to produce certain distinctive markers, the basic points of contention have remained. Re-invigorated by contemporary social and political interest in the phenomenon of trafficking for sexual purposes, feminists on one 'side' of this debate have insisted upon the inevitably coercive and exploitative nature of commercial sex work, and its objectifying implications for female sexuality, to condemn the practice, and to call for more urgent responses as the scale of the industry expands and popular condemnation of it (or at least of certain manifestations of it) diminishes (see, for example, Coy, Horvath and Kelly 2007, Coy 2008, Jeffreys 2009). At the same time, feminists on the other 'side' have campaigned just as vehemently for a recognition that many of those involved in prostitution have 'chosen' to sell sex, albeit often against a context of limited alternatives and other circumstantial constraints, and have maintained that the best way to ensure the well-being of those involved is not through criminalization or abolition strategies, but rather through a well-managed system of regulation within which participants could be assured of a minimum level of safety and protection (see, for example, Brooks-Gordon 2006, Campbell and O'Neill 2006, Scoular and O'Neill 2007). Though the existence of this divide, and the hostility that it has frequently given rise to, has been lamented, the terrain upon which recent critical engagement and policy interventions have taken place in this context has remained deeply marked by these binary affiliations. This has arguably had significant ramifications upon the ability of divergent feminist campaigners to create coherent strategies for reform, which in turn has hampered the prospects for meaningful change and improvement in women's lives.

Clearly related to the developments outlined above has been another important shift in recent decades, which also has implications in terms of the construction of feminist analyses of, and responses to, violence against women. Signified most prominently perhaps in international law, but also reflected in domestic contexts, the concept of 'gender-based' violence has increasingly been deployed alongside, and in some instances as a preferred replacement for, the concept of 'violence against women'. The UN Declaration on the Elimination of Violence against Women, which was adopted in 1994, defines violence against women as 'any act of gender-based violence that results in, or is likely to result in, physical, sexual, or psychological harm or suffering to women, including threats of such acts, coercion or arbitrary deprivation of liberty, whether occurring in public or private life' (Article 1). Under Article 2, it stipulates that this includes forms of physical, sexual or psychological violence that occur both within the family (including battery, sexual abuse of girls, dowry-related violence, marital rape, female genital mutilation, and violence related to exploitation) and within the general community (including rape, sexual abuse, sexual harassment, trafficking and forced prostitution), as well as any such violence perpetrated or condoned by the State, wherever it occurs. Though offering, in many respects, a broad interpretation, this definition has been criticized by some feminist commentators for conflating violence against women with gender-based violence. To the extent that it positions gender difference as the *cause* of violence, and thus embeds a male–female comparator approach, Alice Edwards (2009 and 2010) has argued that it can be read as entailing a disinterest in forms of violence which do not contain an overt element of sex discrimination, arguably sidelining those other types of structural or systemic harm that are disproportionately experienced by women. At the same time, however, the benefit of this approach remains that it enables a conceptualization of violence against women as one manifestation of a broader phenomenon of gender-based violence, which can be experienced by and issued upon men as well as women, depending on context.

Again, this development has not been welcomed as an unqualified good by all commentators. Indeed, some of the ways in which this resistance has played out are well-illustrated in the specific context, outlined above, of responses to domestic abuse and sexual assault in England and Wales. In relation to domestic abuse, for example, certain theorists of violence against women have been at pains to point out the limits of any analysis that incorporates without distinction the experiences of male victims or that uses the fact of their experiences to question the applicability of conventional explanations grounded in patriarchal structures and a male proclivity for violence (see, for example, Dobash and Dobash 2004). Such theorists have focused attention on claims that much of women's violence is in fact preceded by a period of abuse at the hands of a male partner, and have relied heavily on evidence which suggests that repeat victimization is less common for men and that the negative experiences associated with abuse – as reported by male victims – are less physically and psychologically acute (Walby and Allen 2004, Home Office 2009, Dobash and Dobash 2004). Meanwhile, in the context of sexual assault, though significant strides have been made in England and Wales in terms of recognizing male rape as a serious offence that merits criminalization on a par with its female counterpart, a reluctance to conceive of rape as an offence that can be committed other than with a penis and other than by a man testifies to its ongoing association with a particular form of male sexual aggression, which by definition cannot be replicated by women. Though such an approach is at odds with developments in several other jurisdictions – including Canada and certain Australian states – it has been strongly supported by many UK feminists on the basis that a definition that encompassed women as potential perpetrators could 'detract from the core of the crime and its motivations' (Regan and Kelly 2003: 15). As a result, when this more restricted definition was supported by the Home Office (2000: para 2.8.2) and instantiated within the 2003 Sexual Offences Act in England and Wales, it was widely welcomed (although, for a more critical evaluation of this approach, see Cowan 2010).

In fact, although this challenge to the more entrenched dualism of male perpetrator/ female victim, which has been embedded in many conventional violence against women models, demands some careful reflection, it does not necessarily obliterate the merits of an explanatory approach that situates violence in the context of patriarchal structures. The defensiveness that it has generated from some quarters may, therefore, be rather misplaced, not to mention counter-productive. In providing a more fluid model for understanding the complex, and often contradictory, impulses of gender power and its violent manifestations, this shift in nomenclature offers a way beyond the more essentialist and monolithic accounts that have often dominated the theoretical frame, acknowledging diversity of experiences and perspectives, as well as of identities, without detaching discussion from broader structural and institutional contexts and without robbing us of the opportunity to continue to talk about violence against women as a particular – and no doubt particularly problematic – manifestation of this phenomenon.

## The Master's House, the Master's Tools?
## The Role of the State in Responding to Violence

Feminist activism and critique have played an important role in highlighting the fundamentally political nature of violence against women, including that which occurs in the private sphere, and in rendering this an object of legitimate concern for governments and official agencies, such as the police. At the same time, it is clear that such violence continues to be perpetrated, and too often with impunity. Recent legislative and policy interventions in the UK (and elsewhere) have marked an ongoing commitment to protecting victims and punishing perpetrators. Initiatives have recently been designed, for example, to encourage a more rigorous no-drop policy among police forces in relation to complaints of domestic abuse and to impose more severe criminal penalties in the event of breach of domestic violence protection orders; to impose a reasonable rather than merely honest belief in consent standard in relation to sexual offences and to establish a more expansive regime of protection in relation to other forms of sexual abuse; and to criminalize the purchase of sex from 'controlled prostitutes' while proactively pursuing strategies designed to facilitate (with a backstop of coercive threat) the exit of those convicted of soliciting from the commercial sex industry. Significantly, the state has framed and justified these initiatives through explicit reliance on feminist analyses that position violence against women as a symbol and strategy of patriarchy. To the extent that this has been supported by (some) feminist campaigners, it can thus be seen to reflect a changing consciousness regarding the contentious issue of engagement with legal reform and centralist state structures.

In this section, I will reflect on the implications of this development. Drawing on recent work exploring the neo-liberal state's engagement with the violence against women agenda in particular, I will call for caution lest feminist analytical frames become co-opted and deployed in the service of regressive agendas. Such agendas rely on punitive, carceral interventions that extend the surveillance and control to which citizens – including vulnerable women – are subject, while reducing the state's responsibility to provide the socio-economic conditions required for genuine safety and empowerment.

Particularly during the late 1980s and 1990s, a number of commentators expressed concerns regarding the potential for law, as a fundamentally masculinist medium, to secure genuine feminist victories and abiding, progressive social change. It was argued that legal method may be impervious to feminist critique (Mossman 1991) and that 'the analytical frames of patriarchal law are not the spaces within which to create visions of feminist futures' (Wishik 1985: 77). By failing to de-centre law and state, it was suggested that feminists risked becoming co-opted by it, and ceding to it even greater power (Smart 1989). While such cautionary warnings are important, critics have equally emphasized that the dangers associated with a turn away from law and legal reform should not be underestimated. As MacKinnon explains, 'one result of this turning away, however realistic its reasons, is that male power continues to own law unopposed' (2005: 107). It is perhaps for this reason that, despite her trenchant criticism of the liberal legal order as thoroughly saturated with patriarchy, MacKinnon has continued to campaign for legal reform as a strategy to respond to the experiences of violence that she locates in women's daily lives, whether in the domestic context in relation to pornography or in the international context in relation to wartime rape.

While Carol Smart's insistence that 'in accepting law's terms in order to challenge the law, feminism always concedes too much' (1989: 5) provides a useful antidote against an overly-optimistic faith in the power of law to secure change, where it is taken to demand an abandonment of law and legal reform, it risks going too far. As Nicola Lacey has observed, not all legal reform strategies are equally flawed and what feminism needs 'is not an abandonment of the legal and political project, but rather the development of more sophisticated understandings of legal practices, their strengths as well as their evident and important limitations' (1998: 180). It is precisely such a close examination that reveals, however, the difficulties and dangers associated with contemporary state responses to violence against women, and the role of feminist campaigning therein.

A growing body of recent feminist work has explored the ways in which contemporary legal responses to violence against women have extended beyond the conventional juridical model of sovereign command in order to invoke a range of disciplinary mechanisms, which are intimately bound up with strategies of neo-liberal governmentality. Building on a critique of the kind of 'universalizing victim' approach that they see to be typified by MacKinnon's work, Kerry Carrington and Paul Watson have insisted that 'the government of sexual violence is not a problem reducible to some underlying structure of masculinist domination, locatable in its state institutions, judiciaries and formal laws' (1996: 267). For them, this requires policing and control mechanisms that operate 'through the ethical constitution of the self, personhood and citizenship itself' (1996: 268). The focus of government, under this model, becomes one of providing men with the means to self-regulate their own conduct, and thereby 'recasting the normative content of badly disposed masculinities' (1996: 268). This analysis highlights the more disciplinary nature of responses to violence against women that may be deployed by the modern state, as well as their more subtle, and self-regulatory, functioning, and ties this effectively to neo-liberal strategies for the governance of responsible citizenship. But other, more recent, feminist commentators have begun to question the extent to which, in their concrete deployment and application, these strategies have 'back-fired' by turning the gaze of surveillance firmly back upon the woman rather than the man.

Situating her analysis primarily in the US context, Kristin Bumiller has launched a powerful argument which insists that, over recent decades, the conjunction of a growing awareness of the problem of violence against women, together with a rise in both 'penal populism' and 'cultures of control' (for further discussion see, for example, Garland 2001, Pratt 2007, Simon 2007), as well as an expansion of the reach of the 'therapeutic state', has led to the feminist movement becoming 'a partner in the unforeseen growth of a criminalized society, a phenomenon with negative consequences not only for minority and immigrant groups of men, but also for those women who are subject to scrutiny' (2008: xii). As the conventional parameters of the state's command have gradually but incrementally been curtailed, strategies employed to help victims of violence against women have been focused increasingly upon individualistic forms of problem-solving, detached from the broader contexts that frame experiences of violence and prospects for recovery or redress. The locus for this problem-solving has been positioned, moreover, not at the feet of men, as Carrington and Watson suggest, but rather at the hands of women. Indeed, as Michelle Fine and Lois Weis have noted, also in the US contemporary context, 'public sites of help have been appropriated into sites of surveillance', thrusting responsibilities – which are, at base, impossible to satisfy solely at the personal level – onto 'the bodies and souls of girls and women' (2000: 1144).

Victims of violence have become the focus of penal/welfare apparatuses. In the name of victims, calls have been made (and heard) for harsher penalties for perpetrators, serving a broader agenda of crime control and carceralism, irrespective of the wishes of the victim, or the impact that such forms of punishment may have on her – for example, in cases of domestic violence, where punishment of the perpetrator may provoke further violence or disrupt the parental contact and financial support provided to children (Hoyle and Sanders 2000); or in cases of prostitution, where punishment of clients may promote hastier negotiations with a riskier client base and may imperil the safety and financial security of the sex worker (Scoular and O'Neill 2008, Brooks-Gordon 2010, Munro and Scoular 2013). At the same time, the victim-focused agenda has facilitated a growth in the regulatory power of quasi-state, therapeutic institutions, which are wielded to 'protect' women, once again irrespective of their own perspectives. Women – whether through being compelled to comply with the rules and procedures of battered women's shelters, being required to prove themselves to be 'respectable' and 'credible' witnesses in their cooperation with criminal justice officials, or being diverted, under the threat of more coercive sanction, into supervisory programmes designed to ensure their exit from sex work – are trained to be 'successful survivors', who are presumed, once trained, to be able to protect themselves from future violence (Bumiller 2008: chapter 4). Across both arms of this contemporary response, then, the state is enabled to increase its surveillance, normalization and capacity for regulatory control, while at the same time absolving itself of any responsibility for providing the material and social conditions that are required in order to truly improve safety and protection against violence.

Reflecting on previous decades of feminist knowledge about, and responses to, violence against women in the UK context, Sandra Walklate has recently raised similar concerns. She has cautioned that victim advocates have often been placed in an 'uneasy alliance with criminal justice professionals – alliances that may have unintended consequences' (2008: 43). The voices of women themselves, and their desired outcomes from engagement with criminal justice, have often been lost in the rush towards responses that are simultaneously more protectionist and interventionist in relation to victims, and more punitive (at least at the level of official policy rhetoric) towards perpetrators. Feminist organizations have found themselves co-opted by the state as it implements these initiatives, and have found the frames of analysis they have traditionally relied upon being deployed in the service of unfamiliar, and potentially regressive, agendas.

In these regards, both Bumiller's and Walklate's commentaries provide an important counter to recent claims by Halley which maintain that feminism – or, more specifically, the genre of 'governance feminism' which she associates with the kind of asymmetrical accounts of patriarchal violence against women provided by theorists like MacKinnon – has gained power and privilege 'from the White House and the corporate boardroom through to the minute power dynamics ... [included in] the governance of the self' (2006: 22). While it may be true that the rhetoric of these radical accounts has increasingly infused the frames of official policy on violence against women – in the UK, the US and other domestic jurisdictions, as well as at the international level – this should not in itself be taken to evidence the 'success' of this analysis or the 'acceptance' of its advocates. On the contrary, as Bumiller has demonstrated, 'feminists have not been in total command of the "sexual violence agenda"' as it has proliferated, and as it has been utilized by the neo-liberal state in the service of more coercive and regressive forms of intervention, legitimated in the interest of ensuring women's security (2008: 2).

Though the dangers of co-option by the state, or by more regressive elements therein, are by no means novel terrain for feminist commentators, in moving forward, it is necessary, therefore, to engage in a more complex analysis of these dynamics in the context of neo-liberal governance. The fact that agents of the state have afforded an increased priority to the practices of violence against women and have sought to understand these practices in ways that transcend the merely inter-personal level may be seen to reflect a success for the demands initiated by second-wave feminism. At the same time, the challenge for contemporary feminists is to be vigilant regarding the motivations behind these developments, as well as their implications for women's agency and safety. If we are to ensure more positive interventions, we must not blind ourselves to the ways in which these developments can also serve broader state agendas of 'punitive correctness' (McGlynn 2011) and responsibilization, which entrench rather than redress the vulnerability to violence that too many women endure.

# Concluding Remarks

While the complexity of the concept, the diversity of the experience, and the malleability of the frames within which it can be understood continue to provide significant challenges, the issue of gender violence – and of violence against women as a specific manifestation thereof – remain, quite rightly, a cornerstone of feminist critique and activism. Although there is more work yet to be done in these regards, improvements have been made in recent decades in a number of jurisdictions, both in terms of public awareness of the scale of the problem and the willingness of the state and its agencies to intervene. As 'victim-centred' criminal justice agendas have gained prominence, particularly but by no means exclusively in the UK and US, the state has increasingly cited the protection of the vulnerable and the punishment of perpetrators as among its key objectives. At the same time, the parameters of what constitutes violence, of what marks someone as vulnerable, and of who counts as a victim have remained heavily contested. Though contemporary feminist work has often sought to develop more nuanced analyses that transcend the sharp dualism of agency/ victimhood, the threat that this is perceived to pose to conventional, asymmetrical accounts of patriarchal dominance and shared female oppression has generated considerable resistance; and in many applied contexts, for example, in relation to prostitution, this has mapped onto a terrain of feminist debate that has remained highly divisive and polarized. This lack of clarity and consensus has also had consequences beyond the context of feminist theorizing, since it has ensured that the broad and inclusive definitional approaches adopted by the state at the level of formal policy are often permitted to revert to a far narrower, and more limited, response at the level of operational practice (Munro 2010). Notwithstanding this, the ways in which such responses have been crafted – relying on self-regulation and compliance by 'responsible' citizens – have often imposed greater burdens on those at risk of harm, while excusing the state from proactive assistance. Moving forward, this will present ongoing challenges for feminist theory and activism. But in a context in which the issues at stake are too important, both personally and politically, to be ignored, 'taking a break' (Halley 2006) is simply not an option.

# References

Brooks-Gordon, B. 2006. *The Price of Sex: Prostitution, Policy and Society*. Cullompton: Willan Publishing.

Brooks-Gordon, B. 2010. Bellwether Citizens: The Regulation of Male Clients of Sex Workers. *Journal of Law and Society*, 37(1), 145–170.

Brown, J., Horvath, M., Kelly, L. and Westmarland, N. 2010. *Connections and Disconnections: Assessing Evidence, Knowledge and Practice in Response to Rape*. London: Government Equalities Office.

Brownmiller, S. 1975. *Against Our Will: Men, Women and Rape*. New York: Simon & Schuster.

Bumiller, K. 2008. *In an Abusive State: How Neoliberalism Appropriated the Feminist Movement against Sexual Violence*. Durham & London: Duke University Press.

Campbell, R. and O'Neill, M. (eds), 2006. *Sex Work Now*. Cullompton: Willan Publishing.

Carrington, K. and Watson, P. 1996. Policing Sexual Violence: Feminism, Criminal Justice and Governmentality. *International Journal of the Sociology of Law*, 24(3), 253–272.

Cook, D., Burton, M., Robinson, A. and Vallely, C. 2004. *Evaluation of Specialist Domestic Violence Courts/Fast Track Systems*. London: Crown Prosecution Service & Department of Constitutional Affairs. Available at: www.cps.gov.uk/publications/docs/specialist dvcourts.pdf.

Cornell, D. 1991. Sexual Difference, the Feminine and Equivalency. *Yale Law Review*, 100(7), 2247–2275.

Cowan, S. 2010. All Change or Business as Usual? Reforming the Law of Rape in Scotland, in *Rethinking Rape Law: International and Comparative Perspectives*, edited by C. McGlynn and V. Munro. London: Routledge, 54–169.

Coy, M. 2008. The Consumer, the Consumed and the Commodity: Women and Sex Buyers Talk about Objectification in Prostitution, in *Demanding Sex: Critical Reflections on the Regulation of Prostitution*, edited by V. Munro and M. Della Guista. Aldershot: Ashgate Publishing, 181–198.

Coy, M., Horvath, M. and Kelly, L. 2007. *It's just like going to the supermarket': Men Buying Sex in East London*. London: CWASU.

Dobash, R. and Dobash, R. 1994. *Women, Violence and Social Change*. London: Routledge.

Dobash, R. and Dobash, R. (eds), 1998 *Rethinking Violence Against Women*. London: Sage.

Dobash, R. and Dobash, R. 1998. Violent Men and Violent Contexts, in *Rethinking Violence Against Women*, edited by R. Dobash and R. Dobash. London: Sage, 141–168.

Dobash, R. and Dobash, R. 2004. Women's Violence to Men in Intimate Relationships. *British Journal of Criminology*, 44(3), 324–349.

Edwards, A. 2009. Violence against Women as Sex Discrimination: Judging the Jurisprudence of the United Nations Human Rights Treaty Bodies. *Texas Journal of Women and the Law*, 18(1), 101–165.

Edwards, A. 2010. Everyday Rape: International Human Rights Law and Violence Against Women in Peacetime, in *Rethinking Rape Law: International and Comparative Perspectives*, edited by C. McGlynn and V. Munro. London: Routledge, 92–108.

Ellison, L. and Munro, V. 2009. Of 'Normal Sex' and 'Real Rape': Exploring the Use of Socio-Sexual Scripts in (Mock) Jury Deliberation. *Social and Legal Studies*, 18(3), 291–312.

Finch, E. and Munro, V. 2007. The Demon Drink and the Demonised Woman: Socio-Sexual Stereotypes and Responsibility Attribution in Rape Trials Involving Intoxicants. *Social and Legal Studies*, 16(4), 591–614.

Fine, M. and Weis, L. 2000. Disappearing Acts: The State and Violence Against Women in the Twentieth Century. *Signs: Journal of Women in Culture & Society*, 25(4), 1139–1146.

Finley, L. 1988. The Nature of Domination and the Nature of Women: Reflections on Feminism Unmodified. *Northwestern University Law Review*, 82(2), 352–386.

Garland, D. 2001. *The Culture of Control*. Oxford: OUP.

Halley, J. 2006. *Split Decisions: How and Why to Take a Break from Feminism*. New Jersey: Princeton University Press.

Hekman, S. 1995. 'Subjects and Agents – The Question for Feminism', in J. Gardiner (ed.), *Provoking Agents*. Chicago: University of Illinois Press, 194–207.

Hester, M., Kelly, L. and Radford, J. 1996. *Women, Violence and Male Power*. Buckingham: Open University Press.

HMCPSI and HMIC. 2007. *Without Consent: A Report on the Joint Review of the Investigation and Prosecution of Rape Offences*. London: Central Office of Information.

Home Office. 2000. *Setting the Boundaries: Reforming the Law on Sexual Offences*. London: HMSO.

Home Office. 2008. *Justice with Safety: Specialist Domestic Violence Courts Review*. London: HMSO.

Home Office. 2009. *Together We Can End Violence Against Women and Girls*. London: HMSO.

Home Office. 2010. *The Stern Review: A Report by Baroness Vivien Stern CBE of an Independent Review into How Rape Complaints are Handled by Public Authorities in England and Wales*. London: HMSO & The Government Equalities Office.

Home Office. 2011. *Crime in England and Wales 2010/11 – Findings from the British Crime Survey and Police Recorded Crime*, edited by R. Chaplin, J. Flatley and K. Smith. London: HMSO. Available at: www.homeoffice.gov.uk/publications/science-research-statistics/research-statistics/crime-research/hosb1011/hosb1011?view=Binary.

Hoyle, C. and Sanders, A. 2000. Police Responses to Domestic Violence: From Victim Choice to Victim Empowerment? *British Journal of Criminology*, 40(1), 14–36.

Jeffreys, S. 1997. *The Idea of Prostitution*. Melbourne: Spinifex Press.

Jeffreys, S. 2009. *The Industrial Vagina: The Political Economy of the Global Sex Trade*. London: Routledge.

Jordan, J. 2004. *The Word of A Woman: Police, Rape and Belief*. London: Palgrave.

Kelly, L. 1988. *Surviving Sexual Violence*. Oxford: Polity Press.

Kelly, L. 2002. *A Research Review on the Reporting, Investigation and Prosecution of Rape Cases*. London: HMCPSI.

Kelly, L. and Radford, J. 1998. Sexual Violence Against Women and Girls: An Approach to an International Overview, in *Rethinking Violence Against Women*, edited by R. Dobash and R. Dobash. London: Sage, 53–76.

Kelly, L. Temkin, J. and Griffiths, S. 2006. Section 41: An Evaluation of New Legislation Limiting Sexual History Evidence in Rape Trials, Home Office Report 20/06. London: HMSO.

Krug, E., Dahlberg, L., Merch, J., Zwi, A. and Lozano, R. 2002. *World Report on Violence and Health*. Geneva: World Health Organisation.

Lacey, N. 1998. *Unspeakable Subjects: Feminist Essays in Legal and Social Theory*. Oxford: Hart Publishing.

MacKinnon, C. 1987. *Feminism Unmodified*. Cambridge, MA: Harvard University Press.

MacKinnon, C. 1989. *Toward a Feminist Theory of State*. Cambridge, MA: Harvard University Press.

MacKinnon, C. 2005. The Power to Change, in *Women's Lives, Men's Law's*. Cambridge, MA: Harvard University Press.

McGlynn, C. 2011. Feminism, Rape and the Search for Justice. *Oxford Journal of Legal Studies*, 31(4), 825–842.

Meyers, D. 1989. *Self, Society and Personal Choice*. New York: Columbia University Press.

Mohanty, C. 1988. Under Western Eyes: Feminist Scholarship and Colonial Discourses. *Feminist Review*, 30, 61–88.

Mossman, M. 1991. Feminism and Legal Method: The Difference It Makes, in *At the Boundaries of Law: Feminism and Legal Theory*, edited by M. Fineman and N. Thomadsen. London: Routledge, 283–300.

Munro, V. 2007. *Law and Politics at the Perimeter: Re-Evaluating Key Debates in Feminist Theory*. Oxford: Hart Publishing.

Munro, V. 2010. An Unholy Trinity? Non-Consent, Coercion and Exploitation in Contemporary Legal Responses to Sexual Violence in England and Wales, in *Current Legal Problems*, edited by G. Lestas and C. O'Cinneide. Oxford: OUP, 45–71.

Munro, V. and Scoular, J. 2013. Harm, Vulnerability and Citizenship: Constitutional Concerns in the Criminalisation of Contemporary Sex Work, in *The Constitution of Criminal Law*, edited by A. Duff, L. Farmer, S. Marshall and V. Tadros. Oxford: OUP, 30–52.

O'Donovan, K. 1991. Defences for Battered Women Who Kill. *Journal of Law and Society*, 18(2), 219–240.

Pratt, J. 2007. *Penal Populism*. London: Routledge.

Regan, L. and Kelly, L. 2003. Rape: Still a Forgotten Issue. London: CWASU.

Scoular, J. and O'Neill, M. 2007. Regulating Prostitution: Social Inclusion, Responsibilisation and the Politics of Prostitution Reform. *British Journal of Criminology*, 47(5), 764–778.

Scoular, J. and O'Neill, M. 2008. Legal Incursions into Supply/Demand: Criminalising and Responsibilising the Buyers and Sellers of Sex in the UK, in *Demanding Sex: Critical Reflections on the Regulation of Prostitution*, edited by V. Munro and M. Della Guista. Aldershot: Ashgate Publishing, 13–34.

Simon, J. 2007. *Governing Through Crime: How the War on Crime Transformed American Democracy and Created a Culture of Fear*. Oxford: OUP.

Smart, C. 1989. *Feminism and the Power of Law*. London: Routledge.

Smith. K., Coleman, K. Eder, S. and Hall, P. 2011. *Homicides, Firearm Offences and Intimate Violence 2009/10 – Supplementary Volume 2 to Crime in England and Wales 2009/10*. London: HMSO. Available at: www.homeoffice.gov.uk/publications/science-research-statistics/research-statistics/crime-research/hosb0111/hosb0111?view=Binary.

Temkin, J. and Krahe, B. 2008. *Sexual Assault and the Justice Gap: A Question of Attitude*. Oxford: Hart Publishing.

Walby, S. and Allen, J. 2004. *Domestic Violence, Sexual Assault and Stalking: Findings from the British Crime Survey*. London: Home Office Research, Development and Statistics Directorate.

Walklate, S. 2008. What is to be done about Violence against Women? Gender, Violence, Cosmopolitanism and the Law. *British Journal of Criminology*, 48(1), 39–54.

Wells, C. 1994. Battered Woman Syndrome and Defences to Homicide: Where Now? *Legal Studies*, 14(2), 266–276.

Wishik, H. 1985. To Question Everything: The Inquiries of Feminist Jurisprudence. *Berkeley Women's Law Journal*, 1, 64–77.

Žižek, S. 2008. *Violence*. London: Profile Books Ltd.

# The Body, Bodies, Embodiment: Feminist Legal Engagement with Health

## Marie Fox and Thérèse Murphy[1]

An invitation to write can be counted on to provoke a response. One can feel flattered, intimidated, overwhelmed or, perhaps, obliged. The invitation we received was to write a chapter on the ways in which feminist legal scholarship (FLS) has engaged with the issue of health. It was a welcome invitation. Writing such a chapter would not be a problem, we thought. We began by making a decision to focus on FLS in the United Kingdom, while noting the migration of key ideas from elsewhere. Next we turned to health; this proved more difficult to pin down. It clearly meant more than the absence of illness, more than a focus on cures. But how, for instance, did it relate to disability? Was there a non-discriminatory way to understand that relationship, one that would not biomedicalize difference, seeing the need for a cure when neither illness nor suffering was present? There was also the question of how we should handle the social determinants of health. Equally, how should we handle the wide range of newer discourses – on genetics, vulnerability, well-being and pandemic preparedness – that have been altering both planning priorities and individual choices? Moreover, when viewed through FLS, wasn't it medical and, later, health *law* that should be the core concern rather than health itself?

All too soon we were on a slippery slope. How, for instance, was 'feminist legal' to be defined? Specifically, to what – and whom – could this descriptor be applied? Presumably, feminist scholarship that presented itself as, say, bioethics, political theory, anthropology or sociology could be excluded, but what if it had (or should have) influenced FLS? (see, for example, Martin 1987, Petchesky 1987, Strathern 1993). Similarly, in a chapter that is examining scholarship, what place is there for practitioners, activists, policy-makers and judges? For example, should the judgments of UK Supreme Court Justice Brenda Hale count as FLS, or just her extra- and pre-judicial writings? Or the influential judgments of Dame Elizabeth Butler-Sloss? Equally, what of the range of women policy-makers and advisers on health? It is an impressive list; one that includes Ruth Deech, Suzi Leather and Lisa Jardine, former and current chairs of the Human Fertilisation and Embryology Authority,[2] as well as the philosophers, Mary Warnock and Onora O'Neill,[3] and the academic lawyers, Margot Brazier and Sheila McLean (Brazier et al. 1998, McLean 1997, 2002). The latter, of

1    Thanks to Marie-Andrée Jacob, Julie McCandless and Ralph Sandland for thought-provoking comments, and to Katie Cruz for research assistance.
2    www.hfea.gov.uk/689.html, accessed 6 November 2012.
3    Warnock chaired the influential committee which established the legal framework for regulation of assisted reproduction and embryo research (see Warnock 1985). O'Neill is a founder member and former chair of the Nuffield Council on Bioethics: www.

course, have been trailblazers in legal publishing too, producing core medical law texts and occupying key editorial roles. Furthermore a number of male authors have influenced how the discipline has developed and have engaged to varying degrees with feminist theory and arguments (see, for example, Morgan 1998, Sandland 2000, Thomson 2007).

We also faced the question of where to start. Accepting that health law, rather than health per se, has been the focus of FLS, we were looking at a relatively young field of law. Ian Kennedy's 1980 Reith Lectures are widely acknowledged as the field-forming moment for medical law (Kennedy 1981, cf. Brazier 2008), a field which focused on tort law and negligence, and it was some time thereafter before *health care law* came properly into focus. All of this pointed to a short history, little more than 30 years. On the other hand, however, feminist histories generally read rather differently to their official counterparts. So, were we looking for a lost history?

Clearly we had to halt the questions. To do so, we chose a trilogy that for us best captures the key debates in FLS on health. It runs as follows: first, the body; then bodies; and finally embodiment. We flesh it out more fully below, and in order to map out possible future directions, we conclude with some comments on what we see as the most pressing issues now facing FLS on health. One final preliminary note: as the trilogy unfolds, bear in mind that it is a chronology in the very crudest sense and its component parts are both individual frames and deeply interconnected.

## The Body, Bodies, Embodiment

### The Body

The body is a perennial in feminism, present in feminist politics, in scholarship and, of course, in the feminism of 'lived experience'. In FLS, engagement with the body has taken many forms, from women's bodies and the law, to law and the body and, more recently, men's bodies and the law. In FLS on *health* – in effect, FLS on medical and health care law – such engagements focused at first on making women appear (Bottomley 2002). The aim, in other words, was to bring women into the body of the law in ways that would challenge extant representations, exclusions and omissions.

There was certainly no shortage of work. Questions such as what had been medicalized (rather than, say, criminalized), in what ways and with what effects, meant that early FLS opened up a vast territory. Initially, however, it was rare for research to go beyond reproduction. Two reasons, we think, explain this: first, reproduction was an important and remarkably rich terrain – in part because there was legislation (notably, the Abortion Act 1967) and proposed legislation (on surrogacy, and on assisted reproductive technologies (ARTs)) to be considered. Second, both health law and medical law, its leaner predecessor, were fields in formation: throughout the 1970s, into the 1980s and even the early 1990s, neither was established in legal scholarship or in law school curricula. To pursue a feminist perspective in such fields was not, then, the most obvious of moves. Making such a move invited 'double trouble': neither one's choice of

---

nuffieldbioethics.org/, accessed 6 November 2012. And for one example of work that has influenced health lawyers, see O'Neill 2002.

perspective, nor one's site of study, was widely recognized (Sheldon and Thomson 1998: 7–8). Legitimacy, in other words, was twice removed.

FL scholars were not deterred, however. Feminist perspectives were pursued, focusing mostly on the power of law and, relatedly, the power of professionals. In FLS on the latter, neither nurses nor midwives got much of a look-in (Montgomery 1992, 1998). It was the 'medical men' – doctors – who colonized the attention of both legal and FL scholars: to be more precise, it was the ways in which judicial practice indulged its medical counterpart that drew critical comment from scholars of different stripes. The *Bolam* test,[4] which so dominated medical negligence at this juncture, was a key target (Sheldon 1998). Within FLS, there was also concern that male-dominated medicine and science had contributed to a shift of power over reproduction from women to medical men, and that new reproductive techniques such as *in vitro* fertilization would only 'consolidate and continue that tradition' (McLean 1999: 6). Fegan and Fennell (1998), meanwhile, highlighted a comparable tradition of male dominance within the psychiatric profession, while cautioning against reductionist critiques of psychiatry as a patriarchal tool, which they argued would harm the interests of women in need of better treatments inspired by feminist politics.

The power of law was, however, a bigger draw than the power of professionals. Here, two FL scholars – Carol Smart and Catharine MacKinnon – proved particularly influential. Mostly however one had to choose: Smart and MacKinnon were both concerned with the power of law, but in radically different ways. Moreover, MacKinnon's influence was in part the product of opposition to her work – caused perhaps by its 'paradoxical mix of debilitating pessimism and unfathomable optimism' (Jackson 1992: 211). Let's look briefly at each in turn, beginning with Smart. Her 1989 book, *Feminism and the Power of Law*, influenced a generation of FLS on health care law. It brought the work of Michel Foucault into the FL frame, configuring law not just as command-and-control but as regulation too. In so doing it prefigured later work on governmentality and biopower. Its more immediate effect in FL circles flowed from Smart's attention to the 'Woman of legal discourse' (1990, 1992). Influenced by this, a new generation of FL scholars produced striking critiques of the construction of women found *inter alia* in the Abortion Act 1967, the Surrogacy Act 1985 and the Human Fertilisation and Embryology Act 1990 (see, for example, Bridgeman and Millns 1995, 1998, Sheldon 1997).

Catharine MacKinnon pioneered a very different form of legal feminism. For her, law was male through-and-through; at the same time, however, she was deeply committed to law reform – to making and remaking the law in women's name. Sexual harassment and pornography are probably the best-known sites of her early work, but she took on privacy too (MacKinnon 1983, 1987, 1991). The latter (alongside autonomy, its broader counterpart) has been a deeply productive seam within FLS on health law (see, for example, Jackson 2001), mostly with the aim of reconceiving these foundational concepts of medical law and ethics. MacKinnon played a part in this, but others did too: notably, Carol Gilligan (1982) who produced an evocative contrast between an ethic of justice and, what she called, an ethic of care, and Jennifer Nedelsky (1989, 1990, 1993, 2012) whose striking notion of 'relational autonomy' continues to resonate today. For many women (FL scholars included) the lived experience of pregnancy and family life was a major influence too.

MacKinnon and other US legal feminists, including Patricia Williams (1991), may also have been influential in focusing FLS in the UK on the pros and cons of rights claims (see,

---

4    *Bolam v Friern Hospital Management Committee* [1957] 1 WLR 582.

for example, Brazier 1998, De Gama 1993, Fox and Murphy 1992, Kingdom 1991). Certainly *Re S*, a 1991 decision of the High Court of England and Wales giving the go-ahead to a forced caesarean, reverberated strongly in rights terms (see, for example, Thomson 1994, Wells 1998). The Court's decision was subsequently overturned,[5] and it is now contrary to law to carry out a caesarean against the wishes of a competent woman. Furthermore, the fact that the woman's wishes seem odd or morally repugnant, or come with no supporting reason at all, cannot be used as a conclusive indication of lack of capacity (Morris 2002). But *Re S* aside, rights language did not take hold in any deep way in FLS, and neither the coming into force of the Human Rights 1998 (which incorporated the European Convention on Human Rights into domestic law) nor the obvious effects of EU free movement rights have countered this.

Early FLS on health also considered the question of property, specifically whether the body should be treated as property. Initially, however, non-lawyers seemed more interested in this issue than their FL counterparts (see, for example, Petchesky 1995, Dickenson 1997; cf Radin 1987, Williams 1991). For the latter it was more a nod in passing, en route towards discussion of autonomy or bodily integrity. But the rise of the reproduction business, including markets in reproductive services and a global trade (both legal and illicit) in body parts and products, has changed that (Fox and McHale 2000, Richards et al. 2002, Ford 2005). So too has the drive towards 'humans as medicine' (Brazier 2006). Increasingly, the question is not just is it legitimate to permit the body to be used as a resource or possession, but also where precisely is the body being constructed as marketable property and where, by contrast, is altruism the dominant frame? And how does gender play out in the contrast?

What was *not* part of early FLS is interesting too. By today's standards, the widespread silence on death and dying seems a striking omission.[6] Engagement with the limits of consent, with actual consenting practices, and with the distortions produced by prioritizing consent, was in short supply too (cf Murphy 1998, 2009, Jacob 2012). Resource allocation was also under the radar (cf Whitty 1998) and has only been taken up sporadically by FLS in subsequent years (Biggs and MacKenzie 2000, Bridgeman 2007a). Most interesting of all was the position of the body. It was both absolutely central yet radically absent. To explain: what concerned early FLS was not the body or even bodies, but the female body. More precisely, it was the female reproductive body – not the young female body, nor its ageing or aged counterpart, or indeed the naming of the just-born body as female or male (though cf. on latter topic, O'Donovan 1985).

Put differently, early FLS on health dealt with difference, not with differences. The body that appeared was, by and large, the female body; a body that represented all female bodies, all women.[7] The girl-child was mostly absent; surprising perhaps given the centrality of the *Gillick* case to early medical law (though cf Bridgeman and Mills 1998, Lewis and Cannell 1986).[8] Men, too, were absent. They were present as the 'responsible body of medical men' and as judges and legislators, but as fathers or as reproductive bodies they were absent from FLS (cf Smart 1987). True, the 'need for a father' – part of the welfare principle

---

5     *St George's Healthcare NHS Trust v S* [1998] 3 All ER 673 (CA).
6     On a similar gap in feminist bioethics, see Wolf 1996.
7     Race and disability were particularly striking omissions (Roberts 1998, Kallianes and Rubenfeld 1998).
8     *Gillick v West Norfolk and Wisbech AHA* [1986] 1 AC 112 wherein a mother unsuccessfully challenged the power of doctors to prescribe contraception for under 16s without parental consent.

governing access to ARTs under the original Human Fertilisation and Embryology Act 1990[9] – did garner comment (see, for example, Jackson 2002, Millns 1995), but largely because it functioned to regulate *female* reproduction. Citations to *Paton v BPAS*, and later *C v S*, were also commonplace: these cases established that a decision to carry out an abortion could not be challenged either by a woman's husband or by the putative father of the child.[10] Yet there was no sense that once an embryo was *outside* a woman's body, her right to reproduce or not to reproduce might be no stronger than that of, say, a former male partner with whom the embryo had been created.[11] Or, indeed, that the right to know one's genetic identity would assume the significance it has today (Smart 2010).

Early FLS on health was, one might say, feminism without flesh (Murphy 1997). That changed, however, with a turn towards *bodies* and, more recently, towards *embodiment*. The influences on FLS changed too: continental theory was more widely cited (notably Luce Irigaray, as well as far more Foucault than had been commonplace). A wider range of US feminism also came to the fore, especially the work of Donna Haraway and Judith Butler.

## Bodies

As health law developed its own identity as a field it was accompanied by an emerging strand of FL commentary which sought not only to account for women's condition but to address the body itself as a contested site. The body of medicine, which was claimed to be no body in particular, was exposed as a very specific kind of body. The bodily analyses used in early FL work, which focused on how the female body was used to legitimate women's subordinate position in society, were also shown to be limited. New feminist work opened up a *range of bodies* to the scrutiny of health lawyers who explored not only how different bodies are legally regulated in differing ways, but how the same body is regulated differently at different stages of its life course (Evans and Lee 2002). Dependency and vulnerability also began to come into view as a universal characteristic of the human condition (Fineman 2010).

In the reproductive context, feminist commentators engaged more explicitly with male bodies (Fox 1998, Murphy 2000, Sheldon 1999).[12] The potential of ARTs to alter the different stakes of women and men in reproduction became a key concern (Sheldon 2004, Thomson 2007, Jackson 2008), as did ideologies of fatherhood (Collier and Sheldon 2008). ARTs seemed to offer women the prospect of autonomous reproduction (Firestone 1980) but, as FL scholars highlighted, law ensured that women succeeded only where they operated in accord with the values of what Martha Fineman (1995) has termed the 'sexual family'. Hence, while Diane Blood eventually succeeded in her legal quest to use the sperm of her deceased husband, Stephen (which was retrieved by auto ejaculation without his consent

---

9     Human Fertilisation and Embryology Act 1990, s13(5).
10    See *Paton v BPAS* [1979] QB 276; *Paton v UK* (1980) 3 EHRR 409; *C v S* [1987] 1 All ER 1230.
11    *Evans v UK* (2007) 46 EHRR 34. See Ford 2008, Harris-Short 2010.
12    A number of litigated cases also brought male corporeality more sharply into view: e.g. *Re A (medical treatment: male sterilization)* [2000] 1 FCR 193 – the first application before a UK court to sterilize a man in the wake of a series of cases where women and girls has been sterilized. The application was refused; a decision that could be read as vindicating the bodily integrity of male subjects (Savell 2004). Cf. Keywood who argues that, irrespective of gender, the subjects of sterilization cases were all 'figured either as asexual, child-like eternal beings who must be protected from sexual advances or as predatory creatures with animalistic sexual appetites' (2001: 192).

as he was dying),[13] her actions were explicitly cast as undertaken in his name (Biggs 1997, Morgan and Lee 1997). As Brazier (1994) noted at the time, it is doubtful that a grieving widower who sought to retrieve eggs from his dying wife would have attracted the same degree of judicial sympathy as Mrs Blood.

Disputes about embryonic bodies proved still more contentious than debates over gestational bodies. In the *Evans* case[14] conflicts over whose wishes should prevail in the case of embryos stored outside the woman's body provoked FL debate on what reproductive justice between the sexes entails (Sheldon 2004, Priaulx 2008). Elsewhere FLS seemed to be impacting on legislative reform – for instance in changes to the determination of legal parenthood in Part 2 of the Human Fertilisation and Embryology Act 2008, which expand the range of those who count as parents in the eyes of the law. Thus, same-sex couples are now recognized as legal parents of children conceived via donated eggs, sperm or embryos. Yet, while broadening the category of parent (Jones 2009), the legislation continues to restrict legal maternity to one woman and, in stipulating that there can only be one 'other legal parent', it reinforces a traditional dyadic, heteronormative family form (McCandless and Sheldon 2010a, 2010b, Murphy and Ó Cuinn 2013).

Increasingly the body of the actual child attracted greater FL attention, although here the boundaries between child law and health law are particularly hard to delineate.[15] From *Gillick* onwards some of the most high-profile child law cases have concerned medical interventions (including sterilization and genital cutting) which raise in acute form the question of how far children can have rights separable from those of their parents. Such questions have served to reinforce feminist scepticism about the extent to which liberal rights theories premised on individualized and bounded conceptions of the body are applicable in the context of families and decision-making by and within families. Some FL scholars, drawing on earlier work applying relational approaches to autonomy to women's reproductive and other bodily rights (Jackson 2001), suggested such approaches may also have resonance in the context of decision-making by and on behalf of children (Bridgeman 2007b). Not only do relational perspectives query traditional legal understandings of authority, status and power (Fox and Thomson 2005), but they may also be invoked to valorize the views of parents when their position conflicts with those of health professionals (Bridgeman 2005). On this view children's rights are understood as a matter of relationships and moral responsibilities rather than formal rules (Sabatello 2009). Other FL scholars argue that a consideration of children's rights to participate in decision-making regarding their health has effected a 'paradigm shift' within health law, away from reasoning from abstract principles to being attentive to the experiences of those receiving health-care (Bridgeman 2002, Donnelly and Kilkelly 2011).

Yet, notwithstanding the diversity of bodies which now populate FLS on health law, law and legal processes display a continuing preoccupation with regulating and signposting *female* bodies. This is evident in the forced caesarean cases discussed earlier, and can also be traced in case law concerning forced treatment of those with eating disorders. For instance,

---

13    *R v HFEA, ex p Blood* [1997] 2 All ER 687 (CA).
14    (2007) 46 EHRR 34.
15    Given the growing preoccupation within the discipline with newer rights claims, such as that for a right to know one's genetic identity, and the overlaps between crime and public health, family/child law and criminal law are increasingly pertinent to and perhaps even indistinguishable from 'health' law.

in *B v Croyden Health Authority*,[16] Neil LJ declared himself satisfied that s. 63 of the Mental Health Act 1983 which permits medical treatment of the patient 'for the mental disorder from which he is suffering' could encompass 'treatment given to alleviate the symptoms of the disorder as well as treatment to remedy its underlying cause', thus permitting forced feeding of anorexic patients. However, since '[t]he anorexic's holy grail is control', forced treatment in this context not only denies autonomy but is counter-productive in terms of curing the patient (Lewis 1997: 32). FL scholars have also suggested that law too uncritically endorses the perspective of psychiatric medicine in declaring forced feeding lawful, while deeming the wishes of the adolescent or adult woman to be unintelligible. Thus, Keywood (2003) argues that *B v Croyden* illustrates 'the imperfect and contingent alliance between femininity and mental disorder that is sustained in the courtroom', exemplifying English law's deployment of psychiatric discourse as part of the regulatory apparatus which produces female identity (see also Bridgeman 1993). Equally, feminist scholars have shown how the fat body – also often gendered female – has been pathologized by medical cultures (Murray 2008), although the disciplining of fat bodies has to date attracted little FL scrutiny in the UK.

There is also growing, albeit still limited, recognition of the centrality of capacity and its definition to FLS. The anorexia and forced caesarean cases, for instance, illustrate the need for an integrated, more *embodied* approach of the kind we discuss below. Indeed a key contribution of FLS has been to stress the need to integrate physical and mental dimensions of health (Boland and Laing 2002, Cain 2009). In the UK the codification of legal tests for capacity in the Mental Capacity Act 2005 directed attention to this issue, but FLS which explicitly engages with issues of capacity, and how tests for capacity may be gendered, remains sparse (cf. Keywood 2003, Doyle 2010). Questions of capacity and choices over one's body are, of course, also raised in acute form at the end of life: significantly, many of the UK cases have concerned women's refusal of life-prolonging treatment (Biggs 1998, 2003, Williams 2005).

In the 'bodies' era, FLS also began to engage more directly with bodies which had hitherto been marginalized or deemed anomalous in health law, including infected (Weait 2007) and trans bodies – whether transgendered (Cowan 2005, Sharpe 2002), intersex (Grabham 2012), transpecies (Fox 2005) or conjoined (Munro 2001, Sharpe 2009). Such anomalous bodies were conventionally regarded as needing correction, modification or prohibition. Thus, procedures which served to settle disrupted or abnormal boundaries have been sanctioned by law, for instance in the case of operations to separate conjoined twins or to surgically fix the sex of intersex children. Simultaneously other bodies were seen increasingly as modifiable, posing questions about the extent to which choices such as cosmetic surgery are legitimate choices. In seeking to problematize the legal 'solutions' adopted in many of these cases, FL scholars have engaged with the trope of the monster, analysing how bodies seen to be excessively feminine or to transgress normal bodily boundaries are brought within the purview of legal regulation and discipline. In much of this work Michel Foucault's influence has been apparent. Equally influential has been Donna Haraway's cyborg metaphor, which has been employed in FLS to examine the conjoining of human bodies with those of non-human animals or machines, and to call into question conventional understandings of the nature of kinship and what it means to be human (Lim 1999, Fox 2005, Karpin 2006).

---

16    [1995] 1 All ER 683.

Transgender and other elective surgeries challenge the notion of health law as principally concerned with treatment of illness, yet it seems that such bodies can be accommodated by law provided they fit into the natural order of things (for instance by conforming to a gender script). Thus FL scholars have highlighted the minimal regulation of cosmetic surgery which typically is undertaken to conform with an idealized female aesthetic (Latham 2008). Where bodily transformations are depicted as *challenging* the natural order they have been much less readily tolerated, as the anorexia cases demonstrate. Similarly, attempts by post-menopausal women to access ARTs have been seen as posing a radical challenge that ought to be discouraged; by contrast, late, and even posthumous, fatherhood is legally tolerated (Fisher and Somerville 1998).

## Embodiment

Feminist work focusing on the body and bodies has been crucial in contesting the dominance of bioethical approaches grounded in abstract notions such as 'personhood' which too often erase the corporeality of humans (cf. Naffine 2009). However, having brought bodies back into view, FLS is now faced with the challenge of scholarship which advocates moving 'beyond bodies'. Such work takes two broad directions. Some scholars have adopted transhumanist or posthumanist perspectives, which are explicit about the need to transcend the human body and perhaps even to discard 'the human' (see, for example, Harris 2011). In this strand of work, bodies are seen as infinitely malleable and improvable and perhaps eventually redundant, since technology has the potential to enable humans to evolve into a superior – physiologically and cognitively enhanced – species. Critics have, however, contested these benign depictions of enhancement technologies and their application, arguing that their likely effect in an ill-divided world would be to exacerbate existing injustice and inequalities. FL voices have been largely absent from such debates, aside from some engagement with enhancement technologies (Karpin and Mykitiuk 2008, see also Zylinska 2009), perhaps because transhumanist and posthumanist approaches seem to deny the material reality of bodies and exhibit the same contempt for the flesh of which law stands accused. Instead, recent FL interventions, drawing on the proliferation of bodies which now figure in contemporary health law, have advocated *embodiment*, rather than *the* body or *bodies*, as an organizing concept.

Focusing on embodiment shifts attention from the singular body, or even multiple bodies, as objects of analysis by mandating a broader focus on lived experience and the question of how we inhabit and experience the world through our bodies. As Ruth Fletcher notes, the concept of embodiment 'emerged from a desire to avoid mind/body dichotomies and to capture the interactive process by which mind and body respond to each other in producing knowledge' (2009: 316–317). Thus, embodiment directs FL attention to which bodies, and which embodied choices, law values and validates. It also allows FLS to contest representations of legal subjectivity as universal and disembodied, and 'to explore possible modes of resistance to dominant conceptions of the female subject' (Keywood 2002: 321). Feminist interventions have also highlighted how embodied difference encompasses, but moves beyond, sexual difference to facilitate exploration of the interaction and intersection of various bodily differences. In this regard the turn to embodiment marks a shift within FLS 'from exploring women's rights *over* their bodies, to analysing how social regulation has gendered the body and embodied experiences' (Fletcher, Fox and McCandless 2008: 335). Starting with embodiment therefore allows for different approaches to the ethical questions that have engaged health lawyers, and for critical interrogation of how embodied choices are variously cast as socio-culturally legitimate or transgressive. In these ways it requires us to think through the corporeal consequences of legal decision-making (though what this means in practice may vary considerably).

Significantly, an emphasis on embodiment has become prominent just as bodies are increasingly capable of fragmentation, and as the worth of component bodily parts to pharmaceutical companies and others becomes ever more apparent. As we noted above, early FLS largely eschewed property-based approaches, but interest in property discourse was reinvigorated when cases such as *Moore v Regents of California*[17] alerted individuals to the worth of human materials previously regarded as waste. As Roxanne Mykitiuk observed, 'the scientific dissection of human biology challenges the integrity of human identity and compels us to examine the meaning and significance of our own embodiment' (1994: 66). In similar vein, Catherine Waldby and others have noted that the research potential, and hence commercial value, of human tissues has forced law to mediate between the interests of individuals and biotechnology companies (2006, 2010). Donna Dickenson and others have, in turn, taken up this analysis to show how the bodies of women may be particularly vulnerable to exploitation in this environment: their reproductive labour, in addition to their eggs and tissues, may be appropriated. By unpacking narratives which proclaim the value of cord blood banking, Dickenson reveals how these simultaneously devalue the embodied labour of the pregnant woman by eliding the risks the practice poses to both the woman and child, and construing organisms as 'sets of replaceable parts' (2008: 86).

For some FL scholars, the need to contest such fragmentation and commodification has pointed to the logic of re-engaging with property discourse: Dickenson and others have attempted to reclaim the concept of property to dispute claims by others over women's bodies and have stressed its potential for progressive ends (Ford 2005, Davies 2007). Others have urged caution (Fletcher, Fox and McCandless 2008) given the tendency of dominant property discourses to themselves promote commodification and exploitation of bodies. In any event, there is a need for other paradigms as well as property. Drawing on examples such as experiential accounts of patients who have had hand transplants, Emily Grabham (2012) has proposed that propertied understandings of the body grounded in the notion of individuals having autonomy over their sovereign bodies can be augmented by alternative visions of embodied selfhood which might see embodiment and bodily integrity in terms of functional cohesion or cellular coexistence, thus embracing more fluid conceptions of the body.[18] Such embodied approaches may in the future also prove valuable in rethinking some of the questions prompted by mental capacity and mental health, as we discuss below.

Like property, however, it should be recognized that the discourse of embodiment is not without pitfalls for FLS. For instance, if we claim to value different types of embodiment, and if embryos and foetuses are seen both as embodied and as relational products of human reproductive labour, then questions may arise regarding how feminists should value the embryo or foetus. Indeed, much recent FL work has engaged with the question of how new forms of embryos have been constructed in law, and sought to frame new ways of thinking about embryos and their relationships to us (Karpin 2006, Fox 2009, Jacob et al. 2010). It

---

17  270 Cal Rptr 146 (1990) (California SCt).
18  Such understandings might also be productive for FL scholars who have advocated new paradigms for understanding the pregnant body as intimately connected to the foetus and politically situated (Karpin 1992: 3).

may well be important to constitute embryos as more than raw materials to be exploited; on the other hand, the dangers of thinking of them as *embodied* can be traced in some recent US scholarship which co-opts strands of feminist theory to depict embryos and foetuses as the most vulnerable and dependent forms of embodied life (Bachiochi 2011). The risk of such arguments for a pro-choice politics and law are clear. Faced with such challenges, it is apparent that FLS treads a fine line in formulating approaches which seek to ascribe some form of value to the embryo or foetus (or to limit what may be done to them) without thereby undermining the pro-choice arguments that animated much early FLS on health.

## Future Directions

We hope that this typology – the body, bodies, embodiment – has succeeded in capturing a flavour of the vibrancy and richness of FL engagements with health. Our account is partial of course and cannot do justice to the range of FLS in the field. Furthermore, there are signs that FLS on health is already moving in new directions as it draws from a new variety of disciplines (Sullivan and Murray 2009) and promotes newer methodologies, such as ethnography (Jacob 2012, Murphy 2013). At the same time, however, there are health questions that hitherto have not been taken up in FLS: it is to these that we now turn.

Issues of human rights or resource allocation, for instance, have garnered only sporadic attention within FLS in the UK. However recent case law on resource allocation which has addressed normative questions of embodiment and body modification[19] is ripe for FL analysis. Ongoing activism at the global level around access to medicines merits FL attention too. The global stage is also notable for increasing engagement with the relationship between sexual rights, reproductive rights and health (Roseman and Miller 2011). Two other areas that have been neglected within FLS in the UK are elder care and dementia. Feminist analyses based on caring and relationality, coupled with newer concepts now being taken up in health law scholarship, such as vulnerability (Fineman 2010) and capabilities approaches (Fox and Thomson 2013), do however have the potential to be utilized in contemporary health policy discussions about how we care for and medicate those who live longer and suffer associated debility (Harding and Peel 2013). Similarly, a feminist reconfiguration of all bodies as unbounded, always dependent and subject to the other (Karpin and Mykitiuk 2010) could contribute to debates about interdependency, bodily integrity and the geneticization of bodies – issues which take us beyond the individuated self and body which continue to dominate health law.

Public health, too, calls out for more FLS. While lawyers have increasingly engaged in public health debate, thereby further consolidating the shift from medical to health law, feminist voices to date have been somewhat muted (cf. Murphy and Whitty 2009, Fox and Thomson 2012, 2013). By widening its focus to public health and thus to populations, FLS could also engage more fully with other contemporary practices. For instance, topics such as crossing geographical borders, not being able to cross them, and more generally the effects

---

19   *R (ota AC) v West Berkshire PCT* [2011] EWCA Civ 247 concerned judicial review of a decision not to fund breast augmentation for a male to female transsexual while *R (ota Condliff) v North Staffordshire PCT* [2011] EWCA Civ 910 involved a challenge to a refusal to fund bariatric surgery.

of movements and markets on states, non-state actors and individuals need to be explored in greater depth (Fletcher 2013, McGuinness 2012).

It will also be important for FLS to engage more fully with law's place; that is, law's place in the regulatory environment. Being a feminist *legal* scholar means having a view on this matter: a view that reaches beyond law reform, beyond dismay or despair at 'the law', and beyond both the 'big' legal actors (notably legislatures and courts) and the ones that have most preoccupied FLS (that 'responsible body of medical men'). FLS needs also to have a position on 'public bioethics' (as conducted by, say, the Nuffield Council on Bioethics), on NGOs, religious groups and charities that do health work (and in places act as, or instead of, the state), on informal decision making, on the prioritization of citizen participation in science and technology decision making, and on increased recourse to law by groups of active biocitizens, all of whom want access to treatment or to funding for the research for their particular illness. FLS, in short, faces a future where not just law but also governance must be an object of inquiry. One might even say that the broader field of feminist governance studies rather than FLS is where we ought to be headed.

# References

Bachiochi, E. 2011. Embodied Equality: Debunking Equal Protection Arguments for Abortion Rights. *Harvard Journal of Law and Public Policy*, 44, 889–950.

Biggs, H. 1997. Madonna Minus Child or Wanted: Dead or Alive! The Right to Have a Dead Partner's Child. *Feminist Legal Studies*, 5(2), 225–234.

Biggs, H. 1998. 'I Don't Want to be a Burden!' A Feminist Reflects on Women's Experience of Death and Dying, in *Feminist Perspectives on Health Care Law*, edited by S. Sheldon and M. Thomson. London: Cavendish, 279–295.

Biggs, H. 2003. A *Pretty* Fine Line: Life, Death, Autonomy and Letting it B. *Feminist Legal Studies*, 11(3), 291–301.

Biggs, H. and MacKenzie, R. 2000. Viagra is Coming: The Rhetoric of Choice and Need, in *Law and Medicine*, edited by M. Freeman. Oxford: OUP, 341–361.

Boland, F. and Laing, J.M. 2002. Care, Control or Coercion? Women in the Mental Health System in Ireland, England and Wales, in *Well Women: The Gendered Nature of Health Care Provision*, edited by A. Morris and S. Nott. Aldershot: Ashgate, 117–144.

Bottomley, A. 2002. The Many Appearances of the Body in Feminist Scholarship, in *Body Lore and Laws*, edited by A. Bainham et al. Oxford: Hart, 127–148.

Brazier, M. 1994. Hard Cases Make Bad Law? *Journal of Medical Ethics*, 23(6), 341–343.

Brazier, M. 1998, Reproductive Rights: Feminism or Patriarchy?, in *The Future of Human Reproduction: Ethics, Choice, and Regulation*, edited by J. Harris and S. Holm. Oxford: Clarendon, 66–96.

Brazier, M. 2006. Humans as Medicines, in *First Do No Harm: Law, Ethics and Healthcare*, edited by S. McLean. Aldershot: Ashgate, 187–202.

Brazier, M. 2008. The Age of Deference: A Historical Anomaly, in *Law and Bioethics*, edited by M. Freeman. Oxford: OUP, 464–475.

Brazier, M. et al. 1998. *Surrogacy: Review for Health Ministers of Current Arrangements for Payments and Regulation*, Cmnd. 4068. London: Department of Health.

Bridgeman, J. 1993. Old Enough to Know Best? *Legal Studies*, 13(1), 69–80.

Bridgeman, J. 2002. Learning from Bristol: Healthcare in the 21st Century. *Modern Law Review*, 65(2), 241–255.

Bridgeman, J. 2005. Caring for Children with Severe Disabilities: Boundaried and Relational Rights. *International Journal of Children's Rights*, 13, 99–120.

Bridgeman, J. 2007a. Exceptional Women, Healthcare Consumers and the Inevitability of Caring. *Feminist Legal Studies*, 15(2), 235–245.

Bridgeman, J. 2007b. *Parental Responsibility, Young Children and Healthcare Law*. Cambridge: CUP.

Bridgeman J. and Millns, S. (eds), 1995. *Law and Body Politics: Regulating the Female Body*. Aldershot: Dartmouth.

Bridgeman, J. and Millns, S. 1998. *Feminist Perspectives on Law: Law's Engagement with the Female Body*. London: Sweet & Maxwell.

Cain, R. 2009. 'A View You Won't Get Anywhere Else'? Depressed Mothers, Public Regulation and 'Private' Narrative. *Feminist Legal Studies*, 17(2), 123–143.

Cowan, S. 2005. Gender is No Substitute for Sex: A Comparative Human Rights Analysis of the Legal Regulation of Sexual Identity. *Feminist Legal Studies*, 13(1), 67–96.

Collier, R. and Sheldon, S. 2008. *Fragmenting Fatherhood: A Socio-Legal Study*. Oxford: Hart.

Davies, M. 2007. *Property: Meaning, Histories, Theories*. New York: Routledge-Cavendish.

De Gama, K. 1993. A Brave New World? Rights Discourse and the Politics of Reproductive Autonomy. *Journal of Law and Society*, 20(1), 114–130.

Dickenson, D. 1997. *Property, Women and Politics*. Cambridge: Polity Press.

Dickenson, D. 2007. *Property in the Body: Feminist Perspectives*. Cambridge: CUP.

Dickenson, D. 2008. *Body Shopping: Converting Body Parts to Profit*. Oxford: One World.

Donnelly, M. and Kilkelly, U. 2011. Child Friendly Health Care: Delivering on the Right to be Heard. *Medical Law Review*, 19(1), 27–54.

Doyle, S. 2010. The Notion of Consent to Sexual Activity for Persons with Mental Disabilities. *Liverpool Law Review*, 31(2), 111–135.

Evans, M. and Lee, E. (eds), 2002. *Real Bodies: A Sociological Introduction*. New York: Palgrave.

Fegan, E. and Fennell, P. 1998. Feminist Perspectives on Mental Health Law, in *Feminist Perspectives on Health Care Law*, edited by S. Sheldon and M. Thomson. London: Cavendish, 73–96.

Fineman, M.A. 1995. *The Neutered Mother, the Sexual Family and other Twentieth Century Tragedies*. London: Routledge.

Fineman, M.A. 2010. The Vulnerable Subject and the Responsive State. *Emory Law Journal*, 60, 251–275.

Firestone, S. 1980. *The Dialectic of Sex: The Case for a Feminist Revolution*. London: Women's Press.

Fisher, F. and Sommerville, A. 1998. To Everything there is a Season? Are there Medical Grounds for Refusing Fertility Treatment to Older Women, in *The Future of Human Reproduction: Ethics, Choice, and Regulation*, edited by J. Harris and S. Holm. Oxford: Clarendon, 203–220.

Fletcher, R. 2009. Embodied Practices. *Feminist Legal Studies*, 17(3), 315–318.

Fletcher, R. 2013. Peripheral Governance: The Crisis Pregnancy Agency and the Administration of a Cross-Border Flow for Abortion Care. *International Journal of Law in Context*, 9, 160–191.

Fletcher, R., Fox, M. and McCandless, J. 2008. Legal Embodiment: Analysing the Body of Healthcare Law. *Medical Law Review*, 16(3), 321–345.

Ford, M. 2005. A Property Model of Pregnancy. *International Journal of Law in Context*, 1(3), 261–293.

Ford, M. 2008. *Evans v United Kingdom*: What Implications for the Jurisprudence of Pregnancy? *Human Rights Law Review*, 8(1), 171–184.

Fox, M. 1998. Abortion Decision-Making: Taking Men's Needs Seriously, in *Abortion Law and Politics Today*, edited by E. Lee. London: Macmillan, 198–215.

Fox, M. 2005. Rethinking the Animal/Human Boundary: The Impact of Xeno Technologies. *Liverpool Law Review*, 26(2), 149–167.

Fox, M. 2009. Legislating Interspecies Embryos, in *Transformation/Transgression: The Legal, Medical And Cultural Regulation Of The Body*, edited by S.W. Smith and R. Deazley. Aldershot: Ashgate, 95–126.

Fox, M. and McHale, J. (eds), 2000. Special Issue: Regulating Human Body Parts and Products. *Health Care Analysis*, 8(2), 83–86.

Fox, M. and Murphy, T. 1992. Irish Abortion: Seeking Refuge in a Jurisprudence of Doubt and Delegation. *Journal of Law and Society*, 19(4), 454–466.

Fox, M. and Thomson, M. 2005. Short Changed? The Law and Ethics of Male Circumcision. *International Journal of Children's Rights*, 13, 161–181.

Fox, M. and Thomson, M. 2012. The New Politics of Male Circumcision: HIV/AIDS, Health Law and Social Justice. *Legal Studies*, 32(2), 255–281.

Fox, M. and Thomson, M. 2013. Realising Social Justice in Public Health Law. *Medical Law Review*, 21(2), 278–309.

Gilligan, C. 1982. *In a Different Voice: Psychological Theory and Women's Development*. Cambridge: Harvard University Press.

Grabham, E. 2012. Bodily Integrity and the Surgical Management of Intersex. *Body & Society*, 18(2), 1–26.

Harding, R. and Peel, E. 2013. 'He was Like a Zombie': Off-label Prescription of Anti-Psychotic Drugs in Dementia. *Medical Law Review*, 21(2), 243–277.

Harris, J. 2011. Taking the 'Human' out of Human Rights. *Cambridge Quarterly of Healthcare Ethics*, 20(1), 9–20.

Harris-Short, S. 2010. A Feminist Judgment in *Evans v Amicus Healthcare Ltd and Others*, in *Feminist Judgments: From Theory to Practice*, edited by R. Hunter et al. Oxford: Hart, 64–82.

Jackson, E. 1992. Catharine MacKinnon and Feminist Jurisprudence: A Critical Reappraisal. *Journal of Law & Society*, 19(2), 195–213.

Jackson, E. 2001. *Regulating Reproduction: Law, Technology and Autonomy*. Oxford: Hart.

Jackson, E. 2002. Conception and the Irrelevance of the Welfare Principle. *Modern Law Review*, 65(2), 176–203.

Jackson, E. 2008. Degendering Reproduction. *Medical Law Review*, 16(3), 346–368.

Jacob, M.-A. 2012. *Matching Organs with Donors: Legality and Kinship in Transplants*. Philadelphia: University of Pennsylvania Press.

Jacob, M.-A. et al. 2010. Embryonic Hopes: Controversy, Alliance, and Reproductive Entities in Law and the Social Sciences. *Social and Legal Studies*, 19(4), 497–517.

Jones, C. 2009. The Identification of 'Parents' and 'Siblings': New Possibilities under the reformed Human Fertilisation and Embryology Act, in *Rights, Gender and Family Law*, edited by J. Wallbank et al. London: Routledge, 219–238.

Kallianes, V. and Rubenfeld, P. 1997. Disabled Women and Reproductive Rights. *Disability and Society*, 12(2), 203–222.

Karpin, I. 1992–3. Legislating the Female Reproductive Body: Reproductive Technology and the Reconstructed Woman. *Columbia Journal of Gender and Law*, 3, 325–349.

Karpin, I. 2006. The Uncanny Embryos: Legal Limits to the Human and Reproduction without Women. *Sydney Law Review*, 28, 599–623.

Karpin, I. and Mykitiuk, R. 2008. Going Out On a Limb: Prosthetics, Normalcy and Disputing the Therapy/Enhancement Distinction. *Medical Law Review*, 16(3), 391–436.

Karpin, I. and Mykitiuk, R. 2010. Feminist Legal Theory as Embodied Justice, in *Transcending the Boundaries of Law: Generations of Feminism and Legal Theory*, edited by M.A. Fineman. Abingdon: Routledge-Cavendish, 115–130.

Kennedy, I. 1981. *The Unmasking of Medicine*. London: Allen & Unwin.

Keywood, K. 2000. More than a Woman: Embodiment and Sexual Difference in Medical Law. *Feminist Legal Studies*, 8(3), 319–342.

Keywood, K. 2001. 'I'd Rather Keep Him Chaste': Retelling the Story of Sterilisation, Learning Disability and (non)Sexed Embodiment. *Feminist Legal Studies*, 9(2), 185–194.

Keywood, K. 2002. Disabling Sex: Some Legal Thinking about Sterilisation, Learning Disability and Embodiment, in *Well Women: Women's Access to Health Care*, edited by A. Morris and S. Nott. Aldershot: Ashgate, 21–39.

Keywood, K. 2003. Re-thinking the Anorexic Body: How English Law and Psychiatry 'Think'. *International Journal of Law and Psychiatry*, 26(6), 599–611.

Kingdom, E. 1991. *What's Wrong with Rights?* Edinburgh: Edinburgh University Press.

Latham, M. 2008. The Shape of Things to Come: Feminism, Regulation and Cosmetic Surgery. *Medical Law Review*, 16(3), 437–457.

Lewis, P. 1997. Feeding an Anorexic Patient Who Refuses Food. *Medical Law Review*, 7(1), 21–37.

Lewis, J. and Cannell, F. 1986. The Politics of Motherhood in the 1980s: Warnock, Gillick and Feminists. *Journal of Law and Society*, 13(3), 321–342.

Lim, H. 1999. Caesareans and Cyborgs. *Feminist Legal Studies*, 7(2), 233–249.

MacKinnon, C.A. 1983. Feminism, Marxism, Method, and the State: Toward Feminist Jurisprudence. *Signs*, 8(4), 635–658.

MacKinnon, C.A. 1987. *Feminism Unmodified: Discourses on Life and Law*. Cambridge: Harvard University Press.

MacKinnon, C.A. 1991. *Feminist Theory and the State*. Cambridge: Harvard University Press.

Martin, E. 1987. *The Woman in the Body*. Boston: Beacon Press.

McCandless, J. and Sheldon, S. 2010a. 'No Father Required?' The Welfare Assessment in the Human Fertilisation and Embryology Act 2008. *Feminist Legal Studies*, 18(3), 201–225.

McCandless, J. and Sheldon, S. 2010b. The Human Fertilisation and Embryology Act (2008) and the Tenacity of the Sexual Family Form. *Modern Law Review*, 73(2), 175–207.

McGuinness, S. 2012. A, B and C Leads to D for Delegation. *Medical Law Review*, 19(3), 476–491.

McLean, S. 1997. *Consent and the Law: Review of the current provisions in the Human Fertilisation and Embryology Act 1990 for the UK Health Ministers – Consultation Document and Questionnaire*. London: Department of Health.

McLean, S. 1999. *Old Law, New Medicine: Medical Ethics and Human Rights*. London: Pandora.

McLean, S. 2002. *Legal and Ethical Issues in Xenotransplantation*. London: Department of Health.

Millns, S. 1995. Making 'Social Judgements That go Beyond the Purely Medical': The Reproductive Revolution and Access to Fertility Treatment Services, in *Law and Body*

*Politics: Regulating the Female Body*, edited by J. Bridgeman and S. Millns. Aldershot: Dartmouth, 79–105.

Montgomery, J. 1992. Doctors' Handmaidens: The Legal Contribution, in *Law, Health and Medical Regulation*, edited by S. McVeigh and S. Wheeler. Aldershot: Dartmouth, 142–169.

Montgomery, J. 1998. Professional Regulation: A Gendered Phenomenon?, in *Feminist Perspectives on Health Care Law*, edited by S. Sheldon and M. Thomson. London: Cavendish, 33–51.

Morgan, D. 1985. Making Motherhood Male: Surrogacy and the Moral Economy of Women. *Journal of Law and Society*, 12(2), 219–238.

Morgan, D. 1998. Frameworks for Analysis for Feminism's Accounts of Reproductive Technology, in *Feminist Perspectives on Heath Care Law*, edited by S. Sheldon and M. Thomson. London: Cavendish, 189–210.

Morgan, D. and Lee, R.G. 1997. In the Name of the Father? *Ex parte Blood*: Dealing with Novelty and Anomaly. *Modern Law Review*, 60(6), 840–856.

Morris, A. 2002. The Angel in the House: Altruism and the Pregnant Woman, in *Well Women: The Gendered Nature of Health Care Provision*, edited by A. Morris and S. Nott Aldershot: Ashgate, 97–115.

Munro, V. 2001. Square Pegs in Round Holes: The Dilemma of Conjoined Twins and Individual Rights. *Social and Legal Studies*, 10(4), 459–482.

Murphy, T. 1997. Feminism on Flesh. *Law and Critique*, 8(1), 37–59.

Murphy, T. 1998. Health Confidentiality in the Age of Talk, in *Feminist Perspectives on Health Care Law*, edited by S. Sheldon and M. Thomson. London: Cavendish, 155–172.

Murphy, T. 2000. Gametes, Law and Modern Preoccupations. *Health Care Analysis*, 8(2), 155–169.

Murphy, T. 2009. The Texture of Reproductive Choice, in *New Technologies and Human Rights*, edited by T. Murphy. Oxford: OUP, 195–221.

Murphy, T. 2013. *Health and Human Rights*. Oxford: Hart.

Murphy, T. and Ó Cuinn, G. 2013. Taking Technology Seriously: STS as a Human Rights Method, in *European Law and New Health Technologies*, edited by M. Flear et al. Oxford: OUP, 285–308.

Murphy T. and Whitty N. (2009), Is Human Rights Prepared? Risk, Rights and Public Health Emergencies. *Medical Law Review*, 17(2), 219–244.

Murray, S. 2008. *The 'Fat' Female Body*. London: Palgrave.

Mykitiuk, R. 1994. Fragmenting the Body. *Australian Feminist Law Journal*, 2, 63–98.

Naffine, N. 2009. *Law's Meaning of Life: Philosophy, Religion, Darwin and the Legal Person*. Oxford: Hart.

Nedelsky, J. 1989. Reconceiving Autonomy: Sources, Thoughts and Possibilities. *Yale Journal of Law and Feminism*, 1, 7–36.

Nedelsky, J. 1990. Law, Boundaries and the Bounded Self. *Representations*, 30, 162–189.

Nedelsky, J. 1993. Property in Potential Life: A Relational Approach to Choosing Legal Categories. *Canadian Journal of Law and Jurisprudence*, 6, 343–365.

Nedelsky, J. 2012. *Law's Relations: A Relational Theory of Self, Autonomy, and Law*. Oxford: OUP.

O'Donovan, K. 1985. *Sexual Divisions in Law*. London: Weidenfeld and Nicholson.

O'Neill, O. 2002. *Autonomy and Trust in Bioethics (Gifford Lectures)*. Cambridge: CUP.

Petchesky, R.P. 1987. Fetal Images: The Power of Visual Culture in the Politics of Reproduction. *Feminist Studies*, 13(2), 263–292.

Petchesky, R.P. 1995. The Body as Property: A Feminist Re-vision, in *Conceiving the New World Order: The Global Politics of Reproduction*, edited by F.D. Ginsburg and R. Rapp. Berkeley: University of California Press.

Priaulx, N. 2008. Re-thinking Progenitive Conflict: Why Reproductive Autonomy Matters. *Medical Law Review*, 16(2), 169–200.

Radin, M. 1987. Market Inalienability. *Harvard Law Review*, 100(8), 1849–1979.

Richards, M., Sclater, S. and Bainham, A. (eds), 2002. *Body Lore and Laws: Essays on Law and the Human Body*. Oxford: Hart.

Roberts, D. 1998. *Killing the Black Body: Race, Reproduction and the Meaning of Liberty*. New York: Pantheon Books.

Roseman, M.J. and Miller, A.M. 2011. Normalizing Sex and Its Discontents: Establishing Sexual Rights in International Law. *Harvard Journal of Law & Gender*, 34, 313–375.

Sabatello, M. 2009. *Children's Bioethics: The International Biopolitical Discourse on Harmful Traditional Practices and the Right of the Child to Cultural Identity*. Leiden: Martinus Nijhoff.

Sandland, R. 2000. 'Feminist Theory and Law: Beyond the Possibilities of the Present?' in *Feminist Perspectives on Law and Theory*, edited by R.P. Sandland and J. Richardson. London: Cavendish, 89–115.

Savell, K. 2004. Sex and the Sacred: Sterilization and Bodily Integrity in English and Canadian Law. *McGill Law Journal*, 49(4), 1093–1141.

Sharpe, A. 2002. *Transgender Jurisprudence: Dysphoric Bodies of Law*. London: Cavendish.

Sharpe, A. 2009. *Law's Monsters*. London: Routledge-Cavendish.

Sheldon, S. 1997. *Beyond Control: Medical Power and Abortion Law*. London: Pluto.

Sheldon, S. 1998. 'A Responsible Body of Medical Men Skilled in the Particular Art...': Rethinking the *Bolam* Test, in *Feminist Perspectives on Health Care Law*, edited by S. Sheldon and M. Thomson. London: Cavendish, 15–32.

Sheldon, S. 1999. ReConceiving Masculinity: Imagining Men's Reproductive Bodies in Law. *Journal of Law and Society*, 26(2), 129–149.

Sheldon, S. 2004. Gender Equality and Reproductive Decision-Making. *Feminist Legal Studies*, 12(3), 303–316.

Sheldon, S. and Thomson, M. (eds), 1998. *Feminist Perspectives on Health Care Law*. London: Cavendish.

Smart, C. 1987. 'There is of course the distinction dictated by nature': Law and the Problem of Paternity, in *Reproductive Technologies: Gender, Motherhood and Medicine*, edited by M. Stanworth. London: Polity, 98–117.

Smart, C. 1989. *Feminism and the Power of Law*. London: Routledge.

Smart, C. 1990. Law's Power, the Sexed Body, and Feminist Discourse. *Journal of Law and Society*, 17(2), 194–210.

Smart, C. 1992. The Woman of Legal Discourse. *Social and Legal Studies*, 1(1), 29–44.

Smart, C. 2010. Law and the Regulation of Family Secrets. *International Journal of Law, Policy and the Family*, 24(3), 397–413.

Strathern, M. 1993. *Reproducing the Future: Anthropology, Kinship and the New Reproductive Technologies*. Manchester: Manchester University Press.

Sullivan, N. and Murray, S. (eds), 2009. *Somatechnics: Queering the Technologisation of Bodies*. Aldershot: Ashgate.

Thomson, M. 1994. After *Re S. Medical Law Review*, 2(2), 127–148.

Thomson, M. 1997. Legislating for the Monstrous: Access to Reproductive Services and the Monstrous Feminine. *Social and Legal Studies*, 6(3), 401–424.

Thomson, M. 2007. *Endowed: Regulating the Male Sexed Body*. Abingdon: Routledge-Cavendish.

Waldby, C. and Cooper, M. 2010. From Reproductive Work to Reproductive Labour: The Female Body and the Stem Cell Industries. *Feminist Theory*, 11(1), 3–22.

Waldby, C. and Mitchell R. 2006. *Tissue Economies: Blood, Organs and Cell Lines in Late Capitalism*. Durham: Duke University Press.

Warnock, M. 1985. *A Question of Life: The Warnock Report on Human Fertilisation and Embryology*. Oxford: Basil Blackwell.

Weait, M. 2007. *Intimacy and Responsibility: The Criminalisation of HIV Transmission*. Abingdon: Routledge/Cavendish.

Wells, C. 1998. On the Outside Looking In: Perspectives on Enforced Caesareans, in *Feminist Perspectives on Health Care Law*, edited by S. Sheldon and M. Thomson. London: Cavendish, 237–257.

Whitty, N. 1998. 'In a Perfect World': Feminism and Health Care Resource Allocation, in *Feminist Perspectives on Health Care Law*, edited by S. Sheldon and M. Thomson. London: Cavendish, 135–152.

Williams, M. 2005. Death Rights: Assisted Suicide and Existential Rights. *International Journal of Law in Context*, 1(2), 183–198.

Williams, P.A. 1991. *The Alchemy of Race and Rights*. Cambridge: Harvard University Press.

Wolf, S.M. (ed.), 1996. *Feminism and Bioethics: Beyond Reproduction*. Oxford: OUP.

Zylinska, J. 2009. *Bioethics in the Age of New Media*. Cambridge: MIT Press.

# Motherhood and Law: Constructing and Challenging Normativity

## Susan B. Boyd[1]

An extensive feminist literature explores how law interacts with the social institution of motherhood and with the ideological frameworks that contribute to women's oppression in western, liberal states. This chapter's main concern is with feminist theories about law's role in relation to motherhood, which reflects both coercive and ideological aspects. That is, women can be coerced into normative ideals of motherhood and penalized for failure to conform, but women can also 'consent' or choose to conform to ideological norms, raising far more complex questions for feminists and for feminist legal strategy. The chapter also explores the degree to which law and feminist legal strategies reinforce and/or challenge dominant ideologies of motherhood, which are rooted in the histories of race, class, gender and sexuality.

Another theme of this chapter is the differential impact of legal regulation, depending on whether a mother is working class or middle class, racialized or non-racialized, lesbian or straight, disabled or able-bodied, and so on. All women can be detrimentally affected by dominant legal norms, but women who depart from normative white, middle-class, heterosexual motherhood are likely to be scrutinized more heavily and treated more coercively than those who are able to conform. The question of law's differential impact on women whose social location differs from this standard also poses important questions about feminist legal strategies, including whether they lapse into essentialist or 'maternalist' modes of analysis.

This chapter proceeds on the premise that motherhood is socially constructed through the interaction of complex structures and ideologies. The first part explains this process and is then followed by two illustrative case studies on criminal law and family law. The risk of essentialism is taken up in the next part on legal strategy. The last part of the chapter uses examples of 'transgressive motherhood' to suggest future directions for feminist legal theory and concludes with questions that continue to challenge feminist legal engagement with motherhood.

1    Thanks to my SSHRC-funded research team on 'autonomous motherhood', Dorothy Chunn, Fiona Kelly and Wanda Wiegers, for comments on an earlier draft and to Vanessa Munro and Margaret Davies for their graceful editorial work.

# The Social Construction of Motherhood: Law's Ideological Role

Despite women's biological potential to conceive, gestate, give birth and lactate, '[m]otherhood is not a natural condition' (Smart 1996: 37). Numerous feminist scholars have shown how the *institution* of motherhood is socially constructed in different historical periods, yet is presented ideologically as a natural consequence of biological differences between women and men. Indeed, in their review of feminist approaches to motherhood, Katherine O'Donovan and Jill Marshall (2006: 107) found that social construction is the most common approach within second wave feminism's analysis of motherhood. Adrienne Rich (1976) is often credited as the first feminist to have presented a scholarly analysis of motherhood as an institution and to deconstruct the notion of an inherent maternal instinct. Motherhood, mothering, and family structures are all shaped by social, economic and cultural contexts, which in turn are framed by the interlocking structures of gender, race, class and sexuality. As Martha Fineman puts it, motherhood is a colonized concept, something physically occupied and experienced by women, but defined, controlled, and given legal content by patriarchal ideology (1995: 38).

Early feminist treatments of motherhood often drew on materialist feminist approaches to the family within capitalist patriarchy, including the work of sociologists and political economists about the (hetero)sexual division of labour within both public and private spheres that developed within the context of industrial capitalism (Boyd 1997). For instance, Michèle Barrett and Mary McIntosh (1982) showed that the traditional, nuclear, 'anti-social' or privatized family plays a particular role within capitalism as a socio-economic institution and an ideology. Among other things, the family provides 'free' reproductive labour by women in relation to the care of children and workers which, in turn, allows productive labour to be pursued on the assumption that the 'private' sphere of family is handling care work. Feminist historians have shown that as fathers became increasingly linked with the public world of paid work in the nineteenth and twentieth centuries, and children became an economic cost to families, mothers were constructed as the 'divinely appointed guardians of the family' (Backhouse 1981: 239). Ironically, this idealized and deeply gendered role for mothers did not necessarily translate into legal rights in relation to children (Boyd 2003). These structural insights about the material basis for motherhood have been adopted by many authors (see, for example, Fineman 1995), often combined with attention to the role of ideology.

The concept of ideology has been deployed to refer to the ways in which law both constructs and normalizes a set of ideas about motherhood, often distracting attention away from its material roots. This concept has facilitated an increasingly complex understanding of law's roles in the social construction of motherhood. The notion of ideology also assists in understanding the dynamics through which women are regulated by law across and through their differences and, specifically, how mothers are constructed as 'good' or 'bad', depending on their adherence to the expectations of the 'normative mother' (Boyd 1996, Fineman 1995, Kline 1993). Marlee Kline evocatively summarized the significance of ideology in the regulation of motherhood and highlighted its relationship to traditional family structures during a period of proliferation of literature on the ideology of motherhood (see, for example, Fineman and Karpin 1995).

> *By the dominant ideology of motherhood, I mean the constellation of ideas and images in western capitalist societies that constitute the dominant ideals of motherhood*

*against which women's lives are judged. The expectations established by these ideals limit and shape the choices women make in their lives, and construct the dominant criteria of "good" and "bad" mothering. They exist within a framework of dominant ideologies of motherhood, which, in turn, intersect with dominant ideologies of family. (Kline 1993: 310)*

The key normative expectations associated with the ideology of motherhood are that (1) a woman must be a mother before she will be considered a proper adult woman, thus tying motherhood with femininity; (2) a 'good' mother will be selflessly available to her children, taking primary care of them; (3) a 'good' mother will do so in the context of a heterosexual, nuclear family model premised on privatized female dependence and domesticity. These expectations may shift over time and even countenance working mothers (Boyd 2003, Murphy 1998), but those who deviate may still be constructed as unfit, which in turn can compromise their legal ties with their children. At best, mothers may 'win' a legal claim, but in a manner that reproduces oppressive dominant norms about women and mothers. For instance, arguments from both prosecution and defence in relation to mothers who are charged with murdering their infants often reinforce dominant norms of motherhood (Cunliffe 2011). Whereas the prosecution typically attempts to portray the woman as a bad mother because she departs from those norms, the defence offers evidence of the woman's conformity with maternal ideals.

The requirement that mothers behave selflessly in relation to children in their primary care has important consequences, not least by limiting their ability to take up paid work. As well, mothers' rights are often constructed in opposition to the rights of their children, which may undermine 'the fundamental bond that exists between most mothers and their children' (Murphy 1998: 691). This oppositional treatment of mothers and children is manifested particularly in relation to child protection law, where women can be defined as failing to adequately protect their children even if the risk to the child is generated by other factors, such as poverty (Kline 1993). Even more acute are situations where a pregnant woman is positioned as a risk to the health of her fetus (Diduck 1993).

This example illustrates that law is not the only institution that reproduces the ideology of motherhood through its discursive power: 'discourses such as feminism, modern rationality, science, social work and psychology' interact with law 'in a kind of shifting hierarchy' and also 'are imbued with such factors as race, class and sexuality' (Diduck 1993: 462). In combination with other professional discourses, such as science or medicine or psychiatry, law can be particularly powerful in scrutinizing maternal conduct, particularly in relation to child protection and criminal law (Cunliffe 2011, Diduck 1993, Raitt and Zeedyk 2004). For example, state removal of children from mothers labelled as mentally ill reflects processes through which laws on mental health and child protection interact with the power of the psychiatric paradigm (Langer 2009, Mosoff 1997). In these processes, the ideology of motherhood can facilitate law's coercive aspect.

Mothers who are already marginalized, notably as a result of poverty, race or aboriginality, are most vulnerable to being labelled 'unfit'. For instance, due to the correlation between race and poverty in the United States, which has a high percentage of poor Black families headed by women, a particularly pathological representation of Black single motherhood prevails: 'Ideologically, in America, single motherhood is Black' (Roberts 1993b: 25). Single and African-American mothers have been demonized in poverty and child welfare discourses, the mainstream solution often being a patriarchal one of locating absent fathers and returning them to the family, particularly to make a financial contribution (Fineman 1995).

Child protection disputes between a parent and state authorities graphically reveal the ways in which poverty and race are implicated in the regulation of motherhood. Modern child protection legislation relies on the assessment of risk, based on a belief in the ability to predict future harm to children. As Karen Swift (2010) has shown, the ideology of risk can distort and deflect attention away from the relations of race, class and gender that are structured into child welfare processes, stripping them of their ideological baggage. Single mothers especially are constructed as a 'risk class', 'who can legitimately be intruded upon, scrutinized indefinitely and held to account for their daily activities' (Swift 2010: 143). The experience of aboriginal mothers in Canada's child welfare system similarly highlights a history of colonialist and racist processes of regulation of indigenous families and yet simultaneously erases this history through the application of the best interests of the child standard (Kline 1993). Whether actual harm to children is effectively prevented through these intrusive regulatory processes is questionable.

As these examples suggest, it is not only individual mothers who may be deemed to have fallen short of ideological expectations; rather, entire groups of women may be judged as unfit for motherhood based on their social location (Kline 1993: 312–313). Moreover, as the historical antecedents of the ideology of motherhood (including highly problematic race and class-based eugenics-derived birth control discourses) have faded, its roots and its problematic impact on some groups of women are rendered invisible so that the construct of the 'bad mother' is presented as unbiased or 'innocent'.

That said, the normative frameworks surrounding motherhood are not static but shift in form and content through history and across cultures. The legal system has been one key way in which those norms have been communicated and reinforced and, sometimes, challenged. For example, although procreation by contemporary Black mothers is often devalued and discouraged, at earlier points in American history, procreation by Black slave women was desirable, albeit for problematic reasons (Roberts 1993b: 7–10). Their children replenished the master's supply of slaves, yet slave mothers were deprived of any legal claim to their children. Although this severing of maternal ties was eventually abolished, parallels have been drawn with the modern system of state intervention in the homes of Black mothers, who are more likely to be under scrutiny and have their children removed (Murphy 1998: 708, Roberts 1993b: 13–15).

In addition to shifts in ideological frameworks, women's experiences of motherhood can vary widely. These variations may correlate to the interaction of factors such as class, race, sexuality and immigration status, but also to women's different approaches to motherhood, including some women's resistance to normative expectations or to the experience of motherhood altogether (Arendell 2000). A mother's definition of her own experience may differ radically from the socio-legal construction of her mothering. For example, an 'unwed Black teenager … may experience motherhood as a rare source of self-affirmation, while society deems her motherhood to be illegitimate and deviant' (Roberts 1993b: 4).

Class too plays a key role in mediating the operation of the ideology of motherhood. Middle class women are exhorted to be stay-at-home mothers and criticized for engaging in work outside the home, but single mothers and the working poor receive contradictory messages; they might be expected to take paid work to avoid unemployment and being categorized as lazy, yet still be criticized for taking paid work (Gavigan and Chunn 2007: 749). As well, paid domestic or care work, too often performed by racialized, 'othered' women who may well be mothers themselves, and based on exploitative conditions, enables middle- and high-income mothers to mediate the contradictions between paid work and the conventional expectations of motherhood (Blackett 2011). Poor, racialized mothers in the United States have been caught in impossible situations under policies of no-fault evictions from public housing based on drug-related activity by their children, where mothers are held responsible for their children in circumstances offering them little material ability to rectify the problem (Austin 2002).

The social construction of motherhood is also related to concepts of men and masculinity, fatherhood, gender, heteronormativity, and the division of labour (Smart and Sevenhuijsen 1989). On the one hand, motherhood is held up as the ultimate definition of what it means to be a woman; on the other hand, for women who do not become mothers in the expected context, motherhood can be discouraged (Kline 1993). Even lesbian mothers, parenting intentionally outside the heterosexual mainstream, can be measured against (potentially contradictory) expectations that children should have fathers or that lesbian mothers should adhere to a nuclear family model (Kelly 2011).

Even as traditionalist ideologies on patriarchal authority within the family dissipated in the late twentieth century and women entered the labour force in increasing numbers, dominant norms about motherhood were still reinforced in much popular culture and in the media, generating difficulties for individual women. Women continue to be expected to provide care for children and others, yet these expectations of 'domesticity' generate economic dependency in most mothers (Williams 2000). With the costs of 'inevitable dependency' being privatized within the family, and with women typically being allocated the burden of caring for inevitable dependency, a 'derivative dependency' arises in mother/caretakers (Fineman 1995: 161–164). Mothers become economically dependent on either a wage-earning partner or on (diminishing) state assistance. This dependency is not necessarily resolved when mothers participate in the workforce, where they tend to earn less money than other women and fathers, even controlling for the fact that they work fewer hours due to the demands of their care responsibilities: 'being a mother is incompatible with being an ideal worker' (Becker 2002: 68). The depression in mothers' wages is lifelong, as are its consequences, including poverty among elderly women (Crittenden 2001).

Because ideological expectations have shifted over time, any clear dichotomy between good and bad mothers is now difficult to sustain. Ideological frameworks have been complicated as equality has become a dominant norm, as fathers have been expected to participate more fully in the lives of their children (Boyd 2003) and as mothers are expected to be responsible market citizens (Gavigan and Chunn 2007). The rise of gender symmetry in relation to legal parenthood must, however, be contrasted with the ongoing disproportionate responsibility that women still bear for child care, and the extent to which 'mother work' has been rendered invisible in the face of legal trends promoting paternal rights (Fineman 1995).

Two case studies on criminal law and family law will next serve to illustrate the shifting nature of the social construction of motherhood.

## Case Study: Criminalizing Mothers

The 'bad' or 'unfit' mother is a powerful, yet over-simplified figure in Western law and literature, which identify her 'as the woman whose neglectful, abusive, reckless, or murderous behavior threatens or destroys her children' (Ashe and Cahn 1993: 80). Dorothy

Roberts (1993a) suggests that women's criminal conduct can often be explained through a focus on their refusal to mother or failure to care properly for their children; these mothers are penalized largely for their violation of gender norms and studying them illuminates the mechanisms through which the institution of motherhood confines women and punishes them if they resist. The criminal law both contributes to the construction of dominant norms of motherhood and reveals the complexities of women's struggle against a 'self-annihilating role' under which she must take on any risk to ensure her child's safety (Roberts 1993a: 96, 100). For instance, the punishment of mothers who fail to protect their children from abuse by a male partner holds women, often battered themselves, responsible for violence in the family and enforces the notion that mothers must be selfless. Marie Ashe and Naomi Cahn (1993) argue for more contextualized accounts that counter portrayals of bad mothers as either autonomous, fully responsible evildoers or helpless victims.

Law coercively reinforced the notion that motherhood is an inevitable by-product of heterosexual activity by criminalizing women's efforts to control their reproductive lives through the use of contraceptives and abortion (Smart 1996). Even once the coercive aspect of criminal law prohibitions are removed in relation, say, to abortion, women's struggles to retain control over pregnancy and access to abortion services continue (Gavigan 1992), illustrating the intersection between law and other normative frameworks such as medicine. Racialized differences can also be identified in struggles for women's reproductive autonomy: whereas white, middle class women have historically concerned themselves primarily with contesting criminal laws that restrict their ability to choose *not* to become pregnant, such as contraception or abortion, poor women of colour are often more concerned with challenging restrictions that constrain their choices *to* procreate in a healthy, supported manner, including coercive measures such as sterilization (Roberts 1993b: 32–33).

More complex are the laws on maternal neonaticide. 'Draconican' seventeenth-century English laws on infanticide, later adopted in Canada, regulated women's sexuality by applying only to unmarried mothers, working with a presumption of guilt and imposing capital punishment (Smart 1996: 43). Juries often refused to convict, however, acknowledging the lack of alternatives facing many women (see also Backhouse 1984). In the face of this juror leniency, lesser offences such as concealment were added as a way to secure convictions. In the twentieth century, sex-specific offences were introduced in some jurisdictions, with a focus on a mother's failure to fully recover from the effects of childbirth or lactation and a disturbance to the balance of her mind. Some (see, for example, Smart 1996) see this modern incarnation as a medical-legal category that constructs women's 'deviance' in bio-psychological terms rather than in relation to socio-economic difficulties facing women. Others challenge the notion that infanticide law straightforwardly reflects the medicalization of women's crime or the construction of 'bad' mothers. Based in part on the fact that Canadian law created a separate offence rather than England's mitigation approach, Kirsten Johnson Kramar (2005) argues that this law recognized women's unique experiences of pregnancy and childbirth, including socio-economic hardship.

Since the early 1990s, a moral panic has arisen and the medical-legal system has taken a more punitive approach to mothers whose children die. This harsher approach must be understood against the backdrop of women's attainment of formal legal equality and enhanced reproductive rights, which inculcate a notion that women must be reproductively responsible for their actions in relation to newborns, who have become 'wholly deserving victim[s]' (Kramar 2005: 14). Indeed, a combination of adversarial legal processes, erroneous representations of relevant medical knowledge, and deviation from some normative expectations of motherhood likely combined to generate a wrongful conviction of an Australian mother for murdering her infants (Cunliffe 2011). Kathleen Folbigg was a competent mother, but her occasional resistance to mothering overshadowed the positive indicia. Fiona Raitt and Suzanne Zeedyk (2004) similarly link wrongful convictions to assumptions that murderous mothers can be identified through their standard of childcare and their emotional reactions to children's death or illness. They also suggest that contemporary legal cases of unexplained infant deaths are haunted by the spectre of a diagnosis of Munchausen Syndrome by Proxy, under which mothers are suspected of deliberately causing harm to their children in order to gain attention. Mothers who are suspected of criminal behaviour may well be subjected to more rigid standards (Cunliffe 2011: 203–204), with a 'retributive impulse' towards women labelled as 'bad' mothers (Langer 2009: 218).

## Case Study: Child Custody Law

Child custody law exemplifies the use of ideology to analyse a field that some view as *privileging* motherhood and also illustrates the relational nature of the ideology of motherhood with other ideologies, for example on fatherhood. Mothers have been constructed as the favoured darlings of the law when engaged in disputes over their children. However, whereas a mother who conforms to the ideological expectations of the middle class, heterosexual, stay-at-home mother might be favoured in an adjudication, her sister who, say, works outside the home and delegates aspects of her child's care to another might be viewed as a less worthy candidate because she selfishly placed her own interests above those of the child (Boyd 2003, Mason 1999, Murphy 1998). In some periods, mothers who betrayed their marriage vows by adulterous conduct or, worse still, for lesbian relationships, were assessed as unsuitable for custody.

By reading a child's best interests against the mother's degree of conformity to ideological norms, the legal system reinforces dominant expectations of mothers both in situations where a mother 'wins' custody and where she 'loses'. While this ideology quite clearly operates against the interests of women who fail to conform to it and has a particular impact on women whose mothering is viewed as marginal or threatening to dominant norms (for example, lesbian mothers), it by no means privileges in any absolute manner women who appear to conform by being, say, heterosexual or able-bodied. Even when a form of maternal presumption dominated the legal system, it was easy for a woman to fall from grace (Boyd 2003: 41–101, Murphy 1998: 695). The ideology of motherhood structures and therefore limits the lives of all women: any woman who appears at a given time to conform to the norms can lapse and lose a privileged status. This insight challenges any efforts to draw stark contrasts between 'good' and 'bad' mothers in reality, as opposed to ideology, and illustrates the disciplining effects of ideological norms on all mothers (Boyd 1996).

Child custody law also reveals the dilemmas of feminist inspired law reform. The apparently progressive move to emphasize a child's best interests rather than parental conduct or assumptions about maternal care produced negative consequences for many mothers. The late twentieth-century focus on gender neutrality and no-fault divorce rendered less visible the social and economic forces that reinforce women's responsibility for children (Boyd 2003, Fineman 1995, Mason 1999). Moreover, the rise of fathers' rights advocacy was embedded in this formal equality approach to parenthood, contributing to the trend towards 'gender symmetry'. As a result, the language of maternal care became discredited, depriving women of a legitimate voice with which to express their experience of caring for children. Fineman coined the term 'the neutered mother' to denote the multiple ways in which the concept of Mother has been taken out of context by being de-gendered, de-raced and de-classed (1995: 67). Although the dominance of the ideology of motherhood in earlier periods did not empower mothers as such, instead reinforcing an image of mothers as selfless, pure, full-time carers of children within the heterosexual nuclear family, the resonance of this norm lost its power in law near the end of the twentieth century, as mother love became an increasingly 'exhausted script' (Smart 1991: 486) and claims of 'father love' and fathers' rights prevailed.

Carol Smart's empirical work revealed that mothers more often express their taken-for-granted caregiving responsibility for children as 'caring for', whereas fathers talk about 'caring about' (loving) children, which 'can produce a sentimental rush of concern and can be instrumental in producing legislative reforms' (1991: 489). The evolving family law system values 'caring about' above 'caring for' in the moral register, meaning that fathers' claims are heard positively while mothers' claims appear self-interested. Moreover, mothers who fail to facilitate paternal contact with children after divorce have become identified as bad or vindictive mothers, giving birth to the image of the 'no contact mother', whose anxieties about contact are read as selfishness (Rhoades 2002). Being a 'bad' mother was never really about a mother's relationship with her child, but rather about her conduct in relation to norms about family; now an important aspect of a mother's role is her responsibility to foster a child's relationship with a father.

Having explored the social construction of motherhood and the role of ideology in legal processes, the next section turns to questions of feminist legal strategy.

## Legal Strategy: Reinforcing or Challenging the Ideology of Motherhood?

Feminists have debated whether feminist legal strategies reinforce or challenge dominant ideologies of motherhood. To the extent that legal arguments emphasize the uneven playing field between mothers and fathers, notably, women's ongoing responsibility for care of children and related economic difficulties, the ideology of motherhood can be reinforced, producing negative repercussions for mothers who cannot meet the normative model (see, for example, Kline 1993, Mosoff 1997). This strategic impulse can also be charged with essentialism and 'fix[ing] women as second-class citizens in a patriarchal structure' (Mason 1999: 15). That said, the history of feminist engagement in this field illuminates why feminists often emphasize the specificity of motherhood rather than gender neutrality. To the extent that this strategy is rooted in an appreciation of the social construction of motherhood as embedded in stubbornly entrenched socio-economic structures, it can be viewed as realist rather than essentialist. Nevertheless, negative or unintended consequences can be identified.

Many nineteenth- and early twentieth-century feminists embraced a maternal feminism that correlated motherhood with a special capacity for nurturing, but this approach was largely rejected in the campaigns for equal rights in the 1960s and 1970s (Fineman 1995: 36–37, 77). The liberal feminism that characterized the early second wave of the women's movement was optimistic about involving men as equal parents and moving mothers into the labour force. Gender-based assumptions related to parenthood should be eliminated and men should behave more like women – by participating equally in child care in the 'private' sphere of the family. A common argument was that gender-specific statutory language, for instance, maternal presumptions in custody law, should be eliminated because they reinforced assumptions that mothers should care for children and fathers need not (Mason 1999: 3). Some feminists favoured a joint custody norm for that reason, and others did so because it might better take account of the fact that some women parent within extended networks and recognize that mothers are differently located according to factors such as race and class (Bartlett and Stack 1986).

Optimism about eliminating sex roles through law reforms such as joint custody waned as feminists realized that significant social and economic forces impeded the equal sharing of parental responsibilities and any major shifts in the public/private divide (Boyd 1997). A substantive equality analysis emerged both to explain the apparent failure of formal equality and to argue for a more nuanced understanding of women's inequality in relation to family and child care; an inequality that too often leads to poverty (Becker 2002). The sexual division of labour prevails not only in heterosexual families, but in workplace practices favouring workers who are unimpeded by care responsibilities. Feminists began to argue more strenuously for jobs to be restructured to accommodate mothers and for more systemic changes to acknowledge the 'derivative dependency' of mothers/caregivers (Fineman 1995). Rena Uviller recognized early on that the move towards equal custody rights for fathers could result in equality with a vengeance against mothers: 'under the guise of sex-neutrality, women who want their children may be at a distinct disadvantage in custody disputes due to their inferior earning capacity and an enduring social bias against working mothers' (1978: 109). In addition, when the economic roles of mothers are considered, an (often false) assumption of equality quickly comes into play based on a notion that women can compete equally in the workplace. When applied to both financial responsibilities such as child support and child custody decisions, mothers are placed in a bind: they are penalized in child custody assessments for working outside the home and yet are expected to financially provide on an equal basis for their children (Boyd 2003: 115–120, Murphy 1998).

In child custody law, a strategy focused around a primary care presumption emerged (see, for example, Mason 1999, Smart and Sevenhuijsen 1989), with arguments for a revamped maternal presumption being in the minority (Mason 1990–91, Uviller 1978). Under a primary care presumption, the parent who was the primary caregiver in the past should obtain custody in contested cases, unless proven unfit, or if all other factors were equal. This ostensibly gender-neutral feminist focus on primary care has been the subject of much debate due to its potential to reinforce problematic assumptions about women's essential capacity for caregiving. As Jane Murphy notes (1998: 692), 'protecting children is often best achieved by protecting their caretaker parent – their mother', but this strategy can reinforce maternal stereotypes. Proponents of the care presumption do not promote essentialism per se, yet their work can be read as buttressing the sexual division of labour because it seeks acknowledgement of women's more onerous responsibilities. Mary Anne Case (2001) even argues against policies such as enhanced support for caregivers from government or employers, in part because increasing such benefits would generate more discrimination against women in the labour force. Her proposed solution is a formal equality approach to parenting and services directed to children rather than parents. Others defend the care argument on the grounds that it is necessary to highlight a key source of women's inequality and is sometimes transgressive (e.g. Becker 2002, Kessler 2005).

Feminists who adopt a care approach can also be charged with failure to take account of differences related to race, sexuality, and class – overlooking differences among women as mothers and men as fathers. The primary care presumption is critiqued for its reinforcement of maternal care within the nuclear family, its failure to recognize alternative family structures of care such as extended families, and its potential to permit challenges to custody claims by mothers with disabilities, given they can easily be cast as unfit or unable to take primary responsibility for care (see, for example, Mosoff 1997). The presumption can also be portrayed as regressive in comparison to liberal feminist and fathers' rightists' claims for equal roles for men and women as parents.

Fathers' rights advocates have taken up the formal equality argument for equal treatment of mothers and fathers, suggesting that law is biased in favour of mothers and rests on sexist stereotypes (Boyd 2003: 102–129). They have demanded legal presumptions of joint custody and, more recently, have successfully challenged laws related to the (sur)naming of children, which in turn is often based on whether a father is named by a mother on the birth registration. As Hester Lessard (2004) demonstrates, the apparently benign construction of mothers and fathers as formally equal draws on a bio-genetic model of parenthood that erases the deeply political and ideological nature of the legal ordering of parent–child, and parent–parent relationships.

Despite such insights, feminist approaches to motherhood have not had marked impact on legal policy, perhaps because the arguments are complex and can be misunderstood as reinforcing gendered roles within the family. In many countries, shared parenting has won the day as the dominant normative framework, with an attendant heteronormative emphasis on gender symmetry between fathers and mothers (Boyd 2010). That said, it is difficult to see what better strategy might have been pursued. Arguably, feminist discourse in this field has been misunderstood in a climate that reflects a 'backlash' to social and legal initiatives that appear to favour mothers (Sheldon 2001).

The next section asks whether a focus on transgressive mothering can enrich feminist legal scholarship on motherhood.

## Transgressive Motherhood

We have seen that normative expectations of mothers are tied to the notion that proper motherhood occurs within the context of the white, heterosexual, nuclear, middle class family and to gender roles. Lively debates continue about how feminists should approach motherhood. Legal moves to encourage gender symmetry before socio-economic forces enable it have been aptly critiqued (see, for example, Boyd 2003, Fineman 1995). Nevertheless it is risky for feminists to be perceived as resisting men's equal involvement with children or to argue for maternal autonomy in fields where children's interests are central (Boyd 2010).

Feminists who focus on care and motherhood have, however, importantly complicated liberal individualist approaches to autonomy by emphasizing the nexus between relationships and autonomy (Boyd 2010, Nedelsky 1989, O'Donovan and Marshall 2006). Specifically, the care relationships between mothers and children enable children to become autonomous persons. Yet, due to still powerful societal expectations that mothers will provide primary care and the strong sense of responsibility that many/most mothers feel towards their children, child-rearing imposes significant material constraints on female autonomy. Women's 'pregnant embodiment' (Young 1990) – their more continuous physical experience in relation to children as a result of pregnancy, breastfeeding, and care responsibility – prevents them from being able to opt in and out of involvement with children as men can choose to do. Despite long-standing feminist calls for men to share parenting and for society to support work–life balance, this constraint remains entrenched. While care is not inevitably women's work, the choices that most women make to embrace motherhood, despite the disincentives (Becker 2002), imply ongoing gendered consequences into the future. The challenge is how to recognize the gendered dynamics of care without overemphasizing heteronormative birth and genetic ties and ignoring the significance of social parenting and families of choice.

Gender asymmetry persists in both the social realities of parenthood highlighted above and the social construction of genetic ties, and mothers are by no means favoured. Many feminists have cautioned about an increasing emphasis on the genetic tie (Lessard 2004), which seems to be invoked more easily in favour of legal fatherhood, especially to enforce financial obligations (Sheldon 2001), but also in other contexts. Whereas in earlier periods, mothers had exclusive rights and responsibilities in relation to 'illegitimate' children and fathers garnered legal rights mainly through marriage to a birth mother, that degree of maternal autonomy has been eroded (Smart and Sevenhuijsen 1989: 8–9). Although reproductive technologies open opportunities to move beyond traditional notions of filiation and the two-parent hegemony, maternity remains a naturalized concept that too often fuses genetic, gestational and caregiving roles (Mykitiuk 2001). As a result, maternal legal status tends to be accorded to women only if they fulfil both biological and behavioural requirements. For instance, a birth mother's failure to properly care for a child 'denaturalizes' her, rendering her unfit. Yet a lesbian non-biological co-mother is often not viewed as a legal parent, despite her care and intention (Kelly 2011, Millbank 2008) even if she is a caregiver.

This part of the chapter explores whether a focus on 'transgressive motherhood' can disrupt the over-emphasis on genetic ties and imprisonment of many feminist conversations about motherhood within tropes of heteronormativity, including the notion that fathers should be equal parents. Laura Kessler (2005) argues that feminists have been overly critical or pessimistic about the relationship between caregiving and women and notes that 'transgressive caregiving' can be a form of political resistance, even a subversive practice. This idea holds potential because it focuses on elements of resistance within a traditionally gendered terrain. Lessons can be drawn from feminist work on women who transgress the normative ideals of motherhood, for instance, lesbian, surrogate, Black, single and criminalized mothers.

Lesbian motherhood clearly disrupts the focus on genetic ties, given that most lesbian birth mothers rely on sperm donors for conception, yet donors rarely act as social parents. Very often, a lesbian co-mother without a genetic tie assumes that role (Kelly 2011, Millbank 2008). Lesbian co-mothering also challenges any automatic connection between birth mothers and primary care, with empirical studies on lesbian mothers revealing a focus on intentional and care relationships rather than genetic ties (see, for example, Kelly 2011). At a more general level, O'Donovan and Marshall suggest, drawing on Sara Ruddick (1989: 51) that all women who choose to mother might be regarded as 'adoptive', in the sense that even birth mothers must make a commitment to protect, nurture and train a child after the act of birth (2006: 109). Given still strong expectations that birth mothers undertake mothering, they argue that the distinction between birthing and mothering must be more clearly drawn, noting that it is even less acceptable now than it once was for an unmarried mother to 'give away' her child. A distinction might accordingly be drawn between birthing labour and mothering, as well as sperm donation and parenting.

The challenge is how to devise a system that recognizes care relationships and under which donors are not automatically regarded as legal parents, unless intended, and also to recognize intended lesbian co-mothers. Ruthann Robson (1992) suggests that legal arguments in relation to (lesbian) motherhood can have a deeply problematic 'domesticating' effect and that the very category of 'mother' as a *legal* category may domesticate lesbians under the power of law and restrict lesbian choice. Indeed, early innovative efforts to use the idea of functional parenthood to recognize lesbian mothers (see, for example, Polikoff 1990) often resulted in legal outcomes contrary to their original intention (Millbank 2008). In other words, the transgressive potential of lesbian motherhood has been difficult to translate in the legal realm. Both Fiona Kelly (2011) and Jenni Millbank (2008) propose reforms that rely on intentionality rather than functionality to ascribe legal parentage. Presumptions of legal parenthood would be made upon the occurrence of certain events, such as consent by a non-birth mother to her partner's attempt to conceive through assisted conception. Consensual opt-in methods would exist for third parties, thus disrupting the nuclear model. This line of thought is reminiscent of Fineman's proposal (1995) to place the mother/child relationship at the centre of socio-legal policy, but allow for opt-in relationships. The marital unit is displaced in favour of an emphasis on care relationships, using the metaphor of the mother/child dyad, which could be expanded via contract.

Possibly in tension with the emphasis on intention in determining legal parenthood is surrogate motherhood, given earlier feminist support for the birth mother when considering whether surrogacy contracts should be honoured (e.g. Shanley 1993). They were concerned that surrogate mothers could not give meaningful consent prior to birth, that the potential for exploitation was significant based on factors such as age, class and race as well as emotional vulnerability, and that exchange of money for women's reproductive services would commodify women and children. More recently, these concerns have been tested against empirical research and found to be largely unfounded (Busby and Vun 2010). The focus has shifted to regulatory measures that can ensure women's autonomy and minimize the potential for exploitation and commodification, yet women's unique capacity for pregnancy has not been erased. As in adoption statutes, birth mothers might retain the right to reverse a decision to relinquish a child within a short period after birth (Busby and Vun 2010: 89). The specificities of pregnancy and birth are taken into account even as the ability of women to exercise reproductive autonomy is honoured. Both forms of maternal labour – birthing and (intentional) mothering – are respected, but distinguished (O'Donovan and Marshall 2006).

As we have seen, the history of Black motherhood also challenges dominant constructions of motherhood, with women often having to fight to control their fertility and for legal rights to their children. As well, the practice in many African-American communities is for 'othermothers' to assist blood mothers (Kessler 2005, Roberts 1993a: 132–133). Othermothers need not be blood relatives so, as with practices of parenting within some indigenous communities, their role in parenting challenges the nuclear family model (Kline 1993). As with intentional parenting, these practices highlight relationships in parenting and downplay biological connections. Similarly, single mothers by choice often rely on support networks outside family ties (Kelly 2012, Kessler 2005: 24–25). The challenge for feminists is how to recognize this direction while not erasing women's role in pregnancy and birth.

Kessler (2005) suggests that law could recognize multiple parents for one child, but other feminists suggest risks in using this method to disrupt the nuclear model. Many mainstream law reforms over-emphasize the need to find fathers for children, with particular troubling consequences for the families of single, divorced and lesbian mothers (Fineman 1995, Kelly 2011, Robson 1992). Proposals to move in this direction must be done carefully, with respect both for birth mothers and for intentional parenting relationships. Still, not all legal parents need to be designated as primary (Kessler 2005).

Placing single motherhood, another form of transgressive mothering, at the heart of feminist analysis can assist and potentially build bridges across racial divides. Despite social and legal efforts to persuade Black women to marry, 'white mothers' lives are becoming structurally more similar to the lives of Black mothers' (Roberts 1993b: 27), with unmarried single motherhood on the rise. Black single motherhood can be seen as an example of resistance against suggestions that a return to patriarchal family structures will improve the welfare of women and their children.

Taking this resistance further may be difficult, in part because the overt nature of patriarchal definitions of motherhood has given way to more 'innocent' mechanisms. Shelley Gavigan and Dorothy Chunn (2007) dispel any notion of an evolutionary progression away from a stigmatized treatment of single mothers. Having once been regarded as the most deserving recipients of public assistance, sole-support mothers have been rendered undeserving during the restructuring of welfare law in most liberal states. Single mothers might have had to meet difficult eligibility hurdles (being a 'fit and proper' person to care for children) or attempt to obtain support from putative fathers, but the original welfare system was designed to compensate – minimally – for the failure or inability of a male breadwinner to provide. With the rise of neoliberalism, however, single mothers are constructed as employable market citizens with responsibility for their own support. Meanwhile the unpaid labour performed by mothers 'becomes less visible and less articulated' (Gavigan and Chunn 2007: 767) and single mothers who do not engage in paid work are constructed as a drain on the public purse.

Despite these disincentives and the fact that women's ability to define legal motherhood autonomously from men is constrained by the impetus to 'find fathers' for children, planned single motherhood is on the rise (Kelly 2012). This form of transgressive mothering also raises questions about the discourse of neoliberal responsibility. Many single mothers by choice have planned their motherhood, often using assisted reproduction or adoption, in what might be regarded as a 'responsible' manner. Many are well-educated, middle-class and financially secure. Despite their relative privilege, the legal system has not made it easy for these single mothers to establish themselves as the sole legal parent of a child or to escape accusations that they are depriving children of fathers (Kelly 2012). In the future, a challenge may be for feminists to ensure that arguments for social and legal support for single mothers do not favour only the more privileged or responsible women, just as some progressive legal changes accommodated only exemplary lesbian mothers (Robson 1992: 177–178).

Roberts has said that '[i]t may be in the lives of those most outcast by patriarchy that we will catch a glimpse of a liberated motherhood' (1993b: 28). When mothers who have harmed their children are brought into the frame, more difficult but important transgressive mothering issues arise. Roberts sees child abuse inflicted by mothers as connected to the contradictory role of children as both the source of mothers' vulnerability, with their children being held hostage to both individual men and to society, and also a source of their power and resistance. For instance, slave women sometimes committed crimes against their children in an attempt to defy their masters' exploitation of their reproduction (Roberts 1993a: 134). An approach to liberated motherhood that identified with (some) criminal mothers, with a focus on oppositional actions that are subversive and liberatory rather than subjugating of children, would not excuse all mothers who hurt their children, but rather ask feminists to confront the complexity of women's subordination and the radical measures required to eradicate it (Roberts 1993a: 141).

Ashe and Cahn (1993) similarly emphasize consideration of the figure of the 'bad' mother, including taking seriously the fact that some mothers harm their children. In resisting a notion that mothers must inevitably be good, and avoiding a polarized view of women as either fully responsible moral agents or the victims of individual men and patriarchy, these authors put mothers who engage in child abuse into context. For instance, maternal abuse must also be seen against the backdrop of women's disproportionate care responsibilities as well as their own abuse by male partners. Ashe and Cahn (1993) ask how lawyers who defend mothers who have fallen short of the ideals of motherhood can find moral worth in their clients, challenging feminists to always place a woman's acts and choices into context. As always, the problem is that more ambivalent and complex accounts of motherhood are not necessarily comprehensible in law or legal advocacy. Nevertheless, many criminalized mothers have struggled with material constraints, including poverty and their own abuse, on their ability to provide for or protect their children.

These contextual insights raise a final point highlighted by many feminists: that it is more crucial than ever in neoliberal times favouring a shrunken state, to emphasize that care is a public good and that material support for caregivers is necessary. To the extent that mothers continue to carry and suffer the consequences of disproportionate responsibility for care (Boyd 2003, Fineman 1995, Kessler 2005), public recognition and compensation for their care labour is required. In the longer term, revisioning the relationship between labour in the home and the public sphere of work and politics (including adequate childcare choices, a sort of public 'othermothering') remains necessary in order to support the choices that women as mothers ought to be able to make – and yet, so rarely are able to in a world that relies on their unpaid care labour. Nancy Hirschmann (2010) suggests that the call for state and employer support for family and care responsibilities must be taken with a grain of salt, and that gender equality relies on men sharing equally in child rearing. This point may hold water for heterosexual mothers in relationships, but public support remains essential for transgressive mothers who do not have partners. Making it possible for women to undertake mothering outside of traditional relationships empowers all mothers and allows them to explore non-oppressive ways of parenting.

## Conclusion

Despite the joys and transgressive potential that it offers, motherhood remains an institution that contributes to women's systematic inequality and, therefore, forms a crucial site of debate and struggle for feminists engaged with law. Many questions persist. How can more robust social and economic supports for the work of motherhood be sought without falling into essentialist reductions of women to motherhood, or mothers to mothering? What space for autonomy exists for mothers, in an historical period where the importance of fathers to children's well-being is regarded as key? Should all women's choices be honoured in feminist legal strategies, even if a choice (for example, to be a stay at home mother) embeds a woman in oppressive social formations? Do women's differences as mothers outnumber what they hold in common and can a common legal strategy be contemplated? Can anti-essentialist approaches be recognized without undermining feminist struggles to legally recognize the significance of maternal relationships with children? Does a focus on care-giving or intentional relationships rather than bio-genetic ties provide a constructive direction or is a combination of the two needed? No one feminist theory can answer all such questions, but the literature reviewed in this chapter provides a basis for addressing them in the future.

# References

Arendell, T. 2000. Conceiving and investigating motherhood: the decade's scholarship. *Journal of Marriage and the Family*, 62(4), 1192–1207.

Ashe, M. and Cahn, N. 1993. Child abuse: a problem for feminist theory. *Texas Journal of Women and the Law*, 2(1), 75–112.

Austin, R. 2002. Step on a crack, break your mother's back: poor moms, myths of authority, and drug-related evictions in public housing. *Yale Journal of Law and Feminism*, 14(2), 273–289.

Backhouse, C.B. 1981. Shifting patterns in nineteenth-century Canadian custody law, in *Essays in the History of Canadian Law Volume 1*, edited by D.H. Flaherty. Toronto: The Osgoode Society, 212–248.

Backhouse, C.B. 1984. Desperate women and compassionate courts: infanticide in nineteenth-century Canada, *University of Toronto Law Journal*, 34(4), 447–478.

Barrett, M. and McIntosh, M. 1982. *The Anti-Social Family*. London: Verso.

Bartlett, K.T. and Stack, C.B. 1986. Joint custody, feminism and the dependency dilemma. *Berkeley Women's Law Journal*, 2(1), 9–41.

Becker, M. 2002. Care and feminists. *Wisconsin Women's Law Journal*, 17(1), 57–110.

Blackett, A. 2011. Introduction: Regulating Decent Work for Domestic Workers. *Canadian Journal of Women and the Law*, 23(1), 1–45.

Boyd, S.B. 1996. Is there an ideology of motherhood in (post)modern child custody law? *Social and Legal Studies*, 5(4), 495–521.

Boyd, S.B. (ed.), 1997. *Challenging the Public/Private Divide: Feminism, Law, and Public Policy*. Toronto: University of Toronto Press.

Boyd, S.B. 2003. *Child Custody, Law, and Women's Work*. Don Mills: Oxford University Press.

Boyd, S.B. 2010. Autonomy for mothers? Relational theory and parenting apart. *Feminist Legal Studies*, 18(2), 137–158.

Busby, K. and Vun, D. 2010. Revisiting the handmaid's tale: feminist theory meets empirical research on surrogate mothers. *Canadian Journal of Family Law*, 26(1), 13–93.

Case, M.A. 2001. How high the apple pie? A few troubling questions about where, why, and how the burden of care for children should be lifted. *Chicago-Kent Law Review*, 76(3), 1753–1788.

Crittenden, A. 2001. *The Price of Motherhood*. New York: Metropolitan Books.

Cunliffe, E. 2011. *Murder, Medicine and Motherhood*. Oxford: Hart Publishing.

Diduck, A. 1993. Legislating ideologies of motherhood. *Social and Legal Studies*, 2(4), 461–485.

Fineman, M. 1995. *The Neutered Mother, The Sexual Family, and Other Twentieth Century Tragedies*. New York and London: Routledge.

Fineman, M.A. and Karpin, I. (eds), 1995. *Mothers in Law: Feminist Theory and the Legal Regulation of Motherhood*. New York: Columbia University Press.

Gavigan, S.A.M. 1992. Morgentaler and beyond: abortion, reproduction and the courts, in *The Politics of Abortion*, edited by J. Brodie, S.A.M. Gavigan and J. Jenson. Toronto: Oxford University Press, 117–146.

Gavigan, S.A.M. and Chunn, D.E. 2007. From mothers' allowance to mothers need not apply: Canadian welfare law as liberal and neo-liberal reforms. *Osgoode Hall Law Journal*, 44(4), 733–772.

Hirschmann, N.J. 2010. Mothers who care too much. *Boston Review*. [Online]. 35(4). Available at: http://bostonreview.net/BR35.4/hirschmann.php [accessed: 22 January 2012].

Kelly, F. 2011. *Transforming Law's Family: The Legal Recognition of Planned Lesbian Motherhood*. Vancouver: UBC Press.

Kelly, F. 2012. Autonomous from the start: single mothers by choice. *Child and Family Law Quarterly*, 24(3), 257–283.

Kessler, L.T. 2005. Transgressive caregiving. *Florida State University Law Review*, 33(1), 1–87.

Kline, M. 1993. Complicating the ideology of motherhood: child welfare law and First Nation women. *Queen's Law Journal*, 18(2), 306–342.

Kramar, K.J. 2005. *Unwilling Mothers, Unwanted Babies: Infanticide in Canada*. Vancouver: UBC Press.

Langer, R. 2009. A dignified and caring mother: an examination of Munchausen Syndrome by Proxy case law. *Psychiatry, Psychology and Law*, 16(2), 217–239.

Lessard, H. 2004. Mothers, fathers, and naming: reflections on the law equality framework and Trociuk v. British Columbia (Attorney General). *Canadian Journal of Women and the Law*, 16(1), 165–211.

Mason, M.A. 1990–1991. Motherhood v. equal treatment. *Journal of Family Law*, 29(1), 1–50.

Mason, M.A. 1999. *The Custody Wars*. New York: Basic Books.

Millbank, J. 2008. The limits of functional family: lesbian mother litigation in the era of the eternal biological family. *International Journal of Law, Policy and the Family*, 22(2), 149–177.

Mosoff, J. 1997. A jury dressed in medical white and judicial black: mothers with mental health histories in child welfare and custody, in *Challenging the Public/Private Divide: Feminism, Law, and Public Policy*, edited by S.B. Boyd. Toronto: University of Toronto Press, 227–252.

Murphy, J.C. 1998. Legal images of motherhood: conflicting definitions from welfare reform, family and the criminal law. *Cornell Law Review*, 83(3), 688–766.

Mykitiuk, R. 2001. Beyond conception: legal determinations of filiation in the context of reproductive technologies. *Osgoode Hall Law Journal*, 39(4), 771–816.

Nedelsky, J. 1989. Reconceiving autonomy: sources, thoughts and possibilities. *Yale Journal of Law and Feminism*, 1(1), 7–36.

O'Donovan, K. and Marshall, J. 2006. After birth: decisions about becoming a mother, in *Feminist Perspectives on Family Law*, edited by A. Diduck and K. O'Donovan. New York: Routledge, 101–122.

Polikoff, N. 1990. This child does have two mothers: redefining parenthood to meet the needs of children in lesbian-mother and other nontraditional families. *Georgetown Law Journal*, 78(3), 459–576.

Raitt, F. and Zeedyk, S. 2004. Mothers on trial: discourses of cot death and Munchausen's Syndrome by Proxy. *Feminist Legal Studies*, 12(3), 257–278.

Rhoades, H. 2002. The no contact mother: reconstructions of motherhood in the era of the new father. *International Journal of Law, Policy and the Family*, 16(1), 71–94.

Rich, A. 1976. *Of Woman Born: Motherhood as Experience and Institution.* New York: W.W. Norton & Company.

Roberts, D. 1993a. Motherhood and crime. *Iowa Law Review*, 79(1), 95–141.

Roberts, D. 1993b. Racism and patriarchy in the meaning of motherhood. *American University Journal of Gender and the Law*, 1(1), 1–38.

Robson, R. 1992. Mother: the legal domestication of lesbian existence. *Hypatia*, 7(4), 172–185.

Ruddick, S. 1989. *Maternal Thinking.* New York: Ballantine Books.

Shanley, M.L. 1993. Surrogate mothering and women's freedom: a critique of contracts for human reproduction. *Signs*, 18(3), 618–639.

Sheldon, S. 2001. Sperm bandits, birth control fraud and the battle of the sexes. *Legal Studies*, 21(3), 460–480.

Smart, C. 1991. The legal and moral ordering of child custody. *Journal of Law and Society*, 18(4), 485–500.

Smart, C. 1996. Deconstructing motherhood, in *Good Enough Mothering*, edited by E. Silva. London: Routledge, 37–57.

Smart, C. and Sevenhuijsen, S. (eds), 1989. *Child Custody and the Politics of Gender.* London: Routledge.

Swift, K. 2010. Risky women: the role of risk in the construction of the single mother, in *The Legal Tender of Gender: Law, Welfare and the Regulation of Women's Poverty*, edited by S.A.M. Gavigan and D.E. Chunn. Oxford: Hart Publishing, 143–163.

Uviller, R.K. 1978. Fathers' rights and feminism: the maternal presumption revisited, *Harvard Women's Law Journal*, 1(1), 107–130.

Williams, J. 2000. *Unbending Gender: Why Family and Work Conflict and What to do About it.* New York: Oxford University Press.

Young, I.M. 1990. Pregnant embodiment: subjectivity and alienation, in *Throwing Like a Girl and other Essays in Feminist Philosophy and Social Theory*, edited by I.M. Young. Bloomington: Indiana University Press, 160–174.

# Marriage and Civil Partnership: Law's Role, Feminism's Response

### Rosemary Auchmuty

Marriage cannot be spoken of as a fixed legal concept since it has meant different things at different times and in different places. Today, even within a single country, there may be different cultural conceptions of marriage and people may have very different motives for marrying. Nevertheless, politicians, churches and courts tend to speak of 'marriage' as if we all understand and all agree on what is meant by the term. Take, for instance, the pronouncement by the President of the Family Division in England and Wales in *Wilkinson v Kitzinger* [2006] EWHL 2022:

> It is apparent that the majority of people, or at least of governments, not only in England but Europe-wide, regard marriage as an age-old institution, valued and valuable, respectable and respected, as a means not only of encouraging monogamy but also the procreation of children and their development and nurture in a family unit (or "nuclear family") in which both maternal and paternal influences are available in respect of their nurture and upbringing. (para. 118)

Recognizing that marriage plays an important part in disciplining citizens, governments endow the institution with prophylactic qualities against crime, poverty, loneliness and all forms of social disorder, including challenges to established gender roles, thus justifying the provision of financial incentives for the married. These incentives, such as tax benefits or access to health care, not only add an important practical impetus to marry, but help to define the institution itself. For this reason, this chapter will approach the subject from a historical perspective and, for reasons of space and my own expertise, will focus on feminist legal theorizing in the UK, with some reference to influential contributions from other common law jurisdictions.

## Nineteenth-century Marriage

In the nineteenth century, and well into the twentieth, marriage played a fundamental role in the substantive law of England and Wales; whole textbooks were devoted to the law of 'Husband and Wife' (e.g. Grant-Bailey 1933), while marriage occupied at least one separate chapter in volumes on property law, criminal law and obligations. Marriage then, unlike now, made a huge difference to a woman's legal status. When Queen Victoria came to the throne in 1837, women were obliged to relinquish their property and earnings to their husband on marriage and, with this, their ability to contract, sue or be sued, except against any 'separate' property they might possess under a trust. A husband had the right to 'chastise' (even with force) and imprison his wife and had free access to her body. After 1857, he could divorce her on the sole ground of her adultery but, such was society's acceptance of male promiscuity, if *she* wanted a divorce she would have to prove his adultery plus some other offence (Stetson 1982, Shanley 1989).

Why then were women so keen to marry? First, marriage was assumed to be a woman's *only* respectable career, an assumption reinforced by church, education, cultural forces and family expectations. It followed that *not* to marry spelt social disaster. Marriage provided the only acceptable context for heterosexual love, sex and children. It was a refuge from the servitude of the daughter-at-home or maiden aunt role. The wish to marry was fostered then, as now, by a flourishing culture of romance that obscured the disadvantages of the institution. For all the women who carefully weighed the pros and cons of marrying, many more entered into a union totally unaware of the legal ramifications: Caroline Norton, for example, was astonished to discover that she had no right of custody of her young children or even access to them when her husband took them away from her (Norton 1839).

The final, clinching reason for women to marry was economic. The great majority of women were poor, and their poverty was structural: well-off fathers provided less generously for daughters in the expectation that husbands would support them; girls were not educated for careers because, again, they were only going to be wives and mothers; if obliged through family circumstances to go out to work, they earned little in the menial jobs open to them. Even those with some independent means found that marriage would usually offer them a higher standard of living than they could otherwise attain (Hamilton 1909).

That marriage was woman's sole vocation constituted so embedded a truth it was inarguable. For nineteenth-century feminists, then, the challenge was to expose the injustices of the marriage laws, both substantively and in their operation, while (in public at least) never questioning the primacy of marriage and its overwhelming appeal for women. As Mona Caird put it: 'We must not look for destruction, but for re-birth' (Caird 1897: 110). At the same time, marriage was subjected to criticism from outside feminism, and some of those critiques were more radical. Many early-nineteenth-century Utopian socialists rejected the institution, advocating – and practising – free love and birth control; Fanny Wright and Anna Wheeler specifically addressed married women's property and divorce, and Frances Morrison called for the abolition of *all* the marriage laws (Perkin 1989: 208). These more extreme critiques should not be forgotten even as they were sidelined by feminist activists anxious to focus on winnable campaigns that would not alienate public sympathy.

Privately, however, many prominent feminists chose not to marry, and were even prepared to declare that the single life had many advantages. In an essay frankly entitled *Celibacy v Marriage*, Frances Power Cobbe pointed out that 'while the utility, freedom, and happiness of a single women's life have become greater, the *knowledge* of the risks of an unhappy marriage (if not the risks themselves) has become more public' (Cobbe 1862: 81). The existence of these contented spinsters was an important aid to feminist critics, not only in demonstrating that there were alternatives to marriage, but practically, since the growing army of unsupported women provided feminists with objects of social concern for whom educational and employment opportunities *must* be improved, else they might starve to death.

Victorian feminists were keenly aware of the interconnectedness of the various forms of women's subjection, and many were active in several different causes. But marriage was central to all debates. The fact that marriage was conceived as women's inevitable goal and destiny justified the denial of an academic education, the exclusion from remunerative employment, the argument that the vote was unnecessary (since wives were represented by their husbands) and undesirable (what if husband and wife disagreed?), and the sexual double standard. It enabled society to treat poor unmarried women with contempt and 'fallen' women – unmarried mothers and prostitutes – with cruelty. Feminists recognized that women's financial dependence within marriage made them vulnerable to all kinds of exploitation, including violence and sexual abuse. As a result, changing the law to allow married women to keep their own property was an early goal which feminists viewed as essential to alleviating married women's exploitation (Holcombe 1989).

Yet, by simultaneously working to improve women's education and opportunities for employment, feminists almost inadvertently created alternatives to marriage so that middle-class women for the first time enjoyed a choice as to whether to marry or not and the conditions they would be prepared to settle for. And if marriage remained the more attractive option for most, they did not now have to marry just anybody who came along, but could afford to pick and choose. Feminists boasted that, in an era when the falling marriage rate was causing official anxiety, they were helping to raise the institution's status by making it more attractive. In reality, by introducing options, they caused the marriage rate to fall still further.

## Theoretical Approaches of First-wave Feminism

Nineteenth-century or 'first-wave' feminism is often characterized as *liberal*, which tends to be interpreted these days as equality-based. This may be due to a mistaken identification with Mary Wollstonecraft, whose *A Vindication of the Rights of Woman* (1792) long pre-dated the organized women's movement, and whose primary argument was that there should be no distinction between the education and opportunities for employment available to men and women – indeed, that the sexes should be taught and work alongside each other. Her thesis was that, if women were properly educated, they would be worthy of civil rights, and if they could do the kinds of jobs that men did, they 'would not then marry for support' (222). In truth, however, Wollstonecraft's writings were largely ignored by first-wave feminists, anxious not to damage the movement by association with her 'irregular' life: by choosing to live in sin with two men in succession, to each of whom she bore a child, Wollstonecraft offered a lived critique of the institution that would have deprived her of the very civil rights she prized.[1]

Perhaps, alternatively, the characterization of first-wave feminism as 'liberal' is due to the influence on many mainstream accounts of the distinguished liberal philosopher John Stuart Mill, who is sometimes portrayed as the beginning and end of feminist activity in the nineteenth century. Yet even Mill identified the source of women's oppression in a relationship of 'subjection' of one sex to the other, not simply inequality. Using a metaphor employed by many earlier writers including Wollstonecraft, Mill showed how the marriage laws of England reduced women, whatever their actual lived conditions, to a state of legal slavery (Mill 1869: 158, 175). He further explained how women voluntarily entered this

---

1    Under pressure she married William Godwin just before the birth of her second daughter, Mary (later Shelley), but died of puerperal fever soon after.

condition not, as was claimed, because it was their 'natural vocation', but because they had no realistic alternatives, because they were barred from 'any other means of living, or occupation of their time and faculties, … which has any chance of appearing desirable to them' (155).

When one examines the feminist claims for married women to have rights to their property, to their children, and to education and employment, it is clear that the basis of their claim was not equality; what they wanted was the removal of unjust and oppressive restrictions on women not because they kept them unequal but because they *gave men power over them*. While their analysis can be seen as liberal in that it sought the removal of restrictions on their personal liberty, it was really closer to modern radical feminism. Radical feminism is a twentieth-century theory that sees gender as the primary organizing principle of society, and men and women as separate classes (neatly matching the Victorian notion of 'separate spheres') in a relationship of dominance and oppression (Douglas 1990). Male power is exercised both structurally, through institutions like law and religion, and personally, through individual male–female interactions, particularly in the family. It is now generally recognized that such views were shared by many nineteenth-century feminists. As Valerie Bryson notes, in both the UK and the US at this time we find 'a well-developed analysis of the ways in which women's subordination extends beyond a lack of legal political and economic rights and is rooted in family life and personal relationships' (1999: 25).

Cobbe's wide-ranging analysis of marriage demonstrates this point. Contributing to the campaign for married women's property, Cobbe depicted the English wife as a chained bird in a heavily barred cage: 'As to its rudimentary wings, we always break them early, for greater security; though I have heard Professor Huxley say' [a dig at opponents of higher education for women] 'that he is convinced it could never fly far with them, under any circumstances' (Cobbe 1868: 119). Yet, in systematically refuting all justifications for the common law position – justice, expediency and sentiment – she still stopped short of criticizing the institution of marriage itself (Auchmuty 2008a). In an equally influential article on 'Wife-Torture in England', Cobbe tackled the law's indifference to women's sufferings and even death as a result of domestic violence (Cobbe 1878) – a subject often thought to have been newly revealed by second-wave feminists, but a significant focus of first-wave feminism.

## New Theoretical Insights in the 1890s/1900s

With the inclusion of provisions for separated wives in the Matrimonial Causes Acts of 1857 and 1878 (which enabled wives to leave brutal marriages and receive financial maintenance) and the passing of the Married Women's Property Acts of 1870 and 1882, nineteenth-century feminists in England and Wales could congratulate themselves on the transformation of 'the law of husband and wife', and a huge shift in social attitudes. Yet these reforms, instead of calming social unease, seemed only to open the door to more. The publication of Mona Caird's essay 'Marriage' in the *Westminster Review* in 1888 led to a correspondence on the theme 'Is Marriage a Failure?' in the *Daily Telegraph*, in which 27,000 letters were received before the editor called a halt (Caird 1897: 61).

Caird joined the debate at a time when marriage was not only a hot topic – with huge publicity surrounding the *Clarence*[2] and *Jackson*[3] cases in 1888 and 1891 – but when many of the earlier feminist claims had been won. A new theme had emerged: men's sexual licence. Where most feminists demanded further curbs on men's behaviour (an approach epitomized by Christabel Pankhurst's famous slogan, 'Votes for women and chastity for men'), others, including Caird as well as Olive Schreiner and Edith Lees, called for greater sexual freedom for women and tolerance of pre- and extra-marital sex, a topic also explored by writers – female *and* male – in the genre known as the 'New Woman' novel (Cunningham 1978).

Caird also pursued the financial exploitation of marriage that earlier writers had identified. Using the language of economists, she observed that, where women's only 'capital' lay in their youth and attractiveness, they were obliged to 'invest' it in marriage, as no other socially acceptable destiny was open to them. But, Caird warned, there were signs that this arrangement no longer suited women *or* men. Both sexes disliked 'the commercial element' and more and more women, she noted, were 'refusing a life of comparative ease in marriage rather than enter upon it as their means of livelihood, for which their freedom has to be sacrificed' (Caird 1897: 109).

Cicely Hamilton's *Marriage as a Trade* (1909) bore out the truth of this claim. Its uncompromising argument was that an independent working life was a better one for women than the economic subjection and intellectual boredom of marriage. Hamilton's goal thereafter (and that of other equal-rights feminists between the wars) was to improve the position of working women to the extent that single independence would be as attractive a choice as marriage. Yet, even as they campaigned for women's right to paid employment, equal-rights feminists did not question the sexual division of labour or women's primary responsibility for housework and childcare. For them it was an either/or choice; working wives were assumed to have some form of domestic help (not, however, from their husband) in the home. This reveals the middle-class bias of the philosophy: Hamilton's liberal call for the removal of all restraints on women's work was not echoed by working-class women whose trade unions sought *more* state regulation of the workplace (a point made by Lewis in her introduction to the reissue of Hamilton 1909: 8).

Caird, herself married, did not share the view that women must choose between work and marriage. Rather, she called for wages for housework and professional childcare to free married women for activity in the public sphere (Caird 1897). Such claims, which required state intervention, had much in common with the first demands of the Women's Liberation Movement in 1970. Indeed, Ann Heilman contends that 'Caird's conceptual framework anticipates elements of 1970s and 1980s feminism, especially radical but also psychoanalytic thought' (Heilman 1996: 68). The demands noted here were in many ways closer to socialist feminism, though Caird was hardly a socialist; but her analysis as a whole was radical-feminist in that it located marriage within a 'whole social drift' (Caird 1897: 110) organized to sustain men's exploitative power, both economic and physical, over women. Prostitution was part of this system and so, in a remarkably modern vision, was motherhood. Decades before Adrienne Rich (1977) and Nancy Chodorow (1978) demonstrated the structural role

---

2   *The Queen v Clarence* [1889] 22 QBD 23, in which an extended court held 9:4 that a husband had not inflicted grievous bodily harm on his wife by having sexual intercourse with her, knowing he was suffering from gonorrhoea, and causing her (in ignorance of this) to be infected.

3   *The Queen v Jackson* [1891] 1 QB 671, in which the court held that a husband could not detain his wife against her will.

of motherhood in women's oppression, Caird showed how it not only seduced women away from rebellion – 'An appeal to the maternal instinct had quenched the hardiest spirit of revolt' (Heilman 1998: xxv) – but also conditioned women to a self-destructive femininity (this is the part Heilman identifies as psychoanalytic). A further modern touch is added by Caird's advocacy of private marriage contracts in preference to the one-size-fits-all state-defined marriage. The fact that her critique is so comprehensive and so radically theorized may account for her almost complete disappearance from intellectual history until recently.

## Between the Waves

Though the period between 1920 and 1970 is generally thought to have been a fallow period for feminist achievement, it was not for want of trying. Feminist activity in those 50 years took the form of what looked like a set of diverse, separate and even contradictory campaigns, but which in fact all derived from a common understanding across the feminist spectrum that without financial means of their own, women – even and especially *within* marriage – would never be free.[4]

It is noteworthy that almost all feminists looked to law – and specifically to the legislature – to ameliorate women's situation. We can hardly be surprised at this: so recently admitted to the law-making process, feminists had all the confidence and optimism of those who could at last influence, even as MPs *make*, the laws affecting their sex.[5] It goes without saying that they were to be cruelly disappointed by their faith in the law, for very little progress was made in these 50 years. This led not so much to a more sophisticated grasp of the difference between *formal* and *substantive* equality – this came later – as to disillusionment with and, in the case of many second-wave feminists, rejection of law – and of marriage – as a means to women's liberation (Smart 1984, Smart 1989).

The largest single focus of feminist concern between 1920 and 1970 was the position of the married woman, even though (as before) the debates never focused on the *idea* of marriage, but rather on its lived experience. The primacy of marriage for women was as much assumed as it had been in the nineteenth century – more so, really, because it was much more universal in these years. Although the census of 1921 recorded the lowest proportion of married women in recorded history (due not simply to the huge loss of young men in the first world war but to the steady fall in the marriage rate in the second half of the nineteenth century), its popularity was reinstated after the war, celebrated and then propelled by a new, modern range of women's magazines promoting romance, marriage and motherhood rather than independence and careers. When Ethel Snowden wrote in 1913 that: 'The destiny of the normal woman is undoubtedly marriage and motherhood', she spoke a truth that was to remain uncontested until the 1970s; and when she declared, doubtless to reassure critics that 'feminism does not stand for the abolition of the marriage laws, but for the equality of man

---

4   Only some socialist women stuck to a class-based agenda that prioritized better conditions for men at work, to enable them to earn a wage genuinely capable of supporting a family; they viewed women's aspirations for money of their own as threatening this goal.

5   The Representation of the People Act 1918 gave women of 30+ the vote; a similar Act of 1928 extended the vote to women on the same terms as men (i.e. 21+); the Parliament (Qualification of Women) Act 1918 enabled women to stand for Parliament; the Sex Disqualification (Removal) Act 1919 opened the legal professions to women.

and woman in the married state', she summed up the movement's primary objective during that period (Snowden 1913: 204, 247).[6]

The feature of marriage that feminists agreed was central to women's oppression was *money* – or, rather, their lack of it. The Married Women's Property Acts may have permitted wives to keep their property and earnings, but the law was of no use to women who had none of their own to keep. Both 'equal rights' and 'new' feminists agreed that all the worst features of the married woman's situation could be traced to her enforced financial dependence, which facilitated men's exercise of power over her. They only differed as to the means of tackling this. The 'equal rights' feminists, exemplified by the 'Six-Point Group' and the journal *Time and Tide*, focused on women's duty to undertake paid work as the only way to raise the value of women generally. They blamed girls' expectation of eventual marriage and consequent withdrawal from the labour market for deterring them, their parents and employers from taking women's work seriously. They campaigned for equal pay and an end to marriage bars in the workplace to enable married women to combine motherhood and paid employment; special privileges for working wives and mothers were rejected (Welsh 1927: 205). The 'new' feminists, on the other hand, sought to raise the status of motherhood, and to this end campaigned for state endowment of the family in the form of allowances paid directly to mothers, which would provide them with some money of their own (Rathbone 1924).[7]

## Second-wave Feminism

The advent of the women's liberation movement around 1970 coincided with the greatest popularity of marriage. Up to this point, marriage had occupied a fixed and unchallengeable place at the top of the hierarchy of social relationships and the centre of women's lives, and feminists had focused on reforms which they confidently hoped would iron out any remaining flaws in the institution (Earengey 1953: 23). In the 1970s, however, marriage ceased to be an institution with a few problems and became the problem itself. 'Shorn of its more obviously oppressive features, it is often thought that marriage is now a harmless or neutral institution,' observed Michele Barrett and Mary McIntosh in *The Anti–Social Family*. 'Yet this is far from being the case' (1982: 54). Such indeed was revealed in studies by Hannah Gavron (1966), Ann Oakley (1974), Jessie Bernard (1972) and Lee Comer (1974).

The pioneers of the women's liberation movement in the UK were mostly 'graduate wives' from a socialist background who had come to realize both intellectually and experientially that their male associates ignored, indeed disparaged, women's contribution to the means of production in childbearing and unpaid work in the home. It is a measure of how deeply entrenched was the assumption that women would perform this work *within marriage* that the critiques rarely distinguished marriage from women's domestic labour generally, except to identify the institution as the state's main way of controlling women and perpetuating gender inequality. For this reason, if the goal was 'to transform the basis of the family structure, and those of our personal relationships' (Wandor 1974: 206), socialist

---

6    That is not to say that there were no rebels against conventional morality; but even these women – Dora Russell is a well-known example – usually married eventually, generally for the sake of the children.

7    Eventually won in the Family Allowances Act 1944.

feminists quickly concluded that women must as a first step abandon marriage. They called on feminists to create viable, desirable, alternatives to marriage and for the state to provide free public childcare, partly because this was the socialist solution, but also because they recognized that current employment structures and men's obvious reluctance to assume domestic responsibilities made role-sharing in individual homes a less easily won goal (Auchmuty 2012).

If radical feminists, too, started by assuming that women performing gendered work in heterosexual relationships would be doing this within marriage, they soon dropped this model and focused instead on the problem of *men* (Friedman and Sarah 1982). Then, when lesbian feminists named *heterosexuality*, rather than marriage, as the institution centrally responsible for women's oppression (Rich 1980), attention was drawn to the fact that many marriage refuseniks found living in a cohabiting relationship with a man not so very different from marriage in terms of its potential for sexual exploitation, domestic violence and gender role assumptions. Materialist feminists brought both the radical-feminist focus on the *sexual* and the socialist-feminist focus on the *economic* together to identify society's construction of gender as the root of both forms of women's exploitation, and called for an end to a social organization based on gender (Delphy and Leonard 1992, Jackson 1999).

Katherine O'Donovan was the first legal scholar in the UK to address the specific contribution of *law* to women's dependence and exploitation in marriage. She pointed out that gender lay at the heart of marriage law and its associated legal regimes, such as tax and social security: 'In marriage the rules, both constitutive and behavioural, are based on gender and their sum constitutes the rule of husband or wife' (O'Donovan 1979: 135). However much individuals might hope to modify or avoid their institutionalized gender role, they could not: 'legal rules cannot be changed by personal redefinition' (136). As a wife, therefore, you might feel completely equal to your husband but the state would enforce dependence upon you. The law's reach went even further than this, as those who lived outside marriage were still treated as if married or marriageable – as in the social security rules based on household income, which assumed if you lived with a man he would maintain you.

Carol Smart's *The Ties That Bind* (1984) appeared just when women were beginning to suffer the full effects of easier divorce under the Divorce Reform Act 1969, effects which were about to get worse with the enactment of the 'clean-break' provisions of the Matrimonial and Family Proceedings Act 1984. 'The extent of the poverty of women and children is often not revealed until the family unit breaks down' (Smart 1984: 12). It was clear that the 'many hard-won legal reforms' of past feminists had achieved little in terms of tackling married women's vulnerability (4). Smart showed how the official approach to marriage throughout the twentieth century had always been to reinforce women's domestic role, and thus their economic dependence, largely for ideological reasons, but also to save the state money (Smart 1984: 21). If divorce law reform 'averted a large-scale dissent from legally-controlled marriage', it still perpetuated the legal regulation of sexual and reproductive relationships (56–57). Likewise, when cohabitation increased, judges strove to find solutions for 'deserving' women, but not with any view to strengthening women's structural position. Rather, these developments 'can only be understood as the law's response to a shifting social practice which is to accommodate to the change, rather than to resist it, and to thereby achieve some degree of authority over these extra-marital or unlawful relations' (112).

For Smart, the contribution of second-wave feminism was to reject the assumption that marriage and the family were 'natural pre-givens which can and should be improved upon to provide the desired haven-in-a-heartless world' (Smart 1984: 142). Instead, marriage and the family were shown to be the site of the most powerful gender subordination. Marriage must be resisted for its ideological significance and because it was there that the most serious abuses, like lawful marital rape, took place:

> *The aim is not to extend the legal and social definition of marriage to cover cohabitees or even homosexual couples, it is to abandon the status of marriage altogether and to devise a system of rights, duties or obligations which are not dependent on any form of "coupledom" or marriage or quasi-marriage. (146)*

## Beyond Marriage

Marriage lost its centrality in feminist theory in the final years of the twentieth century, partly because it was subsumed into the wider lens of the family, heterosexuality, or 'the problem of men', and partly because marriage itself went into steep decline (Lewis 2001). Bearing out Smart's observation that law adjusts to social change, many marital privileges in law were removed (such as the marital rape exemption) and marital *obligations* extended to marriage-like relationships. This led to a blurring of the line between the two states, a process exacerbated by the courts' increasing concern with divorced women, the children of unmarried unions, cohabiting victims of domestic violence and unmarried women claiming a share in the family home. While still purporting to support and encourage marriage, the law could no longer ignore or condemn those outside it, and this led to a paradox. As Brenda Hoggett put it: 'The modern preoccupation with such protection has led to the virtual abandonment of any attempt to "buttress" the stability of marriage, and thus called in question the usefulness of the institution itself' (Hoggett 1980: 94).

As the marriage rate continued to fall, the principle that marriage and cohabitation were distinct statuses requiring separate legal regimes came under pressure from arguments that, since many cohabitants *believed* they had the same rights as wives, and since their relationships were functionally similar, they should in fact be granted them, or something like. These arguments often came from feminists whose research or practice had demonstrated the depth of respondents' ignorance of their legal position and who therefore concluded that women would be better off married (Barlow et al. 2005). This suggestion was based not on the earlier understanding that husbands would provide for their wives but on the recognition that courts had greater powers on divorce to redistribute assets to the weaker party than they had on the breakdown of a cohabiting relationship. Their advice was thus essentially practical rather than an argument in favour of marriage.

Ruth Deech was an early opponent of this protective approach. Already by 1980 she was arguing forcefully that the way forward for women was to *avoid* the dependence trap rather than to try to negotiate it to their best advantage. Law should treat family members as individuals rather than as a unit which, she pointed out, tends to meet the interests of the strongest (men) at the expense of the weakest (women). Deech took a resolute equality line. Men and women should have the same opportunities to do the same work for the same value, in the workplace *and* at home. She ridiculed the idea, put forward by some feminists, that housewives should be paid for their domestic labour. Housework and childcare were not the preserve of one sex, and there was no reason why responsibility for them should not be shared among the members of the household. In her vision, moreover, this household might consist (as many did) of something other than a heterosexual couple with or without children: 'To single out heterosexual unions for the compensation of the "weaker" partner is to reveal the most important basis for monetary rewards to women: domestic and sexual services rendered' (Deech 1980: 303).

With a liberal respect for people's 'choices', Deech contended that the law should not assume that women would necessarily have embraced the institution of marriage if they had understood its economic benefits. Many people lived outside of marriage to keep benefits they would lose if they married (such as maintenance from a former husband), because they did not want the law to interfere in their relationship, or as a trial before committing themselves legally. 'Women in particular may wish to avoid what they see as a male-dominated legal institution and to preserve their mobility for a career and as much independence and freedom as possible' (Deech 1980: 302). While her opposition to legal protection for same-sex couples could not be explained in terms of choice, it was in line with her general refusal to privilege *couples* above other relationships and, indeed, individuals. 'Why is the elderly widow or cohabitant more deserving of support than the elderly spinster?' she asked (306).[8] Yet she stopped short of suggesting that marriage should be abolished. A true liberal, she kept open the choice to marry, but foresaw that marriage would cease to make much practical difference and would, in fact, become more like cohabitation than the other way round (303) – as it has done.

Deech's analysis was seen as callous and unrealistic by other feminists working in family law, who doubted that many cohabitants made an informed choice not to marry and felt that feminist energies were better directed at helping women *now* rather than working towards a (possibly Utopian) legal realignment of gender relations. Deech's view, however, was that we should stop using law to correct past faults but should legislate (or not – much of her argument was based on legal *non*-interference) for a feminist vision (310): 'the day of equality is highly unlikely to dawn until stimulated by changes in family law that presuppose equality' (307).

## Debates Outside the UK

Marriage is in decline in North America just as it is in Europe. It is from the US, however, where it has more symbolic and, often, economic significance than elsewhere, that we see the most radical dialogue among feminist legal scholars on marriage. In Canada, where the rights and responsibilities of marriage have been broadly distributed to marriage-like relationships (with feminists divided as to whether this is a good thing), the focus has been more on the creeping privatization of care and the state's continued adherence to gender and couple norms as its basis (Boyd 1999, Young and Boyd 2006).

American feminists have long understood that women are vulnerable in marriage, where dependency is privatized even more than in Europe, which means that the needs of individual family members must be met through their relationship with a breadwinner (Okin 1989: 134–169). One body of feminist legal thought would, therefore, abolish the institution, replacing it by individually negotiated contracts (Weitzman 1981) or recourse to normal principles of private law governing interactions between unrelated individuals (Fineman 1998). A drawback with this approach is that, in order to avoid exploitation, the parties must be of equal bargaining power – which is often not the case. It also assumes that

---

8    An argument later put forward in *Burden v the UK* (2008) 47 EHRR 38. See Auchmuty 2009.

we all act rationally and independently, even when 'in love'. Following Carole Pateman's *The Sexual Contract* (1988), such feminists have increasingly recognized that such a solution must be combined with changes in other areas of law and public policy to bring about this equal agency.

Other feminist legal scholars contend that marriage retains a special value that is worth defending, albeit in revised form, stripped of its enforced gender roles and dependency. For them, the definition of marriage has been transformed as a result of second-wave feminism from its original conception of male dominance and female subjection to something approaching equality. Mary Lyndon Shanley believes that marriage plays an important social role in promoting stability and personal happiness and should thus be protected in law. But she too admits that further shifts in the law's construction of marriage are necessary: 'Addressing women's poverty by attaching them to men who can support them reinforces inequality and vulnerability within marriages' (Shanley 2004: 24).

If the state has a stake in protecting any relationship, however, it is hard to see why it should be marriage. Critics ask why 'the presence of a sexual relationship [should] be the dividing line between those relationships that are recognized and those that are not' (Cossman 2004: 96). Martha Fineman has powerfully argued that the primary relationship requiring legal protection is the mother/child bond, so she would confer legal protection upon care-giving relationships rather than marriage (Fineman 1995). Nancy Cott takes issue with Shanley's assumption that public benefit necessarily follows from state support of marriage and points out that this leads to massive privileging of an institution to which only half the population belong (Cott 2004: 34–35). Wendy Brown adds that privileging marriage renders less visible 'other ways of committing ourselves to the well-being of others', given that many people's most important support comes not from spouses but from friends or siblings (Brown 2004: 91). Drucilla Cornell's solution is for state recognition (as 'marriage') of all forms of caring relationship, including adult friends and plural relationships (Cornell 2004: 84–85).

## Same-sex Marriage and Civil Partnerships

Once legal protection for heterosexual cohabitants had been mooted, and civil rights and social acceptance extended to gays and lesbians (a process which began in the 1970s), it was inevitable that attention would be drawn to the unprotected status of homosexual couples. In the UK, both Deech and Smart, from their very different perspectives, rejected the idea of same-sex marriage, focusing instead, as did most politicized lesbians and gays in the 1980s, on the many and varied family and community forms that gays and lesbians had evolved, that might serve as *better* models than marriage. Lesbian feminists in particular emphasized the greater equality possible in a relationship not subject to socially-imposed gender roles (Dunne 1998). It was not until the new century that same-sex marriage received any serious attention in the British lesbian and gay 'community'. The chief impetus came from north America and specifically from middle-class white men who had most to gain from the financial benefits that flowed from the married state. American lesbian feminists were not at first interested – *Since When is Marriage a Path to Liberation?* is the title of Paula Ettelbrick's celebrated reaction.

The basis of the gay male claim, sustained through a substantial literature, was that same-sex couples were 'just like' heterosexual married couples and posed no threat to marriage;

rather the reverse. Andrew Sullivan's book on the subject was called *Virtually Normal* (1995), and this summed up the conservative plea for inclusion. Its premise was the opposite of what lesbian feminists had always stood for. 'It rips away the very heart and soul of what I believe it is to be a lesbian in this world', wrote Ettelbrick. 'It robs me of the opportunity to make a difference' (Ettelbrick 1989: 166). As the campaigns progressed, however, some lesbian feminists came out in favour of marriage; and, following legislation to allow same-sex couples to marry in Canada, some continental jurisdictions, some US states and (in the slightly different form of the civil partnership) the UK, feminists have been divided – and often conflicted – in their response.

Arguments in favour of same-sex marriage fall into two categories: its benefits for gays and lesbians and its benefits for marriage. Almost everyone, conservative gay or feminist, agrees that state acceptance and recognition of same-sex relationships, after centuries of denial and oppression, is a positive thing for gays and lesbians. We all accept that formal and substantive equality for gays and lesbians with heterosexuals is a *sine qua non*;[9] and as same-sex relationships are (or are portrayed as) structurally and functionally similar to heterosexual marriage, it makes sense that they should be treated in the same way. The publicity accorded to celebrity weddings has increased gay visibility and made it easier to be 'out' at our workplaces and in our families. However much we might deplore the uncritical enthusiasm with which many gay and lesbian couples have embraced the ideologies and symbols of romance and the commercial trappings of the marriage industry, these very symbols and discourses speak to the general public and make our relationships intelligible (Peel and Harding 2004).

These, then, are the benefits of marriage for gays and lesbians. *Their* contribution to the institution of marriage, in the view of its advocates, is twofold. First, the social acceptance and recognition of legal marriage would have a 'domesticating' effect on same-sex couples, giving them the public support that heterosexual couples enjoy and promoting stability and monogamy (for this last, read: curbing gay male promiscuity, with its associations with AIDS). This is not a feminist argument. It is the second justification that is central to the claim of pro-marriage lesbian feminists: that the admission of same-sex couples to marriage will disrupt its gendered nature to such an extent that marriage must be transformed into something different and *better*. With no gendered role expectations, no enforced gender inequality, gays and lesbians will carve out new conceptions of what it means to be a spouse and serve as models for heterosexual couples of how marriage should be (Hunter 1995, Bevacqua 2004). 'What is at stake is not the right to participate in a traditional form of family life', explains Cheshire Calhoun. Because homosexual oppression has historically centred on *exclusion* from the family (unlike heterosexual women's oppression, located *within* the family), lesbians and gays have to get inside to be able 'to *define* what counts as a family' (Calhoun 2000: 132).

As the legal revolution to extend marriage rights to same-sex couples gathered pace, it became difficult for feminist critics of marriage to express their reservations for fear of being lumped together with conservative or religious opponents. This was especially true for *heterosexual* feminists who might be labelled homophobic even though it was marriage they opposed, not gays and lesbians. Nevertheless there is now a substantial body of feminist legal theorizing that problematizes same-sex marriage. The principal objection is that, *pace*

---

9    As Kitzinger and Wilkinson pointed out, one need not approve of marriage to believe that exclusion from it is unjust (2004: 134).

Calhoun, letting same-sex couples into the privileged status of marriage does nothing to improve the position of all those diverse family forms – miscellaneous groupings of friends, relatives, step-relatives, ex-lovers, multiple current lovers and single-parent families – as well as single people. Lesbians and gays have been proud of the 'families we choose' which, though often the result of ostracism from families of origin, have come to be seen as *better* supports; heterosexuals, too, increasingly live in non-nuclear ways. In privileging the monogamous couple, same-sex marriage would diminish these alternative forms, as well as conceding the conservative argument that casual sex is socially irresponsible. This severely limits the potential for same-sex marriage to re-define family; as Nicola Barker puts it, personal transgression, without redistribution of social resources, cannot be transformative (Barker 2012: 15, Donovan 2004, Josephson 2010).

For feminist critics of same-sex marriage, even the argument that it will avoid or confound gender roles is only true up to a point, for it takes no account of the structured inequalities that attach to *roles* in couple relationships. As second-wave feminists demonstrated, gender does not always map directly on to biological sex; same-sex couples with inequalities of income or with children or other care-giving responsibilities will tend to evolve gendered roles. Such roles will be taken for granted by the state in its allocations of benefits, leading to the same inequality of finances and, therefore, power in same-sex couples as heterosexual couples experience.

Lesbian feminists reject the conservative 'domestication' function of marriage which institutionalizes 'family values' and constrains our behaviour. They fear that the appeal of bourgeois respectability implicit in the idea of marriage (Marso 2010: 148) will deflect same-sex couples from any radical project: they will 'be too busy registering at Harvey Nicholls to transform the institution from within' (Clarke 2003: 524). Rather than seek admission into what they see as a legal and social straitjacket, some lesbian feminists call for the *abolition* of the institution (Robson 1998, Jeffreys 2004).

Others, doubtful that this can be realized, point to the decline of marriage across the Western world and counsel simply waiting till it dies out of its own accord (Finlay and Clarke 2003, Auchmuty 2008b). For such feminists, the contention by Celia Kitzinger and Sue Wilkinson that marriage has 'immense legal and symbolic power' (2004: 141) seems anachronistic and out of line with public opinion and practice. Lesbian feminists point out that most of the collateral privileges attaching to marriage – such as the right to adopt children or name their partner as next-of-kin – can be provided, or *already are*, by existing legislation (Auchmuty 2004, Polikoff 2008): they are not (and should not be) dependent on marriage. Equally, they point out that rights that ought to be available – such as adequate support for care-givers – are *not* bestowed by marriage. Rather the reverse: extending marriage to same-sex couples simply increases the pool of unpaid care-givers so that the state need not provide (Young and Boyd 2006, Wilson 2010).

The same-sex marriage debates have revealed just how problematic it is to invoke law in the context of marriage. As Barker points out, marriage has no agreed content or 'fixed essence'. Drawing on Judith Butler, Barker suggests that we might view it as an institution that is constantly being performed and recreated. 'If same-sex couples perform marriage differently, perhaps this creates an opening to transgress or subvert the heteronormative boundaries of the institution as they are currently interpreted' (Barker 2012: 165). The problem lies in assuming that *law* can provide a solution. When Wilkinson and Kitzinger sought to have their Canadian marriage recognized as a marriage in the UK, rather than a civil partnership, they found that in order to harness the symbolic content of the legal status of marriage they were expected to embrace the normative values associated with that status. It was clear that the judge in this case could not imagine a marriage stripped of its gender roles and traditional purposes.[10]

In the UK, the peculiar form of the civil partnership has given rise to a smaller body of legal critique. Many feminists, while recognizing the possible economic disadvantages and increased surveillance that legal regulation brings, broadly welcome the legislation for giving rights to formerly oppressed groups. Some like the fact that though the civil partnership bestows almost all the substantive rights and obligations of marriage it is a civil rather than religious status and it avoids the name, with its historical 'baggage' (Peel and Harding 2004: 593).[11] Yet for other feminists, as long as the name is different, the civil partnership will never equate to marriage, and there will be no true equality (Kitzinger and Wilkinson 2004). And those opposed to the privileging of couples feel about civil partnerships as they do about same-sex marriage: that it can only have a partial, discriminatory and conservative effect and is irrelevant to the radical project of women's liberation (Auchmuty 2007).

## Conclusion

Today much social concern in the UK is directed at 'forced marriage'. This highly political issue is generally depicted as an outsider practice foreign to Western ideas of marriage, the implication being that British women have always freely chosen their husbands and married for love. As we have seen, however, marriage has rarely been a free choice for British women. Decisions to marry have always lain along a continuum from forced (no choice) to lifestyle (free choice), with few brides located at either extremity. Choice has been constrained by class, religion, race, nationality, family and social pressure, ideas of morality and respectability and, above all, financial considerations. Feminism's contribution to the debates on the deplorable practice of forced marriage is to point out that Western marriage has much more in common with it than we would like to think (Gill and Anitha 2011).

The true measure of 'choice' is whether one can choose *not* to do the relevant act; and it is not without significance that historically, women who 'choose' not to marry have almost always had their own incomes and independence from family pressures. The other prerequisite for a free choice is the ability to undo an action – to get divorced. Once again, even where Western women have not been forced *into* marriage, they may well have been obliged to *stay* in an unhappy union because of the absence of accessible divorce provisions or alternative means of support. Moreover, as feminists remind us, 'force' in the shape of domestic violence and marital rape has not been absent from British marriages and, indeed, was condoned by law until the late twentieth century (Gangoli et al. 2011).

In Western societies where marriage is regarded as freely chosen, the institution's coercive power is easily lost sight of. Its association with gender and sexuality oppression becomes displaced on to other people in other places or at other times – and now on to minority cultural groups in the UK. It remains to be seen whether marriage can survive in some new 'equal' form or whether it will be overtaken by other living arrangements which the law will feel obliged to respond to, and to regulate.

---

10   See the quotation from the judge in the case at the start of this chapter.
11   This argument has been rather weakened by the gay and lesbian community's appropriation of the language of marriage like 'wedding', 'husband' and 'wife'.

# References

Auchmuty, R. 2004. Same-sex marriage revived: Feminist critique and legal strategy. *Feminism and Psychology*, 14(1), 101–126.

Auchmuty, R. 2007. Out of the shadows: Feminist silence and liberal law, in *Sexuality and the Law: feminist engagements*, edited by V. Munro and C. Stychin. London: Glasshouse, 91–124.

Auchmuty, R. 2008a. The Married Women's Property Acts: Equality was not the issue, in *Rethinking Equality Projects in Law: Feminist Challenges*, edited by R. Hunter. Oxford: Hart, 13–40.

Auchmuty, R. 2008b. What's so special about marriage? The impact of *Wilkinson v Kitzinger*. *Child and Family Law Quarterly*, 20(4), 475–498.

Auchmuty, R. 2009. Beyond couples. *Feminist Legal Studies*, 17(2), 205–218.

Auchmuty, R. 2012. Law and the Power of Feminism: How marriage lost its power to oppress women. *Feminist Legal Studies* 20(2), 71–77.

Barker, N. 2012. *Not the Marrying Kind: A Feminist Critique of Same-sex Marriage*. Basingstoke: Palgrave Macmillan.

Barlow, A., Duncan, S., James, G. and Park, A. 2005. *Cohabitation, Marriage and the Law: Social Change and Legal Reform in the 21st Century*. Oxford: Hart.

Barrett, M. and McIntosh, M. 1982. *The Anti-social Family*. London: Verso.

Bernard, J. 1972. *The Future of Marriage*. New York: World Publishing.

Bevacqua, M. 2004. Feminist theory and the question of lesbian and gay marriage. *Feminism and Psychology*, 14(1), 36–40.

Boyd, S.B. 1999. Family, law and sexuality: Feminist engagements. *Social and Legal Studies*, 8(3), 369–390.

Brown, W. 2004. After marriage, in *Just Marriage*, edited by M.L. Shanley. Oxford: Oxford University Press, 87–92.

Bryson, V. 1999. *Feminist Debates: Issues of Theory and Political Practice*. Basingstoke: Macmillan.

Caird, M. 1897. *The Morality of Marriage and Other Essays on the Status and Destiny of Woman*. London: George Redway.

Calhoun, C. 2000. *Feminism, the Family, and the Politics of the Closet: Lesbian and Gay Displacement*. New York: Oxford University Press.

Chodorow, N. 1978. *The Reproduction of Mothering: Psychoanalysis and the Sociology of Gender*. London: University of California Press.

Clarke, V. 2003. Lesbian and gay marriage: Transformation or normalization? *Feminism and Psychology*, 13(4), 519–529.

Cobbe, F.P. 1995 (orig. 1862). Celibacy v Marriage, in *'Criminals, Idiots, Women, and Minors': Nineteenth–century writing by women on women*, edited by S. Hamilton. Peterborough, Ont: Broadview Press, 74–84.

Cobbe, F.P. 1995 (orig. 1868). 'Criminals, Idiots, Women, and Minors': Is the Classification Sound?, in *'Criminals, Idiots, Women, and Minors': Nineteenth-century writing by women on women*, edited by S. Hamilton. Peterborough, Ont: Broadview Press, 108–131.

Cobbe, F.P. 1995 (orig. 1878). Wife-Torture in England, in *'Criminals, Idiots, Women, and Minors': Nineteenth-century writing by women on women*, edited by S. Hamilton. Peterborough, Ontario: Broadview Press, 132–170.

Comer, L. 1974. *Wedlocked Women*. Leeds: Feminist books.

Cornell, D. 2004. The public supports of love, in *Just Marriage*, edited by M.L. Shanley. Oxford: Oxford University Press, 81–86.

Cossman, B. 2004. Beyond marriage, in *Just marriage*, edited by M.L. Shanley. Oxford: Oxford University Press, 93–98.

Cott, N.F. 2004. The public stake, in *Just Marriage*, edited by M.L. Shanley. Oxford: Oxford University Press, 33–36.

Cunningham, G. 1978. *The New Woman and the Victorian Novel*. London: Macmillan.

Deech, R. 1980. The case against the legal regulation of cohabitation, in *Marriage and Cohabitation in Contemporary Societies*, edited by J.M. Eekelaar and N. Katz. London: Butterworths, 300–312.

Delphy, C. and Leonard, D. 1992. *Familiar Exploitation: A New Analysis of Marriage in Contemporary Western Societies*. London: Polity.

Donovan, C. 2004. Why reach for the moon? Because the stars aren't enough. *Feminism and Psychology*, 14(1), 24–29.

Douglas, C.A. 1990. *Love and Politics: Radical Feminist and Lesbian Theories*. San Francisco: Ism Press.

Dunne, G. 1998. *Living Differences: Lesbian Perspectives on Work and Family*. Binghamton, NY: Haworth Press.

Earengey, F. 1953. *A Milk-white Lamb: The Legal and Economic Status of Women*. London: National Council of Women.

Ettelbrick, P. 1989. Since when is marriage a path to liberation?, in *Same-sex Marriage: The Moral and Legal Debate*, edited by R.M. Baird and S.E. Rosenblum. Amherst, NY: Prometheus, 164–168.

Fineman, M. 1995. *The Neutered Mother, The Sexual Family and Other Twentieth Century Tragedies*. New York: Routledge.

Fineman, M. 1998. Contract, Marriage and Background Rules, in *Analyzing Law: New Essays in Legal Theory*, edited by B. Bix. Oxford: Clarendon Press, 183–195.

Finlay, S.J and Clarke, V. 2003. 'A marriage of convenience?' Feminist perspectives on marriage. *Feminism and Psychology*, 13(4), 415–420.

Friedman, S. and Sarah, E. 1982. *On the Problem of Men*. London: The Women's Press.

Gangoli, G., Chantler, K., Hester, M. and Singleton, A. 2011. Understanding forced marriage, in *Forced Marriage: Introducing a Social Justice and Human Rights Perspective*, edited by A.K. Gill and S. Anitha. London: Zed books, 25–45.

Gavron, H. 1966. *The Captive Wife: Conflicts of Housebound Mothers*. London: RKP.

Gill, A.K. and Anitha, S (eds), 2011. *Forced Marriage: Introducing a Social Justice and Human Rights Perspective*. London: Zed books.

Grant-Bailey, S.N. 1933. *Lush on the Law of Husband and Wife*, 4th edn. London: Stevens.

Hamilton, C. 1909. *Marriage as a Trade*. London: The Women's Press, 1981.

Heilman, A. 1996. Mona Caird (1854–1932): Wild Woman, New Woman, and Early Radical Feminist Critic of Marriage and Motherhood. *Women's History Review*, 5(1), 67–95.

Heilman, A. 1998. *The Late-Victorian Marriage Question, Vol 1: Marriage and Motherhood*. London: Routledge.

Hoggett, B. 1980. Ends and means: The utility of marriage as a legal institution, in *Marriage and Cohabitation in Contemporary Societies*, edited by J.M. Eekelaar and N. Katz. London: Butterworths, 94–101.

Holcombe, L. 1983. *Wives and Property: Reform of the Married Women's Property Law in Nineteenth Century England*. Toronto: Toronto University Press.

Hunter, N.D. 1995. Marriage, law and gender: A feminist inquiry, in *Sex Wars: Sexual Dissent and Political Culture*, edited by L. Duggan and N.D. Hunter. New York: Routledge, 107–122.

Jackson, S. 1999. *Heterosexuality in Question*. London: Sage.

Jeffreys, S. 2004. The need to abolish marriage. *Feminism and Psychology*, 14(2), 327–335.

Josephson, J. 2010. Romantic weddings, diverse forms. Special issue of *Politics and Gender: Whatever happened to feminist critiques of marriage?*, 6(1), 119–153.

Kitzinger, C. and Wilkinson, S. 2004. The re-branding of marriage: why we got married instead of registering a civil partnership. *Feminism and Psychology*, 24(1), 127–150.

Lewis, J. 2001. *The End of Marriage: Individualism and Intimate Relations*. Cheltenham: Edward Elgar.

Marso, L.J. 2010. Marriage and bourgeois respectability. Special issue of *Politics and Gender: Whatever happened to feminist critiques of marriage?*, 6(1), 145–153.

Mill, J.S. 1869. *The subjection of women*, in *Essays on Equality*, edited by A.S. Rossi. Chicago: University of Chicago Press, 1970, 123–242.

Norton, C. 1839. *A Plain Letter to the Lord Chancellor on the Infant Custody Bill*. London: James Ridgway.

Oakley, A. 1974. *Housewife*. Harmondsworth: Allen Lane.

O'Donovan, K. 1979. 'The male appendage: Legal definitions of women', in *Fit Work for Women*, edited by S. Burman. London: Croom Helm, 134–152.

Okin, S.M. 1989. *Justice, Gender, and the Family*. New York: HarperCollins.

Pateman, C. 1998. *The Sexual Contract*. Cambridge: Polity Press.

Peel, E. and Harding, R. 2004. Divorcing romance, rights and radicalism: Beyond pro and anti in the lesbian and gay marriage debate. *Feminism and Psychology*, 14(1), 588–599.

Perkin, J. 1989. *Women and Marriage in Nineteenth-Century England*. London: Routledge.

Polikoff, N. 2008. *Beyond (Straight and Gay) Marriage: Valuing all Families under the Law*. Boston: Beacon Press.

Rathbone, E. 1924. *The Disinherited Family*. London: Falling Wall Press, 1986.

Rich, A. 1977. *Of Woman Born: Motherhood as Experience and Institution*. London: Virago.

Rich, A. 1980. *Compulsory Heterosexuality and Lesbian Existence*. London: Onlywomen.

Robson, R. 1998. *Sappho goes to Law School*. New York: Columbia University Press.

Shanley, M.L. 1989. *Feminism, Marriage, and the Law in Victorian England, 1850-1895*. Princeton, N.J.: Princeton University Press.

Shanley, M.L. (ed.), 2004. *Just Marriage*. Oxford: Oxford University Press.

Smart, C. 1984. *The Ties that Bind: Law, Marriage and the Reproduction of Patriarchal Relations*. London: RKP.

Smart, C. 1989. *Feminism and the Power of Law*. London: Routledge.

Snowden, E. 1913. *The Feminist Movement*. London: Collins.

Stetson, D.M. 1982. *A Woman's Issue: The Politics of Family Law Reform in England*. Westport, CT: Greenwood Press.

Sullivan, A. 1995. *Virtually Normal: An Argument about Homosexuality*. Basingstoke: Macmillan.

Wandor, M. 1974. The conditions of illusion, in *Conditions of Illusion: Writings from the Women's Movement*, edited by S. Allen, L. Sanders and J. Wallis. Leeds: feminist books, 186–207.

Weitzman, L. 1981. *The Marriage Contract: Spouses, Lovers, and the Law*. London: Collier Macmillan.

Welsh, C. 1984 (orig. 1927). The married woman wage-earner, in *Time and Tide wait for No Man*, edited by D. Spender. London: Pandora, 202–206.

Wilson, A. 2010. Feminism and same-sex marriage: Who cares?. Special issue of *Politics and Gender*: *Whatever happened to feminist critiques of marriage?* 6(1), 134–145.

Wollstonecraft, M. 1967 (orig. 1792). *A Vindication of the Rights of Woman*, edited by C.W. Hagelman. New York: Norton.

Young, C.F.L. and Boyd, S.B. 2006. Losing the feminist voice? Debates on the legal recognition of same-sex relationships in Canada. *Feminist Legal Studies*, 14(2), 213–240.

# Gendered Power Over Taxes and Budgets

## Åsa Gunnarsson

Revenue-raising systems and public budgets shape almost every aspect of economic and cultural life. The power to raise and spend public revenues remains fundamentally associated with the nation state (Levi 1989, Lahey 2011), but the fiscal systems and welfare regimes in welfare economies are also challenged by a world of unstable, mobile and integrated markets (Philipps et al. 2011). While no clear consensus has emerged about what the ideal revenue system looks like, major international financial and development organizations, such as the Organisation for Economic Co-operation and Development (OECD), the World Bank Group (WBG) and the International Monetary Fund (IMF) have increasingly promoted more competitive fiscal environments under the overall objective of stimulating economic growth. This promotion takes the form, for example, of encouraging investment, risk-taking, entrepreneurship and an increased incentive to take on paid work. The dominant ideology of tax design that has been promoted by these international organizations is to reduce the degree of progressivity in tax systems, reduce total revenues, and shift some of the tax burden from income tax to consumption taxation (Piper and Murphy 2005, Owens 2006, Lahey 2011). As men in general have higher incomes from paid work, and own more wealth both as capital assets and business shares, they also benefit more from this type of tax design.

Economic inequality between men and women is deeply rooted in legal cultures and economic structures, most importantly, in the division of labour. Traditionally, men's labour has been valued publicly in the market, while women's reproductive labour inside the private domain of the family or household has not been afforded any economic recognition. Transplanting this normative pattern has also shaped the gender-segregation of men's and women's work in the labour market, and contributed to assigning a lower value to women's work once they entered that market (Gunnarsson 2003, Gunnarsson 2011a).

Welfare economies are facing massively gendered social risks (Bonoli 2005) created by the transformations of labour markets, demographic aging, and family structures, which will put additional pressure on the organizing and financing of care work and reproduction, with enormous implications for the gendered division of paid and unpaid work. However, no government or other norm- and policy-producing political body in the OECD-sphere of Western welfare economies has ever seriously considered the gendered nature of taxation and public expenditures. Within this international frame, the following issues will be explored in this chapter:

- Basic ontological challenges for gender studies in the area of taxation and budgeting; and
- how structural choices in tax policy design and social transfers contribute to gender inequality.

Gender research from various parts of the OECD world has shown that even though taxation is not the original source of the economic structures of inequality between men and women, it contains some tools with the power to change the gendered economic gap. Ann Mumford describes the importance of gender perspectives on taxation in the closing of her latest book as follows:

> ... this book began by stating that the problem of women's economic inequality is universal, and cannot be solved by tax law, in any state, or through any tax-based international agreement. It stated that, simply, tax law is not a capable forum for redressing gender equality. And it is difficult to identify which provisions of tax law, exactly, benefit women, because every aspect of a tax system has the potential to affect women. This book, ultimately, suggests that the tax system puts women on the margin. The challenge of a coherent, revised tax policy, informed by the important development of gender budgeting, would be to move women from the margin, to the economic mainstream. (Mumford 2010: 192)

## Ontological Challenges in Gender Studies of Taxation

One aspect of citizenship in the nation state that women have very seldom been denied is the status of taxpayer. In many welfare economies, women were obliged to pay taxes even before they achieved the right to vote (Lahey 2011, Gunnarsson 2011b), resulting in civil disobedience and protests in many countries. For instance, inspired by the use of tax resistance as a means to an end in the American Revolution, British suffragettes initiated the Women's Tax Resistance League (1909–1918). The protest against the duty on tea at the iconic Boston Tea Party was a protest against England's tax sovereignty over the American colonies, and the British suffragettes recycled the slogan 'no taxation without representation' to convey the simple message that without political representation women would refuse to pay tax (Gross 2008).

It is obvious that the power to tax is an important part of democracy and the legitimacy of governments, but it is also constitutive in nature (Lahey 2011: 14–15). As the conservative philosopher Edmund Burke once so aptly formulated the matter: 'The revenue of the state is the state' (Prior 1988). How a state chooses to structure its fiscal base thus has a strong influence on economic and social attitudes and the behaviour of the citizens, which feeds the demands for tax equity. On an aggregated level tax fairness is also related to a just and equitable connection between fiscal obligations and social benefits and rights (Gunnarsson 1995, 2003).

Economic inequalities between men and women bring a gendered dimension to policy issues concerning tax equity and social justice. Generalizations about the socio-economic conditions of women are, of course, difficult to make. However, despite the intersections of sex with other demographic factors such as age, race and class, inevitable common traits exist in statistical differences between men and women regarding economic status. In general, it is possible to state that men earn more and are wealthier than women. Another notable difference is that women tend to be clustered in lower income groups and have higher poverty rates than men. One variable of significance for differences in accumulating wealth is that women are less likely to have capital gains income and a financial cushion (Skatteverket 2007, Kornhauser 2011, Abramovitz and Morgen 2006, Young 2000). Nordic studies have also shown that quite separately from the issue of women being underrepresented as company owners, managers and entrepreneurs, the type of business they manage differs from those of men. Normally, women's companies are livelihood businesses, which produce services and do not attract risk capital. The description 'livelihood companies' refers to enterprises that are established with the objective of making a living rather than building a business empire. These types of companies produce a modest profit and have low expectations of wealth accumulation (Vada 2007, Skatteverket 2007, Andersson-Skog 2007).

Given these variables regarding differences between men and women one can see that the socio-economic realities of women's lives must be a part of policy making concerning the manner in which work, entrepreneurship and investments are taxed. But analysis cannot be limited to the income side of the public budget if the full context of women's economic subordination is to be grasped. The structures of revenue and social transfers are intertwined in welfare state policies (Young 2000). A further important gender aspect is that tax and social security regulations also mirror what the state regards as the preferred way of organizing families and paid productive work on the market and unpaid reproductive or care work in the home, and which social spheres of work should be male and female (Apps 2009, Apps and Rees 2009, Gunnarsson 2007, 2011a, Pfau-Effinger 2004).

Gender studies of taxation provide a critical epistemology which challenges the basic ontological categories, concepts and presumptions upon which tax laws and public budgets are built. Central presumptions about tax fairness and tax efficiency are particularly contested by feminist tax scholars (Brooks et al. 2011).

## Tax Ability, Family Configurations and Market Participation

One of the oldest tax theory debates is occupied with the question of what constitutes tax ability. Much feminist revenue research has focused both on the relative merits of the individual versus the spousal couple as the appropriate tax unit from an ability-to-pay perspective, and on the impact of the choice of the tax unit as either an incentive or disincentive for women to participate in paid work in the labour market. A gender-equality view of joint taxation maintains that the marital tax unit is both a defective indicator of ability to pay and a disincentive for women's economic autonomy and their opportunity to participate in the labour market (Apps 1984, Lahey 1985, Kornhauser 1997, Grbich 1990–91, Dulude 1985, Young 1997, Gunnarsson 2003).

Taxation of wealth and income also affects family configurations. Broadly, comparative studies show two main normative positions regarding tax and social policies concerning spouses, families and children. One is the male breadwinner family model linked to a traditional female, care regime, which fosters a housewife ideal – as in the case of Germany, the US and Spain. Consequently, the legal system rests on a normative base where the family or the marriage is the unit of assessment for social entitlements and taxation, in which the carer has only supplementary and no individual rights. Looking back on empirical facts, the model is representative for the traditional male breadwinner regime that is distinctively sexually segregated. The earner has, with very few exceptions, been the husband and the carer has been the wife (Sainsbury 1996: 44–45, Sainsbury 1999: 77–80, 314, Lahey 2011, Wersig 2011).

The other is the dual-earner family model for which the Nordic countries are renowned. Social entitlements and income taxation are based on the individual's work performance, citizenship or residence, not marital status. The lack of sex equality produced by the division of labour is recognized by the Swedish welfare state and is officially resisted by a strategy to promote the reconciliation of paid work and family life in a dual breadwinner family. Individual obligations via income tax, and individual social rights based on earnings-related social security schemes are measures that, as one of several objectives, aim to increase economic autonomy for married women. Parallel to individualization, and the goal of achieving gender neutralization of social rights and tax obligations, a new insight that public intervention needs to equalize the burden of caring and unpaid work between the sexes has slowly gained acceptance. Caring, principally in the form of parenting, as the basis for entitlements has become an individual right, not a supplementary right, and the financial costs of children are shared by public childcare and general child allowances available to all families (Gunnarsson 2003, Sainsbury 1999: 77–80).

In economic research, the impact of taxation on the labour supply of households is based on the assumption that households make rational choices between labour and leisure on the basis of economic self-interest. This assumption can lead, for example, to the simple conclusion that the primary earner in a family governs the labour supply of the second earner. If the costs, in the form of taxes, become too high for the primary earner he or she (though it is usually a male) will choose to spend more time on leisure than work, which will promote an increase of labour supply from the secondary earner. This is typically the case in a progressive income tax system where spouses and cohabitant partners with children file individually. The effective marginal tax rate[1] is higher for the primary earner, which makes an increase in working hours for women more beneficial for the family. In contrast, if the taxes are reduced for the primary earner, the best economic choice for the family is to reduce the labour supply of the secondary earner. This is the situation where income tax is not individualized in a progressive income tax system, where the breadwinner model is supported by extensive tax reductions for family support, or where tax credits are based on family income and similar structures. Even though the assumption of rational choice is problematic from a gender perspective, there is no doubt that families consist of primary and secondary earners, which is a deeply gendered family form. One can also see that the choice does not usually lie between time for work and time for leisure in a family, particularly not in a family with care obligations. Instead, the choice is between paid work on the market and unpaid work in the household. It is a gendered choice and it is a central incentive for women's labour supply (Apps and Rees 2009, Grbich 1993, Nyberg 1997, 2005).

## Exchange of Time, Care and Economic Resources

The gender order in tax law is deeply influenced by the division of production in public and private spheres. Going back to ancient legal texts such as the Roman law, one can see how the constitution of the family unit under the control of a husband was a central issue. This legal frame is representative of how law in general has been used to capture and control women's productive work and contribution to wealth accumulation within the domestic sphere. It has had a crucial impact on the division of labour between the public and the private sphere, and marginalized women as passive and dependant citizens in relation to the public economy (Lahey 2011: 15).

One effect of the gendered separation of productive work is that the whole picture of the production and distribution of welfare in a triangular relation between the market, the state

---

1   The effective marginal tax rate (EMTR) is the tax paid on the last part of earned income.

and the household is not recognized in tax law. The common view in tax policies and tax scholarship is that market production and public budget transfers are the sources of welfare for households. However, to grasp the whole gendered context of social welfare, one has to consider that the exchange of time, care and economic resources within the household is also a source of welfare production. The opposite of welfare valued in money terms is that valued in time. Households contribute to welfare production by adding the value of time for care work and other domestic services (Ketscher 2008, Stang Dahl 1988).

Official neglect of the value of household production underpins both sides of the public budget. Women continue to do the majority of household and care work, and this is outside what is considered to be societal responsibility in law reforms concerning taxation and social transfers. An effect is that taxation and social welfare reforms often contribute to the reproduction of relational dependency in the family or traditional notions of the productivity of women's labour and their contribution to the economy (Grbich 1990–91, Staudt 1996, Young 1997).

## Optimal Taxation and a Global Economic Order

The power to raise and spend public revenues remains fundamentally associated with the nation state at a time when states increasingly set their fiscal directions in response to pressures associated with global economic integration, capital mobility and market deregulation. Nation states have also agreed to collaborate on matters of fiscal governance and policies in the OECD, the WBG and the IMF. Apart from having a strong global influence on world trade, these organizations also have a worldwide influence on multinational commitments to engage in stimulus budgeting and on cooperating in preventing tax evasion. A global economic order has been on the agenda for a while as a means for fighting harmful tax competition. Tax law reforms are regarded as valuable instruments for achieving this aim (Mumford 2010, 36–37). The series of economic crises starting with the global economic crisis in 2008 has also led to new multinational commitments. The interventions of international organizations in the economic and fiscal governance of national states is exposed, for example, in the way Greece has been forced to submit to massive budgets cuts and fiscal restraint.

Many OECD countries have reformed their income tax over the last 20 years. Even though a common understanding of the ideal income tax system has never been expressed openly, there are common strands in the various tax reforms. Based on a neoliberal tax ideology, a special interpretation of what constitutes an optimal taxation has guided the international trend in redesigning national budgets and fiscal systems. A line between fiscal purposes and social justice has been drawn, meaning that tax regulations with redistributive intentions are seen as political interventions in the market economy. Such economic interventions are believed to create excess burdens or welfare losses, which hinder economic growth. As redistribution of wealth and income are based on political ideals concerning economic equality, such interventions are seen as creating inefficiency in the economy. This has resulted in a normative standard whereby distributional neutrality is a part of the concept of fiscal taxation, which aims to preserve the status quo (Hayek 1956, Korpi and Palme 1993, Prop. 1989/90:110: 620–632). Subjecting all forms of income and consumption to tax fulfils the principle of distributional neutrality. The Swedish tax reform of 1991, for instance, expanded the income tax base by almost one per cent by including a large group of previously tax-free fringe benefits and income in kind in the category of labour income (Birch Sørensen 2010: 70).

The principles of tax neutrality and tax horizontal equity have been invoked to justify uniform taxation in conjunction with the goal of ensuring that taxation should only fulfil a neutral, fiscal purpose. The fiscal purpose is to raise revenue without any intervention that will distort an efficient allocation of resources in the market economy. The overall objective in the OECD community is to promote economic growth by reducing tax regulations that have a negative influence on entrepreneurship, labour supply and investments. When applied in national tax reforms a normative pattern emerges of reduced progressivity, financed by a broadening of the tax base for income taxation and higher consumption taxation. Some experts describe this policy as a shift from income tax to consumption taxes. Another element is the abandoning of the global personal income tax structure[2] and movement towards a dual income tax system, in which labour income and various types of capital incomes are taxed separately. As an example of this international trend, the Nordic countries have combined progressive taxation of labour and social transfer incomes with a linear, flat rate tax on income from capital at a level equal to the corporate income tax rate (Gunnarsson 1995, Piper and Murphy 2005, Owens 2006, Birch Sørensen 2010).

It is evident that, in the past, welfare economies have used taxes as part of social programmes to protect an income level that can support a family, in both the male breadwinner family model and in the dual-earner family model. However, when social justice is excluded as a guiding principle for tax policies, the revenue side of public budgets becomes detached from social programmes with redistributive aims. Again, a new type of deeply gendered logic of separation becomes visible, in which taxes are merely fiscal and all social programmes are implemented by public budget expenditures (Gunnarsson 2003). Another aspect of this new type of separation between taxation and social programmes for family support is the new policy trend, promoted at least by the European Union, which individualizes the income protection to each worker citizen. The policy does not take any account of the new social risks that changes in labour markets and family structures have created. Magnified in many countries by demographic aging, difficulties in reconciling work and family life from many angles, this creates social risks that put additional pressure on the organizing and financing of care work and reproduction, with enormous implications for the gendered division of paid and unpaid labour (Lewis 2002, Bonoli 2005, Åmark 2005, Lister 2009, Brooks et al. 2011).

## Gender Budgeting

The public budget is a blueprint of a government's priorities. It represents the aims and ambitions of a nation state (Levi 1989). Traditionally economic and fiscal policies concerning the income side have been separated from the social policies governing the spending side of budgets. A new insight into the relation between tax measures and spending programmes emerged when Stanley Surrey presented his theoretical concept of tax expenditures at the beginning of the 1970s. Surrey saw tax expenditures as those tax regulations that deviate

---

2    A global or comprehensive personal income tax is the income tax that aggregates income from all sources at the level of an individual or a family unit. The sum of the aggregated income is taxed at a single income tax rate.

from the benchmark. The 'benchmark' is the ideology of the tax system, and identifying it is inherently normative. Tax expenditure analysis of budgets is valuable in understanding and targeting those tax measures that are actually spending programmes (Surrey 1973, Young 2000).

Tax expenditure analysis has been used by the gender budgeting movement to demonstrate the gender blindness in conventional budget policies. Fiscal policies and government budgetary allocations have done little to promote women's equality. Activists have agitated about the need to identify the differential impact that expenditures and revenues have on men and women (Walby 2005, Budlender et al. 2002). Gender budgeting gained worldwide recognition when, in 1995, the Declaration and Platform for Action was adopted at the UN's Fourth World Conference in Beijing. The Platform calls for a wide range of actions in national-level policies to be used to identify and eliminate discrimination against women in taxation, expenditure programmes and government budgets. It clearly declares that fiscal policies are critical for the achievement of progress towards equality between men and women. An integrated gender perspective in budgetary decisions is stated as being a necessary prerequisite for gender equality. Disaggregated analysis and systematic reviews of the gendered outcome of fiscal and budget policies are also mandated.[3]

Member States of the European Union are now legally required to undertake a form of gender budgeting (EU Gender Directive, Council Directive 2004/113/EC). Accounting by governments to explain the impact of their expenditures on gender equality is required as a means of implementing the principle of equal treatment of men and women in access to and supply of goods and services. The European Commission recognizes gender-based assessment of budgets as an application of gender mainstreaming. The Commission also regards gender budgeting as a proactive bureaucratic tool that can be used to restructure revenues and expenditures in order to promote gender equality (Mumford 2010: 23, Walby 2005).

Gender budgeting analysis in the more than 50 countries which apply the Platform confirms that budget decisions are not neutral. In general, men benefit from government budgetary allocations. Economic priorities in budgets are normally based on the preferences of men and their socio-economic realities. Economic values implying the preservation of economic gender inequality are obviously embedded in budgets. For instance, one fundamental issue is how budgetary allocations draw upon the division of productive work. Paid work and the supply of goods and services in a market is the only economy recognized. The integrated relation between the market economy and the economy of unpaid, domestic production is left outside budgetary consideration. The consequence is that a large part of women's work is excluded (Mumford 2010, Lahey 2010, Villagomez 2004). A report from the European Parliament highlighted the need for an analysis of the impact of public expenditures on time use in order to consider the implications of budgetary policies for unpaid work such as social reproduction, domestic work and family and community care (European Parliament 2003).

The statement of the European Parliament is a confirmation of the need to recognize all sources of welfare production in the budget. Women's productive work in the household does not give them any individual social rights. It does not provide for intra-generational rights, such as pension rights or social rights, to cover income losses over the lifecycle. For

---

3    The Platform at: www.un.org/womenwatch/daw/beijing/platform/plat1.htm [accessed 20 November 2012].

most women, tax deductions for supplementary pensions plans, a common tax expenditure in many OECD countries, is not an option for compensating for the loss of economic rights consequential upon household work. This is because, in the majority of tax systems, the deductions for pension plan savings mostly benefit high-income groups. A taxable income above a minimum level is necessary before the taxpayer can contribute to a pension plan. Even though the lack of social security from public welfare regimes for household work still remains deeply hidden in the shadows of welfare policies in many countries, extensive tax expenditure programmes exist that indirectly compensate for unpaid household work. This is the case in those countries which promote the breadwinner model family (Staudt 1996, Young 1997, 2000, de Villota and Ferrari 2004, Spangenberg 2011, Wersig 2011). In the next section I will show how joint taxation, income splitting and family support through the tax system function as expenditure programs.

Recently a new type of tax expenditure has been introduced in several EU countries which indirectly recognizes that household production is a part of the market economy. As part of job growth policies, stimulation of the domestic services sector has led to reforms that in different ways subsidize paid domestic work. The Nordic countries – Sweden, Denmark and Finland – have used tax credits in the form of tax reductions.[4] Germany has applied a mini-job model, which is a specific category of employment for the household sector with low wages and low social contribution costs. Belgium, France and Austria have introduced a voucher model, which at least France combines with a tax credit provision. The voucher is a pre-paid service cheque that the user of domestic services can purchase and use as a salary for the domestic worker. It aims to simplify the process of hiring and paying salaries as well as social contributions for domestic workers. If the vouchers model is combined with a tax credit, the employers of domestic workers also can claim an income tax reduction of parts of the costs for the voucher (Kvist 2011). It seems as though domestic services vouchers are a more common policy option in breadwinner model countries that practise joint income taxation of spouses, and that tax credits are the common tax policy for the Nordic individual income tax systems (Gunnarsson and Kvist 2011).

## The Tax/Benefit Unit and Family Taxation

Since the time of Roman law the economic unit of a breadwinner household has constituted the basic tax unit for income and wealth in many jurisdictions. The legal concept of *unitas personae* in Roman law meant a unit under which the male heads of households legally gained control over women's and other dependent's productive capacity. Free men, the only social category who could be citizens of the state and uphold the legal status of a 'unitary person', had the authority under the law to represent all members of the household. This legal concept has had a strong normative influence over joint taxation of spouses and families until the present day (Lahey 2011).

Family taxation, in which joint taxation of spouses is traditionally the basic element, can be defined in many ways. However, two normative structures are rather obvious. One

---

4    The definition of a tax reduction is that it reduces the amount of tax paid. It is different from a tax deduction which only reduces the taxable income. Tax reductions can be both refundable and non-refundable. When tax reductions are refundable it means that they can amount to a greater sum than the total tax liability. The excess is then paid as an allowance.

is the taxable capacity approach and the other is the social welfare approach. The taxable capacity approach aims to preserve horizontal equity. It is based on principles such as equal treatment, non-discrimination, protection of the family and the ability to pay. Under the liberal, rule-of-law tradition, these are all recognized as outcomes of the state's obligation to protect freedoms and rights of citizens. In some states these principles are established in the constitution and in other states they are considered to be fundamental general principles. The social welfare approach aims to achieve vertical equity concerning socio-economic issues of redistribution (Soler Roch 1999). The tax unit is not isolated from the benefit unit as family taxation is regarded as part of the welfare programme. Tax measures can be used as replacements for direct social entitlements in cash or in kind or used as a complement to social benefit programmes directed to the support of families (Gunnarsson 2003).

One representative example of how redistributive, family policy issues span between the tax and the social security system is how different jurisdictions have solved the support of child costs. Since the birth of modern family policy, both tax deductions and child benefits have been used to subsidize the costs of raising children. In Sweden and elsewhere, before 1947, child costs were subsidized mainly as a tax deduction for maintenance support for the breadwinner of the family, a system which also recognized in part the family care work of housewives. However, after the Second World War, many European countries chose to subsidize child costs as a universal child allowance independent of parental income or employment status. Germany, on the other hand, did not abandon the tax deduction regime for child costs. As a part of the breadwinner family model, Germany combines child benefits and child-related tax deductions. A system with universal, residence-based social transfers to support maintenance costs for children individually granted to the caregiver would be preferable from a gender equality perspective as it is not related to the level of earned income and not jointly assessed income of a household (Gunnarsson 2003, Scheiwe 2011).

## Gender Equality Perspectives on Joint and Individual Taxation

The underlying policies of joint taxation regimes are that households constitute economic units and that joint taxation combined with income splitting in a progressive income tax system is a guarantee of neutral treatment for single- and dual-earner families. Joint taxation also preserves traditional family configurations such as the male breadwinner model, or the so-called 'housewife marriage' model (Grbich 1990–91). On the other hand, a basic argument in favour of individual taxation is that the control of the money is the appropriate test for ability to pay. The tax burden should be distributed according to the control over economic resources that the individual taxpayer possesses (Stewart 2011, Gunnarsson 1995, Simons 1938).

Today, joint filing of the aggregated marital income is normally voluntary in those countries which construct their income tax system on a joint fiscal model. However, the freedom is illusory as choosing not to exercise it often means that the family will lose a substantial amount of disposable income after tax. As long as the income tax is progressive, the technique of splitting the aggregated income of both spouses and filing half the income for each spouse will reduce the total tax burden as the spouse with the highest income will pay a lower marginal tax rate. Single-earner families will benefit more than dual-earner families from this tax relief. As the income structures in heterosexual families follow gendered lines, income taxation of the marital unit results in the overtaxing of married women. This is truly a disincentive for housewives to enter the workforce, which is the case, for example, for women in Germany and in Spain. It also traps many of those married women who work in the position of secondary earner in the family. Contrary to the claimed neutrality between one-earner and dual-earner families, joint income and wealth taxation favours the marital tax unit. Experiences from Germany, Japan, Spain and the United States show that the joint taxation of spouses contributes to a patriarchal, asymmetrical division of unpaid household work and paid work on the labour market (Lahey 2011, de Villota 2011, de Villota and Ferrari 2004, Wersig 2011, Gottfried and O'Reilly 2002).

In contrast to joint taxation, the experiences from Sweden and the other Nordic countries show that individual taxation is a prerequisite for improving economic gender equality. Studying the integrated development of gender equality and welfare state regimes in Sweden shows that the individual income tax reform from 1971 opened the way for what has been defined as the women-friendly welfare state. The reform was unique as it addressed gender equality objectives. It was based on knowledge of the correlation between the labour-market participation of women living in partnerships and the income of their cohabitant partner. When the reform was introduced, the income tax rating scale was massively progressive, thus it benefited those households where women increased their working hours in the labour market (Gunnarsson 2003: 57–62).

In contemporary tax systems, income-splitting between conjugal partners almost always has negative consequences for gender equality. Normally, tax regulations allowing income splitting reduce tax for the transferor and are used as an element in tax planning. The splitting is merely a technique and the transfer of income is just a fiction. The tax liability of the receiving spouse will not correspond to a legal claim on the assets or income for which she will be taxed. However, as Lisa Philipps argues, income splitting could very well be designed in such a way that, instead of trapping married women in the household, it could resource them. This can be accomplished by transforming tax avoidance and income-splitting regulations into real intra-household transfers serving as compensation for various forms of assisting and caring performances by the receiving spouse (Philipps et al. 2011). Such tax regulations on income-splitting have the potential to capture the value of time for care work and other domestic services that add to household production of welfare.

## Family Support in the Tax System

An extension of the idea of joint taxation and splitting of income between spouses are systems which promote family taxation and splitting of income across extended families. Such family policies expressed through the tax system exist in many countries. Family benefits delivered over the tax system are regulated in numerous ways. France, for instance, represents the patriarchal model of family taxation. The French state is renowned for its history of supporting large, male-breadwinner families through an extensive form of joint taxation, which can be defined as a family-splitting system (Hantrais and Letablier 1996, Wersig 2011).

*Foyer fiscal* is the family tax unit, including everyone sitting around the 'fireplace', which symbolizes economic dependency on the breadwinner. The tax unit strongly resembles the 'unitary person' of ancient Roman law. It includes spouses, cohabitant French civil union partners, children and other family members claimed as dependants. Income-splitting in relation to family size is called *quotient conjugal* for income-splitting between spouses and civil union partners, and *quotient familial* for income splitting between children and other dependant members of the household. Since French family taxation is based on a combined taxable capacity and social welfare approach, the *quotient conjugal* is mainly based on the same reasoning as the German joint taxation of spouses. That is, the primary objective is to ensure neutrality between single persons on the one hand and cohabiting partners on the other. The *quotient familial* (which is a form of extended joint taxation) has been linked to two objectives: one fiscal and one non-fiscal. The objective considered to be fiscal is to achieve neutrality between tax units with and without children, based on the ability-to-pay principle, and the non-fiscal is the distributive motive to support parts of the families' child costs (David 1999, Gunnarsson 2003: 72–82, Thévenon 2008).

A trend in tax policy among OECD countries since the 1990s has been the use of various types of tax credits as a part of an active labour market policy to incentivize particularly low-earning families' but also middle-income families' labour supply. Many of these working family tax credits are assessed on the basis of spouses' or partners' conjugal income. The idea is that the family will get a tax credit if they increase their hours of paid work on the labour market (Brewer et al. 2008). New Zealand introduced working family tax credits as early as 1986 through the Family Support Tax Credit (FSTC) and Guaranteed Minimum Family Income (GMFI) which targeted poor families. The tax credits, however, proved counter-productive as the effective marginal tax rate became very high for every extra working hour. A new tax credit, the Independent Family Tax Credit (IFTC), was introduced in 1996 to equalize the effect of the marginal tax rates. The New Zealand tax credits have all used the aggregated parental income to determine the size of the tax reduction, which has conflicted with the individual-based income tax system. In short, the working family tax credits introduced income-targeted support for families, which increased the marginal tax rate for the secondary earner in the family (Gunnarsson 1999, Chan 1993).

Similarly, the UK introduced a Working Family Tax Credit (WFTC) at the beginning of the 1990s, aimed at stimulating increased labour market participation for families with small children, focusing particularly on single parents. The WFTC was later replaced by a Working Tax Credit (WTC), embracing all low-earning families, and an additional subsidy for families with children in the form of a Child Tax Credit (CTC). The tax credits are administered by Her Majesty's Revenue and Customs, but are technically much more of a social cash benefit transfer as they do not reduce the tax liability of the receiver and are paid directly into the bank account of the taxpayer. Both WTC and CTC are assessed on the basis of family income, number of children and working hours per week (Brewer et al. 2008).

Australia also introduced a version of family tax credit in the 1990s, assessed on the basis of joint, family income. It is delivered as a Family Tax Benefit A (FTB-A) and a Family Tax Benefit B (FTB-B). FTB-A provides a cash transfer per child under 13 years of age. It elaborates with a span of a basic and maximum rate withdrawn from the joint family income. FTB-B is a cash transfer for a child under five years deducted from the income of the second earner income if the yearly income of the primary earner does not exceed a certain threshold. As a consequence of the joint income-testing for the FTB, both the marginal and the average income tax rates have increased for secondary earners (Apps 2009, Stewart 2011).

There are many other examples of how reforms of earned income tax credits and tax-delivered benefits, particularly for child subsidies, have introduced a joint tax-benefit unit. This means that individual taxation has become eroded in many OECD countries. Several of these reforms have also raised the tax rates for the secondary earner (Lahey 2005, Philipps et al. 2011, Apps 2006, Apps 2009 Stewart 2011). Again, the Swedish working tax credit reform does not follow this trend. When it came into force in 2007, each individual taxpayer became the unit of assessment for the earned income tax credit (Prop. 2006/07:1, Vol. 1:

137). In summary, tax credits that are based on joint, family income have the same lock-in effect on women's labour market supply as joint taxation and income splitting of spouses or cohabitant heterosexual partners.

## 'Gender-Based' Income Taxation: Optimal Taxation for Gender Equality

The neoliberal understanding of the correlation between economic growth and the need to reduce taxes on income draws upon the view that high-income earners and the capital they control are very mobile. As described earlier, the OECD countries share the view that optimal income taxes should have a broad income base and a flat or linear tax rate. Many of the transfer economies in Eastern Europe, such as Russia and Slovakia, have served as something of a laboratory for the most consistent reforms in the direction of linear personal income taxes. Nevertheless, distributive adjustments are also present in the reforms as tax exemptions for basic income in the form of basic reductions and targeted tax credits. These elements often produce an inverted U-shaped progressivity, shifting the income tax burden to the middle of the income brackets (Apps 2009, Piper and Murphy 2005). Similarly, neoliberal corporate income tax policies have followed a tax-cutting trend. Canada, for example, introduced a federal programme of gradual income tax rate cuts in 1998, which reduced the federal corporate rate to as low as 15 per cent. The revenue losses are expected to reach a total of $47.7 billion during the period 2010–2014 (Lahey 2010).

OECD tax policies are based on the belief that what is best for the dominant market participants is also best for economic growth. Optimal taxation is thought to result from less interventionist tax regulations, but it is obvious that this also means less distribution and less income equality. The question is whether this really is an optimal tax strategy (Apps 2009).

What matters from an optimal tax theory perspective are the economic costs for distributive, social justice considerations. The costs are the dead-weight welfare losses that arise as an effect of disincentives to work. In short, optimal tax analyses have been occupied with the impact different tax structures have on labour supply. Basically, given that the salary corresponds to the employer's marginal utility for the worker, taxation affects labour supply in two ways. One is the income effect which simply means that the worker will have less means available for private consumption after tax is taken. The other is the substitution effect where work becomes less attractive relative to the alternative use of time. The standard view regarding economic behaviour of one-person households mean that the substitution and income effects pull in different directions; the choice is either to work harder to compensate for the taxation or to spend more time on leisure (Mirlees 1971, McCaffrey 1997: 170–178).

Transplanting this analysis to a dual-income-earning household with children, one discovers one of the core issues of economic gender equality. Even though the standard assumption is that choices are based on rational economic self-interest, it is obvious that decisions about labour supply are an interdependent issue in the household. Women in traditional relations have much greater income elasticity than men, which probably has to do with the traditional division of paid labour market work and unpaid household work between men and women. From this it follows, based on optimal tax theory, that men ought to pay a higher rate of income tax than women as they have a low income elasticity. Higher income tax on men's labour incomes has a much lower impact on their labour supply than it has on women. Another observation is that what women substitute for work is not leisure but unpaid household work. A woman's reallocation from paid work in the labour market to household production is determined by her net market income after tax in relation to the net income of her male partner. As the incomes of women are generally lower than those of men, tax reforms that increase this difference also indirectly put a price on women's household work. Given that men have a constantly lower income elasticity and that women's lower labour supply is reallocated to household production, women ought to be taxed at a lower income tax rate than men (McCaffrey 1997: 180–181, Apps 2009). This is, of course, a generalized theoretical conclusion based on the parameters given in the theorem of optimal tax theory. Empirical studies and theoretical elaborations are solely focused on the 'standard' couples, which are heterosexual couples, normally married and normally with common children. However, one could very well expect similar outcomes in terms of labour market supply and income elasticity in other types of relations where there exists some kind of breadwinner or primary- and secondary-earner stereotypes in combination with a care obligation of some sort.

The optimality of 'gender-based' taxation in respect of providing substantial welfare and employment gains seems to be a quite obvious result of these analyses. The question is what could constitute an adequate tax policy recommendation? In a frequently cited article, Michael Boskin and Eytan Sheshinski claim that, based on certain fixed parameters such as the cross elasticities of labour supply between men and women and heterogeneous households, optimal income taxation for labour supply would be a gender based income tax system that taxes men twice as much as women (Boskin and Sheshinski 1983). When adding in the gendered aspect of how families organize family duties, in which the possible comparative advantages of women taking on a larger share of family duties are considered, optimal tax analysis presents the same conclusions. 'Gender-based' taxation with lower tax rates for females is superior to gender-neutral tax rates in respect to levelling out those intra-household income elasticities that restrains women's labour supply (McCaffery 1997, Alesina et al. 2008). From an optimal tax theory point of view, a tax policy directed to gender-based tax rates is the best policy alternative for economic growth. It may very well be that this incentive to indirectly put a price on gender equality will have stronger influence than other gender and family policy measures where the aim is affirmative actions such as forced parental leave, work tax credits and other public subsidies directed to families' labour supply. Optimal tax analyses indicate that a personal, progressive individual income tax promotes gender equality in heterosexual families with children (Alesina et al. 2008, Gustafsson and Bruyn-Hundt 1991, Kornhauser 1997, 2004).

## The Need for a Theoretical Reorientation of Tax Systems from a Gender Perspective

In this chapter, I have tried to show how the gender inequalities connected to the division of paid work in the market and unpaid work in households is largely reproduced by tax systems and public budgets. Tax reforms that reduce redistributive elements, such as progressive income tax rates and reduced capital and corporate income taxes, will be systematically more beneficial for men than women. Joint assessments of taxes and social transfers have the same effect. The message in the OECD tax reform trend is that the formula for economic growth is less progressivity and more jointness, which seems to contradict the correlation between the increases in women's labour supply and the increase of economic growth. The increase in women's labour supply is also at the core of what improves economic gender equality. There are clear indicators from gender statistics that the OECD tax and welfare policies are moving in the opposite direction to what would be preferred from a gender equality perspective, which means that the OECD countries violate the mainstreaming of substantive equality as regulated by the Convention on the Elimination of All Forms of Discrimination against Women (CEDAW).

These backlashes in economic gender equality in many countries show, as Kathleen Lahey puts it, the fragility of equality gains. Her recommendation, based on experiences from the gender equality backlashes in Canada, is to confront the deep structures of our tax systems in order to arrive at a more solid frame for economic gender equality. She argues:

> Women do not fit the models imposed on them by abstract categorical thought, but their variability and their capabilities cannot be "seen" among the images used in the dominant discourse. The problems caused for women by tax laws of all kinds have common elements: they do not take seriously women's persistently low incomes, high levels of responsibilities and constrained mobility. Nor do they give sufficient weight to society's responsibility for sharing those burdens fairly, or the unacceptability of constructing male wealth out of those unequal burdens. The unrelenting focus on gender-neutral categories like "the poor" or "single parents" or "children living in poverty" has made it seem as if women, whether contained in the couple, in the social assistance system or in parenting, do not matter unless they and their containers are "poor" and serve worthy purposes. Thus, the greatest challenge may be to find ways to reveal the artificiality of the containers and to see women as being too variable, too self-defining, to be contained – to imagine women as fully human subjects with equal entitlements to all the opportunities life can offer. (Lahey 2011: 29–30)

However, before we can achieve a comprehensive revision of the foundations of present tax systems from a gender perspective there are still some policy recommendations that could be made about best practice for an income tax system that promotes gender equality. Based on the Swedish experience, the income tax system should be broad-based, individual, global and progressive. Broad-based in the sense that the income tax base ought to embrace all income in cash and in kind. The individual should be the tax unit with no exemptions for tax credits or tax deductions. The tax unit should correspond with the benefit unit, which means that the benefit unit also has to be the individual. A global income tax is a tax where the same tax rate scale is applied on the collected incomes of the tax subject. And finally a progressive income tax scale is distributive in a way that is generally more beneficial for women than men.

# References

Abramovitz, M. and Morgen, S. 2006. *Taxes are a Women's Issue*, with the National Council for Research on Women. New York: The Feminist Press.

Alesina, A., Ichino, A. and Karabarbounis, L. 2010. *Gendered-Based Taxation and the Division of Family Chores*. [Online]. Available at: www2.dse.unibo.it/ichino/gbt16.pdf [accessed: 20 November 2012].

Andersson-Skog, L. 2007. In the Shadow of the Swedish Welfare State: Women and the Service Sector. *Business History Review*, 81(3), 451–470.

Apps, P. 1984. *A Theory of Inequality and Taxation*. Cambridge: Cambridge University Press.

Apps, P. 2007. The New Discrimination and Childcare, in *Kids Count: Better Early Childhood Education and Care in Australia*, edited by E. Hill, B. Pocock and A. Elliot. Sydney: Sydney University Press, Chapter 4.

Apps, P. 2009. *Tax Reform, Targeting, and the Burden on Women*. Paper prepared for National Foundation for Australian Women for submission to the Review of Australia's Future Tax System. [Online]. Available at: http://taxreview.treasury.gov.au/content/submissions/post_14_november_2008/National_Foundation_for_Australian_Women_Sub01_20090505.pdf.

Apps, P. and Rees, R. 2009. *Public Economics and the Household*. Cambridge: Cambridge University Press.

Birch Sørensen, P. 2010. *Swedish Tax Policy: Recent Trends and Future Challenges*. Report to the Expert Group on Public Economics 2010: 4. Stockholm: Fritzes.

Bonoli, G. 2005. The Politics of New Social Risks: Providing Coverage Against New Social Risks in Mature Welfare States. *Policy and Politics*, 33(3), 431–439.

Boskin, M. J. and Sheshinski, E. 1983. Optimal Tax Treatment of the Family: Married Couples. *Journal of Public Economics*, 20, 281–297.

Brewer, M., Saez, E. and Shephard, A. 2008. *Means-testing and tax rates on earnings*. Report of a Commission on Reforming the Tax System for the 21st Century, Chaired by Sir James Mirrlees. Available at: www.ifs.org.uk/mirrleesreview.

Brooks, K., Gunnarsson, Å., Philipps L. and Wersig, M. 2011. *Challenging Gender Inequality in Tax Policy Making: Comparative Perspectives* Oxford: Hart Publishing.

Budlender, D., Elson, D., Hewitt, G. and Mukhopadhya, T. 2002. *Gender Budgets Makes Cents: Understanding Gender Responsive Budgets*. Gender Budget Initiatives. London: Commonwealth Secretariat.

Chan, W. 1993. Taxing the Female – as Woman or Wife, in *Women and Taxation*, edited by C. Scott. Wellington, Victoria: Institute of Policy Studies, 53–73.

David, C. 1999. France, in *Family Taxation in Europe*, edited by S. Ross and M. Teresa. Dordrecht: Kluwer Law, 27–54.

Dulude, L. 1985. Taxation of the Spouses: A Comparison of Canadian, American, British, French and Swedish Law. *Osgoode Hall Law School Law Journal*, 23(1), 67–129.

European Parliament Session Document. 2003. *Report on Gender Budgeting – Building Public Budgets from a Gender Perspective*. [Online]. Available at: www.europarl.europa.eu [accessed 20 November 2012].

Gottfried, H. and O'Reilly, J. 2002. Reregulating Breadwinner Models in Socially Conservative Welfare Systems: Comparing Germany and Japan. *Social Politics*, 9(1), 29–59.

Grbich, J. 1987. The position of women in family dealing: the Australian case. *International Journal of the Sociology of Law*, 15, 309–332.

Grbich, J. 1990–91. The Tax Unit Debate Revisited: Notes on the Critical Resources of a Feminist Revenue Law Scholarship. *Canadian Journal of Women and the Law*, 4, 512–538.

Grbich, J. 1993. Writing Histories of Revenue Law: The New Productivity Research. *Law in Context*, 11, 57–77.

Gross, D.M. (ed.), 2008. *We Wont Pay! A Tax Resistance Reader*. London: CreateSpace.

Gunnarsson, Å. 1995. *Skatterättvisa*. Uppsala: Iustus Förlag AB.

Gunnarsson, Å. 1999. Equity Trends in Taxation – with Examples from Swedish and New Zealand Tax Reforms, in *Liber Amicorum Leif Mutén*, edited by Gustaf Lindecrona, Sven-Olof Lodin and Bertil Wiman. Amsterdam: Kluwer, 141–168.

Gunnarsson, Å. 2003. *Fördelningen av familjens skatter och sociala förmåner*. Uppsala Iustus: Förlag AB.

Gunnarsson, Å.2007. Gender Equality and the Diversity of Rights and Obligations, in *Exploting the Limits of Law. Swedish Feminims and the Challenge to Pessimism*, edited by Gunnarsson, Å,Svensson, E.-M. and Davies, M. Aldershot: Ashgate, 191-211.

Gunnarsson, Å. 2011a. Challenging the Benchmarks in Tax Law Theories and Policies from a Gender Perspective – The Swedish Case, in *Challenging Gender Inequality in Tax Policy Making: Comparative Perspectives*, edited by K. Brooks, Å. Gunnarsson, L. Philipps and M. Wersig. Oxford: Hart Publishing, 75–92.

Gunnarsson, Å. 2011b. Genus– och kvinnoperspektiv på rätten. I en internationell och tvärvetenskaplig belysning, in Svensson, Eva-Maria, Andersson, Ulrika, Braekhus, Hege, Burman, Monica, Hellum, Anne, Jörgensen, Stine (eds), *På Vei, Kjönn og Rett I Norden*. Makdam förlag: Göteborg, Stockholm, 146–178.

Gunnarsson, Å. and Kvist, E. 2011. Public Expenditure for Domestic Work Challenges Swedish Gender Equality, in *Equal is Not Enough: Challenging Differences and Inequalities in Contemporary Societies*, edited by J. Motmans, D. Cuypers, P. Meier, D. Mortelmans and P. Zanoni Patrizia. Conference Proceedings. Antwerpen: Policy Research Centre on Equal opportunities, University of Antwerpen – Hasselt University, 156–172.

Gustafsson, S. and Bruyn-Hundt, M. 1991. *Incentives for women to work: A comparison between the Netherlands, Sweden, and West Germany*. The Hague: Netherlands Scientific Council for Government Policy.

Hantrais, L. and Letablier, M. 1996. *Families and Family Policies*. London: Longman.

Hayek, F. 1956. Progressive Taxation Reconsidered, in *On Freedom and Free Enterprise. Essays in Honour of Ludwig von Mises*, edited by M. Sennholz. Princeton, New Jersey, Toronto, London: Nostrands Company, 265–284.

Ketscher, K. 2008. *Socialret: Principper, rettigheder, værdier*, 3 udg, Thomson, København.

Kornhauser, M. 1993. Love, Money, and the IRS: Family, Income-Sharing and the Joint Income Tax Return. *Hastings Law Journal*, 45, 63–75.

Kornhauser, M. 1997. What Do Women Want: Feminism and the Progressive Income Tax. *American University Law Review*, 47, 151–163.

Kornhauser, M. 2004. The Rhetoric of the Anti-Progressive Income Tax Movement: A Typical Male Reaction. *Michigan Law Review*, 86, 465–523.

Kornhauser, M. 2011. Gender and Capital Gains Taxation, in *Challenging Gender Inequality in Tax Policy Making: Comparative Perspectives*, edited by K. Brooks, Å. Gunnarsson, L. Philipps and M. Wersig. Oxford: Hart Publishing, 275–291.

Korpi, W. and Palme, J. 1993. *Socialpolitik, kris och reformer: Sverige i internationell belysning*. Stockholm: Universitet, Institutionen för social forskning.

Kvist, E. 2011. Changing social organizations of care through tax laws – European tax reforms promoting paid domestic work. *European Journal of Ageing*, 9(2), 111–117.

Lahey, K. 1985. The Tax Unit Income Tax Theory, in *Women the Law, and the Economy*, edited by D. Pask. Toronto, Boston: Butterworths.

Lahey, K. 2005. *Women and Employment: Removing Fiscal Barriers to Women's Labour Force Participation*. Ottawa: Status of Women Canada.

Lahey, K. 2010. Women, Substantive Equality, and Fiscal Policy: Gender-Based Analysis of Taxes, Benefits, and Budgets. *Canadian Journal of Women and the Law*, 22(1), 27–106.

Lahey, K. 2011. The 'Capture' of Women in Law and Fiscal Policy: Implications for the Tax/Benefit Unit, Gender Equality and Feminist Ontologies, in *Challenging Gender Inequality in Tax Policy Making: Comparative Perspectives*, edited by K. Brooks, Å. Gunnarsson, L. Philipps and M. Wersig. Oxford: Hart Publishing, 11–35.

Lewis, J. 2002. Gender and Welfare State Change. *European Societies*, 4(4), 331–357.

Levi, M. 1989. *Of Rule and Revenue*. Berkley: University of California Press.

Lister, R. 2009. A Nordic Nirvana? Gender, citizenship, and social justice in the Nordic Welfare State. *Social Politics*, 16(2), 242–278.

McCaffrey, E. 1997. *Taxing Women*. Chicago and London: University of Chicago Press.

Mirlees, J. 1971. An Exploration in the Theory of Optimum Income Taxation. *The Review of Economic Studies*, 38(2), 175–208.

Mumford, A. 2010. *Tax Policy, Women and the Law*. Cambridge: Cambridge University Press.

Nyberg, A. 1997. *Women, Men and Incomes. Gender Inequality and Economic Independence*.

Nyberg, A. 2005. Har den ekonomiska jämställdheten ökat sedan början av 1990-talet?, in *Forskarrapporter till Jämställdhetspolitiska utredningen. SOU 2005: 66*, 13–84.

Owen, F. 1997. *The Tax Practitioner*. Wellington.

Owens, J. 2006. Fundamental Tax Reform: The Experience of OECD Countries, Centre for Tax Policy & Administration, OECD. Presented at the 67th Annual Meeting of Tax Foundation Washington DC. OECD. *Tax Policy Studies* No. 13: Fundamental Reform of Personal Income Tax.

Philipps, L. 2001. Income Splitting and Gender Equality: The case for Incentivizing Intra-household Wealth Transfers, in *Challenging Gender Inequality in Tax Policy Making: Comparative Perspectives*, edited by K. Brooks, Å. Gunnarsson, L. Philipp and M. Wersig. Oxford: Hart Publishing, 235–254.

Philipps, L., Brooks, K., Gunnarsson, Å. and Wersig, M. 2011. Introduction, in *Challenging Gender Inequality in Tax Policy Making: Comparative Perspectives*, edited by K. Brooks, Å. Gunnarsson, L. Philipps and M. Wersig. Oxford: Hart Publishing, 235–254.

Piper, S. and Murphy, C. 2005, Flat personal income taxes: systems in practice in Eastern Europe economies, *Economic Roundup*, Spring 2005, Treasury, Canberra, 37–52.

Pfau-Effinger B. 2004. Socio-historical paths of the male breadwinner model – an explanation of cross-national differences. *British Journal of Sociology*, 55(3), 377–399.

Platform for Action. 1995. Geneva: United Nations. Available online at www.un.org/womenwatch/daw/beijing/platform/plat1.htm [accessed 20 November 2012].

Prior, J. (ed.), 1988. *The Works of the Right Honourable Edmund Burke, vol. 2 – Reflections on the Revolution in France*. London: George Bell and Son.

Prop. 1989/90:110, *Om reformerad inkomst – och företagsbeskattning*.

Prop. 2006/07:1, *Budgetpropositionen för 2007*.

Sainsbury. D. 1996. *Gender, Equality, and Welfare States*. Cambridge: Cambridge University Press.

Sainsbury, D. (ed.), 1999. *Gender and Welfare State Regimes*. Oxford: Oxford University Press.

Scheiwe, K. 2011. Income Redistribution through Child Benefits and Child-Related Tax Deductions: A Gender-Neutral Approach? in *Challenging Gender Inequality in Tax Policy*

*Making: Comparative Perspectives*, edited by K. Brooks, Å. Gunnarsson, L. Philipps and M. Wersig. Oxford: Hart Publishing, 195–211.

Simons, H. 1938. *Personal Income Taxation: The Definition of Income as a Problem of Fiscal Policy*. Chicago: University of Chicago Press.

Skatteverket Rapport 2007: 2, *Enklare skatter för ökad jämställdhet*.

Soler Roch, M. 1999. Introduction in *Family Taxation in Europe*, edited by M. Soler Roch. The Hague, London, Boston: Kluwer Law International.

Spangenberg, U. 2011. Indirect Discrimination in Tax Law: The Case of Tax Deductions for Contributions to Employer-provided Pension Plans in Germany, in *Challenging Gender Inequality in Tax Policy Making: Comparative Perspectives*, edited by K. Brooks, Å. Gunnarsson, L. Philipps and M. Wersig. Oxford: Hart Publishing, 253–273.

Stang Dahl, T. 1988. *Women's Law*. Oslo: Norwegian University Press.

Staudt, N. 1996. Taxing Housework. *Georgetown Law Journal*, 84(5), 1571–1647.

Stewart, M. 2011. Gender Equity in Australia's Tax System: A Capabilities Approach, in *Challenging Gender Inequality in Tax Policy Making: Comparative Perspectives*, edited by K. Brooks, Å. Gunnarsson, L. Philipps and M. Wersig. Oxford: Hart Publishing, 53–73.

Surrey, S. 1973. *Pathways to Tax Reform*. Cambridge: Harvard University Press.

Thévenon, O. 2008. *Does Fertility Respond to Work and Family-life Reconciliation Policies in France?* CESifo Conference on Fertility and Public Policy: How to Reverse the Trend of Declining Birth Rates, 1–2 February 2008.

Vada, R. 2007. *Satsning på kvinner som naeringsutövere*. Fagbokforlaget, Bergen.

Villagomez, E. 2004. *Gender Responsive Budgets: Issues, Good Practices and Policy Options.'* Regional Symposium on Mainstreaming Gender into Economic Policies. NNNUU Comisón Económica para Europa.

Villota de, P. and Ferrari, I. 2004. *Reflexiones sobre el IRPF la perspectiva de género: La Discriinación fiscal del/de la segundo/a preceptor/a*. Instituto de Estudios Fiscales, Universidad Complutense de Madrid.

Villota de, P. 2011. A Gender Perspective Approach Regarding the Impact of Income Tax on Wage-earning Women in Spain, in *Challenging Gender Inequality in Tax Policy Making: Comparative Perspectives*, edited by K. Brooks, Å. Gunnarsson, L. Philipps and M. Wersig. Oxford: Hart Publishing, 109–133.

Walby, S. 2005. Gender Mainstreaming: Productive Tensions in Theory and Practice. *Social Politics: International Studies in Gender, State and Society*, 12(3), 321–343.

Wersig, M. 2011. Overcoming the Gender Inequalities of Joint Taxation and Income Splitting: The Case of Germany, in *Challenging Gender Inequality in Tax Policy Making: Comparative Perspectives*, edited by K. Brooks, Å. Gunnarsson, L. Philipps and M. Wersig. Oxford: Hart Publishing, 213–231.

Young, C. 1997. Taxing Times for Women: Feminism Confronts Tax Policy, in *Tax Conversations. A Guide to the Key Issues in the Tax Reform Debate*, edited by R. Krever. London, The Hague, Boston: Kluwer Law International, 261–292.

Young, C. 2000. *Women, Tax and Social Programs: The Gendered Impact of Funding Social Programs through the Tax System*. Ottawa: Status of Women Canada

Åmark, K. 2005. *Hundra år av välfärdspolitik. Välfärdens framväxt i Norge och Sverige*. Umeå: Boréa Bokförlag.

# From Women and Labour Law to Putting Gender and Law to Work

## Judy Fudge

My goal in this chapter is to reconstruct the main themes and key debates that have threaded through the 'feminist theoretical project' in labour law. I will begin by defining my terms, and setting out the scope of the endeavour. I am borrowing the phrase 'feminist theoretical project' from Joanne Conaghan (1999: 17) who laid out some of the theoretical foundations of feminist labour law scholarship. She identified three core features of this project: first, that feminist scholarship ought to highlight and explore the gendered nature of accounts of the social world; second, that it should focus on disadvantage and change; and finally, that it should place women at the centre of the analysis. Like Conaghan, I believe that the scope of what counts as labour law is ideological and not conceptual (Conaghan 1999: 21, Fudge 2011a: 136).[1] A distinctive contribution of much recent feminist scholarship is that it has expanded the reach of labour law's domain, to include women's unpaid work that takes place in the household, and, thus, feminists have expanded labour law's normative concerns beyond redistribution to include recognition of identity and status (Conaghan 1999).

In this chapter I use the term 'reconstruct' advisedly when referring to the feminist theoretical project in labour law because it is simply not possible to summarize the key theoretical debates. In the 1970s and 1980s, feminists who wrote about labour law were not very explicit about their theoretical approaches and commitments. In fact, early attempts to classify feminist approaches used fairly traditional political labels such as 'liberal', 'integrative', 'socialist' and 'radical' feminism (Conaghan 2000: 357). It was only in the 1990s that a more explicitly theoretical, specifically epistemological, classificatory system was adopted (Conaghan 2000). Carol Smart (1995), for example, identifies 'feminist empiricism', 'standpoint feminist' and 'postmodern feminist' approaches to law, and to this list 'materialist feminism' can be added (Conaghan 2000, Fudge and Cossman 2002, Fudge and Owens 2006). At the same time as feminist legal scholars became increasingly self-reflective about feminist theoretical approaches, we also became more conscious of theoretical debates about how 'labour' is conceived and about how 'law' is understood. While a distinctively feminist approach to labour, one which extends the boundaries of the field beyond paid work to unpaid caring labour, has developed (Rittich 2002b), feminist approaches to law

---

1   'Labour law' is conventionally defined to denote a specific subject of regulation, employment relations, and law to encompass a variety of legal forms. It refers to the legal regulation of individual and collective employment via contract, statute and collective bargaining, and it includes the application of legislation and common law by administrators, statutory adjudicators, private arbitrators and the courts.

have tended to adapt other theoretical approaches, such as liberal, critical legal studies and postmodernist.

My reconstruction of the key theoretical themes and debates in feminist labour law scholarship will historicize the scholarship (Fraser 2005) in order to reveal how it was 'shaped by social milieu, political background, and theoretical debates of the time' (Sangster 2010: 2). My goal is to re-contextualize and re-interpret feminist labour law scholarship in light of the concepts and questions that have percolated beneath the surface. Using this approach I argue that it is possible to discern three conceptual shifts in the feminist legal literature on employment and labour law over the past 30 years. The first shift is away from focusing on women as a unified category of analysis and object of study to exploring gender as a constructed, contested and differentiated social relationship. The second shift broadens the scope of inquiry beyond formal employment contracts to the labour market in general and the relationship between unpaid and paid work in particular. The third shift is from an instrumental conception of law in which law is seen as a tool for remedying sex discrimination to a more complex and multi-dimensional understanding of the relationship between law and society. These shifts in feminist legal writing about employment and work both reflect and are informed by changes in feminist and legal theory. They also track profound changes in the structure and operation of labour markets, the organization of production and the politics and power of the nation state.

The chapter begins by showing how the literature in the 1970s and the 1980s concentrated on identifying and remedying women's employment inequality. This work tended to focus on specific dimensions of, or topics relating to, women's inequality, such as unequal pay, occupational segregation, sexual harassment and discrimination on the basis of pregnancy. The overarching debate during this period was whether an approach to equality that emphasized women's sameness to men or one that emphasized women's differences, especially women's role as child bearers and carers, was more effective in redressing women's subordination. Most of the literature was oriented towards law reform. Law was regarded as instrumental, and theoretical approaches tended to map on to political claims. Feminist concerns with labour law were deeply linked with the second wave of the feminist movement.[2]

In the 1990s, feminist concerns about addressing various axes of subordination that influenced a women's social location combined with the erosion of the standard employment relationship to reveal differences between women and the profoundly gendered nature of employment norms. The third section discusses how feminist legal researchers attempted to develop both a transformative conception of equality and a postmodern understanding of law that appreciated its discursive and ideological effects. Following this discussion, the chapter focuses on some key themes – the relationship between gender and intersectionality, the conflict between employment and unpaid, but socially necessary, work and the shift from instrumental to discursive conceptions of law – that have shaped contemporary feminist labour law literature. The chapter concludes by summarizing some of the major achievements in feminist theorizing about labour law and identifying some of the key issues with which feminists who study labour law continue to grapple.

---

2    For a discussion of second wave feminism, see Fraser 2005.

## Using Law to Achieve Women's Equality in Employment: 1970s and 1980s

In the 1970s, a literature that focused on women in labour law emerged in the United States (Williams 2000: 204–226). It tended to concentrate on topics that specifically pertained to women such as pregnancy and maternity leave, wage discrimination, occupational segregation and sexual harassment. The focus was not on the broad field of labour law; instead, it was on what, from a labour law perspective, is a narrower subfield – anti-discrimination law.[3] The primary question was how to redress women's unequal treatment in employment. Law was primarily viewed as instrumental, a tool to remedy a social problem. However, although there was general agreement among feminist scholars who focused on women as the key subjects of labour law that the problem was women's inequality and law was a solution, there were profound disagreements about whether the best strategy for improving women's employment situation was to emphasize their sameness with or difference from men.[4]

The rise of a feminist legal literature on women's equality in employment was fuelled by the increase in women's labour force participation that took off in the mid-1960s and continued throughout the 1970s. Marriage bars in the civil service (many of which took the form of subordinate legislation such as regulations) that prohibited the employment of married women were repealed throughout the 1960s as women joined the ranks of the expanding public sector (Fudge 2002). Legislation outlawing sex discrimination in employment began to be enacted in advanced industrialized countries in the mid-1960s. The second wave of the women's movement demanded women's autonomy and equality and, despite political divisions between social, liberal and radical feminists, there was general agreement that anti-discrimination law could be used to improve women's situation (Fredman 1997, Fudge 2002, Williams 2010).

Initially, there was little explicit theorizing in feminist labour law scholarship. However, the selection of the topic or dimension of women's inequality in employment reflected important distinctions in broader theoretical approaches, especially in the United States. Feminists who examined the legal treatment of pregnancy in employment were worried that a focus exclusively on women's sameness with men would disadvantage women because of their biological difference from men. They wanted legislation that enabled a woman to take leave to give birth and care for an infant, and then return to her job. These feminists focused on women's differences from men (see, for example, Krieger and Cooney 1983, Littleton 1987). Yet at the same time, feminists who were concerned with occupational segregation and women's unequal pay emphasized the similarities between men and women, and challenged employment practices and laws that treated women differently than men (see, for instance, Ginsberg 1975, Williams 1992). Feminists who emphasized equality and sameness were concerned that protective legislation stressed women's roles as mothers at the expense of their need to earn an adequate income for themselves, their children and others, and that this emphasis would stigmatize women. The problem with this approach is that it tackles

---

3    I recognize that from an anti-discrimination perspective, labour law and women are specific areas within a broader field.

4    For a discussion of the debate in the US literature see Williams 2000: 204–226, Williams 2010: 109–138, Albitson 2009: 1130.

the symptoms but not the causes of women's inequality, which are the household division of labour, violence against women and sexism.

Feminist legal scholars have characterized these approaches to women's inequality as caught on the horns of the sameness/difference dilemma, which is a version of what political theorist Carole Pateman labelled the 'Wollstonecraft dilemma'. According to Pateman (1989: 196), the 'two routes towards citizenship that women have pursued are mutually incompatible within the confines of the patriarchal welfare state, and within that context they are impossible to achieve'.[5] On the one hand – mostly liberal – women have demanded that the ideal of citizenship be extended to them and they have insisted on gender-neutrality. For women to achieve this form of 'universal' citizenship they must participate in paid employment in the same way that men do. However, to do that they must abandon the domestic and private sphere of women's distinctive work. On the other hand, women have demanded that women's unpaid domestic work, especially their tasks as mothers, be recognized as productive and, therefore, a contribution to the welfare state. The problem with the sameness/difference dilemma is that it:

> *belies the hard choices that women must make when they choose between social policies that emphasize their differences from men and those that insist that men and women be treated as alike for workplace purposes. These choices are often blurred. (Wikander et al. 1995: 2)*

Some feminist legal scholars found a way out of this dilemma by changing how they conceptualized law; instead of regarding it as a neutral instrument, they saw law's so-called neutrality as embodying a male bias (MacKinnon 1987). The goal of this strand of feminist legal scholarship is to show how laws that are gender neutral on their face impact on men and women differently. Conaghan (1986: 377) observed that, apart from sex discrimination law, equal pay legislation and the maternity provisions in which women were explicitly recognized, 'labour law is a world made up of full-time male breadwinners and the legal rules reflect this conception of the male worker'. Similarly, in a review of textbooks and casebooks on Australian labour law, Rosemary Hunter (1991) looked at how the law fails to take into account the experiences and values that seem more typical of women than men. Her goal was to reveal the 'masculinist bias' in labour law by tracing how gender is implicated in rules and practices that otherwise appear to be neutral. She also drew upon Pateman's theory of the 'sexual contract' to illustrate how the non-regulation of the private sphere of the household really means the freedom for men to exercise untrammelled patriarchal power in that domain.

## Gender at Work: The 1990s

The concern to 'unmask the male perspective in law' in order to enable 'us to give due weight to that of women' was a central theme of feminist approaches to labour law during the 1990s (Fredman 1997: 3). Ranging over a broad historical canvass, in *Women and the Law*, Sandra Fredman sought to identify and deconstruct male bias when it comes to the legal regulation of employment. She examined the social reality of women's lives and

---

5    By citizenship, Pateman (1989) is referring to full participation in all realms of social life.

contrasted it with the idealized male worker embodied in employment norms. In doing so, she recognized that 'the business of revealing perspectives has its own momentum' (Fredman 1997: 3). Referring to Elizabeth Spelman (1991: 3), Fredman acknowledged that there is no unitary female perspective, and that 'the nature of subordination differs between women depending on other factors such as race, class, sexual orientation, marital status and parenthood'. Despite this caveat, she argued that 'gender is an important and at times determinative feature in the pattern of domination' that needs to be studied in conjunction with other forms of domination (ibid.).

Fredman's book exemplifies the three-fold shift in the theoretical commitments of feminist labour law scholarship described in the introduction: from women to gender, from employment to work and away from an instrumental view of law to one that sees law as ideological and institutional. Yet, although Fredman deploys the concept of gender, and understands the significance of socially constructed norms in justifying the different treatment of men and women, she does not elaborate upon it. By contrast, she developed the relationship between women's 'private' unpaid caring and domestic duties and women's paid employment, illustrating how the former shapes the latter, which embodies the male norm of the unencumbered worker. Moreover, Fredman illustrated the tension in law between the 'tenacious status ascriptions to which the law continues to subscribe and the liberal tenets which underpin much of the legal framework' (Fredman 1997: 36). She maintained that equality claims reify and reinforce the male employment norm and alternatively argued that:

> real change requires far more radical intervention, in which legal forms are complemented by wide-ranging social measures opening the door to balanced participation by women in paid work and facilitating balanced participation by men in family work. Such measures require changes in working time for both men and women, a high level of child-care provision, and parental leave for both parents on sustainable levels of pay. (Fredman 1997: 415)

In the 1990s, feminist labour law scholars and theorists, especially those of a materialist persuasion, also specifically linked the broader feminist challenge to the male breadwinner norms embedded in labour law to changes in the structure and operation of labour markets (Conaghan 1999, Fudge 1991a, Fudge 1997). From the end of World War II, the normative focus of labour law had been the standard employment relationship, which was an ongoing and full-time job that was regulated by a mixture of collective bargaining and statutory standards and provided the male head of the household with sufficient income to support a dependent wife and children throughout the lifecycle. The standard employment relationship and its male breadwinner ideal assumed, and depended upon, a female-housewife gender contract in which women did not work for wages and took care of domestic and household responsibilities (Fudge and Vosko 2001). In the early 1980s, the two-fold feminization of labour (the increase in the labour force participation rates of women and the deterioration in jobs caused by economic restructuring) and a policy emphasis on flexible labour markets undermined the male employment norm (Fudge 1991b). The restructuring of wages reduced the capacity of households to live on a single-male wage. At the same time, because women continued to perform a disproportionate share of caring and household responsibilities, they were unable to compete equally in the labour market for good jobs. Women tended to work in atypical and non-standard forms of precarious work (Fudge and Owens 2006), which enabled them to supplement the declining male wage but did not provide them with full independence (Owens 2002).

Conaghan (1999: 26) noted that it 'is only as the male norm of full-time, long-term employment has broken down, following a growing economic demand for more flexible working arrangements, that labour law has properly begun to recognize and address the situation of the "atypical" (predominantly female) worker who does not correspond to the legally enshrined one'. Changes in the structure and operation of the labour market, combined with a more sophisticated approach to inclusive equality (Sheppard 2010) presaged a recognition of the significance and contingency of the boundary between production – the domain of men and paid employment – and reproduction – women's domestic realm of the family. As women's employment rate rose and promoting women's paid employment became an increasingly desirable public policy goal in advanced welfare states, reconciling the conflict between work and family life came to be seen as an important goal of labour law. Feminists, however, used the conflict as an aperture to re-imagine the scope of labour law, broadening it to encompass the law of work. According to Joanne Conaghan and Kerry Rittich (2005: 1), the 'application of a feminist lens to the world of work has served simultaneously to highlight and problematize the structural and discursive boundaries between work and family, production and reproduction, paid and unpaid work'.

Feminist labour law scholarship in the 1990s was also much more explicitly theoretically self-conscious than that of its forebears. It was no longer so tightly linked with political positions and became more epistemological as feminists explicitly examined the discursive and political foundation of conventional understandings of labour law and gender (Conaghan 2002: 357 referring to Smart 1995). This epistemological turn incorporated several further developments. There was a shift from an initial, and important, concern to reveal the masculinist bias at work to discussion of how gendered norms operated in the labour market. At the same time the admonition not to essentialize women (Spelman 1991) fuelled scholarship that looked at how various social relations of subordination – especially race and gender – intersected. Attempts to expand the activities that count as work to unpaid caring and household labour (Waring 1988) and the increased recognition of paid work in the home (Prügl 1996) troubled the traditional work–family divide that has long been at the heart of labour law. Simultaneously, feminist legal scholars began to explore the discursive, and not simply the instrumental, power of law. The remaining sections of the chapter deal with these three matters in turn.

## From Women to Gender

A common feature of feminist labour law scholarship is its 'women-centredness'. However, the enduring focus on 'women' obscures both changes in, and debates over, how 'women' was conceptualized. The focus on women was closely related to feminist standpoint theory, which starts from the assumption that because women's lives and roles in almost all societies are significantly different from men's, women have a different type of knowledge. According to Nancy Hartsock (1983), women's contributions to subsistence and childrearing result in a systematic difference of experience for women and men: women's location as a subordinated group allows women to see and understand the world in ways that are different from, and challenging to, the existing male-biased conventional wisdom. In the field of labour law, both Marion Crain (1991, 1992) and Gillian Lester (1991) focused on women's experience of collective bargaining in the United States and Canada to show how the dominant 'masculinist' model of collective bargaining disadvantaged women. Each drew upon women's experience of work and unions to suggest strategies to empower women,[6] and both critiqued male-centred notions of power as adversarial and hierarchical, and contrasted them with women-centred views.

This feminist labour law scholarship was important not only because it was explicitly theoretical, but also because it focused on the centre of labour law – collective bargaining – and not the margin, which is anti-discrimination law. Moreover, Crain cautioned feminists not to 'essentialize' women, and to recognize that other oppressions – such as race and class – intersect with sex (Crain 1992: 1824). She also claimed that law was not simply a tool to remedy discrimination, since law itself 'articulates and reflects patriarchy' (Crain 1991: 489).

Although standpoint feminism revealed the structural bias in labour law in favour of men's work, especially paid employment in the manufacturing sector, it was criticized for failing to recognize the many differences that divide women. There were two strands of the criticism that standpoint feminism assumed a universal 'women's experience'. The first complained of the failure of standpoint feminists to appreciate other systems of domination such as capitalism, racism, homophobia and colonialism. In response, feminists absorbed this criticism, and developed the idea of 'intersectionality'. Building on the work of Kimberly Crenshaw (1989) in the United States, Nitya Duclos (1993) and Diamond Ashiagbor (1999) demonstrated how anti-discrimination law in Canada and the United Kingdom, respectively, systematically ignored the claims of Black women.

The feminist scholarship that emphasized intersecting forms of discrimination in the labour market was a step away from treating women's experience as the touchstone of feminist analysis towards a social relations approach to understanding women's position in the labour market. Instead of concentrating on experience and identity, feminists increasingly focused on status and social relations and were careful to avoid the claim that all categories of subordination had the same ontological status (Fudge and Cossman 2002).

The second strand of the critique of standpoint feminism was from postmodern feminists, who argued that there is no concrete 'women's experience' from which to construct knowledge. However, instead of emphasizing the need to incorporate other social relations into an analysis of women's subordination, they challenged the categories of 'man' and 'woman', arguing that they are discursive and socially constructed, and not ontological categories. In order to stress the discursive nature of these social relations, feminists increasingly referred to 'gender' instead of 'women' in their analyses.

Feminists writing about labour law tended to conceive of gender as the social process by which significance and value is attributed to sexual difference through symbols, concepts and institutions (Fudge 1997: 253). They drew upon the work of feminist historians, some of whom were influenced by postmodernism (Scott 1986). According to this view, gender discourses naturalize sexual differences through family relations, sexuality, state institutions and work practices that organize procreation and maintain the population (Lerner 1997, Scott 1986). Labour markets, because they 'operate at the intersection of ways in which people make a living and care for themselves', are bearers and reinforcers of gender (Elson 1999: 612). Joan Williams (2010) noted that the beauty of the market is its ability to transmit

---

6    Crain specifically considered the potential and basis for building an alliance between the feminist and labour movements. Lester focused on changes to collective bargaining law that were more women-friendly.

socially created preferences efficiently, including those pertaining to racial and gender norms, for example.

Gender is both material, in the sense that it is crucial to how work and families are organized and human life is reproduced in the short and long term in any society, and cultural, in that gender signifies values that permeate society. What the concept of gender does is provide an explicitly historical, relational and dynamic understanding of how inequality in the labour market is configured, refashioned and challenged. A feminist-inspired gender analysis explicitly recognizes that gender is a socially constructed relationship and, thus, departs from feminist standpoint theory that treats women's experience as an ontological and epistemological touchstone. A gender analysis is sensitive to how gender relations change over time and to how gender is intertwined with other social relations such as age, class and race, for example.

Feminist labour law scholars from the 1990s onwards have shown how employment relations are gendered (Conaghan 1999, Fredman 1997, Fudge 1997, Fudge and Owens 2006). Norms about the forms and role of law and types of worker shape labour markets, labour institutions and labour law. These norms select, organize and describe salient features of the social environment and emerge out of and in relation to particular historical processes. Moreover, they have a power beyond their verisimilitude. For example, immediately after World War I, although one-quarter of Canadian women were the sole breadwinners for dependent children, the norm of male breadwinning obscured this social and economic reality when it came to setting minimum wages for women, where the assumption that women had no dependents prevailed (McCallum 1986, Fudge 1991a). The power of legal and employment norms is ideological and discursive, and these norms can develop a life of their own that is quasi-independent of actually existing social relations.

Feminists have demonstrated the gendered nature of the standard employment relationship, which has been the fulcrum of labour law and regulation since the end of World War II.[7] Not only has the standard employment relationship pertained – initially exclusively and now predominantly – to men, it rested upon a gendered division of labour in which women had the primary responsibility for the socially necessary, but generally unpaid labour that occurred within the household. Some feminists who write about labour law have referred to a gender contract, which blends Pateman's (1989) notion of a sexual contract with the idea of social contract, a concept that aims to capture social, legal and political norms surrounding the exchange between breadwinning and caregiving, protection and freedom, and public and private responsibility (Fudge and Vosko 2001, Vosko 2010). The notion of gender contract seeks to capture how the gendered division of labour in the public sphere of employment is deeply connected to the gendered division of labour within the private sphere of the family and household.

The erosion of the standard employment relationship and the proliferation of feminized forms of employment, which are poorly paid, part-time and insecure, have eaten away at the basis of the traditional gender contract (Fudge and Vosko 2001). But, although the material basis for the traditional gender contract has been eroded, especially since the 1980s, with the decline in male wage and the increase in women's labour force participation, the continued gender division of labour within the family has undermined women's employment equality.

---

7    The standard employment relationship is a full-time year-round employment relationship with a single employer that is highly regulated by labour law and/or unions (Fudge and Vosko 2001).

Feminist legal scholars have shown how masculine and feminine norms and roles that were designed for the 1950s and 1960s no longer pertain today (Williams 2010). In most industrialized countries, the majority of women, including those who live in a household with another adult and have young children, work for wages. However, despite the increase in women's labour force participation, which is known as the feminization of employment, work – both in the public and private spheres – remains a deeply gendered activity. Women work at jobs that are different from those of men. Labour markets are hierarchically segmented according to gender (Rittich 2002b). Thus, feminists have argued that labour markets, the family and welfare policy are witnessing the simultaneous intensification and erosion of gender (Fudge and Cossman 2002: 25).

Walby (1997: 2), for example, identified a convergence and polarization in the contemporary restructuring of gender relations. In some ways, the visibility and relevance of gender difference is disappearing as the employment experiences of men and women converge. Yet, in other ways, the relevance of gender in the labour market is increasingly marked. Although the employment history of many women increasingly resembles that of men as women continue to work after childbirth and while they are raising children, women remain overrepresented in precarious employment (jobs that are temporary, part-time, insecure, lacking in benefits, and poorly paid) in order to accommodate their disproportionate share of unpaid caring and domestic labour. These processes of intensification and erosion, of convergence and divergence, are occurring both within labour market and family institutions and discourses.

## Broadening the Conception of Work

Women's precarious position in the labour market is inextricably bound up with the gendered division of labour in the family. Feminist legal scholars have deployed the concept of gender to probe the permeable and changing boundary of what counts as work. They have focused in particular on the relationship between paid employment and family. Conaghan (2005: 19) claims that a 'focus on the operation of the work/family dichotomy in labour law offers a window through which to (re)view and (re)consider labour law's fundamentals'. She challenges traditional labour law theory's emphasis on disciplinary unity and coherence, and calls instead for an approach that draws on feminist standpoint theory that incorporates the postmodern insight that labour law does not have a unitary subject but one that is fluid and fragmentary (ibid.: 36). She endorses a critical and reflexive theoretical stance that advocates surveying 'the field from a marginalized point of view' (ibid.: 35). Conaghan argues that 'labour law is beset by boundaries' that rest on:

> dichotomized pairing of concepts hierarchically positioned in relation to one another: public/private; work/family; paid/unpaid; employed/unemployed; formal/ informal economy; typical/atypical workers; standard/nonstandard work; regulation/ deregulation; citizens/aliens, to name but a few. (Conaghan 2005: 38)

The problem with these boundaries is that they create hierarchies and exclusions. A crucial disciplinary boundary for labour law has been that between work and family or paid and unpaid labour. These boundaries are profoundly gendered. Thus, Conaghan (2005: 40) warns: '[u]nless, and until, labour lawyers confront the full consequence of the gender division of labour in terms of effective and entrenching inegalitarian work relations, any project of progressive transformation through labour law is likely to founder.'[8]

Recent labour law scholarship has sought to widen the ambit of the field of labour law beyond employment to cover the labour market more generally (Fudge 2011a). This expanded conception of labour law's domain, which has been driven by the breakdown of the standard employment relationship, is congruent with recent feminist labour law scholarship, although, generally, most labour law scholars have not adopted a feminist approach to understanding the labour market. The concept of social reproduction, which is drawn from political economy literature, has been used by feminists to illuminate the significance of women's unpaid labour for the functioning of labour markets. 'Social reproduction' refers to the social processes and labour that go into the daily and generational maintenance of the population. It also involves the reproduction of bodies and minds located in historical times and geographic spaces. It 'includes the provision of material resources (food, clothing, housing, transport) and the training of individual capabilities necessary for interaction in the social context of a particular time and place' (Picchio 2003: 2). Social reproduction is typically organized by families in households and by the state through health, education, welfare and immigration policies (Fudge 2011a). It can also be organized through the market and through voluntary organizations such as churches. Production and reproduction are highly gendered. However, as Rittich (2002b: 129) notes, 'there is nothing natural or inevitable about the boundaries between productive and reproductive activity or the ability of different parties to pass on or absorb greater or lesser parts of the costs of production'.

Traditional accounts of work and labour law have ignored all of the unpaid domestic work, overwhelmingly performed by women, that is involved in maintaining living spaces, buying, and transforming the commodities used in the family, supplementing the services provided to family members by the public and private sectors, caring for people and managing social and personal relationships. Feminists have emphasized how the gendered division of paid and unpaid work has negative distributive consequences for women (Rittich 2002a). Some have claimed that 'the reconciliation of paid work to unpaid care is arguably the most pressing problem currently facing labour law', and have argued for the need to shift the emphasis from the employment rights of carers to the provision of caring rights for those who engage in paid work (Busby 2011: 1). However, in doing so, feminists have been careful to caution against an 'institutional and political preoccupation with family-friendly policies', and instead to broaden the focus to appreciate the extent to which the gender contract has been destabilized (Conaghan 2005: 40, see also Fudge 2005: 266). Feminists have also observed that the instability in the current gender contract presents an opportunity for a more egalitarian division of reproductive and productive labour.

While many feminist labour law scholars have begun to stress the importance of unpaid care work and rights for care providers in order to achieve substantive equality for women in the labour market, other feminist labour law scholars, such as Vicki Schultz, for example, continue to emphasize the significance of paid work to the good life and women's equality. Although Schultz (2000) agrees that it is vitally important to create society-wide mechanisms in order both to allocate the costs of household labour and to enable people to realize their

---

8   Similarly, Rittich (2002b: 124) observes had there been serious engagement with the situation of women in the labour market, it seems highly unlikely that the world of production would have been defined as it is, and the intersection of unpaid work and market work would have been placed beyond the concerns of labour law.

preferences, unlike other feminist labour law scholars, she does not acknowledge the limits to the commodification of care (Busby 2011, Fudge 2011a, 2011c). Referring to work of the economist Jean Gardiner (1997), Linda McDowell (2001: 460) has argued that 'those aspects of domestic provision that entail the giving of care are particularly resistant to commodification as the relations of exchange are not susceptible to monetary evaluation'. Shultz's sensitivity to the institutional contexts in which household work is valued and individual choices are realized does not fully appreciate the distinctive features of caring activities. Care is more than a task that can be performed in exchange for wages; it is embedded in personal relationships of love and obligation, and is a crucial part of identity formation (Fudge 2011a: 132). Treating care work as work, that is, as a socially necessary activity that is a matter of obligation and initiative, rather than women's natural role, results in a profound reconceptualization of labour law (Fudge 2011a: 132). I have argued that:

> in societies that value paid employment as the primary path to "citizenship", treating
> unpaid care work, the socially necessary labour predominantly performed by women,
> as a matter of social or family law, and not labour law, reinforces the idea that such
> work is not only a woman's natural role, but also that in the social hierarchy it is of
> lower value than paid employment. (Fudge 2011a: 136)

A feminist reconceptualization of labour law requires scholars to comprehend that the relations of social reproduction are as important as employment relations (and productive relations more generally) for individual development as well as viable and sustainable societies. The conflict between the competing demands of employment and social reproduction cannot be resolved through the wholesale commodification of care.

The commodification of caring labour has been characterized as the new Wollstonecraft dilemma – does it strengthen or weaken the gendered division of labour? (Lister 1997). This dilemma is particularly acute in the current era of globalization. Feminist political economists have argued that gender inequalities are constitutive of contemporary patterns of intensified globalization, and that gender differences in migration flows often reflect the way in which gender divisions of labour are incorporated into uneven economic development processes (Herrera 2008: 94). They have emphasized the connection between migrant care work, globalization and the privatization of social reproduction. They note that many of the women who leave the South to work in the North are temporary migrant workers who do not enjoy either the right to become permanent residents in their host country or the right to circulate freely in the labour market. Given the basic gender division of labour in destination countries, women migrants are often restricted to traditionally 'female' occupations – such as domestic work, care work, nursing, work in the domestic services and sex work – that are frequently unstable jobs marked by low wages, the absence of social services and poor working conditions (Antonpoulos 2008: 38).

Arlie Hochschild (2000: 131) coined the term the 'global care chain' to refer to 'a series of personal links between people across the globe based on the paid or unpaid work of caring'. Global care chains are transnational networks that are formed for the purpose of maintaining daily life; these networks comprise households that transfer their caregiving tasks across borders on the basis of power axes as well as employment agencies, governments and their departments, and other agents, institutions and organizations (Orozco 2009). Ann Stewart (2011) combines the notion of global care chain with a feminist relational framework of ethics of care to explore the relationship between gender, justice and law in a global market. She notes that commodifying care work may solve the care crisis in the North at the expense of creating a care crisis in the South (see also Fudge 2011b, 2011c). Global care chains exemplify the globalization of services.

The globalization of services helps to create a new international division of immaterial labour. 'Immaterial labour' is a term coined by Michael Hardt and Antonio Negri (2001: 290) to describe labour that 'produces an immaterial good, such as a service, a cultural product, a knowledge or communication'. They identify three forms of immaterial labour: the first involves industrial production that has incorporated information technologies; the second is analytic and symbolic labour involved in computer and communication work, which can either involve creative manipulation or be routine; and the third is affective labour that has traditionally been regarded as women's caring work. Not only are these 'categories infused with class relations', they are profoundly gendered (Kelsey 2008: 189). The gender-saturated nature of immaterial labour is particularly true of 'affective' labour, which is associated with women and care.

Global care chains illustrate the shift from industrial to immaterial, especially affective, labour, and expose 'the conceptual limitations of labour law within the present context of globalisation' (Stewart 2011: 312). The first limitation is the territorial scope of labour law (Mundlak 2009), which is starkly revealed by migrant labour (Williams 2002). In this context, the precarious migrant status of migrant workers undermines labour rights and standards initially for migrant workers and, in the longer term, for all but those few workers whose credentials and skills are officially recognized and valued (Fudge 2012).

The second conceptual limitation of labour law is its:

> *failure to recognize fully the changed nature of the labour relations that occurs when caring is performed in the market through relationships that are personalised, less time bound and conducted in "private" workplaces. As a result, the conditions in which the content – "affect" – is performed can result in more extraction of the workers' labour than is acceptable.* (Stewart 2011: 313)

Feminist political economists and labour law scholars have argued that not only do global care chains illustrate the ways in which unequal resources are distributed globally (Hassim 2008: 397), they also reveal the gendered nature of this inequality. Thus, they claim that it is not possible to consider gender equality in a comprehensive manner without considering global redistribution (Hassim 2008, Stewart 2007). As a result, feminist labour law scholars have broadened the scope of labour law in two important ways. The first is to expand the scale of labour law so that it is no longer unquestionably identified with the territory of the nation state, and the second is to expand it materially, so that it includes the processes of social reproduction, which include both immigration and unpaid work in the household. The partial de-territorialization, the recognition that labour law operates beyond the boundaries of the nation state, challenges feminists, and other labour law scholars, to develop normative foundations for labour law that are not confined to narrow conceptions of national citizenship. Simultaneously, by expanding the material scope of labour law to include caring labour, whether paid or unpaid, feminist labour law scholars are at the forefront of grappling the specific dynamics governing affective or embodied labour. For example, focusing on the conflict between the obligation to care and the need to work for an income, Emily Grabham (2011) has examined how flexibility in the context of work–life balance debates is discursively created through legal documentation, such as case reports, that operate within prescribed networks and practices. Increasingly, contemporary feminists tend to emphasize the discursive power of law.

## From Law as Instrumental to Law as a Gendering Practice

The least explicitly theorized aspect of feminist labour law scholarship is how law is conceptualized. Law is no longer understood as a neutral tool or instrument that can 'solve' the problem of women's inequality. Nor do most feminists accept the positivist tenet that law can be understood as autonomous from society (Lacey 1998: 9). Feminist labour law scholars appreciate that law has both institutional and normative dimensions. Law is an important site for the production of discourses that play a powerful role in shaping consciousness and behaviour. Some feminists consider law to be a gendering practice, which constitutes 'male' and 'female' subject positions and contributes to identity formation. According to Conaghan (2000: 363), '[w]ithin such a theoretical framework, law is relocated as one of a range of practices through which gender is acquired, a *process* of which gender and gender differences are an *effect*'. Conaghan and Rittich (2005: 3), for example, consider how the terrain of work is legally constituted and regulated though the creation and deployment of distinctions such as public and private, work and family, production and reproduction. Rittich (2002a, 2002b) is also attentive to the distributional consequences of gender at work. Other feminists emphasize the coercive force of law that distinguishes it from other discourses (Fudge and Cossman 2002: 5).

Recently, Grabham (2011) has focused on how legal technologies and texts, such as adjudication and case reports, create discourses and subjectivities that result in a specific understanding of flexibility at work in which women's labour is seen as infinitely elastic. She elucidates how legal networks of actors and texts orient themselves in time, and she cautions against prevailing conceptions of work–life balance that condemn women to precarious work and require women to adapt to employer-driven flexibility.

Other feminist legal scholars have broadened the notion of law beyond standard legal texts and officials to regard it as a system of enacted norms that operates outside of the 'official' state legal system (Lacey 1998: 9). Stewart (2011: 61) adopts a 'strong' legal pluralist account of law, which assumes that there are multiple forms of ordering beyond state law that govern legal subjects. Focusing on the impact of globalization on legal discourse, she emphasizes the extent to which law is porous and how it interacts with other social fields. Stewart treats law as a system of thought or discourse rather than a system of rules, and, thus, she identifies one of the tasks of feminist labour law scholars as mapping the relationship between 'interpenetrating legalities' that operate at a number of scales from the local, through the regional and national, to the transnational and international.[9] She also recognizes that legal discourses are not stable, but are constantly changing.

Most contemporary feminist labour law scholars accept legal pluralism, at least in the weak variety, and recognize that discourses of legality are deeply entwined with other social discourses.[10] They also recognize that legal discourses have a distinctive relationship

---

9  Stewart (2010: 61) refers to Melissaris (2004), who, in turn, refers to De Sousa Santos (2002).
10 Weak pluralism accepts the centrality of state law, but recognizes the existence of customary and Islamic law, for example, in post-colonial contexts. Strong pluralists recognize multiple forms of ordering that are not dependent upon the state (Stewart 2010: 60–61).

to the state. Moreover, by and large, feminist labour law scholars accept that that law has no 'essential' meaning; although there are structural and institutional biases, there are contradictions in law that can be exploited with a view towards contesting existing gender roles and relations. The challenge is to developed nuanced accounts of law that are not confined to the nation state, while, at the same time, appreciating the specific power of legality, which is its close proximity to both justice and coercion, and harnessing this view of law with the overall goal of redressing women's material inequality and discursive difference.

## Conclusion

The erosion of the standard employment relationship, the male breadwinner and female housewife gender contract, the vertically integrated firm and the hegemony of the nation state have created a crisis for labour law as its norms have been weakened and its ability to protect workers has been undermined. Despite a flourishing feminist labour law scholarship that challenges the traditional boundaries of labour law, it has proven difficult to move gender from the margin to the centre of the discipline. As Conaghan and Rittich (2005: 2) note, 'while virtually all labour regulation strategies are necessarily shaped and informed by encounters at the boundaries of productive and reproductive realms, labour law fails to acknowledge or take account of this in large part because of the lack of conceptual apparatus to identify and chart such encounters'. Feminists have long claimed that women's location in the labour market should be addressed as a moral matter of substantive inequality; now we are also arguing that it is a conceptual necessity to attend to the specificity of women's paid and unpaid work in order to understand how labour markets operate. Excluding unpaid care work from the scope of labour law is an example of what the philosopher Elizabeth Anderson (1999: 311–312) characterizes as a 'perfect reproduction of Poor Law thinking, including its sexism and its conflation of responsible work with market wage-earning'. Feminist labour law scholarship is now at the forefront of the discipline in reconceiving the material scope of labour law to include all of the processes that make up the labour market, including social reproduction (Fudge 2011a, Stewart 2011).

Moreover, feminist legal scholars who concentrate on global care chains are challenging the nation state as the appropriate frame of labour law and the methodological nationalism (Wimmer and Schiller 2002) with which it is associated. Public policies in developed countries that emphasize increasing women's employment rates without simultaneously stressing the obligations of men to engage in care activities are likely to perpetuate global care chains in which women from poor countries migrate to richer countries to perform care work (Fudge 2011c, Stewart 2011). Such policies not only reinforce the gendered nature of care work, they perpetuate global inequality. More generally, Lucie Williams (2002: 95) has argued that 'privileging nation-state waged work as the site for redistributive politics ignores and devalues the needs and concerns of millions of low and non-waged workers in a globalized economy'.

And finally, feminist labour law scholars are questioning whether the traditional normative basis of labour law, which is to mediate the unequal power relations between employers and employees, provides sufficient grounding for the discipline. Some, like Stewart (2011), are drawing upon the ethic of care, which is based on relationship and connection, rather than on individualism, to ground normative positions. Others, like Nicole

Busby (2011) and Fudge (2011), are turning to modified versions of the capabilities approach (Nussbaum 2000, Sen 1999), to provide the conceptual tools for a robust understanding of substantive equality.

However, despite the conceptual and normative advances of feminist labour law theory, there is more work to be done. Understanding the role and characteristics of immaterial and affective labour as labour markets globalize, challenging the binary opposition between male and female in order to convey and appreciate the full array of sexualities and gender relations (Chapman 2005, Conaghan and Grabham 2007), and attending to the nuanced and contradictory roles of legal institutions and discourses, and how they interact with other forms of social-ordering discourses, are some of the intellectual and political tasks with which feminist labour law scholars continue to grapple.

# References

Albitson, C. 2009. Institutional inequality. *Wisconsin Law Review*, 29(5), 1093–1168.

Anderson, E. 1999. What is the point of equality? *Ethics*, 109(2), 287–337.

Antonpoulos, R. 2008. The Unpaid Care Work–Paid Work Connection. The Levy Economics Institute of Bard College, Working Paper No. 541. Available at: www.levyinstitute.org/publications/?docid=1081.

Ashiagbor, D. 1999. The intersection between gender and 'race' in the labour market: lessons for anti-discrimination law, in *Feminist Perspectives on Employment Law*, edited by A. Morris and T. O'Donnell. London: Cavendish, 139–160.

Busby, N. 2011. *A Right to Care? Unpaid Work in European Employment Law*. Oxford Monographs on Labour Law, Oxford University Press.

Chapman, A. 2005. Challenging the Constitution of the (White and Straight) Family in Work and Family Scholarship. *Law in Context*, 23(1), 65–87.

Conaghan, J. 1986. The invisibility of women in labour law: gender-neutrality in model-building. *International Journal of the Sociology of Law*, 14, 377–392.

Conaghan, J. 1999. Feminism and labour law: contesting the terrain, in *Feminist Perspectives on Employment Law*, edited by A. Morris and T. O'Donnell. London: Cavendish, 13–42.

Conaghan, J. 2000. Reassessing the feminist theoretical project in law. *Journal of Law and Society*, 27(3), 351–385.

Conaghan, J. 2002. Women, work and family: a British revolution? in *Labour Law in an Era of Globalization: Transformative Practices and Possibilities*, edited by J. Conaghan, R.M. Fischl and K. Klare. Oxford: Oxford University Press, 54–73.

Conaghan, J. 2006. Time to dream? Flexibility, families and the regulation of working time, in *Precarious Work, Women, and the New Economy: The Challenge to Legal Norms*, edited by J. Fudge and R. Owens. Oxford: Hart, 101–130.

Conaghan, J. and Grabham, E. 2007. Sexuality and the Citizen-Carer: The 'Good Gay' and the Third Way. *Northern Ireland Legal Quarterly*, 58(3), 325–342.

Conaghan, J. and Rittich, K. 2005. Introduction: interrogating the work/family divide, in *Labour Law, Work, and Family: Critical and Comparative Perspectives*, edited by J. Conaghan and K. Rittich, Oxford: Oxford University Press, 1–18.

Crain, M. 1991. Images of power in labor law: a feminist deconstruction. *Boston College Law Review*, 33(3), 481–538.

Crain, M. 1992. Feminism, labor, and power. *Southern California Law Review*, 65(4), 1819–1886.

Crenshaw, K. 1989. Demarginalizing the intersection of race and sex: a black feminist critique of antidiscrimination doctrine, feminist theory and antiracist politics. *University of Chicago Legal Forum*, 1989, 139–168.

Duclos, N. 1993. Disappearing women: racial minority women in human rights cases. *Canadian Journal of Women and the Law*, 6(2), 25–51.

Elson, D. 1999. Labour markets as gendered institutions: equality, efficiency and empowerment issues. *World Development*, 27(3), 611–627.

Fraser, N. 2005. Mapping the feminist imagination: from redistribution to recognition to representation. *Constellations*, 12(3), 295–307.

Fredman, S. 1997. *Women and the Law*. Oxford: Clarendon Press.

Fudge, J. 1991a. *Labour Law's Little Sister: The Employment Standards Act and the Feminization of Labour*. Ottawa: Canadian Centre for Policy Alternatives.

Fudge, J. 1991b. Reconceiving employment standards legislation: labour law's little sister and the feminization of labour. *Journal of Law and Social Policy*, 7, 73–89.

Fudge, J. 1997. Rungs on the labour law ladder: using gender to challenge hierarchy. *Saskatchewan Law Review*. 60(2), 237–263.

Fudge, J. 2002. From segregation to privatization: equality, law and women public servants, 1908–2000, in *Privatization, Law and the Challenge to Feminism*, edited by B. Cossman and J. Fudge. Toronto: University of Toronto Press, 86–127.

Fudge, J. 2005. The new duel-earner gender contract: work–life balance or working-time flexibility?, in *Labour Law, Work and Family: Critical and Comparative Perspectives*, edited by J. Conaghan and K. Rittich. Oxford: Oxford University Press, 261–288.

Fudge, J. 2011a . Labour as a 'fictive commodity': radically reconceptualizing labour law, in *The Idea of Labour Law*, edited by G. Davidov and B. Langille. Oxford: Oxford University Press, 120–135.

Fudge, J. 2011b. Global care chains, employment agencies and the conundrum of jurisdiction: decent work for domestic workers in Canada. *Canadian Journal of Women and The Law*, 23(1), 235–264.

Fudge, J. 2011c. Gender, equality and capabilities, in *The Role of Labour Standards in Sustainable Development: Theory in Practice*, edited by T. Novitz and D. Mangan. London: Oxford University Press/The British Academy.

Fudge, J. 2012. Precarious Migrant Status and Precarious Employment: The Paradox of International Rights for Migrant Workers. *Comparative Labor Law and Policy Journal*, 34(1), 101–137.

Fudge, J. and Cossman, B. 2002. Privatization, law and the challenge to feminism, in *Privatization, Law and the Challenge to Feminism*, edited by J. Fudge and B. Cossman. Toronto: University of Toronto Press, 3–37.

Fudge, J. and Owens, R. (eds), 2006. *Precarious Work, Women, and the New Economy: The Challenge to Legal Norms*. Oxford: Hart Publishing.

Fudge, J. and Vosko, L. 2001. Gender, segmentation and the standard employment relationship in Canadian labour law and policy. *Economic and Industrial Democracy*, 22(2), 271–310.

Gardiner, J. 1997. *Gender, Care and Economics*. Basingstoke: Macmillan.

Ginsberg, R. 1975. Gender and the Constitution. *University of Cincinnati Law Review*, 44, 1–42.

Grabham, E. 2011. Doing things with time: flexibility, adaptability, and elasticity in UK equality cases. *Canadian Journal of Law and Society*, 26(3), 485–508.

Hardt, M. and Negri, A. 2001. *Empire*. Cambridge: Harvard University Press.

Hartsock, N. 1983. The feminist standpoint, in *Discovering Reality*, edited by S. Harding and M.B. Hintikka. Dordrecht, Holland: D. Riedel Publishing Company, 283–310.

Hassim, S. 2008. Global constraints on gender equality in care work. *Politics and Society*, 36(3), 388–402.

Herrera, G. 2008. States, work and social reproduction through the lens of migrant experience: Ecuadorian domestic workers in Madrid, in *Beyond States and Markets: The Challenges of Social Reproduction*, edited by I. Bakker and R. Silvey. London: Routledge, 93–107.

Hochschild, A.R. 2000. Global care chains and emotional surplus value, in *On the Edge: Living with Global Capitalism*, edited by W. Hutton and A. Giddens. London: Jonathon Cape, 131–146.

Hunter, R. 1991. Representing gender in legal analysis: a case/book study in labour law. *Melbourne University Law Review*, 18(2), 305–327.

Kelsey, J. 2008. *Serving Whose Interests: The Political Economy of Trade in Services Agreements.* Abingdon: Routledge-Cavendish.

Krieger, L.J. and Cooney, P.N. 1983. The Miller-Wohl controversy: equal treatment, positive action and the meaning of women's equality. *Golden Gate University Law Review*, 13(3), 513–572.

Lacey, N. 1998. *Unspeakable Subjects: Feminist Essays in Legal and Social Theory.* Oxford: Hart Publishing.

Lester, G. 1991. Toward the feminization of collective bargaining law. *McGill Law Journal*, 36(4), 1181–1221.

Lerner, G. 1997. *Why History Matters: Life and Thought.* New York: Oxford University Press.

Lister, R. 1997. *Citizenship: Feminist Perspectives.* Basingstoke: Macmillan.

Littleton, C. A. 1987. Reconstructing sexual equality. *California Law Review*, 75(4), 1279–1337.

MacKinnon, C. 1987. *Feminism Unmodified: Discourses on Life and Law.* Cambridge: Harvard University Press.

McCallum, M. 1986. Keeping women in their place: the minimum wage in Canada. *Labour/ Le Travail*, 17, 29–56.

McDowell, L. 2001. Father and Ford revisited: gender, class and employment change in the new millennium. *Transactions of the Institute of British Geographers*, 26(4), 448–464.

Melissaris, E. 2004. The more the merrier: a new take on legal pluralism. *Social and Legal Studies*, 13(1), 57–79.

Mundlak, G. 2009. De-territorializing labor law. *Law and Ethics of Human Rights*, 3(2), 189–222.

Nussbaum, M. 2000. *Women and Human Development: the Capabilities Approach.* Cambridge: Cambridge University Press.

Orozco, A. P. 2009. *Global Care Chains (Gender, Migration and Development Series).* The United Nations International Research and Training Institute for the Advancement of Women, Working Paper No. 2. Available at: www.un-instraw.org/data/media/documents/GCC/WORKING%20PAPER%202%20%20INGLES.pdf.

Owens, R. 2002. Decent work for the contingent workforce in the new economy. *Australian Journal of Labour Law*, 15(3), 209–234.

Pateman, C. 1988. *The Sexual Contract.* Cambridge: Polity Press.

Pateman, C. 1989. *The Disorder of Women: Democracy, Feminism and Political Theory.* Cambridge: Polity Press.

Picchio, A. 1992. *Social Reproduction: The Political Economy of the Labour Market.* Cambridge: Cambridge University Press.

Picchio, A. 2003. A Macroeconomic Approach to an Extended Standard of Living, in *Unpaid Work and the Economy: A Gender Analysis of the Standard of Living*, edited by A. Picchio. New York: Routledge, 1–10.

Prügl, E. 1996. Biases in labor law: a critique from the standpoint of home-based workers, in *Homeworkers in Global Perspective: Invisible No More*, edited by E. Boris and E. Prügl. New York: Routledge, 203–218.

Rittich, K. 2002a. *Recharacterizing Restucturing: Law, Distribution and Gender in Market Reform*. Boston: Kluwer Law International.

Rittich, K. 2002b. Feminization and contingency: regulating the stakes of work for women, in *Labour Law in an Era of Globalization: Transformative Practices and Possibilities*, edited by J. Conaghan, R.M. Fischl and K. Klare. Oxford: Oxford University Press, 117–136.

Sangster, J. 2010. *Through Feminist Eyes: Essays on Canadian Women's History*. Edmonton: Athabasca University Press.

Santos, B. 2002. *Toward a New Legal Common Sense: Law, Globalisation and Emancipation*. London: Butterworths.

Schultz, V. 2000. Life's Work. *Columbia Law Review*, 100(7), 1881–1964.

Schultz, V. 2010. Feminism and workplace flexibility. *Connecticut Law Review*, 42(4), 1203–1222.

Scott, J. 1986. Gender: a useful category of historical analysis. *The American Historical Review*, 91(5), 1053–1075.

Sen, A. 1999. *Development as Freedom*. Oxford: Oxford University Press.

Sheppard, C. 2010. *Inclusive Equality: The Relational Dimensions of Systemic Discrimination in Canada*. Montreal: McGill-Queen's University Press.

Smart, C. 1995. *Law, Crime and Sexuality: Essays in Feminism*. London: Sage Publications.

Spelman, E. 1991. *Inessential Woman: Problems of Exclusion in Feminist Thought*. Boston: Beacon Press.

Stewart, A. 2007. Who do we care about? Reflections on gender justice in a global market. *Northern Ireland Legal Quarterly*, 58(3), 358–374.

Stewart, A. 2011. *Gender, Law and Justice in a Global Market*. Cambridge: Cambridge University Press.

Vosko, L. 2010. *Managing the Margins: Gender, Citizenship, and the International Regulation of Precarious Employment*. Oxford: Oxford University Press.

Walby, S. 1997. *Gender Transformations*. London: Routledge

Waring, M. 1988. *If Women Counted: A New Feminist Economics*. San Francisco: Harper and Row.

Wikander, U., Kessler-Harris, A. and Lewis, J. 1995. Introduction, in *Protecting Women: Labor Legislation in Europe, the United States, and Australia, 1880–1920*, edited by U. Wikander, A. Kessler-Harris and J. Lewis. Urbana and Chicago: University of Illinois Press, 1–28.

Williams, J. 2000. *Unbending Gender Why Family and Work Conflict and What To Do About It*. Oxford: Oxford University Press.

Williams, L. 2002. Beyond labour law's parochialism: a re-envisioning of the discourse of redistribution, in *Labor Law in an Era of Globalization: Transformative Practices and Possibilities*, edited by J. Conaghan, R.M. Fischl and K. Klare. Oxford: Oxford University Press, 93–116.

Williams, J. 2010. *Reshaping the Work Family Debate: Why Men and Class Matter*. Cambridge: Harvard University Press.

Williams, W.W. 1992. The equality crisis: some reflections on culture, courts and feminism. *Women's Rights Law Reporter*, 14(2), 151–174.

Wimmer, A. and Schiller, G. 2002. Methodological nationalism and beyond: nation-state building, migration and the social sciences. *Global Networks*, 2(4), 301–334.

# Gender, Justice and Law in a Global Market

## Ann Stewart

Recognition of women's human rights has been a focus for international activism for over 30 years. Political campaigns, such as those to confront tolerance of myriad forms of violence against women, have been successful in forcing the position of women on to the international stage. These battles were hard fought and fraught with tensions but nonetheless the 'culturally sensitive' universalism (Engle 2005) that emerged laid the cornerstones for creative use of rights by women's activist groups throughout the world. The positive momentum of this movement was reflected in the UN conferences of the 1990s, a period of optimism. However, the rights framework emerged against the backdrop of the profound economic, social and political changes associated with the collapse of the Soviet system and the triumph of neoliberal economic development, which has resulted in the contemporary forms of globalization of the twenty-first century.

Until recently, feminist engagement with the theories and practices of development has followed a different path. Rooted in the wider discourse of development, practitioners have tackled the gender blind nature of much economic development theory and practice, and highlighted the consequent impact of the unequal distribution of economic and social resources within Global South communities and states. Gender and development campaigners succeeded in ensuring that gender concerns have been 'mainstreamed' into normative frameworks and multilateral and state based development policies. Does this represent another success story?

The first half of this chapter traces the contribution of rights and development discourse to the achievement of women's wellbeing. Until the late 1990s, these were separate stories to a large extent. However, since then a rights approach to development, involving advocacy and empowerment strategies, has permeated development discourse and policy, resulting in a seeming merger of the two. Arguably, the importation of rights into development provides a powerful new 'tool' for gender activists because of the normative centrality of equality and non-discrimination to the concept of rights. Equally, the engagement of human rights activists with those who work with the effects of economic and social processes can enrich the jurisprudence of rights.

However, the guarded optimism of the 1990s has been replaced in the twenty-first century with a growing realization that feminism has lost its emancipatory edge in an era of globalization. It is, of course, important not to forget that for the many whose everyday lives are not conducted within states and communities in which rights have any resonance, the power of its language can hold out some hope. However, it is clear that the language of rights has been accommodated within neoliberal economic policies and that a concept which has been influenced by feminist analysis can, however unwittingly, underpin such policies. Rights may have addressed some deficits in recognition but they have not delivered a more equal world or significant benefits to the vast majority of women. Rights based approaches to development are not used as a means by which to implement the distribution of resources from the Global North to the South but as a top-down bureaucratic prescription for Global South governments or 'failing states' which need aid or arms.

The second half of the chapter further develops this theme. It considers, in particular, the implications for feminist legal analysis of the rapidly changing relations of production and social reproduction (the broad ranging processes needed to nurture and reproduce us all such as the provision of food, clothing, shelter, social and cultural values) associated worldwide with the development of global consumer based market economies. Traditionally, such care and nurture have been undertaken within families and have been the primary responsibility of women. Market based economies increasingly commodify such nurture, transforming relationships of interdependence, mutuality and trust into bought goods and services. These developments, coupled with the continued undervaluation of unpaid care place new strains on gender relations and a more general loss or depletion in what can be called socially reproductive capital. This section draws upon the feminist analysis associated with the ethics of care to explore these changes and to argue that this approach offers a basis for a politics of redistribution in an era of globalization. However, it also highlights the way in which the concept of care is increasingly being resignified within market discourses in the context of the rise of service economies. The challenge, therefore, is to ensure that care continues to be a feminist concept which does not 'go rogue'.

The present period of relatively uncontained global crisis reaffirms the need for a 'structural turn' in feminist analysis, which is not reductionist, but which places it more firmly within political economy. The contribution of Karl Polanyi and in particular the feminist rewriting of his approach by Nancy Fraser suggests a way of doing this. Polanyi, in his historical account of the rise of the market economy in England, argued that the modern market economy and the modern nation state are inextricably linked human inventions. The resulting market society is a combination of economic processes and social actions. The 'market' is not separate from society. Fraser, while using his frame of analysis, injects concepts drawn from feminism, in particular those of emancipation and non-discrimination, to provide an analysis which addresses the crises in contemporary market societies which include the deep problems relating to caring. The second part of this chapter assesses the extent to which such an approach can be put to work to address issues relating to women's involvement in global markets and the depletion in socially reproductive capital. More broadly, it also explores the extent to which it can operate to realign feminism with global gender justice.

## International Development

Development as a concept, although rooted in a long history of colonialism and imperialism, came into being to mark out the West from the 'underdeveloped' other in the immediate aftermath of the Second World War. The knowledge underpinning the scientific advances and industrialization that formed the foundations for progress in the West was to be transferred to underdeveloped areas to tackle the misery in which half the world was living. As Shirin Rai points out (2011a: 14–18) 'development' appeared in the context of the divide between the socialist and capitalist world orders, the consolidation of post-war hierarchies of power and nationalist struggles. The Third World emerged in contradistinction to the Western First World and Soviet Bloc Second World. Third World countries, as they emerged as postcolonial states, found it difficult to carve out their own approaches to development in the Cold War era. However, despite differences of position and ideology, members of all three Worlds (with the exception of China in this period) considered that economic growth was linked to industrialization and urbanization and with the mechanization of agriculture.

Today, the dominant discourse of development is still economic, as is indicated by the way in which development is measured in the annual reports of the World Bank (the key multilateral development agency). However, the more recent influence of a 'human development' approach, championed by the United Nations Development Programme, has stretched the boundaries of the 'economic' to include indices on education and health and a gender equality index. Nonetheless, political development has always played a part in international development policies although such assistance is generally understood to be 'technical' rather than an intervention in local politics.

The failure of development assistance to produce economic 'lift off' in 'underdeveloped' countries led some development bodies to focus on the need for democratization, which it was assumed would lead to greater efficiency and accountability. At the same time, it led others to re-characterize the relationship between First and Third Worlds as one of maintaining dependency within peripheral states to advantage those at the core. For the Bretton Woods institutions[1] in the first camp, the answer was better and smaller government; meanwhile, for some Third World/Global South[2] states in the second camp, the answer was reduced dependence on the capitalist world order. However, the debt crises which resulted in the economic rescue of Global South states by the Bretton Woods institutions in the 1980s put an end to this movement towards autonomy. Structural Adjustment Policies (SAPs) required states to implement neoliberal policies which involved state withdrawal from economic activity to enable markets to develop and national growth to be stimulated by reduction in state debt. These policies, which included privatization of some services and payment for others, such as health and schooling, had deeply detrimental impacts on vulnerable groups in society, particularly women, whose responsibilities revolve around caring.

The hardships inflicted on citizens by what were clearly seen as external agencies, coupled with their failure to produce the goods – that is, to stimulate sustainable growth – produced a rethink in the 1990s. SAPs were replaced by Poverty Reduction Strategy Papers (PRSPs), which recognized that the state had a role in supporting good governance and poverty alleviation. PRSPs required citizen participation, although such involvement tended to become consultation conducted by external agents.

The context in which such top-down development strategies function has changed significantly in recent years. Globalization, based upon neoliberalism, coupled with the collapse of the Soviet bloc and rise in the economies of the 'emerging markets' (Brazil, Russia, India, China, South Africa) has destabilized an already shaky concept of international

---

1   The Bretton Woods agreement in 1944 established the rules and institutions, which included the International Monetary Fund (IMF) and the International Bank for Reconstruction and Development (IBRD), now part of the World Bank Group, to regulate the international monetary system among the major industrial states at the time.

2   There is a range of terms used within development discourse to describe the recipients of its attention: Third World, developing, Global South. My preference is for Global South but the other terminology is used here where appropriate.

development. An ideological distinction between First, Second and Third Worlds is increasingly meaningless. India, for instance, is described as an 'economic superpower' with markets to which First World states are desperate to gain access, while still receiving development aid from the same states to assist the third of its massive population which lives in abject poverty. New types of states described as 'failed and post conflict' have emerged and are associated with the politics of security and the rise of the ideology of terrorism. Development assistance is increasingly tied, although with dismal evidence of impact, to international security agendas rather than on indices directly associated with GDP or wellbeing.

It is therefore not surprising that there are critiques from a number of different ideologically placed constituencies which argue for an end to development on the basis that it causes more harm than good, reduces entrepreneurial agency and encourages dependency, wastes taxpayers' money due to corruption, inefficiency and failures to deliver, or leads to anti-democratic, unaccountable top-down state interventions that stifle counter hegemonic social movements.

## Moving to Gender and Development

Rai (2011b) identifies the now familiar strands of feminist analysis that have contributed to critiques of dominant development discourses. The 'Women in Development' (WID) approach argued powerfully that women must benefit equally from modernization while not questioning the modernization agenda. This critique focused on the inefficiency as well as lack of equality when women are marginalized from all aspects of the economy. So, for instance, feminists adopting this approach have exposed the gendered nature of policies such as those relating to the mechanization of agricultural production and now the securitization of land as an economic asset, which do not consider the impact on women who produce food using minimal technology for family security (Williams 2003, Manji 2006). In contemporary contexts, this is the 'business case' for women's inclusion.

The 'Basic Needs' approach challenged the assumption that wealth would eventually 'trickle down' to the majority of the population. Championed by the International Labour Organisation (ILO), the specialist UN agency concerned primarily with (paid) employment, this approach argued that the goal of development should be the 'satisfaction of an absolute level of basic needs' (ILO 1977: 31). The understanding of needs encompassed not only tangible essentials such as food but also political essentials such as participation and community life. Its association with the ILO, however, meant that, while the needs of all humans are covered, little attention was given to the marginality of women's paid work and the centrality of family relations to women's wellbeing.

The more recent 'human capabilities' approach is rooted in the same soil, although much more aware of the relationship between the world of the family and work. Amartya Sen (1999) argues that human beings require entitlements in order to realize the capabilities that constitute the basis of a life worth living. It is essential that human beings are free to maximize these entitlements. Freedom supported by rights, therefore, is a development goal in itself. Labour remains a core capability for the vast majority of people so 'the conditions of labour should be central to any analysis of entitlements' (Rai 2011b: 30). Nevertheless, Martha Nussbaum (1999a and b) has torn through the ideological public/private divide to insist that women (as well as men) are entitled to choose to be emotional, playful and desiring individuals and that power relationships within families cannot deny access to choice on these and other entitlements. Family relationships therefore can be of concern to development policy makers.

Materialist feminists provided critiques of these liberal approaches (Elson and Pearson 1981, Beneria 2003). They highlighted the similarities between the position of women and that of the Third World in international and national capital accumulation and pointed to the way in which women's labour is devalued, for instance treated as housework or undertaken informally as homework (Mies 1982), and therefore exploited both by men and by capital through its association with the social reproductive sphere of the family.

Perhaps the most trenchant criticism of strategies predicated upon growth and modernization came from the eco-feminist movement and its understanding of sustainable development (Shiva and Mies 1993). Highlighting the assumed relationship between women and nature this movement has linked women's position with the degradation of the environment associated with the relentless (and patriarchal) pursuit of economic growth. While this link between women and nature worries many, the debate over how to meet needs sustainably is now centre stage (for further discussion, see Morrow in this collection).

By 1990, feminist engagements had shifted from a focus on 'women' to analyses of the 'gender contract' based up the division of labour within the home and in waged work and to assessments of the power relations that control access to resources. The discursive power of this 'gender and development' (GAD) approach is generally acknowledged: '"Gender" has been foundational, both as an organizing principle and a rallying call, for [a wide range] of discourse coalitions' (Cornwall et al. 2007: 5). It became a political force in the transnational civil society arena provided by a number of UN conferences of the 1990s. As a result, it found its way into international discourse on environment, rights, population, social development, human habitat, women, food, trade and finance at a time when the focus was moving to 'politicized concerns with delivering human rights and more holistic concepts of development' (Harcourt 2009: 27). Accordingly, gender was 'mainstreamed' into a wide variety of development institutions including those responsible for international human rights implementation (Charlesworth 2005).

While the 'landslide' of GAD *discourse* might have been celebrated as a success story (Cornwall et al. 2007: 5), subsequent lack of progress, epitomized by the contrast between the Beijing Platform for Action in 1995, which set out a wide range of gender based development objectives and the anaemic counterparts in the Millennium Development Goals, has provoked a reassessment. Mainstreaming has not led to visible effects on institutional policies and practices (Charlesworth 2005) despite enormous efforts to develop frameworks, tools and mechanisms to implement gender sensitive policies. Women have undoubtedly become subjects of development. However 'poor women with an expertly understood set of needs and rights' who were once victims 'in need of aid' have along the way been transformed into 'working subjects with productive potential, willing and useful agents for development'; but they are still impoverished (Harcourt 2009: 28).

When such gender mainstreaming is imposed externally upon states, it can become the stick with which to beat recipient government bureaucrats leading to inertia at best and backlashes at worst. It can become 'governance feminism'. It may privilege the voices of funded 'gender compliant' NGOs over women's social movements (Jad 2007) such as in relation to human trafficking (O'Connell-Davidson and Anderson 2006). GAD's emancipatory potential has been almost completely dissipated, leading to another widely held view that 'gender' has 'fallen from favour and has a jaded, dated feel to it' (Cornwall et al. 2007: 5).

## From Legal to Rights Based Approaches to Development?

Law has its own history within development theory and practice (Tamanaha 2008) and legal feminists have engaged in similar struggles to shape content and implementation (Stewart 2011: chapter 2). The early law and development movement was rooted in an emancipatory project. Although disillusion with the limits to this project soon set in, lawyers sought to use law as a tool to assist newly emerged postcolonial states in achieving social justice (Trubeck and Galanter 1974). Thereafter, law's contribution to development became the subject of academic critiques which revealed the complex nature of law in postcolonial states and the ways in which law supported hierarchies of power both within states but also between the Global North and South (Ghai et al. 1987, Shivji 1993). Analysis focused upon the ideology of the rule of law and of rights, constitutionalism, and the plurality of law in postcolonial societies, influenced by the work of anthropologists, sociologists and historians (Griffiths 1986, Chanock 1985).

Not surprisingly, given the marginal position of women within the legal academy in the Global North and even more so in the Global South, much of this early work was gender blind. However, since the 1980s, scholarship on gender within law in development has emerged. It has reshaped understandings through its focus on the impact of family, community and religious institutions on the distribution of assets (Armstrong 1992, Griffiths 1997, Nyamu-Musembi 2002, Patel 2007), analysis of the impact of legal pluralism on women's lives (Griffiths 2002, Hellum et al. 2007, Manji 2006), on violence against women in public and private spheres (Merry 2006, Kannibaran 2005), women's access to justice (Tsanga 2004, 2007, Mehra 2007), and more recently for the recognition of sexual identities (Kapur 2005, Tamale 2008, 2011). There is a close relationship with local women's organizations and with regional and trans-national activist networks where the discourse of rights, rather than development, tends to feature more prominently.

This gender and law scholarship had, however, little impact on the institutional development context partly because law itself was marginalized. The role for law within neoliberal development policies of the 80s and early 90s tended to be limited to providing the infrastructure to support markets and security for investors. This discourse of good governance and the rule of law involved the reduction of state regulation to a minimum (Faundez 1997, Faundez et al. 2000) but afforded it no role in facilitating social or redistributive justice. The destabilizing effects of these policies, including the sheer misery imposed on sections of populations, led to a certain rehabilitation of the state to provide the necessary social safety nets. Thereafter, there has been an expanded role for the state and law in tackling issues relating to security and terrorism in post conflict and failed states. Newly defined 'rule of law' projects have proliferated (Trubeck 2006) but seemingly learned little from critical law in development analyses (Trubek 2009, Hammergren 2010).

These projects have mainstreamed a limited gender analysis resulting in a lack of practical impact on women's lives. In particular, feminist analyses of the impact of the power relationships associated with the plurality of institutions – customary, religious and familial – which structure women's lives have been incorporated into some forms of development discourse as 'non state institutions' (ICHRP 2009). Yet these analyses have little resonance with the discourse of good governance, democratization and *formal* women's rights described by Deniz Kandiyoti as the 'trinity' of contemporary international development policy. This trinity is deployed in a context of 'armed "democratization" and regime change' (Kandiyoti 2007: 191) and in 'failing' and failed states 'which are war torn, lacking almost any governance institutions' and 'whose political economies are based on illegal trade in drugs, arms and high value commodities' (Kandiyoti 2007: 191).

Since the last decade of the twentieth century, the struggle for discursive power within the various development institutions has centred on the now dominant 'rights based approach' (RBA) which seeks to connect the power of a legally constructed concept of rights to development theory and practice. Given the range of meanings attached to the term, it is more appropriate to describe these in the plural – as approaches (that is, as RBAs) (Tsikata 2007). However, they all share a common legal basis in the normative framework of international and regional human rights instruments and therefore place accountability on states and international actors to ensure the implementation of policies which uphold the human rights of vulnerable groups. They all seek empowerment, participation and non-discrimination and are directed at redressing injustice rather than relieving suffering. They champion agency by individuals rather than victimhood.

It could be argued that what we are seeing here is the success of the international human rights movement, including that associated with women's rights, to deploy its discursive power in support of more emancipatory forms of development. The central importance of equality and non-discrimination, therefore, should benefit women. But how emancipatory are these approaches? Few acknowledge any link to the Declaration on the Right to Development 1986 (Cornwall and Nyamu-Musembi 2005). This Declaration, instigated by Global South states, heralded as a collective solidarity right, requires inter alia 'sustained action to promote more rapid development of developing countries' and 'effective international co-operation [to provide] countries with appropriate means and facilities to foster their comprehensive development' (Article 4 (2)). Proponents use the Declaration to argue for regulation of the global economy to ensure greater equality between states, for state duties to provide aid and assistance and as a means by which the human rights of all can be realized (Marks 2008). Few seek to tackle the 'roots of structural injustices rather than their effects' (Tsikata 2007: 215, Cornwall and Molyneux 2006).

In general, those implementing RBAs ignore analyses of the complex relationship between women, state and law (described briefly above). They fail to understand that rights are not easily attached to the activities of many international actors, such as the International Financial Institutions and Multinational Enterprises, but can be used by dominant development agencies to transfer responsibilities to Global South states. Southern governments are expected to guarantee more rights to citizens while transnational economic policies oblige them to restrict access to services. RBAs are also 'empowerment lite'. An effective right to participate in development would require a radical rethink in the practices of democracy (Benhabib 1996, An-Naim and Hammond 2002, Santos and Rodriquez-Gavarito 2005) and produce unpalatable outcomes for international development policy makers.

## Women's Human Rights and Culturally Sensitive Universalism

Other chapters in this collection address the issue of rights and international law so the discussion here will not rehearse the many conceptual reasons why rights may disappoint (see also Lacey 2004). This section confines itself to a consideration of the way in which the international women's rights discourse has emerged to reflect briefly on the consequences of the engagement between rights and development.

In her review of feminist critiques of international human rights law, Karen Engle identifies three approaches associated roughly with three time periods: in order, they are liberal inclusion, structural bias and third world (Engle 2005). The first sought to add women to the existing human rights protections; the second critiqued this approach arguing that international law and institutions permitted, even required, women's subordination; and the third critiqued both approaches for their 'exclusion or false representation of third world women' (2005: 49). Engle, echoing the earlier discussion here, argues that liberal inclusion has secured a place in mainstream discourse and that proponents of structural bias critiques, who argue that 'women's bodies constitute the locus of women's oppression', have 'compromised' with third world feminists to champion a new discourse – 'culturally sensitive universalism'. In the process, the cultural has become separated from the economic. The discourse thereby loses its ability to address issues of global injustice and to support redistributive strategies (Engle 2005: 50, Stewart 2011).

As we have seen, the international practice of 'women's human rights' is heavily associated with the UN system and its language (Merry 2006). This 'talk' is translated by women's legal activists into state based demands to tackle: many forms of violence against women; discrimination within customary, personal and religious laws relating to marriage and inheritance; and access to land and to political representation. However, this talk often fails to translate because it ignores the alternative understandings and power relationships operating within such contexts. Despite examples to the contrary, it is associated with individualism and elite concerns. It is also perceived as donor driven and therefore externally imposed. There has been much less focus on the core concerns of gender and development, which address the social and economic injustices that flow from the neoliberal macroeconomic development paradigm.

While 'gender' has been absorbed into the discourses of rights and development, and mainstreamed into the institutions most associated with them, its power in relation to the legal discourse associated with the global market is still much weaker. Gender based legal critiques of any sort relating to trade and finance have been resisted, despite growing scholarship in the area of international economic law (Beveridge 2005, Kelsey 2006, Rittich 2002, Bedford 2011) and attempts to develop human rights audits (Harrison 2007). There has been no equivalent mainstreaming into such institutions as the World Trade Organization (WTO) or the International Monetary Fund (IMF).

## The Argument So Far

To summarize the key points so far, we have witnessed long-term struggles to ensure that the interests of women are of central concern to both international development and human rights discourse and practice. On one level there has been considerable success: women's rights are recognized as human rights and 'gender' has been incorporated into development discourse. Development discourse has adopted concepts drawn from the domain of rights such as empowerment and agency. Yet this seemingly powerful combination of an institutionally supported gendered rights based approach to development has not resulted in significant improvements in women's lives (UNRISD 2005, UN Women 2011). Feminist critical engagement within development has faltered because this concept has lost any salience it might once have had. The ideological vanquishing of the Second World fuelled the form of market based globalization which has come to prominence in the last 30 years. The gender and development critique which linked social, economic and gender justice with institutional practice has been decoupled: recognition of women's entitlement to development has not resulted in redistribution of power and resources within a global market. Gender concerns have become the soft issues of development: 'the micro level adjuncts to the hard macro development issues of war, failed states, internal conflict, economic crisis, the restructuring and liberalizing of markets, security and trade agreements' (Harcourt 2009: 29).

The rights based approach has tackled concerns relating to culturally constructed differences, associated with what men do to women, but not economically determined disadvantages, associated with what economic processes do to women and men. States are now obliged through the development and rights discourse to tackle culturally based oppression – within families and communities – which is seen as bad for women *and* for market based development. Women can then join 'economic man' who has been freed to pursue his interests in the market.

## Do Women Benefit from Global Consumer Markets?

Feminists as well as economists recognize the importance of paid work: involvement in the 'productive' sphere of the economy provides income and supports values of independence, autonomy and choice. Opportunities for women to engage in the market have increased significantly: 60 per cent of women in developing countries (70 per cent in developed countries) are now involved in forms of paid labour (ILO undated). Women's engagement in the labour market challenges oppressive assumptions relating to the division of labour within family and community. Implicit gender contracts which do not value, but allocate socially reproductive, caring activities to women become more transparent. The development of a market in caring services and products potentially frees women from this unvalued familial labour and provides remuneration for those who undertake it. Feminist critiques of developmental (Global South) and bureaucratic (Global North) welfare states as often reinforcing existing familial and community patriarchal assumptions are recognizable to neoliberal economists who view overblown governments as obstacles to the entrepreneurial freedom of everyone.

Is the consequence of this 'fellow travelling' of feminism and proponents of contemporary forms of globalization (Fraser 2009) that all of us will benefit from engagement in the global market? That the state's role is to facilitate these processes? Somehow, the crucial theoretical insights gained from feminism have been lost – in particular, the relationship *between* productive and reproductive spheres of activity and the role played by the state in the provision of social welfare support which is so crucial to women's work and caring activities (Stewart 2011: chapter 2).

The relationship between social reproduction and production is being profoundly affected by contemporary globalization. Although differently constituted, socially constructed gender contracts (reflecting the gender division of labour) are under pressure across the globe as women are drawn into global markets while expected to maintain socially reproductive activities with limited and often shrinking social systems of support. Women's engagement with this market at present can result in triple burdens; undertaking paid work, family labour and compensating for the lack of social provision. Women (and men) are increasingly involved in survival migration and working in precarious conditions. As Ruth Pearson points out, 'being exploited by capital is the fate of virtually all women in today's global economy' (2007: 211, 2009). She argues that increasing wages will not on their own make women less poor or more powerful. Like others with roots in socialist feminism, she argues that it is essential to combine a guaranteed minimum income with labour regulation and supportive social policy.

The depletion in social reproductive capital which results from these global changes has profound effects not only for women but also for communities and societies (Pearson 2007, 2009, Hoskyns and Rai 2007). For instance, care 'deficits' in the Global North, in part produced by the unavailability of women's labour and the lack of a socially provided alternative, are met by commodification of care, which is provided by the commodified labour of migrant women body workers whose legitimacy as 'immigrants' is increasingly challenged politically. Migrant women care for the vulnerable in host societies, often working with minimal legal protection and for low wages, thereby keeping costs down in host societies, while endeavouring to support their families, emotionally and financially, at home. This transnational transfer of caring deeply affects the provision of care in labour exporting societies. More generally, it is questionable whether the market can provide a satisfactory replacement for caring relationships and provision based upon the values of solidarity, mutuality and love.

There is clearly a need to repoliticize feminist engagement (Cornwall et al. 2007: 15) and reunite the cultural with the economic. It is not about '"empowering" economic female or male subjects of global capitalism but creat[ing] conditions that allow lived bodies with diverse social, cultural and political expressions to flourish' (Harcourt 2009: 32).

It involves drawing on the insights from the materialist tradition of feminism, which brings the gendered relationship between production and social reproduction to the forefront. I have argued elsewhere that it also involves recognizing the contribution of ethical care analyses which focus upon the way in which identities are moulded through relationships and which privileges the values associated with caring – responsibility, attentiveness, responsiveness (Stewart 2011). It involves asking, in a global market, who do we care about? Only the proximate few (family, friends, fellow members of clans or those sharing ascribed identities)? Or wider cohorts (fellow citizens or non-citizens living alongside us, global citizens)? Does care extend to those upon whom we rely or who are linked with us in often invisible ways? We need to ask who benefits, in what ways and to what extent, by the social and economic processes of globalization. These questions are in contrast to, but do not preclude, such rights focused questions as: do others have the same rights as me? Or what are the barriers to realizing these rights?

## An Integrated Global Feminist Analysis

Here, however, I would like to consider the insights provided by the revival of interest in the work of Polanyi in the *Great Transformation*, first published in 1944 (2001) – and in particular,

Fraser's feminist re-reading,[3] which she uses to tackle the 'fellow travelling' of feminism and neoliberalism, discussed above (Fraser 2009).

The bare bones of Polanyi's argument are as follows. Historically, the economy was embedded in society (reliant upon social relationships) but developments in nineteenth-century Britain led to attempts to dis-embed the economy (to divorce it from social relationships) so that it functions as a self-regulating market. However, Polanyi stresses that the state is a constitutive element of a self-regulating market because it is required by those seeking to dis-embed the economy to provide the framework through which entrenched interests can be overcome. These moves provoked a counter movement (landed interests, workers, local/small business) for social protection which sought to use the state to re-embed the economy. This protection could be at both international and state level. He points, therefore, to a double movement; the first seeks to create the market which provokes the second, demanding social protection, although this is not necessarily progressive in form. It resulted in fascism in the 1930s. This double movement is the 'actor' element in his analysis. The 'system' element revolves around his concept of fictitious commodities. Polanyi argued that the process of creating a self-regulating market involves the incorporation of land, labour and money as commodities which, in his view, is a conceptual impossibility because they are not created through a market. The commodification of land, labour and money (the last of which he viewed as a social construct) destroys the very basis upon which the market depends – the social foundations of society – thereby setting the seeds of its own destruction.

The contemporary attraction of Polanyi's work is that it reveals the relationship between the 'economy' (global markets) and social relationships. The efforts to construct the first as 'self-regulating' have met with major problems in recent times. His concept of fictitious commodities can easily be transposed into three obvious contemporary areas of crisis – ecological, financial and that pertaining to socially reproductive labour. We can see the movements associated with each demanding social protection at national and international levels. Fraser, however, argues that Polanyi needs a feminist makeover (Fraser 2009). She introduces a third movement, associated with emancipatory struggles such as feminism and anti-imperialism (overlooked by Polanyi) to add to those associated with the struggle for a self-regulating market and for social protection. Their interest is, she argues, in non-domination. These movements are not wholly located within the spheres of activity of the other two – economy or society. Both feminism and anti-imperialist movements offer a critique of the market while recognizing its role in freeing up those who have been enslaved or confined within family and community institutions, as well as a critique of the role played by developmental and welfare state protectionism, which can replicate such hierarchies of power. She sees the value of the fictitious commodity concept but argues that in contemporary contexts it is essential to integrate the three rather than treat them as separate. She is wary of the potential to essentialize – to consider that non-commodification of land, labour and money can be the basis for a sustainable and progressive society. Feminism has revealed the extent to which the social construction of economic relations is gendered – how 'non-commodified' work of women in community and home is unvalued economically and takes place in conditions of unequal power relations. She rightly argues

---

3    Three lectures given at The Centre for Research in the Arts, Social Sciences and Humanities (CRASSH) University of Cambridge on 'A Polanyian Feminism? Re–reading The Great Transformation in the 21st Century' Tuesday, 8, 9 and 16 March 2011. Available at www.crassh.cam.ac.uk/events/1534/.

that it is not possible to return to or create non-commodified forms given the degree to which, in contemporary capitalism, the concepts have been commodified (for example body parts or genes). We need, therefore, to resist a communitarian, essentialist response in the movements for social protection to avoid 'doxa' or common-sense based responses which can reproduce women's lack of emancipation. What is needed instead, Fraser maintains, is a political process which is not statist, top-down and bureaucratic but which involves bottom-up democratic, participatory processes – identified as the space of civil society – to provide the basis for social protection designed to re-embed the market. In effect, to make the market work for the wellbeing of people rather than the reverse.

The strength of Fraser's approach is that she uses the triple movement concept to facilitate an assessment of the role of the market and social protection from the perspective of emancipation and an interest in non-domination. The market might not be all bad and social protection not all good. The latter can re-entrench hierarchies and mis-frame protection. This mis-framing can involve non-recognition of those upon whom citizens rely – undocumented workers for example. At the same time, she is able to use the framework to interrogate emancipation from the perspective of social protection and the movement for self-regulating markets. It becomes possible to assess the extent to which emancipation takes a form which reinforces the claims of the self-regulating market – individualism, autonomy and the destruction of social solidarity – or aligns itself with those of social protection, which seek to re-embed (regulate) economies to achieve an egalitarian gender and socially just world.

## Applying Polanyian Feminism

In this section, I intend to apply this approach to one example which distributes the benefits of globalization to the Global North in part by its ability to exploit both women's productive and reproductive labour in the Global South. By necessity, this discussion will be somewhat schematic (see Stewart 2011 for more detailed discussion of this and other examples).

Fruit and flowers are produced in Kenya to supply supermarkets in the UK to meet consumer demands for exotic or luxury items. This process takes place within a global value chain. The retailers determine every aspect of the product through detailed specifications which are passed down the supply chain. These specifications are designed to meet the exacting price and quality standards demanded by global north consumers while minimizing the suppliers' exposure to risk. Suppliers seek maximum flexibility through just in time ordering. These measures retain as large a slice of the total value of the product as possible for retailers. Other actors in the supply chain play their parts and take their slice of the value. Large commercial farmers in Kenya employ predominately women workers to pick, prepare and pack these products on farms and in packing houses near the airport. Farmers must absorb the risks associated with the ordering. There is every incentive to minimize these risks through 'flexibility' of labour, in other words to use casual and seasonal labour, which is women's work, due to culturally ascribed divisions of labour. The formal labour market is very small. Jobs in agribusiness are therefore sought after although women maintain their heavy responsibilities for social reproduction within the families and communities. Significant numbers of women provide for their families through semi-subsistence agriculture and/or informal activities in Kenya. The state provides minimal levels of social protection. Labour laws have recently been updated to provide rudimentary protections to casual workers but bestow greatest entitlements upon full-time employees.

Polanyi's first movement would involve the creation of a self-regulating market in food. A global dis-embedded market in food, built through the power of the giant retailers, has developed. The market in agricultural commodities has itself been subsumed within a speculative market in food futures. The incorporation of agriculture into the world trading system through the Agreement on Agriculture came relatively late but has led to reductions in trade barriers, although the European Union can resist in ways that Kenya cannot. The Kenyan state has been required to support the commodification of land, labour and finance to facilitate this market. Dominant neoliberal development policies have dismantled state marketing boards in Kenya, as elsewhere, to facilitate the development of a private market assisted by the wider fiscal measures associated with Structural Adjustment Policies. Land reform policies, which have encouraged privatization and securitization of land, challenge community held land systems. Kenya has established Export Processing Zones, which offer wide-ranging fiscal benefits for those located within them. As noted above, until recently, labour laws were rudimentary and union activity curtailed.

The attempts to establish a self-regulating dis-embedded food market has provoked moves for social protection from a number of constituencies. Within the world trading system, organized labour in association with other human rights activists have sought to introduce a social clause which would take account of workers' rights. This has been resisted by Southern states, keen to protect competitive advantage. Labour organizations have sought more rights for workers using international labour standards. The Kenyan state has modernized its labour laws to increase social protections, including extending maternity rights and benefits, under pressure from the ILO, but also to facilitate the development of a regional economic market – through the East African Economic Partnership Agreements. It has introduced a new constitution which offers more formal rights to women. EU and British farmers lobby for measures to protect themselves against cheap imports and many have resisted reductions in European subsidies. They support the enforcement of internationally developed phyto-sanitary standards (regulating plant disease, pests and contaminants) which require substantial investment to meet.

Applying Fraser's approach, these labour based and work-related social protection laws have been mis-framed and have not reflected the principle of non-domination. They have incorporated the 'doxa' of the male wage hierarchy based on the full-time employee model, which does not adapt well to Global South economic contexts, agricultural production or female patterns of work. They are also territorially limited. Anti-imperialist, feminist inspired measures would consider the provision of equal protections for all workers involved in the global value chain and extend social protections to support women (and men) who undertake socially reproductive responsibilities. This would involve recognizing the challenges involved in the development of appropriately framed social protections in a 'non-welfarist' postcolonial state – that is where rights are state provided but the costs of their implementation are not socialized. In Kenya, for instance, individual local employers bear the full cost of maternity rights. If women exercise these rights they become too costly.

Kenyan agribusiness incorporates very clearly the three fictitious commodities. Land is commodified to produce food crops that are alienated from their local social and economic context – the products cater to Global North tastes not local needs. The production places unsustainable pressures on the environment – use of water, pesticides, and an 8,000-mile round trip. Women's farming labour, when transformed into commodified employment, remains undervalued while their socially reproductive time is not replaced, leading to a depletion in socially reproductive capital (children cannot be cared for; community cohesion is eroded). However, if non-domination/emancipation is 'tested' against the need for social protection and for market access, it could be argued that what women small farm producers need is access to markets and to be able to protect values of social solidarity within local land systems which themselves must reflect non-domination principles. What they need is an ability to negotiate in civil space to ensure that they can shape land and environmental policies, labour rights and collective progressive social measures which resist the erosion of social and caring relationships.

The counter movement to re-embed the market must be more directly organized around care thinking. Coalitions of NGOs, worker organizations and northern consumers, within the space of civil society have used market forms of intervention based upon concepts of corporate social responsibility to develop 'soft law' or private standards in relation to ethical trading. Although supported by development agencies associated with the state, these measures have proven in some instances more open to recognizing principles of non-domination and therefore better gender framed protections. However, the far stronger progressive movement is that associated with fair trade. Here consumers, in coalition with Global South producers and civil society organizations, care about the social effects of production. They recognize to some extent that Global South production is built on the fictitious commodity of socially reproductive labour as well as land. They seek to identify who loses out and to pay a social premium that contributes toward social solidarity.

A Polanyian feminist approach would, therefore, involve supporting the development of co-operatively based fair trade movements, which maximize the civil space for negotiation for the full recognition of schemes based upon principles of non-domination, rather than encouraging schemes which involve the branding of Fair Trade production by multinational enterprises.

## Conclusion

This chapter has reviewed the way in which approaches to gender and law have been tackled within the discourse of international development and identified the convergence between these two fields. Both gender and rights approaches have permeated institutional development discourse since the 1990s. This is undoubtedly a reflection of the success of the women's movement in forcing the position of women on to the international stage and the influence of feminism within the academy. The 1990s were not only a period of optimism for this movement but also, prompted by the ending of the Cold War, for neoliberalism in the Global North, even though such approaches had failed to produce the expected economic growth in the Global South states who adopted these measures. The reduction in the role of the developmental state deeply affected the position of women, in particular because of their roles both within the productive and reproductive spheres.

A rights based approach (RBA) to development offered possibilities to a number of differently positioned constituencies holding varying understandings of freedom. The international women's rights movement, closely associated with the UN institutional framework, has an understanding of rights which has taken some account of Southern critiques but in the process decoupled the cultural identities of women from their economic positioning within a global economy. The tendency, therefore, has been to make demands of Southern states to deliver a framework for the empowerment of women to free them from oppressive family and community based institutions. The marginalization of the devastating impact of Structural Adjustment Policies (SAP) on Southern populations within the measurement of progress led to a reassessment of the goals of development. The 'capabilities approach' places the empowerment of the individual at its core: development as freedom to live a fully human life of one's choosing. This approach expects all those involved in development, including Southern states, to provide the necessary conditions to enable these capabilities. Rights have a significant role to play to enable women to flourish as individuals, unfettered by family and community restrictions. The reassessment of the effectiveness of SAPs within the dominant discourse led to a view that good governance and the ability to deliver a rule of law were important. In order to take 'ownership' of policies, a state needs the legitimacy gained through participatory processes, including those associated with Poverty Reduction Strategy Papers. A rights framework offers a way of framing these processes.

The shifts in geopolitics in the twenty-first century associated with the spectre of terrorism subsumed much of the RBAs into its concerns. Armed democratization, interventions in conflict and post-conflict states, often defined as failed or failing states provided the new 'hard' security discourse into which the earlier 'softer' RBAs must now fit. Women's rights formed an important element in the justification as well as the goal of these security discourses, which focus on formal constitutionalism and formal institution building to replace the exercise of power by warring clans, tribes, religious groups or other factions.

The radical analysis shared by gender and development and many Global South feminists that economic and social processes construct gender relationships and profoundly disadvantage many women has been drowned out in the contemporary context of globalization. Meanwhile, global capitalism thrives through its use of gendered identities to sell products and services, enthusiastically using rights and care concepts in the process. It increasingly draws on women's embodied labour to produce commodities and services which undoubtedly offer women opportunities to access monetized resources. Women's labour is increasingly used as a factor of production. At the same time, the ability of organized labour to win back some protection for workers is undermined by the same processes of globalization. Efforts to maintain or gain more social provision through states to support women in their continuing socially reproductive roles as mothers and carers with wider community based obligations are undermined by lack of resources and capacity within states. While Global South states are the site for rights discourse, the capacity to deliver or to facilitate delivery is severely curtailed.

This chapter has also assessed the salience of Fraser's reinterpretation of Polanyi's analysis in this context. Can it be used to wrest the discourse of feminism and care back from the domain of the market, not for the purpose of retreating into the traditional spheres of authority such as the family, but to harness some of the power it has achieved outside feminism to move forward? An example of the way in which this may be done has been provided here in the discussion of Kenyan agricultural production. Certainly, a materialist analysis which combines structure and agency and takes full account of feminist contribution to this form of analysis offers possibilities for future developments in integrated feminist approaches to gender justice.

# References

An Na'im, A. and Hammond, J. (eds), 2002. *Cultural Transformation and Human Rights in Africa*. London: Zed books.

Armstrong, A. 1992. *Struggling over Scarce Resources: Women and Maintenance in Southern Africa*. Harare: University of Zimbabwe Publications.

Bedford, K. 2011. *Developing Partnerships: Gender, Sexuality and the Reformed World Bank*. Minneapolis and London: University of Minnesota Press.

Beneria, L. 2003. *Gender, Development, and Globalization*. London: Routledge.

Benhabib, S. 1996. *Democracy and Difference: Contesting the Boundaries of the Political*. Princeton NJ: Princeton University Press.

Beveridge, F. 2005. Feminist Perspectives in International Economic Law, in *International Law: Modern Feminist Approaches*, edited by D. Buss and A. Manji. Oxford and Portland: Hart Publishing, 173–201.

Charlesworth, H. 2005. Not Waving but Drowning: Gender Mainstreaming and Human Rights in the United Nations. *Harvard Human Rights Journal*, 18, 1–18.

Chanock, M. 1985. *Law, Custom and Social Order: The Colonial Experience in Malawi and Zambia*. Cambridge: Cambridge University Press.

Cornwall, A. and Molyneux, M. 2006. The Politics of Rights-Dilemmas for Feminist Praxis: an introduction. *Third World Quarterly*, 27(7), 1175–1191.

Cornwall, A. and Nyamu-Musembi, C. 2005. What is the "Rights–based approach" all about? Perspectives from International development agencies. *Sussex University: Institute of Development Studies*, Working paper no. 234.

Cornwall, A., Harrison, E. and Whitehead, A. (eds), 2007. *Feminisms in Development: Contradictions, Contestations and Challenges*. London and New York: Pluto Books.

De Sousa Santos, B and Rodriquez-Garavito, C.A. (eds), 2005. *Law and Globalization from Below: Towards a Cosmopolitan Legality*. Cambridge: Cambridge University Press.

Elson, D. and Pearson, R. 1981. The subordination of women and the internationalization of factory production, in *Of marriage and the Market*, edited by K. Young et al. London: CSE Books, 18–40.

Engle, K. 2005. International Human Rights and Feminisms: When Discourses Keep Meeting, in *Feminist Perspectives on International Law*, edited by D. Buss and A. Manji. Oxford: Hart Publishing, 47–66.

Faundez, J. (ed.), 1997. *Legal Technical Assistance in Good Government and Law: Legal and Institutional Reform in Developing Countries*. London: Macmillan.

Faundez, J., Footer, M.E. and Norton, J. (eds), 2000. *Governance, Development and Globalization*. London: Blackstones.

Fraser, N. 2009. Feminism, Capitalism and the Cunning of History. *New Left Review* 56, 97–117.

Ghai, Y., Luckham, R. and Snyder, F. (eds), 1987. *The Political Economy of Law: A Third World Reader*. New Delhi: Oxford University Press.

Griffiths, A. 1997. *In the Shadow of Marriage: Gender and Justice in an African Community*. Chicago and London: University of Chicago Press.

Griffiths, A. 2002. Legal Pluralism, in *An Introduction to Law and Social Theory*, edited by R. Banakar and M. Travers. Oxford: Hart, 289–310.

Griffiths, J. 1986. What is legal pluralism? *Journal of Legal Pluralism*, 24, 1–55

Hammergren, L. 2010. 'With friends like these can multilateral development banks promote institutional development to strengthen the rule of law?, in *Law in Pursuit of Development: Principles into Practice?*, edited by A. Perry-Kassaris. London and New York: Routledge, GlassHouse, 202–233.

Harcourt, W. 2009. *Body Politics in Development: Critical debates in gender and development*. London: Pluto Press.

Harrison, J. 2007. *Human Rights Impact of the World Trade Organisation*. Oxford: Hart.

Hoskyns, C. and Rai, S.M. 2007. Recasting the Global Political Economy: Counting Women's Unpaid Work. *New Political Economy*, 12(3), 297–317.

Hellum, A., Ali, S.S., Stewart, J. and Tsanga, A. (eds), 2007. *Human Rights, Plural Legalities and Gendered Realities: Paths are Made for Walking*. Harare: Weaver Books.

International Council on Human Rights Policy. 2009. *When Legal Worlds Overlap: Human Rights, State and Non State Law*. Geneva: ICHRP.

International Labour Office. 1977. *Employment, Growth and Basic Needs: A One World Problem*. London: Praeger.

International Labour Office. undated. *Facts on Women at Work*. Geneva: ILO.

Jad, I. 2007. The NGO-ization of Arab women's movements, in *Feminisms: Contradictions, Contestations and Challenges*, edited by A. Cornwall, E. Harrison and A. Whitehead. London and New York: Zed Books, 177–190.

Kandiyoti, D. 2007. Political fiction meets gender myth: post-conflict reconstruction, 'democratization' and women's rights, in *Feminisms: Contradictions, Contestations and Challenges*, edited by A. Cornwall, E. Harrison and A. Whitehead. London and New York: Zed Books, 191–200.

Kannabiran, K. (ed.), 2005. *The Violence of Normal Times: Essays on Women's Lived Realities*. New Delhi: Women Unlimited in association with Kali for Women.

Kapur, R. 2005. *Erotic Justice: Law and the New Politics of Postcolonialism*. London: Glasshouse Press.

Kelsey, J. 2006. *Taking Nurses and Soldiers to Market: Trade Liberalisation and Gendered Neo-colonialism in the Pacific*. Opening Plenary Paper to the 15th annual conference on feminist economics, Sidney, 2006.

Lacey, N. 2004. Feminist Legal Theory and the Rights of Women, in *Gender and Human Rights*, edited by K. Knopp. Oxford: Oxford University Press, 13–55.

Manji, A. 2006. *The Politics of Land Reform in Africa: From Communal Tenure to Free Markets*. London: Zed Books.

Marks, S. (ed.), 2008. *Implementing the Right to Development: The Role of International Law*. Geneva: Friedrich-Ebert-Stiftung.

Mehra, M. 2007. Women's Equality and Culture in the Context of Identity Politics. *Journal of Comparative Law*, 2(2), 1–32.

Merry, S.E. 2006. *Human Rights and Gender Violence: Translating International Law into Local Justice*. Chicago: The University of Chicago Press.

Mies, M. 1982. *The Lace Makers of Narsapur: Indian Housewives Produce for the World Market*. London: Zed Press.

Nussbaum, M. 1999a. Women and Equality: The capabilities approach. *International Labour Review*, 138(3), 227–245.

Nussbaum, M. 1999b. *Sex and Social Justice*. Oxford: Oxford University Press.

Nyamu-Musembi, C. 2002. Are local norms and practices fences or pathways? The example of women' property rights' in An Na'im, in *Cultural Transformation and Human Rights in Africa*, edited by A.A. An-Na'im and J. Hammond. London: Zed books, 126–150.

O'Connell Davidson, J. and Anderson, B. (eds), 2006. The Trouble with 'Trafficking', in *Trafficking And Women's Rights Series – Women's Rights In Europe*, edited by C.L. van den Anker and J. Doomernik. London: Palgrave Macmillan, 11–26.

Patel, R. 2007. *Hindu Women's Property Rights in Rural India: Law Labour and Culture in Action*. Aldershot: Ashgate.

Pearson, R. 2009. Reassessing paid work and women's empowerment: lessons from the global economy, in *Feminisms: Contradictions, Contestations and Challenges*, edited by A. Cornwall, E. Harrison and A. Whitehead. London and New York: Zed Books, 201–213.

Pearson, R. 2007. Beyond Women Workers: Engendering CSR. *Third World Quarterly*, 28(4), 731–439.

Polanyi, K. 2001. *The Great Transformation: The Political and Economic Origins of Our Time*. Foreword by J.E. Stiglitz. New introduction by Fred Block. Boston, Mass: Beacon Press.

Rai, S. 2011a. The history of international development: concepts and contexts, in *The Women, Gender and Development Reader* (second edition), edited by N. Visvanathan, L. Duggan, N. Wiegersma and L. Nisonoff. Halifax (Canada): Fernwood Publishing and London: Zed Press, 14–21.

Rai, S. 2011b. Gender and development: theoretical perspectives, in *The Women, Gender and Development Reader* (second edition), edited by N. Visvanathan, L. Duggan, N. Wiegersma and L. Nisonoff. Halifax (Canada): Fernwood Publishing and London: Zed Press, 28–37.

Rittich, K. 2002. *Recharacterizing Restructuring: Law, Distribution and Gender in Market Reform*. The Hague: Kluwer Law International.

Sen, A. 1999. *Development as Freedom*. Oxford: Oxford University Press.

Shiva, V. and Mies, M. 1993. *Ecofeminism*. Zed Books: London.

Shivji, I. 1993. *The Concept of Human Rights in Africa*. London and Dhaka: CODESRIA.

Stewart, A. 2004. *Aspirations to Actions: 25 years of CEDAW*. London: British Council.

Stewart, A. 2011. *Gender, Law and Justice in a Global Market*. Cambridge: Cambridge University Press.

Tamale, S. 2008. The Right to Culture and the Culture of Rights: A Critical Perspective on Women's Sexual Rights in Africa. *Feminist Legal Studies*, 16(1), 47–69.

Tamale, S. (ed.), 2011. *African Sexualities: A Reader*. Oxford: Pambazuka Press.

Tamanaha, B.Z. 2008. Understanding Legal Pluralism: Past to Present, Local to Global. *Sydney Law Review*, 30, 375–411.

Trubek, D. and Galanter, M. 1974. Scholars in Self-Estrangement: Some Reflections on the Crisis in Law and Development Studies in the United State. *Wisconsin Law Review*, 4, 1062–1101.

Trubek, D. 2006. The Rule of Law in Development Assistance, in *The New Law and Economic Development: A Critical Appraisal*, edited by D. Trubek and A. Santos. Cambridge: Cambridge University Press, 74–94.

Trubek, D. 2009. The Political Economy of the Rule of Law: The Challenge of the New Developmental State. *Hague Journal on the Rule of Law*, 1(1), 28–32.

Tsanga, A. 2004. *Taking Law to the People: Gender, Law Reform and Community Legal Education*. Harare: Weaver Press.

Tsanga, A. 2007. Reconceptualising the role of legal information dissemination in the context of legal pluralism in African settings, in *Human Rights, Plural Legalities and Gendered*

*Realities: Paths are made by walking,* edited by A. Hellum, S.S. Ali, J. Stewart and A. Tsanga. Harare: Weaver Books, 437–460.

Tsikata, D. 2007. Announcing a new dawn prematurely? Human rights feminists and the rights-based approaches to development, in *Feminisms: Contradictions, Contestations and Challenges,* edited by A. Cornwall, E. Harrison and A. Whitehead. London and New York: Zed Books, 214–226.

UNRISD. 2005. *Gender Equality: Striving for Justice in an Unequal World.* Geneva: UNRISD. Available at: www.unrisd.org/unrisd/website/document.nsf/0/1FF4AC64C1894EAAC12 56FA3005E7201?OpenDocument

UNWomen. 2011. *In Pursuit of Justice: Progress of the World's Women 2011–12.* New York: United Nations.

Williams, M. 2003. *Gender Mainstreaming in the Multilateral Trading System.* London: Commonwealth Secretariat.

# Women, Migration and the Constitutional Underpinning of the European Union

## Patricia Tuitt

The migration of people is an age-old phenomenon. Few countries would have reached their current state of social and economic advancement without having acted as host to individuals seeking to escape poverty or violence or seeking merely to expand their knowledge of the world. Indeed, one can hardly conceive of constructs such as country, state or border absent the activity of migration, nor can one speak meaningfully of any distinction between nation and the international sphere. Such constructs flow from the many so-called voyages or journeys of discovery that shaped the modern world. Not surprisingly, the phenomenon of migration has been accompanied by an extensive literature, spanning a host of disciplines but particularly marked within the various sub-disciplines of the social sciences: sociology, economics, anthropology and law. This literature has produced statistics on migration flows, accounts of the experience of migration, and theories concerning the factors that encourage or compel individuals to migrate (see, for example, Bhabba and Shutter 1994, Indra 1999, Kofman 2000).

As many have noted before me, until recently, that literature largely presented migration as a gender-neutral phenomenon. Data concerning the migration of women was poorly collated and analysed, the experience of women migrants played little or no role in the development of migration theories and, to the extent that the literature could not entirely ignore the fact that some women migrated across international borders, their role as active agents in the migration process certainly was not acknowledged. Until the late eighties/early nineties, women appeared in migration discourses largely as wives or other family members entirely suborned to the enterprise of the male (see, for example, Kaplan 1996, especially chapter 4).

Today, women are reported to make up around 49 per cent of individuals migrating across international borders.[1] Precisely when women began to appear more and more in statistical literature on migration is difficult to say, but the early nineties onwards has seen a slow realization among commentators on migration that gender determines both the event and the experience (psycho-social) of migration (see, for example, van Walsum

---

1    United Nations, Department of Economic and Social Affaire, Population Division (2011). Trends in International Migrant Stock: Migrants by Age and Sex (United Nations Database, POP/DB/MIG/Stock/Rev.2011).

and Spijkerboer 2007). Women have not entirely escaped their dependent status but it is now more generally understood that migration presents women with viable options in the face of restrictive social policies at home, ethnic tensions and forms of sexual and familial violence. Moreover, the significance of gender on the type of migration enjoyed – illegal/ legal, temporary/permanent – is a growing feature of discourses. Finally, the fact that many women are placed in the paradoxical position whereby their flight from harm results in an exchange for sometimes more extreme exploitation or abuse is now a strong theme within contemporary literature.

That this literature does not recount women's role in contemporary journeys of discovery – those journeys that contribute to the shaping of the World – is perhaps not surprising, since the function of migration in bringing about political transition or transformation is not an evident feature of contemporary migration literature *per se* – whether trained towards the situation of men or women. It is with the objective of bringing to the forefront of migration studies the role of migration in inaugurating, shaping and refining the political systems within which we live that I write this chapter. In this way, I seek also to contribute to research that examines the intersections between gender and race (see, for example, Brah 1996, Da Silva 2004, 2007, Moller Okin 2008). Migration is the human activity that links the colonial past to a possible post-colonial future – one in which the spaces of the world can be put to uses other than those proscribed by white, European men. The migration of women has played a significant role in the development of a polity that has emerged in the latter half of the twentieth century – the European Union. By focusing on this example, I will argue that we may begin to see how far women migrants might alter the terms in which political community comes into being.

The argument in this chapter offers, then, an important intervention in the current phase of research on women migrants, which by and large receives women's increased share in the statistics on international movement and asylum in a positive light. That more women can migrate to places of asylum, seek reunion with family members and search for job and educational opportunities beyond their countries of origin or domicile would seem, on first sight, to constitute a welcome paradigm shift. It suggests a greater exercise of independent agency on the part of women, notwithstanding the evidently gendered nature of immigration law documented in detail by feminist legal theorists (see, for example, Webber 2012: 72–82, Bhabba and Shutter 1994, Crawley 2001). Yet, the development which has seen women cross international borders in numbers equal to men and that has inspired more policy oriented and academic work devoted to an account of their experiences – a development which is often referred to as the 'feminization of migration' – could equally be seen in a less positive, or at least more complex, light. This is not only because migrants, and in particular women, are often vulnerable in their new places of residence and have precarious connections to work and community. It is also because migration in the service of a new legal order almost invariably comes about at the expense of individuals or groups whose continued survival or flourishing is not considered conducive to the new order. Is violence and dispossession an inevitable result of the kind of migration that inaugurates new political and legal communities? The instance of women's migration may suggest not. Women migrants may not only have impacted differently in relation to their male counterparts on the social, cultural and political norms of the host state, they might also have brought about a different (less hostile) relation between the new polity and what remains of the old.

It is inconceivable that the advent of new legal and political entities will cease to be a function of the migration and settlement of people. As more and more women migrate across international borders, it is inevitable that they will play a part in inaugurating the new. My purpose in this chapter is to look beyond discussions about the gendered nature of particular immigration laws, to the question of how, if at all, women's migration has altered the manner in which such new legal entities acquire their force.

Such an exploration as I have set for myself cannot ignore the fact that one way of interpreting the various developments that allow commentators to speak of the feminization of migration is that a more diverse range of social actors (especially women) are embracing the status that was integral to the new sovereign entities that emerged during the period of European discovery. In his 1961 publication, the *Wretched of the Earth*, Frantz Fanon was to designate the European discoverers as settlers. For Fanon, the settler was the 'unceasing cause' (1961: 40) of the violence and dispossessions of the current age; a violence that is exemplified in colonialism. The settler's violence was evident not in his mere settlement on foreign lands but in his desire to exclude others from a share of those lands. Above all, the settler's violence was evident in his contempt for – and his disavowal of – all that existed prior to his arrival and all who could not, or would not, acquire the status of settler. The settler is juxtaposed by Fanon with that of the native, whose 'petrification' (1961: 70) contrasts starkly with the settler's freedom and mobility.

Fanon oscillates between two possible responses to the native's wretchedness or damnation. The first sees the native (or at least a privileged class of natives) eventually taking the settler's place or, in a sense, *becoming* the settler by acquiring freedom, economic power, and education. The second response sees the end of the logic of settlement as a result of a political invention or revolution that the native inaugurates.

But Fanon's text is effectively silent on the question of how women might disrupt the binary of co-option or revolution that he outlines in *Wretched of the Earth* and a reading of *Wretched* with this corrective in view is, to my mind, long overdue.

Two particular features of Fanon's texts merit the effort of such a reading. The first is that he exposes the violent impositions that often flow from migration. Second, although Fanon's text is not explicitly attentive to the position of women, his category of 'the native' has much to offer critical theory – certainly it can usefully be deployed to speak to the position of women. At the very least we can say that, as more and more women are able to migrate within and across borders, those women migrants are, like Fanon's natives, challenged to either critique or instantiate the logic of settlement.

The European Union is offered here as an instance of a polity shaped through migration. That is, migration in the European Union has created *new* law in the form of a new legal and political community, the shaping of which, I argue, owes much to the migration of women during its early development. While not all migration is law-creating, I suggest that commentary on the migration of women typically fails to bracket off those law-creating moments from other modes of migration. Without purporting to resolve the conundrum at the heart of Fanon's revolutionary thesis, such a bracketing off is needed in order to allow commentators on the position of women migrants to fully appreciate the problematic raised in the possibility of the native/settler substitution – a problematic to which Fanon was alive, even though it was one he could not ultimately resolve.

Migration is always violent when it inaugurates *new* law, in the sense that it displaces old law as well as – to varying degrees – the people and ways associated with the old law. The possibility that women migrants are bringing about new law, and what this might mean for a critical theory and practice relating to the position of women, are questions that are not sufficiently aired in existing discourses. For these questions to be addressed, commentators must first acknowledge what I will call – paraphrasing Walter Benjamin (1921) – the 'law-creating' character of certain patterns of migration. It is these 'law-creating' migration patterns from which Fanon's settler is constituted. In other words, I will argue that discussions about women and migration need to address not only the ways in which women interact with positive legal norms, but also the effects of migration on the shape, identity and form of law.

The discussion in this chapter begins with a summary of the fundamental logic of the law–migration nexus before turning to a consideration of the feminization phenomenon. I start with this more abstract theoretical material because it is important to delineate the argument that migration is constitutive of law, rather than simply a response to, or engagement with, existing law. The chapter is ordered in four parts. In the first part, I outline the forms of intervention that I see as law-creating patterns of migration – that is, a form of migration that continues the norm of settlement that Fanon indicts. In the second part, I summarize the current position as regards women and international migration in an effort to show that the law-creating character of women's migration is too often unstated/understated in contemporary commentary. In the third part, I advance the argument that the migration of women around the spaces of which the European Union is now comprised is an instance of law-creating migration. In the fourth and final part, I attempt to explore the value and limitations of Fanon's analysis in *Wretched of the Earth* on the position of women within what we have come to call the bio-political order.

## Part One: Law Creation and Migration

The question of migration is always – and first and foremost – a question of law. Migration both creates and preserves law. When positive legal norms are deployed in order to enable or facilitate the movement of persons within and beyond state boundaries (increasingly unstable as these boundaries are becoming), such migration occurs in a more or less critical engagement with the already constituted order within which those positive norms exist. Such migration is law-preserving, because it simply utilizes the existing frameworks of states and the international order. However, as the emergence of the so-called 'new world' attests to, certain patterns and modes of migration have the effect of bringing about new legal entities. When a polity is created substantially through the migration and settlement of people, we witness the inauguration (creation) of law through migration. The most obvious illustration is the creation of new legal entities through colonialism but, as I will explain, the modern era has seen migration operate in a less explicit but equally powerful way to create new law.

Since Walter Benjamin wrote his *Critique of Violence* in 1921, the idea that law makes its first and fundamental appearance in the more or less violent inauguration of political community has generally gained acceptance. Law and the most visceral form of violence – force – are related at this most basic sense, since it is through war, conquest, civil revolt or other forceful means that many legal entities have, and continue to be, created. Migration modes and patterns must, therefore, be firmly placed within Benjamin's scheme of law-creating and law-preserving violence. On the face of it, migration in the service of a new polity is a less violent imposition of the law than civil upheaval or external conquest. It only appears so, however, until one examines the communities and cultures damaged and dispossessed during the age of discovery – histories that critical race and post-colonial theories in particular have done much to uncover. While Benjamin (and later Derrida (2002)) appear to elide migration when addressing the forceful events or acts that create or preserve law, through the work of Carl Schmitt (1950; reprinted 2006) and Frantz Fanon (1961) we can fully appreciate the *force* of migration.

Carl Schmitt's *Nomos of the Earth* examines the creation of a European public law largely through the so-called discovery of the new world. Discovery – that now disputed process of imposing order upon inhabited as well as uninhabited land – was a mode of establishing new sovereigns and depended crucially on human movement and settlement. Schmitt begins his treatise with a very compelling account of how what we might call the primary law (what Schmitt calls the *nomos*) is frequently imposed/established through migration. For Schmitt, political existence commences with a 'land appropriation' (2006: 48) and this act constitutes the primary law against which all positive norms owe their existence – the first measure of all subsequent measures (2006: 67). From Schmitt, then, we understand that the basic law is essentially a law of the earth, created, that is, in the moment of appropriating earth. A land-appropriation is a particular form of enclosure of earth that quite evidently produces forms of social organization radically different to that which existed before. Such enclosures, as we shall see, are usually effected through the migration and settlement of people over a relatively short and intense period – such as during the early emergence of the European Union.

Not every land-appropriation creates a *nomos*, since – like instances of migration – land appropriation can be conducted within the framework of an existing *nomos* or – foreseeably – it could be regarded as simple occupation outside any legal framework (new or existing). Moreover, not every instance of migration involves a land-appropriation capable of enacting a *nomos*. But, as I have explained above, every instance of migration has a relationship with law in the law-creating or the law-affirming sense. In addition, some form of migration precedes the form of land-appropriation that inaugurates Schmitt's law of the earth (law-creating migration) and the positive norms that the basic law creates are the principal facilitators of the migration patterns that sustain a legal and political system (law-preserving migration). Thus, migration is always a question of law, and migration inaugurates new law specifically through the violent bracketing of territory.

Eleven years after Schmitt wrote his thesis, Fanon intervened in a way which does not fundamentally challenge Schmitt's ideas, but focuses on the extreme forms of deprivation and violence meted on those wretched individuals whose degradation upon the earth was a necessary corollary of European territorial ambition (1961: see in particular 27–119). Neither Fanon nor Schmitt paint a scene in which women had any integral place, but Fanon's work at least offers something to the analysis of the position of women, provided that it can be plausibly extended, as I think it can be, beyond its racialized sense of personhood and colonial sense of place.

In its primary, essential, basic form, law can be identified, then, in all that is comprised in the various activities of travel and settlement – and in the varying labels of host, guest, visitor and stranger, who collectively enact the forms of closure that have always marked the advent of modern law. From the example of colonial settlements, we might say that we can recognize law-creating moments in the migration that enables a polity to be radically represented – that is, re-presented (in the colonial instance) on the precise terms of the colonizer, and as no longer recognizable by the colonized. In modern times, the emergence of the European Union can be seen to correspond in many ways to the political communities settled through migration and, as will be discussed below, female migration was an important part of that settlement process.

Because of the displacement, destruction, or re-presentation of prior peoples and their social forms, migration in the service of a new polity produces a relation with law that is inevitably malign. Migration within an already constituted space is not an activity free from violence. Indeed, the original settlement – the non-juridical beginning – is, to deploy Derrida, a violent force that grounds *itself*, justifies *itself* (2002: 242). It is a force that cannot be judged against positive legal norms and the institutions that enforce these, since all positive norms and institutions are dependent for their authority on the original settlement. Equally, nor can moral precepts such as right or wrong be brought into play to judge this malign law. And yet, as Derrida maintains, that malign law is not immune to challenge or contestation – it is deconstructable (2002: 243). Those whom history has written outside the norm of sovereign constituting – women and the colonized native, for instance – are now faced increasingly with the choice of being involved in this forceful means of bringing about new political beginnings or of interrogating it.

It is within this framework of creation of new *nomoi* that I think we need to understand migration. Although not couched in such terms, prevailing discourses around the 'feminization of migration' suggest that women's share in international migration is primarily critical and progressive – having the effect, if not the intention, of unsettling gender roles in particular. In this discourse, and as I will explain, women are increasingly regarded as active subjects making strategic use of law. The dominant narrative, therefore, is one in which women migrants use positive norms to traverse already constituted spaces that would not have yielded to them without the benefit of access to those legal tools. Read thus, the period marked out as manifesting the feminization of migration is one in which legal norms, and the deployment of those norms, have *lessened* the violence of a constituted settlement that in all places over the globe excluded or marginalized women. Yet, as I hope to show, the second half of the twentieth century saw women migrants involved in what seems remarkably like a process of discovery and production of spaces that were to form what is now the European Union. Whether the role of women in the European Union is in any way critical of the processes in which the world is constituted is the key question posed in this chapter.

## Part Two: The Feminization of Migration

At its most basic level, the fact that more women can move about the earth is all that is comprised in the phenomenon that has come to be known as the feminization of migration. Amie Gaye and Shreyasi Jha write of this phenomenon:

> *Since 1950 the female share of international migration has been more than 40 per cent. Initially, women moved as accompanying family dependents, however, currently more women are migrating independently in search of jobs.* (2011: 50)

To understand more clearly how this share of international migration is translated into particular forms of action on the earth requires some discussion of what factors are generally presented as facilitating women's increasing mobility. Among these factors, developments in fundamental rights principles hold a prominent place. For example, behind the feminization of migration is thought to lie the unravelling of the gender bias of international norms, compellingly outlined by Hilary Charlesworth, Christine Chinkin and Shelley Wright in their influential 1991 journal article. Article 8 of the European Convention of Human Rights and Fundamental Freedoms, which endorses the right to private and family life, is but one of a number of international norms that have placed restraints upon states desirous of impeding migration. The feminization of migration owes itself also to the gamut of legislation that outlaws discrimination on grounds of gender, which has enabled more women to combine paid work with family life – a goal towards which much feminist engagement has been directed – with, in the main, far-reaching and positive results (Caracciolo di Torella and Masselot 2010). Also not to be overlooked among the developments around human rights norms is the expanded meaning of the concept of 'social group' and 'political opinion' within Articles 1A(2) and 33 of the Convention Relating to the Status of Refugees, 1951. These developments have offered territorial protection to women facing sexual violence in times of war or serious political upheaval and seeking protection from recognized forms of gender harm, such as female genital circumcision (see, for example, *Shah and Islam v SSHD* 1999 and *Fornah v SSHD* 2006, Webber 2012: 72–82).

I pause here to acknowledge that the factors that have caused international migration to undergo the process of feminization extend well beyond positive legal norms. I do not overlook, therefore, the endless political campaigns and personal sacrifices of women, without which the legal developments outlined in the preceding paragraph would not have happened. However, the impact of positive norms – international human rights, equality legislation and domestic immigration laws – on the ability of commentators to claims that migration structures and practices have been feminized cannot be overlooked. As presented by dominant narratives, the feminization of migration is a result of women gaining increasing command over particular areas of substantive law. It is in this sense that women are perceived as engaged in law in its more benign guise – engaged, in other words, in the law simply as a set of norms, rather than in its fundamental form, or *nomos*. The focus on women's negotiation with substantive laws naturally presupposes that the period of constituting the *nomos* that produced those substantive norms has now passed, leaving women largely able to claim innocence in the violence of that constituting – at least insofar as the constituting is instigated by acts of migration.

It is, I suggest, against the background of a narrative in which women have opened a space, using positive norms, to enable them to contribute to the maturing and development of the social and political order, that commentators are – by and large – able to applaud the feminization of migration phenomenon. On the face of it, there is much to feel optimistic about in the share of women in international migration – conferring, as it has, rights that enable women to challenge traditional gender roles, often through a move from family dependency towards independent worker or wage earner status (Gaye and Jha 2011). Equally, however, such optimistic accounts underplay the deeper ways in which the increasing share of women in international migration has a law-creating character, which has significantly structured the bio-political. In the next section, I will explore the implications of this insight with the specific example of the contemporary constituting of the European Union.

## Part Three: Women, Migration and the European Union

As anyone familiar with the principle of the free movement of workers would know, the Court of Justice of the European Union (formerly, the European Court of Justice) has directed its most revolutionary jurisprudence toward the instance of female migration. Whether one takes the case of *Levin* (1982) concerning a British citizen living and working in the Netherlands in a part-time capacity of chambermaid, or *Raulin* (1992) whose very informal waitress contract was the subject of litigation, or the highly significant decision in *Martinez Sala* (1998) where workers' rights were, for the first time, eclipsed by citizenship status per se, it is hard to dismiss the role of female migration in the shaping of the EU's legal norms.

The story of these instances of women migrating around the EU has been resolutely advanced as examples of women making use of positive legal norms. Indeed, from the vantage point of dominant readings of the character of the European Union, to suggest anything other than that the women migrants involved in these litigated disputes were simply exercising legal norms within a constituted polity would be to challenge the popular conception of the European Union as a system co-extensive with its positive norms (see, for example, MacCormick 1993, Weiler 1991, Ward 1995). Within this frame, one could only attribute the prominent role that women played in developing jurisprudence around the notion of worker – or in elaborating the meaning of European citizenship – to the enlightened outlook of the European Union and its various institutions, especially its Court. The fact that the principle of equal pay between men and women was (like the free movement of workers) one of the earliest of the fundamental rights enshrined within the original Treaty of Rome (now Treaty on the Functioning of the European Union) certainly seems to support this reading.

However, as I have intimated throughout this chapter, and have argued elsewhere, another way of looking upon the movement of persons (specifically, women) within the territories that now comprise the European Union is not as the simple exercise of a legal right attached to an established polity – the existence of which cases like *Levin* (1982) simply declare – but, instead, as constitutive acts of land-appropriation. Migration sits behind many acts of land appropriation, although, as stated earlier, not all migratory events are capable of appropriating – that is, closing off – land in the service of a new political order.

Few now doubt that the European Union constitutes a political revolution. Whether couched in terms of a polity that exceeds the nation state, as a polity co-extensive with its positive norms, or even as a postmodern space, consensus generally surrounds the view that the EU boasts significant differences to other international legal systems.

Historical accounts of the development of the European Union are remarkably consistent in attributing the idea of European integration to the vision of Jean Monnet who long sought to find ways in which to avoid simply reproducing the political and economic conditions that led to two World wars (Urwin 1995, Pinder 1998). According to Monnet and his supporters, what Europe needed was an overarching system of governance that would act as a barrier to any one country in Europe assuming a position of economic and political dominance. Against the nation state form, which simply incentivized inward looking and protectionist policies, his dream could not be realized.

The early beginnings of the European Union were modest indeed. It began with the establishment in 1951 of the European Coal Steel Community under the Treaty of Paris. Far more significant to the shaping of the European Union was the Treaty of Rome, signed in 1957. This established two new community frameworks: the European Economic Community and the European Atomic Energy Community. The latter of these has no relevance to the current analysis and was, in any event, later disbanded, but the EEC remains one of the founding Treaties of the European Union. On ratification of the most recent amending Treaty (the

Reform Treaty/Treaty of Lisbon) in 2009, it was rather tellingly re-named the Treaty on the Functioning of the European Union.

The Rome Treaty contains what is today still considered to constitute the core or mainstay of European integration. This core consists of the movement of workers, goods, capital and services across European spaces. Until 2004, such movement was unrestricted, save in the interests of health and safety, public morality and other compelling considerations. States that joined the EU in 2004 and since have not been able to secure unrestricted free movement for their nationals – a factor which, much more than the recent economic instability of some member states, signalled a crisis of the European integration project.

The European Community became the European Union in 1992, following ratification of the Maastricht Treaty. This gave legal affirmation to what was a reality at least since the Rome Treaty – member states were joined through much more than economic structures and ambitions. This trajectory has continued since, such that the competences of the European Union are now wide-ranging – spanning foreign affairs, culture and security matters, among others.

It is important to understand that the EU has a legal existence independent of the sovereign states – nation states – from which it emerged. It is a product of a process in which the territorial divisions between member states of the European Union have been erased or at least significantly weakened. Amidst the violent overthrowing of political and legal orders that have occurred in every epoch, it is dangerously simple to view the emergence of the European Union as indicative of a means of settling a political community in a composition that transcends or exceeds the bio-political order. However, the twentieth-century emergence of the European Union carries stark resemblances to earlier polities settled through migration and, lying under the surface of dominant narratives of progress and citizenship, I maintain that its case law betrays the currency of age-old modes of sovereign constituting.

While the EU is typically, and somewhat misleadingly, presented as a de-territorialized space, the unmaking of the territorial borders that structured the nation state could only have occurred through an appropriation of territory. The European Union has partially de-coupled citizenship and some of the entitlements associated with it from territorial belonging. Over areas within its legislative competence, the European Union can promulgate and enforce laws, regardless of the domestic jurisdiction of its member states, and persons and goods can circulate within the territories of the European Union relatively free of immigration, fiscal or customs controls. In these ways, it is correct to speak of the European Union as a deterritorialized space, but otherwise, the classic territorial closures of which Schmitt speaks are strongly evident in the shaping of the European Union. Indeed, in the early development of the European Union, it took personal ambition, unstoppable curiosity about other people and other ways of life, as well as the common push factors that make some journeys around the earth less than voluntary, to bring about the re-presentation of the debased territories and arcane political and social structures of the old order of Europe. I do not seek here to argue anything like a reverse colonialism behind the EU's emergence, but I do argue that it was inaugurated from a dramatic representation of the old territories. The free movement of persons (as well as of goods and capital) was a key law-creating and *nomos*-constituting element of this re-presentation.

The places and spaces of the earth have long been populated and structured according to some form of governance. We cannot invent new territory on which to build/invent new political community, and instead must create our new worlds upon old territory. A major part of Schmitt's thesis concerns the discovery of the so-called 'new world'. The new world was, so the story goes, the product of the migration and settlement of European people in foreign territories. Is it merely coincidence that that which was created from the Rome Treaty – a Treaty which announced another period of European free movement –was, until recently, characterized as the 'new' Europe?

What role then did women play in the territorial undoing of the spaces upon which was to be inaugurated the European Union? To the cases cited above that tell of the migration of women around the EU territories many others can be added that relate ground-breaking changes through which the new polity claims distinction. While the women protagonists in *Levin* and *Kempf* re-presented crucial aspects of the organization of social life within European states, and among European people in general, *Carpenter* (2002) and *Chen* (2004) were to blur the distinction between the inside and outside of Europe – its citizens and its third country outsiders. Most ordinary people will know of the European Union – and will understand its claim to uniqueness – through its famed four freedoms of the movement of people, goods, services and capital. Recent limitations on the free movement of persons – relating to those member states who acceded to the European Union in 2004 and in later years – notwithstanding, the free movement of persons holds a foremost place in the presentation of the EU as *suis generis*; and the movement of women has, from the early beginnings of the polity, determined the forms of transaction that the ideal citizen will engage in, in the service of the new order.

The cases of *Levin*, *Kempf* and *Raulin*, and the speculative journeys around the European space that their female protagonists embarked on, recall to mind how well other equally speculative journeys of discovery have served other settled communities. Returning to the beginning of this part, one might read the decisions in the Court of Justice as an endorsement of the exploratory journeys that the women had embarked on *in fact*. By endorsing such journeys, the Court encouraged other equally speculative journeys. But in order to reveal the law-creating character of certain patterns and modes of migration, it is necessary to look behind the achievements that cases like *Levin* are commonly read as marking. We are informed that such cases produced an expansive reading of the concept of worker and that the broad notion of worker has assisted women in combining paid work with family life. I do not question this achievement but would urge instead that we look for something more behind the constitution of the European Union than the largely interpretative exercise that the Court engaged in. Behind that exercise we see many individuals – we are concerned here particularly with women – expressing a willingness to explore the emerging spaces of Europe.

Not only do we witness speculative, exploratory journeys around the European space, such journeys have prompted an equally speculative approach to significant aspects of the organization of social life common to the old nation state form that the European Union was developed in opposition to. As postcolonial theorists have informed us, the radical re-presentation of forms of social life was one of the key impulses behind various colonial impositions (see, for example, Hall 2000). The expansive notion of worker is indeed a striking feature of the court's jurisprudence. Indeed, so liberal is the notion, that individuals can claim worker status while being required to do very little actual work. It was reported that *Raulin* (1992), for example, was engaged on a contract which did not guarantee even a minimum number of working hours. She could go for days or weeks without work and indeed after a period of eight months residing in the Netherlands had only worked for a reported 60 hours. The Court nevertheless construed her as a worker for the purposes of the free movement provisions. In the case of *Levin*, the Court asserted the 'right of all workers to pursue the activity of their choice within the Community, irrespective of whether they are permanent, seasonal or frontier workers ...'. The Court would be prepared to exclude from the scope of the concept 'only work on such a small scale as to be regarded as purely marginal or ancillary'.

I have absolutely no quarrel with the Court's conclusions in relation to the individual cases, but the obvious and, I think, significant implication of its approach is that many individuals who, according to the interpretation of the court, are workers cannot conceivably settle into work in the sense of ever forming part of a stable workforce. During her time in the Netherlands, *Raulin* engaged in work for around 10 working days. But was her time spent away from formal labour idle time from the vantage point of the constituting of Europe? What we learn from Schmitt is that seizure alone can have a compelling force and transformative effect – in this case, the seizure of space *per se*, irrespective of what activities are performed in those spaces. Work, leisure and education are some of the currencies which individuals are prepared to exchange to embark on a sometimes uncertain existence in an unfamiliar world. But these private journeys must be in exchange for something that exceeds the private transactions themselves. In the case of *Morson v Jharjan* (1992) the British citizens evinced no desire at all to make use of the right that their citizenship conferred on them to move and reside freely in another member state. Such disinterest was soon to reveal its negative effects as their citizenship was to prove insufficient currency to exchange for a non-EU family member to reside with them in the UK. Such a basic right of family reunion was reserved only for those *true* citizens of the Union and that *authentic* citizenship could only be acquired through migration – with the ostensible objective of work or other economic interest in mind. Had the applicants just once exercised their free movement rights, family reunion would have been guaranteed under European law.

The European Union is marked out as *sui generis* – an invention in a class of its own. In part this is because it has developed its own conception of citizenship within which, unlike other international entities, its citizens can invoke its legal principles directly in national courts (*van Gend en Loos v Netherlands* 1963). But more significantly, it is because, like so many legal entities that have preceded it, the EU commenced with a declaration of the sovereign importance of the free movement of European citizens, thereby enabling women (and others) to mark out the new polity through important social transformations. It is these forms of movement that, to me, intimate migration of a kind that has a law-creating character.

Some of the most critical work on women and migration has taken the European Union as a key context, and writers have begun to examine the role of gender within a broad constitutional, institutional and international frame (see, for example, Shaw 2002, Ackers 1996, 1998). However, the balance of analysis is still towards women's interaction with substantive laws. In most of these accounts, the conclusion has been that women have been very much marginalized from the constitutional development of the European Union (Shaw 2002). By contrast, Louise Ackers has produced some interesting empirical work which could lay the foundation toward a re-imagining of the role of women in the emergence of the European Union. In particular, Ackers' demonstrates that women make up some 50 per cent of EU migration flows and suggests that this calls for a closer examination of the nature and longer term impact of such migrating patterns. Ackers and other writers, such as Isabella Moebius and Erika Szyszczak (1998), have challenged a particular aspect of the standard narratives of women's movements, which tend to read these as motivated by family related matters, downplaying, therefore, the extent to which women deploy migration as economic actors or market citizens.

Cases like *Levin* can be read, alongside the dominant narrative, as reflecting instances of migration that work in the service of the development of the EU. Such migration reflects a decisive constitutional act or event, and the individuals engaged in it are accorded the highest form of citizenship – that which Fanon identifies as the status of 'settler'. That this point is not fully appreciated is because everywhere scholars who comment upon the European Union – its development, its substantive areas of competence and especially its free movement provisions – insist on removing the political from market activity. However, as I have argued elsewhere, such a separation is unsustainable. Indeed, I have gone so far as to suggest that an individual's exercise of so-called market freedoms has always been the primary marker of the political, as distinct from an individual's involvement in mere politics (Tuitt 2011a).

Jo Shaw has identified a tension between the 'reality of migration' of women in the European Union and the 'historic focus' within the internal market on 'economic status' (2002: 222), thereby highlighting values within the market that are opposed to the interests of women. Shaw's statement is one of many that assert the innocence of women in the inauguration of the malign law that makes its appearance in migration. This claim to innocence may cease to hold, however, as more and more women acquire command over intra-border movement and thus, I suggest, begin to embrace the status of settler.

On this point, I move to the fourth and final section of the chapter, which examines the application of Fanon's notions of settler and native in the increasingly complex scene in which women migrate.

## Part Four: Women and Native – Considering Frantz Fanon

The core of Frantz Fanon's treatise in the *Wretched of the Earth* explores how, in the service of settlement (that is, in the pursuit of what Schmitt designated the makings of a European public law), the oppositional categories of settler and native were produced. The settler asserted command over the earth and thereby established the primary law, while the native was made wretched before that very earthly law. Fanon's native does not bring about new political beginnings through migration, for he is static – or, to deploy Fanon's terminology, 'petrified' (1961: 73). It is the settler who seizes the earth and in that seizure is able to enjoy the label 'host', while the native is the stranger, the foreigner, the guest. This opposition of native/settler, as Fanon elaborates it in *Wretched*, speaks of the relation between the law of the white man and its governance of the native black man, but today the notion of settler/native has purchase to explore the varying degrees of relation to law of a whole range of social actors. As such, *Wretched* offers a framework for the examination of the role women migrants have played in further shaping or extending the European public law that Schmitt wrote of and which I argue has been extended with the emergence of the European Union.

Writing in 1950, Schmitt opined that the period of sovereign-constituting of the law had passed (2006: 341). On this point, I differ from Schmitt – indeed, I would question whether the making of the European public law will ever be complete. If, as I believe is the case, this shaping of a European public law is still in process, then both Schmitt and Fanon hold important insights for the contemporary moment. As far as Fanon is concerned, his work must be made to extend beyond its specific colonial context. It is crucial to conceive of his native as not merely a racialized category but as a gendered one also. The history of colonial settlement is not just a history of race but a history of gender too. It is a history of men who appropriated land through conquest, occupation and settlement and of women who either did not exist in the matrix at all or who occupied passive or subordinate roles. Yet, as indicated above, Fanon was ever equivocal over the nature of the native's challenge to the settler, and in particular whether the native becomes the settler in structural terms, or whether the native can challenge the very logic and existence of colonization through revolutionary means. His ambivalence over this question is evident throughout the text. At certain places, Fanon appears to call for a simple and violent exchange between settler and native; at others, he urges a deconstructive turn that expels the settler entirely from the scene of the political and the social. This latter position would, of course, constitute a major challenge to the bio-political condition.

The structure of Fanon's native/settler opposition may be made to speak meaningfully of the experience of women but if Fanon's more explicit yearning is for the native to take the settler's place, then his ambitions are desperately in tension with the aims of much feminist critique which insists instead that the native (if we can use the term to address the position of women in the context of international migration) *remain* native (see, for example, Gordon et al. 1996, especially part four). The law-creating mode of migration – that which transforms the old to the new – has very different ends and effects than that implied in the notion of the feminization of migration. In terms of that latter narrative, women merely have a *share* of international migration. However, the migration that enables the re-presentation of a polity cannot, by definition, readily cede a share in the imagining of the new entity to any individual not similarly engaged in the process of sovereign emergence.

Of course, women can enjoy migration without becoming settlers. With the more extensive use of positive norms to aid migration, the female migrant is hardly the petrified native in the most debased state that Fanon describes, but she is equally not desirous (or capable?) of simply entering uncritically the category of settler. The stratagems and tools within which the native emerges from their petrified stance are what may take us beyond the bio-political dispensation, provided that movement does not simply ground *new* law.

These tools include positive norms that enable the migration of women and other natives. Such norms, although authorized by the primary mode of land appropriation, can always extend beyond that sovereign moment and (to an extent) interrogate and challenge it. Feminist critique, by and large, does not purport to operate outside systems. It is alive to the reality that women can/must enter violent places and spaces, but must not seek to be comfortable in those places and spaces. Understood thus, it is not merely Fanon's overtly misogynist moments that render his political critique in *Wretched of the Earth* problematic for many feminists, it is precisely the possibility that Fanon can imagine the native as comfortable in the settler's place which leaves him at odds with the basic tenets of feminist theory and practice.

Early on in this piece, I provided an intimation of how women (and others previously subordinated in migration patterns and discourses) might move across international borders, thereby improving their economic and social existence, and yet avoid simply embracing the category of settler. A central feature of colonial imposition was the treatment of all that came before the act of settlement as debased, backward or barbaric. Elsewhere I have shown how important it was to the development of the European Union for discourses surrounding its emergence to constantly impugn the nation state form – to repeatedly outline its violent and obsolete political and economic structures (Tuitt 2011b). The past and all those individuals or groups who represent or recall the past are – to the settler – a barrier to the economic, social and political advancement that he or she seeks. However, the settler's logic need not prevail and in the comfortable co-existence of past/present and future we might begin to erase the settler from the scene of migration.

## Conclusion

I have hinted all along that what is really at stake in the feminization of migration debate is the ways and means, and – importantly – the agencies through which the bio-political order is placed in contestation. Migrating women should not be burdened with the task of radically altering the ends of migration but nor should they be ruthlessly engaged in the service of the kind of sovereign constituting that largely retraces the steps taken by other putative settlers during Europe's colonial past. Thus, the increasing share of women in international migration may be considered a feature of contemporary social and political life which is much less desirable than it, at first sight, appears. The status of settler is the highest form of citizenship that a law of the earth can produce and thus in migration, as with all forms of social action, women are faced with the age old question of whether full citizenship – full belonging – is hostile to critique. What this might intimate is that the tools for contestation lie only in the position of the native – no longer petrified, but still native – in stark opposition to the settler's unceasing demands.

People migrate to spaces and places prompted by a variety of motives and imperatives. It cannot be denied that always, in migration, a certain transformation takes place, but the most traumatic changes to landscape occur in relation to those migratory movements that occur in the service of a new polity. Such migration is traumatic because it invariably involves an enclosure of space and place, and a more or less violent expulsion of or encroachment upon persons in prior occupation. Schmitt's critique provides us with an insight into two types of law that migration both produces and preserves – the relatively benign positive norms and the malign non-juridical and non-justiciable primary law, which makes its appearance at the beginning of every settled community and people. Set against this frame, it is apparent that involvement in the former mode of law's operation is the only form of engagement that offers the possibility of critique and does not, conversely, risk simply repeating the violence of all political beginnings. In this chapter, I have argued that these insights hold a particular relevance when set against the dual context of the increasing 'feminization of migration' and the emergence of the European Union as a new political, legal and spatial order. What ultimately emerges from this analysis, then, is that feminism's desired break from the bio-politics that govern women's lives cannot occur simply by setting the native forth on a voyage of discovery.

## References

Ackers, L. 1996. Internal Migration and the Negotiating of citizenship; the Struggle for Reproductive Self-determination in Ireland. *Journal of Social Welfare and Family Law*, 18(4), 5413–5428.

Ackers, L. 1998. *Shifting Spaces – Women, Citizenship and Migration in the European Union*. Bristol: Policy Press.

Benjamin, W. 1921. Critique of Violence, 1921 in Reflections: Essays, Aphorisms, Autobiographical Walter Benjamin, Trans. E. Jephcott. New York: Schocken Books.

Bhabba, J. and Shutter, S. 1994. *Women's Movements: Women under Immigration, Nationality and Refugee Law*. Stoke on Trent: Trentham Books.

Brah, A, 1996. *Cartographies of Diaspora: Contesting Identities*. London and New York: Routledge.

Caracciolo di Torella, E. and Masselot, A. 2010. *Reconciling Work and Family Life in EU Law and Policy*. Basingstoke: Palgrave Macmillan.

Charlesworth, H. Chinkin, C. and Wright, S. 1991. Feminist Approaches to International Law. *American Journal of International Law*, 85(4), 613–645.

Crawley, H. 2001. *Refugee and Gender: Law and Process*. Bristol: Jordon Publishing.

Da Silva, D. 2004. Mapping Territories of Legality: An Exploratory Cartography of Black Female subjects, in *Critical Beings: Race, Nation, and the Global Subject*, edited by P. Fitzpatrick and P. Tuitt. Aldershott: Ashgate, 203–222.

Da Silva, D. 2007. *Toward a Global Idea of Race*. Minneapolis: University of Minnesota Press.

Derrida, J. 2002. Force of Law: The Mystical Foundations of Authority, in *Acts of Religion*, edited by G. Anidjar. London and New York: Routledge, 228–299.

Fanon, F. 1961. *The Wretched of the Earth*, Trans. C. Farrington. London: Penguin Books.

Gaye, A. and Jha, S. 2011. Measuring Women's Empowerment through Migration. *Diversities*, 13(1), 49–66. UNESCO. ISSN 2079–6595. Available at: www.unesco.org/shs/diversities/vol13/issue1/art4

Gordon, L., Sharpley-Whiting, T. and White, R. (eds), 1996. *Fanon: A Critical Reader*. Oxford: Blackwell.

Hall, C. 2000. *Cultures of Empire: Colonisers in Britain and The Empire In Nineteenth and Twentieth Centuries*. New York: Routledge.

Indra, D. 1999. *Engendering forced migration: Theory and practice*. Oxford: Berghahn Books.

Kaplan, K. 1996. *Questions of Travel: Postmodern Discourses of Displacement*. Durham: Duke University Press.

Kofman, E. 2000. *Gender and International Migration in Europe: Employment, Welfare, and Politics*. New York: Routledge.

Lacey, N. 1998. *Unspeakable Subjects: Feminist Essays in Legal and Social Theory*. Oxford: Hart Publishing.

MacCormick, N. 1993. Beyond the Sovereign State. *Modern Law Review*, 56(1), 1–18.

Moebius, I. and Szyszczak, E. 1998. Of Raising Pigs and Children. *Yearbook of European Law*, 18(1), 124–144.

Moller Okin, S. 2008. Is Multiculturalism Bad for Women, in The Global Justice Reader, edited by T. Brooks. Oxford: Wiley-Blackwell, 587–597.

Pessar, P. and Mahler, S. 2003. Transnational Migration: Bringing Gender In. *International Migration Review*, 37(3), 812–846.

Pinder, J. 1998. *The Building of the European Union*. Oxford: Oxford University Press.

Schmitt, C. (1950) *The Nomos of the Earth in the International Law of the Jus Publicum Europaeum*. (Reprinted 2006) New York: Telos Press.

Shaw, J. 2002. The European Union and Gender Mainstreaming: Constitutionally Embedded or Comprehensively Marginalised? *Feminist Legal Studies*, 10(3), 213–226.

Spijkerboer, T. 2000. *Gender and Refugee Status*. Aldershot: Ashgate.

Tastsoglou, E. and Dobrowolsky, A. 2006. *Women, Migration, and Citizenship: Making Local, National, and Transnational Connections*. Aldershot: Ashgate.

Tuitt, P. 2011a. From the State to the Union: International law and the Appropriation of the New Europe, in *Events: the Force of International Law*, edited by F. Johns, R. Joyce and S. Pahuja. London and New York: Routledge/Cavendish, 177–191.

Tuitt, P. 2011b. Narratives of Origin and the Emergence of the European Union, in *Storied Communities: Narratives of Origin, Contact and Arrival in Constituting Political Community*, edited by H. Lessard, R. Johnson, and J. Webber. Vancouver: UBC Press, 229–245.

Unwin, D. 1995. *The Community of Europe: a History of European Integration*. Essex: Longman.

van Walsum, S. and Spijkerboer, T. 2007. *Women and Immigration Law: New Variations on Classical Feminist Themes*. Routledge-Cavendish.

Ward. I. 1995. Identity and Difference: European Law as a Postmodern Legal Text, in *New Legal Dynamics of the European Union*, edited by J. Shaw and G. More. Oxford: Clarendon Press, 15–26.

Webber, F. 2012. *Borderline Justice: the Fight for Refugee and Migrant Rights*. London and New York: Pluto Press.

Weiler, J. 1991. The Transformation of Europe. *Yale Law Journal*, 100(8), 2403–2483.

## Case Law and Conventions

Convention Relating to the Status of Refugees, 28 January 1951, 189 UNTS

Case 26/26 van Gend & Loos v Netherlands [1963] ECR 105

Case 139/85 Kempf v Staatssecretaris van justitie [1982] ECR 1035

Case 35 and 36/82 Morson and Jhanjan v Netherlands [1982] ECR 3723

Case 53/81 Levin v. Staatssecretaris van Justitie [1982] ECR 103

C–357/89 Raulin v Minister van onderwijis en wetenschappen [1992] ECR1–1022

Case C–85/96 Martinez Sala v. Freistaat Bayern [1998] ECR I–2961

Shah and Islam v SSHD [1999] 2 A.C. 629

Case C–60/00 Carpenter v. Secretary of State for the Home Department [2002] ECR I–6279

Case C–200/02 Zhu and Chen v. Secretary of State for the Home Department [2004] ECR 1–9925

# Ecofeminism and the Environment: International Law and Climate Change

## Karen Morrow

This chapter will introduce the reader to feminist theory as it has been applied to environmental issues. It will take as its focus the concept of ecofeminism, which is founded on both the recognition of a shared societal classification of women and the environment and the application of feminist scrutiny to the particularized impacts of environmental degradation on women. Ecofeminism is best understood as a very broad church. It is rooted in and accommodates diverse (if often contested) areas of social praxis and scholarship, and thus comprises an extensive range of approaches to a wide variety of issues concerning gender and the environment.

Women, in many guises, including as farmers, mothers, workers and members of indigenous communities are among the most seriously affected in social and economic terms by environmental degradation. In light of this, coupled with its characteristic inclusiveness, embracing both activist and theoretical perspectives, ecofeminism is a particularly vibrant and dynamic area of inquiry. As a result, it offers a wealth of insight and creativity that can be channelled into engaging with imperative environmental challenges and beyond. In order to give a flavour of the broad spectrum of ecofeminism, this chapter will begin with a brief discussion of the main schools of ecofeminist thought, ranging from essentialist to social ecofeminism. It will then outline the core components of ecofeminist methodology by identifying the foundational principles which it promotes, and considering their application. The chapter will then briefly consider the contribution that women, gender and nascent ecofeminist approaches have made to the development of the foundational international law concept of sustainable development. Discussion will conclude by focusing on ongoing developments in that most pressing of problematic areas in environmental sustainability, climate change, in order to evaluate the potential and actual contribution that women and ecofeminism stand to make to developing international law and policy in this area.

## A Brief Introduction to Ecofeminism

As a development of the latter part of the twentieth century, ecofeminism applies many of the elements discussed elsewhere in this collection, albeit in a characteristically pragmatic fashion. In particular, ecofeminism strongly features intersectionality (notably addressing considerations of race, religion, motherhood, citizenship and human rights) and it is by its very nature interdisciplinary (with close links to anthropology, sociology, ecology and legal theory). This polycentric and porous conception of ecofeminism goes some way towards engaging with the inevitable contestability of any such assertion of commonality/common identity (Ferguson 2007). It also offers a sophisticated conception of the multiple and interwoven layers of both individual and group identity: thus a woman/group of women may identify themselves with reference to gender, but also by a host of other elements, for example – nationality, ethnicity and socio-economic status.

The feminist movement has long espoused recognition of the pervasive impact of gender on all aspects of social praxis. Thus, as environmental matters gained increased social currency, it was inevitable that the multiple impacts of environmental degradation on women would become subject to feminist scrutiny, and would contribute to the wider debate in numerous ways, not least in exposing gaps in emerging analytical frameworks, for example in development studies. The application of feminist analysis, employing core feminist methodologies to environmental exploitation, therefore spawned the development of ecofeminism, the term itself being first coined by Francoise d'Eaubonne (d'Eaubonne 1974). These core methodologies have included unmasking patriarchy, applying concrete, contextual, case-by-case reasoning as the basis of developing theory from practice, and consciousness raising (Verchick 1996).

The foundation of ecofeminist methodology involves identifying and tackling the manifold implications of philosophical dualisms, such as that between nature and culture, through questioning the status quo in terms of a multi-faceted understanding of oppression. While the common oppression of women and nature is most definitely the foundational consideration here, it is by no means the sole one. For example, while the origins of ecofeminism lay with white Western women, it was rightly criticized for the false universals that were posited on this basis in its early days, and its response was to accommodate a broad diversity of perspectives from indigenous women, women of colour and women of the developing world (Morrow 2006, Shiva 1993). The synthesis of perspectives from the developing world added an intensely practical dimension to ecofeminism and significantly augmented the development of its methodology. This synthesis ultimately came to represent one of the hallmarks of ecofeminism: it is as much a product of grassroots activism as of academic enquiry, which is both a source of vitality and (normally) creative tension. As a result of this inclusive and flexible approach there was a rapid expansion in ecofeminist concerns through conscious endeavours to engage with what may be characterized as a web of mutually reinforcing, interpenetrating, multiple oppressions, extending to encompass race (embracing the concerns of people of colour and indigenous peoples), class, sexual orientation, age, disability, and non-human nature. As it has developed, ecofeminism has, therefore, in its turn, contributed, and continues to add, to both the ever-developing richness of feminist ontology, epistemology and practice and to environmental discourse. Furthermore, in synthesizing feminist and ecological concerns, ecofeminism is more than the mere sum of its parts, developing distinctive features that take it beyond both mainstream feminism and environmentalism.

Ecofeminism is broadly rooted in radical feminism, focusing for the most part on gender difference, the domination/oppression of women by men, and resulting hierarchical social structures to '… serve as conceptual paradigms for understanding other oppressions, including the oppression of nature' (Hughes 1995: 504). It views the shared oppression of women and nature as giving rise to both negative and positive features. Most commonly, negative connotations are viewed as the result of applying post-Enlightenment dualisms to both women and nature, in which they are each constructed as 'other' to the male and rational. This facilitates the designation of the former as inferior to the latter, thus rendering them ripe for objectification, instrumentalization and ultimately exploitation. At the same time, a minority of commentators (Shiva 1993, see also McGuire and McGuire 2003) argue that positive ramifications can also be drawn from such dualisms, through embracing the conscious and mutually sustaining identification of the female with the natural world, recognizing the nurturing status of 'mother' nature or even extending into worship of nature as a goddess. This perspective is very much at odds with the views of many within the main body of feminist thought that has spent decades attempting to dissolve the 'damaging' association of woman and nature (Norgaard and York 2005). On the other hand, this aspect of ecofeminism sits well with an ecological understanding of the biosphere and the place of humanity within it (Mellor 1997, Plumwood 1993, Merchant 1981), as they share an understanding of humanity as an integral part of the biosphere, rather than in some way superior to or separate from it.

The inherent inclusivity and malleability of ecofeminism necessarily fosters immense diversity within its bounds; thus, what we are actually dealing with here is not so much a monolithic ecofeminism but rather 'ecofeminisms' (Plumwood 1993: 36). As a result, in this chapter, I can only provide a glimpse of its myriad manifestations. Nonetheless, the broad range of the ecofeminist spectrum can be represented as falling along a continuum ranging from essentialist to socialist ecofeminism. While all versions of the theory are of course open to cogent criticism (Twine 2001), an outline consideration of these two widely divergent positions, and some of the points that lie positioned between them, serves to provide both a flavour of the internal debates involved and a viable starting point for wider discussion.

Essentialist (also referred to as affinity ecofeminism) perspectives grew in the first instance from the work of US theologians and artists (Mellor 1997). Proponents of this species of ecofeminism basically take a radical feminist line. Specifically, they argue that as a result of biology and/or spirituality (Marina 2002, Hughes 1995), women are necessarily more identified with nature than men and that they therefore enjoy/endure an inherent affinity with the environment (Shiva 1993). This is however widely regarded as, at best, a highly contestable notion. Victoria Davion, for example, actually goes so far as to refute the idea that such 'uncritical' (idealized would seem a better term) perspectives on women and the environment are ecofeminist at all, referring to them instead as 'ecofeminine' (Davion 1994, 9). Such an exclusionary approach sits ill with the pluralism that characterizes ecofeminism and may therefore go too far.

Moving along the spectrum from 'pure' essentialism, but sharing some of its characteristics, is cultural ecofeminism. This type of ecofeminism focuses on personal transformation and also on seeking to reverse exclusion by according value to the previously devalued (in this case, women and nature). This approach is based on the recognition and accommodation of equality/difference within the current societal context, and is therefore essentially a manifestation of liberal feminism (Plumwood 1993: 31).

Current approaches to ecofeminism, however, tend more often to fall under the umbrella of socialist ecofeminism. As such, they are based on the core premise that a special relationship exists between women and the environment due in part to the reproductive functions of the former, in the broadest sense of the word, which encapsulate the full range of activities necessary to sustain life. This demonstrates the radical ecofeminist roots of socialist ecofeminism; it has, however, grown beyond this, developing an approach founded on an ontological understanding that extends the personal into the surrounding world, reflecting also the complex interrelating influences that situate women in a variety of ways. Most significant among these are race/ethnicity, class and age and the interplay between them as expressed through the concept of compound disadvantage. Thus, socialist ecofeminism thought accommodates the view that relationships between women and the environment are rooted, enforced and reinforced by a complex, interlinked web of societal mechanisms. Broadly, socialist ecofeminism approaches view the concerns of cultural ecofeminism as valid but too narrow. Focusing instead on collective change as their goal, they require a profound societal re-ordering, dismantling the ideology and structures of patriarchy and the dualism on which it is founded and replacing them with ideology and structures based on egalitarianism which can accommodate both non-gendered humanity and nature (Hughes 1995, Plumwood 1993). This approach finds practical expression in a number of ways, not least in promoting women's participation in environmental law and policy-making processes, as discussed below.

In its various forms, ecofeminism may be viewed as a necessary component in a gendered understanding of human relationships with the environment. It acknowledges that both female and male perspectives require consideration in viable decision-making processes and (in its prevalent form) it stresses both difference and equality in methodology and outcomes. In attempting to articulate those areas of concern that are particularly relevant to women and nature, ecofeminism provides a necessary corrective to the dominant patriarchal and anthropocentric world view, the structures that it inhabits and the unsustainable practice that it endorses. Ecofeminism understands the relationship between humanity and the environment as both embodied by, and embedded in, our dependence upon the biosphere for life itself and for its subsistence. This dependence of course manifests itself for all of us, though its exact nature is dependent on interaction with a multitude of other factors, ranging from geography and economics through culture, politics and law; and for women these can, individually or in combination, reveal themselves in additional distinctly gender-specific ways. Crucially, then, ecofeminism insists that gender is a cross-cutting issue that touches upon all aspects of our being and agency. Thus the response that ecofeminism offers to environmental challenges is founded not only on the recognition that women feature prominently among those subjected to the greatest burdens by all classes of environmental degradation but also on the understanding that women are potentially powerful agents of change in tackling such problems.

## Constituting a Core Ecofeminist Methodology

It is evident that ecofeminist priorities, principles and values are expressed in the core methodology that it employs to address specific environmental problems. Underpinning this, and foundational to its viability, is the central awareness of the location of humans within an inescapable (though mutable, for good and ill) ecological context and the constraints that this places on human activity. Using Katharine Bartlett (1990) as a starting point, discussion here will focus on identifying the central methodological elements of ecofeminism as currently practiced in an international context.

To address multiple but intertwined oppressions, ecofeminism advocates societal transformation through an inclusive approach, made manifest in expansive, participatory decision-making that accords respect to lay experience in addition to scientific and technical knowledge. It also promotes consensus building and ultimately the mainstreaming of previously excluded perspectives. This process is pursued by the aggregation of experiential narratives (which in modern praxis goes well beyond the notion of 'story-telling' and speaks not only to individual but also collective experience) to build a knowledge base, broaden understanding and construct campaign coalitions. This embracing of pluralism, is not, however, to be equated with relativism, as it necessarily engages a critical dialogue that sees claims contested and evaluated (Gruen 1994: 124, 130). In fact, the goal of achieving broad-based participatory debate (Tinker 1999) that this process of assimilating and digesting the import of lived experience involves is as much a feature of ecofeminism as the positions that emerge from it (Morrow 2011). An example of this type of approach being adapted to good effect is found in the grassroots women's conference held in the run-up to the UN's climate change negotiations in Durban in 2011 (Gendercc IV).

It is important to consider here that, contrary to what is often suggested, ecofeminism need not seek to fashion internal consensus. The need for total agreement is not central to an approach that makes it its business to accommodate diverse perspectives clustered around shared areas of concern (Walby 2000) and which eschews the idea of a hegemonic theory. When ecofeminism is pursued in an international context, its goal is to import this paradigm-shifting approach to accommodating alternative/additional procedural and substantive expertise and experience, from the periphery to the mainstream. In this way, it seeks to provide a corrective to an important constituent of the systemic failure that characterizes much current endeavour in this regard. The way in which ecofeminist methodology actually operates in an international context will be considered in subsequent discussion of ongoing developments in the area of climate change.

## Making an Impact: Gender, Environment and International Law

While ecofeminism is a comparative newcomer to the international arena, this is because international environmental law itself only emerged consistently in the latter part of the twentieth century. Ecofeminism has, however, been well placed in principle to exploit the rising prominence of environmental matters, as it has benefitted from the inclusion of gender issues in international law and policy more generally (Prugl and Meyer 1999). This laid a foundation in three broad stages. The first stage involved the recognition of gender equality issues 'in principle' resulting in the inclusion of women's rights within the wider provision of the Universal Declaration of Human Rights 1948. While of undoubted symbolic significance, this development generated relatively limited progress on the ground (Morrow 2006). In response to the gap between women's rights as acknowledged in principle and enjoyed in practice, the second stage of international action saw a shift towards specific policies focused on women. This move was supported by further important legal developments, notably the 1979 Convention on the Elimination of all forms of Discrimination Against Women (CEDAW). This strategy too was, however, ultimately found wanting as, once again, the existence of legal rights and entitlements on paper failed to consistently deliver gender equality in practice (Morrow 2006).

In consequence, a third stage of initiatives to address gender concerns is now finding expression in a more holistic and systematic methodology. Known as 'gender mainstreaming', this approach is built on experience wrought from its predecessors. This latest tranche of activity had its theoretical genesis in the UN's 1995 Beijing Conference on Women, and, in a more developed fashion, in the Beijing +5 Conference, Women 2000: Gender, Equality, Development and Peace for the twenty-first century. These gave rise to a high-level, systemic UN policy commitment to addressing gender issues, subsequently expressed through significant structural and institutional initiatives, such as System-Wide Plans for the Advancement of Women. While progress has undoubtedly been made under gender mainstreaming, it too is not without its own problems and limitations (Bhatta 2001), notably in terms of generating changes in institutional culture and substantive impacts (Benschop and Verloo 2006). In sum, while it must be acknowledged that the coverage offered to gender equality issues in international law more broadly has been, and often continues to be, problematic in some respects, such interventions are still hugely significant. Among other things, as will be discussed in this section, they have laid a useful foundation for the development of ecofeminism at this level.

Environmental issues rose to prominence in the mainstream international arena later than gender, with most commentators attributing the genesis of modern environmental law to the United Nations Conference on Environment and Development (UNCED) in Stockholm, 1972 (popularly known as the first earth summit). Progress was however retarded by the oil crisis that began the following year and it was arguably not until the second earth summit, the UNCED in Rio in 1992, that modern international environmental law really began to mature. The Rio Summit also provided the opportunity for a dovetailing of gender and environmental concerns under the auspices of the core underpinning notion that emerged from the Conference: sustainable development. This is usually defined as: 'development which meets the needs of the present without compromising the ability of future generations to meet their own needs' (Brundtland 1987) and involves seeking a notional balance of economic development, social equity and environmental protection in human activity.

The ambition of sustainability is considerable (and possibly overweening). It ultimately seeks to re-orientate the relationship between humanity and the environment and to this end requires an unprecedented re-envisioning and re-fashioning of the global polis and governance, specifically through harnessing bottom-up, grassroots activity to established top-down political and legal processes (Brundtland 1987). The international community endorsed sustainable development at the Rio Earth Summit most notably by adopting the Rio Declaration and Agenda 21 (which was to provide the 'blueprint' for progressing sustainability). Being soft law documents, neither the Declaration nor Agenda 21 is legally binding, but they are nonetheless influential in political terms as statements of intent and as bases for developing state practice. Among the many policy and practical issues that Agenda 21 covers, facilitating the radical degree of societal engagement that the 'bottom up' approach of sustainability requires is a recurring priority. Nurturing and developing the role of civil society, an area in which women are traditionally very active (Verchick 1996), is a key strategy in this regard. The dominant role of women in grassroots environmental organization membership and (to a lesser degree) leadership also makes this area a fertile one for women's action. The opportunities offered were enthusiastically exploited in the run-up to the Rio Summit itself, not least through the World Women's Congress for a Healthy Planet in Miami in 1991, which was run by the Women's Environment and Development Organisation (WEDO), a leading women's environmental NGO. WEDO took full advantage of existing women's networks and further augmented them to ensure that a broad spectrum of opinion was represented at the event. Among the outputs of the Congress was the comprehensive revision of the original 'gender neutral' text of Agenda 21, resulting in a thoroughgoing integration of gender in the final document (Morrow 2006). Women also obtained 'major group' status under Agenda 21, enabling them to play a continuing role in advancing the sustainability agenda through the ongoing work of the UN's Commission for Sustainable Development (CSD) (Kaasa 2007). As demonstrated in the Rio process, the women's movement (as a broad coalition) is an established actor within the UN system which draws support and influence from established global grassroots networks and enjoys honed repeat-player expertise in engaging with international policy and legal agendas. Thus, in principle at least, the women's movement was notionally relatively well positioned to promote its priorities to the fore in advancing sustainable development. In practice, however, the impact of gender on the rhetoric and practice of sustainable development remains, as we shall see below, sporadic (Morrow 2006).

## Gender, Climate Change and the International Climate Change Regime

Arguably the most pressing sustainability challenge that currently faces humanity is anthropogenic climate change which has progressed from highly contested theory into something approaching broadly accepted orthodoxy (Burleson 2009–2010). Like sustainable development, climate change burst on to the international legal landscape at the Rio earth summit in 1992 with the adoption of the United Nations Framework Convention on Climate Change (FCCC). Climate change is complex, cross-cutting and multi-scalar (with impacts ranging from local through global) in nature and it is having, and will continue to have, a disproportionate impact on the most vulnerable in society, notably women. Climate change is complicated by being enmeshed and entangled with other established areas of societal concern including health, resource (notably water) scarcity, food security, environmental disasters, conflict and migration. To cut the Gordian knot that this creates will require unprecedented energy and imagination, involving scaling up and out responses to discrete problems in a more coordinated and holistic way than ever before. Effectively addressing climate change issues therefore requires an innovative, cross-cutting synthesis of approaches in order to develop viable policy and law responses.

On this basis, there would appear to be significant potential synergies in harnessing ecofeminist approaches among the strategies for tackling climate change, yet this is an area in which, despite the expectations raised by recent history, the impact of gender has thus far proved unexpectedly limited. The case for active participation by women in the climate change arena is made in practical terms by the fact that women are, as a consequence of wide-ranging and deep-set societal inequalities, prominent among those most disadvantaged by its impacts. Women suffer in this respect both as a discrete group and through 'double disadvantage' as the most impacted members within other disadvantaged categories, notably indigenous peoples and refugees (Brody et al. 2008). Yet women are not just victims of climate change; they are also drivers of and contributors to the societal practices that generate it. This means that, through gendered societal roles and responsibilities, women are also potentially powerful agents for change, possessing considerable (though often latent or under-exploited) facilities to offer insights into addressing core climate change issues, and in particular issues relating to mitigation, adaptation, sustainability, participation (Alber 2009: 61–62) and capacity building. For example, in many parts of the world women dominate in the practice of subsistence agriculture and have valuable practical contributions to make to mitigation, adaptation and sustainability issues in this area.

Despite the significance of women's agency in this area, a search of the Intergovernmental Panel on Climate Change (IPCC) website, representing the acme of expert opinion across the range of climate change issues, and providing significant underpinning for the FCCC regime, reveals only limited and fairly recent engagement with gender, notably in relation to mitigation, adaptation and disasters (IPCC 2007). It would seem, then, that while it appears obvious that climate change is an area that would benefit from the contribution of minimally gender aware (if not fully ecofeminist) analysis, this view has taken quite some time to emerge within the UN system. This has been true not only of the FCCC regime but also of gender-specialist bodies, and the combined result has been a lacuna in the climate change context. This has, until comparatively recently, prevented effective engagement with gender issues to the detriment of both women and the development of an effective regime.

The UN has, however, latterly made a degree of progress in both introducing gender into the international climate change debate and resourcing women's groups to better equip them for participation in some areas. UN bodies with gender mandates, such as the Commission on the Status of Women, have actively underlined the under-representation of women in climate change decision-making (CSW 2008). The Committee on the Elimination of Discrimination Against Women has drawn attention to the 'absence of a gender perspective' in the FCCC regime, highlighting the need to address a number of issues including gender mainstreaming and participation (CEDAW 2009). Progress is also apparent in other elements of the UN system, extending beyond those with vested interests in women's issues, which are also actively promoting gender issues in the context of climate change. Notable examples include the UN Development Programme (UNDP 2009) and the World Conservation Union (Aguilar 2003). Thus it would seem that it is now recognized within the wider UN system, in principle at least, that if we are to marshal all of the resources at our command to tackle climate change, we must see meaningful participation by women (Brody et al. 2008).

Sadly, realizing gender issues in the FCCC regime has remained problematic. There are a number of possible explanations for this. While the FCCC was spawned contemporaneously with Agenda 21, it is not a gender literate instrument. On one level, this is perhaps to be expected in a framework treaty concerned with an extremely complex and scientifically (IPCC 1990, 1992) and politically contested area. At the same time, the relevant institutional actors missed opportunities to proactively engage with the women's movement, taking a largely reactive approach in this regard. This problem was exacerbated by the fact that the FCCC was not a substantial focus for the activities of the women's movement at the Rio summit, where its energies were poured into Agenda 21. Given the nature of the provisions involved, in particular in seeking to harness grassroots organizations in the development of sustainability praxis, the Rio Declaration and Agenda 21, in stating applicable principles and applying a 'blueprint' for sustainability respectively, were apt targets for the women's movement's activism at that time, fitting readily into the template of its previous engagement with the UN. Furthermore, the women's movement was knocking on an open door, as the UN needed to co-opt grassroots support for the sustainability project to be viable. It would, however, be fair to say that, while the UNCED saw gender issues being harnessed to the emerging sustainability agenda, they were effectively ghettoized in the Rio Declaration and Agenda 21; neither gender nor women were mentioned in the FCCC. This regime was State focused, highly technical, and the subject of such pronounced wrangling between states and powerful industrial actors that there was arguably little or no viable opportunity at this stage for any influence beyond the political and the technocratic to be made manifest. The same could be argued in relation to the 1997 Kyoto Protocol (KP) to the FCCC (UN 1997), which imposed initial (and politically expedient rather than environmentally warranted) greenhouse gas emissions targets on developed countries. Nonetheless, it was inevitable that this neglect of gender issues in the FCCC regime would prove problematic (Nelson et al. 2002).

In the period since the adoption of the FCCC, climate change has arguably been mainstreamed (albeit with varying degrees of accuracy and impact) in popular consciousness (Ungar 2000). As a result, the need to critically consider how to have an input that will shape the successor to the Kyoto Protocol (the first commitment period of which ran its course in 2012) has become a conscious concern for civil society, women's groups included (Re/Sisters for Climate Justice 2007). There are a number of enabling factors and constraints, several of which directly concern legal matters that specifically affect women's participation in climate change governance (Brody et al. 2008). These broadly comprise awareness of rights and how to access them, access to both general and specific legal and policy information, and last, but by no means least, the presence or absence of

> ... an enabling environment, meaning a political, legal, economic and cultural climate that allows women to engage in decision-making processes in a sustainable and effective way. (Brody et al. 2008: 17)

This explains in part why, despite the overtures from the women's movement outlined here, the development of the status of the women and gender constituency in the FCCC has been an extremely lengthy process, with formal recognition from the UNFCCC Secretariat finally being accorded to it only in April 2010 (Alber 2010). Achieving special observer status is important to a constituency in a number of ways – it augments the position of those groups to whom it is accorded in general terms and allows them to access various intervention rights in Convention processes. It is hugely significant that Environmental, Business and Industry NGOs, Local Government and Municipal Authorities, Indigenous Peoples, and Research and Independent Organisations and Trade Unions constituencies all gained constituency status under the FCCC regime before women.

Gendering the FCCC climate change debate however got off to a fairly slow start, with an early attempt to develop a women's NGO forum at the first FCCC Conference of Parties (COP1) (Berlin) in 1995 foundering in fairly short order (Wamukonya and Skutsch 2001). The issue was only reinvigorated by the general gender focus adopted in the World Summit on Sustainable Development (WSSD) in Johannesburg in 2002 and the run-up to it (Okello 2002), and found specific expression in FCCC COP7 (Marrakech) in 2001 which finally saw the adoption of a draft resolution advocating improved representation for women among participants (FCCC/CP 2001). However, the first FCCC women's caucus was only held at COP 11 (Montreal) in 2005. Once the caucus had been established, however, momentum built comparatively swiftly and debate on an application for special observer status emerged at COP13 (Bali) in 2007, and this was agreed at COP 14 (Poznan) in 2008.

The FCCC secretariat accorded provisional recognition to the gender constituency headed up by Gendercc – Women for Climate Justice (a global network of women, gender activists and experts from all world regions focusing on gender and climate justice) in 2009, with formal approval being granted the following year in good time for COP17 (Durban) in December 2011. The process of gaining FCCC recognition in many ways encapsulates the lessons garnered from over half a century of engagement with IGOs in complex and cross-cutting fields. This often necessitates fighting the battle on a number of disparate fronts and drawing on a range of tools to pursue specific priorities, which again are reflected and advocated in ecofeminist models of engagement. Key among these is the characteristic ecofeminist strategy of coalition building, in a way that accommodates diverse women's perspectives. As part of the bid for special observer status, a Charter was drafted through dialogue, again exhibiting ecofeminist tactics, undertaken by a coalition of women's groups including Women in Europe for a Common Future (WECF), ENERGIA (International Network on Gender and Sustainable Energy), Gendercc, and WEDO for the Women and Gender Constituency. Article 2 of the Charter promotes a number of the core ecofeminist principles referred to above including use of democratic and participatory governance, respect for divergent positions, broad, equitable and representative (in terms of age, region, ability, affiliation) membership and inclusive and enabling procedures (notably utilizing electronic communications). Likewise, the Charter's Objectives, as laid out in Article 3, which include making women's voices and experiences heard, feeding these views into ongoing discourse, and co-operating with the women's and gender caucuses and other constituencies and caucuses, fit with the ecofeminist perspective of confronting gender and other oppressions on the basis of identified 'common ground' (Gendercc III).

The ambition of the women's agenda in climate justice continues to expand, driving toward a more directional role (Jackson 2010). This was evident in the establishment of an informal women's leadership network, drawing together representatives from the UN, governments, civil society, philanthropy and the private sector, under the auspices of the Mary Robinson Foundation's Climate Justice Initiative (MRFCJ) in the run-up to the COP16 Cancun in 2010. The approach that emerged from the MRFCJ project exhibits clear ecofeminist credentials (Jackson 2010: 6), notably promoting gender equality in FCCC sub-programmes, full participation for women in decision-making, collaborative sharing and extrapolation of good practice and networking.

Further progress in adopting a strategic approach to gender issues in the FCCC process was made at Cancun by the setting up of a troika (Sebastian and Ceplis 2010) constituted by the three women ministers holding the relevant ministerial portfolios from the states hosting COPs 15, 16 and 17. Its purpose was to further promote the women's agenda in Durban.

In her statement given on behalf of the women and gender constituency in the High Level Segment of COP16 (Cancun), Ana Agostino reiterated the need to respect women's rights (in particular insofar as full participation in the deliberations was concerned) and recognize their knowledge in order to effectively address climate change. In so doing, she employed several concepts that feature prominently in ecofeminism, advocating societal transformation through

> ... reducing inequalities, enhancing human rights and agreeing collectively on a comprehensive approach to combat climate change and save ecosystem integrity and humanity's future. (Agostino 2010)

This sits well with the core ecofeminist principles of highlighting gender and nature issues, identifying multiple oppressions, and seeking to remedy problems by broad-based inclusive and participatory decision-making in order to build consensus.

The outcomes of COP16 in Cancun, while disappointing in many respects, not least in the failure to generate an environmentally viable, legally weighty replacement for the Kyoto Protocol in the face of a political impasse, were at least something of an improvement on the extremely limited outcomes of the COPs following the Bali conference in 2007. For present purposes, Cancun did feature some progress insofar as women's issues were concerned, with significantly improved visibility for gender concerns (Gendercc II, WEDO). For example, in the COP's statement of its 'shared vision for long-term co-operative action', women were numbered among the recognized stakeholders who needed to be engaged. More significantly, 'gender equality and the effective participation of women' were identified as necessary to 'effective action on all aspects of climate change' (FCCC/CP/2010/7/Add.1, 2010: I (7)).

Though it might have reasonably been expected that the engagement of the women's movement with the global climate change regime would benefit from the foundations laid by established women's activism in the international arena and from the precedent set in the context of sustainability in particular, this appears not to have been the case. Indeed it would seem instead that some of the problems experienced in these areas are being replicated and perhaps even amplified in the realm of climate change. It should be noted that permanent recognition for the women's constituency when it finally came in 2010 was not a gift – it was earned, based as it is on proving that it can make a sustained and significant contribution to the ongoing institutional process. It must also be borne in mind that gaining special observer status is no panacea: participation without commensurate influence represents a mere illusion of progress, exhibiting only superficial engagement with the issues rather than actually addressing them. In addition, the exercise of participation rights may be hampered by a host of structural and procedural factors including lack of representation, lack of access to information, lack of technical capacity to engage with scientific materials, and financial constraints. Furthermore, women continue to experience an additional range of gendered social, economic, cultural, legal and educational barriers that serve to make their participation particularly problematic (Brody et al. 2008).

While developments to date fall far short of mainstreaming gender concerns in the context of climate change, they at least indicate a developing profile for these issues and there are multiple signs of continuing work in progress. In the run-up to COP 17, the cultivation of grassroots activity continued, for example through a joint conference held by Gendercc and the Land Access Movement of South Africa in Durban in November 2011 (Gendercc IV). Early indications from COP 17 itself show the constituency making full use of special observer status through interventions. The Durban meeting also featured an unprecedented 36 gender-themed events (Gendercc V) and saw continued dissemination of gender constituency activities and views through social media. The COP also featured further high level cross-cutting gender-awareness raising activity from key women players including Mary Robinson (Lefton 2011).

Gratifying as recent developments undoubtedly are, it is as yet too early to fully assess their impact. The general outcomes at Durban were however, once again, less than impressive; though this must be viewed in light of the very real danger that no agreement would be reached at all. Talks will now begin to make a binding treaty to replace the Kyoto Protocol and set up a regime that is agreed to apply to all countries by 2020 (Vidal and Harvey 2011), though based on past experience delivering meaningful progress is by no means a given. Furthermore, the international community's continuing ability to stall on meaningful action in respect of climate change in the teeth of increasingly compelling scientific evidence continues to place all at risk; and the time when limited progress in tackling aspects of the problem could be enthusiastically applauded is long past – rather it serves to show just how far we have yet to go. This is not only true of climate change but also of broader attempts to fashion more sustainable governance mechanisms. Thus, despite developments made in the latter part of the twentieth century, the core issue of women's participation in the international polis continues to prove problematic rather than a given.

This is the case despite its recognition of the political and legal concept of good governance as a key tool for effective engagement in all substantive contexts. The goal here extends beyond tokenism, supporting the inclusion of women's views and perspectives and resulting in their effective expression in policies, processes and procedures. Nonetheless, it remains the case that despite developments in gender activism, environmentalism and ecofeminism, women continue generally to lack power in respect of both policy and decision-making processes (Bhatta 2001). This acts not only to the detriment of women's equal citizenship but goes to the failure to adequately address environmental degradation.

It seems increasingly obvious that traditional top-down approaches to international law are unable to effectively address the pervasive nature of climate change. It would therefore seem logical to suggest that a synthesis of top-down and bottom up approaches, including those drawing on ecofeminist methodology, will be required in order to attempt effective action. This type of strategy is necessary to cultivate the organized, active and collaborative agency of women's and other NGOs, offering a potential mechanism to tackle the need for grassroots engagement and continuing participation problems. While formal recognition for the women and gender constituency in the FCCC process is a small step in the right direction, the next will be much more demanding, extending beyond formal recognition of the value of women's contribution to the integration of their perspectives in policy, law and practice. This is necessary to develop coherent and connected strategies to generate new, sustainable (in the fullest sense of the word) societal responses to climate change. Rising to this challenge will not be easy, but then again, it would be naive to think that such complex problems are likely to be adequately addressed by simplistic solutions. In tackling them, we need to act in full recognition of the universal nature of the gender gap which applies across all areas of state-craft and international governance, not least climate change (OECD 2008). However, lest it be thought that addressing the issues involved is merely a narrow sectoral concern, it is also the case that women's involvement in governance improves the ability of policies to deliver for all citizens (OECD 2008).

The late Nobel Prize winner, Wangari Maathi, who did so much to bring the combined concerns of gender and environment into the public eye, remarked that:

> As women and men continue this work of clothing this naked earth, we are in the company of many others throughout the world who care deeply for this blue planet. We have nowhere else to go. Those of us who witness the degraded state of the environment and the suffering that comes with it cannot afford to be complacent … If we carry the burden, we are driven to action. We cannot tire or give up. We owe it to the present and future generations of all species to rise up and walk! (Maathai 2007: 295)

The societal transformation that this would require may, for now, still be a choice, though it could soon become an ecological necessity. Heeding not only the critical perspective provided by ecofeminism on the status quo but also its positive promotion of inclusive participation representing alternative viewpoints in climate change law and policy making processes offer constructive means by which to engage with the environmental challenges that are already beginning to be made manifest and will, perhaps, forestall catastrophe. However the continuing, relatively peripheral role accorded to gender considerations thus far gives scant cause for optimism. Having said this, albeit late in the day, moves are clearly being made in the right direction. The lengthy quest to obtain official recognition of a specific role for women in the context of the FCCC must, however, give pause for thought about what continues to represent an overly simplistic, ill-developed and under-nuanced response to policy debate in the most complex international governance issue that we have yet to face. If the lessons of the past had truly been understood and mainstreamed by both the women's movement and the international polity, and their implications for the future in light of unprecedented global environmental threat fully appreciated, women would not have been seeking formal status under the FCCC 'cap in hand' almost two decades after that regime came into existence. Rather it would have had it accorded as of right *ab initio*. One can but wonder how (or indeed if) a different tack would have been taken in the development and operation of the FCCC regime to date had this been the case. At the very least, the distinctive and valuable perspective that women bring to the table in environmental governance contexts more generally (Jahan 1995) would have been integrated into the FCCC process. Evidence suggests that the approach adopted would have been mediated in a number of other significant ways: women are, on the whole, unconvinced by technological optimism and the resultant belief that science can solve all of the problems that we face. As a result, they place a premium on individual responsibility and tend to view behaviour change as central to addressing environmental degradation (Hemmati 2005). This is particularly apposite as climate change is set, even on the most conservative predictions, to challenge not just international and national governance, but ultimately individual lifestyle choices. Starting with the successor to the Kyoto Protocol, which will not now be fully in place before 2020, the central question that needs to be posed is: how are we rising to the challenges posed by the changing global environment? Experience thus far, with the collapse of the Copenhagen negotiations and the relatively weak Cancun and Durban agreements, has not been encouraging. That said, for the purposes of this chapter, the delay may actually prove fortuitous in facilitating the adoption of a more mainstreamed approach to gender in the next generation of climate change law. This should serve to improve any outcomes generated. For now, it is worth underlining that, despite developments to date, overall women continue to be among the least well placed socially, legally and economically, to resist and/or address and adapt to the impacts of climate change (Parikh 2009). That must change along with the prevailing view of women as mere victims of climate change: female agency must be harnessed as a positive force for change.

# References

Agostino, A. 2010. *Statement by Women and Gender NGOs Constituency in the High Level Segment*, Cancun, 10 December 2010. Available at: www.gendercc.net/fileadmin/inhalte/Dokumente/UNFCCC_conferences/COP16/COP16_Women_gender_final_intervention_.pdf [accessed 12 May 2011].

Aguilar, L., Araujo, A. and Quesada-Aguilar, A. 2003. *Gender and Climate Change*, International Union for Conservation of Nature. Available at: www.gdnonline.org/resources/IUCN_FactsheetClimateChange.pdf [accessed 24 June 2011].

Alber, G. 2009. The Women and Gender Constituency in the Climate Negotiations. *Women in Action*, 2, 59–62. Available at: www.gendercc.net/fileadmin/inhalte/Dokumente/Network/2wia09_15talkpoints_gotelind.pdf [accessed 23 June 2011].

Alber, G. 2010. *Recognition of Women and Gender* [Online]. Available at: www.goalber.eu/2010/recognition-of-women-and-gender/ [accessed 9 December 2011].

Bartlett, K.T. 1990. Feminist Legal Methods. *Harvard Law Review*, 103(4), 829–888.

Benschop, V. and Verloo, M. Sisyphus' Sisters: Can Gender Mainstreaming Escape the Genderedness of Organizations? *Journal of Gender Studies*, 15(1), 19–33.

Bhatta, G.,2001. Of Geese and Ganders: mainstreaming gender in the context of sustainable human development. *Journal of Gender Studies*, 10(1), 17–32.

Brody, A., Demetriades, J. and Esplen E. 2008. *Gender and climate change: mapping the linkages*, BRIDGE, Brighton, 2008. Available at: www.bridge.ids.ac.uk/reports/Climate_Change_DFID_draft.pdf [accessed 24 June 2011].

Brundtland, G. (ed.), 1987. *Our Common Future*. Oxford: Oxford University Press.

Burleson, E. 2009–2010. Climate Change Consensus: Emerging International Law. *William and Mary Environmental Law and Policy Review*, 34, 543–588.

CEDAW. 2009. *Statement of the CEDAW Committee on Gender and Climate Change*, 44th session of CEDAW, New York, 20 July to 7 August 2009, Available at: www2.ohchr.org/english/bodies/cedaw/docs/Gender_and_climate_change.pdf [accessed 24 June 2011].

CSW. 2008. *Gender Perspectives on Climate Change*, 52nd session of the Commission on the Status of Women, 28 February 2008, Available at: www.un.org/womenwatch/daw/csw/csw52/issuespapers/Gender%20and%20climate%20change%20paper%20final.pdf [accessed 24 June 2011].

Davion, V. 1994. Is Ecofeminism Feminist?, in *Ecological Feminism*, edited by K.J Warren. London: Routledge, 8–28.

D'Eaubonne, F. 1974. *La Feminisme ou la mort*. Paris: Pierre Horay.

FCCC. 2010, *Report of the Conference of the Parties on its sixteenth session*, Cancun, 29 November to 10 December 2010. Available at: http://unfccc.int/resource/docs/2010/cop16/eng/07a01.pdf#page=2 [accessed 24 June 2011].

Ferguson, M.L. 2007. Sharing without Knowing: Collective Identity in Feminist and Democratic Theory. *Hypatia*, 22(4), 30–45.

Gendercc. 2010. *Women and Gender Constituency in the UNFCCC* [Online]. Available at: www.gendercc.net/about-gendercc/activities/women-gender-constituency-in-the-unfccc.html [accessed 22 June 2011].

Gendercc (II). *Women and Gender – References in the Outcome of the work of the Ad Hoc Working Group on long-term Cooperative Action under the Convention*, advance Unedited version, Draft Decision -/CP.16 [Online]. Available at: www.gendercc.net/fileadmin/inhalte/Dokumente/UNFCCC_conferences/COP16/references_Cancun.pdf [accessed 13 May 2011].

Gendercc (III). *Charter of the Women's and Gender Constituency under the UNFCCC* [Online]. Available at: www.gendercc.net/fileadmin/inhalte/Dokumente/UNFCCC_conferences/Constituency/Women_Gender_Constituency_Charter_final.pdf [accessed 24 June 2011].

Gendercc (IV). *Grassroots Women's Conference on Climate Change* [Online]. Available at: www.gendercc.net/network/forum-news-and-debates/news-details/article/grassroots-womens-conference-on-climate-change-1/83.html?no_cache=1 [accessed 12 December 2011].

Gendercc (v). *Gender Related Events at COP17* [Online]. Available at: www.google.com/calendar/embed?src=c2FsbHkuai53aWxraW5zb25AZ21haWwuY29t&gsessionid=OK [accessed 12 December 2011].

Gruen, L. 1994. Towards and Ecofeminist Moral Epistemology, in *Ecological Feminism*, edited by K.J. Warren. London: Routledge, 120–138.

Hemmati, M. 2005. Gender & Climate Change in the North: Issues, Entry Points and Strategies for the Post-2012 Process and Beyond. *Genanet/Focal Point Gender Justice and Sustainability* [Online], 1–31. Available at: www.gendercc.net/fileadmin/inhalte/ Dokumente/UNFCCC_conferences/Gender_Post-Kyoto.pdf [accessed 24 June 2011].

Hughes, E.J. 1995. Fishwives and Other Tails: Ecofeminism and Environmental Law. *Canadian Journal of Women and Law*, 8, 502–530.

IPCC. 1990. *First Assessment Report* [Online]. Available at: www.ipcc.ch/ipccreports/1992%20 IPCC%20Supplement/IPCC_1990_and_1992_Assessments/English/ipcc_90_92_ assessments_far_contents.pdfit [accessed 13 May 2011].

IPCC. 1992. *Supplement: Scientific Assessment* [Online]. Available at: www.ipcc.ch/ipcc reports/1992%20IPCC%20Supplement/IPCC_Suppl_Report_1992_wg_I/ipcc_wg_I_ 1992_suppl_report_scientific_assessment.pdf [accessed 8 December 2011].

IPCC. 2007. *Fourth Assessment (Synthesis) Report Climate Change: Impacts, Adaptation and Vulnerability* [Online]. Available at: www.ipcc.ch/publications_and_data/ar4/syr/en/ main.html [accessed 13 May 2011].

Jackson, S. 2010. *Women's Leadership on Climate Justice: Planning for Cancun and Beyond*. Mary Robinson Foundation: Climate Justice and Realizing Rights: The Ethical Globalization Initiative [Online]. Available at: www.mrfcj.org/pdf/Meeting_Report_Womens_Leader ship_on_Climate_Justice_17Sep2010.pdf [accessed 16 May 2011].

Jahan, R. 1995. *The Elusive Agenda: Mainstreaming Women in Development*. London: Zed Books.

Kaasa, S.M. 2007. The UN Commission on Sustainable Development: Which Mechanisms Explain Its Accomplishments? *Global Environmental Politics*, 7(3), 107–129.

Lefton, R. 2011. *Gender and Climate Change: Durban Explores the Intersection* [Online]. Available at: http://thinkprogress.org/romm/2011/12/05/381664/gender-and-climate-change-durban/ [accessed 12 December 2011].

Maathai, W. 2007. *Unbowed: One Woman's Story*. London: William Heinemann.

McGuire, C. and McGuire, C. 2003. Ecofeminist Visions. *Feministezine* [Online]. Available at: www.feministezine.com/feminist/ecofeminism/What-is-Ecofeminism-Anyway.html [accessed 6 December 2011].

Marina, L. 2002. 'Woman & the Land' [Online]. Available at www.ecofem.org/journal at www.lancs.ac.uk/staff/twine/ecofem/linda.pdf [accessed 19 June 2011].

Mellor, M. 1997. *Feminism and Ecology*. Cambridge: Polity Press.

Merchant, C. 1981. *The Death of Nature: Women, Ecology and the Scientific Revolution*. London: Wildwood House.

Morrow, K. 2006. 'Gender, International Law and the Emergence of Environmental Citizenship', 33–61 in S. Buckingham-Hatfield et al. *In the Hands of Women – Women, Human Rights and the Environment*, Manchester University Press: Manchester.

Morrow, K. 2011. Perspectives on Environmental Law and the Law Relating to Sustainability: A Continuing Role for Ecofeminism?, in *Critical Environmental Law: New Environmental Foundations*, edited by A. Philippopoulos-Mihalopoulos. London: Routledge, 126–152.

Nelson, V., Meadows, K., Cannon, T., Morton, J. and Martin, A. 2002. Uncertain predictions, invisible impacts, and the need to mainstream gender in climate change adaptations. *Gender and Development*, 10(2), 51–59.

Norgaard, K. and York, R. 2005. Gender Equality and State Environmentalism. *Gender and Society*, 19(4), 506–522.

Okello, D. 2002. *WEDO's Analysis of the WDDS Plan of Implementation* [Online]. Available at: www.pamoya.com/node/1131 [accessed 13 May 2011].

Parikh, J. 2009. *Towards a Gender-Sensitive Agenda for Energy, Environment and Climate Change* [Online]. Available at: www.un.org/womenwatch/daw/egm/impact_bdpfa/EP10%20-%20Parikh_final.after%20track.pdf [accessed 24 June 2011].

Plumwood, V. 1993. *Feminism and the Mastery of Nature*. London: Routledge.

Prugl, E. and Meyer, K.M. 1999. Gender Politics in Global Governance, in *Gender Politics in Global Governance*, edited by K.M. Meyer and E. Prugl. Lanham: Rowan & Littlefield, 3–16.

Thomas-Pellicer, R. and Pepper, M. 2007. *A Jubilee for Climate Justice* [Online: Re/sisters for Climate Justice]. Available at: www.ecopaxmundi.org/docs/jubilee-for-climate-justice.pdf [accessed 12 May 2011].

Sebastian, J. and Ceplis, D. 2010. *Perspective on Gender and Climate Change at Cancun* [Online: CARES]. Available at: www.aic.ca/gender/pdf/Gender_and_Climate_Cancun.pdf [accessed 16 May 2011].

Shiva, V. 1993. The Impoverishment of the Environment: Women and Children last, in *Ecofeminism*, edited by M Mies and V. Shiva. London: Zed Books, 70–90.

Tinker, I. 1999. Non-Governmental Organisations: An Alternative Power Base for Women?, in *Gender Politics in Global Governance*, edited by K.M. Meyer and E. Prugl. Lanham: Rowan & Littlefield, 88–104.

Twine, R.T. 2001. Ecofeminisms in Process. www.ecofem.org/journal [Online]. Available at: www.lancs.ac.uk/staff/twine/ecofem/ecofem2001 [accessed 21 June 2011].

UNDP. 2009. *Resource Guide on Gender and Climate Change* [Online]. Available at: www.un.org/womenwatch/downloads/Resource_Guide_English_FINAL.pdf [accessed 23 June 2011].

UN. 1992. *Earth Summit: Agenda 21: The United Nations Programme of Action from Rio* [Online]. Available at: www.un.org/esa/dsd/agenda21/res_agenda21_00.shtml [accessed 23 June 2011].

UN. 1992. *Framework Convention on Climate Change (FCCC)* [Online]. Available at: http://unfccc.int/resource/docs/convkp/conveng.pdf [accessed 13 May 2011].

UN. 1997. *Kyoto Protocol to the Framework Convention on Climate Change* [Online]. Available at: http://unfccc.int/kyoto_protocol/items/2830.php [accessed 16 June 2011].

Ungar, S. 2000. Knowledge, ignorance and the popular culture: climate change versus the ozone hole. *Public Understanding of Science*, 9(3), 297–312.

Verchick, R.R.M. 1996. In a Greener Voice: Feminist Theory and Environmental Justice. *Harvard Women's Law Journal*, 19(3), 23–88.

Vidal, J. and Harvey, F. Durban climate deal struck after tense all-night session. *The Guardian* [Online, 11 December]. Available at: www.guardian.co.uk/environment/2011/dec/11/durban-climate-deal-struck [accessed 12 December 2011].

Walby, S. 2000. Beyond the Politics of Location: The Power of Argument in a Global Era. *Feminist Theory*, 1(2), 189–206.

Wamukonya, N. and Skutsch, M. 2001. Is there a Gender Angle to the Climate Change Negotiations [Online], *Energy & Environment*, 13(1), 115–124. Available at: www.unep.org/roa/amcen/Projects_Programme/climate_change/PreCop15/Proceedings/Gender-and-climate-change/IsthereaGenderAngletotheClimateChangeNegiotiations.pdf [accessed 12 May 2011].

WEDO. 2010. *Gender Equality Language in the Cancun Agreements Outcome of the work of the Ad Hoc Working Group on long-term Cooperative Action under the Convention Draft decision*

*[-/CP.16]* [Online]. Available at: www.wedo.org/wp-content/uploads/W+G-compilation_ Cancun-Agreements_advance-version.pdf [accessed 24 June 2011].

# Index